W9-BRY-983

Law for Business

14th Edition

John D. Ashcroft, J.D.
Member of the Missouri Bar

Janet E. Ashcroft, J.D.
Member of the Missouri Bar

Australia · Canada · Mexico · Singapore · Spain · United Kingdom · United States

Law for Business, 14e by John D. Ashcroft & Janet E. Ashcroft

Senior Acquisitions Editor: Rob Dewey
Senior Developmental Editor: Susanna C. Smart
Marketing Manager: Nicole Moore
Production Editor: Elizabeth A. Shipp
Media Developmental Editor: Peggy Buskey
Media Production Editor: John Barans
Manufacturing Coordinator: Sandee Milewski
Internal Design: Ramsdell Design/Craig Ramsdell, Cincinnati
Cover Design: Imbue Design/Kim Torbeck, Cincinnati
Cover Image: © PhotoDisc, Inc.
Production House: Pre-Press Company, Inc.
Printer: R.R. Donnelley & Sons—Willard Manufacturing Division

Printed in the United States of America
1 2 3 4 5 04 03 02 01

For more information contact West Legal Studies in Business, South-Western College Publishing, 5101 Madison Road, Cincinnati, Ohio, 45227 or find us on the Internet at http://www.westbuslaw.com

Library of Congress Cataloging-in-Publication Data

Ashcroft, John D., 1942–
Law for Business / John D. Ashcroft, Janet E. Ashcroft.—14th ed.
p. cm.
Includes index.
ISBN 0-324-06053-X (alk. paper)
1. Commercial law—United States. 2. Business law—United States. I. Ashcroft, Janet E. II. Title.

KF889.3 .A84 2002
346.7307—dc21

2001027811

Brief Contents

Contents

Preface

Why Study Business Law?

Newspapers, magazines, television, radio—and even our computers—relate business information to us almost by the minute. Behind the scenes of business activity—from startups of new businesses to corporate mergers, marketing, advertising, technology, and employment—laws governing business play a vital role. The study of business law is necessary to provide students with an overview of the law of commercial transactions and other business legal issues. ***Law for Business, Fourteenth Edition,*** focuses on these laws to prepare students to conduct business in our dynamic world marketplace.

Purpose of the Text

Law for Business, Fourteenth Edition, is a practical approach to law that emphasizes current and relevant topics students need to understand about business transactions and issues, such as contracts, property, employer/employee relations, and insurance. The basic concepts of business law are covered without the excessive theory that often makes law seem incomprehensible. Practical coverage of law pertaining to business, without the detailed treatment of a law school text, is the hallmark of this text. The substantial breadth of this text, complete with examples and cases, is an effective introduction to a variety of legal topics.

New and Successful Features

INTEGRATED LEARNING OBJECTIVES

Each chapter begins with learning objectives that outline what the students will accomplish after reading the chapter. Margin icons indicate where learning objectives are first discussed in the text. Each objective is briefly restated as reinforcement, so students need not refer to the beginning of each chapter. These learning objective icons create a natural outline to help students easily comprehend the information.

ACTUAL U.S. COURT CASES

This book contains no make-believe cases. Every case example, problem, and summary is an actual U.S. court case, transferring theory into practice. These exciting actual cases help students relate to the subject as they learn about real-world legal situations that can occur in business.

ETHICAL POINTS

In order to give greater focus to ethical considerations in various business situations, the text contains ethical point questions and comments interspersed in the margins. These questions highlight pertinent ethical issues, show the relationships between law and ethics, and serve as a basis for class discussion.

INTERNET MATERIAL

A part opening screen from the Internet highlights a topic from a chapter in that part, and sends students to the Internet address for further information or study. In addition, addresses at the end of each chapter direct students to sites that provide additional or relevant information related to chapter topics. The Internet search also helps students become familiar with the use of the World Wide Web, a skill that can be useful on the job.

REAL DOCUMENTS

Real documents from the Quicken® Business Lawyer 2000® CD-ROM, available separately, provide students with samples of forms and letters commonly used in financial and other business transactions. These documents also include a related exercise if students have access to Quicken® Business Lawyer 2000®; if not, they can still complete the part of the exercise that sends them to relevant Internet sites. Other documents are prepared especially for this text, and some are from government sources.

Enhanced Content and Other Important Features

In the Fourteenth Edition, we have maintained the format of the previous edition, but of course, have updated the content as needed throughout. This edition contains many new cases, some of which are listed here:

- *Granse & Associates, Inc. v. Kimm,* 529 N.W.2d 6 (Minn. App.)
- *Chiaro v. Chiaro,* 623 N.Y.S.2d 312 (A.D.)
- *Golt by Golt v. Sports Complex, Inc.,* 644 A.2d 989 (Superior Ct. Del.)
- *AIG Europe, S.A. v. M/V MSC Lauren,* 940 F. Supp. 925 (E.D. Va.)
- *Skelton v. Chicago Transit Authority,* 573 N.E.2d 1315 (Ill. App.)
- *Catlett v. Steward,* 804 S.W.2d 699 (Ark.)
- *Sebastian v. Dist. of Columbia,* 636 A.2d 958 (D.C. App.)
- *Carter v. Innisfree Hotel, Inc.,* 661 So.2d. 1174 (Ala.)
- *Hariscom Svenska,* AB v. Harris Corp., 3 F.2d 576 (2nd Cir.)
- *Farmers' Elec. V. Mo. Dept. of Corrections,* 977 S.W.2d 266 (Mo.)
- *Murray v. Crest Const., Inc.,* 900 S.W.2d 342 (Tex.)
- *Brandis v. Lightmotive Fatman, Inc.,* 443 S.E.2d 887 (N.C. App.)
- *McBride v. Wausau Ins. Companies,* 500 N.W.2d 387 (Wis. App.)
- *SMS Financial, L.L.C. v. ABCO Homes, Inc.,* 167 F.3d 235 (5th Cir.)
- *Shawmut Bank, N.A. v. Miller,* 614 N.E.2d 668 (Mass.)
- *Kruser v. Bank of America NT & SA,* 281 Cal. Rptr. 463 (Cal. App.)
- *Guarantor Partners v. Huff,* 830 S.W.2d 73 (Tenn. App.)
- *Florida Nat. Bank v. Isaac Industries,* 560 So.2d 1203 (Fla. App.)

In addition, in response to our users and reviewers, we have made significant revisions to the chapters in Part 4 on sales to simplify these complex topics and help students to understand them better. These and other changes include:

- Chapters 18 and 19 have been totally reorganized and further explanations have been added to make the material easier to understand.
- Because electronic fund transfers are so widely used, potential liabilities for customers are explained in greater detail in Chapter 20.
- Explanation of the reasons for the acceptability of bank drafts or tellers' checks is given in Chapter 22.
- Because negotiable instruments are frequently issued to more than one payee, a section discussing the requirements for negotiation of such instruments has been added to Chapter 23.
- Explanation of how check clearinghouses operate, and a section explaining who bears the loss when there is a forged signature, has been added to Chapter 24.
- Chapter 27 explains how a principal may terminate an agency.
- Since more and more employers publish and distribute handbooks to employees, the impact of such handbooks is mentioned in Chapter 28.
- A discussion of the ability of a partnership to continue when one partner departs has been added to Chapter 33.
- Chapter 35 has been revised to reflect the fact that in many cases, actual stock certificates are not issued when stock is purchased.
- The material in Chapter 38 dealing with the obligation of an insurer to defend the insured from liability to others has been reorganized and expanded.

We have improved upon existing features as well:

Ample Questions and Cases

The end-of-chapter materials include questions and case problems. This gives the teacher and the student the opportunity to check how well the student understands the material.

Key Terms and Definitions

Key terms and their definitions, critical to students' understanding of business law, are printed in the margins for easy identification and mastery. The terms are also compiled into a glossary at the end of the text.

Improved Readability

In *Law for Business*, special attention has been given to improving the readability of the text and cases by using such techniques as shortened sentences, active voice, and more information presented in list format rather than in paragraph form.

Short Chapters

Long chapters tend to dilute the critical points and confuse the reader. *Law for Business* is set up in short, easy-to-understand chapters so that critical points stand out.

Chapter Opening Preview Case and Preview Case Revisited

The beginning of every chapter has a "Preview Case" to involve students in the issues to be discussed in the chapter. Each preview case ends with a question that is answered by the court's decision in the "Preview Case Revisited."

For the Instructor

Law for Business comes with a complete and integrated teaching package. The following supplements are available to aid the instructor:

Instructor's Manual with Transparency Masters

This manual, by the text authors, acts as a guide to the text and course, providing teaching suggestions, lesson outlines, explanations and citations for the example cases, and answers to the problems contained in the text. It also contains answers to the achievement tests and exams, and transparency masters.
ISBN: 0-324-06055-6

Achievement Tests and Exams

These tests provide an assessment opportunity for the instructor to show what students have learned by using this text.
ISBN: 0-324-06056-4

Test Bank

Written by Janet Ashcroft, this supplement provides more than 900 objective and case questions by chapter, giving the instructor additional assignments and questions for student testing.
ISBN: 0-324-06060-2

ExamView Computerized Testing

A computerized version of the test bank allows the instructor to quickly and efficiently produce professional-quality tests.
ISBN: 0-324-06062-9

PowerPoint 4.0 Presentation Slides

A PowerPoint presentation package, prepared by Jimidene Murphey of South Plains College, provides enhanced lecture materials for the instructor, as well as study aids for students. Available online at http://ashcroft.westbuslaw.com or on the Instructor's Resource CD-ROM.

Instructor's Resource CD-ROM

This CD-ROM (the IRCD) for instructors contains all non-salable supplements for ease-of-use.
ISBN: 0-324-11679-9

WEST BUSINESS LAW MULTI-MEDIA SUPPLEMENTS

West is committed to providing you, our educational partners, with the finest educational resources available, including the full complement of West resources. Because we prepare our instructor resources with a variety of teaching environments in mind, it is likely that you will need only a portion of these for your course. Before you request an item, we ask that you please read thoroughly the description of each resource. If you still need more information about resources, we urge you to contact your local West/Thomson Learning sales representative or visit our web site at http://www.westbuslaw.com. Many teaching and learning resources can be downloaded directly from this site.

Ten Free Hours of WestLaw

West's computerized legal research gives instructors and students access to U.S. Code, federal regulations, and numerous special libraries.

Court TV Trial Stories

In courtrooms across America, dramatic stories of people in conflict unfold every day. Since 1991, *Court TV* has covered hundreds of these cases, each one a balance of right and wrong, fact and fiction, truth and lies. *Court TV's "Trial Story"* series features highly relevant cases condensed into one-hour programs. Each "Trial Story" captures the whole story of a trial, including news footage, courtroom testimony and interviews with defendants, plaintiffs, witnesses, lawyers, jurors and judges. Each *"Trial Story"* video engages students while presenting important legal concepts.

CNN Legal Issues Video Update

You can update your coverage of legal issues, as well as spark lively classroom discussion by using the *CNN Legal Issues Video Update.* This video update is produced by Turner Learning, using the resources of *CNN,* the world's first 24-hour, all-news network.

South-Western's Business Law Video Series

This set of situational videos covers a range of topics for the full business law course, including the Uniform Code Council, employment law, and the business law portion of the CPA exam.

Business Law and Legal Environment Video Library

The Video Library includes seven different types of professionally produced legal videos: *Drama of Law* and *Drama of the Law II; The Making of a Case; Law and Literature; Ethics in America;* American Bar Association mock trial videos; *Equal Justice Series;* and West's *Business Profiles.*

For the Student

Also available are supplementary materials for the student that provide further opportunities to learn and review business law. Some of the supplements are specific to this text, while others are part of the extensive offering of West's Business Law Multimedia supplements. These materials include:

Study Guide and Workbook

Written by Ronald L. Taylor, from Metropolitan State College in Denver, the *Study Guide* provides chapter outlines, general rules and limitations on the rules, examples, and study hints. In addition, objective questions and case problems assist students in reviewing terms and applying concepts learned in each chapter. Students' comprehension is reinforced by reviewing the concepts and applying them to factual situations and through a variety of learning exercises including true/false questions, fill-in-the-blank statements, yes/no questions, questions referring to fact situations, and definition exercises. This edition's *Study Guide* includes all answers.
ISBN: 0-324-06054-8

Quicken® Business Lawyer 2000® CD-ROM

The Quicken® Business Lawyer 2000® CD-ROM is a valuable product that contains numerous sample documents, including forms and letters that are common to the workplace and used for personal business.
ISBN: 0-324-03737-6

A Handbook of Basic Law Terms: Black's Dictionary Series

A Handbook of Basic Law Terms is a guide to the most important and most common words and phrases used it he law today. Students can keep this comprehensive and helpful dictionary for both their professional and personal lives.
ISBN: 0-324-03737-6

Business Law: The Game, by S. Andrew Ostapski

Students develop a heightened focus on topics in a business law course through teamwork, self-directed research into legal issues, detailed written records, tem competition, interpersonal skills and evaluation of other team members.
ISBN: 0-324-07059-4

The New York Times Guide to Business Law and Legal Environment, by Marianne M. Jennings and Jamie Murphy

This guide is a collection of the best business law related articles from the *New York Times,* and includes access to an online collection of the most current articles, continually posted as news breaks.
ISBN: 0-324-04160-8

WebTutor and Personal WebTutor

Available on WebCT or Blackboard, this teaching and learning aid features chat discussion groups, testing, student progress tracking, and business law course materials. See http://webtutor.swcollege.com.

Acknowledgments

We would like to thank the following reviewers who helped with the revision of this and other editions of the text, as well as the many reviewers whose assistance was invaluable throughout numerous past editions. It is your suggestions and comments that have helped make this text what it is today.

Gretchen Carroll
Owens Community College

Marilyn S. Chernoff
Sawyer School

Robert D. Colestock
Indiana Vocational Technical College

Elizabeth Cummings
Mississippi Delta Community College

Linda B. Davis
Vance-Granville Community College

Paul Davis
Cincinnati Technical College

Jennie Dehn
Bryant and Stratton Business Institute

Gamewell Gantt
Idaho State University

Julie A. Goodwin
Heald Business College

Timothy R. Hart
College of the Sequoias

Jay S. Hollowell
Commonwealth College, Virginia Beach

Jeff Holt
Tulsa Community College

Susan Johnson
Central Wesleyan College

Joanna Jones
Vance-Granville Community College

J. Franklin Lee
Pitt Community College

Louie J. Michelli
Belmont Technical College

Lee Miller
Indiana Business College

Jimidene Murphey
South Plains College

Clovie C. Quick
Columbus Technical Institute

Michael L. Ramsey
Sanford Brown Business College

John Sedensky
Newbury College

Alan L. Sheets
Indiana Business College

Esther M. Tremblay
Duff's Business Institute

Timothy G. Wiedman
Thomas Nelson Community College

Hugh L. Wink
Kilgore College

Allen Young
Bessemer State Technical College

Betty Young
Washington State Community College

John Zahar, Jr.
Heald Business College

We would also like to thank Ronald L. Taylor of Metropolitan State College, preparer of the *Study Guide,* and Jimidene Murphey of South Plains College, preparer of the PowerPoint Presentation Package and online quizzes, for their assistance with these supplements to the text. In addition, we thank the staff at West for their work on the preparation of this edition for publication, especially Susanna Smart, Senior Developmental Editor, Rob Dewey, Senior Acquisitions Editor, and Libby Shipp, Production Editor.

John D. Ashcroft
Janet E. Ashcroft

About the Authors

JOHN ASHCROFT served one term in the United States Senate from 1995 to 2001. He previously served as governor of Missouri for two terms. As governor, Ashcroft balanced eight consecutive budgets during his terms, and *Fortune* magazine rated him one of the top 10 education governors.

In the Senate, Ashcroft took a leading role on key issues such as welfare reform, juvenile crime, and reform of the civil justice system, while authoring significant changes to federal law. He served on the Judiciary, the Commerce, Science, and Transportation, and the Foreign Relations committees and was also the chairman of subcommittees on the Constitution, consumer affairs, and Africa, respectively.

Ashcroft, widely recognized for his innovative use of technology and the Internet, has taught students in Missouri and across the country about using the Internet and online information as a tool of citizenship. Ashcroft is currently the Attorney General of the United States.

Prior to entering public service, Ashcroft taught business law at Southwest Missouri State University in Springfield. He graduated with honors from Yale University in

1964, met his wife, Janet, at the Law School of University of Chicago where they each received law degrees in 1967, and later co-authored two college textbooks together. Both have been admitted to practice law in the U.S. Court for the Western District of Missouri.

JANET ASHCROFT has been a full-time faculty member at Howard University, teaching business law, taxation, and accounting, and serving on the Judiciary Committee at the university. She has taught at Central Bible College in Springfield, Missouri, and at Stephens College in Columbia, Missouri. She is a member of the Board of Trustees of Patrick Henry College and has served on the Visiting Committee of the University of Chicago, chair of the Alzheimer's disease Task Force for the State of Missouri and as state liaison for the National Alzheimer's Association. In these capacities, Janet Ashcroft has authored numerous reports and articles relating to Alzheimer's disease. In addition, she has been a general counsel for the Missouri Department of Revenue.

Part 1 The Legal System and the Legal Environment of Business

United States • Copyright Office
The Library *of* Congress

"To promote the Progress of Science and useful Arts, by securing for limited Times to Authors and Inventors the exclusive Right to their respective Writings and Discoveries"
(U.S. Constitution, Article 1 Section 8)

What's New
- Current Developments
- **Webcasting**
- Anticircumvention Rulemaking
- Digital Millennium Copyright Act §104 Study
- Napster *Amicus* Brief
- Digital Transmissions
- Copyright Regulations
- Fee Changes
- Press Releases

About the Office
- Welcome
- Hours and Location
- Contact Information
- History and Overview

Library of Congress
Visit the Library of Congress to access information and materials from its collections.

General Information
Copyright Basics
Registration Procedures
(FAQ) Frequently Asked Questions
CORDS (Copyright Office Electronic Registration, Recordation & Deposit System)
CARP (Copyright Arbitration Royalty Panels)
Licensing
Freedom of Information Act Requests
Fax on Demand
Mandatory Deposit

Copyright Office Records
Search Registrations/Documents
On-line Service Provider Agents
NIE Lists (Notices of Intent to Enforce)
Vessel Hull Design

Announcements
Federal Register Notices
Press Releases
NewsNet Information Service

Publications
Forms
Information Circulars
Form Letters/Factsheets
Federal Regulations
Compendium II Copyright Office Practices
Office Reports and Studies

Legislation
Copyright Law
New/Pending Legislation
Register's Testimony
Digital Millennium Copyright Act Summary (version: pdf)

International
International Copyright
URAA amends U.S. law (Uruguay Round Agreements Act)
WIPO (World Intellectual Property Organization) Diplomatic Conference--
Preparatory Documents
New Treaties

http://www.loc.gov/copyright

Copyrights and trademarks are covered in Chapter 3, "Business Torts and Crimes." You can learn more about copyright laws, registration, fees, international issues and regulations, and the latest on digital transmissions at the Web site of the U.S. Copyright Office. A similar Web site at the U.S. Patent Office provides many links to information about trademarks and patents, fees, laws, how to apply, and more. For more information, see http://www.uspto.gov and http://www.loc.gov/copyright.

1 Introduction to Law

Learning Objectives

1 Define law.

2 Explain why we have laws.

3 List four sources of law.

4 Distinguish among crimes, torts, and ethics.

LO1
Define law

Law
Governmental rule prescribing conduct and carrying a penalty for violation

Many authors have tried to define law. Blackstone's definition is famous: "**Law** is a rule of civil conduct, commanding what is right and prohibiting what is wrong." Many rules of civil conduct command what is right and condemn what is wrong, but rules are not necessarily laws. Only when a sovereign state issues rules prescribing what is right and what is wrong can a rule be called a law. Even then rules are not effective unless penalties are applied when the rules are broken. Thus a law is a rule that prescribes conduct and that is enacted and enforced by a government.

Religious teachings, social mores, habit, and peer pressure all contribute to social control of conduct, but only the rules of law are all-pervasive, applying with equal force to every member of society. A breach of some of these rules is a crime, for which the penalty is a fine, a jail sentence, or both. A breach of other rules is a civil wrong, for which the penalty most often is payment of a sum of money called **damages**. Every deviation from prescribed rules of conduct has a penalty.

Damages
A sum of money a wrongdoer must pay to an injured party

Business Law
Rules of conduct for the performance of business transactions

Business law is a class of laws that are concerned primarily with those rules of conduct prescribed by government for the performance of business transactions. The laws governing business transactions in the United States did not come into existence overnight. Laws result from society's changing concepts of what is right and what is wrong. Laws may be created or modified to deal with new technology or circumstances. For example, for several centuries in England and America an individual who owned land owned the soil and minerals below the topsoil and the air above the land "all the way to heaven." The law prohibited trespassing on a person's land or air. A telephone company that wanted to string a telephone wire through the air had to buy a right of way. When airplanes were invented, this law became a millstone around society's neck. Under this law, a transcontinental airline would have to buy a right of way through the air of every property owner in its path from New York to San Francisco.

The modification of this rule by judicial decree shows how the law changes when circumstances change.

Objectives of Law

LO2
Why we have laws

We live in a complex society. Every time we have business dealings with others—working, making a purchase, starting a business, traveling, renting an apartment, or trying to insure against loss—we have the potential for a dispute. The law seeks to establish rules so that we will be able to resolve those disputes that arise. The law also sets the rules of conduct for many transactions so we will know how to avoid disputes. The law thus tries to establish a stable framework to keep society operating as smoothly as possible.

Roots of Our Legal System

When the European colonists settled in this country, they instituted legal systems similar to what they had in their native lands. Therefore English, French, and Spanish colonists set up legal systems similar to those in England, France, and Spain. The 13 original colonies that became the United States were all English colonies, so they adopted a legal system like England's. Although additional territory was added and the influence of other legal systems was felt, the system we have today is still based heavily on the English legal system of common law and equity.

The Common Law

Common Law
English custom recognized by courts as binding

Common law is custom that has come to be recognized by the courts as binding on the community and therefore law. In medieval England, there were no laws prescribing the proper rule of conduct in hundreds of situations. When a dispute came before a judge, the court prescribed a rule of its own based on the customs of the time. Over a period of several centuries, these court decisions developed into a body of law. The colonists brought this body of law from England to America. After the United States became a sovereign nation, most of these common laws were either enacted as statutory laws or continued as judge-made laws. Much of our current law is based on this common law.

Facts: A court ordered that Dupuy Warrick be awarded $125,000 for his efforts in negotiating the settlement of a claim by Missouri-Kansas Pipe Line Company (Mokan) against Columbia Companies. Stockholders and Mokan objected to the size of the award, and several years of litigation passed before Warrick was finally paid. Warrick also moved to be paid interest on the award. The company alleged that neither the state common law nor any statutes required the payment of interest on awards.

Outcome: The court did not find the right to interest in state statutes, but looked to rules derived from the custom of antiquity. It found that under such ancient custom in England, a creditor could demand and receive interest on awards. Therefore, the common law did allow the awarding of interest.

Equity

Uniformity in the common law spread throughout England because judges tended to decide cases the same way other judges had decided them. But some wrongs occurred for which law provided no remedy except for money damages. In some cases, this was not an appropriate remedy. To obtain suitable relief, the parties began to petition the king for justice. The king delegated these matters to the chancellor, who did not decide the cases on the basis of the recognized legal principles, but on the basis of *equity*—what in good conscience ought to be done. Eventually an additional system of justice evolved that granted judicial relief when no adequate remedy at law existed. This system is called **equity**.

Equity
Justice system based on fairness; provides relief other than merely money damages

Courts of equity, although they sometimes recognized legal rights, also provided new types of relief. For example, instead of merely ordering a person who had breached a contract agreeing to sell real estate to pay money damages, they would order "specific performance"—that is, require the seller to comply with the terms of the contract and sell the real estate. They also provided for preventive action to protect individuals from likely harm. In this type of case a court with equity powers might initially issue a **restraining order**, a temporary order forbidding a certain action. Upon a complete hearing, the court might issue an **injunction**, a permanent order forbidding activities that would be detrimental to others. Today only a few states maintain separate equity courts or, as they are also called, *chancery courts*. In most states, courts apply legal and equitable principles to each case as the facts justify, without making any formal distinction between law and equity.

Restraining Order
Court's temporary order forbidding an action

Injunction
Court's permanent order forbidding an action

Sources of Law

LO3
Sources of law

Our laws come from several sources. They include judges' decisions, federal and state constitutions, statutes, and administrative agency orders.

JUDICIAL DECISIONS

Judicial interpretation is an important element of the legal process. Because courts can interpret laws differently, the same law might have somewhat different consequences in different states. Interpretations by the highest courts have the effect of setting **precedents**. A precedent is a decided case or court decision that determines the decision in a subsequent case because the cases are so similar. Under the doctrine of **stare decisis** (stand by the decision) these precedents bind the lower courts. These interpretations may concern a situation not previously brought before the court, or the

Precedent
Court decision that determines the decision in a subsequent, similar case

Stare Decisis
Principle that a court decision controls the decision of a similar future case

Facts: An accident involving a power lawnmower operated by his father, Alan Clark, injured Paul Clark, age 5. Paul sued the lawnmower's manufacturer and Alan and his insurer. Alan said the doctrine of "parental immunity" prevented him from being sued by his dependent son. The state supreme court had held in a case two years previously that parental immunity was abolished, thus a child could sue a parent.

Outcome: The state supreme court said that it was the policy of courts to stand by previous decisions because judges, lawyers, and citizens have a right to rely on previous holdings. Thus stare decisis required that parental immunity not prevent the suit.

court may decide to reverse a previous decision. Any state supreme court or the Supreme Court of the United States can reverse a decision of a lower court. For legal stability and so that we can know our rights before we undertake a transaction, courts must generally adhere to the judicial precedents set by earlier decisions. However, changing situations or practices sometimes make it necessary for the previous case law to be overturned and a new rule or practice to be established.

CONSTITUTIONS

Constitution
Document that contains fundamental principles of a government

A **constitution** is the document that defines the relationships of the parts of the government to each other and the relationship of the government to its citizens or subjects. The U.S. Constitution is the supreme law of the land. State constitutions, as well as all other laws, must agree with the U.S. Constitution. The Supreme Court of the United States is the final arbiter in disputes about whether a state or federal law violates the U.S. Constitution. A state supreme court is the final judge as to whether a state law violates the constitution of that state.

In 1791, after the U.S. Constitution had been adopted, it was amended by the addition of the Bill of Rights. The Constitution contained no specific guarantees of individual liberty. The **Bill of Rights** consists of 10 amendments specifically designed to protect the civil rights and liberties of the citizens and the states. It is a part of the U.S. Constitution.

Bill of Rights
First 10 amendments to U.S. Constitution

STATUTES

Statutes
Laws enacted by legislative bodies

Ordinances
Laws enacted by cities

Statutes are laws enacted by legislative bodies. The federal Congress, state legislatures, and city councils, all made up of persons elected by the voters, comprise the three chief classes of legislative bodies in the United States. City councils make laws called **ordinances**, a specific type of statutory law.

In some cases statutes enacted by one legislative body conflict with statutes enacted by another legislative body. A constitutional federal statute prevails over a conflicting state statute.

Unlike constitutions, which are difficult to amend and are designed to be general rather than specific, statutes may be enacted, repealed, or amended at any regular or special session of the lawmaking body. Thus, statutes respond more to the changing demands of the people.

In the field of business law the most important statute is the Uniform Commercial Code (UCC).[1] The UCC regulates sales and leases of goods; commercial paper, such as checks; secured transactions; and particular aspects of banking and fund transfers, letters of credit, warehouse receipts, bills of lading, and investment securities. Although all 50 states have enacted at least some portions of the UCC, individual states have made some changes. Therefore, variations in the UCC exist from state to state.

ADMINISTRATIVE AGENCY ORDERS

Administrative Agencies
Governmental boards or commissions with authority to regulate matters or implement laws

Administrative agencies set up by legislative bodies carry on many governmental functions today. **Administrative agencies** are commissions or boards that have the power to regulate particular matters or implement laws. At the federal level alone almost 60 agencies are involved in regulatory activity. The legislative branch of government enacts laws that prescribe the powers that may be exercised by administrative

[1] The UCC has been adopted at least in part in every state. The UCC also has been adopted in the Virgin Islands and for the District of Columbia.

agencies, the principles that guide the agencies in exercising those powers, and the legal remedies available to those who want to question the legality of some administrative action.

Administrative agencies may be given practically the same power to make law as the legislature and almost the same power to decide cases as the courts. However, agencies are created by laws and have the power to enact law only if that power has been delegated to them by the legislature.

The president of the United States with the consent of the Senate appoints the heads of federal administrative agencies. The governor appoints heads of state administrative agencies. Administrative agencies are given wide latitude in setting up rules of procedure. They issue orders and decrees that have the force of law unless set aside by the courts after being challenged. If an agency rule conflicts with a statute, the statute takes precedence.

Facts: Herbert Brooks who had served as an apprentice for 21 months, applied to take the funeral director licensing exam. The law setting the qualifications for a funeral director required a person to have completed 12 months as an apprentice. The state board that licensed funeral directors promulgated a rule that required a person to serve 24 months as an apprentice, so the board denied Brooks' application. Brooks appealed the denial.

Outcome: The court said that the agency's rule was in irreconcilable conflict with the law and was therefore void and unenforceable.

Civil Versus Criminal Law

LO4
Distinguish among crimes, torts, ethics

Civil Law
Law dealing with enforcement or protection of private rights

Criminal Law
Law dealing with offenses against society

Crime
Offense against society

Prosecutor or District Attorney
Government employee who brings criminal actions

Felony
A more serious crime

Misdemeanor
A less serious crime

Law may be classified as either civil or criminal law. A person may file a lawsuit in order to enforce or protect a private right by requesting compensation for damage suffered or other action for restoration of his or her property. This action in **civil law** is concerned with private or purely personal rights.

Criminal law is that branch of the law dealing with crimes and the punishment of wrongdoers. A **crime** is an offense that tends to injure society as a whole. A criminal action differs from a civil action in that an employee of the government—usually called the **prosecutor** or **district attorney**—brings a criminal action. The standard of proof required is greater than in a civil case. A person can be convicted of a crime only if proven guilty "beyond a reasonable doubt." If a person accused of a crime is subject to the penalty of imprisonment, the accused has a right to an attorney even if he or she cannot pay for one. In addition, the constitutional prohibition against double jeopardy means that a person can only be tried for a crime once. This protection is not absolute since it allows for retrial, for example, if a conviction is overturned or if there is no decision in a first trial.

Crimes are usually classified, according to the nature of the punishment, as felonies or misdemeanors. Generally speaking, **felonies** are the more serious crimes and are usually punishable by death or by imprisonment in a penitentiary for more than one year. **Misdemeanors** are offenses of a less serious character and are punishable by a fine or imprisonment in a county or local jail. Committing a forgery is a felony, but driving an automobile in excess of the speed limit is a misdemeanor. The criminal statutes define the acts that are felonies and those that are misdemeanors. Criminal statutes vary somewhat from state to state.

Tort Law

Tort
Private wrong for which damages may be recovered

Negligence
Failure to exercise reasonable care

A **tort** is a private or civil wrong or injury for which there may be an action for damages. A tort may be intentional or it may be caused by negligence. **Negligence** is the failure to exercise reasonable care toward someone. It is tort law that allows an innocent motorist who is the victim of a careless or negligent driver to sue the negligent driver for damages. Other torts include fraud, trespass, assault, slander, and interference with contracts. A tort action must be brought by the injured person against the person alleged to be negligent.

Ethics

This chapter has discussed the basis for laws. One of the most important ideas mentioned is that "laws are the result of society's changing concepts of what is right and what is wrong." That means laws are based on our judgment regarding what human conduct is right, and therefore should be encouraged, and what conduct is wrong, and therefore should be discouraged. We thus base our laws on our morals. Those principles that help a person determine the morality of conduct, its motives, and its duties are called our **ethics**.

Ethics
Principles that determine the morality of conduct, its motives, and its duties

BASES FOR ETHICAL JUDGMENT

Everyone has opinions on what behavior and thinking is right and what is wrong, basing these ethical judgments on personal values. We develop our values from our religious beliefs, our experience, our cultural background, and our scientific knowledge. Since people have differing backgrounds, our judgments as to what is right and wrong vary somewhat.

ETHICAL PRINCIPLES

In considering how ethics relates to the law, several principles regarding the application of ethics emerge. These principles include:

1 Seriousness of consequences
2 Consensus of the majority
3 Change in ethical standards

Seriousness of Consequences. Although law is based on what we believe is right and wrong, our laws do not reflect everything we believe is right or wrong. When unethical behavior can harm others—when the matter is of serious consequence to people—laws are usually enacted to regulate that behavior. Less serious matters can be considered wrong, but laws do not address them. For example, rules of etiquette frequently reflect our ethical judgments about behavior, but they do not have serious enough consequences that we pass laws to enforce them.

Consensus of the Majority. Our laws cannot express every individual's ethical principles since everyone does not agree on what is moral. There may be no law reflecting a judgment on a particular matter, or the laws might reflect the judgment of some. For example, vegetarians and nondrinkers may not believe laws permitting the eating of meat or the consumption of alcoholic beverages are ethical. Their morality may not be reflected in law. In a democratic society such as ours, the laws are designed to reflect the ethical view of the majority.

Change in Ethical Standards. Ethical standards change over time. Behavior believed ethical in the past becomes unethical, and behavior previously viewed as immoral becomes acceptable. Consider the matter of cigarette smoking on airplanes. Many years ago airline passengers could smoke no matter where they were seated. Then the law mandated smoking and nonsmoking sections on planes. Now all commercial airlines in the United States prohibit smoking in all sections and the federal government uses the force of law to enforce this rule. This change in government rules reflects the change in the view of most people about the harmful effects of cigarette smoking. Our ethical standards have changed and this is reflected in the law.

BUSINESS ETHICS

Our ethical standards apply to every aspect of life. For businesspeople, this means that ethical standards help determine their business practices. In our competitive economic system, the standard people in business have been expected to follow in determining behavior is "the bottom line." Is the behavior something that will help the business financially? When studying ethics as applied to business, we ask, does a business have obligations other than simply to make a profit or maximize "the bottom line"?

Many types of businesses or professional organizations have adopted codes of ethics to guide the behavior of their members. Variety occurs not only in the types of business that have adopted such codes, but also in the impact of the codes on business. Some codes are legally enforceable, technically making them laws, not ethical rules. Other codes are strictly voluntary and are thus truly rules of ethics.

Legally Enforceable. A number of professions have codes of ethics, usually called *codes of professional responsibility,* which when violated provide the basis for penalties against members of the profession. For example, the American Bar Association has produced a model code and model rules for ethical behavior by lawyers. Although these particular models have not been adopted by every state, each state has adopted an ethical code for lawyers. A violation of legal ethics subjects a lawyer to discipline including suspension from practicing law or even disbarment.

Voluntary. Some businesses have adopted codes of ethics for themselves as guides for individuals employed in these businesses. Since government has not imposed the codes, they do not carry legal penalties for violation. The codes recognize that ethical business conduct is a higher standard than that required by law and encourage behavior that is fair, honest, and, if disclosed, not embarrassing to the individual or the business.

Questions

1. What is the difference between a rule and a law?
2. What is the consequence of the breach of a rule of law?
3. Explain what common law and equity are and how they differ.
4. Why are we justified in classifying law by judicial decision as a source of law? What are three other sources of law?
5. What is the supreme law of the land? What does that mean about other laws?
6. How does the enactment of statutes differ from the issuance of administrative agency orders?

7 Classify the following crimes into felonies or misdemeanors: murder, theft of one dollar, drunkenness, robbery, overtime parking, forgery.
8 Distinguish crimes from torts in as many aspects as possible.
9 Are all persons' ethical judgments the same? Why or why not?
10 If law is based on ethics, explain whether this means that everything unethical is illegal.

Internet Resources for Business Law

Name	Resources	Web Address
'Lectric Law Library's Lawcopedia	The Lawcopedia's 'Lectric Legal Lexicon defines legal words, terms, and phrases.	http://www.lectlaw.com/ref.html
FedLaw	FedLaw, maintained by the U.S. General Services Administration (GSA), includes federal laws and regulations.	http://www.legal.gsa.gov/
WashLaw WEB	StateLaw, maintained by the Washburn School of Law, provides links for state legislative and governmental information—including court cases and statutes—as well as local information.	http://www.washlaw.edu
West's Legal Directory	West's Legal Directory, updated daily, offers over 800,000 profiles of lawyers and law firms in the United States and Canada, including international offices.	http://www.lawoffice.com
De Paul University Institute for Business and Professional Ethics	The De Paul University Institute for Business and Professional Ethics maintains materials on ethics, including articles, professional papers, an online journal, and book reviews.	http://condor.depaul.edu/ethics/
Ethics Updates	Ethics Updates provides updates on current ethics literature, both popular and professional.	http://ethics.acusd.edu/index.html
Institute for Global Ethics	The Institute for Global Ethics, an independent, nonsectarian, and nonpolitical organization, provides general resources on ethics.	http://www.globalethics.org/
Corporate Conduct Quarterly (CCQ)	CCQ provides news concerning corporate ethics and compliance, as well as information on conferences, major decisions, and changes in the field.	http://camden-www.rutgers.edu/~ccq/

2

Courts and Court Procedure

Learning Objectives

1 Explain the function of the courts.

2 Explain the relationships of the various courts in our society.

3 Describe the procedure for filing a lawsuit.

4 Describe the basic procedure for a jury trial.

Each state has two distinct court systems—federal courts and state courts. Federal courts are part of the federal government headquartered in Washington, D.C. There are 50 different state court systems, each part of a state government headquartered at its state capital. Although the federal and state court systems are largely independent of each other, they have similar functions.

Function of the Courts

LO1 Function of courts

A court declares and applies judicial precedents, or case law, and applies laws passed by the legislative arm of the government. This is not the whole story, however. Constitutions by their very nature must be couched in generalities. Statutes are less general than constitutions; however, they could not possibly be worded to apply to every situation that may arise. Thus, the chief function of the courts is to interpret and apply the law from whatever source to a given situation. For example, the U.S. Constitution gives Congress power to regulate commerce "among the several states." This is the power to regulate interstate commerce. Under this power Congress passes a law requiring safety devices on trains. If the law is challenged, the court must decide whether this is a regulation of interstate commerce.

Similarly, an act of Congress regulates minimum wages for the vast majority of workers. A case may arise as to whether this applies to the wages paid in a sawmill located in a rural section of the country. The court must decide whether or not the sawmill owner engages in interstate commerce. The court's decision may become a judicial precedent that will be followed in the future unless the court changes its decision in a subsequent case.

Jurisdiction of Courts

Jurisdiction
Authority of a court to hear a case

The power or authority of a court to hear cases is called its **jurisdiction**. Courts must have jurisdiction over the subject matter of the case and jurisdiction over the persons involved. If a claim is made for damages due to an automobile accident, a probate court does not have jurisdiction over the subject matter since a probate court deals with wills and the distribution of deceased persons' property. The damage action would have to be brought in a court of general jurisdiction. A court may have jurisdiction over the subject matter but not over the person. If a resident of Ohio is charged with trespassing on a neighbor's property in the same state, a court in Indiana does not have jurisdiction over the person of the accused. Nor does a court in Ohio have jurisdiction over the person of the accused if the accused has not been properly served with notice of the trial. Before any court can try a case, it must be established that the court has jurisdiction over both the subject matter and the person in the case at issue.

Classification of Courts

LO2
Relationships of various courts

Courts are classified for the purpose of determining their jurisdiction. This classification can be made in a variety of ways. One classification can be made according to the governmental unit setting up the court. Under this classification system, courts are divided into (1) federal courts, (2) state courts, and (3) municipal courts.

Trial Court
Court that conducts original trial of a case

Appellate Court
Court that reviews decision of another court

The same courts may be classified according to the method of hearing cases. Under this system they are classified as trial courts and appellate courts. **Trial courts** conduct the original trial of cases. **Appellate courts** review cases appealed from the decisions of lower courts. A losing party appeals to the higher court to review the lower court's decision by claiming the lower court made a mistake that caused the party to lose. Appellate courts include courts of appeals and supreme courts. Appellate courts exercise considerable authority over the courts under them. Lower courts are bound by the decisions of their appellate courts.

FEDERAL COURTS

The federal courts have exclusive jurisdiction over bankruptcy matters, claims against the United States, and patent and copyright cases. Federal courts (see Illustration 2-1) include:

1. Special federal courts
2. Federal district courts
3. Federal courts of appeals
4. United States Supreme Court

Special Federal Courts
Federal trial courts with limited jurisdiction

Special Federal Courts. The **special federal courts** are limited in their jurisdiction by the laws of Congress creating them. For example, the Court of International Trade hears cases involving the rates of duty on various classes of imported goods, the collection of the revenues, and similar controversies. The U.S. Court of Federal Claims hears cases involving claims against the U.S. government. The Tax Court hears only cases involving tax controversies. Bankruptcy courts decide bankruptcy cases. Most bankruptcy appeals are to a three-judge appellate panel of bankruptcy judges.

Illustration 2-1 The Federal Court System

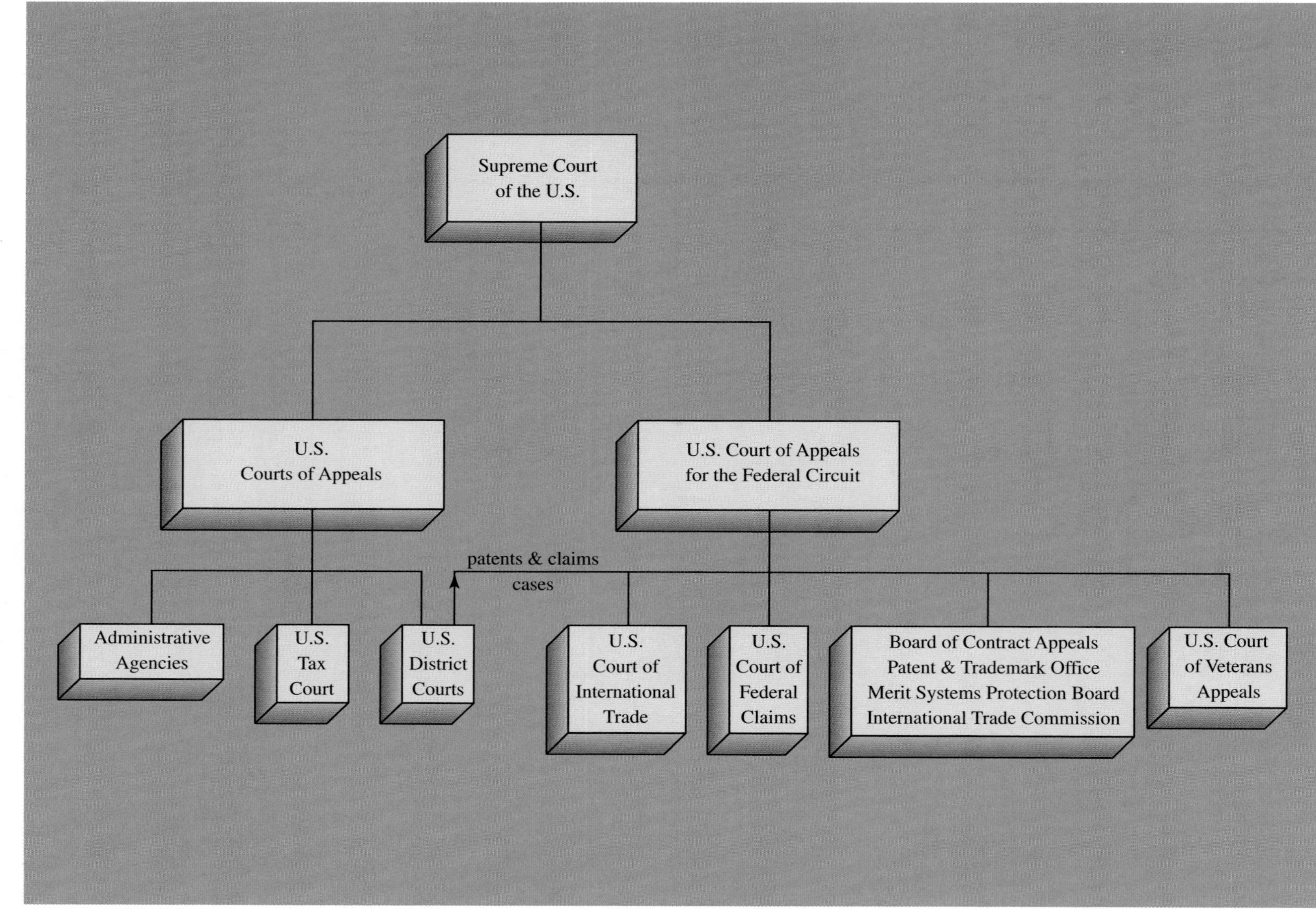

Federal District Court
Trial court of federal court system

Diversity Jurisdiction
Federal jurisdiction based on parties being from different states

Federal District Courts. By far the largest class of federal courts consists of the almost 100 **federal district courts**. These courts are strictly trial courts in which all criminal cases involving a violation of the federal law are tried. The district courts also have jurisdiction over civil suits that: (1) are brought by the United States; (2) arise under the U.S. Constitution, federal laws, or treaties; or (3) are brought by citizens of different states—called **diversity jurisdiction**—or between citizens of one state and a foreign nation or one of its citizens where the amount in controversy is $75,000 or more.

Facts: Arkoma Associates (Arkoma), a limited partnership, sued two Louisiana citizens in a federal district court relying on diversity jurisdiction. The defendants asked the court to dismiss the action because one of Arkoma's limited partners was also a citizen of Louisiana and therefore there was not complete diversity between the defendants and all the plaintiffs.

Outcome: The court held that diversity jurisdiction in a suit by an entity is determined by the citizenship of all its members. Therefore the federal district court lacked jurisdiction.

Federal Court of Appeals
Court that hears appeals in federal court system

Federal Courts of Appeals. The United States is divided geographically into 12 federal judicial circuits. Each circuit has a **court of appeals**, which hears appeals from cases arising in its circuit. The federal courts of appeals hear appeals from federal district courts and from federal administrative agencies and departments. A decision of a federal court of appeals is binding upon all lower courts within the jurisdiction of that circuit.

It is possible that one court of appeals could decide an issue one way and another court of appeals could decide it in another way. Because the lower courts within each court of appeals' jurisdiction must follow the decision of its court of appeals, courts in different circuits might decide similar cases differently. When this occurs, there is a conflict between the circuits. The conflict lasts until one circuit changes its decision or the U.S. Supreme Court rules on the issue.

There is also another court of appeals called the Court of Appeals for the Federal Circuit. It reviews decisions of special federal courts (such as the Court of International Trade and the U.S. Court of Federal Claims), decisions of four administrative agencies, and appeals from district courts in patent and claims cases.

Supreme Court of the United States
The highest court in the United States

United States Supreme Court. The **Supreme Court of the United States** has original jurisdiction in cases affecting ambassadors, public ministers, and consuls, and in cases in which a state is a party. It has appellate jurisdiction in cases based on the U.S. Constitution, a federal law, or a treaty.

The majority of cases heard by the U.S. Supreme Court are cases appealed from the federal courts of appeals. Under certain circumstances a decision of a federal district court may be appealed directly to the Supreme Court. A state supreme court decision may also be reviewed by the U.S. Supreme Court if the case involves a federal constitutional question or if a federal law or treaty has been held invalid by the state court. Unlike the courts of appeals, the Supreme Court does not have to take all cases appealed. It chooses which appealed cases it will hear.

Writ of Certiorari
Order to produce record of a case

The normal way a case gets to the Supreme Court is by application for a **writ of certiorari**. The party asking for the Supreme Court review of a case asks the court to issue a writ of certiorari, which requires the lower court that has decided the case to produce the record of the case for the Supreme Court's review. The court issues a writ for only a small number of the requests.

The U.S. Supreme Court is the highest tribunal in the land, and its decisions are binding on all other courts. Its decisions are final until the Court reverses its own decision or until the effect of a given decision is changed by a constitutional amendment or an enactment by Congress.

The Constitution created the Supreme Court and gave Congress the power to establish inferior courts.

STATE COURTS

State courts (see Illustration 2-2) can best be classified into the following groups:

1 Inferior courts
2 Courts of original general jurisdiction
3 Appellate courts
4 Special courts

Illustration 2-2 Typical State Court System

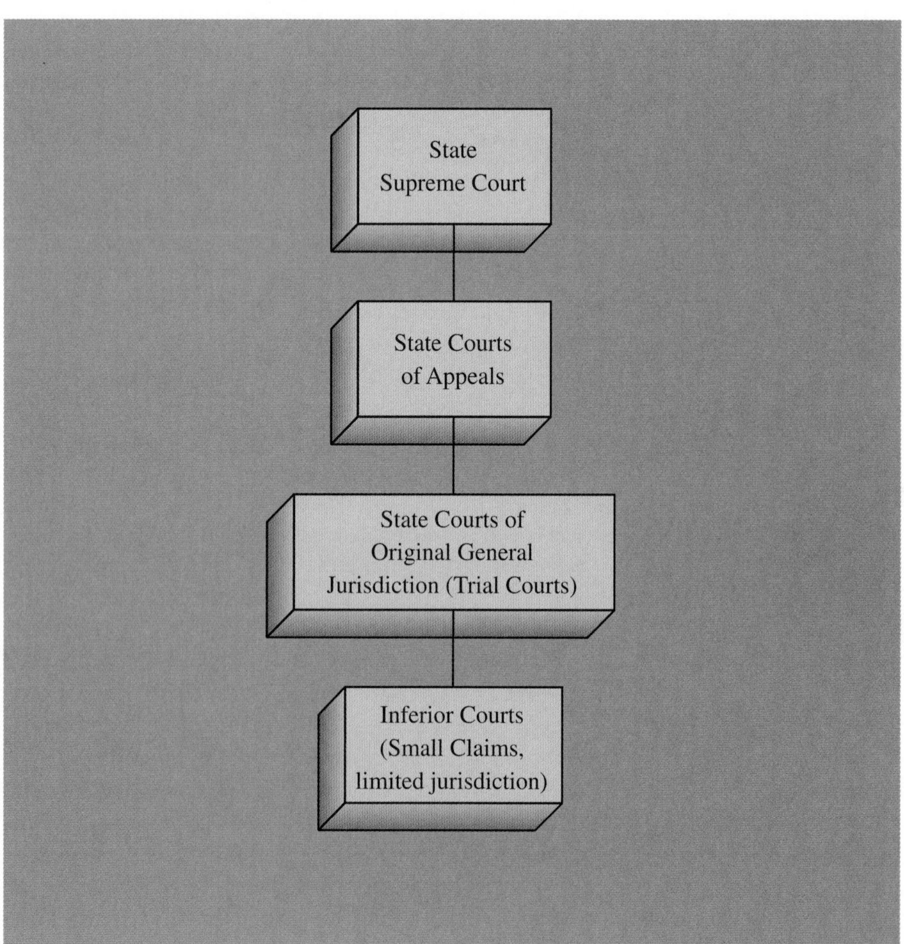

Inferior Courts
Trial courts that hear only cases involving minor offenses and disputes

Inferior Courts. Most states have **inferior courts** that hear cases involving minor criminal offenses and minor disputes between citizens. The names of inferior courts vary greatly from state to state. These courts are most frequently called district, magistrate, county, municipal, small claims, justice, or even taxi courts. Some states have more than one of these named courts. Civil jurisdiction is limited to controversies involving a maximum amount of money, which generally varies from $1,000 to $25,000, or to a particular type of controversy. In addition, these courts may try all criminal cases involving misdemeanors. The loser in any of these courts may normally appeal to a court of original general jurisdiction.

Courts of Original General Jurisdiction
Court of record in which case is first tried

Courts of Original General Jurisdiction. Courts of original general jurisdiction are the most important courts of the state for the average citizen. These courts have broad jurisdiction over disputes between two or more parties as well as criminal offenses against the state. They are called **courts of original general jurisdiction** because the case is first instituted in them. On occasion they hear appeals from inferior courts, but this does not make them true appellate bodies because the entire case is retried at this level. Thus, such an appeal is actually treated as a case of original jurisdiction. These courts are also called trial courts, because they hear witnesses, receive evidence, and try the case.

Court of Record
Court in which an official record of the proceedings is kept

An official, permanent record is kept of the trial showing the testimony, evidence, statements of counsel and the judge, the judgment, and the findings of the court. For this reason these courts are referred to as **courts of record**. The official name of such a court of original general jurisdiction varies from state to state, but in almost every state is one of the following: circuit court, district court, or Superior Court.[1]

State Courts of Appeals
Intermediate appellate courts

State Supreme Court
Highest court in most states

Appellate Courts. All states provide for an appeal to an appellate court by the party dissatisfied with the final judgment of the trial court or any of its rulings and instructions. Most states have a system of intermediate appellate courts usually called **courts of appeals**, as well as one final appellate court. Decisions of the appellate courts bind lower courts. The **state supreme court** is usually the highest appellate court of a state.

Facts: Robert and Margaret Rohde had an insurance policy that protected against loss from vandalism or malicious mischief. A motor was damaged when stored oil used to service it was contaminated with water. In county court, the Rohdes sued their insurance carrier, Farmers Alliance Mutual, when it denied coverage for the damage under the vandalism and malicious mischief coverage.

Outcome: The court found in favor of Farmers, saying the Rohdes had not proved their case. The Rohdes appealed to the district court. The district court found for the Rohdes, so Farmers appealed to the court of appeals. The court of appeals dismissed the case and Farmers appealed to the state supreme court. After the three appeals, the highest court found the Rohdes had proven their case.

Probate Court
Court that handles estates

Juvenile Court
Court that handles delinquent, dependent, and neglected children

Special Courts. Many states have additional special courts, such as **probate courts** that handle wills and estates; **juvenile courts** that are concerned with delinquent, dependent, and neglected children; and **domestic relations courts** that handle divorce and child custody cases. These are not courts of general jurisdiction, but of special jurisdiction. In some states these courts are on the same level as the

[1] In New York this court is known as a Supreme Court, and in Ohio it is known as a Court of Common Pleas.

Domestic Relations Court
Court that handles divorce and related cases

trial courts. When this is the case, they are properly called *trial courts* and are courts of record. In other states they are on the same level as the inferior courts and are not courts of record.

Court Officers

Judge, Justice of the Peace, Magistrate, or Trial Justice
Chief officer of court

Sheriff
Court of record executive officer

Marshal
Executive officer of federal court

Lawyers or Attorneys
Persons licensed to represent others in court

The chief officer of an inferior court is the **judge, justice of the peace, magistrate, trial justice**, or similar officer. The executive officer is the constable or bailiff. In a state court of record the chief officer is the judge, the executive officer is the **sheriff**, and the recorder is the clerk of the court. These titles are the same in the federal courts except that the executive officer is called a **marshal**.

Persons educated in the profession of the law and licensed to practice law, which means they may represent others in legal matters, are known as **lawyers** or **attorneys**. They are officers of the court and are subject to punishment for a breach of duty. Lawyers ordinarily represent the parties in a civil or a criminal action, although many states permit the parties to represent themselves. The practice of presenting one's own case, however, is usually not advisable.

Procedure in Courts of Record

Procedural Law
Law specifying how actions are filed and what trial procedure to follow

Procedural laws are laws that specify how parties are to go forward with filing civil actions and how these actions are to be tried. They must be followed if the parties wish to have the case settled by a court.

FILING SUIT IN A CIVIL ACTION

LO3
Lawsuit procedure

Complaint or Petition
Written request to a court to settle a dispute

Plaintiff
Person who begins a civil lawsuit

Defendant
Person against whom a case is filed

Summons or Process
Notice of suit

Answer or Motion
Response of defendant to a complaint

Discovery
Means of obtaining information from other party before a trial

With few exceptions, courts are powerless to settle disputes between individuals unless one of the parties so requests the court. The written request, called a **complaint** or **petition**, begins a civil suit. The individual who institutes a civil action is called the **plaintiff**, and the individual against whom action is brought is called the **defendant**. The order of events in bringing an action is generally as follows:

1. *Filing suit.* The complaint or petition is filed with the clerk of the court. This petition sets forth the jurisdiction of the court, the nature of the claim, and the remedy sought.
2. *Notice of suit.* As soon as the petition is filed, the clerk issues a **summons** or, as it is sometimes called, a **process**. This gives the defendant notice of the complaint and informs the defendant of the time in which to respond.
3. *Response.* The defendant has a specified number of days available in which to file an **answer** or a **motion**. The answer admits or denies the facts alleged in the complaint. A motion is an application to the judge for an order requiring an act be done in favor of the moving party. The complaint and answer constitute the first pleadings.
4. *Discovery.* To obtain information relevant to the subject matter of the action, the parties may request unprivileged information from another party in a number of ways, called **discovery**, including:

a. Interrogatories: Written questions to be answered in writing.
b. Deposition: Examination of a party or potential witness outside court and under oath.
c. Admissions: Requests to agree that a certain fact is true or a matter of law is decided.
d. Medical examination by a physician.
e. Access to real and personal property.

If a court issues an order compelling discovery, failure to comply can result in punishment. The party who does not comply may be found in contempt of court or the judge may dismiss the case.

The parties may take other actions after a case has been instituted and before it goes to trial. A party may file a wide variety of motions, including a motion to dismiss the case, a motion for a judgment based solely on the pleadings, and a motion to obtain a ruling on the admissibility of certain evidence or to suppress evidence prior to trial.

5 *Fact finding.* If disagreements occur about facts of the case, a jury may be impaneled to decide these facts. If neither party requests a jury, the case may be tried before a judge alone, who would act as both judge and jury.

LO4 Jury trial procedure

TRIAL PROCEDURE

A typical jury trial proceeds in the following order:

1 The jury is selected and sworn in.
2 The attorney for the plaintiff makes an opening statement to the jury indicating the nature of the action and what the plaintiff expects to prove. This is usually followed by the defendant's attorney's opening statement.
3 The plaintiff presents evidence in the form of testimony of witnesses and exhibits designed to prove the allegations made in the plaintiff's petition. The plaintiff has the burden of proving facts adequate to support the petition's allegations. If this burden is not met, the case can be dismissed and the lawsuit ends. The plaintiff's evidence is followed by the defendant's evidence. The defendant tries to disprove the plaintiff's allegations. The defendant may also present evidence excusing the behavior complained of by the plaintiff.
4 The attorneys for each side summarize the evidence and argue their points in an attempt to win the jury to their version of the case.
5 The judge instructs the jury as to the points of law that govern the case. The judge has the sole power to determine the points of law, and the jury decides what weight is to be given to each point of evidence.
6 The jury adjourns to the jury room and in secret arrives at its decision, called the **verdict**. This verdict may be set aside by the court if it is contrary to the law and the evidence. Unless this is done, the judge enters a judgment in accordance with the verdict.

Verdict
Decision of a jury

APPEALS

If either the plaintiff or the defendant is dissatisfied with the judgment and can cite an error of law by the court, an appeal generally may be taken to a higher court. When an appeal is taken, a complete transcript or written record of the trial is given to the appellate court. Rather than hear testimony from witnesses, the appellate court reviews the entire proceedings from the transcript. The attorney for each side files a brief, setting forth the reasons that warrant the appellate court to either affirm or reverse the judgment of the lower court. The decision of the appellate court becomes judicial precedent and is binding upon lower courts. The appellate court may, however, reverse itself in a future case, although this seldom occurs.

Procedure in Small Claims Court

Filing and trying a suit in an inferior court like a small claims court is a much simpler matter than filing and trying a suit in a court of record. A form for the complaint may be obtained from the court and filled out by the plaintiff without help from a lawyer. Frequently court employees will assist in filling out the forms. The defendant is then served with the complaint.

When the case is tried, the procedure is much more informal than in a court of record. The case is tried by a judge, so there is no jury. Since neither party has to be represented by an attorney, and in some courts may not be so represented, the judge asks the parties to state their positions. Witnesses and evidence may be presented, but the questioning is more informal. The judge is likely to ask questions in order to assist in ascertaining the facts. The judge then renders the verdict and judgment of the court. Normally, either party may appeal the judgment to a court of record, in which case the matter is retried there.

Questions

1. What is the function of a court?
2. What types of jurisdiction must a court have in order to hear a case?
3. What must a losing party claim in order to appeal to a higher court?
4. Is it ever possible for cases involving the same issue to be decided differently in different courts of a court system? Explain.
5. Name the court in which the following disputes would be settled:
   a. A claim for an unpaid bill of $100
   b. A dispute between divorced parents about the custody of their child
   c. A damage suit for $2,500
   d. An appeal from a judgment
   e. A case involving the tariff on imported caviar
   f. An allegation that a child has been neglected
6. Who are the officers of
   a. An inferior court?
   b. A state court of record?
   c. A federal court?
7. a. What is the purpose of a summons?
   b. When sued, how must the defendant proceed?
8. In what ways may a party to a lawsuit request unprivileged information from the other party?
9. Which party has the burden of proof and how are allegations proved in court?
10. How does trying a case in a small claims court differ from trying a case in a court of record?

Internet Resources for Business Law

Name	Resources	Web Address
U.S. Federal Judiciary	The U.S. Federal Judiciary site, maintained by the Administrative Office of the U.S. Courts, provides a clearinghouse for information from and about the judicial branch of the U.S. government.	http://www.uscourts.gov/
Local Government	LII, maintained by Cornell Law School, provides links to a variety of local government sites.	http://www.law.cornell.edu/topics/state_statutes.html#government_local
'Lectric Law Library	'Lectric Law Library provides links and materials for legal research, news, and professional activities.	http://www.lectlaw.com/rotu.html
West's Legal Directory	West's Legal Directory, updated daily, offers over 800,000 profiles of lawyers and law firms in the United States and Canada, including international offices.	http://www.lawoffice.com
Trial Behavior Consulting, Incorporated	Trial Behavior Consulting, Incorporated, provides mock trials, case strategy, *voir dire* questions, community surveys, focus groups, witness preparation, and jury selection, among other services.	http://www.trialbehavior.com
Federal Rules of Civil Procedure (1996)	LII, maintained by the Cornell Law School, provides the Federal Rules of Civil Procedure in a hypertext and searchable format.	http://www.law.cornell.edu/rules/frcp/overview.htm

3 Business Torts and Crimes

Learning Objectives

1 Discuss the basis for intentional and negligent tort liability.

2 List and explain the generally recognized business torts.

3 Explain what business crimes are.

4 Describe what computer crimes are and the three types that affect business.

PREVIEW CASE

At a supermarket, a police officer observed Victor Balboni remove two cartons of cigarettes from their rack and place them in an opened bag in his shopping cart. Balboni then put more cartons of cigarettes in the opened bag. The officer walked down the aisle to Balboni's shopping cart and looked into the bag. He saw several cartons of cigarettes in it. The officer arrested Balboni since state law specified that concealing merchandise with the intention of depriving the merchant of its use without payment constituted shoplifting. Balboni was searched and found to have no money. Is he guilty of shoplifting? Do you think he intended to pay for the cigarettes?

How do businesses relate to society and to other businesses? Can the activity of a business unfairly damage another business or even violate a criminal law? With some variations from state to state, courts have found some activities by businesses and some activities against businesses actionable.

Torts

LO1 Basis for tort liability

Chapter 1 defined a tort as a private wrong or injury. The law permits people to sue for injuries caused by the intentional or negligent acts of others. The person who causes the injury is called a **tortfeasor**.

Tortfeasor
Person whose action causes injury

INTENTIONAL TORTS

To recover for an intentional tort, the injured person must show three things:

1. An act by the defendant,
2. An intention to cause the consequences of the act, and
3. Causation—the injury was caused by the defendant's act or something set in motion by the act.

Intentional torts include such actions as assault, battery, trespass, and false imprisonment. Although a business could be involved in these torts, parties involved in these types of cases come from every sector of the community.

Facts: Sears, Roebuck employed Lynn Malanga in the candy department. Sears knew that it had lost merchandise in the department. During Malanga's regular business hours in familiar surroundings, the store manager questioned her about her involvement in a theft ring. Malanga sued Sears for false imprisonment. The manager's act of questioning Malanga was clearly intentional, so Malanga claimed there had been an intentional tort.

Outcome: Since Malanga had not been confined, there was no false imprisonment.

NEGLIGENCE TORTS

To recover for a tort based on negligence, the injured party must show:

1. A duty of the tortfeasor,
2. Breach of that duty,
3. The breach was the actual and proximate cause of the injury, and
4. Injury or damage.

A person may recover in tort for negligence whenever these four elements occur. Courts frequently hear such cases involving automobile accidents, medical malpractice, injuries from products, and injuries resulting from the condition of a landowner's property.

BUSINESS TORTS

LO2
General business torts

The type of tort caused by a business or involving a business is a **business tort**. Businesses become involved in a tort action in several common ways.

Business Tort
Tort caused by or involving a business

Product Liability. Manufacturers of products incur potential liability in tort for injuries caused by the products. A person injured through the use or condition of a product could sue on the basis of the manufacturer's negligence in the preparation or manufacture of the article. The plaintiff must go (figuratively) into the defendant's plant or factory, learn how the article was made, and prove negligence. Unless the plaintiff can show negligence in the design of the manufacturer's product or the general method of manufacture, it is unlikely the plaintiff will be able to prove negligence.

Facts: An overhead guard on a forklift fell and hit John Harper on the head. Harper sued Clark Equipment Co., the manufacturer of the forklift, for negligence in its design. Experts testified that the guard met all the industry standards. It had been tested at the equivalent of 10,000 hours of use for endurance and passed.

Outcome: The court said Harper had not shown negligence in the design so he could not recover.

Whenever a manufacturer, as a reasonable person, should foresee that a particular class of persons would be injured by the product, the manufacturer is liable to an injured member of that class without regard to whether such member purchased from the manufacturer or from anyone else.

Strict Tort Liability Manufacturer of product liable without proof of negligence for dangerous product

The difficulty of proving negligence has helped lead the courts to expand a doctrine called **strict tort liability**. This doctrine makes a manufacturer liable without proof of negligence. It applies to anyone injured because of a defect in the manufacture of a product when such defect makes the use of the product dangerous to the user or persons in the vicinity of the product. The person injured or killed must be a user or person in the vicinity.

Business Activity. Several other business activities have been widely recognized as tortious. They are intentional torts and may be based on state law, federal law, or the common law. While some variation exists among the states, an injured party may recover damages on the basis of conduct that causes two general types of harm:

1 Interference with a contract or economic advantage
2 Confusion about a product

Interference with a Contract or Economic Advantage

Although contracts are not discussed until Chapter 5, the tort of interference with a contract or economic advantage basically occurs when a business relationship has been formed and in some way a third party causes one party to break up that business relationship. If injured, the other party to the business relationship may have a cause of action against the party causing the breakup. This tort could also be the result of unjustified interference with a person's reasonable expectation of future economic advantage.

Traditionally, proof of this tort only required a showing that the defendant knowingly interfered with a business relationship. However, more and more states require that the intentional interference be improper. Improper interference can occur because of an improper motive, an improper means, or by acting other than in the legitimate exercise of the defendant's own rights. A defendant who protects its economic or safety interests or asserts an honest claim is not acting improperly.

In a free market economy, competitors inevitably injure one another. Courts do not hold such injury tortious, even when intentional, if the action was taken to advance a person's economic interest and results from the competitive economic system.

However, if a person unjustifiably interferes with another's business relationship or reasonable expectation of future economic advantage, there is a tort. Interference with leasing opportunities, the opportunity of buying and selling goods or services, and interference with the hiring of employees are examples of the types of interference that can be actionable.

Facts: W. S. Leigh contracted to sell a furniture business to Richard Isom. The contract included a 10-year lease of a floor of the building housing the business. Leigh later wanted to sell the building, but could not because of the lease. Every week Leigh, his wife, and his bookkeeper harassed Isom at the store, sometimes in front of customers. This interrupted sales activities and caused customers to comment and complain, and even to leave the store. Leigh filed two groundless lawsuits against Isom, refused to pay his share of bills, and threatened to cancel the sale contract. Leigh sued to repossess the building and terminate the lease. Isom alleged intentional interference with prospective economic relations.

Outcome: The court said that by forcing Isom to defend groundless lawsuits, Leigh had employed an improper means to interfere with Isom's business. Isom recovered damages.

CONFUSION ABOUT A PRODUCT

A person may commit a tort by intentionally causing confusion about another's product. This could be done by making false statements about another's product or by representing goods or services as being the goods or services of someone else.

Injurious Falsehood
False statement of fact that degrades quality of another's goods or services

Communication
Telling a third person

Injurious Falsehood. When a person makes false statements of fact that degrade the quality of another's goods or services, the tort of **injurious falsehood** occurs. The false statement must be made to a third person. This is called **communication**. The hearer must understand the statement to refer to the plaintiff's goods or services and to degrade their quality. The injured party must also show the statement was a substantial element in causing damage. In some states the plaintiff must identify specific customers lost as a result of the statement.

Facts: In a book, Time-Life Books, Inc. reproduced Charles Atlas, Ltd.'s classic ad about a "97-pound weakling" who becomes a "real man" after using the Atlas exercise system. The caption above the reproduced ad described the Atlas system as isometric. The text of the book warned readers of the extreme dangers of isometric exercises. Atlas sued Time-Life alleging product disparagement.

Outcome: The court found that reading the caption in conjunction with the text, a reasonable reader could conclude that Atlas marketed an isometric exercise program, isometric exercises are dangerous, and therefore, Atlas' exercise program was dangerous. Time-Life falsely described the Atlas system as isometric, so Atlas stated a claim for injurious falsehood.

Finally, the statement must have been made maliciously. Malice can always be shown by proving that the statement was made as a result of ill will, spite, or hostility with the intention of causing harm to the plaintiff. In some jurisdictions, the plaintiff need only show that the false statement was made knowing it was false or with reckless disregard as to the truth or falsity of it.

Confusion of Source
Representing goods or services as those of another

Confusion of Source. The tort that occurs when a person attempts to represent goods or services as being the goods or services of someone else is **confusion of source**. The law assumes customers would be confused as to the source of the goods or services. Actual confusion need not be shown. This tort occurs from trade mark or trade name infringement or unfair competition.

http://
www.uspto.gov

Trademark
Word, symbol, device, or combination of them used to identify and distinguish goods

Trademarks. Federal law defines a **trademark** as a word, name, symbol, device, or any combination adopted and used by a person to identify and distinguish goods, including a unique product, from another's goods and to indicate the source of the goods. A trademark indicates that goods carrying that mark all come from one source. A trademark or trade name gives the owner the exclusive right to use a word or device to distinguish a product or a service (see Illustration 3-1 for a sample trademark violation letter form).

Not all words or symbols qualify for protection as trademarks. Only those marks used by a business in a way that identifies its goods or services and differentiates them from others are entitled to protection. The mark normally must be inherently distinctive, which means the mark is unique, arbitrary, and nondescriptive.

Secondary Meaning
Special meaning of a mark that distinguishes goods

A mark that is not so distinctive may be a trademark if it has acquired a **secondary meaning**. A secondary meaning is a special or trade meaning developed by usage that distinguishes the goods or services in such a way as to warrant trademark protection. A generic term can be protected if it has acquired a secondary meaning. If the right to trademark protection is based on the doctrine of secondary meaning, the geographical area of protection will be limited to the area in which the mark has such a secondary meaning.

Marks that are fanciful, arbitrary, or subtly suggest something about the product can be protected. Protected marks include words such as *Ivory* for soap, the letters *S* and *ECI,* abbreviations and nicknames such as *Coke,* made-up words such as *Exxon* and *Rolex,* and the shapes of packages and products. Generic terms such as *superglue* and *soft soap* cannot be trademarks.

A trademark may be registered or unregistered. A trademark registered under the federal trademark law provides the holder with all the rights and remedies of that law. The holder of an unregistered trademark also has some rights under the federal law and rights provided by the common law. Many states also have trademark laws; however, they vary greatly. In some states the holder of a mark may not get greater protection by registering than the common law affords an unregistered mark.

Trademark or Trade Name Infringement
Unauthorized use or imitation of another's mark or name

Trademark or **trade name infringement** is the unauthorized use or confusingly similar imitation of another person's mark or name. If the imitation is likely to cause confusion or mistake or deceive people, courts will halt use of the imitation. Courts examine a number of factors when deciding whether a likelihood of confusion between two marks exists. Although the various courts do not always use the same factors, those factors most commonly considered include:

1 The similarity of the two marks
2 The similarity of the products represented by the marks
3 The similarity of marketing and customers
4 The similarity and amount of advertising used
5 The area of overlapping use
6 The intent of the parties in adopting the marks
7 The strength of the marks
8 Actual confusion by the public

____
____
______________________, __ ______

November 1, 2000

S A M P L E

____
____
______________________, __ ______

Re: Trademark Violation

To Whom It May Concern:

I am the owner of rights to the mark which is described in the enclosed materials ("mark"). The mark has been registered with the U.S. Patent and Trademark Office, and United States Registration No. ________________ has been issued for the mark. A copy of the registration certificate is enclosed for your information.

I have just learned of your use of this mark, which is described in the enclosed materials. Specifically, your use of the mark is ______________________________. Your continued use is likely to cause confusion.

From the information that I have received regarding your use, my use of this mark has priority over yours based upon my earlier and continuous use, as well as the above federal registration. Therefore, your use is a violation of my rights.

I am demanding that you immediately stop using the mark described in the enclosed materials or any other name or mark confusingly similar. If you promptly contact me and provide written assurance that you have taken steps to discontinue such use, I will not pursue this matter further and will not assert any claim against you for money damages. You must provide me with an acceptable response before ______________ in order to avoid possible legal action against you.

Please contact me if you have any questions or need additional information.

Sincerely,

____

If you have the Quicken Business Lawyer program, open this document. Complete the form as if your company's trademark has been violated.

Now visit the U.S. Patent and Trademark Office and click on Patent & Trademark Depository Libraries, then on Trademark FAQs. What is a certification mark? What is a collective mark? A service mark? How are these different from a trademark? http://www.uspto.gov

Illustration 3-1

Sample Trademark Violation Letter

Facts: The denomination's board of directors disaffiliated the First Church of Christ, Scientist, Plainfield, New Jersey. The church added the word Independent before its former name. The board sued for an injunction to keep the church from using Christian Science or Church of Christ, Scientist, in relation to its church or reading room.

Outcome: The court said that the guidelines to determine the likelihood of confusion in reference to the sale of goods were equally applicable to religious associations. It said that the addition of the qualifying adjective independent to the name of a well-known prior organization was insufficient to avoid confusion. The injunction was granted.

However, the imitation of another's trademark is not always done to cause confusion and does not always lead to infringement. Where the imitation is for the purpose of jest or commentary, the parody is successful only when there is no confusion and therefore no infringement.

Facts: Jim Henson Productions planned to release a movie, "Muppet Treasure Island," which featured a wild boar puppet called *Spa'am.* Spa'am, the high priest of a tribe of wild boars that worshipped Miss Piggy, was intended to poke fun at the luncheon meat, SPAM. Henson also planned to market movie-related merchandise displaying the words *Muppet Treasure Island* with a likeness of Spa'am and the name *Spa'am.* Hormel Foods had a distinctive, widely recognized trademark on the name *SPAM* for its luncheon meat. Hormel also merchandised products featuring SPAM and sued for trademark infringement.

Outcome: In recognizing that the two marks were superficially similar, the court also found that the two marks would appear in very different contexts, be very dissimilar visually, and be used in different merchandising markets. Because the SPAM trademark was such a strong mark the court held there would be no confusion.

When infringement is a tort, rather than a crime, the holder of the trademark or name has the duty of bringing any legal action to stop the alleged infringement and recover damages.

Trademarks identify and distinguish tangible goods; service marks identify and distinguish services. However, the same legal principles govern trademark infringement and service mark infringement.

Trademark or Trade Name Dilution
Lessening the capacity of a famous mark to identify and distinguish goods

The owner of a trademark is protected from unauthorized use of the trademark even when confusion might not result. **Trademark** or **trade name dilution** is "the lessening of the capacity of a famous mark to identify and distinguish goods or services." This could be done either by what is called *blurring* or by tarnishing a trademark. Blurring means to diminish the selling power of a trademark by unauthorized use on noncompeting products. A blurring use would occur if someone produced McDonald's light bulbs or Chrysler tires, for example. Tarnishing a trademark occurs when the mark is used in a disparaging manner or on low-quality goods. The owner of a trademark or name may get an injunction against anyone's commercial use of the trademark or name.

Unfair Competition
Total impression of product results in confusion as to its origin

Unfair Competition. **Unfair competition** exists when the total impression a product gives to the consumer results in confusion as to the origin of the product. The

Facts: Intermatic Incorporated was the exclusive owner of the famous trade name *intermatic.* Dennis Toeppen operated an Internet service provider business. He registered 240 Internet domain names including *intermatic.com* without permission from anyone who had previously used the names registered. He hoped to sell companies the right to use domain names he had registered. At a Web page at intermatic.com he used a map of Champaign-Urbana, Illinois. When Intermatic could not register *intermatic.com* as its domain name, it asked Toeppen to give up the domain name. He refused, so Intermatic sued him for trade name dilution.

Outcome: The court held that Toeppen's registration lessened the ability of Intermatic to identify its goods on the Internet since it could not use its own name as its domain name. The Trademark Dilution Act protected Intermatic from having its federally registered trade name used as a domain name by Toeppen.

impression of a product includes its packaging, size, color, shape, design, wording, any decorative indicia, and name. When unfair competition is claimed, the total physical image conveyed by the product and its name are considered together.

Crimes

The news media report on crimes every day so everyone hears about murders, robberies, assaults, and break-ins. Some of these crimes involve businesses or businesspeople.

LO3
What business crimes are

BUSINESS CRIMES

Business Crimes
Crimes against a business or committed by using a business

Certain criminal offenses, such as arson, forgery, fraudulent conveyances, shoplifting, and embezzlement, closely relate to business activities. **Business crimes** are crimes committed against a business or in which the perpetrator uses a business to commit the crime.

Types of Business Crimes

The types of crimes committed by and against businesses appear to be limited only by the ingenuity of the human mind. Many include stealing or theft from the business. In this age of computers, wire transfers, and organized crime, the range of crime has been growing. Today, crimes affecting business include:

1. Theft
2. RICO cases
3. Computer crimes

Theft
Taking another's property without consent

Theft. **Theft** is the crime of stealing. It involves taking or appropriating another's property without the owner's consent and with the intention of depriving the owner of it. This definition includes taking and depriving another of property even when the thief initially obtains the property lawfully.

Some states use different terms to identify the various possible types of theft. As it relates to business, types of theft include such crimes as shoplifting, embezzlement, and larceny. The elements of each of these offenses differ somewhat from state to state, but the crimes generally consist of the following:

Shoplifting
Taking unpurchased goods from a store

1 **Shoplifting**: Taking possession of goods in a store with the intent to use as the taker's own without paying the purchase price. In some states, merely concealing unpurchased goods while in a store constitutes shoplifting. The intent required for shoplifting is the intent to use the property as the taker's. This crime must be committed in a store by taking store merchandise, so it is always a business crime.

PREVIEW CASE REVISITED

Facts: At a supermarket, a police officer observed Victor Balboni remove two cartons of cigarettes from their rack and place them in an opened bag in his shopping cart. Balboni then put more cartons of cigarettes in the opened bag. The officer walked down the aisle to Balboni's shopping cart and looked into the bag. He saw several cartons of cigarettes in it. The officer arrested Balboni since state law specified that concealing merchandise with the intention of depriving the merchant of its use without payment constituted shoplifting. Balboni was searched and found to have no money.

Outcome: The court held that he was guilty of shoplifting because he concealed the cartons and had no money to pay for them.

Embezzlement
Fraudulent conversion of property lawfully possessed

2 **Embezzlement**: Fraudulent conversion of another's property by someone in lawful possession of the property. Embezzlement requires the intent to defraud the owner of the property. Conversion here means that the defendant handles the property inconsistently with the arrangement by which he or she has possession of it. Since many businesses rely on employees to receive payments and make disbursements, embezzlement is often a crime against a business.

Facts: Gailon A. Joy owned Credit Management Services Corp. (CMS), a debt-collection agency. When CMS made a collection, it would deposit the money in a bank in Barre. CMS also had its own separate account. However, CMS began transferring funds from the Barre account to its own account to cover its expenses. CMS received a collection for Stacey Fuel and Lumber Co., but never even told Stacey the money had been collected. A year later, CMS filed for bankruptcy. The state charged Joy with the crime of embezzling the collection made for Stacey. Joy claimed he intended to repay the money.

Outcome: The court upheld Joy's conviction, saying an intent to repay was irrelevant.

Larceny
Taking and carrying away of property without consent

3 **Larceny**: Taking and carrying away the property of another without the consent of the person in possession and with the intention of depriving the possessor of the property. The intent to deprive the person in possession of the property must exist at the time the property is taken. For larceny to exist, the taker need not take the

property from the owner—merely from the person in possession of it. Larceny can relate to business whenever someone takes any business property, whether inventory, tools, or even office supplies.

Facts: Stephen Murray made false entries in his corporate employer's books and forged 180 of his employer's checks, making them payable to himself. The amounts of the checks ranged from $2,000 to $60,000, and over five years Murray stole more than $4,000,000.

Outcome: The court found him guilty of 180 larcenies because he had taken his employer's property 180 times without consent and with the intention of depriving the employer of the money.

RICO Cases. The Racketeer Influenced and Corrupt Organizations Act, called RICO for short, is a federal law designed to prevent the infiltration of legitimate businesses by organized crime. It prohibits investing income from racketeering to obtain a business, using racketeering to obtain a business (through conspiracy, extortion, and so on), using a business to conduct racketeering, and conspiring to do any of these. The conspirators do not have to do the acts themselves. If they direct the action, they are responsible. The law includes stiff criminal penalties for violation.

However, RICO includes civil sanctions as well as criminal ones. As a result it has been used by one business against another in cases not involving organized crime. The injured party brings the action under RICO based on the perpetration of criminal activity and requests damages. In criminal cases a government brings the action. To find a business violation of RICO, a plaintiff must show all of the following:

1. Conduct
2. Of an enterprise (at least two people)
3. Through a pattern (at least two acts within 10 years)
4. Of racketeering activity

Racketeering activity means activity labeled criminal under state or federal laws. Examples of such activity include murder, kidnapping, arson, robbery, bribery, extortion, distribution of illegal narcotics, prostitution, and white-collar crime such as mail fraud, money laundering, and securities fraud. The defendant does not have to have been convicted; it is enough just to have engaged in activity for which a conviction could be obtained. This makes it easier to win a civil RICO case than a criminal case.

Facts: Sedima and Imrex Company, Inc. formed a joint venture to sell electronic components. Once the buyer ordered parts, Imrex was to procure them and ship them to Europe. Sedima and Imrex were to split the net proceeds. Orders were filled, but Sedima believed that Imrex was inflating expense bills and therefore cheating Sedima out of some of the proceeds. Sedima filed suit asserting claims under RICO.

Outcome: The trial court held that RICO did not apply because Imrex had not been convicted on criminal charges for a racketeering injury. The appellate court said only criminal activity, not a conviction, need be shown.

Civil suits under RICO have been very popular because of the liberal damages available. Rather than allowing merely compensatory damages, RICO provides recovery of three times the damages suffered. It also allows the recovery of attorneys' fees, which can be a substantial sum.

In addition to the federal RICO, many states have passed so-called *Baby RICO* laws. Similar to the federal law, these laws apply to activities in intrastate commerce. The federal law has jurisdiction over interstate commerce.

LO4

What computer crimes are

Computer Crimes
Crimes that are committed with aid of computers or because computers are involved

Computer Crimes. **Computer crimes** are crimes committed with the aid of a computer or because computers are involved. Under this definition, computers can be involved in crimes in various ways:

1. They can be the objects of the crimes—such as when a computer is stolen or damaged.
2. They can be the method of committing a crime—such as when a computer is used to take money from an account.
3. They can represent where the crime is committed—such as when copyrights are infringed on the Internet.

As more and more businesses rely on computers, as computer systems have become more interconnected, and as more businesses and private individuals use the Internet and the information on the Internet, more opportunities exist for criminal behavior. Frequently computer offenses can be successfully prosecuted by using existing criminal laws prohibiting theft, mail fraud, wire fraud, and the transportation of stolen property.

Facts: McGraw operated a computer for the Indianapolis Department of Planning and Zoning. He used the city's computer for his private business of selling a dietary product. City employees did not have authorization to use the computer for private business. McGraw put his customer lists, inventory control, and other business records on the computer. After being fired, he asked another employee to get him a printout of his business records and then erase them. The other employee reported this and McGraw was charged under a traditional theft law with theft of computer services.

Outcome: The court said that computer time was services, which are a valuable asset. Therefore it was property and within the definition of property subject to theft.

Some courts have refused to apply traditional criminal laws to computer offenses. Both the federal government and the states have responded to the need for laws that clearly apply to computer crimes by enacting specific computer crime legislation.

One federal law is called the Computer Fraud and Abuse Act. This act makes it an offense to, without authorization, access a computer or exceed authorized access of a computer used by or for the U.S. government or a financial institution and to (1) fraudulently obtain anything of value; (2) intentionally and without authorization obtain or destroy information; (3) affect the use of the computer; or (4) cause damage. It is also an offense to (1) deal in computer passwords and thereby affect interstate commerce; (2) knowingly access a computer, obtain national defense information and disclose, attempt to disclose, or retain it; and (3) transmit a threat to damage a U.S. government or financial institution computer in order to extort money from anyone. The punishment is a fine and/or up to 10 years imprisonment for the first offense and up to 20 years imprisonment for the second offense.

The federal government has also enacted a law called the *Electronic Communications Privacy Act*. This law prohibits the interception of computer communications, such as e-mail, or obtaining and divulging without permission data stored electronically.

The laws enacted by the states vary considerably. However, they generally prohibit alteration of a computer program or intentional, unauthorized access to a computer regardless of the reason for the access and the disclosure of any information gained by such access.

Facts: Eastman Kodak Corp. employed Versaggi as a computer technician. To perform his job, Kodak supplied him with a security device that allowed him to access the Kodak computer systems. Versaggi accessed the computer system that controlled the telephone system at Kodak and entered specific commands that activated a series of instructions directing the computer system off its existing operation. The result shut down 3,000 phone lines at Kodak for 1½ hours. Versaggi was charged with computer tampering by altering computer programs.

Outcome: Finding that a program's function is to control the computer's activities, the court stated that by disconnecting the normal application programs and ordering the computer to shut down, Versaggi had altered the programs. He was guilty of computer tampering.

Criminal activity relating to computers can be classified as three types: trespass, fraud, and criminal copyright infringement.

Computer Trespass
Unauthorized use of or access to a computer

Trespass. As applied to business crime, **computer trespass** means unauthorized use of or access to a computer. A trespass can range from being harmless to being a threat to national security. Such activities as merely using a computer to play games or prepare personal documents constitute computer trespass. More serious trespasses include learning trade secrets, customer lists, and classified defense information. Computer trespass has been the focus of state computer crime laws.

A computer trespass may be committed in a number of ways, depending on who gains unauthorized access and the use made of the computer. The access might be by:

1. An employee not authorized to use a computer in the business
2. An employee authorized to use a computer who uses it for nonbusiness purposes
3. An unauthorized outsider who gains access to the business's computer system—called a **hacker**

Hacker
Unauthorized outsider who gains access to another's computer system

Since all computer trespass involves the use of computer time without permission, all trespass technically can be classified as theft of computer time. However, computer trespass causes even more serious problems. It ties up computers and prevents employees from doing their jobs and may reveal trade secrets, customers' personal financial records, or confidential medical information. Because computers house so much information, it is helpful that the computer crime laws of the majority of jurisdictions protect the confidentiality of all information stored in computers.

Rogue Program
Set of software instructions that produces abnormal computer behavior

One of the most highly publicized methods of trespass involves damaging computer record systems by using rogue programs. A **rogue program** is a set of software instructions that produces abnormal or unexpected behavior in a computer. Various kinds of rogue programs have such colorful names as viruses, bacteria, worms, Trojan horses, and time bombs. They may cause computer users difficulty, inhibit normal use, or impose injury. The programs can be introduced to a computer by being attached to a useful program or even e-mail and spread to other computers through modems, discs, or network connections. Once introduced, a rogue program can alter the operations of a program, destroy data or screen displays, create false information, display a message, or even damage the computer.

Facts: Robert Morris, a graduate student at Cornell University, had authorization to use computers at Cornell. He wanted to demonstrate that security measures on computer networks were inadequate. Morris released a worm into the Internet from a computer at MIT. The worm was supposed to take up little computer time and be difficult to detect. The worm duplicated and infected computers much faster than Morris expected. An estimated 6,200 computers at universities, military sites, and medical research facilities all over the country crashed or would not work.

Outcome: The court found Morris guilty of violation of the Computer Fraud and Abuse Act.

Rogue programs may not show up for some time, so they can spread without alerting operators to their presence and damage all files in a computer system. One large computer software company inadvertently sent out copies of a software program containing a virus. The product had been accidentally infected after being loaded onto a computer that had received the virus from another program. In this case the virus merely caused a message to flash on computer users' screens. However, the software company had the expense of recalling thousands of copies of its software program.

Fraud. As applied to computer crime, fraud encompasses larceny and embezzlement. It includes causing bank deposits to be credited to just one individual's account. Such an action might be prosecuted under traditional crime statutes or new computer crime statutes.

Facts: Jones and an accomplice altered accounts payable documents fed into a computer. As a result, the computer issued checks to Jones totaling $130,000. They originated in Canada, and Jones cashed them in Maryland. Charged under a statute that made it a crime to transport securities known to be stolen, converted, or taken by fraud in interstate or foreign commerce, Jones argued the securities were forgeries and as such the statute did not apply to them.

Outcome: The court said the checks were genuine but contained a false statement as to the true creditor. Jones was found guilty.

The use of the Internet has made it possible for a wide variety of frauds to be perpetrated on unsuspecting businesses and individuals. Sometimes the Internet provides an easy and inexpensive way to advertise a scam since so many people "surf the Web." A fraud can be easily advertised on the Internet, such as the one in which a 15-year-old advertised computer parts for sale. Customers were required to pay cash upon delivery or by a check on which payment could not be stopped. The box supposedly containing the computer parts would be empty and the perpetrator had the customers' money.

Other Internet fraud has included a long-distance telephone company employee selling more than 50,000 calling card numbers. The employee was convicted and sent to prison. The Federal Trade Commission stopped an illegal pyramid arrangement after it scammed participants of $6 million.

Computer criminals frequently target businesses, particularly large banks. Citibank recently lost $10 million, but recovered all but $400,000 when some Russians broke into its computer system and engaged in fraudulent transactions. Businesses frequently suffer losses quietly in preference to advertising to customers, stockholders, and clients that they are vulnerable to hackers, so it is impossible to accurately measure the dollar amount of loss to business from computer fraud.

http://
www.loc.gov/copyright

Criminal Copyright Infringement. In addition to civil copyright infringement, there exists the crime of criminal copyright infringement. In order to establish the criminal offense, the prosecutor needs to prove that (1) there has been copyright infringement, (2) the infringement was willful, and (3) the infringement was done for business advantage or financial gain.

As anyone who has used the Internet knows, it is relatively easy to copy material found on the "Net." The most serious problems for business occur when software is copied. Software that is copied illegally is called **pirated software**. Pirating software is a worldwide industry because the Internet links people all over the world. Software is sometimes copied without the owner's knowledge and stored in someone else's computer located anywhere else in the world. Within a relatively short time people all over the world can make numerous illegal copies. If the owner of the computer used for storage finds out, the pirated software can be removed from the computer, but the copying has already taken place. Hundreds or thousands of copies of the pirated software could have already been made.

Pirated Software
Software copied illegally

Finding software pirates can be extremely difficult, if not impossible. They could have used fake identification and nicknames or used an anonymous remailer. An **anonymous remailer** is a device that permits a person who has access to a computer and an e-mail account to send messages and software to an e-mail address or a group without the recipient knowing the source of the communication. The person who wants to send an anonymous communication sends it to the anonymous remailer. The remailer removes the identity and address of the sender and then sends, or "remails," the communication to the address indicated by the sender. The recipient receives the communication with the remailer's address on it. Since some remailers keep a record showing the sender's identity, some communications can be traced. However, if the sender uses a remailer who does not keep such a record or uses several anonymous remailers, the communication could be impossible to trace. As a result, computer copyright infringement is, in dollar terms, the most serious crime on the Internet. It has been estimated to cost copyright holders billions of dollars a year.

Anonymous Remailer
Device that permits sending anonymous e-mail messages

Questions

1. What three things must an injured person show to recover for an intentional tort?
2. Explain the benefit to plaintiffs of the doctrine of strict tort liability.
3. What is a trademark and what does it indicate?
4. Why is shoplifting always a business crime?
5. Is it a business crime to take pencils home from the office? Explain.
6. Must the defendant have been convicted of a crime in order for a plaintiff to win a civil RICO case? Explain.

7 Summarize the response of government to the threat of computer crime.
8 In terms of dollars lost, what is the most serious crime on the Internet? Why is it so big a problem?

Case Problems

When the concluding question in a case problem can be answered simply yes or no, state the legal principle or rule of law that supports your answer.

LO3 1 James Gagan and others invested in South Hesperia CATV which proposed to build and operate a cable television system. The construction was to be done by American Cablevision, Inc. (ACI), owned by Sharar, Trimble, and Gouyd. After several years, Hesperia was in financial shambles. The person running Hesperia asked Sharar for help. Sharar, Trimble, and Gouyd agreed they would sell Hesperia and keep the proceeds. They sold Hesperia and wrote the other investors offering to buy their investments in Hesperia. The three planned to use the proceeds of the sale of Hesperia, some of which was clearly the property of the other investors, for the buyout. A financial consultant and an attorney actually sent out the offers to buy and checks to the other investors. Gagan refused to sell his interest and sued the three under RICO. He alleged he lost $350,000 as a result of the misapplication of the sales proceeds. Had Sharar, Trimble, and Gouyd conspired to violate RICO in their sale of Hesperia and the diversion of the sale proceeds even though they had not directly made the offers or sent out the checks?

LO1,2 2 For 30 years, Draper Communications, Inc. operated a television station under the call letters WBOC-TV. It advertised by those call letters, spending $150,000 annually. A new station managed by Delaware Valley Broadcasters chose the call letters WBOT-TV. WBOC and WBOT had some overlapping service area. Draper sued to prevent Broadcasters from using the call letters WBOT-TV. A witness testified that the call letters were overwhelmingly similar phonetically. WBOC had an extremely strong mark. WBOT posed a significant competitive threat, and television viewers were not likely to exercise great care in choosing a station. Could Draper keep Broadcasters from using the call letters WBOT-TV?

LO3,4 3 Anaheim police detective Stockwell asked Diane Terry to help in a sting investigation of wrongful computer access. Terry worked for Trans Union, a credit reporting agency. She created a phony file in her company's credit data bank using the name Diane T. Wolfe, but without supplying any data. She phoned National Credit Service, which advertised as a service to help people with bad credit. Lelas Gentry told her he could create a new credit file for her with false information. She and Stockwell met with Gentry, who gave Stockwell a full credit report on Diane T. Wolfe from Trans Union. Gentry did not have authorization for access to Trans Union's files, and only Gentry, Stockwell, and Terry knew of the fictitious Diane T. Wolfe. Gentry was charged with gaining access to a computer system and obtaining services with fraudulent intent. Was he guilty?

LO1,2 4 Teilhaber Manufacturing Co. produced an industrial storage rack called the *Cue-Rack*. It competed with one sold by Unarco Materials Storage, Inc. Unarco conducted tests on a hybrid rack composed of uprights manufactured by Teilhaber for the Cue-Rack and beams manufactured by another company. Unarco distributed a report on these tests written by Unarco's chief engineer. It stated that the tests were performed on a Cue-Rack "furnished by Teilhaber." Teilhaber sued Unarco for product disparagement. Was the report false?

LO3 5 William Croft, an assistant professor at the University of Wisconsin–Madison, received a $130,000 grant from the Environmental Protection Agency to study cancer in cattle. He wanted to investigate the cancer-causing effects of asbestos. While he was working on the project, the town of Weston hired Croft to test the asbestos content of Weston's water supply. Croft hired Laurel Johnson to test Weston water samples during the summer. Johnson received $2,000 from EPA funds for her work on the Weston project. Croft's report to Weston included calculations prepared by Johnson. Croft was charged with larceny—misappropriating Johnson's services, paid for by the government, for his own personal research project. Was he guilty?

LO2 6 Knaack Manufacturing Company registered the trademark WEATHER GUARD to identify toolboxes and other truck and van equipment (not car covers), which it sold through contractors and industrial supply houses. Rally Accessories, Inc. sold two car covers called SILVERGUARD and GOLDGUARD through mass retailers. It produced a car cover in a weather-resistant fabric and chose the name WeatherGUARD for it. Both Rally's attorney and the U.S. trademark office advised that the name was registerable for car covers. There were 12 registrations and approved applications using "weather guard." Knaack sued Rally for infringement and dilution of its mark. Knaack used its mark in red and Rally used its mark on a four-color box. None of Knaack's distributors carried any Rally car covers and there was no evidence of confusion by customers. Since Knaack's and Rally's products differed in function, price, packaging, method of installation, and use, was Rally guilty of infringement or dilution?

LO2 7 Hawkeye Bank & Trust and affiliated banks agreed to refer bank customers to Financial Marketing Services, Inc. (FMS) for the purchase of life insurance. Hawkeye and FMS shared the commissions. Hawkeye employees and some independent agents licensed through FMS made the actual sales; however, all insurance business was FMS's property. Because of concern about the confidentiality of bank customer information, Hawkeye decided to terminate its contract with FMS and sell insurance directly to its customers. The independent agents claimed Hawkeye terminating the contract with FMS constituted intentional interference with the agents' contracts and prospective business relations. Was it?

LO4 8 Cardservice International, which provided credit and debit card processing, registered the trademark *Cardservice International,* with exclusive right to the word *Cardservice.* Without Cardservice's permission, Webster McGee, who also provided credit and debit card services, registered *cardservice.com* as his domain name with the company that regulates the use of domain names on the Internet. At that Internet site, McGee advertised merchant card services. Cardservice demanded that McGee give up the domain name and he refused. Cardservice had to use the domain name *cardsvc.com* and sued for trademark infringement. McGee was liable if his use of the domain name *cardservice.com* was likely to cause confusion among consumers. Was it?

LO2 9 The TV program "60 Minutes" had a segment titled "Killer Wheels" about the use and safety of multipiece tire rims. It stated that people had been injured and killed when pieces of metal from such rims separated. Redco Corp., a manufacturer of multipiece tire rims, sued CBS for trade libel even though the program did not mention Redco. Redco admitted that some people had been killed in accidents involving multipiece rims, although no one had died in an accident involving its rims. Redco claimed that the rims would not explode if properly serviced. Did Redco state a claim for product disparagement?

LO3 10 As a contact representative in an IRS office, Richard Czubinski, for use in his official duties, had a password that allowed him to access information from IRS computers. He used the password with his office computer to get information about the tax returns of, among others: a prosecutor who had charged Czubinski's father with a felony, a city counselor who had defeated him in an election, and a woman he had dated. Czubinski did nothing more than observe the confidential information he had obtained. He was charged with violating the Computer Fraud and Abuse Act. To be guilty he must have exceeded authorized access of a federal computer and obtained something of value. Is he guilty?

Internet Resources for Business Law

Name	Resources	Web Address
Legal Information Institute (LII)—Torts Law Materials	LII, maintained by Cornell Law School, provides an overview of tort law, including the Federal Torts Claim Act (28 U.S.C. § 2671-80), recent Supreme Court tort decisions, and other information.	http://www.law.cornell.edu/topics/torts.html
Computer Fraud and Abuse Act of 1986, 47 USC § 1030	The Legal Information Institute (LII), maintained by Cornell Law School, provides a hypertext and searchable version of 47 USC § 1030, Computer Fraud and Abuse Act of 1986.	http://www.law.cornell.edu/uscode/18/1030.html
Racketeer Influenced and Corrupt Organizations Act (RICO), 18 USC § 1961	LII provides a hypertext and searchable version of 18 USC § 1961, popularly known as the Racketeer Influenced and Corrupt Organizations Act (RICO).	http://www.law.cornell.edu/uscode/18/1961.html
U.S. Patent and Trademark Office	Patent and Trademark Office (PTO) allows for patent searches; as well, it provides forms, legal materials, and the PTO museum.	http://www.uspto.gov/
Intellectual Property Center	Intellectual Property Center, sponsored by The New York Law Publishing Company, provides daily news and articles, case law, and analysis.	http://www.ipcenter.com/
World Intellectual Property Organization (WIPO)	The World Intellectual Property Organization (WIPO) maintains the Berne Convention, Paris Convention WIPO Copyright Treaty, and WIPO Performances and Phonograms Treaty, among other resources.	http://www.wipo.org/eng/general/copyrght/bern.htm
Copyright Office, Library of Congress	The Copyright Office provides publications and extensive information on copyright topics, including the basics of copyright law.	http://lcweb.loc.gov/copyright/

4

Government Regulation of Business

Learning Objectives

1 Explain why government regulates business.

2 Discuss the types and powers of administrative agencies.

3 List the major antitrust laws.

4 Summarize the areas in which the federal government has enacted legislation for environmental protection.

PREVIEW CASE

Cherokee Resources, Inc. had a wastewater treatment and oil reclamation business. It accepted oil and industrial wastewater and processed the oil for reuse and treated the wastewater that it discharged into the sewer system. Cherokee accepted more oil and wastewater than it could treat and often dumped untreated oil and water into the sewer system. Cherokee, its president, and its vice-president were charged with conspiracy to violate the CWA. They argued the CWA applied only to navigable waters and their discharges were into the sewer system not a navigable waterway. Did it? What was the purpose of the CWA? What difference did it make whether the oil and water was dumped into the sewer system or a river?

Government rules and regulations affect the operation of every business, no matter what type. The areas of business operation affected by government regulation, both state and federal, range from prices and product safety to the relationship of the business to its employees. This chapter discusses some ways in which government regulates the operation of business. Some other aspects of governmental regulation of business are discussed in Chapter 19 (consumer protection) and in Chapters 28 and 29 (employers and employees).

Purpose of Regulation

LO1
Why government regulates

Government regulates business in order to eliminate abuses and to control conduct considered to be unreasonable. The goal is to enhance the quality of life for society as a whole by setting the rules under which all businesses compete.

Administrative Agencies

Chapter 1 defined administrative agencies as governmental boards or commissions with the authority to regulate or implement laws. Most governmental regulation of business is done by administrative agencies.

Most administrative agency regulation occurs because of the complex nature of the area of regulation. Each administrative agency can become a specialist in its particular area of regulation. Agencies can hire scientists and researchers to study industries or problems and set standards that businesses must follow. Agencies conduct research on proposed drugs (the Food and Drug Administration), examine the safety of nuclear power facilities (the Nuclear Regulatory Commission), certify the wholesomeness of meat and poultry (the Food Safety and Inspection Service), and set standards for aircraft maintenance (the Federal Aviation Administration). In all these areas, research has been necessary to determine a safe level for the public.

Some agencies investigate industries and propose rules designed to promote fairness to the businesses involved and the public. This occurs in the area of trading in stocks (the Securities and Exchange Commission), the granting of radio and television licenses (the Federal Communications Commission), and the regulation of banks (the Federal Deposit Insurance Corporation). The legislature thus can set up the guidelines and specify the research to be done by specialists in the field.

STRUCTURE OF ADMINISTRATIVE AGENCIES

Agencies may be run by a single administrator who serves at the pleasure of the executive, either the president of the United States in the case of federal agencies or the governor in the case of state agencies. Alternatively, a commission, the members of which are appointed for staggered terms, frequently of five years, may run agencies.

LO2
Types and powers of agencies

TYPES OF AGENCIES

The two types of administrative agencies are usually referred to as regulatory and nonregulatory. Regulatory agencies govern the economic activity of businesses. They prescribe rules stating what should or should not be done in particular situations. They decide whether a law has been violated and then proceed against those violating the law by imposing fines and, in some cases, ordering that the activity be stopped. Regulatory-type agencies include agencies such as the Environmental Protection Agency, the Securities and Exchange Commission, and the Federal Trade Commission.

Regulatory agencies also regulate a wide variety of professions that serve the public. Those supervised by governmental agencies in an effort to protect the interests of consumers include barbers, doctors, insurance agents, morticians, cosmetologists, fitters of hearing aids, and restaurateurs. In order to be licensed to practice a regulated profession, an individual must meet the requirements set by the appropriate regulatory agency.

Public utility companies, which are granted monopoly status, are regulated to ensure that they charge fair rates and render adequate service. Such businesses include natural gas, electric, and water companies. A Public Service Commission or Public Utilities Commission regulates these companies in most states.

Nonregulatory agencies, also called social regulatory agencies, dispense benefits for social and economic welfare and issue regulations governing the distribution of benefits. Such agencies include the Railroad Retirement Board, the Farm Credit Administration, and the Department of Health and Human Services.

POWERS OF AGENCIES

Different regulatory agencies have different powers. However, the three major areas of regulations include:

1. Licensing power: Allowing a business to enter the field being regulated.
2. Rate-making power: Fixing the prices that a business may charge.
3. Power over business practices: Determining whether the activity of the entity regulated is acceptable or not.

Agencies such as the Federal Communications Commission, the Nuclear Regulatory Commission, and the Securities and Exchange Commission have licensing power. The Civil Aeronautics Board, the Federal Power Commission, and the Interstate Commerce Commission all have rate-making power. The primary powers of the Federal Trade Commission and the National Labor Relations Board are to control business practices.

RULE MAKING

Administrative agencies primarily set policy through the issuance of rules and regulations. When an agency's rule is challenged, the courts primarily focus on the procedures followed by the agency in exercising its rule-making power. The rule-making procedure followed by state agencies resembles that which must be used by federal agencies.

After investigating a problem, an agency will develop a proposed rule. A federal agency must publish a notice of the proposed rule in the *Federal Register*. This allows interested parties the opportunity to comment on the proposed rule. The agency might hold formal hearings, but informal **notice** and **comment rule making** has been more and more common. When an agency uses notice and comment rule making, it publishes a proposed rule, but does not hold formal hearings. After time for comments, the proposed rule could be published as proposed, changed, or entirely abandoned by the agency. Once a rule or regulation is adopted, it has the force of a statute.

Notice and Comment Rule Making
Enacting administrative rules by publishing the proposed rule and then the final rule without holding formal hearings

STATE AGENCIES

Whereas federal administrative agencies affect businesses throughout the country, state administrative agencies affect businesses operated in their states. The most common state agencies include public service commissions, state labor relations boards or commissions, and workers' compensation boards.

Antitrust

LO3
Major antitrust laws

Government also regulates business by means of **antitrust laws** which seek to promote competition among businesses.

The most important antitrust law, the federal Sherman Antitrust Act, declares that, "Every contract, combination in the form of trust or otherwise, or conspiracy, in

Antitrust Laws
Statutes that seek to promote competition among businesses

restraint of trade or commerce among the several states, or with foreign nations is . . . illegal."[1] It further provides that anyone who monopolizes or tries to obtain a monopoly in interstate commerce is guilty of a felony.

The Sherman Act applies to commerce or trade between two or more states and applies to both buyers and sellers. Most states also have antitrust laws, very similar to the Sherman Act, which prohibit restraint of trade within their states.

In interpreting the Sherman Act, the federal courts have said it prohibits only those activities that *unreasonably* restrain trade. The *rule of reason* approach means that the courts examine and rule on the anticompetitive effect of a particular activity on a case-by-case basis. The effect of the activity, not the activity itself, is the most important element in deciding whether the Sherman Act has been violated.

Per Se Violations
Activities illegal regardless of their effect

However, some activities are illegal under the Sherman Act without regard to their effect. Called **per se violations**, they include price fixing, group boycotts, and horizontal territorial restraints.

Many activities may lessen competition. Obviously, every business firm seeks to have cooperation within its firm. This is the basis of economic productivity, and this is lawful under the antitrust laws. Only when separate businesses make a commitment to a common plan or some type of joint action to restrain trade does an antitrust violation occur.

In addition to the Sherman Act, the federal government has enacted three other important antitrust laws. These include the Clayton Act, the Robinson-Patman Act, and the Federal Trade Commission Act.

The Clayton Act amends the Sherman Act by prohibiting certain practices if their effect may be to substantially lessen competition or to tend to create a monopoly. The Clayton Act prohibits price discrimination to different purchasers where price difference does not result from differences in selling or transportation cost. The Clayton Act also prohibits agreements to sell on the condition that the purchaser shall not use goods of the seller's competitors, ownership of stock or assets in a competing business where the effect may be to substantially lessen competition, and interlocking directorates between boards of directors of competing firms.

Facts: The Brown Shoe Co. and the G. R. Kinney Co., which together would have controlled 5 percent of the United States shoe market, attempted to merge. The federal government sought to stop the merger on the grounds that it violated the Clayton Act, which prohibits corporations from acquiring other corporations where the effect of the acquisition might substantially lessen competition or tend to create a monopoly.

Outcome: The U.S. Supreme Court prohibited the merger, holding that the proposed merger would tend to lessen competition.

The Robinson-Patman Act, an amendment to the Clayton Act, prohibits price discrimination generally and geographically for the purpose of eliminating competition. It also prohibits sales at unreasonably low prices in order to eliminate competition.

The Federal Trade Commission Act prohibits "unfair methods of competition in commerce and unfair or deceptive acts or practices in commerce."[2] In addition, this law

[1] 15 U.S.C. §1.
[2] 15 U.S.C. §45 (a) (1).

prohibits false advertising. To prevent these unfair and deceptive practices, a federal administrative agency, the Federal Trade Commission, was established.

Environmental Protection

LO4
Federal environmental protection legislation

In recognition of the fact that the environment is the property of everyone, the federal government and many states have enacted a number of laws to protect our environment. A federal agency, the Environmental Protection Agency (EPA), administers many of these federal laws. The laws the EPA administers include the following:

1. Clean Air Act
2. Water Pollution and Control Act
3. Resource Conservation and Recovery Act
4. Comprehensive Environmental Response, Compensation, and Liability Act

CLEAN AIR ACT

The Clean Air Act was the first national environmental law. Under this law, the EPA sets minimum national standards for air quality and regulates hazardous air pollutants. These standards protect public health and welfare. The states apply and enforce these standards under state implementation plans setting limits on pollutants and approved by the EPA. The law provides civil and criminal penalties for its violation.

Facts: Under authority of the Clean Air Act, the EPA set an air quality standard for ozone. The state of Michigan issued a state implementation plan, and the EPA approved the plan. Later, the United States sued in federal court to enforce the plan. A month later, Ford Motor Company sued the Michigan state pollution control agencies in a state court to keep them from enforcing the plan. The EPA was not a party to that suit. Ford and the state agencies negotiated a judgment in the state court changing the limits and thereby vacating the plan. Ford alleged the plan could not be enforced in the federal suit because the state court judgment invalidated it.

Outcome: The court said since the EPA must approve plans and any revisions to plans, the state court action could not revise the plan.

WATER POLLUTION AND CONTROL ACT

Congress enacted the Water Pollution and Control Act (also referred to simply as the Clean Water Act—or CWA) to restore and maintain the proper chemistry of U.S. waters, including adjacent wetlands. The law seeks to prevent the discharge of pollutants into navigable waters. The EPA has the primary administration and enforcement responsibility under the law. It sets limits on discharges, including pollutants into sewer systems, has the responsibility for wetlands protection, and can block or overrule the issuance of permits under the law. The EPA or private citizens may sue on the basis of the act, which even includes criminal liability for violation.

RESOURCE CONSERVATION AND RECOVERY ACT

The Resource Conservation and Recovery Act regulates the generation, storage, transportation, treatment, and disposal of hazardous waste. The law lists certain

PREVIEW CASE REVISITED

Facts: Cherokee Resources, Inc. had a wastewater treatment and oil reclamation business. It accepted oil and industrial wastewater and processed the oil for reuse and treated the wastewater that it discharged into the sewer system. Cherokee accepted more oil and wastewater than it could treat and often dumped untreated oil and water into the sewer system, which ultimately discharged into rivers and the ocean. Cherokee, its president, and its vice president were charged with conspiracy to violate the CWA. They argued the CWA applied only to navigable waters and their discharges were into the sewer system not a navigable waterway.

Outcome: The court said that the CWA regulates discharges into sewer systems and Congress has the authority to regulate such discharges. The defendants were convicted.

wastes defined as hazardous, but the term includes ignitable, corrosive, reactive, or toxic waste.

The law gives the EPA the duty of setting standards for individuals who own or operate hazardous waste disposal facilities. Anyone who generates or transports hazardous waste, and owners and operators of facilities for the treatment, storage, or disposal of such waste, must obtain a permit and must comply with the requirements of the permit. The law requires individuals handling hazardous waste to keep extensive records in order to track it from generation to disposal. The law provides large civil and criminal penalties for its violation. This law also permits suits by private citizens.

COMPREHENSIVE ENVIRONMENTAL RESPONSE, COMPENSATION, AND LIABILITY ACT

ETHICAL POINT
Is it ethical for the law to impose liability retroactively? Should government force a person to pay for doing something that was legal and carried no penalty at the time it was done?

Perhaps the most discussed federal environmental legislation, the Comprehensive Environmental Response, Compensation, and Liability Act (CERCLA), also called the "superfund" law, seeks the cleanup of waste from previous activities and requires notification of the release of hazardous substances. CERCLA imposes liability for cleanup on past and current owners or operators of facilities where hazardous substances have been released, on anyone who arranged for disposal of substances where released, and on anyone who transported them. CERCLA imposes liability retroactively—acts that occurred before enactment of this law and were not negligent or illegal then can be the basis of liability.

Liability of Multiple Parties. Because CERCLA imposes liability on four groups of people—owners, operators, disposers, and transporters—several parties could be liable for one site. A liable party may take legal action to require other responsible or potentially responsible parties to pay a share of cleanup costs. Courts have stated that when several defendants are responsible under CERCLA, liability should be apportioned according to their contribution to the problem. However, if liability cannot be apportioned or only one liable party has any funds, one party could be liable for the entire cleanup cost. These costs can run into millions of dollars.

Business Costs. These provisions of CERCLA concern businesses and potential business owners because of the possibility of courts imposing huge cleanup costs on them as new owners of facilities who never released hazardous wastes there. If a hazardous substance was released 20 years ago by the then owner of a facility who sold the facility and then there was a series of sales, the current owner, who does not know about the release, might still have to pay for or help pay for the cleanup. Some courts have found everyone in the chain of ownership of contaminated property, from disposal of the substance to the current owner, liable for cleanup. Thus, anyone buying contaminated land is potentially liable for cleanup costs. This can have serious repercussions for all landowners but particularly for businesses since business or manufacturing sites are the most likely to have been the site of a release of hazardous substances.

Business costs could include not only large cleanup costs but also legal fees. Litigation under the superfund law can be extremely expensive. A party responsible for cleanup costs can sue to require other "potentially" liable parties to share in the costs. Just the cost of defending against such a lawsuit can be very expensive. Legal fees have been reported to be 30 percent to 60 percent of superfund costs.

In addition to owners of facilities, courts have imposed CERCLA liability on business employees who had control over disposal decisions. Even lenders have been found liable for cleanup costs if the court found them adequately involved in running the business.

STATE LAWS

A number of states have enacted state superfund laws. They also impose liability for cleanup costs and may require notification of release of hazardous substances to state environmental agencies.

PROTECTION FROM LIABILITY

A person can take some steps to help reduce the potential of liability under CERCLA and state superfund statutes. Banks and other lending institutions should require environmental assessments of properties before making a loan and before foreclosing on property. Before anyone buys or invests in property, an investigation should be made to identify any environmental risks and determine expected costs. Cleanup costs that run in the millions of dollars can be much greater than the value of the property involved.

Questions

1 Give two examples of the areas of business operation affected by government.
2 Why does most administrative agency regulation occur?
3 What do regulatory agencies do and how do they do it?
4 What is the purpose of nonregulatory agencies?
5 What are the three types of powers possessed by regulatory agencies?
6 What are antitrust laws?
7 What is the difference between the rule of reason approach to antitrust and *per se* violations?
8 Who has the power to sue to enforce the Water Pollution and Control Act?
9 What four classes of people are potentially liable under the superfund law?
10 Who is required to obtain and comply with a permit under the Resource Conservation and Recovery Act?

Internet Resources for Business Law

Name	Resources	Web Address
Sherman Antitrust Act—15 U.S.C. §1	LII provides 15 U.S.C. §1–7, popularly known as the Sherman Antitrust Act.	http://www4.law.cornell.edu/uscode/15/1.shtml
Clayton Act—15 U.S.C. §12	LII provides 15 U.S.C. §12–25, popularly known as the Clayton Antitrust Act.	http://www4.law.cornell.edu/uscode/15/12.html
U.S. Department of Justice, Antitrust Division	The Antitrust Division of the U.S. Department of Justice provides press releases, speeches, congressional testimony, antitrust guidelines, court cases since 1994, international agreements and documents, and division status reports.	http://www.usdoj.gov/atr/atr.htm
U.S. Federal Trade Commission (FTC)	The FTC provides news and press releases, speeches and articles, and facts for consumers and businesses.	http://www.ftc.gov/
Antitrust Policy	The Antitrust Policy, maintained by Vanderbilt University, provides antitrust case documents (complaints, opinions, and expert testimony), enforcement guidelines and speeches, economic bibliographies, and current antitrust issues in the news.	http://www.antitrust.org/
U.S. Environmental Protection Agency	The EPA provides educational materials; regulations, publications, and news; and text for the National Environmental Policy Act of 1969.	http://www.epa.gov/
Council on Environmental Quality (CEQ)	The CEQ provides, among other services, NEPANet (National Environmental Policy Act), which includes Environmental Impact Statements (EISs) and a library of environmental resources.	http://www.whitehouse.gov/CEQ/
Comprehensive Environmental Response, Compensation, and Liability Act (CERCLA)—42 USC §9601	LII provides the Comprehensive Environmental Response, Compensation, and Liability Act, 42 USC §9601.	http://www.law.cornell.edu/uscode/42/9601.html

Part 2 Contracts

http://www.fraud.org

Back to Main Menu
Scams Against Businesses
Tips for Spotting Scams
Reporting Scams Against Businesses
SEARCH THIS SITE

Scams Against Businesses

Individual consumers aren't the only victims of fraud. Businesses, from large corporations to small "Mom and Pop" stores, are targets for a variety of illegal schemes. No matter whether the con artist uses the mail, the telephone, or the Internet, the best defense against scams is to follow these basic rules:

- **Do business with companies you know and trust.** If you don't know them, check them out.
- **Understand the offer.** Get all the details and promises in writing.
- **Check all bills and invoices carefully.** It's hard to get your money back once you've paid it to a con artist.
- **Guard your financial or other account information.** Don't provide it to anyone unless there is a legitimate reason to do so as part of a transaction.
- **Educate your employees about avoiding scams.** Make sure they understand their roles and responsibilities.

You can help stop fraud by recognizing these common scams and reporting them.

Advertising Materials	Bogus Invoices	Calling Card Charges	Charitable Solicitations
Cramming	Fax Fraud	Internet Services	Loan Scams
Nigerian Money Offers	Pager Scams	Paper Pirates & Toner Phoner	Pay-Per-Call Scams
PBX Phone Scams	Prize Promotions	Slamming	Y2K Scams

NCL created this Web page with support from the Yellow Pages Publishers Association, a nonprofit trade organization representing both the major utility directory publishers and many independent directory publishers.

SEARCH THIS SITE

Links for Non-Frames Version

Defective agreements—and fraud—are covered in Chapter 9. Businesses can be the target of scams as easily as the average consumer. Educate your employees on what to watch out for, and before you sign on the dotted line, get all of the loan terms in writing, including the payment schedule and interest rate. If the lender isn't familiar to you, contact your state banking department and ask how to confirm that it's licensed and operating properly. More information on fraud can be found at http://www.fraud.org.

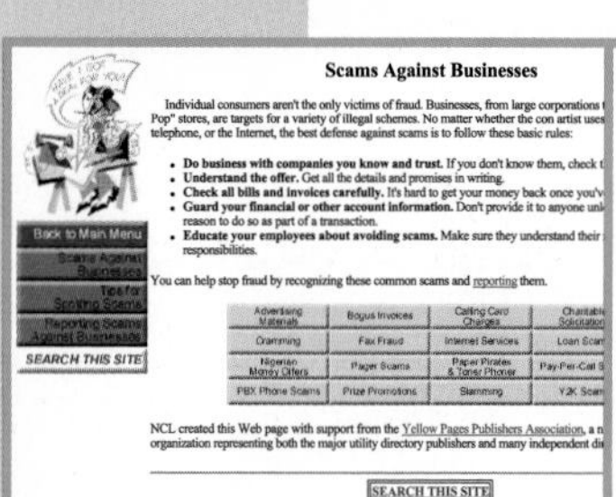

5

Nature and Classes of Contracts

Learning Objectives

1 Describe what a contract is and how it differs from an agreement.

2 List the different types of contracts.

3 State the five requirements for a valid contract.

PREVIEW CASE

Richard Iacomini contracted with Theodore Zadlo to tow, store, and repair a Mercedes. Zadlo said he owned the car and gave Iacomini a state registration certificate bearing his name. The police later notified Iacomini that the Mercedes was stolen. When the real owner wanted to pick it up, Iacomini refused to release the car until he had been paid repair and storage fees. Must the owner pay the fees? Would it be just for the real owner to have the car repaired and pay nothing for the repair?

Contract
Legally enforceable agreement

A **contract** can be defined as a legally enforceable agreement between two or more competent persons. At first glance this seems like a very simple definition. Notice that this definition does not even require a written document. Chapters 5 through 13 are devoted exclusively to explaining and clarifying this definition.

Making contracts is such an everyday occurrence that we often overlook their importance, except when the contracts are of a substantial nature. When one buys a cup of coffee during a coffee break, a contract has been made. When the purchaser agrees to pay 50¢ for the coffee, the seller agrees not only to supply one cup of coffee but also agrees by implication of law that it is safe to drink. If the coffee contains a harmful substance that makes the purchaser ill, a breach of contract has occurred that may call for the payment of damages.

Business transactions result from agreements. Every time a person makes a purchase, buys a theater ticket, or boards a bus, an agreement is made. Each party to the agreement obtains certain rights and assumes certain duties and obligations. When such an agreement meets all the legal requirements of a contract, the law recognizes it as binding upon all parties. If one of the parties to the contract breaches it by failing or refusing to perform, the law allows the other party an appropriate action for obtaining damages or enforcing performance by the party breaching the contract.

Contracts are very important in business because they form the very foundation upon which all modern business rests. Business consists almost entirely of the making and performing of contracts. If the contract is a sale of goods, it is governed by the Uniform Commercial Code (see Chapter 16).

Contracts Contrasted with Agreements

LO1 Contract versus agreement

A contract must be an agreement, but an agreement need not be a contract. Whenever two or more persons' minds meet upon any subject, no matter how trivial, an agreement results. Only when the parties intend to be legally obligated by the terms of the agreement will a contract come into existence. Chapter 6 explains how such agreements are formed. Ordinarily, the subject matter of the contract must involve a business transaction as distinguished from a purely social transaction.

If Mary and John promise to meet at a certain place at 6 P.M. and have dinner together, this is an agreement, not a contract, since neither intends to be legally bound to carry out the terms of the agreement.

If Alice says to David, "I will pay you $25 to be my escort for the Spring Ball," and David replies, "I accept your offer," the agreement results in a contract. David is legally obligated to provide escort service, and Alice is legally bound to pay him $25.

Classification of Contracts

LO2 Types of contracts

Contracts are classified by many names or terms. Unless you understand these terms, you cannot understand the law of contracts. For example, the law may state that executory contracts made on Sunday are void. You cannot understand this law unless you understand the words *executory* and *void.* Every contract may be placed in one of the following classifications:

1. Valid contracts, void agreements, and voidable contracts
2. Express and implied contracts
3. Formal and simple contracts
4. Executory and executed contracts
5. Unilateral and bilateral contracts

VALID CONTRACTS, VOID AGREEMENTS, AND VOIDABLE CONTRACTS

LO3 Requirements for valid contract

Agreements classified according to their enforceability include valid contracts, void agreements, and voidable contracts.

Valid Contract
Contract enforceable by law

A **valid contract** will be enforced by the courts against all parties. Such a contract must fulfill the following definite requirements:

1. It must be based on a mutual agreement by the parties to do or not to do a specific thing.
2. It must be made by parties who are competent to enter into a contract that will be enforceable against both parties.

3. The promise or obligation of each party must be supported by consideration (such as the payment of money, the delivery of goods, or the promise to do or refrain from doing some lawful future act) given by each party to the contract.
4. It must be for a lawful purpose; that is, the purpose of the contract must not be illegal, such as the unauthorized buying and selling of narcotics.
5. In some cases, the contract must meet certain formal requirements, such as being in writing or under seal.

You may test the validity of any contract using these five requirements. If the agreement fails to meet one or more of these requirements, the agreement may be void or the contract may be voidable.

Void
Of no legal effect

Unenforceable Contract
Agreement that is not currently binding

An agreement with no legal effect is **void**. An agreement not enforceable in a court of law does not come within the definition of a contract. A void agreement (sometimes referred to as a void contract) must be distinguished from an **unenforceable contract**. If the law requires a certain contract to be in a particular form, such as a deed to be in writing, and it is not in that form, it is merely unenforceable, not void. It can be made enforceable by changing the form to meet the requirements of the law. An agreement between two parties to perform an illegal act is void. Nothing the parties can do will make this agreement an enforceable contract.

Voidable Contract
Enforceable agreement that may be set aside by one party

A **voidable contract** would be an enforceable agreement; but, because of circumstances or the capacity of a party, one or both of the parties may set it aside. The distinguishing factor of a voidable contract is the existence of a choice by one party to abide by or to reject the contract. A contract made by an adult with a person not of lawful age (legally known as a minor or infant) is often voidable by the minor. Such a contract is enforceable against the adult but not against the minor. If both parties to an agreement are minors, either one may avoid the agreement. Until the party having the choice to avoid the contract exercises the right to set the contract aside, the contract remains in full force and effect.

EXPRESS AND IMPLIED CONTRACTS

Express Contract
Contract with the terms of the agreement specified in words

Contracts classified according to the manner of their formation fall into two groups: express and implied contracts. In an **express contract**, the parties express their intentions by words, whether in writing or orally, at the time they make the agreement. Both their intention to contract and the terms of the agreement are expressly stated or written. Customary business terms, however, do not need to be stated in an express contract in order to be binding.

Facts: The Computer Shoppe, Inc. bid on a computer system for Tennessee sheriffs. After extended testing, state government representatives told the company it would get the contract for the computer system if it would modify its software. The company modified it as requested, and the state gave preliminary approval. The general assembly asked the attorney general to review the procurement process, and ultimately all the bids were rejected. Computer Shoppe filed a claim for its costs for software modification. State law allowed such claims based on an express contract. The state said no written contract existed, therefore no express contract existed. The company said an express oral contract existed to award it the contract if it modified the software.

Outcome: The court held that an express contract could be oral.

Implied Contract Contract with major terms implied by the parties' conduct

An **implied contract** (also called a **contract implied in fact**) is one in which the duties and the obligations that the parties assume are not expressed but are implied by their acts or conduct. The adage "actions speak louder than words" very appropriately describes this class of contracts. The facts of a situation imply that a contract exists. The parties indicate so clearly by their conduct what they intend to do that there is no need to express the agreement in words to make it binding.

Facts: Richardson hired the J. C. Flood Co. to correct a blocked sewer line. When the line was excavated, many leaks were found in a rusty, defective water pipe that ran parallel to the sewer line. Water district regulations required the pipe to be replaced. If the pipe were not replaced while it was exposed for the sewer-line repair, the yard would later have to be redug to replace the pipe. Flood told Richardson this and replaced the line. Richardson objected to paying for it.

Outcome: The court found that since Richardson inspected the work daily, knew the magnitude of the work being done, and made no objection until the work was done, there was an implied contract to replace the water line.

FORMAL AND SIMPLE CONTRACTS

Formal Contract Contract with special form or manner of creation

A **formal contract** must be in a special form or be created in a certain way. Formal contracts include contracts under seal, recognizances, and negotiable instruments.

When very few people could write, contracts were signed by means of an impression in wax attached to the paper. As time passed, a small wafer pasted on the contract replaced the use of wax. The wafer seal was in addition to the written signature. This practice is still used occasionally, but the more common practice is to sign formal contracts in one of these ways:

Jane Doe (Seal); Jane Doe [L.S.]

Today, it is immaterial whether these substitutes for a seal are printed on the document, typewritten before signing, or the persons signing write them after their respective names. In jurisdictions where the use of the seal has not been abolished, the seal implies consideration.

Facts: Marine Contractors Co., Inc. had a trust for its employees, but an employee who quit could not receive trust benefits for five years. When Thomas Hurley notified Marine he was quitting, they agreed upon immediate payment of his $12,000 in benefits in return for his promise not to compete in the Boston area for five years. The agreement stated the parties had "set their hands and seals" to it. Within a few months Hurley was competing. When sued by Marine, Hurley claimed there was no consideration since he was owed the $12,000 anyway. Marine alleged the agreement was a sealed instrument, which in that state implied consideration.

Outcome: The court held it was a sealed instrument.

In some states, the presence of a seal on a contract allows a party a longer time in which to bring suit if the contract is broken. Other states make no distinction between contracts under seal and other written contracts. The Uniform Commercial Code abolishes the distinction with respect to contracts for the sale of goods.

Recognizance
Obligation entered into before a court to do an act required by law

Recognizances, a second type of formal contract, are obligations entered into before a court whereby persons acknowledge they will do a specified act that is required by law. The persons acknowledge that they will be indebted for a specific amount if they do not perform as they agreed, such as the obligation undertaken by a criminal defendant to appear in court on a particular day.

Negotiable Instrument
Document of payment, such as a check

Negotiable instruments, discussed in later chapters, are a third type of formal contract. They include checks, notes, drafts, and certificates of deposit.

Simple Contract
Contract that is not formal

All contracts other than formal contracts are informal and are called **simple contracts**. A few of these, such as an agreement to sell land or to be responsible for the debt of another, must be in writing in order to be enforceable; otherwise they need not be prepared in any particular form. Generally speaking, informal or simple contracts may be in writing, may be oral, or may be implied from the conduct of the parties.

Written Contract
Contract with terms in writing

Oral Contract
Contract with terms spoken

A **written contract** is one in which the terms are set forth in writing rather than expressed orally. An **oral contract** is one in which the terms are stated in spoken, not written, words. Such a contract is usually enforceable; however, when a contract is oral, disputes may arise between the parties as to the terms of the agreement. No such disputes need arise about the terms of a written contract if the wording is clear, explicit, and complete. For this reason most businesspeople avoid making oral contracts involving matters of very great importance. Some types of contracts are required to be in writing and are discussed in Chapter 11.

EXECUTORY AND EXECUTED CONTRACTS

Executory Contract
Contract not fully carried out

Contracts are classified by the stage of performance as executory contracts and executed contracts. An **executory contract** is one in which the terms have not been fully carried out by all parties. If a person agrees to work for another for one year in return for a salary of $3,500 a month, the contract is executory from the time it is made until the 12 months expire. Even if the employer should prepay the salary, it would still be an executory contract because the other party has not yet worked the entire year, that is, executed that part of the contract.

Executed Contract
Fully performed contract

An **executed contract** is one that has been fully performed by all parties to the contract. The Collegiate Shop sells and delivers a dress to Benson for $105, and Benson pays the purchase price at the time of the sale. This is an executed contract because nothing remains to be done on either side; that is, each party has completed performance of each part of the contract.

Facts: Lockheed sent M. B. Electronics a written order to repair a shaker-amplifier system. The order contained an indemnity agreement stating M. B. would indemnify Lockheed from injury arising out of the repair work. While working, Wichman, an employee of M. B., was electrocuted. Lockheed paid Wichman's heirs $115,000 and sued M. B. for reimbursement under the purchase order. Under state law, M. B. was not liable unless the order was fully executed prior to the injury.

Outcome: Since Wichman was killed during the process of repairing the system, the repairs had not been completed nor had they been paid for; therefore, the purchase agreement was not fully executed.

UNILATERAL AND BILATERAL CONTRACTS

Unilateral Contract
Contract calling for an act in consideration for a promise

When an act is done in consideration for a promise, the contract is a **unilateral contract**. If Smith offers to pay $100 to anyone who returns her missing dog and Fink returns the dog, this would be a unilateral contract. It is unilateral (one-sided) in that only one promise is made. A promise is given in exchange for an act. Smith made the only promise, which was to pay anyone for the act of returning the dog. Fink was not obligated to find and return the dog, so only one duty existed.

Bilateral Contract
Contract consisting of mutual exchange of promises

A **bilateral contract** consists of a mutual exchange of promises to perform some future acts. One promise is the consideration for the other promise. If Brown promises to sell a truck to Adams for $5,000, and Adams agrees to pay $5,000, then the parties have exchanged a promise for a promise—a bilateral contract. Most contracts are bilateral because the law states a bilateral contract can be formed when performance is started. This is true unless it is clear from the first promise or the situation that performance must be completed. The test is whether there is only one right and duty or two.

QUASI CONTRACT

ETHICAL POINT
Notice that quasi contracts arise because of strictly ethical considerations.

Quasi Contract
Imposition of rights and obligations by law without a contract

Unjust Enrichment
One benefiting unfairly at another's expense

One may have rights and obligations imposed by law when no real contract exists. This imposition of rights and obligations is called a **quasi contract** or implied in law contract. It is not a true contract because the parties have not made an agreement. Rights and obligations will be imposed only when a failure to do so would result in one person unfairly keeping money or otherwise benefiting at the expense of another. This is known as **unjust enrichment**. For example, suppose a tenant is obligated to pay rent of $300 a month but by mistake hands the landlord $400. The law requires the landlord to return the overpayment of $100. The law creates an agreement for repayment even though no actual agreement exists between the parties. For the landlord to keep the money would mean an unjust enrichment at the expense of the tenant. An unjust enrichment offends our ethical principles, so the law imposes a contractual obligation to right the situation.

PREVIEW CASE REVISITED

Facts: Richard Iacomini contracted with Theodore Zadlo to tow, store, and repair a Mercedes. Zadlo said he owned the car and gave Iacomini a state registration certificate bearing his name. The police later notified Iacomini that the Mercedes was stolen. When the owner wanted to pick it up, Iacomini refused to release the car until he had been paid repair and storage fees.

Outcome: The court said that although Iacomini and the car's owner did not have a contractual agreement, a court could and would impose one so there would not be an unjust enrichment.

Questions

1 If one party to a contract breaches it, what recourse does the other party have?
2 Why are contracts so important to business?

Facts: Lucy said to Zehmer, "I bet you wouldn't take $50,000 for . . ." the Ferguson farm. Zehmer replied, "Yes, I would, too; you wouldn't give $50." Lucy said he would and told Zehmer to write up an agreement to that effect. Zehmer took a restaurant check and wrote on the back that he agreed to sell it. Lucy told him he needed to change the *I* to *We* because Mrs. Zehmer would have to sign, too, and add a provision for having the title examined. Zehmer wrote on another check, "We hereby agree to sell to W. O. Lucy the Ferguson Farm complete for $50,000, title satisfactory to buyer." He and his wife both signed it, and Lucy took it with him. Zehmer later said he and Lucy had been drinking and the discussion about selling the farm was only a joke.

Outcome: The court held that Zehmer's actions appeared to be a good faith acceptance of Lucy's offer, so there was a contract.

THE OFFER MUST BE COMMUNICATED TO THE OFFEREE

Until the offeror makes the offer known to the offeree, it is not certain that it is intended that the offeree may accept and thereby impose a binding contract. Accordingly, the offeree cannot accept an offer until the offeror has communicated the offer to the offeree. If one writes out an offer and the offer falls into the hands of the offeree without the knowledge or consent of the offeror, it cannot be accepted. Furthermore, an offer directed to a specific individual or firm cannot be accepted by anyone else. This is because people have a right to choose the parties with whom they deal.

Facts: Stauffer Chemical Co. had a severance pay policy that was explained in written instructions furnished to its management. The policy was not published or disseminated to other employees. The granting of severance pay was a voluntary, gratuitous benefit to be determined solely by Stauffer. Severance pay was not discussed with prospective employees. When Stauffer sold its plant as a going concern, 33 former employees sued Stauffer for severance pay.

Outcome: The court found that an offer of severance pay had not been made to the employees; thus, there was no contract to pay it.

Invitations to Make Offers

LO2
Offer versus invitation to make offer

In business, many apparent offers are not true offers. Instead, they are treated as invitations to the public to make offers at certain terms and prices. If a member of the public accepts the invitation, and an offer is submitted embodying all the terms set out in the invitation, the inviter may refuse to accept the offer. Ordinarily, however, as a practical matter and in the interest of maintaining goodwill, such an offer will be accepted. The most common types of general invitations are advertisements, window displays, catalogs, price lists, and circulars. If a merchant displays in a store window a coat for $95, there is no binding requirement to sell at this price. Most businesspeople would consider refusing to sell a very poor business policy, but nevertheless merchants may legally do so. Considering advertisements and window displays as invitations to make offers rather than offers provides protection to businesspeople. Otherwise they might find that they were subjected to many suits for breach of contract if they oversold their stock of goods.

Facts: Abraham and Strauss advertised a set of Sango china dishes for sale in Newsday. The ad listed a sale price for a service for 12 as $39.95 and the regular price as $280. Judith Geismar tried to buy the set for $39.95, but the store would not sell it at that price. She sued the store.

Outcome: The court stated that the ad was not an offer but an invitation to negotiate.

The general rule is that circulars are not offers but invitations to the recipients to make an offer. However, it is often difficult to distinguish between a general sales letter and a personal sales letter. The fact that the letter is addressed to a particular individual does not necessarily make it a personal sales letter containing an offer. If the wording indicates that the writer is merely trying to evoke an offer on certain terms, it is an invitation to the other party to make an offer.

An advertisement, however, may be an offer when it clearly shows it is intended as an offer. This is primarily true with advertisements that offer rewards.

PREVIEW CASE REVISITED

Facts: Weldon Hall sponsored a boat race for which the advertised first prize was a 14-foot boat, a trailer, and a 20-horsepower motor. After Gerald Bean called Hall's marina and verified the first prize, he won, but Hall offered a 6-horsepower motor as first prize. Bean sued to recover the advertised first prize.

Outcome: The court found that Hall had made an offer to the public, which Bean accepted by winning the race.

Duration of the Offer

LO3 Rules on duration of offers

Several rules affect the duration of an offer.

1 The offeror may revoke an offer at any time prior to its acceptance. If it has been revoked, the offeree can no longer accept it and create a contract. Normally the offer can be revoked even if the offeror has promised to keep it open.

Facts: L. M. Cater and Daniel Haralson agreed to the sale of some land and Haralson put down a $5,000 deposit. Haralson signed a "contract" that stated, "This instrument shall be regarded as an offer by the party who first executes" it and "is open for acceptance by the other" until a specified date. Cater never signed the "contract." Haralson decided not to buy the land and sued to recover his deposit.

Outcome: The court said the "contract" was an offer, which Haralson was free to withdraw before Cater accepted it; therefore, Haralson could recover his deposit.

Option
Binding promise to hold an offer open

Firm Offer
A merchant's signed, written offer to sell or purchase goods saying it will be held open

2 An option cannot be revoked at will. If the offeror receives something of value in return for a promise to hold the offer open, it is said to be an **option** and this type of offer cannot be revoked.

If the offer relates to the sale or purchase of goods by a merchant, a signed written offer to purchase or sell that states that it will be held open cannot be revoked during the time stated or if no time is stated, for a reasonable time, not to exceed three months. This type of offer is called a **firm offer**. It is valid even though no payment is made to the offeror.

Facts: In April, Mid-South Packers sent a letter to Shoney's listing prices at which Mid-South would supply bacon. The letter, titled "Proposal," stated Shoney's would have 45-days notice of price changes. In July, Shoney's began purchasing meat from Mid-South. In August, Mid-South told Shoney's that the price of bacon would be 7¢ per pound higher. Shoney's next order requested shipment at the old, lower price, but orders were filled and billed at the higher price. Shoney's reduced its payment by what it claimed it was overcharged by the price increase. Mid-South sued for payment. Shoney's argued that the proposal was an offer, which it accepted by placing orders. As a binding contract, it required 45-days notice of price increases.

Outcome: The court said that as a firm offer, the proposal was irrevocable for no more than three months, which expired in July, prior to Shoney's acceptance. Mid-South had the right to raise its price in August and collect full payment.

In states in which the seal has its common-law effect, an offer cannot be revoked when it is contained in a sealed writing that states that it will not be revoked.

3 A revocation of an offer must be communicated to the offeree prior to the acceptance. Mere intention to revoke is not sufficient. This is true even though the intent is clearly shown to persons other than the offeree, as when the offeror dictates a letter of revocation.

Notice to the offeree that the offeror has behaved in a way that indicates the offer is revoked, such as selling the subject matter of the offer to another party, revokes the offer.

Facts: Melvin Ingebretson, the major stockholder of the First State Bank of Thornton, sought to employ Glenn Emmons as manager. Ingebretson agreed to give Emmons an option to purchase his and some other stock if Emmons would work for the bank. Ingebretson signed an option agreement and sent it to Emmons. Before Emmons signed it, Ingebretson called and told him to "hold up on the contract" because he could not get all the stock to sell. Four days later Emmons signed the contract and returned it to Ingebretson with a check for the first payment.

Outcome: The court held that the obvious implication of Ingebretson's statement was that he would not be able to continue the offer to sell the stock and he therefore revoked the offer.

4 An offer is terminated by the lapse of the time specified in the offer. If no time is specified in the offer, it is terminated by a lapse of a reasonable time after being communicated to the offeree. A reasonable length of time varies with each case depending on the circumstances. It may be 10 minutes in one case and 60 days in another. Important circumstances are whether the price of the goods or services involved are fluctuating rapidly, whether perishable goods are involved,

and whether there is keen competition with respect to the subject matter of the contract.

5 Death or insanity of the offeror automatically terminates the offer. This applies even though the offeree is not aware of the death or the insanity of the offeror and communicates an acceptance of the offer. Both parties must be alive and competent to contract at the moment the acceptance is properly communicated to the offeror.

6 Rejection of the offer by the offeree and communication of the rejection to the offeror terminates the offer.

7 If, after an offer has been made, the performance of the contract becomes illegal, the offer is terminated.

The Acceptance

Acceptance
Assent to an offer resulting in a contract

When an offer has been properly communicated to the party for whom it is intended and that party or an authorized agent accepts, a binding contract is formed. **Acceptance** is the assent to an offer that results in a contract. The acceptance must be communicated to the offeror, but no particular procedure is required. The acceptance may be made by words, oral or written, or by some act that clearly shows an intention to accept. Silence does not, except in rare cases, constitute an acceptance; nor is a mental intention to accept sufficient. If the offer stipulates a particular mode of acceptance, the offeree must meet those standards in order for a contract to be formed.

Facts: The check Michael O'Brien used to apply for auto insurance with Nationwide Mutual bounced. On October 2, he mailed a money order with a copy of his original insurance application to Nationwide. Nationwide sent him a letter saying it was not insuring him because the check bounced. When it received the money order, Nationwide deposited it, but immediately returned the payment saying the original policy was still cancelled. On October 27, O'Brien had an auto accident and sued Nationwide saying he had insurance coverage.

Outcome: Sending the application and check was an offer that Nationwide clearly did not accept because the check bounced. Sending the money order and copy of the application was another offer to purchase insurance from Nationwide. However, Nationwide never accepted this offer so there was no contract of insurance.

Counteroffers

LO4
Define counteroffer

Counteroffer
Offeree's response that rejects offer by varying its terms

An offer must be accepted without any deviation in its terms. If the intended acceptance varies or qualifies the offer, this **counteroffer** rejects the original offer. This rejection terminates the offer. This rule is changed to some extent where the offer relates to the sale or purchase of goods. In any case, a counteroffer may be accepted or rejected by the original offeror.

Facts: The Schoonovers offered to sell some real estate to Nance for $17,000 in cash. Nance told the Schoonovers he intended to give them a personal check in the amount of $17,000 to pay for the property.

Outcome: Since the offer specified payment in cash, not by personal check, Nance's statement was a counteroffer. The Schoonovers could either accept or reject this counteroffer.

Inquiries Not Constituting Rejection

The offeree may make an inquiry without rejecting the offer. For example, if the offer is for 1,000 shares of stock for $20,000 cash, the offeree may ask: "Would you be willing to wait 30 days for $10,000 and hold the stock as collateral security?" This mere inquiry does not reject the offer. If the offeror says no, the original offer may still be accepted, if it has not been revoked in the meantime.

Manner of Acceptance

LO5
Acceptance by mail

An offer that does not specify a particular manner of acceptance may be accepted in any manner reasonable under the circumstances. However, the offeror may stipulate that the acceptance must be written and received by the offeror in order to be effective. If there is no requirement of delivery, a properly mailed acceptance is effective when it is posted. This rule is called the "mailbox rule," and it applies even though the offeror never receives the acceptance.

Facts: National Old Line Insurance Company issued a $150,000 life insurance policy on John Bruegger. Premiums were not paid, and the policy lapsed. National sent an offer to reinstate the policy. On June 12, the documents required for reinstatement were properly mailed. The next day, Bruegger was shot. He died on June 24. The beneficiary requested the $150,000.

Outcome: National had to pay. Bruegger's acceptance of National's offer of reinstatement was effective upon mailing.

Similarly, the delivery of an acceptance to the telegraph company is effective unless the offeror specifies otherwise or unless custom or prior dealings indicate that acceptance by telegraph is improper. In former years the courts held that an offer could be accepted only by the same means by which the offer was communicated, called the "mirror-image rule." But this view is being abandoned in favor of the provision of the Uniform Commercial Code, Sec. 2–206(1)(a), relating to sales of goods: "Unless otherwise unambiguously indicated by the language or circumstances, an offer to make a [sales] contract shall be construed as inviting acceptance in any manner and by any medium reasonable in the circumstances." Under this principle, an acceptance can be made by telephone or even by fax. The contract is made on the date and at the place the fax acceptance is sent.

Careful and prudent persons can avoid many difficulties by stipulating in the offer how it must be accepted and when the acceptance is to become effective. For example, the offer may state, "The acceptance must be sent by letter and be received by me in Chicago by 12 noon on June 15 before the contract is complete." The acceptance is not effective unless it is sent by letter and is actually received by the offeror in Chicago by the time specified.

Questions

1 How is a contract created?
2 What are the three requirements of a valid offer?

3 What are common types of invitations to make an offer?

4 a. When may an offer be revoked?
b. What is the effect of death or insanity of the offeror?

5 How is a "reasonable time" after which an offer would "lapse" determined?

6 What are the requirements for an acceptance to the offeror?

7 What is a counteroffer and what is its effect on an offer?

8 What is the "mailbox rule?"

9 How may an offer received by (a) letter, (b) telegraph, or (c) fax be accepted?

Case Problems

LO1

1 Charles Wohltmann of Executive Recruitment, an employee recruitment company, twice talked with a Boston Scientific Corp. sales representative who had no authority to accept offers for hiring employees. Later Thomas Schmidt contacted a friend who worked for Boston and found out that Boston had a job opening in Birmingham where he wanted to work. Schmidt applied and eventually was hired by Boston. Executive Recruitment then claimed it had an oral contract for recruiting with Boston and should be paid for Schmidt's hiring. Should it?

LO1

2 After establishing a retirement system for public school teachers, the state of Maine amended the plan by raising the rate of teachers' required contributions, limiting salary increases that could be included in calculating a teacher's retirement benefit, and delaying the first cost-of-living adjustment. Richard Parker and other teachers sued saying they reasonably relied on and were induced to work by the continued existence of the original retirement benefits. Did the state have a contractual duty to provide the original benefits to those teachers who had worked long enough to meet the eligibility requirements for retirement benefits?

LO4

3 Roy Gilbert was an expert witness in a toxic tort lawsuit. When Gilbert sent his final bill to Akins & Pettiette, lawyers, they did not pay, so Gilbert's lawyer sent a letter demanding $5,448.25. Akins & Pettiette sent a check for $5,448.25 that stated: "Endorsement of this check constitutes . . . indemnity . . . of any and all claims and/or causes of action that arise or may arise out of" the toxic tort case and the present case. Gilbert rejected the check. The lawyers claimed he breached a contract to settle for $5,448.25. Did he?

LO5

4 Medicine Shops Inc. (MSI) offered to allow Jayco to use MSI's trademark, trade name, logo, and services. On January 18, Jayco wrote a letter to MSI accepting its offer. Although properly addressed, stamped, and mailed on January 20, the letter was never delivered. On January 19, MSI wrote and mailed a letter to Jayco revoking the offer. Jayco received this letter on January 21. Was there a contract?

LO5

5 A candidate in the Democratic primary election for the municipal council in Ridgefield, New Jersey, withdrew. A petition nominating Michael Madden was prepared, but because Madden was a student at Purdue University in Indiana he was not in New Jersey to sign the nomination acceptance. He signed the acceptance in Indiana and faxed it to New Jersey where it was properly and timely filed with the borough clerk. The clerk said the acceptance was defective because of the "facsimile" signature and refused to certify Madden as a candidate. Using principles of contract law, what is your opinion about the faxed document?

LO1,2

6 At the request of Nations Enterprises, Process Equipment made a proposal to supply some pumps for a project. Later Process got the specifications for the project and found out the pumps needed to withstand huge shock specifications. Nations sent a purchase order for some of the pumps in Process' proposal. The order said,

"Execute acceptance [copy] . . . and return . . ." and, "This order is not valid until acceptance copy showing shipping date is received." Process never executed or returned the acceptance copy because it was not sure the pumps could meet the shock requirements. After some negotiation, the shock requirements were reduced and Process shipped nine pumps. It did not supply any more. Did Process breach a contract to supply the remaining pumps?

LO1 7 Lynch received a contract to teach for the following school year. She signed the contract and delivered it in a sealed envelope to Chinn, the vice president of the school board. Chinn took it to the school board meeting that evening and gave it to the secretary. Miner, the school superintendent, announced that Lynch had returned the contract unsigned and recommended she be notified that her services would be terminated at the end of the current school year. The board approved that recommendation. After the meeting, the secretary opened the envelope. When sued by Lynch, the board alleged there was no contract because its offer had been withdrawn before it was accepted. Was there a contract?

Internet Resources for Business Law

Name	Resources	Web Address
Uniform Commercial Code §2-205	LII provides a hypertext and searchable version of UCC §2-205, Firm Offers.	http://www.law.cornell.edu/ucc/2/2-205.html
Uniform Commercial Code §2-206	LII provides a hypertext and searchable version of UCC §2-206, Offer and Acceptance in Formation of Contract.	http://www.law.cornell.edu/ucc/2/2-206.html
Uniform Commercial Code §2-207	LII provides a hypertext and searchable version of UCC §2-207, Additional Terms in Acceptance or Confirmation.	http://www.law.cornell.edu/ucc/2/2-207.html

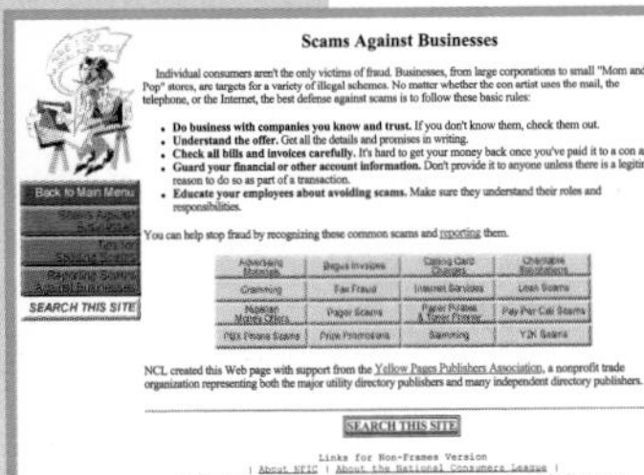

7 Capacity to Contract

Learning Objectives

1 Identify classifications of individuals who may not have the capacity to contract.

2 Define disaffirmance.

3 Explain how a minor's contract can be ratified.

4 Discuss reasons other than age that may impair a person's ability to contract.

PREVIEW CASE

When Jacqueline Flowers was four years old she was severely injured in an automobile accident. She received medical treatment for her injuries from East Tennessee Baptist Hospital, and the unpaid bill for this treatment was $5,271.29. A settlement in the amount of $7,125 was made for Jacqueline with the person alleged to have caused the accident. The hospital tried to subject the settlement to the payment of the hospital bill. Can the hospital recover? Was the medical treatment necessary?

For an agreement to be enforceable at law, all parties must have the legal and mental capacity to contract. This means that the parties must have the ability to understand that a contract is being made, have the ability to understand its general nature, and have the legal competence to contract. The general rule is that the law presumes that all parties have this capacity. This means that anyone alleging incapacity must offer proof of incapacity to overcome that presumption.

LO1 Those lacking capacity

However, in the eyes of the law some parties lack such capacity because of age, physical condition, or public policy. Among those whom the law considers to be incompetent, at least to some degree, are minors, mentally incompetent persons, intoxicated persons, and convicts.

Minors

Minor Person under the legal age to contract

The common-law rule that persons under 21 years of age are **minors** has been abolished by most of the states. Most states have enacted statutes making persons competent to contract at 18 years of age, and a few set the age at 19. In some states, all married minors are fully competent to contract. In still other states minors in business for themselves are bound on all their business contracts.

CONTRACTS OF MINORS

Almost all of a minor's contracts are voidable at the minor's option. That is, if a minor so desires, the minor can avoid the contract. If a minor wishes to treat a contract made with an adult as valid, the adult is bound by it. An adult cannot avoid a contract on the ground that the minor might avoid it. If a contract is between two minors, each has the right to avoid it. Should the minor die, the personal representative of the estate may avoid the contract that the minor could have avoided.

Firms that carry on business transactions in all the states must know the law dealing with minors in each state. Mail-order houses and correspondence schools are particularly susceptible to losses when dealing with minors. The significance of the law is that, with but few exceptions, people deal with minors at their own risk. The purpose of the law is to protect minors from unscrupulous adults, but in general the law affords the other party no more rights in scrupulous contracts than in unscrupulous ones. The minor is the sole judge as to whether a voidable contract will be binding.

CONTRACTS THAT CANNOT BE AVOIDED

Although most contracts made by minors are voidable, a few are not. These include contracts for necessaries, business contracts, and other specially enforced contracts such as student loan agreements.

Necessaries
Items required for living at a reasonable standard

Contracts of Minors for Necessaries. If a minor contracts for **necessaries**, the contract is voidable, but the minor is liable for the reasonable value. Necessaries include items required for a minor to have a reasonable standard of living that are not provided by the minor's parents or guardian. The dividing line between necessaries and luxuries is often a fine one. Historically necessaries included food, clothes, and shelter. With the raising of standards of living, courts now hold that necessaries also include medical services such as surgery, dental work, and medicine; education through high school or trade school, and in some cases through college; working tools for a trade; and other goods that are luxuries to some people but necessaries to others because of peculiar circumstances.

PREVIEW CASE REVISITED

Facts: When Jacqueline Flowers was four years old she was severely injured in an automobile accident. She received medical treatment from East Tennessee Baptist Hospital, and the unpaid bill for this treatment was $5,271.29. A settlement of $7,125 was made for Jacqueline with the person alleged to have caused the accident. The hospital tried to subject the settlement to the payment of the hospital bill.

Outcome: The court found that the treatment was necessary. Because of the inability of Jacqueline's parents to pay for the needed medical treatment, Jacqueline was required to pay the reasonable value of the services from the settlement.

The minor's liability is quasi-contractual in nature. The reasonable value of what is actually received must be paid in order to prevent the minor from being unjustly enriched. The minor is not, however, required to pay the contract price.

LO2
Define disaffirmance

Disaffirmance
Repudiation of a voidable contract

Disaffirmance. The term **disaffirmance** means the repudiation of a contract, that is, the election to avoid it or set it aside. A minor has the legal right to disaffirm a voidable contract at any time during minority or within a reasonable time after becoming of age. If the contract is wholly executory, a disaffirmance completely nullifies the contract.

Upon electing to disaffirm contracts, minors must return whatever they may have received under the contracts, provided they still have possession of it. The fact that the minor does not have possession of the property, however, regardless of the reason, does not prevent the exercise of the right to disaffirm the contract. In most jurisdictions, an adult may not recover compensation from a minor who returns the property in damaged condition.

Facts: Halbman, a minor, agreed to purchase a car from Lemke. He made a down payment and took possession of the car. An engine rod broke, and Halbman had the car repaired at a garage. Lemke endorsed the car's title to Halbman, but shortly thereafter Halbman returned the title to Lemke, disaffirmed the contract, offered to return the car, and demanded the return of all his money. The repair bill had never been paid, so the garage removed the engine and transmission. The car was vandalized, making it unsalvageable. Halbman sued Lemke for the money he had paid him. Lemke argued that he should be entitled to recover for the damage to the vehicle up to the time of disaffirmance.

Outcome: Halbman was entitled to recover his payments without liability for the use, depreciation, or damage to the car.

If an adult purchases personal property from a minor, the adult has only a voidable title to the property. If the property is sold to an innocent third party before the minor disaffirms the contract, the innocent third party obtains good title to the property. However, the minor may recover from the adult the money or the value of property received from the third party. Statutes in some states make minors' contracts void, not merely voidable. In these states, disaffirmance is not necessary.

LO3
Minor's ratification

Ratification
Adult indicating contract made while a minor is binding

Ratification. A minor may ratify a voidable contract only after attaining majority. **Ratification** means indicating one's willingness to be bound by promises made during minority. It is in substance a new promise and may be oral, written, or merely implied by conduct.

After majority is reached, silence ratifies an executed contract.

Facts: William Jones, a minor, signed a contract with Free Flight Sport Aviation allowing Jones to use an airplane ferrying skydivers. The contract included an agreement not to sue and an exemption of liability for Free Flight. A month later Jones attained majority. Ten months after that he was seriously injured when a Free Flight skydiving plane crashed. He sued Free Flight for his injuries.

Outcome: The court held that Jones had ratified the contract by accepting the benefits of it when he used Free Flight's facilities the day of the crash.

A minor cannot ratify part of a contract and disaffirm another part; all or none of it must be ratified. Ratification must be made within a reasonable time after reaching majority. A reasonable time is a question of fact to be determined in light of all surrounding circumstances.

Minors' Business Contracts. Many states, either by special statutory provision or by court decisions, have made a minor's business contracts fully binding. If a minor engages in a business or employment in the same manner as a person having legal capacity, contracts that arise from such business or employment cannot be set aside.

Other Enforceable Contracts. A number of states prevent a minor from avoiding certain specified contracts. These contracts include educational loan agreements, contracts for medical care, contracts made with court approval or in performance of a legal duty, and contracts involving bank accounts.

Facts: When 17 years old, Kate Michaelis came to Dr. Janet Schori for pregnancy care. Michaelis signed an agreement for binding arbitration of disputes regarding the quality of the medical care. When Michaelis went into labor Schori told her another doctor would meet her at the hospital. The other doctor never showed up and the baby, otherwise normal, was stillborn. Michaelis and Bodie Stroud, the baby's father, sued saying Michaelis disaffirmed the arbitration agreement. State law provided that a minor could give binding consent for medical care related to treatment of pregnancy.

Outcome: The court pointed out that consent to medical treatment necessarily includes the resolution of disputes over the quality of care. Further, a minor who had to have a parent consent to pregnancy treatment might forgo prenatal care. Thus Michaelis could not disaffirm the arbitration provision entered into as part of the contract for treatment of her pregnancy.

CONTRACTING SAFELY WITH MINORS

Since in general it is risky to deal with minors, every businessperson must know how to be protected when contracting with minors. The safest way is to have an adult (usually a parent or guardian) join in the contract as a cosigner with the minor. This gives the other party to the contract the right to sue the adult who cosigned. A merchant must run some risks when dealing with minors. If a sale is made to a minor, the minor may avoid the contract and demand a refund of the purchase price years later. Since few minors exercise this right, businesspersons often run the risk of contracting with minors rather than seeking absolute protection against loss.

MINORS' TORTS

As a general rule, a minor is liable for torts as fully as an adult is. If minors misrepresent their age, and the adults with whom they contract rely upon the misrepresentation to their detriment, the minors have committed a tort. The law is not uniform throughout the United States as to whether or not minors are bound on contracts induced by misrepresenting their age. In some states, when sued, they cannot avoid their contracts if they fraudulently misrepresented their age. In some states they may be held liable for any damage to or deterioration of the property they received under the contract. If minors sue on the contracts to recover what they paid, they may be denied recovery if they misrepresented their age.

Facts: The Manasquan Savings and Loan Association loaned Lynn Mayer, a minor, and her husband $22,000 based on her sworn statement that she was of age. Mayer and her husband later separated and defaulted on the loan. When Manasquan sued to recover the collateral, Mayer asserted her minority and demanded that Manasquan return all her funds used to make payments on the note.

Outcome: The court held that minority was no defense to Manasquan's action because Mayer misrepresented her age.

Mentally Incompetent Persons

LO4 Impairment other than by reason of age

A number of reasons beyond a person's control result in mental incompetence. These include insanity or incompetence as a result of stroke, senile dementia, and retardation. In determining a mentally incompetent person's capacity to contract, the intensity and duration of the incompetency must be determined. In most states, if a person has been formally adjudicated incompetent, contracts made by the person are void without regard to whether they are reasonable or for necessaries. Such a person is considered incapable of making a valid acceptance of an offer no matter how fair the offer is. When a person has been judicially declared insane and sanity is later regained and a court officially declares the person to be competent, the capacity to contract is the same as that of any other normal person.

If a person is incompetent but has not been so declared by the court, then the person's contracts are voidable, not void. Like a minor, the person must pay the reasonable value of necessaries that have been supplied. Upon disaffirmance, anything of value received under the contracts and which the person still has must be returned.

Facts: A court found Kathy Hauer incompetent after she suffered a brain injury in an accident and appointed a guardian. Hauer's monthly income was $900 from social security and interest from a mutual fund worth $80,000. About the time the guardianship was terminated based on a letter from Hauer's doctor, Ben Eilbes who was in default on a $7,600 business loan from Union State Bank of Wautoma met Hauer. He learned of her mutual fund and convinced her to "invest" in his business. However, she could only cash in her mutual fund at certain times. Eilbes told Richard Schroeder, an officer of the bank, that Hauer wanted to invest in his business and needed a loan but would put up the mutual fund as collateral. He said Hauer's loan would either bring his payments current or pay off his loan. Schroeder called Hauer's financial consultant who said she had the mutual fund, but needed the income to live on and should not use it as collateral. He also said she suffered from brain damage. Schroeder told Eilbes the bank would loan Hauer $30,000. Schroeder met Hauer for the first time when she signed the loan documents thinking she was cosigning for Eilbes who would pay the money back. Hauer sued the bank stating she had cognitive disabilities and was very gullible—people could convince her of almost anything.

Outcome: The court held that she clearly lacked capacity to understand the loan. Because the bank failed to act in good faith toward Hauer she did not have to return the $30,000 which Eilbes had spent.

Facts: Emanuel Watson, when he was 100 years old and unable to handle his business affairs because of a stroke, sold some land worth $6,750 to Stewart and Gloria Landes for $200. Emanuel's widow, Reather, asked a court to set the transaction aside, saying Emanuel was not competent at the time of the sale. Reather alleged that the inadequate consideration was evidence of Emanuel's incompetence.

Outcome: The court held that such a gross inadequacy of consideration proved Emanuel's incapacity. The sale was set aside.

PART PAYMENT

LO2 Part payment as consideration

A partial payment of a past-due debt is not consideration to support the creditor's promise to cancel the balance of the debt. The creditor is already entitled to the part payment. Promising to give something to which the other party is already entitled is not consideration.

Several exceptions apply to this rule:

1 If the amount of the debt is in dispute, the debt is canceled if a lesser sum than that claimed is accepted in full settlement.

PREVIEW CASE REVISITED

Facts: Richard Runyan, age 53, was told his employment would be terminated. He told his employer that it was age discrimination. His employer said it was because of inadequate job performance. After discussing the termination, Runyan and the employer agreed that Runyan would have a one-year consulting arrangement that provided a minimum monthly compensation. Later Runyan asked that the agreement be extended and the compensation increased. The company agreed to increase the monthly compensation by $1,667 in consideration for Runyan's releasing the company from all other debts and claims relating to his termination. Both parties signed this agreement. After the consulting agreement expired, Runyan sued the company for $450,000, claiming he had been terminated because of age discrimination.

Outcome: The court found a bona fide dispute existed concerning the reason for the termination. Therefore, any greater amount potentially owed by the company because of age discrimination was waived when the increased compensation was given in full settlement of any claims by Runyan regarding his termination.

2 If there is more than one creditor, and each one agrees, in consideration of the others' agreement, to accept in full settlement a percentage of the amount due, this agreement will cancel the unpaid balance due these creditors. This arrangement is known as a **composition of creditors**.

Composition of Creditors
When all of multiple creditors settle in full for a fraction of the amount owed

3 If the debt is evidenced by a note or other written evidence, cancellation and return of the written evidence cancels the debt.

Facts: The Henry B. Gilpin Company agreed to pay David Moxley $56,390 and signed a note to Moxley in that amount. When interest came due, Gilpin could not make the payment. It proposed a composition of creditors by which it would pay 60 percent of all debts owed in full settlement. Moxley and a majority of the creditors agreed. Two months later, Gilpin offered a new plan to ensure that it continued in business. This offer stated it superseded the previous offer, which it withdrew. This offer also precluded Gilpin from paying any creditor under the previous offer. All creditors except Moxley accepted the second offer. Moxley demanded payment of the whole amount due including interest. Gilpin paid only interest, and Moxley sued, claiming Gilpin had breached its agreement.

Outcome: The court found that the first composition was a binding contract, and Moxley was entitled to sue on it.

4 If the payment of the lesser sum is accompanied by a receipt in full and some indication that a gift is made of the balance, the debt may be canceled.
5 If a secured note is given and accepted in discharge of an unsecured note for a greater amount, the difference between the two notes is discharged. The security is the consideration to support the contract to settle for a lesser sum.

INSUFFICIENT OR INVALID CONSIDERATION

LO3 Insufficient and invalid consideration

Many apparent considerations lack the full force and effect necessary to make enforceable agreements. Consideration of the following classes is either insufficient or invalid:

1 Performing or promising to perform what one is already obligated to do
2 Refraining or promising to refrain from doing what one has no right to do
3 Past performance

Performing or Promising to Perform What One Is Already Obligated to Do. If the supposed consideration consists merely of a promise to do what one is already legally obligated to do, consideration is invalid. If the consideration is invalid, the contract is invalid. In such case, the promise gives nothing new to the other contracting party.

Facts: Wendell Anderson purchased a herbicide and applied it to farmland. He later became aware of a weed-control problem on the farm. The company that produced the herbicide offered to settle Anderson's claim by providing an alternative herbicide equal to the value of the original herbicide plus a cash allowance for application. Anderson accepted the offer. He later sued for $10,228 for the failure of the original herbicide to control the growth of weeds. Anderson alleged that the producer's settlement offer was a promise to perform a preexisting duty (weed control), so the compromise agreement was invalid for lack of consideration.

Outcome: The court held that the producer's act of providing an alternative herbicide plus cash and Anderson's promise not to sue provided consideration, and the compromise agreement was valid.

Parties to a contract may at any time mutually agree to cancel an old contract and replace it with a new one. For this new contract to be enforceable, there must be some added features that benefit both parties, though not necessarily to an equal extent. If a contractor agrees to build a house of certain specifications for $80,000, a contract of the homeowner to pay an additional $1,000 is not binding unless the contractor concurrently agrees to do something the original contract did not require as a consideration for the $1,000. The value of the additional act by the contractor need not be $1,000. It merely must have a monetary value.

If unforeseen difficulties arise that make it impossible for the contractor to complete the house for $80,000, these unforeseen difficulties may, in rare cases, be consideration. Unforeseen difficulties include underground rock formations or a change in the law relative to the building codes and zoning laws. The homeowner is not bound to agree to pay more because of unforeseen difficulties; but if such an agreement is made, these difficulties will constitute a consideration even though the contractor does not agree to do anything additional. Strikes, bad weather, and a change in prices are examples of foreseeable difficulties, which would not be consideration.

Forbearance
Refraining from doing something

Refraining or Promising to Refrain from Doing What One Has No Right to Do. When one refrains or promises to refrain from doing something, this conduct is called **forbearance**. If the promisor had a right to do the act, forbearance is a valid consideration. Consideration is invalid when it consists of a promise to forbear doing something that one has no right to do, such as to commit an unlawful act.

Often the forbearance consists of promising to refrain from suing the other party. Promising to refrain from suing another constitutes consideration if one has a reasonable right to demand damages and intends to file a suit. Such a promise is even valid when a suit lacks merit if the promisor mistakenly, but honestly and reasonably, believes a suit would be valid.

Facts: Stanley Spray and others owned houses that bordered and enjoyed an unobstructed view of the Arroyo del Oso Golf Course. The city of Albuquerque began to construct a 7-foot chain link fence topped with barbed wire around the golf course. Spray met with city officials and they agreed to a fence of only 3 to 4 feet. A new city administration later began installing 5-foot fence posts. The homeowners threatened to sue to enforce the prior agreement and the city backed down. Still later, the city began installing a 5-foot fence and the homeowners sued.

Outcome: The court held that the homeowners' forbearance from suing was adequate consideration to support the agreement with the city and ordered the city not to build the 5-foot fence.

Past Performance. An act performed prior to the promise does not constitute valid consideration. If a carpenter gratuitously helps a neighbor build a house with no promise of pay, a promise to pay made after the house is completed cannot be enforced. The promise to pay must induce the carpenter to do the work, and this cannot be done if the promise is made after the work is completed.

A debt that is discharged by bankruptcy may be revived under certain circumstances, usually by the debtor's agreeing, with approval from the bankruptcy court, to pay it. Such promises are enforceable even though the creditor, the promisee, gives no new consideration to support the promise. The debtor is said to have waived the defense of discharge in bankruptcy; and the original debt, therefore, is deemed to remain in force.

Facts: For 30 years Virginia Sigler resided with Helen Mariotte and shared expenses. After Mariotte was hospitalized, Sigler was eager for her to return home and told Mariotte's son she would care for her at no charge. Sigler assisted in caring for Mariotte and paid $200 per month for food and rent. Three years later Mariotte signed a document in which she instructed that from the time of her return from the hospital, Sigler was to be paid $85 per week plus room and board. After a conservator was appointed for Mariotte, Sigler filed a claim for $85 per week and reimbursement for rent and food after Mariotte's return from the hospital.

Outcome: The claim was disallowed. Sigler agreed to care for Mariotte free of charge. Past benefits did not constitute consideration for the subsequent promise by Mariotte.

Exceptions to Requirement of Consideration

LO4 When consideration is not required

As a general rule, a promise must be supported by consideration. Certain exceptions to the rule involve voluntary subscriptions, debts of record, promissory estoppel, and modification of sales contracts.

VOLUNTARY SUBSCRIPTIONS

When charitable enterprises are financed by voluntary subscriptions of many persons, the promise of each person is generally held to be enforceable. When a number of people make pledges to or subscribe to a charitable association or to a church, for example, the pledges or subscriptions are binding. One theory for enforcing the promise is that each subscriber's promise is supported by the promises of other subscribers. Another theory is that a subscription is an offer of a unilateral contract that is accepted by creating liabilities or making expenditures. Despite the fact that such promises lack the technical requirements of ordinary contracts, the courts in most states will enforce the promises as a matter of public policy.

Facts: To encourage doctors to settle in Parkersburg and to provide a medical building, P.H.C.C.C. was formed to solicit contributions. At a meeting P.H.C.C.C. held, B. J. Johnston spoke favorably about the project and said he would give $50,000. He read and signed a subscription card that said "I _____ do hereby subscribe and promise to pay P.H.C.C.C. . . . the total sum of $50,000." Johnston gave only $12,750. The building was completed using borrowed money. Johnston's subscription was used as collateral for the loan. P.H.C.C.C sued for the remainder of the pledge. Johnston claimed the subscription agreement was unenforceable.

Outcome: The court said it was enforceable.

DEBTS OF RECORD

Consideration is not necessary to support an obligation of record, such as a judgment, on the basis that such an obligation is enforceable as a matter of public policy.

PROMISSORY ESTOPPEL

Promissory Estoppel Substitute for consideration when another acts in reliance on promisor's promise

Although not supported by considerations, courts enforce some promises on the basis of **promissory estoppel**. According to this doctrine, if one person makes a promise to another and that other person acts in reliance upon the promise, the promisor will not be permitted to claim lack of consideration. Enforcement is held to be proper when the promisor should reasonably expect to cause and does cause action by the promisee and the promisee would be harmed substantially if the promise is not enforced. The theory has gained support as a means of realizing justice. The elements of promissory estoppel include:

1. A promise is made.
2. The promisor reasonably expects the promise to induce action by the promisee.
3. The promisee does act.
4. Justice requires enforcement of the promise.

Courts will find that justice requires enforcement of the promise when the promisee would be substantially harmed if it were not enforced.

Facts: McNeill and Associates was a general agent for ITT Life Insurance. Insurance Marketing, Inc. (IMI) owed ITT a large amount of money and was failing. ITT asked McNeill to purchase IMI's business. McNeill refused. IMI had ten times as many accounts as McNeill. Later ITT again asked McNeill to purchase IMI's business. A written agreement of sale was signed by IMI, McNeill, and ITT. ITT separately promised McNeill it would not terminate the general agency if McNeill purchased IMI. McNeill purchased IMI's business for $510,000. ITT later terminated the agency. McNeill sued and alleged that promisory estoppel required enforcement of the promise not to terminate the agency.

Outcome: The court said justice required enforcing the promise because of liabilities McNeill incurred by purchasing a much larger business in reliance on ITT's promise.

MODIFICATION OF SALES CONTRACTS

Sales of goods are regulated by the Uniform Commercial Code (see Chapter 16). The Code provides that when a contract for the sale of goods is modified by agreement of the parties, no consideration is necessary to make it enforceable.

Questions

1. What is the importance of consideration?
2. May a conditional promise constitute consideration? Explain.
3. If a boy promises his father that he will not own and operate an automobile until he is 18 in exchange for his father's promise to pay him $2,000, is this a valid contract?
4. What is the relevance of a grossly inadequate consideration given by one part to a contract?
5. If Davis owes Dennis $10,000, and Dennis offers to settle for $7,000, what must be done to make the contract binding?
6. Why does a composition of creditors allow partial payment of a debt to cancel the balance of the debt?

7 If parties to a contract mutually agree to cancel the contract and replace it with a new one what must happen for the new contract to be enforceable?
8 May refraining from suing someone be valid consideration?
9 May the promise of the debtor to pay a debt discharged by bankruptcy be enforceable?
10 Under what theory will courts enforce a promise to pay a voluntary subscription?

Case Problems

LO1

1 After Prudential-Bache Securities signed a confidentiality agreement, Robert Apfel allowed it to review a system he proposed to allow bonds to be traded and held solely by means of computerized book entries. Prudential then contracted with Apfel to pay him to use the system even if the technique became public knowledge. The first year Prudential was the only underwriter using such a system. After paying Apfel for several years, Prudential stopped. By this time investment banks were using computerized systems more and more. Apfel sued. Prudential said no contract existed because Apfel gave no consideration. Had he?

LO1

2 Superior Concrete Pumping contracted to pump concrete for David Montoya Construction for $5 per cubic yard with a guaranteed minimum of 200 yards per pour. The first two pours averaged only 100 yards, so the parties modified the contract. Superior was to bill at $5 per cubic yard, but when the job was completed, Montoya would also pay Superior the difference between that price and an hourly rate. When Montoya did not pay the difference Superior sued. Had Superior just agreed to continue performing as already required so the new agreement lacked consideration?

LO2

3 William Coester had a beer distributorship agreement with H.H.B. Company. The parties entered into a Termination of Business Agreement, which included a full release of H.H.B. from Coester. H.H.B. agreed to purchase all Coester's inventory at retail price and pay off a $44,164.10 mortgage on a warehouse rented by Coester from his mother for use in his business. H.H.B. performed all its obligations under the agreement. Coester sued H.H.B., arguing that the release was invalid because it was not supported by adequate consideration because the retail price of the beer was not much and he did not receive the benefit of the $44,164.10 paid on the mortgage. Was the release valid?

LO1,4

4 Gordon Hayes offered Kathleen Hunter a job, to begin on a specified date, as a flag girl on a construction job. He also told her to quit her job at the telephone company. Hunter did quit her job, but Hayes did not employ her, and she was out of work for two months. She sued Hayes for her lost wages. Hayes said there was no consideration for his promise, therefore it was unenforceable. How should the court decide?

LO2

5 Carl Evans Boyd and Luther Claud Boyd died leaving two sets of wills. The beneficiaries of the earlier wills contested the later wills, claiming the Boyds did not have the testamentary capacity to make them. While the will contest was pending, all the parties entered into written agreements resolving all the questions regarding the distribution of the estates of the Boyds. They then asked the judge to enter an order confirming the agreements and disposing of the will contest in accordance with the agreements. The judge claimed he could not enter a judgment declaring the later wills void without finding that the Boyds lacked capacity to make them. Was there sufficient consideration for the agreements?

LO3

6 After having surgery, Roman Hladun needed personal care upon leaving the hospital. Hladun entered a written agreement with Tender Loving Care Agency to

provide the care. A week later, Hladun's daughter, Vira Goldman, returned from Hong Kong. When Tender Loving Care Agency was not fully paid, it sued Goldman claiming she had orally promised to pay for the care. Was Goldman liable?

LO1,4 7 At a meeting of the board of trustees of the Oral Roberts Evangelistic Association, Nicholas Timko proposed that a building in Detroit be purchased. He stated that a down payment of $25,000 could buy it, and if the association made payments for five years, he would then pay any unpaid balance. The association bought the building with Timko making the arrangements and reiterating his promise to pay the balance remaining after five years. Less than five years after the purchase Timko died having made no payment. The association filed a claim for the unpaid balance against Timko's estate alleging his voluntary subscription was enforceable on the basis of promissory estoppel. Is the promise enforceable?

LO3 8 Walter and Martha Crown agreed, in writing, to buy William and Ann Cole's house and put down $1,500, of which $500 was a note. The Crowns asked the broker to condition their purchase on them selling their own house; however, they knew the agreement did not say that. When they had difficulty selling their house, they sued for return of their $1,500 alleging they had an oral agreement that their purchase was conditioned on selling their house. They claimed the consideration for the oral agreement was that they gave up the legal right to contest the validity of the note and not pay it. Was this a forbearance and valid consideration?

Internet Resources for Business Law

Name	Resources	Web Address
Uniform Commercial Code §2-209	LII provides a hypertext and searchable version of UCC §2-209, Modification, Rescission, and Waiver.	http://www.law.cornell.edu/ucc/2/2-209.html
Legal Information Institute—Contract Law Materials	LII provides an overview of contract law, links to federal government statutes, treaties, and regulations; federal and state judicial decisions regarding contract law (including Supreme Court decisions); state statutes; and other materials.	http://www.law.cornell.edu/topics/contracts.html

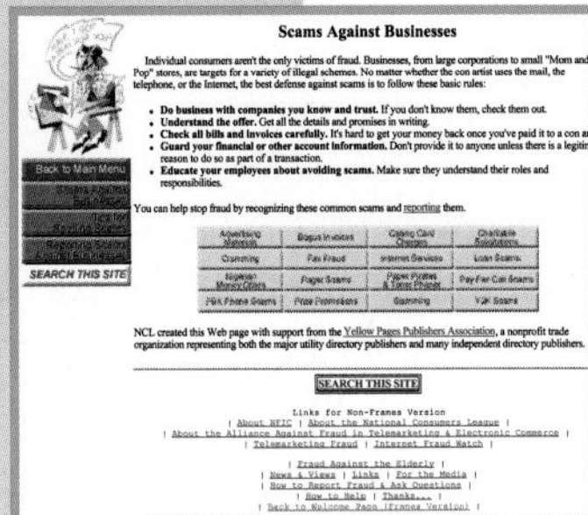

9 Defective Agreements

Learning Objectives

1. Describe the mistakes that do not invalidate a contract.
2. State what types of mistakes normally invalidate contracts.
3. Identify the situations in which fraud, duress, or undue influence are present.
4. Explain the remedies available to the victim of acts rendering contracts voidable.

PREVIEW CASE

Greenspan and Jacobsen built a duplex on a foundation that was constructed in violation of the building code. The foundation could not sustain the weight of the building. Massive cracks and severe settlement ensued. Greenspan and Jacobsen had plasterboard erected in the basement to cover the cracks. They then sold the duplex to Haberman and Ericksen. When the buyers discovered the cracks and settlement, they sought to invalidate the contract. May they? Did Greenspan and Jacobsen try to hide the fact that there were cracks in the foundation?

Even when an offer and an acceptance have been made, situations exist in which the resulting contract is defective. Some mistakes make contracts defective. In addition, fraud, duress, or undue influence makes contracts voidable because they are defective. A victim of an act rendering a contract defective has a choice of remedies.

Mistakes

Unilateral Mistake
Mistake by one party to a contract

Mutual Mistake
Mistake by both parties to a contract

Whether a mistake affects the validity of a contract normally depends on whether just one of the parties or both parties have made a mistake. A **unilateral mistake** occurs when only one party makes a mistake without the knowledge of the other. When both parties to a contract make the same mistake, a **mutual mistake** occurs.

UNILATERAL MISTAKES

LO1
Noninvalidating mistakes

As a general rule, a unilateral mistake made at the time of contracting has no effect on the validity of a contract. This is true, for example, if a unilateral mistake occurs as to price or quantity. Even if the unilateral mistake as to price results from an error in typing or in misunderstanding an oral quotation of the price, the contract is valid.

Facts: Easy Parking, through its president, Vincent Smith, contracted with John Bachman to lease a parking lot at 1102 Dodge Street without ever meeting with Bachman at the property. Bachman supplied the legal description of the property which was ". . . the south 54 feet of Lot 1 and all of Lot 8 . . ." even though a building occupied most of Lot 8. Smith did not check the location of the described lot and had flyers announcing the new management of the lot put on cars in a parking lot on Lot 7. Smith was told the next day that Bachman did not own the parking lot on Lot 7, but had the parking lot just north of the building on Lot 8. Easy Parking then claimed the lease was void because of mutual mistake and a lawsuit ensued.

Outcome: It was apparent to the court that the only mistake was made by Easy Parking. As a unilateral mistake, it did not void the contract.

MUTUAL MISTAKES

When the mutual mistake concerns a material fact, some courts say such a contract is void because no genuine assent by the parties exists. Other courts say the contract is voidable. Some courts are not precise about whether the contract is void or voidable. However they classify a mutual-mistake contract, courts do not find them enforceable.

Facts: When contracting to buy the Last Chance Allotment—a ranching operation—from Robert Langston, neither Gurr McQuarrie, the buyer, nor Langston knew exactly how many cattle were involved in the sale. The contract provided for a cattle count to determine the exact number; however, both parties thought the total number was 285, and at the agreed price per head, the total price would be $240,000. The cattle count showed only 246 head, so the total price was much less than $240,000.

Outcome: The court found a mutual mistake as to the number of cattle and the price. In this jurisdiction the contract was voidable, and Langston had it voided.

The area of mistake is one in which significant variations exist among the states and also where exceptions to the general rules have been established in order to avoid harsh results. In some states it is much easier than in other states to get the courts to agree with a party that a contract should not be enforced when there has been a mistake.

CONTRACT TERMS GOVERN

It is important to remember that no matter what the law provides when a mistake occurs, the parties may specify a different outcome in their contract. And when the contract specifies what is to happen in the case of a mistake, the contract provision will apply even if the law would be otherwise. The contract could also indicate which party assumes the risk that the facts are not as believed. The law as to mistake applies only in the absence of a governing provision in the contract, so long as that governing provision is not unconscionable.

Facts: A. Cushman and Beresha Atkins purchased a residential lot from E. F. and Janice Kirkpatrick. Their contract stated that "this property is purchased 'as is.' " The Atkins tried to have a house built on the lot, but when the contractor dug footings, ground water seeped into the holes making it impossible to use them. The Atkins sued the Kirkpatricks claiming mutual mistake as to the suitability of the lot for use as a residential building lot.

Outcome: The court found mutual mistake of fact, but said the contract clearly allocated the burden of loss on the purchasers and the contract terms governed.

A contract could specify that it will be void if a specified fact is not as believed. *A*, owning a stone, could believe it to be worth very little money. However, if *A* wants to sell the stone to *B* for $100, the contract could recite that it is void if the stone is actually a valuable diamond. This applies in spite of the general rule announced above that a unilateral mistake does not invalidate a contract.

The contract could also make the realization of certain expectations a condition of the contract. If those expectations were not realized, even if only one party was mistaken about them, the contract would not be binding.

Frequently contracts are entered into orally and then reduced to writing. If, through an error in typing, the written form does not conform to the oral form, then the written form does not bind the parties. The contract is what the parties agreed to orally.

EXCEPTIONS TO GENERAL RULE

It is said that every rule has an exception, and the rule regarding unilateral mistake and mutual mistake of fact also has exceptions. Most states recognize the exceptions to the rule on mutual mistake; however, significant variation occurs among the states regarding whether exceptions to the unilateral-mistake rule are recognized.

LO2
Invalidating mistakes

Unilateral Mistakes. When there has been a unilateral mistake of a fact, the mistaken party sometimes receives relief. Courts will generally allow a unilateral mistake of fact to impair the enforceability of a contract if the nonmistaken party has caused the mistake or knew or should have known of the other party's mistake. Courts show extreme unwillingness to allow one party to hold the other to a contract if the first party knows that the other one has made a mistake.

Facts: Svalina, foreign-born and poorly educated, paid $5,160.40 to Big Horn National Life Insurance Co. Agents of the company had told him he could make an investment. He asked what would be paid in interest and they told him 10 percent. He thought that the contract was primarily for the purchase of stock. It was solely for the purchase of insurance. When Svalina found out he had purchased insurance and no stock, he sued for the return of his money.

Outcome: The court found Svalina made a unilateral mistake caused and known by the agents. This entitled Svalina to relief.

A small number of states allow a party who has made a unilateral mistake of fact to raise the mistake as a defense when sued on the contract. This is allowed when the party has not been inexcusably negligent in making the mistake, and the other, nonmistaken, party has not taken actions in reliance on the contract so that failure to enforce it would be unconscionable.

To entitle a party to relief, the mistake must be one of fact, not mere opinion. If *A* buys a painting from *B* for $10 and it is actually worth $5,000, even if *A* knows *B* is mistaken as to its value, there is a valid contract. *B*'s opinion as to its value is erroneous, but there is no mistake as to a fact.

Since there are few exceptions to the rule that unilateral mistake does not affect a contract, it is clear that the law does not save us from the consequences of all mistakes. The exceptions cover a very small percentage of mistakes made in business transactions. Knowledge and diligence, not law, protect businesses against losses due to mistakes.

Mutual Mistakes. A mutual mistake will normally make a contract defective except in the case of mistake as to:

1. Value, quality, or price
2. The terms of the contract
3. The law
4. Expectations

Mistakes as to Value, Quality, or Price. A contract is not affected by the fact that the parties made mistaken assumptions as to the value, quality, or price of the subject matter of the contract. Normally the parties assume the risk that their assumptions regarding these matters can be incorrect. If buyers do not trust their judgment, they have the right to demand a warranty from the seller as to the quality or value of the articles they are buying. Their ability to contract wisely is their chief protection against a bad bargain. If Snead sells Robinson a television set for $350, Robinson cannot rescind the contract merely because the set proved to be worth only $150. This is a mistake as to value and quality. Robinson should obtain as a part of the contract an express warranty as to the set's quality. Conversely, if the seller parts with a jewel for $50, thinking it is a cheap stone, a complaint cannot later be made if the jewel proves to be worth $2,500.

Mistakes as to the Terms of the Contract. A mistake as to the terms of the contract usually results from failure to read a written contract or failure to understand a contract's meaning or significance. Such mistakes in both written and oral contracts do not affect their validity; otherwise anyone could avoid a contract merely by claiming a mistake as to its terms.

Facts: Lula and Martin signed a property settlement agreement giving Lula all the couple's property in California and Martin all the couple's property in Missouri. Martin's lawyer had drawn up the agreement. Martin later wanted the agreement voided because he had intended a note and a bank account in California to be his. Lula said she thought that property was to be hers.

Outcome: The court found Martin's mistake regarding the terms of the contract did not invalidate it.

Mistakes of Law. Ordinarily, when the parties make a mutual mistake of law, the contract is fully binding. The parties are expected to have knowledge of the law when making a contract.

Facts: George Bruner was paid $32,000 in settlement of a lung disease claim against Illinois Central Gulf Railroad. He signed a release that forever discharged the railroad "from any and all claims, demands, damages, actions, . . . or suits of any kind" which he had or might later have from his employment with the railroad. The release specifically included damages arising from any hearing loss. Nine months later Bruner sued Illinois Central for hearing loss from working for the railroad. He said he did not intend the release he signed to release the railroad from a hearing loss claim. He just wanted to release it from his lung disease claim.

Outcome: The court held that Bruner's mistake was one of law, not of fact. He could not avoid the contract because of a mistaken opinion as to its legal effect.

Mistakes as to Expectations. When the parties to a contract are mutually mistaken as to their expectations, the contract is binding.

Fraud

LO3

Situations of fraud, duress, or undue influence

http://

www.fraud.org/

One who intends to and does induce another to enter into a contract as a result of an intentionally or recklessly false statement of a material fact commits **fraud**. The courts recognize two kinds of fraud relating to contracts. These are fraud in the inducement and fraud in the execution.

Fraud
Inducing another to contract as a result of an intentionally or recklessly false statement of a material fact

Fraud in the Inducement
Defrauded party intended to make a contract

Fraud in the Execution
Defrauded party did not intend to enter into a contract

FRAUD IN THE INDUCEMENT

When the party defrauded intended to make the contract, **fraud in the inducement** occurs. Fraud in the inducement involves a false statement regarding the terms or obligations of the transaction between the parties and not the nature of the document signed. The false statement might relate to the terms of the agreement, the quality of the goods sold, or the seller's intention to deliver goods. A contract so induced is voidable.

FRAUD IN THE EXECUTION

The defrauded party might also be tricked into signing a contract under circumstances in which the nature of the writing could not be understood. The law calls this **fraud in the execution** or fraud in the factum. In this case the victim unknowingly signs a contract. A person who cannot read or who cannot read the language in which the contract is written could be a victim of this type of fraud. When fraud in the execution occurs, the contract is void.

Fraud also may be classified according to whether a party engages in some activity that causes the fraud or does nothing. A party who actually does something or takes steps to cause a fraud commits active fraud. Sometimes a party may be guilty of fraud without engaging in any activity at all. Passive fraud results from the failure to disclose information when there is a duty to do so.

ACTIVE FRAUD

Active Fraud
Party engages in action that causes the fraud

Active fraud may occur either by express misrepresentation or by concealment of material facts.

Express Misrepresentation. Fraud, as a result of express misrepresentation, consists of four elements, each of which must be present to constitute fraud:

Misrepresentation
False statement of a material fact

1. **Misrepresentation:** a false statement of a material fact.
2. Must be made by one who knew it to be false or made it in reckless disregard of its truth or falsity.
3. Must be made with an intent to induce the innocent party to act.
4. The innocent party relies on the false statement and makes a contract.

If these four elements are present, a party who has been harmed is entitled to relief in court.

Facts: Brown was the administrator of a health care clinic and a member of the board of directors of the corporation that owned the clinic. Knowing that the statement was false, Brown told several stockholders that pursuant to a corporate resolution they were required to sell their stock for $500. This amount was less than fair market value. After the corporation purchased the stock, Brown and the other remaining stockholders enjoyed a favorable income tax advantage and the retained earnings of the corporation were distributed to them.

Outcome: Brown was guilty of fraud.

ETHICAL POINT
Refraining from disclosing pertinent facts may not be fraud, but is it ethical behavior?

Concealment of Material Facts. If one actively conceals material facts for the purpose of preventing the other contracting party from discovering them, such concealment results in fraud even without false statements.

Merely refraining from disclosing pertinent facts unknown to the other party is not fraud as a rule. There must be an active concealment.

PREVIEW CASE REVISITED

Facts: Greenspan and Jacobsen built a duplex on a foundation constructed in violation of the building code and inadequate to sustain the weight of the building. Massive cracks and severe settlement ensued. Greenspan and Jacobsen had plasterboard erected in the basement to cover the cracks. They then sold the duplex to Haberman and Ericksen. When the buyers discovered the inadequate foundation, they sued.

Outcome: The contract was invalidated. The sellers' active concealment of the cracks constituted fraud.

PASSIVE FRAUD

If one's relationship with another relies on trust and confidence, then silence may constitute fraud. Such a relationship exists between partners in a business firm, an agent

Passive Fraud
Failure to disclose information when there is duty to do so

and principal, a lawyer and client, a guardian and ward, a physician and patient, and in many other trust relationships. In the case of an attorney-client relationship, for example, the attorney has a duty to reveal anything material to the client's interests, and silence has the same effect as making a false statement that there was no material fact to be told to the client. The client could, in such a case, avoid the contract.

Silence, when one has no duty to speak, is not fraud. If Lawrence offers to sell Marconi, a diamond merchant, a gem for $500 that is actually worth $15,000, Marconi's superior knowledge of value does not, in itself, impose a duty to speak.

INNOCENT MISREPRESENTATION

Innocent Misrepresentation
False statement made in belief it is true

When a contract is being negotiated, one party could easily make a statement believing it to be true when it is in fact false. Such a statement, made in the belief that it is true, is called an **innocent misrepresentation**. Courts generally hold that if it was reasonable for the misled party to have relied on the innocent misrepresentation, the contract is voidable.

STATEMENTS OF OPINION

Statements of opinion, as contrasted with statements of fact, do not, as a rule, constitute fraud. The person hearing the statement realizes or ought to realize that the other party is merely stating a view and not a fact. But if the speaker is an expert or has special knowledge not available to the other party and should realize that the other party relies on this expert opinion, then a misstatement of opinion or value, intentionally made, would amount to fraud.

Such expressions as "This is the best buy in town," "The price of this stock will double in the next 12 months," "This business will net you $25,000 a year" are all statements of opinion, not statements of fact. But the statement "This business has netted the owner $25,000" is not an opinion or a prophecy, but a historical fact.

Duress

Duress
Obtaining consent by means of a threat

For a contract to be valid, all parties must enter into it of their own free wills. **Duress** is a means of destroying another's free will by one party obtaining consent to a contract as a result of a wrongful threat to do the other person or family members some harm. Duress causes a person to agree to a contract he or she would not otherwise agree to. Normally, to constitute duress, the threat must be made by the other party and must be illegal or wrongful. A contract made because of duress is voidable.

Facts: One Saturday Carrie Ekl called James Knecht's plumbing company to fix a slow tub drain. Knecht and his helper, Reginald Wagner, cut open a pipe in the basement and removed the obstruction. They replaced the sawed-off pipe and installed a PVC trap and tail assembly in case of future blockage. They spent 60 to 90 minutes. Knecht's bill was $480. Ekl said it was ridiculous and the amount outrageous. Knecht said if Ekl did not pay, he would undo the work and turn off the water in her home. Because she was afraid of Knecht, Ekl wrote a check to him for $480. Carrie and her husband sued Knecht claiming it was a contract entered into under duress.

Outcome: The court said it would have been illegal for Knecht to turn off the water, therefore there was duress.

Duress is classified according to the nature of the threat as physical, emotional, or economic.

PHYSICAL DURESS

When one party makes a threat of violence to another person who then agrees to a contract to avoid injury, physical duress occurs. Holding a gun to another's head or threatening to beat a person clearly risks injury to a human being and is unlawful.

EMOTIONAL DURESS

Emotional duress occurs when one party's threats of something less than physical violence result in such psychological pressure that the victim does not act under free will. Courts will consider the age and health of the victim in determining whether emotional duress occurred.

Facts: Barrett financed the purchase of cars, which Sovine then sold. They divided the profit. After Sovine gave Barrett two worthless checks, Barrett had two warrants issued against Sovine. Barrett repeatedly visited Sovine's 70-year-old mother, waving the two checks at her and saying Sovine would go to jail. On February 20, Mrs. Sovine signed a note and mortgage on her home to Barrett. On March 5, the warrants were dismissed. Barrett sought to foreclose on the home.

Outcome: Mrs. Sovine successfully alleged duress by Barrett.

ECONOMIC DURESS

When one party wrongly threatens to injure another person financially in order to get agreement to a contract, economic duress occurs. However, duress does not exist when a person agrees to a contract merely because of difficult financial circumstances that are not the fault of the other party. Also, duress does not exist when a person drives a hard bargain and takes advantage of the other's urgent need to make the contract.

Undue Influence

Undue Influence
Person in special relationship causing another's action contrary to free will

One person may exercise such influence over the mind of another that the latter does not exercise free will. Although there is no force or threat of harm (which would be duress), a contract between two such people is nevertheless regarded as voidable. If a party in a confidential or fiduciary relationship to another induces the execution of a contract against the other person's free will, the agreement is voidable because of **undue influence**. If, under any relationship, one is in a position to take undue advantage of another, undue influence may render the contract voidable. Relationships that may result in undue influence are family relationships, a guardian and ward, an attorney and client, a physician and patient, and any other relationship where confidence reposed on one side results in domination by the other. Undue influence may result also from sickness, infirmity, or serious distress.

In undue influence there are no threats to harm the person or property of another as in duress. The relationship of the two parties must be such that one relies on the other so much that he or she yields because it is not possible to hold out against the superior position, intelligence, or personality of the other party. Whether undue influence exists is a question for the court (usually the jury) to determine. Not every influence is regarded as undue; for example, a nagging spouse is ordinarily not regarded as exercising undue influence. In addition, persuasion and argument are not per se undue influence. The key element is that the dominated party is helpless in the hands of the other.

Facts: David Thomsen, who was borderline mentally retarded, leased the buildings on his farm to Francis Petersen. Thomsen worked for Petersen as a farm laborer and truck driver. When he and Petersen were together they were almost always drunk or drinking. Petersen also managed a number of business matters for Thomsen and made loans and unexplained payments without keeping records. Thomsen agreed to sell 240 acres of land to Petersen. When Thomsen later refused to sell he was sued.

Outcome: The court held that Petersen was in a confidential relationship with Thomsen and that there was undue influence by Petersen.

Remedies for Breach of Contract Because of Fraud, Duress, or Undue Influence

LO4
Remedies when contract is voidable

Since some mistakes, such as fraud in the inducement, duress, and undue influence, render contracts voidable, not void, you must know what to do if you are a victim of one of these acts. If you do nothing, your right to avoid the contract's provisions may be lost. Furthermore, you may ratify the contract by some act or word indicating an intention to be bound. After you affirm or ratify the contract, you are as fully bound by it as if there had been no mistake, fraud, duress, or undue influence. But still you may sue for whatever damages you have sustained.

Rescind
To set a contract aside

If the contract is voidable, you might elect to **rescind** it or set it aside. Recission seeks to put the parties in the position they were in before the contract was made. In order to rescind, you must first return or offer to return what you received under the contract. After this is done, you are in a position to take one of four actions depending upon the circumstances:

1 You may bring a suit to recover any money, goods, or other things of value, plus damages.
2 If the contract is executory on your part, you may refuse to perform. If the other party sues, you can plead mistake, fraud, duress, or undue influence as a complete defense.
3 You may bring a suit to have the contract judicially declared void.
4 If a written contract does not accurately express the parties' agreement, you may sue for **reformation**, or correction, of the contract.

Reformation
Judicial correction of a contract

In no case can the wrongdoer set the contract aside and thus profit from the wrong. If the agreement is void, neither party may enforce it; no special act is required for setting the agreement aside.

Questions

1 What is the effect on the validity of a contract of a mutual mistake of a material fact?
2 When does the law of mistake apply to a contract?

3 If an oral contract is made and then incorrectly reduced to writing, which contract is binding—the oral or the written one?
4 Under what circumstances does a unilateral mistake invalidate a contract?
5 Explain the difference between fraud in the inducement and fraud in the execution of a contract.
6 May an innocent misrepresentation make a contract defective?
7 Can a misstatement of opinion ever amount to fraud?
8 Can a threat of something other than physical violence constitute duress?
9 What is the key element in finding a contract was entered into by undue influence?
10 What remedies are available to victims of acts that render contracts voidable?

Case Problems

LO3,4 1 Larry and Shirley McDaniel paid American Independent Management Systems, Inc. (AIMS) $1,500 to open an AIMS agency. AIMS had told the McDaniels that it had agencies nationwide; it would provide extensive training for them; it offered a variety of financial management services; and it would provide a monthly management bulletin and advertising material. In fact, AIMS had only 14 agents in seven states; it provided a two-day training session; it supplied no advertising material and only one monthly bulletin; and it did not provide the financial management services. The McDaniels sued for $1,500 and their expenses in setting up the office, alleging fraud. Was AIMS guilty of fraud?

LO1 2 Donna and Clifford Murray, divorced, agreed to a judgment that awarded Clifford their home and custody of the younger of their two sons. The older son attended college in another state. The older son returned home and the two boys fought, so the younger went to live with Donna. She asked the court to set aside the judgment because she had given up her right to the home thinking Clifford would totally support the younger son. Donna claimed the judgment was based on mutual mistake of fact that the younger son would live with Clifford. By law, the judgment was a contract that could only be rescinded on the same grounds as any other contract. Should the judgment be set aside?

LO3 3 After being fired from her job with Hilton Hotels Corp., Marcia Evans filed charges with government agencies and a grievance with Hilton through her union. Evans claimed she was fired because she refused her supervisor's sexual advances. A hearing was held on the grievance. A lawyer represented Evans and an agreement was signed. Evans was to get $2,750 and be allowed to quit. She was to withdraw all her filings. Evans then filed suit against Hilton under the Civil Rights Act. Evans could not sue if the agreement she signed was binding. She alleged undue influence by her attorney caused her to sign the agreement. Was the agreement binding?

LO2 4 After Olga Mestrovic died, the 1st Source Bank was appointed to handle her property. The bank contracted to sell Mestrovic's house to Terrence and Antoinette Wilkin. After closing, the Wilkins complained that the house was cluttered with "junk," "stuff," or "trash." The bank said it would hire a rubbish removal service to clean the house or the Wilkins could clean it out and keep any items they wanted. The Wilkins chose to clean the property and found eight drawings and a sculpture created by Mestrovic's husband, a well-known artist. The Wilkins said they cleaned the house, so they had ownership of the art works. The bank said the parties shared the assumption that the items were "junk" and therefore were both mistaken about a vital fact on which the agreement was made. Who owned the art works?

LO1 5 As an employee at the New Hampshire State Prison, Catherine Barney made contributions to the New Hampshire Retirement System (NHRS). Several years later her employment was terminated. Under financial pressure, Barney withdrew her retirement contributions after reading and signing an application which stated that she waived all her rights to any funds from NHRS. When she later believed she would have been eligible for disability benefits Barney claimed her withdrawal constituted a unilateral mistake. Was it?

LO3 6 When Nancy and William Blodgett divorced, the court ordered Nancy to be paid $2,765,000 as her share of the marital assets if she agreed to a judgment in that amount promptly. Nancy appealed, claiming she should get more money. While the appeal was pending, Nancy asked the appellate court to order that either $2,765,000 be released to both her and William or some other amount that would put them on an equal financial footing during the appeal. The court refused. While the appeal was pending, Nancy signed the judgment, so $2,765,000 was released to her and William deeded her the family home. William asked the court to dismiss Nancy's appeal since such a payment takes away the right to appeal. Nancy argued that she signed the judgment involuntarily as the victim of economic duress. Who wins, William or Nancy?

LO2 7 D.R. was a multihandicapped student needing special education. D.R.'s parents and the school board signed an agreement that required the board to pay the placement costs for D.R. at a residential school, the Benedictine School, at the current annual rate of $30,000. The agreement required the board to pay, for the next year, 90 percent of any increase over the previous rate. The board was to pay no other costs for D.R.'s placement. Several months later the board received an estimate of $62,487 for the next year's cost at Benedictine for D.R. The $62,487 included the services of a one-to-one aide for D.R. during his waking hours. The board refused to pay for the aide. In the proceedings that followed, D.R.'s parents asserted that because the need for the aide was not anticipated when the agreement was signed, there was a mutual mistake of fact and the agreement was defective. Was it?

LO1 8 A partnership defaulted on a note given to South Washington Associates for the purchase of a building, so Washington foreclosed. The foreclosure recovered $1.2 million less than was owed, so Washington sued the partners. Before trial the parties agreed to arbitration. The agreement provided that for the purpose of any appeal, the arbitrators' award should be reviewed like a trial court's decision. Washington did not like the arbitrators' award and appealed to the state court of appeals. The court stated that the law did not give it jurisdiction to review such an award. Washington argued that the agreement to arbitrate was then based on mutual mistake and was invalid. Was the agreement to arbitrate valid?

LO2 9 The Sweetwater County School District had a rule incorporated in its contracts that read, "New teachers being hired by the district will be expected to reside in the community at least five days a week. . . ." Joseph Roush was hired to teach and did live in the community. In a subsequent year he moved to another town and commuted. Two other teachers also commuted. The district tried to terminate Roush, saying that the rule dealing with "new teachers" was meant to apply to teachers hired after the adoption of the rule. Roush had assumed that the rule applied only to first-year teachers. The superintendent testified that the rule had not been enforced. Was Roush's mistake justified?

LO3,4 10 Dimou advertised for sale a used car "in very good condition." McGregor took the car for a short test drive and discovered it could start only in reverse. Dimou said it was an electrical problem and denied that the car had ever been in an accident. McGregor bought the car and took it to an auto dealer for a complete inspection and evaluation. He was told it was seriously defective, hazardous, and not repairable. The car had been "totaled" in an accident. Dimou had purchased it from a salvage operator and had done extensive work on it. Can McGregor rescind the contract of sale?

Internet Resources for Business Law

Name	Resources	Web Address
Uniform Commercial Code §2-201	The Legal Information Institute (LII), maintained by Cornell Law School, provides a hypertext and searchable version of UCC §2-201, Formal Requirements; Statute of Frauds.	http://www.law.cornell.edu/ucc/2/2-201.html
Uniform Commercial Code §2-208	LII provides a hypertext and searchable version of UCC §2-208, Course of Performance or Practical Construction.	http://www.law.cornell.edu/ucc/2/2-208.html
National Fraud Information Center	National Fraud Information Center, a project of the National Consumers League, provides a daily report and other information on fraud, as well as the opportunity to report fraud.	http://www.fraud.org/

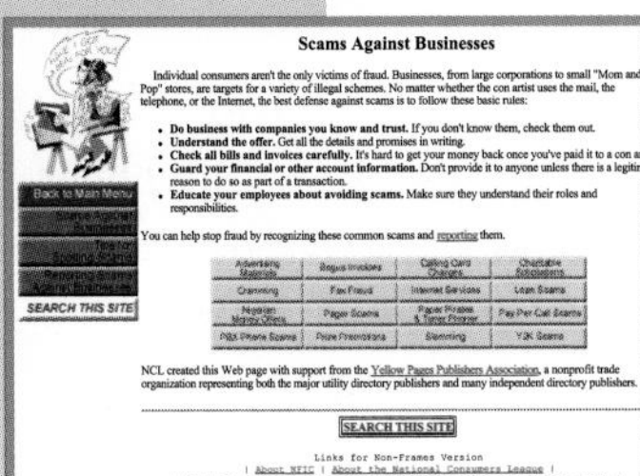

10

Illegal Agreements

Learning Objectives

1. Explain the consequences of a contract for an unlawful purpose or a purpose achieved illegally.
2. Explain what types of contracts are void for illegality.
3. Identify the types of contracts that are contrary to public policy.

PREVIEW CASE

Before their marriage, Richard J. Reynolds executed a prenuptial agreement with Marianne O'Brien. In it he conveyed all the common stock of Sapelo Plantation, Inc., by bill of sale and agreed to transfer the stock upon the books of the corporation in consideration of $10 and O'Brien's agreement to marry him. At the time he was married to Elizabeth Dillard Reynolds. The stock was not transferred on the books of the corporation. After Richard's death, Marianne Reynolds claimed title to the stock. Was the agreement to marry another when already married valid? Is it public policy to encourage divorce in order to marry another?

LO1
Unlawful contracts

A contract must be for a lawful purpose, and this purpose must be achieved in a lawful manner. Otherwise the contract is void. If this were not true, the court might force one party to a contract to commit a crime. If the act itself is legal, but the manner of committing the act that is called for in the contract is illegal, the contract is void.

Facts: In a letter to Gerald Horn, Morris Frydman outlined an arrangement for Frydman to be employed as president of Horn's medical corporation. Horn was a physician and Frydman was not. After his employment with Horn was terminated, Frydman sued alleging the terms in the letter constituted a contract. State laws forbid a person who was not a physician from being president of a medical corporation.

Outcome: The court held that the alleged contract violated state law and was therefore illegal and unenforceable.

LO2
Contracts void for illegality

A contract that is void because of illegality does not necessarily involve the commission of a crime. It may consist merely of a private wrong—the commission of a tort—such as an agreement by two persons to slander a third. A contract contrary to public policy is also illegal.

If the parties are not equally guilty, courts may assist the less guilty party.

If the contract is indivisible, that is, it cannot be performed except as an entity, then illegality in one part renders the whole contract invalid. If the contract is divisible, so that the legal parts can be performed separately, the legal parts of the contract are enforceable. For example, when one purchases several articles, each priced separately, and the sale of one article is illegal because the price was illegally set by price-fixing, the whole contract will not fall because of the one article.

Facts: Savin Corporation entered into a contract with Copy Distributing Company to sell Copy copiers, parts, and supplies. In paragraph 3(a), Copy agreed to sell Savin products "only to bona fide retail end users." Wayne Marcy agreed to pay under the contract if Copy did not. All payments were not made, and Savin sued. The provision to sell only at retail was illegal under state antitrust law, so Copy was not required to pay. Savin argued Marcy was still liable.

Outcome: The court disagreed. An agreement to pay on an illegal contract was not enforceable.

Contracts Prohibited by Statute

There are many types of contracts declared illegal by statute. Some common ones include:

1. Gambling contracts
2. Sunday contracts
3. Usurious contracts
4. Contracts of an unlicensed operator
5. Contracts for the sale of prohibited articles
6. Contracts in unreasonable restraint of trade

GAMBLING CONTRACTS

Gambling Contract Agreement in which parties win or lose by chance

A **gambling contract** is a transaction wherein the parties stand to win or to lose based on pure chance. What one gains, the other must lose. Under the early common law, private wagering contracts were enforceable, but they are now generally prohibited in all states by statute. In recent years certain classes of gambling contracts regulated by the state, such as state lotteries and pari-mutuel systems of betting on horse races and dog races, have been legalized in many states.

In general the courts will leave the parties to a private gambling contract where it finds them and will not allow one party to sue the other for the breach of a gambling debt. If two parties to a gambling contract give money to a stakeholder with instructions to pay the money to the winner, the parties can demand a return of their money. If the stakeholder pays the money to the winner, then the loser may sue either the winner or the stakeholder for reimbursement. No state will permit the stakeholder, who is considered merely a trustee of the funds, to keep the money. The court in this event requires the stakeholder to return each wagerer's deposit.

Facts: During a campaign to fluoridate the water in Codahy, James Quirk was opposed and the Jaycees in favor. Quirk challenged the Jaycees by offering to give them $1,000 if four daily glasses of fluoridated water could not "cause 'dermatologic, gastrointestinal, and neurological disorders.'" He added that he would also pay $1,000 if the Jaycees found he had misrepresented matters. The Jaycees checked up somewhat and were satisfied fluoridation was not so harmful and demanded the $1,000.

Outcome: The court said the challenge was a bet or wager—essentially Quirk was gambling his $1,000 against the Jaycees proving him wrong. Since the court will not settle a dispute for the participants in a wager, the Jaycees lost.

Closely akin to gambling debts are loans made to enable one to gamble. If *A* loans *B* $100 and then wins it back in a poker game, is this a gambling debt? Most courts hold that it is not. If *A* and *B* bet $100 on a football game and *B* wins, and if *A* pays *B* by giving a promissory note for the $100, such a note may be declared void.

Trading on the stock exchange or the grain market represents legitimate business transactions. But the distinction between such trading and gambling contracts is sometimes very fine.

Alewine and Goodnoe could form a contract whereby Alewine agrees to sell Goodnoe 10,000 shares of stock one month from the date at $42 a share. If they do not actually intend to buy and sell the stock, but agree to settle for the difference between $42 a share and the closing price on the date fixed in the contract, this is a gambling contract.

However, Ripetto could agree to sell Bolde 10,000 bushels of wheat to be delivered six months later at $1.70 a bushel. Ripetto does not own any wheat, but intends to buy it for delivery in six months. They agree that at the end of the six-month period the seller does not actually have to deliver the wheat. If the price of wheat has gone up, the seller may pay the buyer the difference between the current price and the contract price. If the price of wheat has gone down, the buyer may pay the seller the difference. Such a contract is legal because the intention was to deliver. The primary difference between the Alewine case and the Ripetto case is the intention to deliver. In the case of trading, the seller (Ripetto) intended at the time of the contract to deliver the wheat and the buyer to accept it. In the gambling case, the seller (Alewine) did not intend to deliver.

SUNDAY CONTRACTS

The laws pertaining to Sunday contracts resulted from statutes and judicial interpretation. They vary considerably from state to state. Most states have repealed their statutes that had made Sunday contracts illegal.

The violators of Sunday acts are seldom prosecuted. For this reason the types of transactions one observes being carried on Sunday do not necessarily indicate restrictions imposed by these laws.

USURIOUS CONTRACTS

Usury
Charging higher rate of interest than law allows

Maximum Contract Rate
Highest legal rate of interest

State laws that limit the rate of interest that may be charged for the use of money are called **usury** laws. Frequently there are two rates, the maximum contract rate and the legal rate. The **maximum contract rate** is the highest rate that may be charged; any rate above that is usurious. In some states this rate fluctuates depending on the

Legal Rate
Interest rate applied when no rate specified

prime rate. The **legal rate**, which is a rate somewhat lower than the contract rate, applies to all situations in which interest may be charged but in which the parties were silent as to the rate. If merchandise is sold on 30 days' credit, the seller may collect interest from the time the 30 days expire until the debt is paid. If no rate is agreed upon in a situation of this kind, the legal rate may be charged.

The courts will treat transactions as usurious when there is in fact a lending of money at a usurious rate even though disguised. Such activities as requiring the borrower to execute a note for an amount in excess of the actual loan and requiring the borrower to antedate the note so as to charge interest for a longer period than that agreed on could make a loan usurious.

The penalty for usury varies from state to state. In most states the only penalty might prohibit the lender from collecting the excess interest. In other states the entire contract is void, and in still others the borrower need not pay any interest but must repay the principal. If the borrower has already paid the usurious interest, the court will require the lender to refund to the borrower any money collected in excess of the contract rate.

In all states special statutes govern consumer loans by pawnbrokers, small loan companies, and finance companies. In some states these firms may charge much higher rates of interest.

Facts: In an attempt to evade the official exchange rate of Nigerian currency for dollars, Christopher Ekwunife contracted to loan Emmanuel Erike $3,000. Within a few weeks, Erike was to give Ekwunife's relative in Nigeria 66,000 Nira. At the official exchange rate the relative should have received only 27,000 Nira. When a lawsuit was brought, Erike argued the loan was usurious because at the official exchange rate he was paying 200 percent interest.

Outcome: Such a huge profit in interest was found by the court to be usurious.

CONTRACTS OF AN UNLICENSED OPERATOR

Statutes make it illegal to operate certain types of businesses or professions without a license. Most of these statutes are made to protect the public from incompetent operators. The most common types of professional persons who must be licensed to operate include doctors, lawyers, certified and licensed public accountants, dentists, and insurance and real estate salespeople. A person who performs these services without license not only cannot sue to collect for the services but also may be guilty of a crime.

Facts: Cebe Loomis and her sons, Andrew, Christian, and Just, signed an agreement for Lange Financial Corporation (LFC) to find a buyer for real estate the Loomises owned. The agreement required the Loomises to pay LFC a 10 percent commission on the sale. William Lange signed for LFC with John Valentine to market the land, although neither had a state real estate broker's license. Valentine found a buyer who then rescinded its offer. The Loomises finally sold part of the land to Allright Sierra Parking. LFC claimed a commission on the sale. The Loomises asserted LFC could not collect because of violation of the real estate licensing law.

Outcome: The court agreed because the law was enacted to protect people when dealing with individuals in the real estate profession.

A licensing law may be designed solely as a revenue measure by requiring payment of a fee for a license. Contracts made by an unlicensed person operating in one of the fields or businesses covered by such a law are normally held valid. However, the unlicensed operator may still be subject to fine or imprisonment for violating the law.

CONTRACTS FOR THE SALE OF PROHIBITED ARTICLES

If a druggist sells morphine or a similar drug to one who does not have a prescription, a suit to collect the price would not be successful. One who sells cigarettes or alcoholic beverages to a minor when such a sale is prohibited cannot recover on the contract. In such cases, the court will not interfere to protect either party.

CONTRACTS IN UNREASONABLE RESTRAINT OF TRADE

Government policy encourages competition. Any contract, therefore, intended to unreasonably restrain trade is null and void. The dividing line between reasonable and unreasonable restraint of trade is often dim, but certain acts have become well established by judicial decision as being an unreasonable restraint of trade. The most common acts in this class include:

1. Contracts not to compete
2. Contracts to restrain trade
3. Contracts to fix the resale price
4. Unfair competitive practices

Contracts Not to Compete. Normally a contract not to compete is illegal; however, it can be valid when buying a business or making an employment contract (see Illustration 10-1 for a sample form).

When one buys a going business, not only are the physical assets acquired, but also the goodwill, which is often the most valuable asset of the firm. In the absence of a contract prohibiting the seller from attempting to retake the asset *goodwill,* the seller may engage in the same business again and seek to retain former customers. It is customary and highly desirable when purchasing a business to include in the contract a provision prohibiting the seller from entering the same business again in the trade territory for a specified length of time. Such a contract not to compete is legal if the restriction is reasonable as to both time and place.

The restriction as to territory should not go beyond the trade area of the business. Since the restriction is sustained to protect the buyer of the business from competition of the seller, it follows that the restriction should not reach out into areas where the buyer's reputation has not reached, nor should the seller be subjected to the restriction longer than is reasonably necessary for the buyer to become established in the new business. When the restriction goes further or longer than necessary to protect the buyer of the business, it is unlawful not only because it burdens the seller but also because it deprives the business community and society in general of the benefit of the activities of the seller.

Closely allied to this type of contract is one whereby an employee, as a part of the employment contract, agrees not to work for a competing firm for a certain period of time after terminating employment. These contracts must be reasonable as to time and place.

NON-COMPETE AGREEMENT

This Non-Compete Agreement (this "Agreement") is made effective as of ______________, by and between ______________________________, of ______________________, ______________, ______________ ______, and ______________________, of ______________________, __________________, ______________________ ________.

In this Agreement, the party who is requesting the non-competition from the other party shall be referred to as "______________________________," and the party who is agreeing not to compete shall be referred to as "______________________."

1. NON-COMPETE COVENANT. For a period of ______________________ after the effective date of this Agreement, ________________________________ will not directly or indirectly engage in any business that competes with ______________________. This covenant shall apply to the geographical area that includes all of the State of ____________________.

2. NON-SOLICITATION COVENANT. For a period of ________________ after the effective date of this Agreement, ______________________________ will not directly or indirectly solicit business from, or attempt to sell, license, or provide the same or similar products or services as are now provided to, any customer or client of ______________________________. Further, for a period of ________________ after the effective date of this Agreement, ______________________________ will not directly or indirectly solicit, induce or attempt to induce any employee of ______________________________ to terminate his or her employment with ______________________________.

3. PAYMENT. ______________________ will pay compensation to ______________________ for the covenants of ______________________________ in the amount of $0.00. This compensation shall be payable in a lump sum on ________________.

4. CONFIDENTIALITY. ______________________________ will not at any time or in any manner, either directly or indirectly, use for the personal benefit of ________________, or divulge, disclose, or communicate in any manner any information that is proprietary to ______________________. ______________________________ will protect such information and treat it as strictly confidential.

5. ENTIRE AGREEMENT. This Agreement contains the entire agreement of the parties regarding the subject matter of this Agreement, and there are no other promises or conditions in any other agreement whether oral or written.

6. SEVERABILITY. The parties have attempted to limit the non-compete provision so that it applies only to the extent necessary to protect legitimate business and property interests. If any provision of this Agreement shall be held to be invalid or unenforceable for any reason, the remaining provisions shall continue to be valid and enforceable. If a court finds that any provision of this Agreement is invalid or unenforceable, but that by limiting such provision it would become valid and enforceable, then such provision shall be deemed to be written, construed, and enforced as so limited.

7. INJUNCTION. It is agreed that if ______________________________ violates the terms of this Agreement irreparable harm will occur and money damages will be insufficient to compensate ______________________________. Therefore, ______________________________ will be entitled to seek injunctive relief (i.e., a court order that requires ______________________ to comply with this Agreement) to enforce the terms of this Agreement.

8. APPLICABLE LAW. This Agreement shall be governed by the laws of the State of ______________________.

PROTECTED PARTY:

____

By: ______________________________

____

NON-COMPETING PARTY:

____

By: ______________________________

____

Illustration 10-1

Non-Compete Agreement

If you have the Quicken Business Lawyer program, open this document on your computer. Complete the form and the checklist that follows it.

This form is only a sample. Do a search on Yahoo.com or AltaVista.com and see how many different types of noncompete agreements exist. Also check some of the sites that discuss their enforcement. What factors might affect the enforcement of noncompete agreements? http://www.yahoo.com, http://www.altavista.com

Facts: James Dagata was employed by Timenterial, Inc., under a contract that provided that he would not "engage . . . in any business venture having to do with the sale or rental of mobile homes . . . in a 50-mile radius from any existing Timenterial, Inc., sales lot" for one year after leaving Timenterial. He terminated his employment with Timenterial and continued to engage in the mobile home business. Timenterial sued Dagata.

Outcome: The court found that the one-year restriction was reasonable, but the area covered by the 50-mile radius from any Timenterial lots would include parts of six states and was unreasonable.

Contracts to Restrain Trade. Contracts to fix prices, divide up the trade territory, limit production so as to reduce the supply, or otherwise limit competition are void. Such contracts, which affect interstate commerce and which are therefore subject to regulation by the federal government, are specifically declared illegal by the Sherman Antitrust Act and the Clayton Act. Most of the states have similar laws applicable to intrastate commerce.

Contracts to Fix the Resale Price. An agreement between a seller and a buyer that the buyer shall not resell below a stated price is generally illegal as a price-fixing agreement. The original seller (manufacturer) can, of course, control the price by selling directly to the public through outlet stores.

Unfair Competitive Practices. The Robinson-Patman Act attempted to eliminate certain unfair competitive practices in interstate commerce. Under this act it is unlawful to discriminate in price between competing buyers if the goods are of like grade, quantity, and quality. Most states have passed similar laws for intrastate commerce. Some state statutes go further and prohibit the resale of goods at a loss or below cost for the purpose of harming competition.

ADMINISTRATIVE AGENCY ORDERS

As was mentioned in Chapter 4, many government administrative agencies have the authority to issue rules and regulations that have the force of law. A contract that violates such a rule is illegal.

Contracts Contrary to Public Policy

LO3 Contracts against public policy

Contracts contrary to public policy are unenforceable. The courts must determine from the nature of the contract whether or not it is contrary to public policy.

One court, in attempting to classify contracts contrary to public policy, defined them thus: "Whatever tends to injustice, restraint of liberty, restraint of a legal right, whatever tends to the obstruction of justice, a violation of a statute, or the obstruction or perversion of the administration of the law as to executive, legislative, or other official action, whenever embodied in and made the subject of a contract, the contract is against public policy and therefore void and not susceptible to enforcement." (*Brooks v. Cooper,* 50 N. J. Eq. 761, 26 A. 978.)

The most common types of contracts contrary to public policy include:

1 Contracts limiting the freedom of marriage
2 Contracts obstructing the administration of justice
3 Contracts injuring the public service

CONTRACTS LIMITING THE FREEDOM OF MARRIAGE

It is contrary to public policy to enter into any contract the effect of which is to limit freedom of marriage. Such contracts are void. The following provisions in contracts have been held to render the contract a nullity: (1) an agreement whereby one party promises never to marry; (2) an agreement to refrain from marrying for a definite period of time (an agreement not to marry during minority, however, is valid); (3) an agreement not to marry certain named individuals.

PREVIEW CASE REVISITED

Facts: Before their marriage, Richard J. Reynolds executed a prenuptial agreement with Marianne O'Brien. In it he conveyed all the common stock of Sapelo Plantation, Inc., by bill of sale and agreed to transfer the stock upon the books of the corporation in consideration of $10 and O'Brien's agreement to marry him. At the time he was married to Elizabeth Dillard Reynolds. The stock was not transferred on the books of the corporation. After Richard's death, Marianne Reynolds claimed title to the stock.

Outcome: The agreement to marry another when already married is contrary to public policy, which encourages the preservation of marriage. The agreement was void.

Also, in order to preserve and protect marriages it is held that an agreement to seek a divorce for a consideration is void as against public policy. However, property settlement agreements made in contemplation of divorces are valid.

CONTRACTS OBSTRUCTING THE ADMINISTRATION OF JUSTICE

Any contract that may obstruct our legal processes is null and void. It is not necessary that justice actually be obstructed. If the contract has the tendency to do so, the courts will not enforce it.

The following provisions have been held to render contracts void: (1) an agreement to pay a witness a larger fee than that allowed by law, provided the promisor wins the case; (2) an agreement by a candidate for sheriff that a certain individual will be appointed deputy sheriff in return for aid in bringing about the promisor's election; (3) an agreement to pay a prospective witness a sum of money to leave the state until the trial is over; (4) an agreement not to prosecute a thief if the stolen goods will be returned.

Facts: While employed as the credit manager of Smithfield Ford, Alfred Coats embezzled $54,000. Alfred and his mother and stepfather, Ann and William Adams, contracted to pay Smithfield $25,000 over time and Smithfield agreed to "abstain from pursuing any legal remedies . . . including criminal prosecution." After making payments for several years Ann and William sued to invalidate the contract.

Outcome: The court found that a contract made in consideration of refraining to prosecute a crime was void as against public policy.

CONTRACTS INJURING THE PUBLIC SERVICE

Any contract that may, from its very nature, injure public service is void. A person may contract as an attorney to appear before any public authority to obtain or oppose the passage of any bill. But a contract to use improper influence such as bribery to obtain the desired results is void.

Contracts to use one's influence in obtaining a public contract that by statute must be let to the lowest responsible bidder, to obtain pardons and paroles, or to pay a public official more or less than the statutory salary are also void.

Questions

1. Does a contract that is void for illegality necessarily involve the commission of a crime?
2. What difference does it make whether an illegal contract is indivisible or divisible?
3. May one party to a private gambling contract sue the other for breach of contract?
4. Why is it that the transactions one observes being carried out on Sunday do not necessarily indicate restrictions imposed by law?
5. What is the difference between the maximum contract rate of interest and the legal rate of interest?
6. What are the potential consequences if a person operates a business without the required license?
7. When may contracts made by an unlicensed person be held valid?
8. Which contracts not to compete are legal?
9. May manufacturers control the prices at which their products are sold to the public?
10. What types of contracts are contrary to public policy?
11. What are the consequences of a contract to seek a divorce for a consideration?
12. Is it necessary that justice actually be obstructed for a contract to be void? Explain.

Case Problems

LO3 1. Gina Marie Hoffman and Brian Boyd, while both married to others, signed an agreement by which Boyd agreed to marry Hoffman within 12 months or support her indefinitely. Hoffman agreed to give up her job and leave a secure home and marriage. When Boyd stopped supporting her and did not marry her, Hoffman sued. Was this agreement contrary to public policy and therefore void?

LO1 2. Local 369 Building Fund, Inc. operated a function hall business. By written lease, it leased the hall to Hastings Associates. The primary source of revenue for the hall was the sale of alcoholic beverages. Hastings applied for a liquor license, but it was denied, so Hastings used Local 369's license. Several years later, Local 369 terminated the lease and Hastings sued for breach. The law required everyone who sold alcoholic beverages to have a license and did not permit licensees to transfer their licenses to others. May Hastings recover for breach of contract?

LO2 3. George and Linda Vordenbaum contracted to sell a residence to Barry and Patricia Rubin. The contract obligated the Rubins to sign a note that would have been usurious. When the Vordenbaums refused to convey the property, the Rubins asked the court to order them to do so. May the Vordenbaums avoid the contract because of usury?

LO3 4. Barbara Weiss Lurie and Bertram S. Lurie, while married but living apart, entered into a property settlement agreement. Bertram was to give Barbara real and personal property and $23,000 cash, $750 for all attorneys' fees, support prior to any divorce, and child support and alimony thereafter. She was to release certain property rights in jointly or separately owned property and resign as requested by Bertram from any position as "Trustee, Officer and/or Director of any trust, corporation, or other entity" in which he was involved. All of this was "[u]pon and in the event of the entry of issuance of a final decree in divorce. . . ." within four months. The divorce was not final within four months but Barbara asked the court to require Bertram to comply with the agreement. Was the agreement against public policy and therefore illegal?

LO1 5 When preparing a bid for the Re/Max real estate agency he worked for on managing and selling homes for the government, Tom Gibbons asked George Vessell to estimate how much he would charge for upkeep and lawn maintenance on the properties. When Gibbons bid the yardwork at much less, Vessell refused to do the lawns. Gibbons told him to make up the difference by bid-rigging and stealing appliances. Vessell decided to turn Gibbons in to the FBI and cooperated with a sting operation. After the sting was conducted Re/Max still had the government contract, but did not ask Vessell to do the lawn work. Vessell sued alleging he had a contract with Re/Max for the lawn work. Did he?

LO3 6 After being injured in an auto accident, Robert Harris saw Dr. Greg Swafford for treatment of his injuries. Harris and Swafford agreed that Swafford would act as a medical/legal consultant and assist in preparing a personal injury lawsuit by Harris in return for $15\frac{1}{2}$ percent of any recovery. Swafford testified at a deposition and supplied medical consultation and treatment. Harris' personal injury claim was settled for $625,000 and Swafford sued for $15\frac{1}{2}$ percent. The American Medical Association's code of ethics condemns contingency fees for medical services or as payment for a medical witness. The state board that denies, suspends, or revokes doctors' licenses for, among other things, unethical conduct adopted the AMA code as a regulatory policy. Was the agreement a violation of public policy?

LO2 7 Polk County Memorial Hospital entered into a recruitment agreement with Dr. Kenneth Peters. Under the agreement the hospital made an interest-free loan of $30,684 to Peters, provided him free office space, gave him rent and utility subsidies, and reimbursed some malpractice insurance. This assistance was given for Peters using the hospital for his patients who required hospitalization. Federal law prohibited kickbacks from hospitals to doctors. When sued by the hospital for the amount of the loan, Peters raised the defense of illegality. Can the agreement to repay the loan be enforced?

LO1 8 To pay a judgment and other debts, Vernon Ai and Sandra Fukuhara signed a note. The amount of the judgment included an award of attorney's fees. The note stated that if it were not paid, it would be given to an attorney to collect and Ai and Fukuhara would "pay attorney's fees at the rate of $33\frac{1}{3}$ percent of the amount due thereon, whether suit be instituted or not." Ai and Fukuhara asked a court to declare the note void as a violation of the law limiting attorney's fees in these cases to 25 percent after a suit is filed against the debtor. Does the provision regarding attorney's fees make the note void?

Internet Resources for Business Law

Name	Resources	Web Address
Uniform Commercial Code §2-208	LII provides a hypertext and searchable version of UCC §2-208, Course of Performance or Practical Construction.	http://www.law.cornell.edu/ucc/2/2-208.html
National Fraud Information Center	National Fraud Information Center, a project of the National Consumers League, provides a daily report and other information on fraud, as well as the opportunity to report fraud.	http://www.fraud.org/
Uniform Commercial Code §2-201	The Legal Information Institute (LII), maintained by Cornell Law School, provides a hypertext and searchable version of UCC §2-201, Formal Requirements; Statute of Frauds.	http://www.law.cornell.edu/ucc/2/2-201.html

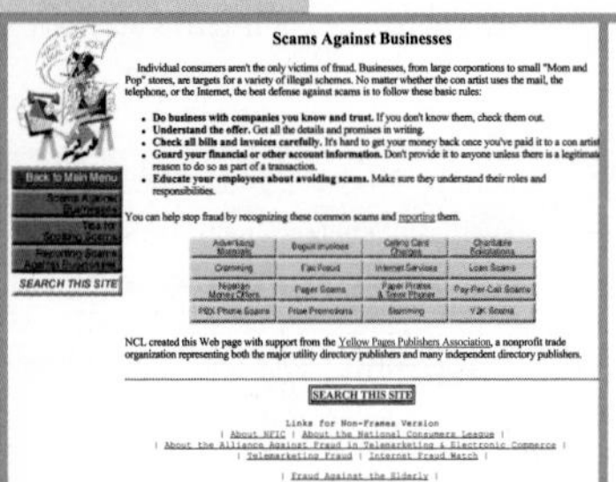

11 Written Contracts

Learning Objectives

1 Identify which contracts the Statute of Frauds requires to be in writing.

2 Distinguish adequate from inadequate writings when a written contract is required.

3 Explain the parol evidence rule.

PREVIEW CASE

General Federal Construction, Inc., was awarded a contract for the construction of a hospital. The project was so large that General expected to use subcontractors for some work. James A. Federline, Inc., submitted a bid to General for the mechanical work. General used Federline's bid in figuring out its bid for the project, but Federline was not awarded the subcontract. Federline sued General, alleging breach of an oral agreement for Federline to do the mechanical work. By the terms of the contract the mechanical subcontractor was to provide all preventive maintenance for the equipment for one year after substantial completion of the contract and a complete water treatment service for one year after acceptance of the condensor water system. Was this contract enforceable? About how long would it take to fully perform this contract?

LO1 Requirement of writing

Contracts may be in written or oral form. All contracts of importance ought to be in writing, but only a few must be written in order to be enforceable. An oral contract is just as effective and enforceable as a written contract unless it is one of the few types specifically required by statute to be in writing.

Reasons for Written Contracts

A written contract has advantages over an oral contract, provided it includes all the terms and provisions of the agreement. In the first place, the existence of a contract cannot be denied if it is in writing. If there were no witnesses when an oral contract was formed, one of the parties might successfully deny that any contract was made. In the second place, one of the parties may die or become insane and therefore be unable to testify as to the terms of an oral contract. The administrator or executor of an estate in case of death, or the committee or guardian in case of insanity, is tremendously handicapped in enforcing an oral agreement that was made by the deceased or insane person. Even when there are witnesses present at the time an oral contract is formed, their testimony may vary considerably as to the actual terms of the contract. Written evidence, composed in clear and unambiguous language, is always better than oral evidence.

For these reasons most businesspeople prefer to have contracts pertaining to matters of importance put in writing, even when not required to do so by law (see Illustration 11-1 for a sample form).

Statute of Frauds

Statute of Frauds
Law requiring certain contracts to be in writing

In the year 1677 the English Parliament enacted a statute known as the **Statute of Frauds**. The statute listed certain classes of contracts that could not be enforced unless their terms were evidenced by a writing. Most of our states have adopted this list with but slight variations.

The Statute of Frauds applies only to executory contracts. If two parties enter into an oral contract that falls under the Statute of Frauds and both parties have performed according to its terms, neither party can seek to set aside the transaction on the ground that there was no writing.

The Statute of Frauds provides that the following types of agreements must be in writing:

1. An agreement to sell land or any interest in or concerning land
2. An agreement the terms of which cannot be performed within one year from the time it is made
3. An agreement to become responsible for the debts or default of another
4. An agreement of an executor or administrator to pay debts of the estate from the executor's or the administrator's personal funds
5. An agreement in which the promise of one person is made in consideration of marriage
6. An agreement to sell goods for $500 or more (This is discussed in detail in Chapter 17.)

AN AGREEMENT TO SELL LAND OR ANY INTEREST IN OR CONCERNING LAND

An agreement to sell any interest in land comes under the Statute of Frauds. The required writing differs from the deed, which will be executed later and by which the seller makes the actual transfer of title to the buyer.

Facts: The Hulbers orally agreed to sell the standing timber on their land to W. S. Hundley for $64,000. They subsequently executed a written agreement to convey the timber to J. T. Butler for $68,500. Hundley sued the Hulbers to require them to comply with the oral contract, alleging that the sale of the timber was the sale of personal, not real, property.

Outcome: The court held that the sale of the timber was the sale of real property. Since the contract was not in writing, it was voidable by the sellers and not enforceable.

Your company wants to sell eight 4-drawer filing cabinets. Since you don't normally sell office furnishings, you have no contracts to sell goods at your disposal. Use the Quicken Business Lawyer program and complete the contract to sell the filing cabinets. Be sure to read through the entire contract and complete the checklist at the end.

For the letter of the law, look up the Statute of Frauds and other sales contract laws on the Cornell Law School Web site. Click on Constitution and Codes, then the UCC, then Article 2—Sales. The Statute of Frauds is Section 2-201, Formal Requirements; Statute of Frauds. http://www.law.cornell.edu/ucc

GENERAL CONTRACT FOR PRODUCTS

This Contract (this "Contract") is made effective as of ______________, between ______________________________, of ______________________, ______________________, ______________________ ____________ ("Seller"), and ______________________________, of ______________________, ______________________, ______________________ ____________ ("Buyer").

1. ITEMS PURCHASED. Seller agrees to sell, and Buyer agrees to buy, the following products (the "Goods") in accordance with the terms and conditions of this Contract:

Description	*Quantity*	*Unit Price*	*Total Price*
________________________	______	$0.00	$0.00
TOTAL:			$0.00

2. PRODUCT STANDARDS. The Goods shall comply with the Seller's quotation dated ________________ and incorporated into this Contract by this reference.

3. TITLE/RISK OF LOSS. The Goods shall be delivered F.O.B. shipping point.

4. **PAYMENT**. Payment shall be made to ______________________________, ______________________, ______________________, ______________________ __________, on or before ________________.

Payment terms are __________% discount within __________ days, net due __________ days from invoice date.

If any invoice is not paid when due, interest will be added to and payable on all overdue amounts at _______ percent per annum, or the maximum percentage allowed under applicable laws, whichever is less. Buyer shall pay all costs of collection, including without limitation, reasonable attorney fees.

In addition to any other right or remedy provided by law, if the Buyer fails to pay for the Goods when due, the Seller at its option may treat such failure to pay as a material breach of this Contract, and may terminate this Contract and/or seek legal remedies.

5. DELIVERY. Time is of the essence in the performance of this Contract. Seller will arrange for delivery by carrier chosen by Seller. Delivery shall be completed by ________________.

(*continued*)

Illustration 11-1

General Contract for Products

One may wish to sell not the land itself, but only an interest in the land. Evidence of this contract also must be in writing. These sales usually involve rights of way, joint use of driveways, mineral rights, or timber. A lease for more than one year must be evidenced by a writing to be binding.

Frequently, oral contracts relative to land are performed before any question of their validity is raised. For example, one leases a building by oral contract for two years. The building is occupied for that period, and then the rent is not paid on the ground that the oral contract is invalid. The law will compel payment of the rent orally agreed to for the time that the premises were occupied. If one has paid money or performed a service under an oral contract, the money or the value of the service may be recovered even though the executory part of the contract cannot be enforced. This recovery is not based on the terms of the contract but on the theory of preventing the unjust enrichment of one party.

AN AGREEMENT THE TERMS OF WHICH CANNOT BE PERFORMED WITHIN ONE YEAR FROM THE TIME IT IS MADE

The terms of a contract that cannot be performed in one year might easily be forgotten before the contract is completed. To minimize the need to resort to the courts, the law requires all contracts that cannot be performed within one year to be in writing.

This provision of the Statute of Frauds means that if the terms of the contract are such that, by their nature, they cannot be performed within one year from the date of the contract, then the contract must be in writing. The contract can be so worded that it may not be completed for 50 years, yet if it is physically possible to complete it within one year, it need not be in writing. If John agrees in consideration of $50,000 to care for Chen for "as long as he (Chen) lives," this contract need not be in writing because there is no certainty Chen will live one year. But an agreement to manage a motel for five years will, by its terms, require more than one year for performance; therefore, it comes under the Statute of Frauds.

PREVIEW CASE REVISITED

Facts: General Federal Construction, Inc., was awarded a contract for the construction of a hospital. The project was so large that General expected to use subcontractors for some work. James A. Federline, Inc., submitted a bid to General for the mechanical work. General used Federline's bid in figuring out its bid for the project, but Federline was not awarded the subcontract. Federline sued General, alleging breach of an oral agreement for Federline to do the mechanical work. By the terms of the contract the mechanical subcontractor was to provide all preventive maintenance for the equipment for one year after substantial completion of the contract and a complete water treatment service for one year after acceptance of the condensor water system by the owner.

Outcome: By the terms of this contract, it could not be performed within one year; therefore, the oral agreement was not enforceable.

AN AGREEMENT TO BECOME RESPONSIBLE FOR THE DEBTS OR DEFAULT OF ANOTHER

Debt
Obligation to pay money

Default
Breach of contractual obligation other than money

The term **debt** refers to an obligation to pay money; **default** refers to a breach of contractual obligations other than money, such as a contract to build a house. An agreement to be responsible for the debts or default of another occurs when the promisor undertakes to make good the loss that the promisee would sustain if another person does not pay the promisee the debt owed or fails to perform a duty imposed by contract or by law. If Allen promises Charlotte to pay Betty's debt to Charlotte if Betty fails to pay, the Statute of Frauds requires Allen's promise to be in writing. Allen's promise is to be responsible for the debt of another. This provision of the Statute of Frauds was designed especially for those situations where one promises to answer for the debt of another person purely as an accommodation to that person.

An exception to the Statute of Frauds occurs if in fact a promise is an original promise by the promisor rather than a promise to pay the debt of another. For example, if Andy buys on credit from Betsy and tells Betsy to deliver goods to Cindy, Andy is not promising to pay the debt of another; the promise is to pay Andy's own debt. Andy's promise does not have to be in writing.

The Statute of Frauds requirement of a writing does not apply if the main purpose of the promise is to gain some advantage for the promisor. Situations exist where one person promises to answer for the debt or default of another because it is in the promisor's personal financial interest to do so.

Facts: Modern Electric Co. contracted with Warren Reese to install heating and air conditioning equipment in Reese's building. The equipment installed was not at all satisfactory and did not meet the specifications in the contract. Air Engineers, Inc., the distributor of the equipment, told Reese that if he would delay suing the installer, it would correct the problem. The heating and air conditioning never became adequate. Nearly two years after the requested delay, Reese filed suit.

Outcome: The court found that the forbearance of suit was beneficial to Air Engineers and so was not within the Statute of Frauds.

The Statute of Frauds does not apply where the promisor promises the debtor that the promisor will pay the debt owed to the third person.

Facts: To pay for his political campaign, George Meeker arranged for the Farmers State Bank of Ingalls to loan up to $25,000 on a note signed by supporters. Meeker told the people getting the signatures to tell the supporters they would have no liability to pay because Meeker would pay any balance remaining after the election. Meeker lost; the note was not paid, and the bank sued. Meeker said he was not liable because under the Statute of Frauds, his oral promise to pay the debt of another was not enforceable.

Outcome: The court held that the promise was made to the debtor to pay a debt to a third person, thus it was not within the Statute of Frauds and it was binding.

AN AGREEMENT OF AN EXECUTOR OR ADMINISTRATOR TO PERSONALLY PAY THE DEBTS OF THE ESTATE

When a person dies, an executor or administrator takes over all the deceased's assets. From these assets the executor or administrator pays all the debts of the deceased before distributing the remainder according to the terms of the decedent's will or, in the absence of a will, to the heirs. The executor or the administrator is not obligated to pay the debts of the deceased out of the executor's personal funds. For this reason, a promise to pay the debts of the estate from personal funds is in reality a contract to become responsible for the debts of another and must be in writing to be enforceable.

AN AGREEMENT IN WHICH THE PROMISE OF ONE PERSON IS MADE IN CONSIDERATION OF MARRIAGE

An agreement by which one person promises to pay a sum of money or to give property to another in consideration of marriage or a promise to marry must be in writing. This requirement of the Statute of Frauds does not apply to mutual promises to marry.

Facts: Before Miles Dutton and Patricia Black were married they signed an agreement in which Black relinquished any rights to Dutton's estate. Dutton agreed to purchase a house that would go to Black upon his death. After Dutton died, his daughter from a previous marriage sued to enforce the agreement.

Outcome: The court found that the agreement was one made in consideration of marriage and was required by the Statute of Frauds to be in writing. Since it was in writing, it was enforceable.

Note or Memorandum

LO2 Adequacy of written contract

The Statute of Frauds requires either that the agreement be in writing and signed by both parties or that there be a note or memorandum in writing signed by the party against whom the claim for breach of promise is made. With the enactment of the federal Electronic Signatures in Global and National Commerce Act, that signature no longer has to be on paper. This law makes electronic signatures legally enforceable.

With the exception of the case of the sale of goods (Chapter 17), the contract and the note or memorandum required by the Statute of Frauds must set forth all the material terms of the transaction. For example, in the case of the sale of an interest in real estate the memorandum must contain the names of the parties, the subject matter of the contract, the basic terms of the contract, including the price and the manner of delivery, and it must be signed by the one to be charged.

The law states that the memorandum must contain all the essential terms of the contract; yet the memorandum differs materially from a written contract. Probably the chief difference is that one may introduce oral testimony to explain or complete the memorandum. The court held that the following receipt was an adequate memorandum: "Received of Sholowitz $25 to bind the bargain for the sale of Moorigan's brick store and land at 46 Blackstone Street to Sholowitz. Balance due $1,975."

Facts: Peoples Bank offered land for sale. William Whatley, a real estate broker, showed the property to James Barnes, who signed a check for $5,500 as a deposit. On the check, Whatley filled in the name of the payee and wrote a notation that it was "earnest money" on the land. He sent a real estate sales agreement to the bank, which the vice president signed. The agreement provided for a real estate commission to Whatley "when the sale is consummated." It also stated it was "an offer by the [person] who first signs . . . and is open for acceptance by the other." Barnes never signed the agreement. The bank sold the land to someone else and Whatley sued Barnes to recover the commission he would have received if Barnes had bought the land.

Outcome: The court said there must be a writing signed by the party to be charged in order to have a binding contract for the sale of land. Barnes did not sign the agreement so he was not liable.

The memorandum need not be made at the time of the contract. It needs to be in existence at the time suit is brought. The one who signs the memorandum need not sign with the intention of being bound. If Jones writes to Smith, "Since my agreement to pay you the $500 Jacobson owes you was oral, I am not bound by it," this is a sufficient memorandum and removes the objection based on the Statute of Frauds.

Other Written Contracts

The five classes of contracts listed by the Statute of Frauds are not the only contracts required by law to be in writing in order to be enforceable. Every state has a few additional requirements. The more common ones are contracts for the sale of securities, agreements to pay a commission to real estate brokers, and a new promise to extend the statute of limitations.

Parol Evidence Rule

LO3
Parol evidence rule

Parol Evidence
Oral testimony

Parol Evidence Rule
Complete, written contract may not be modified by oral testimony unless evidence of fraud, accident, or mistake

Spoken words, or **parol evidence**, will not be permitted to add to, modify, or contradict the terms of a written contract that appears to be complete unless evidence of fraud, accident, or mistake exists so that the writing is in fact not a contract or is incomplete. This is known as the **parol evidence rule**.

If a written contract appears to be complete, the parol evidence rule will not permit modification by oral testimony or other writing made before or at the time of executing the agreement. However, an exception is made when the contract refers to other writings and indicates they are considered as incorporated into the contract.

Facts: Thomas leased a farm from Clark. The lease contained this uncompleted provision: "Lessor does hereby rent and lease to the Lessee the following described property . . . for a term commencing on the __ day of __, 19 __, and ending on the __ day of __, 19 __." Clark later sued to regain possession. Thomas wanted to prove an oral agreement that the lease was to run as long as a note, but the maturity date of the note had not been known when the lease was signed.

Outcome: The court found that the written contract (the lease) was clearly incomplete, so parol evidence was permitted to establish the term of the lease.

The parol evidence rule assumes that a written contract represents the complete agreement. If, however, the contract is not complete, the courts will admit parol evidence to clear up ambiguity or to show the existence of trade customs that are to be regarded as forming part of the contract.

A contract that appears to be complete may, in fact, have omitted a provision that ought to have been included. If the omission is due to fraud, alteration, typographical errors, duress, or other similar conduct, oral testimony may be produced to show such conduct.

Questions

1 What are the advantages a complete written contract has over an oral contract?
2 What is the significance if a contract comes under the Statute of Frauds?
3 What does it mean to say that the Statute of Frauds applies to executory contracts?
4 If there is an oral contract to rent land that the tenant occupies before any question as to the validity of the contract is raised, must the tenant pay any rent?
5 Why must a contract that cannot be performed in one year be in writing to be enforceable?
6 If one assumes an original obligation, even though the benefits go to another party, must the contract be in writing to be enforceable?
7 What must be included in a note or memorandum required by the Statute of Frauds?
8 Must the note or memorandum required by the Statute of Frauds be made at the time of the contract?
9 Are all contracts that must be in writing to be enforced included in the Statute of Frauds?
10 What is the impact of the parol evidence rule on a written contract that appears to be complete?

Case Problems

LO3 1 Lobo, Inc. and Carr Construction Co., Inc. used Frost Construction's proposal for the paving work in bidding on a highway construction project. They were awarded the contract and issued a subcontract to Frost incorporating all the terms and conditions in Frost's proposal. Months later Frost sent a different subcontract to Lobo and Carr which imposed liability on them for consequential damages for delays to Frost's work. They rejected it and insisted Frost adhere to the original proposal. Frost claimed there was an oral condition precedent that it would be able to start the paving by May 1. Lobo and Carr subcontracted the work to someone else. Frost sued alleging its original proposal was a contract that was modified by a later oral condition. Was it?

LO2 2 William Henry Brophy College was given two adjacent commercial properties leased by Oscar and Joe Tovar from a former owner. One of the buildings was later destroyed by fire. Brophy gave notice of termination of the lease as to both properties. The Tovars claimed they had a sufficient written memorandum by virtue of handwritten notations on a written lease to the damaged property to lease the undamaged property. The written notations on the first page were: "367.50 mo inc. tax," and "416, 367.50, 783.50" in a column of figures with a line between 367.50 and 783.50 and several initials. On page 2 was written "These Premises Primarily For Expansion of Empress Theater 2339 E. McDowell" and one set of initials. Was this a memorandum sufficient to comply with the Statute of Frauds?

LO1 3 Howard E. Johnson and Loren Ward orally contracted to form a partnership. Johnson later sued for a dissolution of the partnership. The parties had originally agreed that termination of the partnership would occur on default, withdrawal, or death of Ward or the closing of branches operated by Johnson. Ward asked the court to dismiss the suit because the contract was not in writing and not performed within one year. Was the contract in violation of the Statute of Frauds?

LO1 4 Kenneth Gross, the primary creditor of Wind Surfing, asked White Stag Manufacturing Co. to extend credit to Wind Surfing. White Stag said not until a past-due balance was paid. After negotiations, Gross personally sent $14,000 to White Stag to apply to the past-due account. Gross promised White Stag he had signed a guaranty form, which was in the mail. White Stag shipped goods worth $49,637.87 to Wind Surfing. Gross's guaranty never arrived and Wind Surfing never paid its accounts. White Stag sued Gross, who argued that he was not liable because his agreement to pay the debt of Wind Surfing was not in writing. Was he liable?

LO3 5 Limited partners sued their former law firm. The parties agreed to a written partial settlement that dismissed some of their claims, and agreed to further settlement negotiations on the remaining claims. It also stated, "This agreement . . . constitute[s] the entire agreement of the parties. There are no additional promises . . . except those expressly set forth in this agreement." The law firm finally offered to settle for $80,000 when the partners had expected $275,000 to $550,000. The higher amount expected was a result of an oral promise made by the law firm prior to the signing of the agreement. Should the promise modify the settlement agreement?

LO3 6 The Jabberwock Band contracted in writing with Jeanette Johnson to perform for two months at the Riverbend Lounge. Before the contract was signed, the leader of the band orally promised Johnson she could terminate upon giving two weeks' notice if the band did not draw well. The band failed to draw patrons. Johnson gave two weeks' notice and then fired the band. The band sued her for the amount due for the remaining time under the written contract. Was evidence of the oral two-week termination agreement admissible?

LO2 7 After negotiating about the sale of her cottage to Betty Jean Sprague, Laura Johnson signed a piece of notepaper on which was written:

Check 7414 is for down payment on cottage

42,000.00
−1,000.00
41,000.00

I will relinquish if I don't buy or finish in one month—Aug. 13

Johnson received a check for $1,000 from Sprague on which was written "down payment on cottage." Johnson later tried to return the check, claiming that under the Statute of Frauds they did not make an enforceable contract to sell the cottage. Sprague sued to enforce the sale. Should she win?

LO1 8 Henry and Wilma Tatum married after Henry orally promised Wilma to leave her whatever he owned when he died if Wilma married him. The Tatums signed a joint will leaving all the property of either one to the survivor. A month before he died, Henry revoked his will and made a new one leaving everything to Rupert Tatum and Margie Rodriguez. Wilma sued and Rupert claimed the oral promise was made in consideration of marriage and therefore unenforceable. Was it?

Internet Resources for Business Law

Name	Resources	Web Address
Uniform Commercial Code §2-201	The Legal Information Institute (LII), maintained by Cornell Law School, provides a hypertext and searchable version of UCC §2-201, Formal Requirements; Statute of Frauds.	http://www.law.cornell.edu/ucc/2/2-201.html
Uniform Commercial Code §2-202	LII provides a hypertext and searchable version of UCC §2-202, Final Written Expression: Parol or Extrinsic Evidence.	http://www.law.cornell.edu/ucc/2/2-202.html

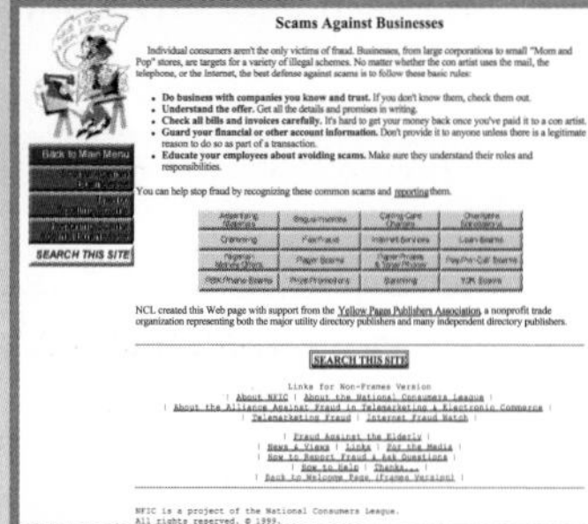

12 Third Parties and Contracts

Learning Objectives

1. Discuss the difference between a third-party beneficiary contract and a novation.
2. Explain the difference between assignment of a contract and delegation of duties under it.
3. Describe the different types of contracts involving more than two people.

PREVIEW CASE

After being injured in an auto accident, Elaine Parker retained attorney Joseph Ohlin to pursue a personal injury action and consulted with Dr. Wi Hsu for treatment. Parker and Ohlin signed a document that authorized Hsu to furnish Ohlin with complete reports of the medical services and directed Ohlin to withhold and pay funds due Hsu from any settlement, judgment, or verdict. Hsu treated Parker, operated on her knee, and furnished Ohlin with the reports. After Parker settled her personal injury claim, she told Ohlin not to pay Hsu's medical fee. Hsu sued Ohlin. Can he recover? Did Parker make an assignment? Did Ohlin know Hsu had a right to part of the settlement?

A contract creates both rights and obligations. Ordinarily, one who is not a party to the contract has no right to the benefits to be derived from the contract nor responsibility for any of the duties or obligations. However, parties may intend to benefit a third person when they make a contract. Also, third parties may acquire rights or assume duties.

Involving a Third Party

A third party can become involved in a contract in several common ways. These include as a third-party beneficiary, by novation, by assignment, and by delegation.

THIRD-PARTY BENEFICIARY

LO1
Third-party beneficiary versus novation

Third-Party Beneficiary
Person not party to contract but whom parties intended to benefit

Creditor Beneficiary
Person to whom promisee owes obligation, which is discharged if promisor performs

Donee Beneficiary
Third-party beneficiary for whom performance is a gift

Incidental Beneficiary
Person who unintentionally benefits from performance of contract

At common law only the parties to a contract could sue upon or seek to enforce the contract. Courts held that strangers to a contract had no rights under it. But courts began to make exceptions to the rule when it seemed evident that the contracting parties intended to benefit a third person, called a **third-party beneficiary**.

The rule today specifies that a third person expressly benefited by the performance of the contract may enforce it against the promisor if the contracting parties intended benefit to the third party. The third person may be either a creditor beneficiary or a donee beneficiary. A **creditor beneficiary** is a person to whom the promisee owes an obligation or duty that will be discharged to the extent that the promisor performs the promise. If *A* makes a contract to pay *B*'s debt to *C*, *C* is the creditor beneficiary of the contract between *A* and *B*. A **donee beneficiary** is one to whom the promisee owes no legal duty but to whom performance is a gift, such as the beneficiary named in a life insurance contract. When an event must occur before the donee beneficiary is benefited, the contracting parties may change the beneficiary.

Not everyone who benefits by the performance of a contract between others is properly considered a third-party beneficiary with rights under the contract. If a person merely incidentally benefits by the performance of a contract, suit for breach or for performance will not be successful. For example, a town contracts with a contractor for the paving of a certain street and the contractor fails to perform. The property owners whose property would have been improved by the paving are not entitled to sue for damages for nonperformance because they were to be only incidentally benefited. The contract for the paving of the street was designed essentially to further the public interest, not to benefit individual property owners. The property owners are merely **incidental beneficiaries**.

Facts: For tax reasons, Paul and Lydia Kalmanovitz executed similar wills and a will agreement binding the survivor to leave everything to a charitable foundation. The agreement did not mention any specific bequests although the wills had bequests of $100,000 each to Alma, Karol, and Stanley Kalmanovitz, and to Ronald Weibelt. Paul died and his $100,000 bequests were paid. Lydia deleted the bequests from her will. After Lydia died, Alma, Karol, Stanley, and Ronald sued for $100,000 each as third-party beneficiaries of the will agreement.

Outcome: The claimants were never intended to be beneficiaries of the agreement and could not recover.

NOVATION

Novation
Termination of a contract and substitution of new one with same terms but new party

The party entitled to receive performance under a contract may agree to release the party who is bound to perform and to permit another party to render performance. When this occurs, it is not just a matter of delegating the duties under the contract; rather, it is a matter of abandoning the old contract and substituting a new one in its place. The change of contract and parties is called **novation**. To be more precise, novation substitutes a new party for one of the original parties at the mutual agreement of the original parties, such that the prior contract terminates and a new one substitutes for it. The terms of the contract remain the same but with different parties. For example, if Koslov and Burnham have a contract, they, together with Caldwell, may agree that Caldwell shall take Koslov's place, and a novation occurs. Koslov is discharged from the contract, and Burnham and Caldwell are bound. It must be shown that a novation was intended. However, a novation does not need to be in writing nor must it be express. It can be implied from the parties' actions. When a novation occurs, the original obligor drops out of the picture, and the new party takes the original obligor's place and is alone liable for the performance.

Part 2 Summary Cases

Contracts

1 Big Red Keno, Inc. operated Keno games at its main location and at a satellite location, Brothers Lounge, through a computer link. The computer link to Brothers went down but an audio link broadcast the winning numbers. Dewey Houghton was at Brothers and heard the winning numbers. He filled out betting slips marked with these numbers. The computer started working and Houghton placed bets. He received a ticket that listed a game already played even though he had not intended to play that game. The computer reported the ticket as a $200,000 winner. Big Red refused to pay on it and Houghton sued claiming he had a contract. Did he? [*Houghton v. Big Red Keno, Inc.*, 574 N.W.2d 494 (Neb.)]

2 General Tire decided to terminate Horst Mehlfedlt's employment and through its employee, Ross Bailey, made several proposals to Mehlfeldt in lieu of the benefits provided in his employment contract. Bailey thought Mehlfeldt had accepted a proposal, while Mehlfeldt expected a larger final figure. In drafting a separation agreement Bailey made a mistake so that General Tire had to pay $494,000—the total Bailey had offered—plus what the employment contract specified. Mehlfeldt thought the larger amount was a result of his request for more money and signed the agreement. General Tire paid him $494,000. When Mehlfeldt asked when he would get the rest, General Tire realized the mistake. It sued alleging mutual mistake. Was it? [*Gen. Tire Inc. v. Mehlfeldt,* 691 N.E.2d 1132 (Ohio App.)]

3 Ristorante Toscano applied for a license to sell beer and wine. Representatives of the Beacon Hill Civic Association told the restaurant they would oppose the application unless it signed an agreement not to apply for an all-alcohol license in the future. Toscano signed the contract. Nine years later it applied for an all-alcohol license. The association sued for breach of contract. Should it succeed? [*Beacon Hill Civic v. Ristorante Toscano*, 662 N.E.2d 1015 (Mass.)]

4 McLeish Ranch signed an agreement to list land for sale with Reinhold Schauer. The agreement stated the terms would be "cash upon delivery of deed. Sale includes ½ of the mineral rights, oil, gas." Erwin Grossman signed a "contract for sale" to purchase the land for the full price in the listing agreement, subject to financing, and stating coal and gravel were included minerals. The ranch would not sell the land. Grossman sued for specific performance alleging the listing agreement constituted an offer to sell that was accepted by Grossman's signing of the "contract for sale." Was there a contract? [*Grossman v. McLeish Ranch,* 291 N.W.2d 427 (N.D.)]

5 Eggers Consulting Company employed Brad Moore as a personnel recruiter under an employment contract with a noncompete clause. Moore agreed not to compete in hiring data processing personnel in the continental United States for one year after leaving Eggers. Moore had concentrated on placements in the Midwest. Within a year after leaving Eggers, Moore did compete in that field in South Dakota. When Moore sued Eggers for unpaid wages, Eggers alleged breach of the noncompete clause. Was the noncompete clause valid? [*Moore v. Eggers Consulting Co., Inc.*, 562 N.W.2d 534 (Neb.)]

6 A schizophrenic and manic-depressive, G.A.S. was recommitted to the state hospital by his wife, S.I.S., on December 23. S.I.S. filed for divorce, and G.A.S. was served with divorce papers on January 10. He did not have his own attorney and had limited

success trying to work days. He was unable to sit or concentrate for any significant time as a result of taking drugs that negatively affected his reasoning powers. While committed, he was dependent on his wife for transportation, cigarettes, money, and permission to leave the hospital. He did not want his wife to get a divorce and therefore was extremely cooperative. On February 20, while still committed, he signed, without reading, a separation agreement prepared by her attorney, at his office. It required G.A.S. to pay $750 a month child support and a $155 mortgage payment from take-home pay of $1,300 and to give S.I.S. their beach property and the use of their home. He complied for several years and then sued to rescind the agreement. Is there any basis on which this contract could be rescinded? [*G.A.S. v. S.I.S.,* 407 A.2d 253 (Del. Fam. Ct.)]

7 American Family Life Assurance Company filed an action to prevent six former employees from violating the nondisclosure covenants in written agreements. Paragraph seven of the agreements, titled "Covenant Not to Compete," contained six subparagraphs, two of which were nondisclosure covenants and two of which were noncompetitive covenants. The two noncompetitive covenants were overly broad and unenforceable. Could the nondisclosure covenants be enforced? [*American Family Life Assurance Company v. Tazelaar,* 468 N.E.2d 497 (Ill. App. Ct.)]

8 Andrew Truebenbach owned two adjoining tracts of land. He sold one to Edward Pick, and the deed stated, "Grantors also guarantee grantees . . . a right-of-way across the 25-acre tract sold to Walter Bartel." The other tract, consisting of 25 acres, was sold to Bartel five days later. Since an easement is an interest in land and therefore subject to the Statute of Frauds, was the language in Pick's deed sufficient to establish an easement? [*Pick v. Bartel,* 659 S.W.2d 636 (Tex.)]

9 After a divorce decree was entered, Richard Pressley was ordered to pay $20-per-week child support. He made payments directly to his ex-wife. A year later she applied for public assistance and was required to assign her right to support to the Commonwealth of Pennsylvania, Department of Public Welfare. Pressley was never notified of the assignment and continued to make payments to his ex-wife. Four years later the Department of Public Welfare sought to collect the support payments from Pressley. Was Pressley bound on the assignment? [*Commonwealth v. Pressley,* 479 A.2d 1069 (Pa. Super. Ct.)]

10 Babylon Associates contracted to build a water pollution control plant for Suffolk County. It hired Lizza Industries, Inc., as subcontractor to install reinforced "102-inch" pipe. Lizza subcontracted with Clearview Concrete Products Corp. to manufacture the "102-inch" pipe. Clearview was convicted of making defective pipe used in the water pollution control plant. The EPA's reduction in its grant for the project and test to determine the soundness of the pipes delayed construction. The contract with Suffolk County provided that the contractor agreed "to be fully and directly responsible . . . for all acts and omissions of his Subcontractors and of any other person employed directly or indirectly by the . . . Subcontractors." In claiming breach of contract the county alleged it was entitled to recission of the whole contract and all the money it had paid Babylon. Is it? [*Babylon Associates v. County of Suffolk,* 475 N.Y.S.2d 869 (N.Y. App. Div.)]

11 In January, Edward Hayes, an employee of Plantations Steel Company, announced his intention to retire in July because he had worked continuously for 51 years. One week before his retirement, an officer of Plantations told him the company "would take care" of him. The following January and for the following three years Plantations paid Hayes $5,000. After the company refused to make any further payments, Hayes filed suit alleging an implied contract to pay him a yearly pension of $5,000. Was there an implied contract? [*Hayes v. Plantations Steel Company,* 438 A.2d 1091 (R.I.)]

12 Arthur Wells agreed to sell the stock he owned in Ramson, Inc., back to the corporation for $52,500. He also agreed not to compete with Ramson in the New Bedford and Fall

River areas, in southeastern Massachusetts, between and not distant from the areas of Ramson's existing business activity. Arthur then formed a corporation that provided the same kind of services as Ramson. Both corporations contracted with regional, nonprofit corporations to provide social services to people. At the time of Arthur's agreement with Ramson no such nonprofit corporations had been organized in the Fall River or New Bedford areas, but they later were. Ramson contracted to provide services with a newly formed New Bedford corporation. Arthur's corporation advertised for a director of a New Bedford office. Ramson sought to have the agreement not to compete enforced. Is the agreement enforceable in Fall River and New Bedford? [*Wells v. Wells,* 400 N.E. 2d 1317 (Mass. App. Ct.)]

Part 3 Personal Property

http://www.consumer.gov/idtheft

When Bad Things Happen
To Your Good Name

Privacy Policy

Home
Minimize Your Risk
If You're a Victim
File a Complaint
Federal Laws
State Laws
Reports & Testimony
Cases & Scams
Links & Publications

FTC Workshop
Victim Assistance

Welcome to the U.S. government's central website for information about identity theft.

This site is maintained by the Federal Trade Commission. Please continue to visit this site often and share the information with your family, friends and colleagues. More information will be added to the site regularly, including government reports and Congressional testimony, law enforcement updates, and links to other sites with helpful information about identity theft.

How can someone steal your identity? By co-opting your name, Social Security number, credit card number, or some other piece of your personal information for their own use. In short, identity theft occurs when someone appropriates your personal information without your knowledge to commit fraud or theft.

Here are some ways that identity thieves work:

- They open a new credit card account, using your name, date of birth, and Social Security number. When they use the credit card and don't pay the bills, the delinquent account is reported on ***your*** credit report.
- They call your credit card issuer and, pretending to be you, change the mailing address on your credit card account. Then, your imposter runs up charges on your account. Because your bills are being sent to the new address, you may not immediately realize there's a problem.
- They establish cellular phone service in your name.
- They open a bank account in your name and write bad checks on that account.

CONSUMER ALERTS!

Internet Account Updates
If you receive an e-mail request that appears to be from your Internet Service Provider (ISP) stating that your "account information needs to be updated" or that "the credit card you signed up with is invalid or expired and the information needs to be reentered to keep your account active," do not respond without checking with your ISP first. According to information received by the FTC, THIS MAY BE A SCAM.

Intangible personal property is covered in Chapter 14. The most personal kind of intangible personal property is your identity, and its theft, through use of your social security number, bank account, or credit card numbers, is not only frightening, but also difficult to solve. Federal and state governments are addressing the problem through various laws and regulations. For information on this issue, visit http://www.consumer.gov/idtheft.

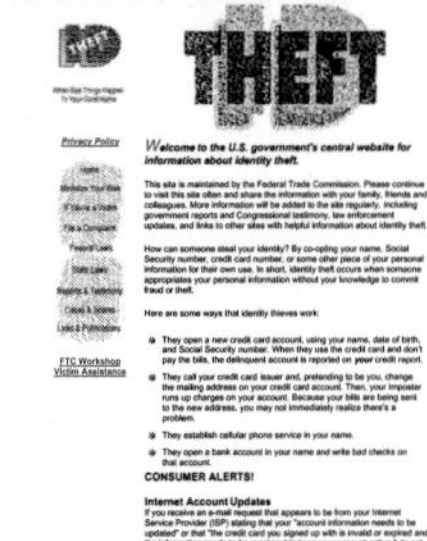

14 Nature of Personal Property

Learning Objectives

1 Define and name the two classes of personal property.

2 Explain the difference between lost and abandoned property.

3 Define and give examples of a bailment.

4 Distinguish the three types of bailments.

PREVIEW CASE

Police in Miami responded to reports of a shooting at the apartment of Carlos Fuentes. Fuentes had been shot in the neck and shoulder and was taken to a hospital. During an ensuing search of Fuentes's apartment, police found assorted drug paraphernalia, a gun, and $58,591 in cash. Fuentes left the hospital and never came forward to claim the property. The police could not find him. Four years later, James Green and Walter Vogel, the owners of the apartment building, sued the city of Miami for the cash. Green and Vogel claimed they were entitled to the money because it had been abandoned on their premises. Was the cash abandoned at the apartment? Do you think Fuentes would return to claim the money?

Property
Anything that may be owned

Anything that may be owned is **property**. A person may enter into a contract with another to use property without becoming the owner of the property. The law protects not only the right to own property but also the right to use it. Property includes not only physical things but also such things as bank deposits, notes, and bonds that give the right to acquire physical property or to use such property.

Personal Property

Personal Property
Movable property; interests less than complete ownership in land or rights to money

Property is frequently classified according to its movability. If it is movable property, it is **personal property**. Thus clothing, food, TVs, theater tickets, and even house trailers are personal property.

LO1
Classes of personal property

Land is not personal property, but an interest in land less than complete ownership, such as a leasehold, is normally classified as personal property.

Facts: When Michael and Judy Kimm were divorced, the court awarded Judy the house subject to Michael's right to 25 percent of the equity, called a lien, when the children became adults or Judy remarried or sold the house. Later Granse & Associates got a judgment against Michael and filed a notice that it was going to have the sheriff sell the house to pay the judgment. If Michael's interest in the house was personal property Granse could do that.

Outcome: The court held that even though Michael's lien was on real property it was not an interest in the land itself. The lien was a claim on the property and personal property.

http://
www.consumer.gov/idtheft

In addition to movable physical property, personal property includes rights to money such as notes, bonds, and all written evidences of debt. Personal property is divided into two classes:

1 Tangible
2 Intangible

TANGIBLE PERSONAL PROPERTY

Tangible Personal Property
Personal property that can be seen, touched, and possessed

Tangible personal property is personal property that can be seen, touched, and possessed. Tangible personal property includes animals, merchandise, furniture, annual growing crops, clothing, jewelry, and similar items.

INTANGIBLE PERSONAL PROPERTY

Intangible Personal Property
Evidences of ownership of rights or value

Intangible personal property consists of evidences of ownership of rights or value. The property itself cannot be touched or seen. Some common forms of intangible personal property include checks, stocks, contracts, copyrights, and savings account certificates.

Facts: When Elizabeth H. Plummer died, her will left her tangible personal property to her brother, Paul Higgins, and sister-in-law, Adelaide Higgins. All property not left to specific persons was left to eight charities. In her safe deposit box were found 240 gold coins—57 Kruggerands, and 183 Canadian maple leaf coins. The executors believed the coins were intangible personal property because they were purchased for investment.

Outcome: The court said the coins could be felt and touched, thus they were tangible property. They went to the Higginses, not the charities.

Methods of Acquiring Personal Property

The title to personal property may be acquired by purchase, will, descent, gift, accession, confusion, and creation.

PURCHASE

Purchase
Ownership by payment

Ownership most commonly occurs through **purchase**. The buyer pays the seller, and the seller conveys the property to the buyer.

WILL

The owner of property may convey title to another by will. Title does not transfer by will until the person who made the will dies and appropriate judicial proceedings have taken place.

DESCENT

When a person dies without leaving a will, that person dies intestate. The person's heirs acquire title to the personal property according to the laws existing in the decedent's state of residence.

Gift
Transfer without consideration

Donor
Person who makes a gift

Donee
Person who receives a gift

GIFT

A **gift** is a transfer made without consideration in return. The person making a gift is called the **donor**. The person receiving the gift is called the **donee**. In order to have a valid gift the donor must have the intention to make the gift and there must be a delivery of the property being given to the donee.

Facts: David Chiro sued his wife, Thecia, for divorce. She claimed the apartment in which they lived during their marriage was a gift to them from David's parents. No stock certificates for the apartment were delivered to David and Thecia, but they voted the unit's stock shares at co-op board meetings, and at some meetings, David's father had voted the shares by proxies signed by David and Thecia. They had made expensive renovations with the parent's knowledge.

Outcome: The court stated that there was an intent to make a gift and delivery.

ACCESSION

Accession
Adding property of another

Accession is the acquiring of property by means of the addition of personal property of another. If materials owned by two people are combined to form one product, the person who owned the major part of the materials owns the product.

CONFUSION

Confusion
Inseparable mixing of goods of different owners

Confusion is the mixing of the personal property of different owners so that the parts belonging to each owner cannot be identified and separated. Grain, lumber, oil, and coal are examples of the kinds of property susceptible to confusion. The property, belonging to different owners, may be mixed by common consent, by accident, or by the willful act of some wrongdoer.

When confusion of the property occurs by common consent or by accident, each party will be deemed the owner of a proportionate part of the mass. If the confusion is willful, the title to the total mass passes to the innocent party, unless it can be clearly proven how much of the property of the one causing the confusion was mingled with that of the other person.

ETHICAL POINT
Why do you suppose a willful confusion results in title passing to the innocent party? Is this result based on the principles of ethics?

CREATION

Creation
Bringing property into being

One may acquire personal property by **creation**. This applies to inventions, paintings, musical compositions, and other intellectual productions. Title to these may be obtained for a period of years through patents and copyrights.

Facts: Wesley West was entitled to a royalty from Humble Oil & Refining Co. on gas produced from certain land. After years of gas production, Humble concluded that the gas reservoir on the land was approaching depletion. It concluded that the injection of extraneous gas was necessary to preserve the reservoir from destruction by water encroachment. A lawsuit between West and Humble resulted. West alleged that injecting extraneous gas into the reservoir resulted in the willful confusion of the two gases. He claimed that Humble must pay a royalty on all gas produced whether native or injected.

Outcome: The court found that the burden was on Humble—the party mingling the goods—to properly identify the share of each owner in the gas. Unless Humble could do so, West was entitled to a royalty on all gas produced from the land.

The one who first applies for and obtains a patent gets title to the production. Creation alone does not give absolute title; it gives only the right to obtain absolute title by means of a patent, which protects the creator for 17 years. Songs, books, and other compositions fixed in any tangible medium of expression are protected by copyright from their creation (see Illustration 14-1 for a sample form). A copyright gives the owner the exclusive right to reproduce, copy, perform, or display the work or authorize another to do so. Although the copyright provides protection from the time of creation of the work, the copyright must be registered for the owner to sue for infringement. Copyrights protect authors for their lifetime plus 70 years, as of January 1, 1978.

LOST AND ABANDONED PROPERTY

LO2
Lost versus abandoned property

Abandon
Discard with no intention to reclaim

The difference between abandoned and lost property lies in the intention of the owner to part with title to it. Property becomes **abandoned** when the owner actually discards it with no intention of reclaiming it.

A person who discovers and takes possession of property that has been abandoned and that has never been reclaimed by the owner acquires a right thereto. The finder of abandoned goods has title to them and thus has an absolute right to possession. The prior owner, however, must have relinquished ownership completely.

PREVIEW CASE REVISITED

Facts: Police in Miami responded to reports of a shooting at the apartment of Carlos Fuentes. Fuentes had been shot in the neck and shoulder and was taken to a hospital. During an ensuing search of Fuentes's apartment, police found assorted drug paraphernalia, a gun, and $58,591 in cash. Fuentes left the hospital, never came forward to claim the property, and the police could not find him. Four years later, James Green and Walter Vogel, the owners of the apartment building, sued the city of Miami for the money. Green and Vogel claimed they were entitled to the money because it had been abandoned on their premises.

Outcome: The court held they had not proven that Fuentes voluntarily gave up his right to the money with the intention of terminating his ownership of it at the time he was taken from the apartment. The money had not been abandoned at the apartment.

Illustration 14-1 Copyright Application Worksheet

Fees are effective through June 30, 2002. After that date, check the Copyright Office Website at www.loc.gov/copyright or call (202) 707-3000 for current fee information.

FORM SR
For a Sound Recording
UNITED STATES COPYRIGHT OFFICE

REGISTRATION NUMBER

SAMPLE

SR SRU

EFFECTIVE DATE OF REGISTRATION

Month Day Year

DO NOT WRITE ABOVE THIS LINE. IF YOU NEED MORE SPACE, USE A SEPARATE CONTINUATION SHEET.

1 TITLE OF THIS WORK ▼

PREVIOUS, ALTERNATIVE, OR CONTENTS TITLES (CIRCLE ONE) ▼

2 a NAME OF AUTHOR ▼ — DATES OF BIRTH AND DEATH Year Born ▼ Year Died ▼

Was this contribution to the work a "work made for hire"? ❑ Yes ❑ No — AUTHOR'S NATIONALITY OR DOMICILE Name of Country OR { Citizen of ▶ Domiciled in ▶ — WAS THIS AUTHOR'S CONTRIBUTION TO THE WORK Anonymous? ❑ Yes ❑ No Pseudonymous? ❑ Yes ❑ No If the answer to either of these questions is "Yes," see detailed instructions.

NATURE OF AUTHORSHIP Briefly describe nature of material created by this author in which copyright is claimed. ▼

NOTE

Under the law, the "author" of a "work made for hire" is generally the employer, not the employee (see instructions). For any part of this work that was "made for hire," check "Yes" in the space provided, give the employer (or other person for whom the work was prepared) as "Author" of that part, and leave the space for dates of birth and death blank.

b NAME OF AUTHOR ▼ — DATES OF BIRTH AND DEATH Year Born ▼ Year Died ▼

Was this contribution to the work a "work made for hire"? ❑ Yes ❑ No — AUTHOR'S NATIONALITY OR DOMICILE Name of Country OR { Citizen of ▶ Domiciled in ▶ — WAS THIS AUTHOR'S CONTRIBUTION TO THE WORK Anonymous? ❑ Yes ❑ No Pseudonymous? ❑ Yes ❑ No If the answer to either of these questions is "Yes," see detailed instructions.

NATURE OF AUTHORSHIP Briefly describe nature of material created by this author in which copyright is claimed. ▼

c NAME OF AUTHOR ▼ — DATES OF BIRTH AND DEATH Year Born ▼ Year Died ▼

Was this contribution to the work a "work made for hire"? ❑ Yes ❑ No — AUTHOR'S NATIONALITY OR DOMICILE Name of Country OR { Citizen of ▶ Domiciled in ▶ — WAS THIS AUTHOR'S CONTRIBUTION TO THE WORK Anonymous? ❑ Yes ❑ No Pseudonymous? ❑ Yes ❑ No If the answer to either of these questions is "Yes," see detailed instructions.

NATURE OF AUTHORSHIP Briefly describe nature of material created by this author in which copyright is claimed. ▼

3 a YEAR IN WHICH CREATION OF THIS WORK WAS COMPLETED — This information must be given in all cases. ◀ Year

b DATE AND NATION OF FIRST PUBLICATION OF THIS PARTICULAR WORK — Complete this information ONLY if this work has been published. Month ▶ Day ▶ Year ▶ ◀ Nation

4 See instructions before completing this space.

a COPYRIGHT CLAIMANT(S) Name and address must be given even if the claimant is the same as the author given in space 2. ▼

b TRANSFER If the claimant(s) named here in space 4 is (are) different from the author(s) named in space 2, give a brief statement of how the claimant(s) obtained ownership of the copyright. ▼

DO NOT WRITE HERE OFFICE USE ONLY: APPLICATION RECEIVED / ONE DEPOSIT RECEIVED / TWO DEPOSITS RECEIVED / FUNDS RECEIVED

MORE ON BACK ▶ • Complete all applicable spaces (numbers 5-9) on the reverse side of this page. • See detailed instructions. • Sign the form at line 8. — DO NOT WRITE HERE — Page 1 of ____ pages

U.S. Copyright Office, Library of Congress (http://www.loc.gov/copyright)

Open this document in your Quicken Business Lawyer program and complete it as if you were applying for a copyright on music you created. Then visit the U.S. Copyright Office Web site to learn more details about copyright issues. You can search the Copyright Office records to find materials that have a copyright. http://www.loc.gov/copyright

A number of states have enacted the Uniform Disposition of Unclaimed Property Act. This law provides that holders of property that the law presumes is abandoned must turn over the property to the state.

Lost Property
Property unintentionally left with no intention to discard

Property is considered to be **lost** when the owner, through negligence or accident, unintentionally leaves it somewhere.

The finder of lost property has a right of possession against all but the true owner as long as the finder has not committed a wrong of some kind. No right of possession exists against the true owner except in instances when the owner cannot be found through reasonable diligence on the part of the finder and certain statutory requirements are fulfilled.

Facts: Leonard and Bernard Kapiloff collected stamps. They purchased two sets of stamps and for years thought the stamps remained in their possession. Then they saw an ad in a nationally circulated catalogue offering the stamps for sale for $150,400. They demanded the stamps back from Robert L. Ganter, the alleged owner. When Ganter refused, the Kapiloffs sued for the stamps. Ganter said that he found them in a dresser he had bought at a used furniture store.

Outcome: The court held that the finder of lost personal property holds it against all except the rightful owner. Once the true owners were determined, Ganter's possessory interest ceased, and the Kapiloffs were entitled to the stamps.

In a few cases the courts have held that if any employee finds property in the course of employment, the property belongs to the employer. Also, if property is mislaid, not lost, then the owner of the premises has first claim against all but the true owner. This especially applies to property left on trains, airplanes, in restaurants, and in hotels.

Bailments

LO3

Nature and examples of bailment

Bailment
Transfer of possession of personal property on condition property will be returned

Bailor
Person who gives up possession of bailed property

Bailee
Person in possession of bailed property

The transfer of possession, but not the title, of personal property by one party, usually the owner, to another party is called a **bailment**. The transfer is on condition that the same property will be returned or appropriately accounted for either to the owner or to a designated person at a future date. The person who gives up possession, the **bailor**, is usually the owner of the property. The **bailee** accepts possession of the property but not the title.

Some typical transactions resulting in a bailment include:

1. A motorist leaving a car with the garage for repairs.
2. A family storing its furniture in a warehouse.
3. A student borrowing a tuxedo to wear to a formal dance.
4. A hunter leaving a pet with a friend for safekeeping while going on an extended hunting trip.

Facts: At an amusement park operated by Sports Complex, Inc., Tabitha Golt bought and used tickets to drive a go-cart. Another go-cart drove into Tabitha's, severely injuring her. She sued Sports alleging it had a mutual benefit bailment with her.

Outcome: The court stated that the arrangement constituted a bailment. Once the driver began to drive a go-cart, Sports had no mechanism to stop the cart, so it was in the possession of the driver.

The Bailment Agreement

A true bailment is based upon and governed by a contract, express or implied, between the bailor and the bailee. When a person checks a coat upon entering a restaurant, nothing may be said, but the bailment is implied by the acts of the two parties. A bailment can be created by the conduct of the parties, whether spoken or written.

Facts: Melvin Delzer leased a paylogger from Rapid City Implement. The lease stated: "Lessee further agrees to protect the Lessor on this contract with full insurance coverage" and "Lessee agrees to pay the Lessor for all loss and damages to the equipment arising from any cause . . . during the life of this lease." During the lease, the paylogger was damaged by fire. It was returned and Rapid City's insurer paid Rapid City for the damage. The insurer then sued Delzer.

Outcome: The court found Delzer liable since he had failed to obtain the insurance required by the agreement.

Delivery and Acceptance

A bailment can be established only if delivery occurs accompanied by acceptance of personal property. The delivery and acceptance may be actual or constructive. Actual delivery and acceptance results when the goods themselves are delivered and accepted. Constructive delivery and acceptance results when no physical delivery of the goods occurs but when control over the goods is delivered and accepted.

Facts: Ovie O. Farmer was employed by Machine Craft as a machinist. As a condition of employment, employees had to furnish their own sets of tools. Farmer's toolbox weighed more than 100 pounds. For the employees' convenience, Machine Craft allowed them to keep the toolboxes at the shop overnight. Although other employees took their tools home, Farmer left his at the shop. Farmer's tools were stolen. Farmer sued Machine Craft for the value of the tools, alleging Machine Craft was the bailee of the tools and had not taken adequate care of them.

Outcome: The judge ruled that to have a bailment, the alleged bailee must have intended to exercise control of the property. Machine Craft never exercised any control so there was no bailment and no liability.

Constructive Bailment
Bailment imposed when a person controls lost property

A **constructive bailment** arises when someone finds and takes possession of lost property. The owner does not actually deliver the property to the finder, but the law holds this to be a bailment. A constructive bailment can also occur when property of one person is washed ashore. The finder becomes a bailee if some overt act of control over the property occurs.

Return of the Bailed Property

In some cases a bailment may exist when the recipient does not return the actual goods.

In the case of fungible goods, such as wheat, a bailment exists if the owner expects to receive a like quantity and quality of goods. If the goods are to be processed in some way, a bailment arises if the product made from the original goods is to be returned.

When a consignment exists, the property may be sold by the consignee and not returned to the consignor. Finally, when property is left for repair, the property returned should be repaired and therefore not be identical to the property left. In each case, a bailment arises although the identical property is not returned.

Facts: Fred Peterson asked Nathan Shay, who was in business as a jeweler, to sell some jewelry. Shay picked up the jewelry at Peterson's house and gave him a receipt listing the items and an estimated value for each. At the bottom of the receipt was written, "To be sold at the agreed prices above." Two days later Peterson told Shay to return the jewelry, but one item had been stolen. Peterson sued his insurance company for the loss. The company denied liability claiming the jewelry had been sold to Shay and was not owned by Peterson when it was stolen.

Outcome: The court held that the transaction was a bailment because any unsold jewelry was to be returned to Peterson.

Types of Bailments

LO4 Types of bailments

The three types of bailments include:

1. Bailments for the sole benefit of the bailor.
2. Bailments for the sole benefit of the bailee.
3. Mutual-benefit bailments.

BAILMENTS FOR THE SOLE BENEFIT OF THE BAILOR

If one holds another's personal property only for the benefit of the owner, a bailment for the sole benefit of the bailor exists. This occurs when a person takes care of a pet for a vacationing friend. The bailee receives no benefits or compensation.

Such a bailment arises when a person asks a friend to store some personal property. For example, a friend may keep a piano until the owner finds a larger apartment. The friend may not play the piano or otherwise receive any benefits of ownership during the bailment. The bailee may only use the property if the use will benefit or preserve it.

A constructive bailment is a bailment for the sole benefit of the bailor. The loser is the bailor, and the finder is the bailee. In a bailment for the sole benefit of the bailor, most states hold that the bailee need exercise slight care and is liable only for gross negligence with respect to the property.

Facts: William and Betty Martin asked Barbara Bell and Ellen Christian to "house sit" while the Martins were on vacation. The Martins left a few dollars for groceries but otherwise did not pay Bell and Christian. Personal property of the Martins was damaged when Christian left a pan of grease unattended on a range burner. The Martins sued Bell and Christian for the damages.

Outcome: The court found that the arrangement was a bailment for the sole benefit of the bailor. It also found that Bell and Christian had not been grossly negligent and were therefore not liable for the damage to the personal property.

BAILMENTS FOR THE SOLE BENEFIT OF THE BAILEE

If the bailee holds and uses another's personal property, and the owner of the property receives no benefit or compensation, a bailment for the sole benefit of the bailee exists. This type of bailment arises when someone's personal property is borrowed.

Facts: Albert Bell and Joseph Lawrence were at the Marriott Hotel to hang banners for a political luncheon. They asked a Marriott employee for a ladder they could use and were directed to one. Bell and Lawrence used the ladder to hang three banners. While on the ladder working on the fourth banner, Bell reached or leaned to work with both hands and fell. Bell sued Marriott for his injuries.

Outcome: The court held that since Marriott was not paid for use of the ladder, it was a bailment for the sole benefit of the bailee. Marriott's only duty was to warn of defects in the ladder.

The bailee must exercise great care over the property. However, any loss or damage due to no fault of the bailee falls upon the owner. If Petras borrows Walker's diamond ring to wear to a dance and is robbed on the way to the dance, the loss falls upon Walker, the owner, as long as Petras was not negligent.

The bailee must be informed of any known defects in the bailed property. If the bailee is injured by reason of such a defect, the bailor who failed to inform the bailee is liable for damages.

MUTUAL-BENEFIT BAILMENTS

Most bailments exist for the mutual benefit of both the bailor and the bailee. Some common bailments of this type include: a TV left to be repaired; laundry and dry cleaning contracts; and the rental of personal property, such as an automobile or furniture. The bailor of rented property must furnish safe property, not just inform the bailee of known defects.

In mutual-benefit bailments, the bailee renders a service and charges for the service. This applies to all repair jobs, laundry, dry cleaning, and storage bailments. The bailee has a lien against the bailed property for the charges. If these charges are not paid after a reasonable time, the bailee may advertise and sell the property for the charges. Any money remaining after paying expenses and the charges must be turned over to the bailor.

A bailee rendering services may receive a benefit other than a fee or monetary payment. For example, a skating rink may offer to check shoes for its customers without charging for the service. A mutual-benefit bailment exists. The customer (bailor) receives storage service and the skating rink (bailee) gains the benefit of a neater, safer customer area.

In mutual-benefit bailments, the standard of care required of the bailee for the property is reasonable care under the circumstances. Such care means the degree of care that a reasonable person would exercise in order to protect the property from harm. The bailee is liable for negligence.

Facts: When John Chambers left his car at Apco Transmission for repair of the transmission, the body of the car was undamaged. When the car was returned, the body was damaged. Chambers sued for the damage.

Outcome: The court found that the transaction was a mutual-benefit bailment. Where goods are in good condition when delivered to a bailee and damaged when returned, negligence is shown. The claim for damages was granted.

Pawn
Tangible personal property left as security for a debt

Pledge
Intangible property serving as security for a debt

SPECIAL MUTUAL-BENEFIT BAILMENTS

A mutual-benefit bailment includes the deposit of personal property as security for some debt or obligation. Tangible property left as security, such as livestock, a radio, or an automobile, is a **pawn**. Intangible property left as a security, such as notes, bonds, or stock certificates, is a **pledge**.

Conversion of Bailed Property by the Bailee

Conversion
Unauthorized exercise of ownership rights

Not being the owner of the property, a bailee normally has no right to convert the property. **Conversion** is the unauthorized exercise of ownership rights over another's property. Thus, the bailee may not sell, lease, or even use the bailed property as security for a loan, and one who purchases such property from a bailee ordinarily does not get good title to it.

However, when the purpose of the bailment is to have the property sold and the proceeds remitted to the bailor, the bailee has the power to sell all goods regardless of any restriction upon the right to sell, unless the buyer knows of the restriction.

A bailor may mislead an innocent third person into believing that the bailee owns the bailed property. In this situation, the bailee may convey good title.

Questions

1 Can an interest in land ever be classified as personal property?
2 How does tangible personal property differ from intangible personal property?
3 What are the two requirements for a valid gift?
4 What difference does it make whether confusion of personal property is willful or by accident?
5 What is the difference between lost and abandoned property?
6 When a bailment occurs, must the same property be returned to the owner? Explain.
7 What standard of care is required of a bailee in a mutual benefit bailment? Explain.
8 If the owner of a car has it in B's garage and gives the keys to C with instructions to get the car, is this a bailment?
9 What use of the bailed property may the bailee in a bailment for the sole benefit of the bailor make?
10 Under what circumstances may a bailee convey good title in the bailed property to a third party?

Case Problems

LO3 1 Richard Gray bought a ticket for an "Alpine Slide" ride owned by Snow King. The ride involved routing a wheeled bob-sled down a winding, trough-shaped slide. Gray was directed to choose a sled and as he went down the slide the sled hit a dip in the slide and became airborne. Gray suffered back injuries from the force of the landing. Gray sued alleging that the transaction was a bailment. Was it?

LO2 2 In 1767 and 1768, while he was the attorney for the king, William Hooper, who later signed the Declaration of Independence, signed and filed two indictments. By an act of the Colonial Assembly the chief justice was authorized to appoint clerks responsible for the safekeeping of records. B. C. West purchased the indictments at an auction more than 200 years later. The state sued to recover possession of them, alleging it was the lawful custodian of and had the right to possess all court records and documents of the state. West alleged the indictments were abandoned, and since he now had possession, he had title to them. Were the indictments abandoned?

LO3,4 3 When Gayle Benz left her husband Jeffrey, she left personal property valued at $10,000 at their residence. After Gayle and Jeffrey got a divorce, she sued for the value of the property. The court found that Gayle had abandoned the property. Gayle appealed. As the appellate judge faced with these facts, how do you decide?

LO1 4 Prior to selling a piece of real estate, Mary Campbell reviewed the documents presented by the real estate agent with her daughter and son-in-law, Trula and Randall Walker. Campbell signed the deed and handed all the documents including a promissory note to be signed by the buyer to Trula and said, "Here, these are yours." After the buyer signed everything he mailed them to a post office box in Campbell's and Trula's names. Walker handed the signed promissory note to Trula and said, "Here, this is yours." The buyer's payments were sent to the post office box and deposited in a bank account in Campbell's and Trula's names. The account was the only one Trula had and she wrote all her checks out of it. After Campbell died Trula's sister alleged Campbell had not given Trula the note. Was there a gift?

LO2 5 Dottie Kitchen had moved her personal belongings out of her mobile home. She told the manager of the trailer park that because she was pregnant, she would be back with help "the next day or over the weekend" to get an air conditioner, a lawn mower, a ladder, and a grill located outside the trailer. Before she returned, the Wachovia Bank and Trust Company repossessed Kitchen's trailer, and the items were taken. Kitchen returned and discovered the loss, so she sued for conversion. The bank alleged she had abandoned them. Had she?

LO1 6 The Elliott System, Inc. hired Fred Adams and promised he would be enrolled in its health insurance plan when he completed three months' work. Adams worked for the required time, but Elliott failed to enroll him. A year later Adams suffered kidney failure requiring hospitalization. Aetna, Elliott's health insurer, refused to cover Adams's expenses, which would have been covered if Adams had been enrolled. Elliott had an insurance policy covering liability for injury to tangible property. Adams sued Elliott, saying loss of the health insurance policy was loss of tangible property. Is health insurance tangible or intangible property?

LO3 7 By written agreement, Clifton Taylor took possession of a Buick from Mark Singleton Buick, Inc., a Buick dealer, for 48 months. The agreement obligated Taylor to make monthly payments, pay the taxes and insurance, make all necessary repairs, and return the car at the expiration of the agreement. The agreement preserved the warranties made by the manufacturer "or its dealers." Singleton repaired and serviced the car numerous times, but after 15 months refused to make any further repairs. The court had to decide if the transaction was a sale or a lease and whether Singleton had any obligation to repair the car. You decide.

LO1 8 Owen Flora got a judgment against Arthur Myles for $1,500. The court ordered Valley Federal Savings and Loan to pay $942.46, which Myles had on deposit, toward the judgment minus $100. State law exempted $100 if the deposit was intangible property. Myles alleged that the deposit was cash and therefore tangible personal property, which was subject to a $4,000 exemption. Was the deposit intangible or tangible personal property, and how much of it was exempt?

LO2 9 In 1776, some American colonists toppled a metal statue of King George III. The statue was hacked apart and the pieces taken to Wilton, Connecticut, where the colonists stopped to imbibe. A group of loyalists stole a load of the pieces, which were scattered in the area of a swamp. Fragments had occasionally turned up since then. Two hundred years later, Louis Miller entered property owned by Fred Favorite without permission and with a metal detector discovered a 15-inch-square statuary fragment 10 inches below the soil. Miller dug it up and removed it. Favorite did not know about the piece found on his property until he read about it in the newspaper. He sued for the fragment. Miller argued that his rights as a finder were superior to those of anyone except the true owner—the British government. Who was entitled to the fragment?

LO3 10 The city of Chicago impounded Bruce Anderson's car after the driver, not Anderson, was arrested. Anderson demanded his car back, but it was stolen from the city's impoundment lot. Since a constructive bailment occurs when the property of one person is voluntarily received by another for a purpose other than obtaining ownership, was the city the bailee of the car and therefore liable for the loss?

Internet Resources for Business Law

Name	Resources	Web Address
Internal Revenue Service	The Internal Revenue Service, and its publication, the Digital Daily, provide tax advice and information on a variety of issues, including personal property issues.	http://www.irs.ustreas.gov/
U.S. Internal Revenue Code—26 USC	LII, maintained by Cornell Law School, provides the U.S. Internal Revenue Code, 26 USC, in a hypertext and searchable format.	http://www.law.cornell.edu/uscode/26/
Legal Information Institute (LII)—Estate and Gift Tax Law Materials	LII provides an overview of estate and gift tax law, including relevant sections from the U.S. Code and Code of Federal Regulation, court cases, and links.	http://www.law.cornell.edu/topics/estate_gift_tax.html

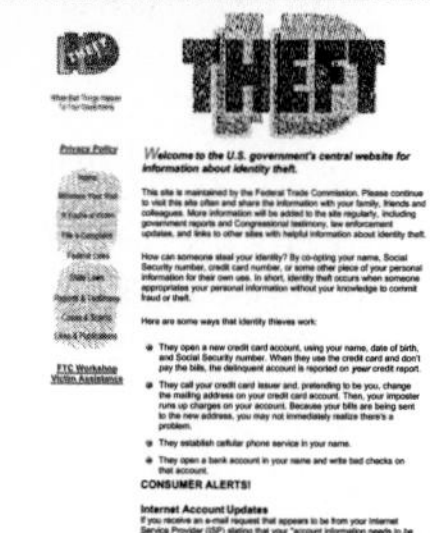

15 Special Bailments

Learning Objectives

1 Explain what a carrier does and name the two categories of carriers.

2 Identify the exceptions to the normal rule of a common carrier being an insurer of the safety of goods.

3 Distinguish a boardinghouse keeper from a hotelkeeper.

4 Name the duties and liabilities of a hotelkeeper.

PREVIEW CASE

Jean King and Miriam Kelley were robbed in Room 821 of the Ilikai Tower Building. Ilikai Properties, Inc. operated the Tower Building of the Ilikai Hotel, as a hotel, but it also contained condominium units. Room 821 was a condominium owned by Melvin Shigeta, who had rented it to King. Kelley was visiting King. King and Kelley sued Ilikai Properties, alleging that their losses were caused by Ilikai's failure to make the premises safe. Did Ilikai have a duty to protect them from robbers? What was the relationship of Ilikai to King and Kelley?

There are several types of mutual-benefit bailments in which the bailor, under the common law, is held to a higher than normal standard of care for the bailed property. These bailments, sometimes called *extraordinary bailments,* include common carriers and hotelkeepers.

Carriers

Carrier
Transporter of goods, people, or both

A **carrier** engages in the business of transporting either goods or persons, or both. A carrier of goods is a bailee. Since a carrier charges a fee for such service, the bailment exists for the mutual benefit of both parties.

LO1 Types of carriers

CLASSIFICATION OF CARRIERS

Carriers are usually classified into two groups:

1 Private carriers
2 Common carriers

PRIVATE CARRIERS

Private Carrier
Carrier that transports under special arrangements for a fee

A **private carrier**, for a fee, undertakes to transport goods or persons. It transports only under special instances and special arrangements and may refuse service that is unprofitable. The most usual types of private carriers are trucks, moving vans, ships, and delivery services. A carrier owned by the shipper, such as a truck from a fleet owned and operated by an industrial firm for transporting its own products, is a private carrier.

Private carriers' contracts for transporting goods are mutual-benefit bailments, and the general law of bailments governs them. They are liable only for loss from the failure to exercise ordinary care. By contract a private carrier may further limit liability for loss to the goods.

COMMON CARRIERS

Common Carrier
One that undertakes to transport without discrimination all who apply for service

Consignor
One who ships by common carrier

Consignee
One to whom goods are shipped

Bill of Lading
Receipt and contract between consignor and carrier

A **common carrier** undertakes to transport goods or persons, without discrimination, for all who apply for that service. The goods to be transported must be proper, and facilities must be available for transport. One who ships goods by a common carrier is called the **consignor**; the one to whom the goods are shipped is called the **consignee**; and the receipt and contract between the carrier and the consignor is called a **bill of lading**.

A common carrier must serve without discrimination all who apply. If it fails to do so, it is liable for any damages resulting from such a refusal. A common carrier may, however, refuse service because the service is not one for which it is properly equipped. For example, an express company does not have to accept lumber for transportation. Also, a common carrier may refuse service if its equipment is inadequate to accommodate customers in excess of the normal demands. A common carrier of persons is not required to transport (1) any person who requires unusual attention, such as an invalid, unless that person is accompanied by an attendant; (2) any person who intends or is likely to cause harm to the carrier or the passengers; or (3) any person who is likely to be offensive to passengers, such as an intoxicated person.

The usual types of common carriers of persons are trains, buses, airplanes, ships, and subways. Common carriers are public monopolies and are subject to regulations as to their prices, services, equipment, and other operational policies. This public regulation is in lieu of competition as a determinant of their prices and services.

Liability of Common Carriers of Goods

LO2 When common carrier is not an insurer

Although common carriers of goods and common carriers of persons are alike in that they must serve all who apply, they differ sharply in their liability for loss. Common carriers of goods are insurers of the safety of the transported goods and are liable for loss or damage regardless of fault, unless the loss arises from:

1 Acts of God
2 Acts of a public authority

3 Inherent nature of the goods
4 Acts of the shipper
5 Acts of a public enemy

These exceptions do not excuse the carrier if the carrier failed to safeguard the goods from harm.

ACTS OF GOD

The carrier is not liable for unusual natural occurrences such as floods, snowstorms, tornadoes, lightning, or fire caused by lightning, since these are considered acts of God. Normal weather such as a rainstorm is not.

Facts: Ozark White Lime Co. shipped a carload of lime from Johnson, Arkansas, to Okmulgee, Oklahoma, by the St. Louis–San Francisco Railway Company. The railway car got as far as McBride, Oklahoma. The train could not proceed beyond McBride because a landslide had covered the tracks. While it was there, excessive rains caused the Grand River to flood the track and the lime was destroyed. Ozark sued the railroad for the value of the lime.

Outcome: The court held that the unprecedented flood was an act of God.

ACTS OF A PUBLIC AUTHORITY

An act of a public authority occurs if public officials seize illicit goods, or if health officials seize goods that are a menace to health. The carrier is not liable for such loss.

INHERENT NATURE OF THE GOODS

The carrier is not liable for damage due to the inherent nature of the goods, such as decay of vegetables, fermentation or evaporation of liquids, and death of livestock as a result of natural causes or the fault of other animals.

ACTS OF THE SHIPPER

Acts of the shipper that can cause loss include misdirection of the merchandise, failure to indicate fragile contents, and improper packing. If improper packing is noticeable, the carrier can refuse to accept the goods.

Facts: Semi Metals, Inc., delivered two cartons of germanium to Pinter Brothers for shipment under a straight bill of lading. The germanium was worth $85 a pound, but to avoid higher freight charges Semi Metals described it as electronic material and no value was stated in the bill of lading. The tariff for electronic materials had a maximum value of $5 a pound. The two cartons were lost. Semi Metals sued Pinter for $19,280, the full value of the germanium.

Outcome: The court held that the intentional misdescription of the shipper to avoid higher shipping charges limited Semi Metals' recovery to $5 a pound.

ACTS OF A PUBLIC ENEMY

Organized warfare or border excursions of foreign bandits constitute acts of a public enemy. Mobs, strikers, and rioters are not classified as public enemies in interpreting this exclusion.

CONTRACTUAL LIMITATIONS ON LIABILITY

A common carrier may attempt to limit or escape the extraordinary liability imposed upon it by law, often by a contract between the shipper and the carrier. As the written evidence of the contract, the bill of lading sets out the limitations on the carriers' liability. Since the shipper does not have any direct voice in the preparation of the bill of lading, the law requires every carrier to have its printed bill of lading form approved by a government agency before adoption.

In addition to uniform limitations set out in the printed form of a bill of lading, additional limitations may be added that the shipper and the carrier may agree upon. The Federal Bills of Lading Act governs this matter as to interstate shipments, and the Uniform Commercial Code controls with respect to intrastate shipments. In general, the limitations upon the carrier's liability permitted by these acts fall into the following classes:

1 A carrier may limit its loss by agreement to a specified sum or to a specified percentage of the value of the goods. However, a carrier must give the shipper the choice of shipping at lower rates subject to the limited liability or at a higher rate without limitation of liability.

Facts: Richard Alteri Jr. shipped two packages containing computer equipment with a declared value of $1,100 from New York to Illinois by Greyhound Lines. Both packages were lost so Alteri sued Greyhound for their alleged true value of $8,000. Greyhound asserted its liability was limited as stated on the bus bills to $100 for a two-package shipment unless the shipper declares and pays for a greater value, not to exceed $1,000, at the time of shipment.

Outcome: The court agreed with Greyhound that its liability was limited to $1,000.

2 Most states permit carriers to exempt themselves from liability due to certain named hazards. The most common named hazards include fire, leakage, breakage, spoilage, and losses due to riots, strikes, mobs, and robbers. Some states specifically prohibit an exemption for loss by fire. These exemptions must be specifically enumerated in the bill of lading or shipper's receipt. The exemptions are not effective if the loss is due to the negligence of the carrier.

3 Delay in transportation of livestock may result in serious losses or extra expense for feed. Most states allow some form of limitation upon the carrier's liability if the loss is due to a delay over which the carrier has no control.

In those cases where the carrier is held liable only for loss due to negligence, the Uniform Commercial Code provides for liability only for ordinary negligence.

DURATION OF THE SPECIAL LIABILITY

The carrier's high degree of liability lasts only during transportation. If the goods are delivered to the carrier ready for shipment and are received from the carrier promptly upon arrival, the goods are regarded as being transported during the entire transaction.

CARRIER AS BAILEE BEFORE TRANSPORTATION

Frequently, goods are delivered to the carrier before they are ready for transportation. The carrier is liable only as a mutual-benefit bailee until the goods are ready for transportation.

CARRIER AS BAILEE AFTER TRANSPORTATION

When the goods arrive at their destination, the consignee has a reasonable time to accept delivery of the goods. Railroads need only place the goods in the freight depot, or, in the case of car lots, set the car on a siding where the consignee can unload the goods. If the consignee does not call for the goods within a reasonable time after being notified by the carrier that the goods have arrived, the carrier is liable only as a mutual-benefit bailee.

CONNECTING CARRIERS

The initial carrier and the final, or terminal, carrier are each liable for a common-carrier loss occurring on the line of a connecting carrier. Whichever of these carriers has been held liable may then compel the connecting carrier to reimburse it.

BILLS OF LADING

The bill of lading not only sets forth the contract between the shipper and the carrier, it is a document of title. Title to the goods described in the bill of lading may be passed by transferring it to the purchaser. There are two types of bills of lading:

1 Straight, or nonnegotiable, bills of lading
2 Order, or negotiable, bills of lading

Straight Bill of Lading Contract requiring delivery of shipped goods to consignee only

Straight Bills of Lading. Under a **straight bill of lading** (see Illustration 15-1), the consignee alone is designated as the one to whom the goods are to be delivered. The consignee's rights may be transferred to another, but the third party normally obtains no greater rights than the shipper or the consignee had. However, if the bill of lading contains a recital as to the contents, quantity, or weight of the goods, the carrier is bound to a bona fide transferee as to the accuracy of these descriptions unless the bill of lading itself indicates that the contents of packages are unknown to the carrier.

The assignee should notify the carrier of the assignment when the original consignee sells the goods before receipt. The carrier is justified in delivering goods to the consignee if it has not received notice of assignment.

Facts: Italian Leather Italy sent shipments of leather skins in a locked, sealed, multimodal shipping container from Italy to the United States. When the container was unloaded from the ship, Marine Freight issued a receipt/bill of lading specifying the weight and trucked the container from Virginia to North Carolina. When Italian Leather opened the container, 20 percent of the skins were missing.

Outcome: Since a common carrier is liable unless damage is caused by one of the recognized exceptions, the court found Marine Freight liable. It was bound by the weight specified on the bill of lading.

Illustration 15-1

Bill of Lading

21040

ALWAYS LIST HAZARDOUS MATERIALS FIRST IN DESCRIPTION OF ARTICLES COLUMN.

STRAIGHT BILL OF LADING - SHORT FORM - Original-Not Negotiable

RECEIVED, subject to the classification and tariffs in effect on the date of issue of this Original Bill of Lading

NOT to be used for ORDER NOTIFY SHIPMENTS. DATE

BIG BEAR Transfer Company

BIG BEAR TRANSFER COMPANY

NOTE: DRIVER AFIX PRO NUMBER LABEL HERE

(NAME OF CARRIER) (SCAC)

CUSTOMER P.O. NO. ROUTE SHIPPER'S NUMBER

TO: CONSIGNEE — on COD Shipments the letters "COD" must appear before consignee's name. FROM: SHIPPER

STREET STREET

(DESTINATION) CITY, STATE, ZIP (ORIGIN) CITY, STATE, ZIP

C.O.D. AMT $ ______ FEE PPD ☐ COL ☐ IS CUSTOMER'S CHECK ACCEPTABLE FOR C.O.D.? YES ☐ NO ☐

NO. SHIPPING UNITS	(X) HM	RATE AND CLASS	KIND OF PACKAGING, DESCRIPTION OF ARTICLES, SPECIAL MARKS AND EXCEPTIONS (LIST HAZARDOUS MATERIALS FIRST)	WEIGHT LBS (Subject to Correcitons)
	◄ TOTAL		TOTAL ►	

NOTE: Where the rate is dependent on value, shippers are required to state specifically in writing the agreed or declared value of the property.

The agreed or declared value of the property is hereby specifically stated by the shipper to be not exceeding

$ ______

per ______

Subject to Section 7 of the conditions, if this shipment is to be delivered to the consignee without recourse on the consignor, the consignor shall sign the following statement:

The carrier shall not make delivery of this shipment without payment of freight and all other lawful charges.

______ (Signature of Consignor

FREIGHT CHARGES

WRITE IN PREPAID OR COLLECT

RECEIVED, subject to the classifications and tariffs in effect on the date of the issue of this Bill of Lading, the property described above in apparent good order, except as noted (contents and condition of contents of packages unknown), marked, consigned and destined as indicated above which said carrier (the word carrier being understood throughout this contract as meaning any person or corporation in possession of the property under the contract) agrees to carry to its usual place of delivery at said destination, if on its route, otherwise to deliver to another carrier on the route to said destination. It is mutally agreed as to each carrier of all or any of, said property over all or any to all the bill of lading terms and conditions in the governing classification on the date of shipment.

Shipper hereby certifies that he is familiar with all the bill of lading terms and conditions in the governing classification and the said terms and conditions are hereby agreed to by the shipper and accepted for himself and his assigns.

This is to certify that the above-named materials are properly classified, described, packaged, marked and labeled, and are in proper condition for transportation according to the applicable regulations of the Department of Transportation	SHIPPER:	BIG BEAR TRANSFER COMPANY	
	PER:	DRIVER	TRAILER
		PIECES	DATE

MARK "X" IN "HM" COLUMN FOR HAZARDOUS MATERIALS.

Order Bill of Lading
Contract allowing delivery of shipped goods to bearer

Order Bills of Lading. The bill of lading may set forth that the goods are shipped to a designated consignee or order, or merely "to the bearer" of the bill of lading. In such case, the bill of lading is an **order**, or negotiable, **bill of lading** and must be presented to the carrier before the carrier can safely deliver the goods. If the goods are delivered to the named consignee and later a bona fide innocent purchaser of the order bill of lading demands the goods, the carrier is liable to the holder of the bill of lading.

Facts: Nissho, a Japanese corporation, ordered hog grease from Amkor Corporation in the United States. Nissho reserved space on Iino Kaiun Kaisha Ltd.'s ship bound for Kobe, Japan, and Amkor purchased the grease from Swift and Company. Amkor asked Chase Manhattan Bank to finance the sale. Chase agreed if it got a signed mate's receipt issued in its name. Grease was pumped aboard Iino's ship, and on May 8 an order bill of lading was issued showing Nissho as owner. While the ship was en route to Japan, Chase was working on the details of financing including receiving a receipt from Swift. It was not until May 26 that Chase wrote Iino claiming to own the goods. Iino replied that upon delivery of the order bill of lading, Iino had released the grease to Nissho. Chase sued.

Outcome: The court said the carrier, Iino, properly delivered the merchandise to the holder when the order bill of lading was presented.

COMMON CARRIERS OF PERSONS

Common carriers of persons have the right to prescribe the place and time of the payment of fares, usually before boarding the plane, train, bus, or other vehicle. They also have the right to prescribe reasonable rules of conduct for transporting passengers. They may stop the vehicle and remove any passenger who refuses to pay the fare or whose conduct offends the other passengers. They also have the right to reserve certain coaches, seats, or space for special classes of passengers, as in the case of first-class seats in the forward cabin of aircraft.

LIABILITY OF COMMON CARRIERS OF PERSONS

The liability of a carrier for the passengers' safety begins as soon as passengers enter the terminal or waiting platform and does not end until they have left the terminal at the end of the journey. Unlike a common carrier of goods, a common carrier of persons is not an insurer. In most states a carrier must provide only ordinary care while passengers are in the terminal; however some states have modified this rule. When passengers board the bus, train, plane, or other vehicle, the highest degree of care consistent with practical operation is required. However, even when the highest degree of care is required a carrier of persons is only liable if it has been negligent.

Facts: At around 1 A.M. Joseph Skelton entered the train platform at a Chicago Transit Authority (CTA) station intending to catch the next train. No ticket agent was on duty and a sign stated "Board Here, Please Pay on Train." He sat and waited. A train passed through without stopping so when he heard a second train he got up to flag it down to make sure it stopped. Standing at the edge of the platform, he leaned over and waved to get the driver's attention. He lost his balance and fell onto the tracks. He was run over by the train and his right arm had to be amputated. Skelton sued the CTA.

Outcome: In this case, the court held that the CTA owed Skelton the highest degree of care because he was a passenger when hit by the train.

DUTIES OF COMMON CARRIERS OF PERSONS

A carrier's duties to its passengers consist of:

1. Duty to provide reasonable accommodations and services.
2. Duty to provide reasonable protection to its passengers.

Duty to Provide Reasonable Accommodations and Services. A carrier is required to furnish adequate and reasonable service. A passenger is not necessarily entitled to a seat; however, the carrier must make a reasonable effort to provide sufficient facilities so that the public can be accommodated, which may be merely standing room. A passenger may make an express reservation that requires the carrier to provide a seat. The carrier must notify the passenger of the arrival of the train, bus, or airplane at the destination and stop long enough to permit the passenger to disembark.

Duty to Provide Reasonable Protection to Its Passengers. Common carriers of passengers need not insure the absolute safety of passengers but must exercise extraordinary care to protect them. Any injury to the passenger by an employee or

Facts: For two weeks during the summer, Burton Fendelman was a passenger on Conrail trains that were late; overcrowded; lacking in air conditioning, water facilities, and electricity; and which had dirty toilets and noxious odors. He sued Conrail and testified that these "atrocious conditions" had existed for years.

Outcome: The court found that as a common carrier, Conrail was required to furnish such service and facilities as shall be safe and adequate and in all respects just and reasonable. This it did not do, and it was required to pay Fendelman damages.

fellow passengers subjects the carrier to liability for damages, provided the injured passenger is without blame. The vehicle must stop at a safe place for alighting, and passengers must be assisted when necessary for alighting.

BAGGAGE

Baggage
Articles necessary for personal convenience while traveling

Baggage consists of those articles of personal convenience or necessity usually carried by passengers for their personal use at some time during the trip. Articles carried by travelers on similar missions and destinations constitute the test. For example, fishing paraphernalia is baggage for a person who expects to go fishing while away, but not for the ordinary traveler. Any article carried for one who is not a passenger is not baggage. A reasonable amount of baggage may be carried as a part of the cost of the passenger's fare. The carrier may charge extra for baggage in excess of a reasonable amount.

The liability of a common carrier for checked baggage historically was the same as that of a common carrier of goods—an insurer of the baggage with the five exceptions previously mentioned. The liability for baggage retained in the possession of the traveler was only for lack of reasonable care or for willful misconduct of its agents or employees. However, today carriers are allowed to limit their liability for loss of baggage to a fixed maximum amount. This amount will be stated on the ticket. Such limitations are binding on passengers.

Facts: On the way to her Delta Airlines flight, Felice Lippert took a handbag containing $431,000 worth of jewelry through a Palm Beach International Airport security checkpoint. She placed the bag on the conveyor belt and walked through the archway magnetometer. The alarm sounded and security personnel briefly inspected her. Lippert then discovered her handbag was missing. She sued Delta and Wackenhut, which operated the security checkpoint for Delta. They asserted that the $1,250 limitation of liability, printed on the back of Lippert's ticket, should apply. It covered "baggage or other property (including carry-on baggage . . . delivered into the custody of [Delta])."

Outcome: The court held that the $1,250 limitation applied because the handbag clearly was delivered into the custody of Delta at the security checkpoint.

Hotelkeepers

LO3
Boardinghouse keeper versus hotelkeeper

A **hotelkeeper** regularly engages in the business of offering lodging to all transient persons. The hotelkeeper may also supply food or entertainment, but providing lodging to transients is the primary business.

Hotelkeeper
One engaged in business of offering lodging to transients

Boardinghouse Keeper
Person in business to supply accommodations to permanent lodgers

A person who provides rooms or room and board to permanent lodgers but does not behave as able and willing to accommodate transients is not a hotelkeeper. Such persons are **boardinghouse keepers** and the laws of hotelkeepers do not apply to them. The owner of a tourist home is not a hotelkeeper if the establishment does not advertise as willing to accommodate all transients who apply. Most people who run hotels and motels are hotelkeepers. A hotel that caters to both permanent residents and transients is a hotelkeeper only with respect to the transients.

WHO ARE GUESTS?

Guest
Transient received by hotel for accommodations

To be a **guest** one must be a transient obtaining lodging, not a permanent resident or visitor. One who enters the hotel to attend a ball or other social function, to visit a guest, or to eat dinner is not a guest. A guest need not be a traveler nor come from a distance. A guest might be a person living within a short distance of the hotel who rents a room and remains there overnight.

The relationship of guest and hotelkeeper does not begin until the hotelkeeper receives the person seeking lodging as a guest. The relationship terminates when the guest leaves or makes arrangements for permanent residence at the hotel.

PREVIEW CASE REVISITED

Facts: Jean King and Miriam Kelley were robbed in Room 821 of the Ilikai Tower Building. Ilikai Properties, Inc. operated the Tower Building of the Ilikai Hotel, as a hotel, but it also contained condominium units. Room 821 was a condominium owned by Melvin Shigeta, who had rented it to King. Kelley was visiting King. King and Kelley sued Ilikai Properties, alleging that their losses were caused by Ilikai's failure to make the premises safe for them as guests.

Outcome: The court found that King and Kelley were not guests of the hotel.

DUTIES OF A HOTELKEEPER

LO4
Hotelkeeper's duties and liabilities

The duties of a hotelkeeper include:

1. To serve all who apply
2. To protect a guest's person
3. To care for the guest's property

DUTY TO SERVE ALL WHO APPLY

The basic test of hotelkeepers is that they hold themselves out as willing to serve without discrimination all who request lodging. However, this does not require hotelkeepers to serve someone who is drunk, someone who is criminally violent, someone who is not dressed in a manner required by reasonable hotel regulations applied to all, or when no rooms are available. If a hotel refuses lodging for an improper reason, it is liable for damages, including exemplary damages, to the person rejected.

In addition, a hotel may be liable for discrimination under a civil rights or similar statutory provision and may also be guilty of a crime if a court has issued an injunction prohibiting such discrimination. By virtue of the Federal Civil Rights Act of 1964, neither a hotel nor its concessionaire can discriminate against patrons nor segregate them on the basis of race, color, religion, or national origin. When there has been improper discrimination or segregation or it is reasonably believed that such action may occur, the federal act authorizes the institution of proceedings in the federal courts for an order to stop such practices.

DUTY TO PROTECT A GUEST'S PERSON

A hotelkeeper must use reasonable care for the guests' personal safety. The same standard applies to the personal safety of a visitor or a patron of a newsstand or lunchroom.

Reasonable care requires that a hotelkeeper provides fire escapes and also has conspicuous notices indicating directions to the fire escapes. If a fire starts due to no negligence of the hotelkeeper or employees, there is no liability to the guests for their personal injuries unless they can show that the fire was not contained because of a failure to install required fire safety features. In one case the court held the hotelkeeper was not liable for the loss of life on the floor where the fire started, but was liable for all personal injuries on the four floors to which the fire spread because of the negligence of the hotel.

If a hotelkeeper knows of prior criminal acts on or near the hotel premises, additional security measures may be required. However, the hotelkeeper is not liable if the guest's behavior increases the risk of criminal attack.

Facts: Merle Fritts, the estranged husband of Erma, an on-duty motel employee, came to the motel and threatened to kill her. Merle had been drinking and had a history of beating Erma and threatening her with a gun. Merle got a shotgun from his truck and returned to the motel. The manager of the business next door saw Merle and asked a customer, Stewart, to help him stop Merle. Merle started shooting in the motel lobby and severely injured Stewart. He sued the motel.

Outcome: The court stated that the motel had a duty to take all precautions for the protection of its guests that reasonable prudence and ordinary care would suggest. Since a reasonable person would have foreseen a risk of harm as a result of Merle's conduct, the motel was liable.

DUTY TO CARE FOR THE GUEST'S PROPERTY

Traditionally, the hotelkeeper had a very high duty and was an insurer of the guest's property except for losses occurring from:

1. An act of God
2. The act of a public enemy
3. An act of a public authority
4. An act of the guest
5. The inherent nature of the property

In every state this liability has been modified to some extent. The statutes vary greatly but most limit a hotel's liability to a designated sum or simply declare that the law of mutual-benefit bailments applies.

Some states permit the hotelkeeper to limit liability by posting a notice in the guest's room. Some of the statutes require that the hotelkeeper, in order to escape full liability, provide a vault or other safe place of deposit for valuables such as furs and jewelry. If a guest fails to deposit valuable articles when notice of the availability of a safe has been posted, the hotelkeeper is released from liability as an insurer.

HOTELKEEPER'S LIEN

A hotelkeeper has a lien on the baggage of guests for the value of the services rendered. This lien extends to all wearing apparel not actually being worn, such as an overcoat or an extra suit.

If hotel charges are not paid within a reasonable time, the hotelkeeper may sell the baggage to pay the charges. Any residue must be returned to the guest. The lien terminates if the property is returned to the guest even though the charges are unpaid.

The lien usually attaches only to baggage. It does not apply to an automobile, for example, in most states. If a hotelkeeper charges separately for car storage, this charge (but not the room charge) must be paid before the car can be removed.

Questions

1 What is an extraordinary bailment?

2 a. What is the liability of a private carrier?
b. What is the liability of a common carrier of goods?

3 Since the law imposes significant liability on a common carrier of goods, is there any way the carrier may limit this liability?

4 What is the difference between a straight bill of lading and an order bill of lading?

5 What is the liability of a common carrier of persons and when does it begin?

6 Must a common carrier of persons provide seats for all the passengers?

7 What is baggage and the liability of a common carrier for baggage carried by a passenger?

8 What are boardinghouse keepers and must they comply with the laws relating to hotelkeepers?

9 What are the duties and liabilities of a hotelkeeper to guests?

10 Is the hotelkeeper liable for the injury to a guest by fire if the hotel was in no way negligent?

11 How may a hotelkeeper frequently limit liability for loss of a guest's property?

12 What is a hotelkeeper's lien?

Case Problems

LO2 1 After Antoinette Sebastian was seriously injured in an automobile accident a District of Columbia ambulance transported her to the hospital. During the ride the ambulance attendant sexually molested her. She sued the district. Should Sebastian recover from the district?

LO4 2 Paul and Wendy Carter rented a room at a Travelodge. While in the room, they heard bumping and scratching sounds that seemed to come from behind a wall covered by a mirror. Later Paul noticed two scratches in the mirror at eye level. He took off the mirror and found scratches on the back of the mirror through which a person could easily see and a large hole in the wall behind where the scratches would be. There was a 1½-foot hollow space between the wall and the wall of the adjoining room. There was also a hole in the adjoining room wall covered by a mirror with scratches. If the mirror in that room was removed one could see into the Carters' room. The Carters sued the hotel. Was the hotel negligent?

LO1,2 3 Accura Systems, Inc. delivered 12 wrapped packages of specially coated aluminum panels to Watkins Motor Lines, Inc. for shipping. Watkins issued a bill of lading that stated the goods were "in apparent good order, except as noted (contents and conditions of contents of packages unknown)." At destination, most of the panels had scratches, gouges and dents. Accura sued Watkins. Is Watkins bound by the statement of "good condition" in the bill of lading?

LO3 4 An individual rented and paid for an efficiency apartment on a weekly basis for four weeks. Apartments were not rented on a daily basis as regular motel rooms were. After leaving some of his belongings in the unit and failing to return the key for two extra days, he was convicted of the crime of theft of services. The law defines theft of services as failure to pay for services rendered as a "transient guest at a hotel, motel, . . . or comparable establishment." The defendant appealed, claiming he was not a "transient guest." The unit had cooking facilities and no maid service as regular motel rooms had. Was the defendant a transient guest?

LO1,2 5 Gensplit Finance Corporation bought the right to collect on three shipments from D.E.C. Western Distributors, Inc., to Corporacion Intercontinental, C.A., in Venezuela. Three Pan American straight air waybills (bills of lading issued by an airline) had been issued and D.E.C.'s rights under them had been transferred to Gensplit. Gensplit relied on these air waybills to advance $117,568 to D.E.C. The shipments never arrived, so Gensplit sued Pan Am. Pan Am had filed tariffs with the government. If they were effective against Gensplit, Pan Am would win the suit. Pan Am alleged that since the tariffs were binding on D.E.C., they would be binding on Gensplit. How should the case be decided?

LO1,2 6 David Lloyd, an independent trucker, contracted with East Texas Motor Freight to haul a load of insulation from California to Ohio. During his trip, Lloyd ran into a severe rainstorm that damaged the load. East Texas sued Lloyd, who argued that an "act of God" was responsible for the damage. He testified that the storm was a little worse than storms he had previously been in. Should Lloyd be excused from liability because of an act of God?

LO4 7 Timothy Augustine attended a seminar at a Marriott hotel. The seminar sponsor, who had rented the meeting room, requested a movable coat rack, which Marriott put outside the room. Augustine hung his coat on the rack and at the noon break found the coat rack had been moved around a corner. His cashmere coat was missing. Augustine sued Marriott as a hotelkeeper for the loss of the coat. Is Marriott liable as a hotelkeeper?

LO1,2 8 During the daytime Phyllis Parlato alighted from a Connecticut Transit bus and started to cross the bus-stop area. She stepped into a hole that was covered by leaves and broke her leg. The bus driver had stopped at the area five or six times previously that day and did not know about the hole. Parlato sued for breach of Connecticut's duty of utmost care for its passengers. Did Connecticut Transit breach its duty?

LO4 9 Mr. and Mrs. Andrew Laubie were guests at the Royal Sonesta Hotel. They locked the doors and windows and secured the chain lock to their room, but during the night burglars opened the door and severed the chain lock. Valuable jewelry was stolen. The hotel provided a safety deposit vault for its guests. State law provided that an innkeeper was not liable to guests for loss of property in any sum exceeding $100 if a copy of the law was conspicuously posted in the guest's room or unless greater liability was contracted for in writing. In a suit brought by the Laubies against the hotel, the question was whether the statute limited the hotel's liability for negligence as well as its liability as a depository. Did it?

LO1,2 10 Iowa Beef Processors, Inc., shipped meat to Standard Meat Company by American Trucking Company, a common carrier. The meat was loaded into a trailer that Iowa sealed. It was Standard's responsibility to break the seal upon arrival. When the shipment arrived, the meat was tendered to Standard but not unloaded for two days because of a lack of freezer space. It was discovered during unloading that much of the meat was spoiled. The shipment was rejected. Iowa sued American for damages, alleging that American was liable as an insurer because the meat was in good condition when it was shipped. Is American liable?

Internet Resources for Business Law

Name	Resources	Web Address
Uniform Commercial Code Article 7, Warehouse Receipts, Bills of Lading and Other Documents of Title	LII provides UCC's Article 7, Warehouse Receipts, Bills of Lading and Other Documents of Title.	http://www.law.cornell.edu/ucc/7/overview.html
Facts for Consumers—Warranties Fast Facts	The FTC Warranties Fast Facts provides guidelines to consumers on different types of warranties, as well as information for resolving disputes over warranties.	http://www.ftc.gov/bcp/conline/pubs/products/warrant.htm
Uniform Commercial Code §2-308	LII provides a hypertext and searchable version of UCC §2-308, Absence of Specified Place for Delivery.	http://www.law.cornell.edu/ucc/2/2-308.html
Uniform Commercial Code §2-609	LII provides a hypertext and searchable version of UCC §2-609, Right to Adequate Assurance of Performance.	http://www.law.cornell.edu/ucc/2/2-609.html

Part 3 Summary Cases

Personal Property

1 Industria Nacional ordered 1,500 tons of soft wood kraft pulp for $569,800. The cargo was loaded onto the M/V *Albert F* which issued a bill of lading. When the ship arrived at the destination it had 505 bales of worthless wastepaper and no wood pulp. Industria sued the ship and its owner claiming it was a common carrier and therefore liable for nonreceipt of the goods or failure of the goods to be as described in the bill of lading. Should the carrier be held liable? [*Industria Nacional Del Papel, CA v. M/V Albert F.,* 730 F.2d 622]

2 Two young men pounded on the door as a bus started and the driver stopped for them. They smelled of alcohol and were stumbling and boisterous. They argued with the driver about the fare and one did not pay. The driver demanded the nonpayer come forward and after an argument he paid. He walked erratically grabbing poles to balance and tripped over a woman's leg. The man yelled at her and threatened to kill her. For at least 10 minutes he walked up and down shouting obscenities. An elderly man, William O'Neill asked the driver to do something, but he refused. The man threatened O'Neill for a minute. When O'Neill got up the man grabbed him. The driver hit the brakes causing them both to fall. The two young men beat O'Neill caving in his face, breaking his nose and jaw, and causing brain and spinal cord injuries. O'Neill sued the bus company. Should the bus company be liable for O'Neill's injuries? [*Washington Metropolitan Area Transit Authority v. O'Neill*, 633 A.2d 834 (D.C. App)]

3 State law provided that all intangible property remaining unclaimed by the owner for more than seven years after it was payable was presumed abandoned. Such intangible property could be claimed by the state. Blue Cross and Blue Shield (BC/BS) held $125,000 in uncashed checks issued by it to pay benefits and premium refunds. The state demanded the funds. Were they intangible property? [*Revenue Cabinet v. Blue Cross and Blue Shield,* 702 S.W.2d 433 (Ky.)]

4 American Cyanamid Co. shipped 12 large boxes of heavy machinery and oil by Seatrain Lines of Puerto Rico, Inc., and then by land with Francisco Vega Otero, a common carrier. The boxes were loaded onto three platforms owned by Seatrain, and the platforms were loaded aboard Seatrain's ship. Upon arrival in Puerto Rico the platforms were unloaded and each mounted on a chassis with wheels. Later they were attached to three Vega Otero trucks. The cargo on the platforms was so high the truck drivers could not pass under a bridge on the normal route. They blocked off a one-way exit ramp and went up the ramp the wrong way, intending to make a U-turn at the top. When the first driver carefully and cautiously tried to turn, the platform tipped onto its side, causing the chassis and truck to overturn and damaging the cargo. It was the custom of the parties for the land carrier to accept goods in the trailers chosen by the sea carrier. Cyanamid's insurance company sued Seatrain and Vega Otero. What is the liability of either or both carriers? [*American Foreign Insurance Association v. Seatrain Lines of Puerto Rico, Inc.,* 689 F.2d 295 (1st Cir.)]

5 The painter Alphonse Mucha had more than 20 of his paintings, including a large one called "Quo Vadis," delivered to the Newcomb-Macklin gallery for the gallery to try to sell for him. Mucha had occasional contact by letter with the gallery, but died 19 years after the delivery. His son, Jiri, thought he had recovered all the remaining paintings after Alphonse's death. Fifty-nine years after receiving the paintings, the gallery was

liquidating and Rupprecht asked the owner for the rolled-up paintings in the basement. One of the paintings was "Quo Vadis," which Rupprecht sold to an art dealer who sold it to Charles King. A year later a friend of King's wrote to Jiri, asking about the symbolism in the painting. Jiri found out King had it and sued for its return, claiming a conversion by the gallery. Was there a 59-year bailment and a conversion of "Quo Vadis"? [*Mucha v. King,* 792 F.2d 602 (7th Cir.)]

6 While she was a passenger in a motor home leased from BCJ Corporation, Jayne Miles was severely burned when the motor home caught fire. It had collided with a guard rail causing the gas tanks to rupture, and the leaking gas caught fire. Miles sued BCJ, alleging it knew the motor home was defectively designed because the only exit door was directly over the gas tanks, and the tires were overloaded and likely to rupture. The trial court dismissed the suit before any evidence was heard. Did Miles allege a cause of action against BCJ? [*Miles v. General Tire & Rubber Co.,* 460 N.E.2d 1377 (Ohio Ct. App.)]

7 After checking into his motel room late at night, Thomas Urbano went to his car in the motel parking lot to get his luggage. He was assaulted and seriously injured by unidentified people. There had been 42 episodes of criminal activity at the motel in the prior three years, and 12 of the episodes had occurred in the previous three and one-half months. The parking lot was not enclosed, and the area of Urbano's room was dimly lighted. Urbano sued the motel, alleging it was negligent in not providing adequate lighting, not fencing the parking lot, not notifying him of criminal activity, and not monitoring and protecting the premises. The motel argued the case should be dismissed. Should it? [*Urbano v. Days Inn of America, Inc.,* 295 S.E.2d 240 (N.C. Ct. App.)]

8 When Thomas Stafford sold some real estate, the purchasers gave him notes made out to him and June Zink (his daughter) "or the survivor." Payments on the notes were put into a bank account in the names of both Stafford and Zink with right of survivorship. The money in the account was spent as Stafford directed. After Stafford died Zink claimed the notes were a gift to her. Were they? [Zink v. Stafford, 509 S.E.2d 833 (Va.)]

Part 4 Sales

http://www.fbi.gov/programs/ifcc/ifccoverview.htm

Overview

As more and more people around the world log onto the Internet, incidents of fraud continue to increase. Many of the fraud schemes already present in the "real" world can now be found on the Internet – fraudulent investment offerings, multi-level marketing schemes and failure-to-render scams (a favorite of unprincipled participants of online auctions). The crucial difference in fraud committed over the Internet is that the perpetrator can "virtually" vanish, pulling down a Web site in seconds, leaving consumers wondering who or where to turn for help.

In response to this growing concern, the Federal Bureau of Investigation (FBI) and the National White Collar Crime Center (NW3C) joined forces in a unique partnership to aid and protect consumers in this largely unregulated environment. The Internet Fraud Complaint Center (IFCC) is the result of that venture. Its Web site provides a mechanism for victims of Internet fraud to report fraud on-line – where it occurred – to the appropriate law enforcement and regulatory authorities.

This part covers topics in Sales, including the process, warranties, product liability, and consumer protection. If you buy a used computer through a newspaper ad, will you have a warranty with it? If you purchase used goods through the Internet—for example through an auction site such as eBay—you may or may not have protection for some aspects of your purchase. As recourse to fraud, trading offenses, illegally auctioned items, and other Internet sales offenses, the Internet Fraud Complaint Center, through the FBI and the National White Collar Crime Center, acts on complaints. Visit eBay to examine their safety measures and then visit the IFCC to see how complaints are handled.
http://www.ebay.com
http://www.fbi.gov/programs/ifcc/ifccoverview.htm

16

Sales of Personal Property

Learning Objectives

1 Define goods.

2 Define a sale of goods and distinguish it from a contract to sell.

3 Distinguish between existing and future goods.

PREVIEW CASE

John Van Sistine contracted with Jan Tollard to install some windows; reposition an air conditioner, a range, and a cabinet; install siding; and perform certain finishing. Van Sistine furnished both goods and services but was referred to in the contract as a contractor, and most of the price was for labor. The parties agreed to add to the job but then disagreed on how much more than the original contract price should be paid. Van Sistine sued Tollard. To determine what law applied the court had to decide whether the contract was the rendition of a service or a sale. Which was it? Was more of the cost of the work for providing goods or for providing labor?

LO1 Define goods

Goods Movable personal property

In terms of the number of contracts as well as the dollar volume, contracts for the sale of **goods**—movable personal property—constitute the largest class of contracts in our economic system. Every time one purchases a package of gum, one makes a sales contract. If the gum contained some harmful substance, the sale could be the basis of a suit for thousands of dollars in damages. Article 2 of the Uniform Commercial Code (UCC), effective in all states except Louisiana, governs sales of movable personal property.

A sales contract that does not meet the requirements of the UCC is unenforceable. However, if both parties—the buyer and the seller—choose to abide by its terms even if they are not legally bound to do so, neither one can later avoid the contract. Both parties must honor the contract.

Property Subject to Sale

Movable Personal Property
All physical items except real estate

Real Property
Land and things permanently attached to land

Intangible Personal Property
Evidences of ownership of personal property

As used in the UCC and in these chapters, *sale* applies only to the sale of movable personal property. Thus, it does not apply to (1) real property or (2) intangible personal property. **Movable personal property** consists of all physical items that are not real estate. Examples include food, vehicles, clothing, and furniture. **Real property** is land, interests in land, and things permanently attached to land. **Intangible personal property** consists of evidences of ownership of personal property, such as contracts, copyrights, certificates of stock, accounts receivable, notes receivable, and similar assets.

Sales contracts must have all the essentials of any other contract, but they also have some additional features. Many rules pertaining to sales of personal property have no significance to any other type of contract, such as a contract of employment.

Sales and Contracts to Sell

LO2 Sale versus contract to sell

Sale
Transfer of title to goods for a price

Contract to Sell
Agreement to transfer title to goods for a price

Title
Ownership

A sale differs from a contract to sell.

A **sale** of goods involves the transfer of title, or ownership, to goods from the seller to the buyer for a consideration called the *price*. The ownership changes hands at the moment the bargain is made regardless of who has possession of the goods.

A **contract to sell** goods is a contract whereby the seller agrees to transfer ownership of goods to the buyer for a consideration called the *price*. In this type of contract individuals promise to buy and to sell in the future.

An important distinction exists between a sale and a contract to sell. In a sale the **title**, or the ownership of the subject matter, is transferred at once; in a contract to sell, the title will be transferred at a later time. A contract to sell is not in the true sense of the word a sale; it is merely an agreement to sell.

Facts: Production Credit Association (PCA) loaned McGraw Farms money and, to secure payment of the loan, McGraw gave PCA an interest in all its crops growing or later planted. A year later, Farm and Town Industries, Inc. (FTI) entered into a contract with McGraw to buy 20,000 bushels of corn then growing. McGraw was to deliver the corn in two months. After McGraw went into bankruptcy a dispute arose between PCA and FTI as to their rights to the corn. If FTI's contract with McGraw was a present sale of the growing corn, PCA had no interest in the corn. If FTI's contract with McGraw was a contract to sell the corn in the future PCA had an interest in the corn and FTI's payment for the corn would have to go to PCA.

Outcome: The court stated that since the contract simply said "20,000 bushels of corn" without identifying the corn or even the land on which it was growing, there could not have been a transfer of ownership. The transaction was a contract to sell, not a sale.

In order to determine who owns goods, a sale must be distinguished from a contract to sell. Ownership always rests with either the seller or the buyer. Since the owner normally bears the risk of loss, the question of whether the seller or buyer has ownership must be answered. Also, any increase in the value of the property belongs to the one who owns it. It is essential, therefore, to have definite rules to aid the courts in determining when ownership and risk of loss pass from one party to another if the parties to the contract have not specified these matters. If the parties specify when title or risk of loss passes, the courts will enforce the agreement.

Sales of Goods and Contracts for Services

An agreement to perform some type of service must be distinguished from a sale of goods since Article 2 of the UCC governs sales of goods but not agreements to perform services. When a contract includes the supplying of both services and articles of movable personal property, the contract is not necessarily considered a contract for the sale of goods. Whether it is a sale or service is determined by which factor is predominant. If the predominant factor is supplying a service, with the goods being incidental, the contract is considered a service contract and is not covered by Article 2. For example, the repair of a television set is not a sale even though new parts are supplied.

PREVIEW CASE REVISITED

Facts: John Van Sistine contracted with Jan Tollard to install some windows; reposition an air conditioner, a range, and a cabinet; install siding; and perform certain finishing. Van Sistine furnished both goods and services but was referred to in the contract as a contractor, and most of the price was for labor. The parties agreed to add to the job but then disagreed on how much more than the original contract price should be paid. Van Sistine sued Tollard claiming the transaction was a sale.

Outcome: Since Van Sistine was referred to in the contract as a contractor, since most of the money claimed was for labor, and since the work was to "install," "reposition," and "finish," the court held the transaction was the furnishing of services not a sale of goods. Van Sistine could not recover.

Price

Price
Consideration in a sales contract

The consideration in a sales contract is generally expressed in terms of money or money's worth and is known as the **price**. The price may be payable in money, goods, or services.

The chapters on contracts explained that an express contract is one in which all the terms are stated in words either orally or in writing. An implied contract is one in which some of the terms are understood without being stated. A sales contract is ordinarily an express contract, but some of its terms may be implied. If the sales contract does not state the price, it will be held to be the reasonable price for the same goods in the market. For goods sold on a regulated market, such as a commodity exchange, the price on that market will be deemed the reasonable price. If the parties indicate that the price must be fixed by them or by a third person at a later date, no binding contract arises if the price is not thus fixed. If the price can be computed from the terms of the contract, the contract is valid.

Facts: A. P. Leonards employed an architect to renovate a building. While Leonards was out of the country, his wife selected bay windows for the building, and the architect ordered them from Benglis Sash & Door Co. The price of the windows was not discussed. When the windows arrived Leonards refused to accept them. Benglis sued for the price of the windows. Leonards argued that there was no contract because the parties had never agreed on the price.

Outcome: Since the parties had a history of dealings in which Leonards ordered things and paid the invoice price, consent to buy at a reasonable price could be implied and the contract was enforceable.

Existing Goods

LO3
Existing versus future goods

Existing Goods
Goods that are in being and owned by the seller

Identified Goods
Goods picked to be delivered to the buyer

In order to be the subject of a sale, the goods must be existing. **Existing goods** are those both in existence (as contrasted with goods not yet manufactured) and then owned by the seller. If these conditions are not met, the goods are not existing and the only transaction that can be made between the seller and the buyer will be a contract to sell goods.

Identified goods are a type of existing goods. They are those that the seller and buyer have agreed are to be received by the buyer or have been picked out by the seller. When the seller specially manufactures the goods to the buyer's order, identification occurs at the time when manufacture begins.

Facts: Matthew Serra agreed to buy a Lincoln Continental Mark V from Suburban Ford Lincoln Mercury. Serra paid a portion of the price, got a title certificate, registered the car, and paid the necessary sales tax. Serra wanted to store the Lincoln for several years because it was in a collectors' series. Since he had no room in his garage, Suburban agreed to keep it on its lot. Suburban had stored the car for more than a year when the car Serra drove was damaged in an accident, and he went to Suburban to get the Lincoln. The car was not there because Suburban was in financial trouble and its main creditor had repossessed all the cars. Serra sued for possession of the Lincoln.

Outcome: Serra was successful because the court said the Lincoln was identified goods.

Future Goods

Future Goods
Goods not both existing and identified

Goods that are not existing goods are **future goods**. The seller expects to acquire the goods in the future either by purchase or by manufacture. For example, if Arnold contracts to buy an antique dresser, he might then contract to sell the dresser to Biff. Since Arnold does not yet own the dresser, he cannot now sell the dresser to Biff. He can only make a contract to sell it in the future, after he acquires title to it. Any contract purporting to sell future goods is a contract to sell and not a contract of sale since the seller does not have title to the goods. Thus future goods are goods that are not yet owned by the seller or not in physical existence. However, title to future goods does not pass immediately to the buyer when the goods come into existence. Some further action, such as shipment or delivery, first must be taken by the seller.

Bill of Sale

Bill of Sale
Written evidence of title to tangible personal property

A **bill of sale** provides written evidence of one's title to tangible personal property (see Illustrations 16-1 and 16-2). No particular form is required for a bill of sale. It can simply state that title to the described property has been transferred to the buyer.

Generally, a buyer does not need a bill of sale as evidence of ownership; but if a person's title is questioned, such evidence is highly desirable. If an individual buys a stock of merchandise in bulk, livestock, jewelry, furs, or any other relatively expensive items, the buyer should demand a bill of sale from the seller. The bill of sale serves two purposes:

1. If the buyer wishes to resell the goods and the prospective buyer demands proof of ownership, the bill of sale can be produced.
2. If any question arises as to whether or not the buyer came into possession of the goods legally, the bill of sale is proof.

BILL OF SALE OF CATTLE

Purchaser Mickey Bedrosian
Address Bedrosian Farms
Rt. 3 Box 1246-A
Miller, KS

Date March 26 20—

Animals	Tattoo#	Sex	Price
Simmental cow with heifer by side	6783	F	$950
Simmental heavy heifer	17302	F	$725

By receipt of above, which is hereby acknowledged, the undersigned grants, bargains, sells and assigns all its rights, title and interest in and to the cattle described above; if check or draft is given in full or part payment of said described animal(s), title and ownership shall remain with Seller until check is cleared by the bank on which drawn.

Seller Cadaret & Co.
Address Rt. 1 Box 1793-C
Wichita, KS
Signed Curt McCaskill

Illustration 16-1
Bill of Sale

BILL OF SALE

________________________(the "Seller"), of
________________________, ____________________,
________________________ ,does hereby sell, assign and transfer to
________________________(the "Buyer"), of
________________________, ____________________,
________________________, the following property.
____

PROPERTY:
AMOUNT: $0.00

for a TOTAL AMOUNT OF $0.00

The Seller warrants that the property is being transferred to the Buyer free and clear of any liens and encumbrances.

The above property is sold on an "AS IS" basis. The Seller makes no warranties, express or implied (except as specifically stated above).

This transfer is effective as of ____________________.

The property is now located at ____________________, ____________________
____________________, and all of such property is in the possession of
______________________________.

Illustration 16-2
Bill of Sale

Use your Quicken Business Lawyer program to open this document on your computer. Complete the form and read the Final Checklist. If there are points in the Checklist you do not understand, look them up in this chapter.

Next, check the Uniform Commercial Code at Cornell Law School's Web site and see how the Bill of Sale conforms to legal requirements of sales agreements.

http://www.law.cornell.edu/ucc/2/overview.html

Facts: Alda Lee Souza signed a bill of sale transferring the contents of her home to Zeuxis Ferreira Neves for several thousand dollars. Neves and Souza agreed that Souza would keep possession and use of the items, but that Neves could take any of the items whenever he wished. After Souza's death, the person handling her estate refused to let Neves have the property. Neves sued, alleging the bill of sale transferred ownership of the property to him.

Outcome: The court agreed with Neves.

Illegal Sales

Many difficulties arise over illegal sales, that is, the sale of goods prohibited by law, such as stolen property. If the sale is fully executed, the court will not intervene to aid either party. If one party is completely innocent and enters into an illegal sale, the court will compel a restoration of any goods or money the innocent party has transferred.

If the illegal sale is wholly executory, that is, has not yet been completed, the transactizon is a contract to sell and will not be enforced. If it is only partially executory, the court will leave the parties where it finds them unless the one who has fulfilled his part of the contract is an innocent victim of a fraud.

If the sale is divisible with a legal part and an illegal part, the court will enforce the legal part. If the individual goods are separately priced, the sale is divisible. If the sale involves several separate and independent items but is a lump-sum sale, then the sale is indivisible. An indivisible sale with an illegal part makes the entire sale illegal.

Facts: A Better Place, Inc. (ABP) manufactured and distributed gifts and souvenirs including pipes and accessories, snuff products, T-shirts, and posters. The state passed a law that made the sale of drug paraphernalia a crime. Giani Investment Co., a retailer, bought items from ABP. Giani's main store was raided by the police. Under the authority of a search warrant for drug paraphernalia, the police seized some of the merchandise purchased from ABP. Giani refused to pay ABP for the seized goods and ABP sued.

Outcome: The court said since the goods were drug paraphernalia, it would not enforce Giani's obligation to pay for them.

International Sales Contracts

Questions may arise about what law governs an international contract for the sale of goods. These questions could present major problems to the parties if any litigation arises on the contract. Of course, the parties may specify in the contract what law governs. However, many international sales contracts are made without such a specification. To help in this type of situation, the United States has ratified the United Nations Convention on Contracts for the International Sale of Goods (CISG). This convention, or agreement, applies to contracts for the sale of goods if the buyer and seller have places of business in different countries that agree to the convention. Several dozen countries have ratified or acceded to the convention.

Businesses may choose to indicate in their international contracts that they will not be governed by the convention. However, unless the parties state that the contract will not be governed by the convention, it will be. The convention does not cover contracts between two parties unless their places of business are in countries that have adopted the convention. It also does not cover personal consumer transactions, but is intended to apply in business-to-business situations. Some provisions of the CISG are similar to the UCC, but many are not.

Questions

1. What type of contract constitutes the largest class of contracts in our economic system and on what basis is that measured?
2. Explain the types of property Article 2 of the UCC applies to and does not apply to.
3. a. What is the difference between a sale and a contract to sell?
   b. Why is it important to make a distinction between a sale and a contract to sell?
4. Must all the terms of a sales contract be express? Explain.
5. What are existing goods?
6. a. What are future goods?
   b. How do future goods differ from existing goods?
7. What two purposes does a bill of sale serve?
8. Will courts enforce or aid either party to a sale of goods prohibited by law?

Case Problems

LO2 **1** During a hip replacement operation on Gordon Porter, the 64 mm acetabular cup portion of a replacement hip broke. Since another cup of the same size was not available a slightly smaller one was used. Porter developed lower back and then elbow and neck pain. Because artifical hip components are expensive, Pfizer Hospital Products, the manufacturer, supplied them to hospitals after surgeons requested them for specific operations. They were basically "loaned" for use during surgery. After surgery Pfizer billed the hospital or surgeon for the pieces used, and the patient would ultimately be billed; however, Porter was not billed for the broken cup. Porter sued Pfizer alleging the 64 mm cup was defective and that there was a completed sale of it because title passed to him. Was there a sale or only a contract to sell?

LO1 **2** KDI Sylvan Pools, Inc. contracted to build an in-ground swimming pool for Fannie Chlan. The pool was built, serious cracks appeared in the walls, and Chlan did not pay the contract price to KDI. In the resulting lawsuit, Chlan argued that under the law of sales she was entitled to a pool in perfect condition. The law of sales applies only if the swimming pool was a "good." Was it?

LO3 **3** Champion Manufacturing Industries ordered from Electrodyne four 104-foot, 210,000-pound masts used in the oil and gas industry. Three masts were completed and accepted by Champion and the fourth was 60 percent complete when Champion canceled the order. The fourth mast was never completed, accepted, or even shipped. Electrodyne sued for the order price of the mast. Under state law, Electrodyne could not recover on its suit unless the mast had been sold to Champion. Analyze the situation and explain whether Electrodyne could recover.

LO2 **4** Lois and Arthur McNeil owned a registered quarter horse named Freckles Beachboy. Arthur executed a note to Doug Brink in the amount of $10,000. Arthur failed to pay it, and Brink sued him to collect. Lois and Arthur began a dissolution of marriage suit, and Lois paid Arthur $5,000 for his interest in the horse. Arthur made out and gave Lois, who had possession, a bill of sale to Freckles Beachboy. Then Brink got a judgment against Arthur, a dissolution of marriage decree was entered, and the sheriff seized the horse. Who owned Freckles Beachboy?

LO2 **5** Hilton Contract Carpet Co. agreed to install carpet in Jane Pittsley's home for $4,402. Hilton paid the installers $700. Pittsley complained about the installation and Hilton tried to correct it, but Pittsley was not satisfied and refused to pay the balance due on the contract. Pittsley sued for rescission of the contract and return of the money she had paid. The case hinged on whether the transaction was a sale of goods or the supplying of a service. Which was it?

LO2 **6** The Plantation Shutter Company contracted with Ricky Ezell to sell and install interior shutters in Ezell's home for $6,000. They signed a written document titled "Terms of Sale." After the shutters were installed Ezell was dissatisfied with 12 of the 37 panels. Plantation remade and installed the panels but Ezell still had complaints and did not like the exposed hinges. Plantation agreed to provide side strips to hide the hinges and reduced the price of the shutters. Plantation made the strips and tried to schedule installation but Ezell would not permit completion of the work. Plantation sued for the balance due on the contract alleging it was a sale of goods. Was it a sale of goods or a services contract?

Internet Resources for Business Law

Name	Resources	Web Address
Uniform Commercial Code §2-711	LII provides a hypertext and searchable version of UCC §2-711, Buyer's Remedies in General; Buyer's Security Interest in Rejected Goods.	http://www.law.cornell.edu/ucc/2/2-711.html
Uniform Commercial Code §2-715	LII provides a hypertext and searchable version of UCC §2-715, Buyer's Incidental and Consequential Damages.	http://www.law.cornell.edu/ucc/2/2-715.html
Uniform Commercial Code §2-718	LII provides a hypertext and searchable version of UCC §2-718, Liquidation or Limitation of Damages; Deposits.	http://www.law.cornell.edu/ucc/2/2-718.html
Uniform Commercial Code §2-513	LII provides a hypertext and searchable version of UCC §2-513, Buyer's Right to Inspection of Goods.	http://www.law.cornell.edu/ucc/2/2-513.html
Lex Mercatoria	Lex Mercatoria provides links to the CISG and the Uniform Law on International Sale of Goods 1964 (ULIS).	http://www.jus.uio.no/lm/index.html

17 Formalities of a Sale

Learning Objectives

1. List the requirements of the Statute of Frauds for sales, and explain the exceptions to it.
2. Define an auction sale, and describe its peculiarities compared to the law of sales.
3. Describe the nature of the writing required by the Statute of Frauds.

PREVIEW CASE

Each fall, Oakland Gin Co. asked Tennessee Valley Cotton Oil Mill what it would pay for seed. Tennessee always said it would pay whatever prices and rebates were paid by its competitors. During two years Oakland was not paid the rebates the other cottonseed oil mills had paid. Oakland requested that Tennessee pay the rebates, but Tennessee refused. A lawsuit was brought over the unpaid rebates. Would Tennessee be required to pay them? What are the exceptions to the Statute of Frauds requirements of a written contract?

LO1 Application of Statute of Frauds to sales

All contracts for the sale of goods must exist in writing when the sale price is $500 or more. This Statute of Frauds' requirement has been included in the UCC. If the sale price is less than $500, the contract may be oral, written, implied from conduct, or a combination of any of these.

Facts: Robert and Virginia Hartley sold irrigation equipment to Robert Cummins, who paid all but $1,000 of the sale price. The Hartleys claimed they orally agreed to repurchase some of the equipment from Cummins in exchange for canceling his debt and therefore claimed ownership of that equipment. A lawsuit ensued to determine the ownership of that equipment. The decision depended on whether the contract to repurchase was valid.

Outcome: The court held that since the alleged contract to repurchase some of the equipment was oral and the price exceeded $500, it was barred by the Statute of Frauds.

Multiple Purchases and the Statute of Frauds

Frequently one makes several purchases from the same seller on the same day. The question may then be raised whether there is one sale or several sales. If one contracts to purchase five items from the same seller in one day, each item having a sale price of less than $500 but, when combined, the total exceeds $500, must this contract meet the requirement of the Statute of Frauds? If the several items are part of the same sales transaction, it is one sale and must meet the requirement of the statute. If all the contracts to purchase are made during the same shopping tour and with the same salesperson, who merely adds up the different items and charges the customer with a grand total, the several items are considered to be part of the same transaction. However, if a separate sales slip is written for each purchase as an individual goes through a store, each transaction is a separate sale.

When Proof of Oral Contract Is Permitted

In some instances, the absence of a writing does not bar the proof of a sales contract for $500 or more.

RECEIPT AND ACCEPTANCE OF GOODS

Receipt
Taking possession of goods

Acceptance
Assent of buyer to become owner of goods

An oral sales contract may be enforced if it can be shown that the goods were delivered by the seller and were received and accepted by the buyer. Both a receipt and an acceptance by the buyer must be shown. **Receipt** is taking possession of the goods. **Acceptance** is the assent of the buyer to become the owner of specific goods. The contract may be enforced only as it relates to the goods received and accepted.

PREVIEW CASE REVISITED

Facts: Each fall, Oakland Gin Co. asked Tennessee Valley Cotton Oil Mill what it would pay for seed. Tennessee always said it would pay whatever prices and rebates were paid by its competitors. During two years Oakland was not paid the rebates the other cottonseed oil mills had paid. Oakland requested that Tennessee pay the rebates, but Tennessee refused. A lawsuit was brought over the unpaid rebates.

Outcome: The court held that although the contract agreeing to pay the rebates was oral, it was enforceable because Tennessee had received and accepted the seed.

PAYMENT

An oral contract may be enforced if the buyer has made full payment on the contract. In the case of part payment, a contract may be enforced only with respect to goods for which payment has been made and accepted.

Some uncertainty occurs under this rule as to the effectiveness of payment by check or a promissory note executed by the buyer. Under the law of commercial paper, a check, draft, or note is conditional payment when delivered. It does not become final and complete until the check, draft, or note is paid by a financial intermediary, such as a bank. However, since businesspeople ordinarily regard the delivery of a check or note as payment, in most states the delivery of such an instrument is sufficient to make the oral contract enforceable. A check or promissory note tendered as payment but refused by the seller does not constitute a payment under the Statute of Frauds.

Facts: Homer Buffaloe orally contracted to buy the five tobacco barns he was renting from Patricia and Lowell Hart. Buffaloe was to pay $20,000 in annual installments of $5,000. Under the rental agreement the Harts had paid the insurance on the barns, but after the contract to purchase them, Buffaloe paid the insurance. He also paid for improvements on the barns. A year after Buffaloe contracted to buy the barns he decided to sell them and found three people who were willing to buy them for $8,000 each. He delivered a check for $5,000 to Patricia. The next day Patricia called Buffaloe and told him she did not want to sell the barns to him. Two days later Hart mailed a letter to Buffaloe containing the check which had been torn up.

Outcome: The court held that the check was an accepted payment for the barns under the contract to sell them. The Harts were liable to Buffaloe.

When the buyer has negotiated or assigned to the seller a negotiable instrument executed by a third person, and the seller has accepted the instrument, a payment has been made within the meaning of the Statute of Frauds.

JUDICIAL ADMISSION

Judicial Admission Fact acknowledged in course of legal proceeding

When a person voluntarily acknowledges a fact during the course of some legal proceedings, this is a **judicial admission**. No writing is required when the person against whom enforcement of the contract is sought voluntarily admits, in the course of legal proceedings, to having made the contract.

NONRESELLABLE GOODS

Nonresellable Goods Specially made goods not easily resellable

Goods that are specifically made for the buyer and are of such an unusual nature that they are not suitable for sale in the ordinary course of the seller's business are called **nonresellable goods**. No writing is required in such cases. For this exception to apply, however, the seller must have made a substantial beginning in manufacturing the goods or, if a middleman, in procuring them, before receiving notice of rejection by the buyer.

Facts: P. N. Hirsch & Co. Stores, Inc., had bought its paper bags from Smith-Scharff Paper Co. for 36 years. The bags were imprinted with the P. N. Hirsch logo. Smith-Scharff kept a supply of the bags in stock so it could promptly fill Hirsch's purchase orders. Hirsch was aware of this practice and even provided a generalized profile of its business forecasts to Smith-Scharff to help it judge how many bags to have on hand. After Hirsch was sold it refused to purchase $20,000 worth of bags left in Smith-Scharff's inventory. Smith-Scharff sued Hirsch for breach of contract. Hirsch argued that it was not liable because there was no written contract.

Outcome: The court held that the bags were nonresellable goods, so the contract did not have to be in writing.

AUCTION SALES

LO2
Auctions and the law of sales

Auction
Sale of property to the highest bidder

Bidder
Person who makes offer at auction

An **auction** is a sale in which a seller or an agent of the seller orally asks for bids on goods and orally accepts the highest bid. A sale by auction for any amount is valid even though it is, by necessity, oral. In most states the auctioneer is the special agent for both the owner and the bidder. When the auctioneer, or the clerk of the auction, makes a memorandum of the sale and signs it, this binds both parties. The **bidder** is the one who makes the offer. There is no contract until the auctioneer accepts the offer, which may be done in several ways. The most common way is the fall of the hammer, with the auctioneer saying, "Sold" or "Sold to (a certain person)." In most auctions the final bid is preceded by several lower bids. When a person makes a bid to start the sale, the auctioneer may refuse to accept this as a starting bid. If the bid is accepted and a higher bid is requested, the auctioneer can later refuse to accept this starting bid as the selling price.

If a bid is made while the hammer is falling in acceptance of a prior bid, the auctioneer has the choice of reopening the bid or declaring the goods sold. The auctioneer's decision is binding.

Without Reserve
Auction goods may not be withdrawn after bidding starts

With Reserve
Auction goods may be withdrawn after bidding starts

Goods may be offered for sale with reserve or without reserve. If they are **without reserve**, then the goods cannot be withdrawn after the bidding starts unless no bid is received within a reasonable time after the auctioneer calls for bids. Goods are presumed to be offered **with reserve**, that is, they may be withdrawn, unless the goods are explicitly put up without reserve.

Nature of the Writing Required

LO3
Requirements of the writing

The UCC does not have stringent requirements that indicate what in a written contract or other writing is adequate to satisfy the Statute of Frauds for sales contracts.

TERMS

The writing need only give assurance that a transaction existed. Specifically, it must indicate that a sale or contract to sell has been made and state the quantity of goods involved. Any other missing terms may be shown by parol evidence in the event of a dispute.

SIGNATURE

When a suit is brought against an individual on the basis of a transaction, the terms of which must be in writing, the writing must be signed by either the person being

Facts: Phil Stillpass and W. E. Walker made a tentative oral agreement with Sidney Whitlock, president of Fortune Furniture Manufacturing Co., for Mid-South Plastic Fabric Co. to sell plastics to Fortune. Walker and Stillpass sent Fortune a letter containing the terms of the contract. The letter stated it was to "confirm the agreement . . . between myself and Phil Stillpass on behalf of Mid-South Plastic Fabric Co., Inc. and you on behalf of Fortune" to supply all the plastic Fortune needed. The letter was signed, "W. E. Walker, President." Mid-South was unable to supply all the plastic Fortune needed and Fortune had to pay considerably more than the contract price elsewhere. To cover its damages, Fortune did not pay Mid-South all it owed. Mid-South sued.

Outcome: The court held that since the letter was signed by Walker as president of Mid-South it satisfied the Statute of Frauds and was binding on Mid-South. Fortune was entitled to damages because Mid-South did not supply the contracted plastic.

sued or an authorized agent of that person. The signature must be placed on the writing with the intention of authenticating the writing. It may consist of initials; it may be printed, stamped, or typewritten. The important thing is that it was made with the necessary intent.

The UCC makes an exception to the requirement of signing regarding a transaction between merchants. It provides that the failure of a merchant to refuse to accept within 10 days a confirming letter sent by another merchant is binding just as though the letter or other writing had been signed. This ends the possibility of a situation under which the sender of the letter was bound, but the receiver could safely ignore the transaction or could hold the sender as desired, depending upon which alternative gave the better financial advantage.

TIME OF EXECUTION

To satisfy the Statute of Frauds, a writing may be made at, or any time after, the making of the sale. It may even be made after the contract has been broken or a suit brought on it. The essential element is the existence—at the time the trial is held—of written proof of the transaction.

PARTICULAR WRITINGS

The writing that satisfies the Statute of Frauds may be a single writing or it may be several writings considered as a group. Formal contracts, bills of sale, letters, and telegrams are common forms of writings that satisfy the Statute of Frauds. Purchase orders, cash register receipts, sales tickets, invoices, and similar papers generally do not satisfy the requirements as to a signature, and sometimes they do not specify any quantity or commodity.

Questions

1 When a sale of goods is for less than $500 what form may the contract take?
2 What facts would be relevant to determining whether the purchase of a number of items is one sale or many sales?
3 With respect to what goods may an oral contract be enforced by showing that those goods were delivered by the seller and received and accepted by the buyer?
4 Does payment by check or promissory note constitute payment for purposes of enforcing an oral contract?
5 How does a contract for goods that are specifically manufactured for the buyer and not suitable for sale to others in the seller's ordinary course of business differ from an ordinary contract of sale?
6 What is an auction sale, and why is it peculiar to the law of sales?
7 In order to satisfy the Statute of Frauds for sales, what must a writing include?
8 When must a writing required by the Statute of Frauds be made?

Case Problems

LO1 1 Bernard Stanfield orally agreed to give Glenn Grove a 1936 car in exchange for Grove doing reupholstering on Stanfield's 1953 car. Grove received the 1936 car, but not its title and the reupholstering was never done. Eight years later Stanfield sued Grove alleging Grove owed $8,000 for the car. Since the contract was oral and came within the

Statute of Frauds, the court had to address the question whether there had been receipt and acceptance of the goods. Had there?

LO3 **2** Abhe & Sxoboda, Inc. and Rainbow, Inc., a joint venture, made a bid to the State of Minnesota to sandblast, repair, and repaint a bridge. Simplex Supplies, Inc. faxed the joint venture an offer to provide an abrasive agent for removing the paint. The offer contained the project number and the contract amount of $362,500. The joint venture submitted to the state a Description of Work, an affidavit signed by Rainbow's president, and a Request to Sublet all saying Rainbow would subcontract to Simplex and listing the project number and the contract amount. After the state awarded the contract to the joint venture, it denied that it had a contract with Simplex. Simplex sued and the joint venture alleged since there was no written contract the statute of frauds barred enforcement of the oral contract. Was there a writing sufficient to satisfy the statute of frauds?

LO1 **3** At a stockholders' meeting, Leonard Pirilla offered to buy all the outstanding shares of stock held by the shareholders in two corporations for $525,000 plus a $15,000 commission. The minutes of the meeting indicated that all the shareholders of the corporations were present in person or by proxy, all voted to accept the offer, and the officers of the corporations were authorized to implement the sale. They signed a Letter of Intent containing the terms of the sale. Pirilla tendered a stock purchase agreement to the shareholders, but some refused to sign it. Pirilla sued for specific performance of the sale. The defense was the Statute of Frauds. Is there an enforceable contract?

LO2 **4** Mary Romani was the successful bidder on a portrait, item number 152, at an auction conducted by Barr Harris. Each prospective bidder was given a paddle displaying a number to hold up to place a bid. Romani's paddle was numbered 170. Harris's clerk made a signed memorandum of each sale and his list showed that item number 152 was sold for $4,600 to number 170. Romani did not pay for the portrait and Harris sued. Must Romani pay?

LO1 **5** Larry Teel wanted to buy a 28-foot cruiser from Peoria Harbor Marina but had a bad credit rating. However, his mother, Wilma McGlasson, agreed to buy the boat if he would pay her. The parties agreed on a price of $19,900, a warranty, the slip rental, $200 deposit, and the balance due. These terms were written on a blank bill of sale form, which also described the boat and which McGlasson and Peoria signed. Teel used the boat every week until it was stored for the winter. McGlasson could not find a bank that would finance the sale, so Teel attempted to pay rental and storage fees as if there had been a rental instead of a purchase. Peoria refused the payment, sold the boat, and sued for the amount it lost on the sale. McGlasson claimed that no written contract existed, therefore the sale was not enforceable. Was there a written contract?

LO3 **6** After negotiations, Quality Oil Co. sent a letter to Pee Dee Oil Co. saying, "We propose to purchase your Shell contract for $75,000.00 and the Fastway station . . . for $140,000.00 . . . [W]e would pay you a reasonable market value for the equipment located at the Rockingham Self Service and Holiday Shell. We would . . . assume the leases on these locations . . . Please contact us as soon as you have made your decision on our proposal." Quality prepared a written contract, which Pee Dee signed and returned to Quality. Four months later, Quality had not signed the contract and Pee Dee had to sell some of the assets at a loss. When Pee Dee sued for breach of contract, Quality said the contract was not binding because Quality had not signed it. Was there an enforceable contract?

LO1 **7** Colorado Carpet Installation was in the business of buying carpet from manufacturers or wholesalers and reselling it to retail buyers. It submitted a proposal to Fred and Zuma Palermo to supply and install carpet in their home for $4,778. Believing Mrs. Palermo orally accepted its proposal, Colorado ordered some carpet, which, although a stock item, was to come from out-of-state suppliers. It was delivered to a warehouse. When the Palermos would not take the carpet, Colorado returned or sold the carpet to others and sued the Palermos for breach of contract. Colorado alleged that the oral contract was enforceable because the carpet was nonresellable goods. Was it?

Internet Resources for Business Law

Name	Resources	Web Address
Uniform Commercial Code (UCC) Article 2, Sales	The Legal Information Institute (LII), maintained by Cornell Law School, provides Article 2, Sales.	http://www.law.cornell.edu/ucc/2/overview.html
Uniform Commercial Code §2-105	LII provides UCC §2-105, Definitions.	http://www.law.cornell.edu/ucc/2/2-105.html
Uniform Commercial Code §2-106	LII provides UCC §2-106, Definitions.	http://www.law.cornell.edu/ucc/2/2-106.html
Uniform Commercial Code §2-201	LII provides UCC §2-201, Formal Requirements; Statute of Frauds.	http://www.law.cornell.edu/ucc/2/2-201.html
National Fraud Information Center	National Fraud Information Center, a project of the National Consumers League, provides a daily report and other information on fraud, as well as the opportunity to report fraud.	http://www.fraud.org/

18

Transfer of Title and Risk in Sales Contracts

Learning Objectives

1. Explain the importance of determining when ownership and risk of loss pass.
2. Distinguish between a sale on approval, a sale or return, and a consignment.
3. Discuss the rule regarding attempted sales by people who do not have title to the goods, and list exceptions to the rule.

PREVIEW CASE

Roger and Sharon Russell agreed to sell Robert Clouser a boat for $8,500. Clouser made an initial payment of $1,700, with the balance to be paid upon possession. The Russells were to retain the boat to replace an engine and drive train, after which Clouser was to take delivery at their marina. No documents of title were required to sell a boat. Prior to delivery to Clouser, while being tested by the Russells' employees, the boat hit a seawall and was destroyed. The Russells' insurance policy with Transamerica Insurance Company did not cover damage resulting from watercraft hazard unless the Russells did not own the watercraft. Transamerica refused to pay, claiming that the Russells owned the boat at the time of the accident. Who owned the boat? Was the boat an existing, identified, or future good?

LO1
When title and risk pass

Title
Evidence of ownership of property

The right of ownership of property or evidence of ownership is called **title**. When a person owns a television set, for example, that owner holds all the power to control the set. If desired, the set may be kept or sold. When sold, title to—and, normally, physical possession of—the set passes to the buyer, who then has control over it. Normally, if the TV set is damaged or lost, the owner bears any loss. In business transactions some problems may arise regarding title to goods and risk of loss. This is because businesses deal in large volumes of goods and often must arrange the sale of goods before they may even exist, both of which may make physical possession of the goods difficult or impossible.

Potential Problems in Sales Transactions

In the vast majority of sales transactions, the buyer receives the proper goods and makes payment, which completes the transaction. However, several types of problems may arise that, for the most part, can be avoided if the parties expressly state their intentions in their sales contract. When the parties have not specified the results they desire, however, the rules in this chapter apply. Some of the potential issues are ownership, insurance, and damage to goods.

OWNERSHIP

Creditors of the seller may seize the goods in the belief that the seller owns them, or the buyer's creditors may seize them on the theory that they belong to the buyer. In such a case ownership of the goods must be determined. The question of ownership is also important in connection with resale by the buyer, liability for or computation of certain kinds of taxes, and liability under certain registration and criminal statutes.

INSURABLE INTEREST

Until the buyer has received the goods and the seller has been paid, both the seller and buyer have an economic interest in the sales transaction. The question arises as to whether either or both have enough interest to entitle them to insure the property involved; that is, whether they have an insurable interest.

RISK OF LOSS

If the goods are damaged or totally destroyed through no fault of either the buyer or the seller, must the seller bear the loss and supply new goods to the buyer? Or must the buyer pay the seller the purchase price even though the buyer now has no goods or has only damaged goods? The essential element in determining who bears the risk of loss is identifying the party who has control over the goods.

Classification of Sales Transactions

The nature of the transaction between the seller and the buyer determines the answer to be given to each question in the preceding section. However, sales transactions may be classified according to

1. The nature of the goods
2. The terms of the transaction

NATURE OF THE GOODS

As explained in Chapter 16, goods may be existing goods, identified goods, or future goods. Goods are existing goods even if the sellers must do some act or complete the manufacture of the goods before they satisfy the terms of the contract.

TERMS OF THE TRANSACTION

The terms of the contract may require that the goods be sent or shipped to the buyer, that is, that the seller make shipment. In that case, the seller's part is performed when the goods are handed over to a carrier, such as a truck line, for shipment.

Warehouse Receipt
Document of title issued by storage company for goods stored

Bill of Lading
Carrier's receipt showing terms of contract transportation

Instead of calling for actual delivery of goods, the transaction may involve a transfer of the document of title representing the goods. For example, the goods may be stored in a warehouse with the seller and the buyer having no intention of moving the goods, but intending that there should be a sale and a delivery of the **warehouse receipt** that stands for the goods. In this case the seller must produce the proper paper as distinguished from the goods themselves. The same is true when the goods are represented by a **bill of lading** issued by a carrier, or by any other document of title.

Ownership, Insurable Interests, and Risk of Loss in Particular Transactions

The kinds of goods and transaction terms may be combined in a number of ways. Only the more common types of transactions will be considered here. The following rules of law apply only in the absence of a contrary agreement by the parties concerning these matters.

EXISTING GOODS IDENTIFIED AT TIME OF CONTRACTING

The title to existing goods, identified at the time of contracting and not to be transported, passes to the buyer at the time and place of contracting.

PREVIEW CASE REVISITED

Facts: Roger and Sharon Russell agreed to sell Robert Clouser a boat for $8,500. Clouser made an initial payment of $1,700, with the balance to be paid upon possession. The Russells were to retain the boat to replace an engine and drive train, after which Clouser was to take delivery at their marina. Prior to delivery to Clouser, while being tested by the Russells' employees, the boat hit a seawall and was destroyed. The Russells' insurance policy with Transamerica Insurance Company did not cover damage resulting from watercraft hazard unless the Russells did not own the watercraft. Transamerica refused to pay, claiming that the Russells owned the boat at the time of the accident.

Outcome: The court said that since the boat had been identified at the time of contracting, no documents were to be delivered, and delivery was to be made without the boat being moved, title passed at the time of contracting.

If existing goods require transporting, title to the goods passes to the buyer when the seller has completed delivery.

The buyer, who becomes the owner of the goods, has an insurable interest in them against risk of loss when title passes. Conversely, the seller no longer has an insurable interest unless by agreement a security interest has been reserved to protect the right to payment.

If the seller is a merchant, the risk of loss passes to the buyer when the goods are received from the merchant. If the seller is a nonmerchant, the risk passes when the seller tenders or makes available the goods to the buyer. Thus, the risk of loss remains longer on the merchant seller on the ground that the merchant seller, being in the business, can more readily arrange to be protected against such continued risk.

The buyer of a motor vehicle bears the risk of loss when the transaction between the buyer and seller is completed even though the state may not yet have issued a new title in the buyer's name.

NEGOTIABLE DOCUMENTS REPRESENTING EXISTING GOODS IDENTIFIED AT TIME OF CONTRACTING

When documents that can transfer title, or ownership, represent existing, identified goods, the buyer has a property interest, but not title, and an insurable interest in such goods at the time and place of contracting. The buyer does not ordinarily acquire the title nor become subject to the risk of loss until delivery of the documents is made. Conversely, the seller has an insurable interest and title up to that time.

FUTURE GOODS MARKING AND SHIPMENT

A buyer may send an order for goods to be manufactured by the seller or to be filled from inventory or by purchases from third persons. If so, one step in the process of filling the order is the seller's act of marking, tagging, labeling, or otherwise indicating to the shipping department or the seller that certain goods are the ones to be sent or delivered to the buyer under contract. This act gives the buyer a property interest in the goods and the right to insure them. However, neither title nor risk of loss passes to the buyer until shipment or delivery, occurs. The seller, as continuing owner, also has an insurable interest in the goods until shipment or delivery.

The seller completes performance of such a contract when the goods are delivered to a carrier for shipment to the buyer. Under such a contract, the title and risk of loss pass to the buyer when the goods are delivered to the carrier; that is, title and risk of loss pass to the buyer at the time and place of shipment.

Facts: Home Liquors ordered whiskey valued at $21,302 from Black Prince Distillery. When the order was ready, Black Prince informed Royal Trucking that the goods were available to be picked up. Home confirmed the order in a writing that asked that the order be released to Royal. There was no direction regarding where the order was to be delivered. While Royal was on the way to a destination directed by Home, the shipment was hijacked. Black Prince sued Home for the contract price.

Outcome: The court said the transaction was clearly a shipping contract so title and risk of loss passed when the whiskey was released to the carrier, Royal.

C.O.D. SHIPMENT

In the absence of an extension of credit, a seller has the right to keep the goods until paid for by the buyer. The seller loses this right if possession of the goods is delivered to anyone for the buyer. However, where the goods are delivered to a carrier, the seller may keep the right to possession by making the shipment C.O.D., or by the addition of any other terms indicating that the carrier is not to surrender the goods to the buyer until the buyer has paid. The C.O.D. provision does not affect when title or risk of loss passes.

AUCTION SALES

When goods are sold at an auction in separate lots, each lot is a separate transaction, and title to each passes independently of the other lots. Title to each lot passes when the auctioneer announces by the fall of the hammer or in any other customary manner that the auction is completed as to that lot.

FREE ON BOARD

F.O.B. (Free on Board)
Designated point to which seller bears risk and expense

A contract may call for goods to be sold **f.o.b. (free on board)** a designated point. Goods may be sold f.o.b. the seller's plant, the buyer's plant, an intermediate point, or a specified carrier. The seller bears the risk and expense until the goods are delivered at the f.o.b. point designated.

Facts: Saul Boyman contracted to buy a boat. The contract required the boat to be delivered "F.O.B. Stuart, Florida." The boat was manufactured in North Carolina and shipped by ocean freight to Stuart, Florida. A dispute about the sale resulted in a lawsuit in which the seller of the boat alleged that Boyman was required to pay the freight charge.

Outcome: The court held that the term "F.O.B. Stuart" required the seller to pay freight charges until the boat reached its destination, Stuart, Florida.

SALES OF FUNGIBLE GOODS

Fungible Goods
Goods of a homogeneous nature sold by weight or measure

Fungible goods are goods of a homogeneous or like nature that may be sold by weight or measure. They include goods of which any unit is treated as the equivalent of any other unit, due to its nature or its commercial use. Fungible goods include wheat, oil, coal, and similar bulk commodities, since any one bushel or other unit of the whole will be the same as any other bushel or similar unit within the same grade.

The UCC provides that title to an undivided share or quantity of an identified mass of fungible goods may pass to the buyer at the time of the transaction. This makes the buyer an owner in common with the seller. For example, when one person sells to another 600 bushels of wheat from a bin that contains 1,000 bushels, title to 600 bushels passes to the buyer at the time of the transaction. This gives the buyer a six-tenths undivided interest in the mass as an owner in common with the seller. The courts in some states, however, have held that the title does not pass until a separation has been made.

The passage of title to a part of a larger mass of fungible goods differs from the passage of title of a fractional interest with no intent to make a later separation. In the former case, the buyer will become the exclusive owner of a separated portion, such as half a herd of cattle. In the latter case, the buyer will become a co-owner of the entire mass. Thus, there can be a sale of a part interest in a radio, an automobile, or a flock of sheep. The right to make a sale of a fractional interest is recognized by statute.

Damage to or Destruction of Goods

Damage to or the destruction of the goods affects the transaction.

DAMAGE TO IDENTIFIED GOODS BEFORE RISK OF LOSS PASSES

When goods identified at the time of contracting suffer some damage, or are destroyed through no fault of either party before the risk of loss has passed, the contract is avoided—or annulled—if the loss is total. If the loss is partial, or if the goods have so deteriorated that they do not conform to the contract, the buyer has the option, after inspecting the goods, (1) to treat the contract as avoided, or (2) to accept the goods subject to an allowance or deduction from the contract price. In either case, the buyer cannot assert any claims against the seller for breach of contract.

DAMAGE TO IDENTIFIED GOODS AFTER RISK OF LOSS PASSES

If partial damage or total destruction occurs after the risk of loss has passed, it is the buyer's loss. However, the buyer may, however, be able to recover the amount of the damages from the person in possession of the goods or from a third person causing the loss. For example, in many instances the risk of loss passes at the time of the transaction even though the seller will deliver the goods later. During the period from the transfer of the risk of loss to the transfer of possession to the buyer, the seller has possession of the goods and is liable to the buyer for failure to exercise reasonable care.

DAMAGE TO UNIDENTIFIED GOODS

So long as the goods are unidentified, no risk of loss has passed to the buyer. If a buyer contracts, for example, to sell wheat without specifying whether it is growing, to be grown, or the land on which it is to be grown, the contract is for unidentified goods. If they are damaged or destroyed during this period, the seller bears the loss. The buyer may still enforce the contract and require the seller to deliver the goods according to the contract. A seller who fails to deliver the goods is liable to the buyer for breach of the contract. The only exceptions arise when the parties have specified in the contract that destruction of the seller's supply shall release the seller from liability, or when the parties clearly contracted for the purchase and sale of part of the seller's supply to the exclusion of any other possible source of such goods.

Facts: Expecting to produce 360,000 bushels of corn, the Bartlett Partnership contracted to sell four shipments of corn amounting to 300,000 bushels to ConAgra at specified times in the future. A hailstorm severely damaged Bartlett's crop in August and it only delivered 108,000 bushels. ConAgra sued and Bartlett alleged its performance was excused because the goods were identified at the time of contracting and therefore the law allowed it to avoid a contract if the goods were damaged without fault of either party before risk of loss passed.

Outcome: The court stated that there was nothing in the contract which identified the corn to be sold by Bartlett except by kind and amount. Since corn is fungible it was not identified to the contract and Bartlett was not excused from performing.

RESERVATION OF TITLE OR POSSESSION

When the seller reserves title or possession solely as security to make certain that payment will be made, the buyer bears the risk of loss if he would bear the loss without such a reservation.

Sales on Approval and with Right to Return

LO2 Distinguish sale on approval, sale or return, consignment

A sales transaction may give the buyer the privilege of returning the goods even though they conform to the contract. In a **sale on approval**, the sale is not complete until the buyer approves the goods. A **sale or return** is a completed sale with the right of

Sale on Approval
Sale that is not completed until buyer approves goods

Sale or Return
Completed sale with right to return goods

the buyer to return the goods and thereby set aside the sale. The agreement of the parties determines whether the sale is a sale on approval or a sale or return. If the parties fail to indicate their intention, a returnable-goods transaction is deemed a sale on approval if a consumer purchases the goods for use. It is deemed a sale or return if a merchant purchases the goods for resale.

Facts: Frederick Prewitt received a shipment of 28 coins with a price of $61,975 from Numismatic Funding Corp. The literature enclosed with the shipment said it was available "on a 14 day approval basis." The invoice said title did not pass until the buyer paid the account. There were no directions on how to return any unwanted coins. Prewitt's wife mailed all the coins to Numismatic within 14 days, but it never received them. Prewitt filed suit for a court declaration that the risk of loss of the returned coins was on the seller.

Outcome: The court said that the transaction was a sale on approval. Since Prewitt placed the coins in the mail within the agreed time he did not accept them and risk of loss was with the seller.

CONSEQUENCE OF SALE ON APPROVAL

Unless agreed otherwise, title and risk of loss remain with the seller under a sale on approval. Use of the goods by the buyer for the purpose of trial does not mean approval. However, an approval occurs if the buyer acts in a manner inconsistent with a reasonable trial, or if the buyer fails to express a choice within the time specified (or within a reasonable time if no time is specified). For example, a "10-day home trial" of a set of encyclopedias allows a consumer to use the books for 10 days. If the consumer does not return the encyclopedias by the 10th day, the books are considered approved. If the buyer returns the goods, the seller bears the risk and the expense involved. Since the buyer is not the "owner" of the goods while they are on approval, the buyer's creditors may not claim the goods.

CONSEQUENCE OF SALE OR RETURN

Commercial Unit
Quantity regarded as separate unit

In a sale or return, title and risk of loss pass to the buyer as in the case of an ordinary sale. In the absence of a contrary agreement, the buyer under a sale or return may return all of the goods or any commercial unit thereof. A **commercial unit** includes any article, group of articles, or quantity commercially regarded as a separate unit or item, such as a particular machine, a suite of furniture, or a carload lot. The goods must still be in substantially their original condition, and the option to return must be exercised within the time specified by the contract or within a reasonable time if not specified. The return under such a contract is at the buyer's risk and expense. As long as the goods are in the buyer's possession, the buyer's creditors may treat the goods as belonging to the buyer.

Special Rules on Transfer of Title

LO3
Attempted sales without title

As a general rule, people can sell only such interest or title in goods as they possess. For example, if property is subject to a **bailment** (personal property temporarily in the custody of another person), a sale by the owner is subject to the bailment. Thus, if the owner of a rented car sells the car to another person, the person who has rented the

Bailment
Temporary transfer of possession of personal property

car, the bailee, may still use the car according to the terms of the bailment. Similarly, bailees can only transfer their individual rights under the bailments, assuming that the bailment agreements permit the rights to be assigned or transferred.

A thief or finder generally cannot transfer legal title to property. Only the actual property in possession (in the case of a thief or finder) can be passed. In fact, the purchaser from the thief not only fails to obtain title but also becomes liable to the owner as a converter of the property. Liability occurs even though the property may have been purchased in good faith.

Facts: Steve Sitton obtained a gold Rolex watch from Nowlin Jewelry by forging a check for $9,000. He asked Eddie Kotis a car salesman who owned a Rolex if he wanted to buy one. Kotis was interested so Sitton came to the car lot and sold him the watch for $3,500. Kotis called Nowlin's and, although initially refusing to identify himself, was told Sitton had purchased the watch the previous day with a check that had not yet cleared. Kotis would not say how much Sitton was asking for the watch and claimed he did not have it and did not want it. Nowlin's found out the check was bad and tried to talk to Kotis who said to talk to his lawyer. When Nowlin sued, Kotis claimed to be a good faith purchaser and entitled to the watch.

Outcome: The court said that Kotis was not a good faith purchaser. He knew the price was exorbitantly low which was evidence the watch was stolen. Kotis could not willfully disregard suspicious facts that would make a reasonable person believe the deal was illegal.

Certain instances occur, however, when because of the conduct of the owner or the desire of society to protect the bona fide purchaser for value, the law permits a greater title to be transferred than the seller possesses. It is important to note that the purchaser must act in good faith which means be unaware the seller does not have title. These situations include:

1. A sale by an entrustee
2. Consignment sales
3. Estoppel
4. When documents of title transfer ownership
5. When documents must be recorded or filed
6. Voidable title

SALE BY ENTRUSTEE

If the owner entrusts goods to a merchant who deals in goods of that kind, the merchant has the power to transfer the entruster's title to anyone who buys in the ordinary course of business. This is true as long as the merchant is not doing business in the entrusting owner's name. Similarly, the goods are subject to the claims of the merchant's creditors.

It is immaterial why the goods were entrusted to the merchant. Hence the leaving of a watch for repairs with a jeweler who sells new and secondhand watches would give the jeweler the power to pass the title to a buyer in the ordinary course of business. The entrustee is, of course, liable to the owner for damages caused by the sale of the goods and may be guilty of a statutory offense such as embezzlement.

If the entrustee is not a merchant, but merely a prospective customer, no transfer of title occurs when the entrustee sells to a third person.

CONSIGNMENT SALES

Consignment Transfer of possession of goods for purpose of sale

A manufacturer or distributor may send goods to a dealer for sale to the public with the understanding that the manufacturer or distributor is to remain the owner and the dealer is, in effect, to act as an agent. This is a **consignment**. Title does not normally pass to the consignee. However, when the dealer maintains a place of business at which dealings are made in goods of the kind in question under a name other than that of the consigning manufacturer or distributor, the creditors of the dealer may reach the goods as though the dealer owned the goods.

A consignment differs from a sale on approval or a sale with right to return. In the absence of any contrary provision, it is an agency and means that property is in the possession of the consignee for sale. Normally the consignor may revoke the agency at will and retake possession of the property. Whether goods are sent to a person as buyer or on consignment to sell for the owner depends upon the intention of the parties.

ESTOPPEL

ETHICAL POINT How is the doctrine of estoppel based on ethical considerations?

The owner of property may be estopped (barred) from asserting ownership and denying the right of another person to sell the property to a good-faith purchaser. A person may purchase a product and have the bill of sale made out in the name of a friend who receives possession of the product and the bill of sale. This might be done in order to deceive creditors or to keep other persons from knowing that the purchase had been made. If the friend should sell the product to a bona fide purchaser who relies on the bill of sale, the true owner is estopped or barred from denying the friend's apparent ownership.

Facts: United Road Machinery Co. leased a truck scale to Consolidated Coal Co. United paid for the scale and told the supplier of the scale that Consolidated would take possession, which it did. United sent a contract for the lease to Consolidated, which never returned the contract. Consolidated took the scale to its place of business in Laurel County, added decking, and then sold it to Kentucky Mobile Homes of Pulaski County. Kentucky had had the records of Laurel and Pulaski Counties checked and found there was no encumbrance shown against the scale. Kentucky then sold the scale to Clyde Jasper, who had also searched the records for an encumbrance on the scale. Neither Kentucky nor Jasper knew of any dispute between United and Consolidated. When it failed to receive any payment from Consolidated, United sued Jasper for the scale.

Outcome: The court found that there was nothing to suggest that Consolidated was not the owner of the scale as against Jasper, a good-faith purchaser. United was estopped from asserting its title against Jasper.

DOCUMENTS OF TITLE

Document of Title Document that shows ownership

Documents that show ownership are called **documents of title**. They include bills of lading and warehouse receipts. By statute, certain documents of title, when executed in the proper form, may transfer title. The holder of such a document may convey the title of the person who left the property with the issuer of the document if all of the following conditions are met:

1 The document indicates it may be transferred.
2 The transferee does not know of any wrongdoing.
3 The transferee has purchased the document by giving up something of value.

In such cases, it is immaterial that the transferor had not acquired the documents in a lawful manner.

RECORDING OR FILING DOCUMENTS

In order to protect subsequent purchasers and creditors, statutes may require that certain transactions be recorded or filed. The statutes may provide that a transaction not recorded or filed has no effect against a purchaser who thereafter buys the goods in good faith from the person who appears to be the owner or against creditors who have lawfully seized the goods of such an apparent owner. Suppose a seller makes a credit sale and wants to be able to seize and sell the goods if the buyer does not make payment. The UCC requires the seller to file certain papers. If they are not filed, the buyer will appear to own the goods free from any interest of the seller. Subsequent bona fide purchasers or creditors of the buyer can acquire title, and the seller will lose the right to repossess the goods.

VOIDABLE TITLE

If the buyer has a voidable title, as when the goods were obtained by fraud, the seller can rescind the sale while the buyer is still the owner. If, however, the buyer resells the property to a bona fide purchaser before the seller has rescinded the transaction, the subsequent purchaser acquires valid title. It is immaterial whether the buyer having the voidable title had obtained title by fraud as to identity, or by larceny by trick, or that payment for the goods had been made with a bad check, or that the transaction was a cash sale and the purchase price has not been paid.

Questions

1. Why is the question of ownership of goods so important in sales transactions?
2. If the terms of a sales transaction require that the seller ship the goods to the buyer, when is the seller considered to have completed performance?
3. Give an example of a transaction in which goods sold are not actually delivered.
4. When does title to existing and identified goods that are not to be transported pass?
5. When existing goods require transporting, when does risk of loss pass when the seller is a merchant and when the seller is a nonmerchant?
6. When a buyer orders goods that will be shipped later when do title and risk of loss pass?
7. When does title to fungible goods pass?
8. Distinguish among a sale on approval, a sale or return, and a consignment.
9. If Holmes leaves a portable television set for repair with Ace TV (repair shop and dealer in new and used sets), and Ace sells the set to Lodder, would the buyer get good title?
10. If a buyer has a voidable title, when may the seller rescind the sale?

Case Problems

LO3 1. Vernon Crum was a merchant in the business of selling used cars to used car dealers. By means of a sight draft, J&T Auto Sales bought some cars for resale from Crum. While keeping the certificates of title for the cars, Crum transferred possession of the cars to J&T. J&T transferred the cars to By-Pass Auto Sales, another used car dealer, which resold the cars in the course of its business to buyers who gave notes for them. By-Pass sold the notes to SouthTrust Bank of Alabama. After By-Pass did not pay J&T for the cars J&T's draft was not paid. The people who had bought the cars from

By-Pass applied for certificates of title but the state would not issue them without the current title certificates which Crum had. SouthTrust sued Crum & J&T for the title certificates. Did ownership of the cars pass to By-Pass' customers?

LO1 2 Stephen Snider bought and paid for an "as is" used car from Berea Kar Co. Snider had trouble with the car and ceased using it a month later. It sat in his driveway for several months and was then stolen. The certificate of title had never been transferred to Snider so he sued Berea for return of his purchase money. He argued he did not bear the risk of loss since he did not have the certificate of title. Did Snider bear the risk of loss?

LO1 3 Andrew Pruitt, a supervisor of the commissary meat department at Fort Lewis, diverted meat ordered for Fort Lewis to his two restaurants. Pruitt instructed Randy's Meats to set aside an order of meat for Fort Lewis in a "will-call" trailer to be picked up later. Randy's marked the top boxes "Fort Lewis" and entered the number on each box on the invoices for Fort Lewis. A person who told Randy's he was acting for Pruitt picked up the meat and delivered it to the restaurants. When charged with conspiracy and theft, the restaurants alleged the meat was not government property. Was it?

LO2 4 Danny Fuller opened a store called Danny's Drapery Outlet. Sixteen days later a fire destroyed its contents. Some of Fuller's inventory had been received from Amcrest Textiles. When sued for the price of the Amcrest goods, Fuller claimed his arrangement with Amcrest was a consignment—that he was to get a percentage of anything he sold. Amcrest had sent Fuller invoices that said, "PAY BY THIS INVOICE" and "no returns will be accepted unless authorized in writing" by Amcrest. If the transaction was a sale, Fuller had title and had to pay for the goods. If it was a consignment, title had not passed to Fuller and Amcrest would bear the risk of loss. What was the transaction?

LO1 5 A & M Engineering Plastics in Pinellas County contracted to supply plastic parts and moldings to Energy Saving Technology in Broward County. The contract called for prices to be f.o.b. Clearwater in Pinellas County. Several shipments were made, but then a machinery breakdown resulted in a shutdown. Technology sued A & M in Broward County. A & M alleged that the suit had to be filed in Pinellas County. The suit had to be filed in the county in which the covenant alleged to have been breached was supposed to be performed. If the breached covenant was failure to supply the parts, where was the contract breached?

LO2 6 Anthony Coppola ordered some coins from First Coinvestors, Inc., under an agreement that the coins would be paid for or returned within ten days. Coppola was not in the business of selling coins but was a collector. The package of coins was delivered to a person on Coppola's property who signed for them, but no one knew who he was or what happened to the coins. Coinvestors sued Coppola for the value of the coins. Is he liable?

LO3 7 A farmer, Carl Davidson, leased 100 head of cattle from Matthew Bauer. Davidson "sold" some of them to R. D. Curran. When sued by Bauer, Curran alleged that Davidson was a merchant who dealt in cattle; therefore, he had the power to transfer title to the cattle. Evidence at the trial was that Davidson had previously sold part of the cattle he leased, but at Bauer's direction and in his name. Davidson had only bought or sold his own cattle occasionally. Who owns the cattle?

LO2 8 Kenneth Stevenson, a car dealer doing business as T & S Enterprises, asked Peter Pan Motors if it could find a certain kind of white BMW. Peter Pan said it could and located and bought one. T & S picked up the car. The parties had made previous deals in which Peter Pan would sell T & S cars and T & S would resell them. T & S deposited payment for the BMW in Peter Pan's bank account, but stopped payment on the check and told Peter Pan it did not want the car. While T & S had the BMW, a creditor, Wayne Minor, claimed it. He said the transaction was a sale or return, so the BMW's title passed to T & S and Minor had a valid claim against it. Was there a sale or return?

Internet Resources for Business Law

Name	Resources	Web Address
Uniform Commercial Code §2-301	The Legal Information Institute (LII) provides UCC §2-301, General Obligations of Parties.	http://www.law.cornell.edu/ucc/2/2-301.html
Uniform Commercial Code §2-303	LII provides UCC §2-303, Allocation or Division of Risks.	http://www.law.cornell.edu/ucc/2/2-303.html
Uniform Commercial Code §2-326	LII provides UCC §2-326, Sale on Approval and Sale or Return; Consignment Sales and Rights of Creditors.	http://www.law.cornell.edu/ucc/2/2-326.html
Uniform Commercial Code §2-327	LII provides UCC §2-327, Special Incidents of Sale on Approval and Sale or Return.	http://www.law.cornell.edu/ucc/2/2-327.html
Uniform Commercial Code §2-401	LII provides UCC §2-401, Passing of Title; Reservation for Security; Limited Application of this Section.	http://www.law.cornell.edu/ucc/2/2-401.html
Uniform Commercial Code §2-402	LII provides UCC §2-402, Rights of Seller's Creditors Against Sold Goods.	http://www.law.cornell.edu/ucc/2/2-402.html
Uniform Commercial Code §2-319	LII provides UCC §2-319, F.O.B. and F.A.S. Terms.	http://www.law.cornell.edu/ucc/2/2-319.html
Uniform Commercial Code §2-320	LII provides UCC §2-320, C.I.F. and C. & F. Terms.	http://www.law.cornell.edu/ucc/2/2-320.html
Uniform Commercial Code §2-509	LII provides a hypertext and searchable version of UCC §2-509, Risk of Loss in the Absence of Breach.	http://www.law.cornell.edu/ucc/2/2-509.html

19

Warranties, Product Liability, and Consumer Protection

Learning Objectives

1 Define a warranty, and distinguish between express and implied warranties.

2 Specify the warranties that apply to all sellers and those that apply only to merchants.

3 Explain how warranties may be excluded or surrendered.

4 Explain the various means the law uses to provide consumer protection.

PREVIEW CASE

Gerard Construction, Inc., executed a bill of sale for a towboat to Phillip Mossesso and Donald Fix. Paragraph 2 of the bill of sale stated, "Seller warrants title to be good and marketable and free of all debts, liens, and encumbrances." Paragraph 5 stated, "Seller states that it is its belief that the vessel is now operative and in a safe condition and is not in violation of any federal regulation." Mossesso and Fix used the boat and then tried to rescind the transaction, claiming Paragraph 5 constituted a warranty. Did the language of Paragraph 5 create a warranty? What is the difference in the language of Paragraph 2 and Paragraph 5?

LO1

Warranties, express and implied

Warranty
Assurance article conforms to a standard

In making a sale, a seller often makes a **warranty** which is an assurance that the article sold will conform to a certain standard or will operate in a certain manner. By the warranty, the seller agrees to make good any loss or damages that the purchaser may suffer if the goods are not as represented.

A warranty made at the time of the sale is considered to be a part of the contract and is therefore binding. A warranty made after a sale has been completed is binding even though not supported by any consideration; it is regarded as a modification of the sales contract.

Express Warranties

Express Warranty
Statement of guarantee by seller

The statement of the seller in which the article sold is warranted or guaranteed is known as an **express warranty**. The UCC specifically provides that any affirmation of fact or promise made by the seller to the buyer that relates to the goods and becomes part of the basis of the bargain creates an express warranty. The seller actually and definitely states an express warranty either orally or in writing. For example, the statement, "the whopper pizza contains one pound of cheese" is an express warranty as to the amount of cheese on the pizza.

However, the seller needs no particular words to constitute an express warranty. The words "warranty" or "guarantee" need not be used. If a reasonable interpretation of the language of a statement or a promise leads the buyer to believe a warranty exists, the courts will construe it as such. A seller is bound by the ordinary meaning of the words used, not by any unexpressed intentions.

The seller can use the word "warrant" or "guarantee" and still not be bound by it if an ordinary, prudent person would not interpret it to constitute a warranty. If the seller of a car says, "I'll guarantee that you will not be sorry if you buy the car at this price," no warranty exists. This is mere sales talk, even though the seller used the word "guarantee."

SELLER'S OPINION

ETHICAL POINT
The law may not define statements of opinion as warranties, but is it ethical for a seller to make such statements when they are not true?

ETHICAL POINT
Is it ethical for a seller to make extravagant claims about merchandise?

Sellers may praise their wares, even extravagantly, without being obligated on their statements or representations. A person should not be misled by "puffing." Such borderline expressions as "best on the market for the money," "these goods are worth $10 if they are worth a dime," "experts have estimated that one ought to be able to sell a thousand a month of these," and many others, which sound very convincing, are mere expressions of opinion, not warranties.

Although an expression by the seller of what is clearly an opinion does not normally constitute either a warranty or a basis for fraud liability, the seller may be liable for fraud if, in fact, the seller does not believe the opinion. Also, a representation by the seller is a warranty if the seller asserts a fact of which the buyer is ignorant so that the buyer has to rely on the seller for information on the matter. If the seller merely states an opinion on a matter of which the seller has no special knowledge and on which the buyer may be expected also to have an opinion and exercise judgment, it is not a warranty.

DEFECTIVE GOODS

If defects are actually known to the buyer, or defects are so apparent that no special skill or ability is required to detect them, an express warranty may not cover them. The determining factor is whether the statement becomes a part of the basis of the bargain. If it does, an express warranty results. This would not be true if the seller used any scheme or artifice to conceal the defect, such as covering the defect with an item of decoration.

PREVIEW CASE REVISITED

Facts: Gerard Construction, Inc., executed a bill of sale for a towboat to Phillip Mossesso and Donald Fix. Paragraph 2 of the bill of sale stated, "Seller warrants title to be good and marketable and free of all debts, liens, and encumbrances." Paragraph 5 stated, "Seller states that it is its belief that the vessel is now operative and in a safe condition and is not in violation of any federal regulation." Mossesso and Fix used the boat and then tried to rescind the transaction, claiming Paragraph 5 constituted a warranty.

Outcome: The court found the language of Paragraph 5 was clearly drafted in pursuance of the UCC provision regarding a seller's opinion and did not create a warranty. Also, Paragraph 2 clearly indicated that the parties knew how to embody a warranty when they wanted to.

Implied Warranties

Implied Warranty
Warranty imposed by law

An **implied warranty** is one that the seller did not make but which is imposed by the law. The implied warranty arises automatically from the fact that a sale has been made. For example, every seller implies that he or she owns the goods being sold and has the right to sell them. Express warranties arise because they form part of the basis on which the sale has been made.

Express warranties do not exclude implied warranties. When both express and implied warranties exist, they should be construed as consistent with each other. When not construed as consistent, an express warranty prevails over an implied warranty as to the same subject matter, except in the case of an implied warranty of fitness for a particular purpose.

Full or Limited Warranties

Full Warranty
Warranty with unlimited duration of implied warranties

Limited Warranty
Written warranty not a full warranty

A written warranty made for a consumer product may be either a **full warranty** or a **limited warranty**. The seller of a product with a full warranty must remedy any defects in the product in a reasonable time without charge, place no limit on the duration of implied warranties, not limit consequential damages for breach of warranty unless done conspicuously on the warranty's face, and permit the purchaser to choose a refund or replacement without charge if the product contains a defect after a reasonable number of attempts by the warrantor to remedy the defects. All other written warranties for consumer products are limited warranties (see Illustration 19-1).

ONE YEAR LIMITED WARRANTY

ABC Company warrants this product, to original owner, for one year from purchase date to be free of defects in material and workmanship.

Defective product may be brought or sent (freight prepaid) to an authorized service center listed in the phone book, or to Service Department, ABC Company, Main and First Streets, Riverdale, MO 65000, for free repair or replacement at our option.

Warranty does not include: cost of inconvenience, damage due to product failure, transportation damages, misuse, abuse, accident or the like, or commercial use. IN NO EVENT SHALL THE ABC COMPANY BE LIABLE FOR INCIDENTAL OR CONSEQUENTIAL DAMAGES. Some states do not allow exclusion or limitation of incidental or consequential damages, so above exclusion may not apply.

This warranty is the only written or express warranty given by The ABC Company. This warranty gives specific legal rights. You may have other rights which vary from state to state.

For information, write Consumer Claims Manager, at the Riverdale address. Send name, address, zip, model, serial number, and purchase date.

Keep this booklet. Record the following for reference:

Data purchased ____________________

Model Number ____________________

Serial Number ____________________

Illustration 19-1
Limited Warranty

Warranties of All Sellers

LO2
Warranties of all sellers

The following warranties apply to all sellers.

WARRANTY OF TITLE

All sellers, by the mere act of selling, make a warranty that they have good titles and make rightful transfers. This means that the seller is confirming ownership of the goods and that ownership is being transferred to the buyer.

Facts: ITT Industrial Credit Company made a loan to Edward McGinn General Contractors, Inc. so McGinn gave ITT a lien on a hydraulic excavator. After McGinn had severe financial problems Vilsmeier Auction Co. sold the excavator at auction. Before the auction Vilsmeier declared that all the equipment being sold had no liens on it. Frank Arnold Contractors bought the excavator at the auction. Later ITT sued Arnold on the basis of its lien on the excavator. Arnold sued Vilsmeier for breach of the warranty of title.

Outcome: The court held that disturbing the buyer's quiet possession of goods is one way in which a breach of the warranty of title can be established. Buyers should not have to participate in a contest over the validity of their ownership.

A warranty of title may be excluded or modified by the specific language or the circumstances of the transaction. The latter situation occurs when the buyer has reason to know that the seller does not claim title or that the seller is purporting to sell only such right or title as the seller or a third person may have. For example, no warranty of title arises when the seller makes the sale in a representative capacity, such as a sheriff or an administrator. For example there is no warranty of title when a country singer's possession are sold to pay an income tax lien. Likewise no warranty arises when the seller makes the sale by virtue of a power of sale possessed as a pledgee or mortgagee.

WARRANTY AGAINST ENCUMBRANCES

Every seller also makes a warranty that the goods shall be delivered free from any security interest or any other lien or encumbrance of which the buyer at the time of making the sales contract had no knowledge. Thus, a breach of warranty exists when the automobile sold to the buyer is already subject to an outstanding claim that had been placed against it by the original owner and which was unknown to the buyer at the time of the sale.

The warranty against encumbrances applies to the goods only at the time they are delivered to the buyer. It is not concerned with an encumbrance that existed before or at the time the sale was made. For example, a seller may not have paid in full for the goods being resold, and the original supplier may have a lien on the goods. The seller may resell the goods while that lien is still on them. The seller's only duty is to pay off the lien before the goods are delivered to the buyer.

A warranty against encumbrances does not arise if the buyer knows of the existence of the encumbrance in question. Knowledge must be actual knowledge as contrasted with constructive notice. **Constructive notice** is information that the law presumes everyone knows by virtue of the fact that it is filed or recorded on the public record.

Constructive Notice
Information or knowledge imputed by law

WARRANTY OF CONFORMITY TO DESCRIPTION, SAMPLE, OR MODEL

Sample
Portion of whole mass of transaction

Model
Replica of an article

Any description of the goods, sample, or model made part of the basis of the sales contract creates an express warranty that the goods shall conform in kind and quality to the description, sample, or model. Ordinarily, a **sample** is a portion of a whole mass that is the subject of the transaction, while a **model** is a replica of the article in question. The mere fact that a sample is exhibited during negotiation of the contract does not make the sale a sale by sample. There must be an intent shown that the sample is part of the basis of contracting. For example, a sample may be exhibited not as a promise or warranty that the goods will conform to it but just to allow the buyer to make a judgment on its quality. A small piece of molded plastic shown to a boat buyer to illustrate the materials and methods used in the construction of boats does not create a sale by sample.

WARRANTY OF FITNESS FOR A PARTICULAR PURPOSE

When the seller has reason to know at the time of contracting that the buyer intends to use the goods for a particular or unusual purpose, the seller may make an implied warranty that the goods will be fit for that purpose. Such an implied warranty arises when the buyer relies on the seller's skill or judgment to select or furnish suitable goods and when the seller has reason to know of the buyer's reliance. For example, where a government representative inquired of the seller whether the seller had a tape suitable for use on a particular government computer system, there arose an implied warranty, unless otherwise excluded, that the tape furnished by the seller was fit for that purpose. This warranty of fitness for a particular purpose does not arise when the goods are to be used for the purpose for which they are customarily sold or when the buyer orders goods on particular specifications and does not disclose the purpose.

The fact that a seller does not intend to make a warranty of fitness for a particular purpose is immaterial. Parol evidence is admissible to show that the seller had knowledge of the buyer's intended use.

Additional Warranties of Merchant

Merchant
Person who deals in goods of the kind or by occupation is considered to have particular knowledge or skill regarding goods involved

A seller who deals in goods of the kind involved in the sales contract, or who is considered because of occupation to have particular knowledge or skill regarding the goods involved, is a **merchant**. Such a seller makes additional implied warranties.

WARRANTY AGAINST INFRINGEMENT

Unless otherwise agreed, a merchant warrants that goods shall be delivered free of the rightful claim of any third person by way of patent or trademark infringement. However this is not true when a buyer supplies the seller with exact specifications for the preparation or manufacture of goods. In such cases the merchant seller makes no implied warranty against infringement. The buyer in substance makes a warranty to protect the seller from liability should the seller be held liable for patent violation by following the specifications of the buyer. For example, a business that orders the manufacture of a machine from blueprints and specifications supplied by the buyer must defend the manufacturer if it is later sued for patent infringement by someone holding a patent on a similar machine.

When the buyer furnishes the seller with specifications, the same warranties arise as in the case of any other sale of such goods by that seller. However no warranty of fitness for a particular purpose can arise since the buyer is clearly purchasing on the basis of a decision made without relying on the seller's skill and judgment.

WARRANTY OF MERCHANTABILITY OR FITNESS FOR NORMAL USE

Unless excluded or modified, merchant sellers make an implied warranty of merchantability (or salability) which results in a group of warranties. The most important is that the goods are fit for the ordinary purposes for which they are sold.

The implied warranty of merchantability relates to the condition of the goods at the time the seller is to perform under the contract by selling the goods. Once the risk of loss has passed to the buyer, no warranty exists as to the continuing merchantability of the goods unless such subsequent deterioration or condition is proof that the goods were in fact not merchantable when the seller made delivery.

Warranty of merchantability relates only to the fitness of the product made or sold. It does not impose upon the manufacturer or seller the duty to employ any particular design or to sell one product rather than another because another might be safer.

Facts: Gina and Douglas Felde bought a new car from Schaumburg Dodge and signed a contract to make 48 monthly payments to Chrysler Credit Corp. Three weeks later, Gina noticed the car occasionally surged forward and accelerated by itself. She took it to the dealer, who replaced the throttle sensor. The problem continued and Gina took the car back two or three times more, but the acceleration continued. Gina took the car to another dealer five times for the problem. The throttle sensor was replaced three times, but the sudden acceleration was not corrected. A year after buying the car, it lurched forward from a stop when Gina took her foot off the brake and it hit a truck. Gina had the car towed to Schaumburg Dodge. The manager called her the next day and told her she would be charged for storage. Gina told him to keep the car. The Feldes sued for breach of the implied warranty of merchantability. At trial a certified mechanic testified that the car was not safe to drive.

Outcome: The court said the warranty of merchantability was breached.

Warranties in Particular Sales

As discussed in the following sections, particular types of sales may involve special considerations.

SALE OF FOOD OR DRINK

The sale of food or drink, whether to be consumed on or off the seller's premises, is a sale. When made by a merchant, the sale carries the implied warranty that the food is fit for its ordinary purpose of human consumption. Some courts find no breach of warranty when a harmful object found in food was natural to the particular kind of food, such as an oyster shell in oysters, a chicken bone in chicken, and so on.

Other courts regard the warranty as breached when the presence of the harm-causing substance in the food could not be reasonably expected, without regard to whether the substance was natural or foreign, as in the case of a nail or piece of glass.

Facts: In good health, William Simpson ate tuna at the Hatteras Island Gallery Restaurant. When he returned home from dinner, Simpson was flushed, short of breath, had rapid pulse, diarrhea and was vomiting. He subsequently died from scombroid fish poisoning. Such poisoning results from an elevated histamine level in fish from mishandling. Simpson's widow sued the restaurant and the supplier of tuna.

Outcome: The appellate court held that the warranty of merchantability was breached and Mrs. Simpson could recover.

In these cases a determination of fact must be made, ordinarily by the jury, to determine whether the buyer could reasonably expect the object in the food.

It is, of course, necessary to distinguish the foregoing situations from those in which the preparation of the foods involves the continued presence of some element such as prune pits in cooked prunes or shells of shellfish.

Facts: Sperry Rand Corp. agreed to convert the record-keeping system of Industrial Supply Corp. so that a computer could maintain it. Sperry Rand also agreed to sell a computer and nine other items necessary for such a record-keeping system. The computer and the equipment were ordered by identified trade name and number. When the system did not work, Industrial Supply sued Sperry Rand for breach of implied warranty of fitness. Sperry Rand raised the defense that no such warranty existed because the equipment had been ordered by trade name and number.

Outcome: The court held that the fact that the equipment was ordered by trade name and number did not automatically extinguish the warranty of fitness. The circumstances showed the sale was made in reliance on the seller's skill, and with appreciation of the buyer's problems, and the sale of the particular equipment to the buyer was made as constituting the equipment needed by it. Under such circumstances, a warranty of the fitness of the equipment for such purpose was implied.

SALE OF ARTICLE WITH PATENT OR TRADE NAME

The sale of a patent- or trade-name article does not bar the existence of a warranty of fitness for a particular purpose, or of merchantability, when the circumstances giving rise to such a warranty otherwise exist. It is a question of fact whether the buyer relied on the seller's skill and judgment when making the purchase. If the buyer asked for a patent- or trade-name article and insisted on it, the buyer clearly did not rely on the seller's skill and judgment. Therefore the sale lacks the factual basis for an implied warranty of fitness for the particular purpose. If the necessary reliance upon the seller's skill and judgment is shown, however, the warranty arises in that situation.

The seller of automobile parts, for example, is not liable for breach of the implied warranty of their fitness when the parts, for example, oil filters, were ordered by catalog number for use in a specified vehicle and the seller did not know that the lubrication system of the automobile had been changed so as to make the parts ordered unfit for use.

SALE OF SECONDHAND OR USED GOODS

No warranty arises as to fitness of used property for ordinary use from a sale made by a casual seller. If made by a merchant seller, such a warranty may exist. A number of states follow the rule that implied warranties apply in connection with the sale of used or secondhand goods, particularly automobiles and equipment.

LEASED GOODS

Rather than purchase expensive goods, many people and businesses lease them. The users of the goods could suffer personal injury or property damage from the use or condition of leased property. Most states have adopted Article 2A of the UCC, which applies to personal property leasing. Article 2A treats lease transactions similarly to the way Article 2 treats sales, which includes express and implied warranty provisions. However, a warranty of possession without interference replaces the warranty of title.

Exclusion and Surrender of Warranties

LO3
Warranty exclusion and surrender

Warranties can be excluded or modified by the agreement of the parties, subject to the limitation that such a provision must not be unconscionable. If a warranty of fitness is to be excluded, the exclusion must be in writing and so conspicuous as to ensure that the buyer will be aware of its presence. If the implied warranty of merchantability is excluded or modified, the exclusion clause must expressly mention the word "merchantability" and if in writing must be conspicuous.

PARTICULAR PROVISIONS

Such a statement as "there are no warranties that extend beyond the description on the face hereof" excludes all implied warranties of fitness. Normally, implied warranties are excluded by the statements "as is," "with all faults," or other language that in normal common speech calls attention to the warranty exclusion and makes it clear that no implied warranty exists. For example, an implied warranty that a steam heater would work properly in the buyer's dry cleaning plant is effectively excluded by provisions that "the warranties and guarantees herein set forth are made by us and accepted by you in lieu of all statutory or implied warranties or guarantees, other than title. . . . This contract contains all agreements between the parties, and there is no agreement, verbal or otherwise, that is not set down herein," and the contract has only a "one-year warranty on labor and material supplied by seller."

In order for a disclaimer of warranties to be a binding part of an oral sales contract, the disclaimer must be called to the attention of the buyer. When the contract as made does not disclaim warranties, a disclaimer of warranties accompanying goods delivered later is not effective because it is a unilateral, or one-sided, attempt to modify the contract.

EXAMINATION BY THE BUYER

No implied warranty exists with respect to defects in goods that an examination should have revealed when, before making the final contract, the buyer has examined the goods, or a model or sample, as fully as desired. No implied warranty exists if the buyer has refused to make such examination.

DEALINGS AND CUSTOMS

An implied warranty can be excluded or modified by the course of dealings, course of performance, or usage of trade. For example, if in the trade engaged in by the parties the words "no adjustment" meant "as is" the words "no adjustment" would exclude implied warranties.

Facts: Standard Structural Steel Co. contracted to remove the truss spans of a bridge. It decided to use a derrick system utilizing a cable to remove the sections of the span. A number of derricks and barges were involved in the system. Standard consulted with Bethlehem Steel Corp. and then telephoned an order for bridge strand cable to Bethlehem. Bethlehem had been a major supplier of Standard's for 62 years. Standard knew it was Bethlehem's policy to sell products only with disclaimers of the warranties of merchantability and fitness for a particular purpose. When Standard was removing the first section of bridge span, some strands of the cable broke and an accident occurred that seriously damaged Standard's equipment. Standard sued Bethlehem for breach of the warranties of merchantability and fitness for a particular purpose.

Outcome: The court held that the oral agreement by telephone included Standard's understanding from the 62-year course of dealing that Bethlehem would not sell products without excluding the implied warranties.

CAVEAT EMPTOR

Caveat Emptor
Let the buyer beware

In the absence of fraud on the part of the seller, or in circumstances in which the law imposes a warranty, the relationship of the seller and the buyer is described by the maxim **caveat emptor** (let the buyer beware). Common law courts rigidly applied this rule, requiring purchasers in ordinary sales to act on their own judgment except when sellers gave express warranties. The trend of the earlier statutes, the UCC, and decisions of modern courts have been to soften the harshness of this rule, primarily by establishing implied warranties for the protection of the buyer. Consumer protection statutes have also greatly softened this rule. The rule of caveat emptor still applies, however, when the buyer has full opportunity to make an examination of the goods that would disclose the existence of any defect, and the seller has not committed fraud.

Product Liability

When harm to person or property results from the use or condition of an article of personal property, the person injured may be entitled to recover damages. This right may be based on the theory of breach of warranty.

PRIVITY OF CONTRACT IN BREACH OF WARRANTY

Privity of Contract
Relationship between contracting parties

In the past, in common law there could be no suit for breach of warranty unless **privity of contract** (a contract relationship) existed between the plaintiff and the defendant. Now, however, a "stranger," one who does not have a contractual relationship, can sue on the theory of breach of warranty. For example, it has been held that a mechanic injured because of a defect in an automobile being fixed may sue the manufacturer for breach of implied warranty of fitness.

In most states an exception to the privity rule allows members of the buyer's family and various other persons not in privity of contract with the seller or manufacturer to sue for breach of warranty when injured by the harmful condition of food, beverages, or drugs.

The UCC expressly abolished the requirement of privity against the seller by members of the buyer's family, household, and guests in actions for personal injury. Apart from the express provision made by the UCC, a conflict of authority exists as to whether other cases require privity of contract. Some states lean toward the abolition of the privity requirement, while many states flatly reject the doctrine when a buyer sues the manufacturer or a prior seller. In many instances, recovery by the buyer against a remote manufacturer or seller is based on the fact that the defendant had advertised directly to the public and, therefore, made a warranty to the purchasing consumer of the truth of the advertising. Although advertising by the manufacturer to the consumer is a reason for not requiring privity when the consumer sues the manufacturer, the absence of advertising by the manufacturer frequently does not bar such action by the buyer. While most jurisdictions have modified the privity requirement beyond the exceptions specified in the UCC, each state has retained limited applications of the doctrine.

Recovery may also be allowed when the consumer mails to the manufacturer a warranty registration card that the manufacturer had packed with the purchased article.

Facts: While William Bernick was playing hockey for Georgia Tech he was struck in the face by a hockey stick. His mouthguard was shattered, his upper jaw fractured, three teeth knocked out, and a part of a fourth tooth broken off. The manufacturer of the mouthguard, Cooper of Canada, Ltd., had promoted it through hockey catalog advertisements and parent guides as giving "maximum protection to the lips and teeth."

Outcome: The language was such as to induce the purchase of the mouthguard by Bernick's mother for his use while playing. Bernick did rely on an express warranty.

WARRANTY PROTECTION

The Magnuson-Moss Warranty and Federal Trade Commission Improvement Act requires that written warranties for consumer goods meet certain requirements. Clear disclosure of all warranty provisions and a statement of the legal remedies of the consumer under the warranty must be a part of the warranty. According to the act, the consumer must be informed of the warranty prior to the sale. In order to satisfy the law, the language of warranties of goods costing more than $15 must not be misleading to a "reasonable, average consumer."

Facts: Roxanne Sadat bought a new car covered by a full written warranty. Unfortunately, the brakes faded or were hard to engage, the steering column vibrated excessively, the transmission slipped from park to reverse, the car leaked oil and dieseled after the engine was turned off, and the passenger compartment smelled of exhaust. Sadat took the car in to the dealer seven times for repair of these problems, but they were never cured. Sadat asked to have her car replaced at no cost. American Motors refused, so Sadat sued for relief under the Magnuson-Moss Act.

Outcome: The court said the law gave Sadat a right to sue for breach of warranty.

The warranty time can be extended if repairs require that the product be out of service for an unreasonable length of time. When this occurs the consumer may recover incidental expenses. If after a reasonable number of opportunities the manufacturer is unable to remedy the defect in a product, the consumer must be permitted to elect to receive a refund or a replacement when the product has been sold with a full warranty.

A significant aspect of the act requires that no written warranty may waive the implied warranties of merchantability and fitness for a particular purpose during the term of the written warranty, or unreasonably soon thereafter. Thus, the previously common practice of replacing the implied warranties of fitness and merchantability with substandard written warranties has been significantly limited. The act also curtails the limitation of implied warranties on items for which a service or maintenance contract is offered within 90 days after the initial sale. The act also extends the coverage of a warranty to those who purchase consumer goods secondhand during the term of the warranty.

EFFECT OF REPROCESSING BY DISTRIBUTOR

Frequently a manufacturer produces a product or a supplier distributes it but believes or expects additonal processing or changes by the ultimate distributor or retailer. Such a manufacturer or supplier is not liable to the ultimate consumer for breach of warranty or negligence if the retailer does not complete the additional processing. For example, a supplier of pork sausage to a delicatessen might advise the delicatessen it would no longer heat the sausage to destroy trichinae. If the delicatessen advises the supplier that it will heat the sausage and does not, a person who becomes ill from eating the sausage can sue the delicatessen, but not the supplier.

Identity of Parties

The existence of product liability may be affected by the identity of the claimant or of the defendant.

THIRD PERSONS

Although the UCC permits recovery for breach of warranty by the guests of the buyer, it makes no provision for recovery by employees or strangers.

A conflict of authority exists as to whether an employee of the buyer may sue the seller or manufacturer for breach of warranty. Some jurisdictions deny recovery on the ground that the employee is outside of the distributive chain, not being a buyer. Others allow recovery in such a case. By the latter view, an employee of a construction contractor may recover for breach of the implied warranty of fitness made by the manufacturer of the structural steel that proved defective and fell, injuring the employee.

MANUFACTURER OF COMPONENT PART

Many items of goods in today's marketplace were not made entirely by one manufacturer. Thus, the harm caused may result from a defect in a component part of the finished product. Since the manufacturer of the total article was the buyer from the component-part manufacturer, the privity rule barred suit against the component-part manufacturer for breach of warranty by anyone injured. In jurisdictions in which privity of contract is not recognized as a bar to recovery, it is not material that the defendant manufactured merely a component part. In these cases, the manufacturer of a component part cannot defend a lawsuit by the final purchaser on the ground of absence of privity. Thus, the purchasers of a tractor trailer may recover from the manufacturer of the brake system of the trailer for damages sustained when the brake system failed to work. Likewise, a person injured while on a golf course when an automobile parked on the club parking lot became "unparked" and rolled downhill can sue the manufacturer of the defective parking unit.

Nature and Cause of Harm

The law is more concerned in cases where the plaintiff has been personally injured rather than economically harmed. Thus, the law places protection of the person of the individual above protection of property rights. The harm sustained must have been "caused" by the defendant.

To prove a case for breach of warranty, only facts of which the plaintiff has direct knowledge, or about which information can readily be learned, need be proven. Thus, the plaintiff must only show that a sale and a warranty existed, that the goods did not conform to the warranty, and that injury resulted from the goods.

A manufacturer or seller may assume by the terms of a contract a liability broader than would arise from a mere warranty.

Facts: Spiegel purchased a jar of skin cream from Saks 34th Street. National had manufactured it. The carton and the jar stated that the cream was chemically pure and absolutely safe. When Spiegel used the cream, it caused a severe skin rash. She sued Saks and National.

Outcome: Judgment was for Spiegel. The statements on the carton and the jar constituted an express warranty binding both the seller and the manufacturer. The statement that it was safe was an absolute undertaking that it was safe for everyone; as distinguished from merely an implied warranty of reasonable fitness, which would be subject to an exception of a particular allergy of a plaintiff.

Consumer Protection

LO4
Consumer protection measures

www.ifccfbi.gov

Consumer protection laws are designed to protect the parties to a contract from abuse, sharp dealing, and fraud. They also strengthen legitimate business interests. Laws requiring fairness and full disclosure of business dealings make it more difficult for unscrupulous businesspeople to operate and thus infringe upon the trade of those with sound business practices.

PRODUCT SAFETY

The range of products affected by safety standards includes toys, television sets, insecticides, and drugs. The federal government has set safety standards for bumpers, tires, and glass. Substandard products are often subject to recall at the instigation of federal agencies. In some instances fines and imprisonment may be imposed on corporate executives whose businesses have distributed clearly hazardous, substandard goods.

In 1972 the federal government implemented the Consumer Product Safety Act, which established the Consumer Product Safety Commission. The commission has broad power to promulgate safety standards for many products. Federal courts have the power to review these standards to make sure they are necessary to abolish or decrease the risk of injury and that they do so at a reasonable cost. The commission may order a halt to the manufacture of unsafe products. Certain products, inherently dangerous or hazardous, may be banned by the commission if there appears to be no way to make the product safe. The law requires manufacturers, distributors, and retailers of consumer products to immediately notify the commission if a product fails to comply with an applicable safety standard or contains a defect that creates a substantial risk of injury to the public.

Facts: A sizable number of people were injured every year from accidental ignition of matchbooks. The Consumer Product Safety Commission issued matchbook safety regulations. They stated that "the friction shall be located on the outside back cover near the bottom of the matchbook." A manufacturer of paper matchbooks, D. D. Bean & Sons, asked for federal court review of the regulations. Although the matchbook industry would have to modify its equipment to put the friction for lighting matches on the back of the covers, it was a one-time cost.

Outcome: The court said that the rule was reasonable in view of the injury likely to be reduced and the relatively small cost to the industry.

TRUTH IN ADVERTISING

The Federal Trade Commission (FTC) has been active in demanding that advertisements be limited to statements about products that can be substantiated. The FTC may seek voluntary agreement from a business to stop false or deceptive advertising and, in some instances, to agree to corrective advertising. Such agreement is obtained by a business's signing a consent order. The FTC also has the power to order businesses to "cease and desist" from unfair trade practices. The business has the right to contest an FTC order in court.

The FTC has the authority to require that the name of a product be changed if it misleads or tends to mislead the public regarding the nature or quality of the product. If an advertisement actually misstates the quality of a product or makes the product appear to be what it is not, the FTC can prohibit the advertising.

Facts: Porter & Dietsch, Inc., marketed "X-11" tablets, which were nonprescription, weight-reduction tablets. Advertisements for the tablets stated, in capital letters, "EAT WELL . . . AND LOSE THAT FAT" and "EAT WHAT YOU WANT—AND SLIM DOWN." They continued to state that "no starvation dieting" was necessary and loss of weight could be accomplished without "suffering through starvation dieting hunger" or "boring reducing diets." In fact, use of the tablets would not cause weight loss unless a severely restricted caloric diet was followed.

Outcome: The FTC found the advertising deceptive and required the phrase "Dieting is required" to be included in future advertising.

PRODUCT UNIFORMITY

A number of required practices give consumers the ability to make intelligent choices when comparing competing products. For years, some states have required certain products to be packaged in specifically comparable quantities.

Unit Pricing
Price stated per unit of measurement

Some local governments require **unit pricing**. In unit pricing the price for goods sold by weight is stated as the price per ounce or other unit of measurement of the product as well as a total price for the total weight. Thus, all products sold by the ounce would be marked with not only a total price but also with a price per ounce that could be compared to competing products even if the competing products were not packaged in an equal number of ounces.

USURY LAWS

Laws that fix the maximum rate of interest that may be charged on loans are called *usury laws*. They recognize that the borrower is frequently in a weak position and therefore unable to bargain effectively for the best possible rates of interest.

Most states provide for several rates of interest. The legal rate, which varies from state to state from about 5 percent to 15 percent, applies when interest must be paid but no rate has been specified. The maximum contract rate is the highest rate that can be demanded of a debtor. This rate varies from about 8 percent to as much as 45 percent. Some states allow the parties to set any rate of interest. A number of jurisdictions have recently adopted a fluctuating maximum rate of interest based on such rates as the Federal Reserve discount rate, the prime rate, or the rate on U.S. Treasury bills. Statutes usually permit a higher rate to be charged on small loans on the theory that the risks and costs per dollar loaned are greater in making small loans.

The laws vary regarding the damages awarded to a person charged a usurious rate of interest. Some laws allow recovery of the total interest charged and others allow recovery of several times the amount charged.

TRUTH IN LENDING

The federal Truth in Lending Act requires lenders to make certain written disclosures to borrowers before extending credit. These disclosures include:

1. The finance charge.
2. The annual percentage rate.
3. The number, amount, and due dates of all payments, including any **balloon payments**—payments that are more than twice the normal installment payments.

Balloon Payment
Payment more than twice the normal one

Finance Charge
Total amount paid for credit

Annual Percentage Rate (APR)
Amount charged for loan as percentage of loan

The **finance charge** is the total dollar amount the borrower will pay for the loan. The finance charge includes all interest and any other fees or charges required to be paid in order to get the loan.

The **annual percentage rate (APR)** is the dollar amount charged for the loan expressed as a percentage of the amount borrowed. The APR must be on a yearly rate. This helps a borrower "comparison shop" among different lenders when seeking credit.

Advertisements indicating any credit terms must also meet substantially the same requirements regarding disclosure. The law provides that when the purchase of consumer products is financed by executing a mortgage on the debtor's principal dwelling, the debtor has three days in which to rescind the mortgage agreement. Both criminal penalties and civil recovery are available against those who fail to comply with the Truth in Lending Act.

STATUTES PROHIBITING UNCONSCIONABLE CONTRACTS

Section 2-302 of the UCC provides courts with authority to refuse to enforce a sales contract or a part of it because it is "unconscionable." If the terms of the contract are so harsh or the price so unreasonably high as to shock the conscience of the community, the courts may rule the contract to be unconscionable.

Facts: The Reynosos purchased a refrigerator-freezer from the Frostifresh Corporation for a cash price of $900 plus a credit charge of $245.88 for a total price of $1,145.88. The contract was negotiated orally in Spanish, and during the conversation Mr. Reynoso stated that he had only one week left on his job and could not afford the appliance. The signed retail installment contract covering the sale was entirely in English. Frostifresh had paid $348 for the appliance. When sued for the contract price the Reynosos argued that the contract was unconscionable.

Outcome: The New York courts set aside the contract price and required the Reynosos to pay only the net cost of the refrigerator-freezer to Frostifresh along with a reasonable profit and trucking and service charges.

FAIR CREDIT REPORTING

The Fair Credit Reporting Act requires creditors to notify a potential recipient of credit whenever any adverse action or denial of credit was based on a credit report. It permits the consumer about whom a credit report is written to obtain from a credit agency the substance of the credit report (see Illustrations 19-2 and 19-3 for sample forms). An incorrect credit report must be corrected by the credit agency. In some cases, if the consumer disagrees with a creditor about the report the consumer may be permitted to add an explanation of the dispute to the report. Certain types of adverse information may not be maintained in the reports for more than seven years. The reports may be used for legitimate business purposes only.

Individuals whose rights under the act have been violated may sue and recover ordinary damages if the harm resulted from negligent noncompliance. If the injury resulted from willful noncompliance with the Fair Credit Reporting Act, the aggrieved party may seek punitive damages.

Facts: Terry Fischl applied for credit. General Motors Acceptance Corp. (GMAC) obtained a consumer report on him. It erroneously referred to one of Fischl's jobs as past employment and an account in good standing with Sears, Roebuck & Co. as a credit inquiry. GMAC sent Fischl a form letter rejecting his application and indicating the reason was "credit references are insufficient." The section of the form designed to report the use of information from outside sources was marked "disclosure inapplicable." When sued for violation of the Fair Credit Reporting Act, GMAC argued that credit was not refused because of what was in the report, but because of what was not in the report.

Outcome: The court held that disclosure under the act was not conditioned on derogatory or negative information in a report, but disclosure was required when a decision is based wholly or in part on information in the report. Since GMAC's denial of credit had been based on a credit report, it violated the act by not disclosing that fact to Fischl.

STATE CONSUMER PROTECTION AGENCIES

Injunctive Powers
Power to issue cease-and-desist orders

A number of states have enacted laws giving either the state attorney general or a special consumer affairs office the authority to compel fairness in advertising, sales presentations, and other consumer transactions. State officials will investigate complaints received from consumers. If the complaint appears valid, efforts will be made to secure voluntary corrective action by the seller. Frequently these agencies have **injunctive powers**,

S A M P L E

____
____
______________________________________ ______ __________

December 05, 2001

____
____
______________________________________ ______ __________

Dear Sir or Madam:

I applied for credit with you on ______________, for ______________________.
I was notified on ________________, that my application had been denied.

Please advise if the adverse action was based in whole or in part on information contained in a consumer credit report or on information obtained from a source other than a consumer reporting agency. If the adverse action was based on information from a source other than a consumer reporting agency, please indicate the nature of the adverse information, such as my credit worthiness, credit standing, credit capacity, character, general reputation, or personal characteristics.

If you have requested an investigative report, please provide me with a complete and accurate description of the nature and scope of the investigation.

Your review of this matter is greatly appreciated. Please respond as soon as possible regarding the results of your review.

Please contact me if you have any questions or need additional information.

Sincerely,

____

Illustration 19-2
Challenge to a Denial of Credit

S A M P L E

____
____
____

December 05, 2001

____
____
____

Re: Credit Report Request

Dear Sir or Madam:

I would like to request a copy of my credit report file. I am providing the following information to obtain the report.

Current address:

____
__________________________________, _____ _________

Previous name or address within the last five (5) years:

Other Information:
Telephone number: ________________________

As proof of identity, enclosed ________________________.

Enclosed is a copy of a letter from ________________________,
denying me credit within the last sixty (60) days. Therefore, the credit report should be provided to me free of charge.

Please contact me if you have any questions or need additional information.

Sincerely,

____

Enclosure

Illustration 19-3

Request for a Credit Report

which means that they may issue cease-and-desist orders similar to those of the FTC. In a limited number of jurisdictions the agencies may prosecute the offending business, and significant criminal penalties may be imposed that substantially augment the operation of these efforts.

Questions

1 What is the effect of a warranty made at the time of a sale and made after a sale is completed?
2 How does an implied warranty differ from an express warranty?
3 What are the obligations of the seller of a product with a full warranty?
4 When does a warranty against encumbrances apply?
5 Distinguish by examples the difference between an implied warranty of fitness for a particular purpose and an implied warranty of merchantability.
6 Explain the difference in the "foreign/natural" test and the "reasonable expectation" test as applied to the sale of food or drink.
7 Does the sale of a patent- or trade-name article bar the existence of a warranty of fitness for a particular purpose or of merchantability?
8 How may warranties be excluded or surrendered?
9 Under what different theories may a person be entitled to recover for personal injury or property damage?
10 How does the Magnuson-Moss Warranty Act assist a consumer?
11 Explain how the disclosure provisions of the Truth in Lending Act benefit consumers.
12 When will a court find a sales contract unconscionable?

Case Problems

LO3 1 By means of long-distance telephone conversations Ace, Inc. agreed to buy an airplane from Unified Technologies of Texas, Inc. subject to a test flight by Thompson Comerford, the sole shareholder of Ace. Comerford arrived in Dallas where the plane was but he did not have time to test fly the plane. He and Ken Gedney, the broker for the plane, agreed Comerford's flight back home would constitute the test flight. In order to take the plane, Gedney required Comerford to sign a "Purchase Agreement" which stated, "the aircraft . . . and accessories, are being sold 'As Is,'" and "there are no representations or warranties, express or implied . . . including . . . merchantability." Comerford found brake, steering, climb, and cruise performance problems with the plane. When Unified refused to repair the problems, Ace sued for breach of warranty including merchantability. Were warranties properly excluded?

LO1 2 John Crow took a ride on a new model sport fishing boat manufactured by Bayliner Marine Corp. but there was no equipment on the boat for determining the speed. The salesman told Crow he had no information about the speed but did have two documents called "prop matrixes" from Bayliner's dealer's manual that listed the maximum speed for each boat model. When equipped with a size "20 x 20" propeller the boat's maximum speed was listed as 30 mph. At the bottom of the prop matrix was the statement: "All testing . . . at full fuel and water tanks and . . . 600 pounds passenger and gear weight." Crow bought the boat, but it had a "20 x 17" propeller. He added equipment weighing 2,000 pounds. The boat only went 13 mph. The dealer's repairs and adjustments got the speed up to 17 mph. Crow sued Bayliner for breach of an express warranty. Did the statements in the prop matrixes create an express warranty?

LO4 3 Ray Vickers owned an automobile pawn business. When a person pawned a car, Vickers issued a standard pawn ticket and required the customer to leave the pawned vehicle at his business. Vickers required each customer to pay a "storage fee" while he kept the vehicle. Wilfred Yazzie pawned his car at Vickers and Vickers charged him a $30 "storage fee." Yazzie later filed suit alleging the "storage fee" was a finance charge under the Truth in Lending Act and therefore Vickers understated the annual percentage rate and the finance charge. Was the "storage fee" a finance charge?

LO1 4 Fuqua Chrysler-Plymouth bought a used Chevrolet from Alfred Dirico, and Fuqua then sold the car at retail. The car odometer showed 50,864 miles, but it had more than 128,000. After being sued by the buyer, Fuqua sued Dirico for breach of express warranty, contending that the odometer mileage statement received when it purchased the car from Dirico formed an express warranty. Since the mileage was incorrect, Fuqua claimed it was a breach of the warranty. After giving the mileage, a box was checked on the mileage statement form by the statement, "I hereby certify to the best of my knowledge the odometer reading . . . reflects the actual mileage." Did the mileage statement create an express warranty?

LO2 5 David Duff bought tongue-and-groove lumber from Bonner Building Supply, Inc., a dealer in lumber products. Bonner represented that the lumber was kiln-dried, which meant its moisture content would not exceed 19 percent and shrinkage would be minimal. Duff installed the lumber as wall paneling and significant shrinkage occurred. Some boards shrank one-half inch, which was enough to pull the wood tongues from their grooves, leaving gaps between the boards. Duff sued Bonner for the cost of repair and replacement, alleging breach of implied warranty of merchantability. Was it?

LO3 6 St. Croix Printing Equipment, in Minnesota, contracted with Tobi's Graphics, in California, to find a used printer for Tobi's to buy "as is." By phone, Deborah Sexton of St. Croix agreed to buy a used Adast press from Rockwell Graphics in Illinois. Sexton wanted the press shipped directly to Tobi's without inspecting it. The press was supposed to be capable of four-color printing, and Sexton was told it was in working condition. The contract between Rockwell and St. Croix conspicuously said the press was sold "as is" and disclaimed any warranties express or implied. After it was shipped to Tobi's, it was found it did not work properly and could not do four-color printing. St. Croix sued Rockwell for breach of warranty. Decide the case.

LO2 7 Ronald and Wyman Robinson did business as Friendly Discount Auto Sales. They bought a classic Chevrolet Camaro and then sold it to Mike Durham. Shortly thereafter, the FBI seized the car. It had been stolen, and the FBI returned it to its original owner. Durham sued for breach of warranty. Did he have a valid claim? Why or why not?

LO4 8 Kenneth McDonald saw an ad for a Hunter 45 sailboat in *Yachting*, a national magazine. The ad had two lists separated by empty space. The first list was headed "Specifications." The second was titled "Cruise Pac." Below both lists appeared the statement, "Specifications subject to change without notice." By written contract, McDonald bought a Hunter 45 for $109,500. The contract listed equipment that came with the boat and stated, "plus . . . all equipment . . . nationally advertising in *Yachting*." Two items listed as included in the Cruise Pac were not included. McDonald sued for false advertising. Was there false advertising?

LO4 9 The Flemings applied to the Federal Land Bank of Columbia for a loan on real estate that they said was not their residence. When they defaulted on the loan, the Land Bank foreclosed on the real estate and then brought an action against the Flemings for a deficiency judgment. The Flemings argued that under the Truth in Lending Act the Land Bank wrongfully denied them the right to rescind the loan transaction since it wasn't on their home. Should they have had the right to rescind within three days following the loan transaction?

Internet Resources for Business Law

Name	Resources	Web Address
Uniform Commercial Code §2-312	LII provides UCC §2-312, Warranty of Title and Against Infringement; Buyer's Obligation Against Infringement.	http://www.law.cornell.edu/ucc/2/2-312.html
Uniform Commercial Code §2-313	LII provides UCC §2-313, Express Warranties by Affirmation, Promise, Description, Sample.	http://www.law.cornell.edu/ucc/2/2-313.html
Uniform Commercial Code §2-314	LII provides UCC §2-314, Implied Warranty: Merchantability; Usage of Trade.	http://www.law.cornell.edu/ucc/2/2-314.html
Uniform Commercial Code §2-316	LII provides UCC §2-316, Exclusion or Modification of Warranties.	http://www.law.cornell.edu/ucc/2/2-316.html
Uniform Commercial Code §2-318	LII provides UCC §2-318, Third Party Beneficiaries of Warranties Express or Implied.	http://www.law.cornell.edu/ucc/2/2-318.html
15 USC §2301-2312 (Magnuson-Moss Warranty Act)	LII provides 15 USC §2301-2312, popularly known as the Magnuson-Moss Warranty Act.	http://www.law.cornell.edu/uscode/15/ch50.html
Facts for Consumers—Warranties Fast Facts	The FTC Warranties Fast Facts provides guidelines to consumers on different types of warranties, as well as information for resolving disputes over warranties.	http://www.ftc.gov/bcp/conline/pubs/products/warrant.htm
Consumer Credit Protection Act—15 USC §1601	Legal Information Institute (LII), maintained by Cornell Law School, provides 15 USC §1601, the Consumer Credit Protection Act, better known as the Truth in Lending Act.	http://www.law.cornell.edu/uscode/15/1601.html
U.S. Consumer Product Safety Commission	U.S. Consumer Product Safety Commission provides consumer news and information, as well as notices on recalls and business contracts.	http://www.cpsc.gov/

Part 4 Summary Cases

Contracts

1 Peck Industries ordered 210,000 custom-manufactured decals from Weisz Graphics to be stored by Weisz and released in increments of 500 decals as requested by Peck. Weisz' acknowledgment of the order stated "On Releases over 12 months." Weisz manufactured the entire order and over the next 12 months released seven shipments as requested by Peck. Weisz then refused to make any more releases until Peck paid the full amount of the remaining balance of the order. When Peck refused to pay, Weisz sued alleging it was entitled to recover the price of the goods since they were identified to the contract. Were the goods identified? [*Weisz Graphics Division of Fred B. Johnson Co., Inc., v. Peck Industries, Inc.*, 403 S.E.2d 146 (Ct. App. S.C.)]

2 After Timothy Garcia was convicted for unlawful distribution of a controlled substance the state sued him for return of the "buy money" used to buy narcotics from him. The state could compel repayment if there was a valid civil basis for recovery. Since the sale of a controlled substance is an illegal sale, does the state have a legal basis for recovery? [*State v. Garcia*, 866 P.2d 5 (Ct. App. Utah)]

3 Songbird Jet Ltd., Inc., and Jet Leasing Corporation, acting together, negotiated with Amax Inc. for the purchase of a jet airplane. Songbird and Jet Leasing claimed that an oral agreement was reached by which they would purchase the jet for $8,850,000. Jet Leasing sent Amax a check for $250,000, which it claimed was a deposit on the sale. Amax later notified Jet Leasing the jet was not for sale and that no contract had been made. Songbird and Jet Leasing sued Amax claiming the $250,000 check was partial performance of the alleged contract. Amax alleged that the claim was barred by the statute of Frauds. Was it? [*Songbird Jet Ltd., Inc. v. Amax Inc.,* 581 F. Supp. 912 (S.D.N.Y.)]

4 Halstead Hospital, Inc., ordered bond forms from Northern Bank Note Company. Northern was advised that the bond closing was scheduled for December 18. Northern accepted the order stating it would complete its work for shipment December 16. It arranged for the delivery of the bond forms to a specific location in New York City, the Signature Company, so that they could be inspected and signed prior to the closing. Northern printed the bonds, boxed them into four cartons, and arranged for a common carrier to deliver them to New York. One of the boxes did not arrive until after December 18, so the closing was canceled for that day. Halstead sued for breach of contract, alleging that the contract required shipment and timely delivery by Northern. Did it? [*Halstead Hospital, Inc., v. Northern Bank Note Co.*, 680 F.2d 1307 (10th Cir.)]

5 Conida Warehouses sold light red kidney bean seed to Larry Mallory. After Mallory planted the seeds, the beans developed halo blight, a disease. Mallory sued Conida for breach of warranty. Conida claimed it had effectively disclaimed the warranty of merchantability by attaching a tag to the bag of seed. That tag showed the word *warranty* in capital letters at the top and the rest of the letters were in standard size type. The disclaimer tag contained no contrasting color or other emphasis. That tag was attached with two other tags at the bottom of the bag and under the other two tags. Was this an effective disclaimer? [*Mallory v. Conida Warehouses, Inc.,* 350 N.W.2d 825 (Mich. Ct. App.)]

6 Lorraine Hinchliffe bought a new Jeep Wagoneer from Lipman Motors, Inc. Hinchliffe had told the seller she wanted a vehicle capable of hauling her camper trailer. The jeep

was advertised as having "full-time four-wheel drive" when it had just a system for transmitting power to the wheels using a limited slip differential mechanism. Hinchliffe had many problems with the Jeep and sued, alleging breach of warranty. Could she establish a case? [*Hinchliffe v. American Motors Corp.*, 440 A.2d 810 (Conn.)]

7 At an auction, Gaylen Bennett bought 55 head of cattle from Tony Jansma. The next day some of the cattle were sick. Eventually 19 of the 55 cattle died. Jansma regularly dealt in the buying and selling of cattle and held himself out as having knowledge peculiar to cattle transactions. Bennett sued for breach of the warranty of merchantability. Was Jansma a merchant? [*Bennett v. Jansma*, 392 N.W.2d 134 (S.D.)]

8 Central Credit Bureau issued a credit report on Barbara Johnson that contained an item relating to Johnson's outstanding obligation to Beneficial Finance Corp. The obligation had been discharged by Johnson's bankruptcy. At Johnson's request, Central had reinvestigated and made a note that the debt had been discharged. It then corrected the report. Johnson sued for damages, alleging a violation of the Fair Credit Reporting Act. Was there such a violation? [*Johnson v. Beneficial Finance Corp.*, 466 N.Y.S.2d 553 (N.Y.)]

20
Nature of Negotiable Instruments

Learning Objectives

1 Discuss how negotiable instruments are transferred.

2 Differentiate between bearer paper and order paper.

3 Describe an electronic fund transfer.

PREVIEW CASE

When Abbott Development Co. (ADCO) defaulted on a note, the FDIC allowed it to refinance by issuing a new note payable to the FDIC. The FDIC made a sale of many notes to SMS Financial L.L.C. including the ADCO note. The FDIC indorsed the ADCO note to SMS but failed to deliver it. Under the sale agreement SMS had the right to ask for a refund of this note which it later did. The FDIC refunded SMS's payment for the note and requested SMS deliver it. Since SMS did not have the note it could not return it. Later the FDIC inadvertently sent the note to SMS in a box with other documents. After receiving the note SMS sued ADCO for payment. ADCO alleged SMS was not the holder of the note. Was SMS in possession of the note? To whom was the note payable?

Commercial Paper or Negotiable Instrument Writing drawn in special form that can be transferred as substitute for money or as instrument of credit

Negotiable instruments or commercial paper are writings drawn in a special form that can be transferred from person to person as a substitute for money or as an instrument of credit. Such an instrument must meet certain definite requirements in regard to its form and the manner in which it is transferred. Two types of negotiable instruments include checks and notes. Since a negotiable instrument is not money, the law does not require a person to accept one in payment of a debt.

History and Development

The need for instruments of credit that would permit the settlement of claims between distant cities without the transfer of money has existed as long as trade has existed. References to bills of exchange or instruments of credit appeared as early as 50 B.C. Their widespread usage, however, began about A.D. 1200 as international trade began to flourish in the wake of the Crusades. At first these credit instruments were used only in international trade, but they gradually became common in domestic trade.

In England prior to about A.D. 1400, all disputes between merchants were settled on the spot by special courts set up by the merchants. The rules applied by these courts became known as the **law merchant**. Later the common-law courts took over the adjudication of all disputes, including those between merchants, but these courts retained most of the customs developed by the merchants and incorporated the law merchant into the common law. Most, but by no means all, of the law merchant dealt with bills of exchange or credit instruments.

Law Merchant
Rules applied by courts set up by merchants in early England

In the United States each state modified in its own way the common law dealing with credit instruments so that eventually the various states had different laws regarding credit instruments. The American Bar Association and the American Banks Association appointed a commission to draw up a Uniform Negotiable Instruments Law. In 1896 the commission proposed a uniform act. This act was adopted in all the states, but it was then displaced by Article 3 of the UCC.

In 1990, a commission that writes uniform laws issued a revised Article 3. Because almost all of the states have adopted the revision, this text explains the law according to the changes made by the revision. The revision uses the term *negotiable instruments* while the original Article 3 uses the term *commercial paper*.

Negotiation

LO1
Transfer of negotiable instruments

Negotiation
Act of transferring ownership of negotiable instrument

Holder in Due Course
Person who acquires rights superior to original owner

Negotiation is the act of transferring ownership of a negotiable instrument to another party. A negotiable instrument owned by and payable to a person may be negotiated by the owner. The owner negotiates it by signing the back of it and delivering it to another party. The signature of the owner made on the back of a negotiable instrument before delivery is called an *indorsement*.[1]

When a negotiable instrument is transferred to one or more parties, these parties may acquire rights superior to those of the original owner. Parties who acquire rights superior to those of the original owner are known as **holders in due course**. It is mainly this feature of the transfer of superior rights that gives negotiable instruments a special classification all their own.

Order Paper and Bearer Paper

LO2
Bearer paper versus order paper

Order Paper
Commercial paper payable to order

Bearer Paper
Commercial paper payable to bearer

Commercial paper is made payable either to the order of a named person, in which case it is called **order paper**, or to the bearer, in which case it is called **bearer paper**. Order paper must use the word *order,* as in the phrase "pay to the order of John Doe," or some other word to indicate it may be paid to a transferee. Order paper is negotiated only by indorsement of the person to whom it is then payable and by delivery of the paper to another person. In the case of bearer paper, merely handing the paper to another person may make the transfer.

Payment is made on a different basis with order paper than with bearer paper. Order paper may be paid only to the person to whom it is made payable on its face or the person to whom it has been properly indorsed. However, bearer paper may be paid to any person in possession of the paper.

[1] Indorsement is the spelling used in the UCC, although endorsement is commonly used in business.

Facts: Rob-Glen Enterprises executed promissory notes for a $46,000 loan and delivered them to the Dolly Cam Corp. Before the notes were due, Dolly Cam indorsed them payable to bearer and delivered them to First National Bank of Long Island. When the notes were due, Rob-Glen refused to pay, claiming it had paid them by paying a third party.

Outcome: The court held that since the notes were payable to bearer and First National had possession of them, it was entitled to be paid.

Classification of Commercial Paper

The basic negotiable instruments are:

1. Drafts
2. Promissory notes

DRAFTS

Draft or Bill of Exchange
Written order by one person directing another to pay sum of money to third person

A **draft** is also called a **bill of exchange**. It is a written order signed by one person and requiring the person to whom it is addressed to pay on demand or at a particular time a fixed amount of money to order or to bearer. Checks and trade acceptances are special types of drafts. When you make out a check on your bank account you are actually writing out a type of draft. (See Chapter 22.)

PROMISSORY NOTES

Promissory Note
Unconditional written promise to pay sum of money to another

A **promissory note** is an unconditional promise in writing made by one person to another, signed by the promisor, engaging to pay on demand of the holder, or at a definite time, a fixed amount of money to order or to bearer (see Illustration 20-1). If the note is a demand instrument, the holder may demand payment or sue for payment at any time and for any reason.

NOTE

$ 7,000.00 Greenfield, Missouri April 1, 20 --

One (1) year after date, for value received I promise to pay to the order of Ana Nieves

the sum of Seven Thousand Dollars ($7,000.00)

with interest thereon from date at the rate of fifteen percent (15%)

per annum, interest payable semiannually and if interest is not paid semiannually to become as principal and bear the same rate of interest.

Payable at Northside Bank

Jan L. Hendricks

Illustration 20-1
Promissory Note
Parties: maker, Jan L. Hendricks: payee, Ana Nieves

Parties to Negotiable Instruments

Each party to a negotiable instrument is designated by a certain term, depending upon the type of instrument. Some of these terms apply to all types of negotiable instruments, whereas others are restricted to one type only. The same individual may be designated by one term at one stage and by another at a later stage through which the instrument passes before it is collected. These terms include *payee, drawer, drawee, acceptor, maker, bearer, holder, indorser,* and *indorsee.*

PAYEE

Payee
Party to whom instrument is payable

The person or persons to whom any negotiable instrument is made payable is called the **payee**.

DRAWER

Drawer
Person who executes a draft

The person who executes or signs any draft is called the **drawer** (see Illustration 20-2).

DRAWEE

Drawee
Person ordered to pay draft

The person who is ordered to pay a draft is called the **drawee**.

ACCEPTOR

Acceptor
Person who agrees to pay a draft

A drawee who accepts a draft, thus indicating a willingness to assume responsibility for its payment, is called the **acceptor**. Drafts not immediately payable are accepted by writing upon the face of the instrument these or similar words: *Accepted, Jane Daws.* This indicates that Jane Daws will perform the contract according to its terms.

MAKER

Maker
Person who executes a note

The person who executes a promissory note is called the **maker**. The maker contracts to pay the amount due on the note. This obligation resembles that of the acceptor of a draft.

$ 450.00 December 22, 20 --

Six months after date PAY TO THE

ORDER OF Community Bank

Four hundred fifty dollars and no/100

FOR CLASSROOM USE ONLY

VALUE RECEIVED AND CHARGE TO ACCOUNT OF DOLLARS

TO Walter Evans

No. 27 Walden, Virginia Lee W. Richardson

Illustration 20-2
Draft
Parties: drawer, Lee W. Richardson; drawee, Walter Evans; payee, Community Bank

Bearer
Payee of instrument made payable to whomever is in possession

Holder
Person in possession of instrument payable to bearer or that person

BEARER

Any negotiable instrument may be made payable to whoever possesses it. The payee of such an instrument is the **bearer**. If the instrument is made payable to the order of *Myself, Cash,* or another similar name, it is payable to bearer.

HOLDER

Any person who possesses an instrument is the **holder** if it has been delivered to the person and it is either bearer paper or it is payable to that person as the payee or by indorsement. The payee is the original holder of an instrument.

PREVIEW CASE REVISITED

Facts: When Abbott Development Co. (ADCO) defaulted on a note, the FDIC allowed it to refinance by issuing a new note payable to the FDIC. The FDIC made a sale of many notes to SMS Financial L.L.C. including the ADCO note. The FDIC indorsed the ADCO note to SMS but failed to deliver it. Under the sale agreement SMS had the right to ask for a refund of this note which it later did. The FDIC refunded SMS's payment for the note and requested SMS deliver it. Since SMS did not have the note it could not return it. Later the FDIC inadvertently sent the note to SMS in a box with other documents. After receiving the note SMS sued ADCO for payment. ADCO alleged SMS was not the holder of the note.

Outcome: The court found that since SMS had possession of the note payable to itself, SMS was the holder.

HOLDER IN DUE COURSE

A holder who takes a negotiable instrument in good faith and for value is a holder in due course.

Indorser
Payee or holder who signs back of instrument

INDORSER

When the payee of a draft or a note wishes to transfer the instrument to another party, it must be indorsed. The payee is then called the **indorser**. The payee makes the indorsement by signing on the back of the instrument.

Indorsee
Named holder of indorsed negotiable instrument

INDORSEE

A person who becomes the holder of a negotiable instrument by an indorsement that names him or her as the person to whom the instrument is negotiated is called the **indorsee**.

Negotiation and Assignment

The right to receive payment of instruments may be transferred by either negotiation or assignment. Nonnegotiable paper cannot be transferred by negotiation. The rights to it are transferred by assignment. Negotiable instruments may be transferred by negotiation or assignment. The rights given the original parties are alike in the cases of negotiation and assignment. In the case of a promissory note, for example, the original parties are the maker (the one who promises to pay) and the payee (the one to whom the money is to be paid). Between the original parties, both a nonnegotiable and a negotiable instrument are equally enforceable. Also, the same defenses against fulfilling the terms of the instrument may be set up. For example, if one party to the instrument is a minor, the incapacity to contract may be set up as a defense against carrying out the agreement.

Facts: Several hundred people invested in a Cayman Islands entity called *Tradecom, Ltd.* They used cashier's checks payable to the order of Tradecom. Tradecom's purported agent, Arvey Drown, indorsed the checks and deposited them in an account at Central Bank and Trust Company. Tradecom deposited one $57,000 check without indorsement into that same account, owned by Equity Trading Corporation. An officer of Central indorsed the check: "For deposit only 072 575 Tradecom by Mark E. Thomson Commercial Loan Officer." Tradecom had no account at Central. The investors lost most of their money. They sued Central, alleging it had permitted Drown to divert checks payable to Tradecom to Equity's account. By state law, a bank could supply an indorsement for a customer.

Outcome: Since the check was order paper it could be negotiated only by indorsement of the holder, Tradecom.

However, the rights given to subsequent parties differ depending on whether an instrument is transferred by negotiation or assignment. When an instrument is transferred by assignment, the assignee receives only the rights of the assignor and no more. (See Chapter 12.) If one of the original parties to the instrument has a defense that is valid against the assignor, it is also valid against the assignee.

When an instrument is transferred by negotiation, however, the party who receives the instrument in good faith and for value may obtain rights that are superior to the rights of the original holder. Defenses that may be valid against the original holder may not be valid against a holder who has received an instrument by negotiation.

Credit and Collection

Negotiable instruments are called *instruments of credit* and *instruments of collection.* If A sells B merchandise on 60 days' credit, the buyer may at the time of the sale execute a negotiable note or draft due in 60 days in payment of the merchandise. This note or draft then is an instrument of credit.

If the seller in the transaction above will not extend the original credit to 60 days, a draft may be drawn on the buyer, who would be the drawee. In this case, the drawer may make a bank the payee, the bank being a mere agent of the drawer, or one of the seller's creditors may be made the payee so that an account receivable will be collected and an account payable will be paid all in one transaction. When the account receivable comes due, the buyer will mail a check to the seller. In this example, the draft is an instrument of collection.

Electronic Fund Transfers

LO3 Electronic fund transfers

More and more transfers of funds occur today in which a paper instrument is not actually transferred and the parties do not have face-to-face, personal contact. An

Electronic Fund Transfer
Fund transfer initiated electronically, telephonically, or by computer

electronic fund transfer (HT) is any transfer of funds initiated by means of an electronic terminal, telephonic instrument, or computer or magnetic tape that instructs or authorizes a financial institution to debit or credit an account. An EFT does not include a transfer of funds begun by a check, draft, or similar paper instrument.

EFTs are popular because they are faster and less expensive than the transfer of paper instruments. EFTs also reduce the risk of problems resulting from lost instruments. If a check, for example, does not have to make the entire trip from the payee to the drawee bank to the drawer customer, costs and delays can be reduced.

A federal law, the Electronic Fund Transfer Act, regulates EFTs and defines them as carried out primarily by electronic means. A transfer initiated by a telephone call between a bank employee and a customer is not an EFT unless it is in accordance with a prearranged plan.

The law requires disclosure of the terms and conditions of the EFTs involving a customer's account at the time the customer contracts for an EFT service. This notification must include:

1 What liability could be imposed for unauthorized EFTs.
2 The type of EFTs the customer may make.
3 The charges for EFTs.

Under this law, a customer's liability for an unauthorized EFT can be limited to $50; however, the customer must give the bank very prompt notice of circumstances that lead to the belief that an unauthorized EFT has been or may be made. Also, a bank does not need to reimburse a customer who fails to notify a bank of an unauthorized EFT within 60 days of receiving a bank statement on which the unauthorized EFT appears.

Several widely used types of EFTs include check truncation, preauthorized debits and credits, automated teller machines, and point-of-sale systems.

CHECK TRUNCATION

Check Truncation
Shortening check's trip from payee to drawer

A system of shortening the trip a check makes from the payee to the drawee bank and then to the drawer is called **check truncation**. Many banks no longer return canceled checks to their customers with the monthly statement. Instead, the form of the statements to customers has been revised to list the check numbers. As before, the dollar amount on the checks is shown, but the transactions are now printed in numerical order. The customer can easily reconcile the account without having the canceled checks. However, banks must be able to supply legible copies of the checks at the customers' request for seven years. This is a type of check truncation.

PREAUTHORIZED DEBITS AND CREDITS

Preauthorized Debit
Automatic deduction of bill payment from checking account

Checking account customers may authorize that recurring bills, such as home mortgage payments, insurance premiums, or utility bills, be automatically deducted from their checking accounts each month, called a **preauthorized debit**. It allows a person to avoid the inconvenience and cost of writing out and mailing checks for these bills.

Preauthorized Credit
Automatic deposit of funds to account

A **preauthorized credit** allows the amount of regular payments to be automatically deposited in the payee's account. This type of EFT is frequently used for depositing salaries and government benefits, such as Social Security payments. It benefits the payor, who does not have to issue and mail the checks. The payee does not have to bother depositing a check and normally has access to the funds sooner.

AUTOMATED TELLER MACHINES

Automated Teller Machine
EFT terminal that performs routine banking services

An **automated teller machine** (HT) is an EFT terminal capable of performing routine banking services. Many thousands of such machines exist at locations designed to be accessible to customers. The capabilities of the machines vary; however, some ATMs do such things as dispense cash and account information and allow customers to make deposits, transfer funds between accounts, and pay bills. ATMs are conveniently found at many locations, even in foreign countries, and are open when banks are not.

POINT-OF-SALE SYSTEMS

Point-of-Sale System
EFTs begun at retailers when customers pay for goods or services

Electronic fund transfers that begin at retailers when consumers want to pay for goods or services with debit cards are called **point-of-sale systems** (POS). These transactions occur when the person operating the POS terminal enters information regarding the payment into a computer system. The entry reduces the consumer's bank account and credits the retailer's account by the amount of the transaction.

Questions

1 How were disputes between merchants settled in England prior to A.D. 1400?
2 What is negotiation?
3 What is the feature that gives negotiable instruments a special classification of their own?
4 What does it mean for a drawee to accept a draft and how is it done?
5 Are the rights given to parties subsequent to the original payee the same whether the instrument is transferred by assignment or negotiation? Explain.
6 How are negotiable instruments transferred?
7 Who is the indorser of a negotiable instrument? Who is the indorsee?
8 What is an electronic fund transfer?
9 Why are EFTs popular?
10 What is the benefit of a preauthorized debit?

Case Problems

LO2 1 Miller Furs, Inc. executed a note that stated it promised "to pay, on demand" to the Shawmut Bank an amount not more than $1,000,000. The note also specified that upon the occurrence of certain events the bank could decide that the note "shall become and be due and payable forthwith without demand, notice of nonpayment, presentment, . . ." Two years later Shawmut demanded payment of the note. In the lawsuit that followed Miller argued that the note was not a demand note due and payable when issued, and the bank could only demand payment in good faith. Was the note a demand note?

LO1 2 Joe Jernigan executed a note payable to Mbank Houston, N.A. Mbank indorsed the note to the Federal Reserve Bank of Dallas. When Mbank became insolvent, the Federal Deposit Insurance Corp. was appointed its receiver. The note and other assets were sold to the Deposit Insurance Bridge Bank, N.A., which changed its name to Bank One, Texas, N.A. Bank One sued Jernigan for the balance due. To recover, Bank One had to show it had received the note by negotiation. Had it?

LO3 3 Lawrence and Georgene Kruser had a joint checking account with Bank of America. The bank had issued each of them ATM cards. The Krusers thought Lawrence's card had been destroyed in September, but their December bank statement showed an unauthorized withdrawal of $20 by someone using Lawrence's card. The next year, the Krusers discovered in September that the statements for July and August showed 47 unauthorized withdrawals totaling $9,020. When the bank refused to reimburse them the Krusers sued. Does the bank have to reimburse them the $9,020?

LO1,2 4 Flight Training Center operated a flight school and aircraft rental business. Russell Lund and William Rubin owned and rented planes to FTC. Lund and Rubin decided to sell two jet planes to FTC. A check drawn on Chemical Bank and payable to FTC for $716,946 was indorsed by FTC and made payable to the order of William Rubin and Russell Lund. FTC's lawyer had prepared a power of attorney purporting to authorize Rubin to indorse the check for Lund. It was a forgery. Rubin indorsed the check in his own name and as attorney-in-fact for Lund. The check was given to Laidlaw Adams & Peck, Inc., which deposited it in its account at Chemical. When he learned of this, Lund sued Chemical. Had there been a negotiation of the check?

LO3 5 June Wachter went to Denver National Bank and paid the bank cash to make a wire transfer to California. Denver's personnel transferred the funds, which were received in California the same day. Wachter later asked for confirmation. Denver gave Wachter a copy of the actual wire transfer and orally advised her the transfer had been made. Denver even provided her with a copy of a letter from the California bank indicating that the intended recipient had received the funds. Wachter was still not convinced and went to California to make sure. She then sued Denver under the Electronic Fund Transfer Act. Did the Act apply?

LO1 6 As limited partner investors, Frank DeSalvo and Anthony Gross executed promissory notes payable to Madison Residential Real Estate Limited Partnership 2013. When Consolidated Capital Corp. loaned it $81.5 million, Madison executed a pledge agreement to cover the notes and transferred them to Consolidated as security. The principal players in the partnership were convicted of fraud and the partnership's real estate lost in foreclosure. Because of the fraud, DeSalvo and Gross stopped paying on their notes and Consolidated ultimately sued them for payment. The case hinged on whether the notes had been transferred to Consolidated by negotiation. Had they?

LO3 7 Melanie Curde tried to deposit a $200 check at Tri-City Bank & Trust Co.'s ATM. Curde canceled the attempt and the ATM produced a receipt whose code showed the attempted deposit had been canceled. Seven months later the check was found behind the front cover of the machine. Curde sued Tri-City and the case hinged on whether the attempted deposit was an electronic fund transfer. Was it?

Internet Resources for Business Law

Name	Resources	Web Address
Uniform Commercial Code (UCC) Article 3, Negotiable Instruments	The Legal Information Institute (LII), maintained by Cornell Law School, provides a hypertext and searchable version of UCC Article 3, Negotiable Instruments. LII also maintains links to Article 3 as adopted by particular states and to proposed revisions.	http://www.law.cornell.edu/ucc/3/overview.html
Legal Information Institute—Negotiable Instrument Law Materials	LII provides an overview of negotiable instruments law, federal and state statutes and regulations, and federal and state court decisions.	http://www.law.cornell.edu/topics/negotiable.html
Uniform Commercial Code §3-104	LII provides a hypertext and searchable version of UCC §3-104, Negotiable Instrument.	http://www.law.cornell.edu/ucc/3/3-104.html
Uniform Commercial Code §3-106	LII provides a hypertext and searchable version of UCC §3-106, Unconditional Promise or Order.	http://www.law.cornell.edu/ucc/3/3-106.html
Uniform Commercial Code §3-107	LII provides a hypertext and searchable version of UCC §3-107, Instrument Payable in Foreign Money.	http://www.law.cornell.edu/ucc/3/3-107.html
Uniform Commercial Code §3-108	LII provides a hypertext and searchable version of UCC §3-108, Payable on Demand or at Definite Time.	http://www.law.cornell.edu/ucc/3/3-108.html
Uniform Commercial Code §3-114	LII provides a hypertext and searchable version of UCC §3-114, Contradictory Terms of Instrument.	http://www.law.cornell.edu/ucc/3/3-114.html
Electronic Fund Transfer Act—15 USC §1693	LII provides a hypertext and searchable version of 15 USC §1693, popularly known as the Electronic Fund Transfer Act.	http://www.law.cornell.edu/uscode/15/1693.shtml

21 Essentials of Negotiability

Learning Objectives

1 List the seven requirements of negotiability.

2 Explain the requirements for issuance and delivery of a negotiable instrument.

3 State whether a negotiable instrument must be dated and whether the location of making payment must be indicated.

PREVIEW CASE

George Werner, Stan Fejta, and August Werner, as well as two witnesses, signed the following document:

Promissory Note

Werner Enterprises, Inc., by resolution and signature acknowledges that a debt of $8,000.00 is owed to Mr. Stan Fejta (Fejta Construction Company) regarding the construction of "Pontchartrain Plaza," 1930 West End Park.

This note is payable at maturity on or before May 19, 19–, plus 10% (percent) interest.

Date: April 4, 19–

After unsuccessful attempts to collect this indebtedness, Fejta filed suit. Werner alleged that the writing was nothing more than an acknowledgment of a preexisting debt since it did not contain an unconditional promise to pay. Was this a note? Did it include a promise to pay?

An important characteristic of negotiable instruments is their transferability or negotiability. However, instruments must meet certain requirements in order to be negotiable.

Requirements

LO1 Requirements of negotiability

An instrument must comply with seven requirements in order to be negotiable. If it lacks any one of these requirements, the document is not negotiable even though it may be valid and enforceable between the original parties to it. The seven requirements are:

1. The instrument must be in writing and signed by the party executing it.
2. The instrument must contain either an order to pay or a promise to pay.
3. The order or the promise must be unconditional.
4. The instrument must provide for the payment of a fixed amount of money.
5. The instrument must be payable either on demand or at a fixed or definite time.
6. The instrument must be payable to the order of a payee or to bearer.
7. The payee (unless the instrument is payable to bearer) and the drawee must be designated with reasonable certainty.

A SIGNED WRITING

Negotiability Transferability

A negotiable instrument must be written. The law does not, however, require that the writing be in any particular form. The instrument may be written with pen and ink or with pencil; it may be typed or printed; or it may be partly printed and partly typed. An instrument executed with a lead pencil meets the legal requirements of **negotiability**. However, a person executing an instrument with pencil takes a risk because of the ease with which the instrument could be altered without detection.

A signature must be placed on a negotiable instrument in order to indicate the intent of the promisor to be bound. The normal place for a signature is in the lower right-hand corner, but the location of the signature and its form are wholly immaterial if it is clear that a signature was intended. The signature may be written, typed, printed, or stamped. It may be a name, a symbol, a mark, or a trade name. The signature, however, must be on the instrument. It cannot be on a separate paper attached to the instrument.

Some odd but valid signatures follow:

1. His
Richard X Cooper
Mark
This type of signature might be made by a person who does not know how to write. The signer makes the X in the center. A witness writes the signer's name, Richard Cooper, and the words *His Mark* to indicate who signed the instrument and that it was intended as a signature.
2. "I, Tammy Morley," written by Morley in the body of the note but with her name typed in the usual place for the signature.
3. "Snowwhite Cleaner," the trade name under which Glendon Sutton operates his business.

The instrument may be signed by an agent—another person who has been given authority to perform this act.

AN ORDER OR A PROMISE TO PAY

A draft, such as a trade acceptance or a check, must contain an order to pay. If the request is imperative and unequivocal, it is an order even though the word order is not used.

A promissory note must contain a promise to pay. The word *promise* need not be used—any equivalent words will answer the purpose—but the language used must show that a promise is intended. Thus, the words *I will pay, I guarantee to pay*, and *This is to certify that we are bound to pay* were held to be sufficient to constitute a promise. A mere acknowledgment of a debt does not suffice.

PREVIEW CASE REVISITED

Facts: George Werner, Stan Fejta, and August Werner, as well as two witnesses, signed the following document:

Promissory Note

Werner Enterprises, Inc., by resolution and signature acknowledges that a debt of $8,000.00 is owed to Mr. Stan Fejta (Fejta Construction Company) regarding the construction of "Pontchartrain Plaza," 1930 West End Park.

This note is payable at maturity on or before May 19, 19–, plus 10% (percent) interest.

Date: April 4, 19–

After unsuccessful attempts to collect this indebtedness, Fejta filed suit. Werner alleged that the writing was nothing more than an acknowledgment of a preexisting debt since it did not contain an unconditional promise to pay.

Outcome: The court held that examination of the entire writing showed a promise to pay. It was titled "Promissory Note" and stated it was "payable at maturity"; therefore, it was intended to be a promise to pay money.

UNCONDITIONAL

The order or the promise must be absolute and unconditional. Neither must be contingent upon any other act or event. If Baron promises to pay Noffke $500 "in 60 days, or sooner if I sell my farm," the instrument is negotiable because the promise itself is unconditional. In any event, a promise to pay the $500 in 60 days exists. The contingency pertains only to the time of payment, and that time cannot exceed 60 days. If the words *or sooner* were omitted, the promise would be conditional and the note would be nonnegotiable. As stated previously, however, an instrument may be binding on the parties even though nonnegotiable.

If the order to pay is out of a particular fund or account, the instrument is still negotiable. For example, "Pay to the order of Leonard Cohen $5,000 out of my share of my mother's estate" would not be a conditional order to pay. The order or the promise need not commit the entire credit of the one primarily liable for the payment of the instrument.

A reference to the consideration in a note that does not condition the promise does not destroy negotiability. The clause "This note is given in consideration of a typewriter purchased today" does not condition the maker's promise to pay. If the clause read, "This note is given in consideration for a typewriter guaranteed for 90 days, breach of warranty to constitute cancellation of the note," the instrument would not be negotiable. This promise to pay is not absolute, but conditional. Also, if the recital of the consideration is in such form as to make the instrument subject to another contract, the negotiability of the instrument is destroyed.

Thus, a mere reference to a separate agreement or a statement that the instrument arises out of a separate agreement does not make the promise or order conditional. However, if the promise or order states it is subject to or governed by another agreement, it is conditional.

Facts: Lloyd Strickland wanted to buy a swimming pool kit from Morgan & Son Pool Company. To be sure Morgan paid his supplier, Kafko Manufacturing Co., Strickland purchased a cashier's check for $4,200 payable to Kafko. The check stated, "for Pool Kit to be delivered to Rt. 1, Box 225, Enterprise, Alabama." Strickland gave the check to Roger Morgan who took the check to Kafko. Morgan & Son owed Kafko $1,000 from a prior pool purchase, and Roger said the check was to pay for that. He asked for the difference in cash, and Kafko paid him $3,200. Morgan & Son never delivered Strickland's pool, and when Strickland found out the check had been cashed he sued Kafko. Kafko had a defense if the check was negotiable.

Outcome: The court said that the language "for Pool Kit to be delivered. . . . " amounted to a recitation of the consideration and did not make the check conditional. The check was negotiable.

A FIXED AMOUNT OF MONEY

The instrument must call for the payment of money. It need not be American money, but it must be some national medium of exchange that is legal tender at the place payment is to be made. Thus it could be payable in dollars, yen, marks, pounds, pesos, or rubles. It cannot be in scrip, gold bullion, bonds, or similar assets. However, the instrument may provide for the payment of either money or goods. If the choice lies with the holder, such a provision does not destroy its negotiability.

The sum payable must be a fixed amount, not dependent upon other funds or upon future profits.

Facts: To buy a new Buick, Susan Kellar executed an installment note to Society National Bank. Kellar stopped making payments on it shortly after making the note. She asked for the payoff balance in order to pay off the loan. The balance was $19,297.87. By mail, Society received a "certified draft" for $19,300 drawn on International Credit Exchange in Acapulco, Mexico. The draft stated, "This draft is redeemable in current funds (credit) when presented. . . ." After forwarding the instrument for payment, Society found out that the draft was returned unpaid and International Credit Exchange did not exist. Society sued Kellar, who claimed the draft was a negotiable instrument.

Outcome: The court held that it was not negotiable because it was not payable in money but in credit.

ETHICAL POINT
Was Kellar behaving in an ethical manner when she tried to pay off a note with credit?

Not only must the contract be payable in money to be negotiable, but the amount must be determinable from the wording of the instrument itself. If a note for $5,000 provides that all taxes that may be levied upon a certain piece of real estate will be paid, it is nonnegotiable. The amount to be paid cannot be determined from the note itself. A provision providing for the payment of interest or exchange charges, however, does not destroy negotiability. Other terms that have been held not to destroy negotiability are provisions for cost of collection, a 10 percent attorney's fee if placed in the hands of an attorney for collection, and installment payments.

A variable rate of interest does not destroy negotiability. Although the UCC requires the instrument to call for payment of a "fixed amount" of money, the fixed amount refers to principal. The Code specifically permits the rate of interest to be a variable one without destroying negotiability.

Sometimes, through error of the party writing the negotiable instrument, the words on the instrument may call for the payment of one amount of money, while the figures call for the payment of another. The amount expressed in words prevails because one is less likely to err in writing this amount. Also, if anyone should attempt to raise the amount, it would be much simpler to alter the figures than the words. By the same token, handwriting prevails over conflicting typewriting, and typewriting prevails over conflicting printed amounts.

PAYABLE ON DEMAND OR AT A DEFINITE TIME

An instrument meets the test of negotiability as to time if it is payable on demand (as in a demand note) or at sight (as in a sight draft). If no time is specified (as in a check), the commercial paper is considered payable on demand.

Facts: Charles and Alice Faulkner signed a promissory note payable to the order of Elmer E. Miller and Ronald Rotert. It provided for 8 percent interest "from the date of death of Elmer E. Miller." Monthly payments of principal and interest were to be made starting one month after Miller's death. The Faulkners made no payments even after Miller's death, and Rotert sued them for payment. The decision in the case rested on whether the note was negotiable.

Outcome: The court held that since payments were to begin one month after Miller's death, the note was not payable at a definite time and therefore not negotiable.

If the instrument provides for payment at some future time, the due date must be fixed.

Promissory notes often include either an acceleration clause or a prepayment clause. An acceleration clause protects the payee, and the prepayment clause benefits the party obligated to pay. A typical acceleration clause provides that in the event one installment is in default, the whole note shall become due and payable at once. This does not destroy its negotiability. Most prepayment clauses give the maker or the drawee the right to prepay the instrument in order to save interest. This also does not affect the negotiability of the instrument.

PAYABLE TO ORDER OR BEARER

The two most common words of negotiability are *order* and *bearer*. The instrument is payable to order when some person is made the payee, and the maker or drawer wishes to indicate that the instrument will be paid to the person designated or to anyone else to whom the payee may transfer the instrument by indorsement.

It is not necessary to use the word *order*, but it is strongly recommended. The law looks to the intention of the maker or the drawer. If the words used clearly show an intention to pay either the named payee or anyone else whom the payee designates, the contract is negotiable. A note payable to "Smith and assigns" was held to be nonnegotiable. If it had been payable to "Smith or assigns," it would have been negotiable.

However, there is an exception in the case of checks. Article 3 provides that a check reading "Pay to Smith" is negotiable. This applies only to checks and not to other drafts or notes.

The other words of negotiability, *payable to bearer*, indicate that the maker or the acceptor of a draft is willing to pay the person who possesses the instrument at maturity. The usual form in which these words appear is *Pay to bearer* or *Pay to Lydia Lester or bearer*. Other types of wording make an instrument a bearer instrument. For example, *pay to the order of cash*, and *pay to the order of bearer*, or any other designation that does not refer to a natural person or a corporation is regarded as payable to bearer.

PAYEE AND DRAWEE DESIGNATED WITH REASONABLE CERTAINTY

When a negotiable instrument is payable "to order," the payee must be so named that the specific party can be identified with reasonable certainty. For example, a check that reads "Pay to the order of the Treasurer of the Virginia Educational Association" is not payable to a specific named individual, but that person can be ascertained with reasonable certainty. Therefore, the check is negotiable. If, on the other hand, the check is payable "to the order of the Treasury of the Y.M.C.A." and the city has three such organizations, it would not be possible to ascertain the payee with reasonable certainty. This check would not be negotiable.

The drawee of a draft must likewise be named or described with reasonable certainty so that the holder will know who will accept or pay it.

Issue and Delivery

LO2
Issue and delivery requirements

Issue
First delivery of negotiable instrument by maker or drawer to give rights to another

Delivery
Intentional transfer of possession and control of something

A negotiable instrument written by the drawer or maker does not have any effect until it is "issued." The UCC defines **issue** as "the first delivery of an instrument by the maker or drawer . . . for the purpose of giving rights on the instrument to any person." By **delivery** is meant the intentional transfer of possession and control of something. So *issue* ordinarily means that the drawer or maker mails it or hands it over to the payee or does some other act that releases possession and control over it and sends it on its way to the payee. Whenever delivery is made in connection with either the original issue or a subsequent negotiation, the delivery must be absolute, as contrasted with conditional. If it is conditional, the issuing of the instrument or the negotiation does not take effect until the condition is satisfied; although, as against a holder in due course, a defendant will be barred from showing that the condition was not satisfied.

To negotiate order paper, it must be both indorsed by the person to whom the paper is then payable and delivered to the new holder. Bearer payer requires no indorsement, and negotiation is effected by a physical transfer of the instrument alone.

Delivery of an Incomplete Instrument

If a negotiable instrument is only partially filled in and signed before delivery, the maker or drawer is liable if the blanks are filled in according to instructions. If the holder fills in the blanks contrary to authority, the maker or drawer is liable to the original payee or an ordinary holder for only the amount actually authorized. A holder in due course, however, can enforce the paper according to the filled-in terms even though they were not authorized.

Facts: Joseph Fasano agreed to an investment which required him to execute a promissory note payable to International Dynergy, Inc. but with the date, principal amount, and dates of payment left blank. Fasano also executed a power of attorney that authorized Dynergy to complete the note if certain conditions occurred. The conditions did not occur, but Dynergy completed the note in the amount of $240,000 and sold it to Equilease Corporation. When Fasano did not pay the note, Equilease sued him.

Outcome: The court stated that a holder in due course, Equilease, could enforce the note even though Dynergy had improperly completed it.

Date and Place

LO3 Requirements of date and place

Various matters not of commercial significance do not affect the negotiable character of a negotiable instrument.

1. The instrument need not be dated. The negotiability of the instrument is not affected by the fact that it is undated, antedated, or postdated. The omission of a date may cause considerable inconvenience, but the date is not essential. The holder may fill in the correct date if the space for the date is left blank. If an instrument is due 30 days after date and the date is omitted, the instrument is payable 30 days after it was issued or delivered. In case of dispute, the date of issue may be proved.
2. The name of the place where the instrument was drawn or where it is payable need not be specified. For contracts in general, the law where the contract is made or where it is to be performed governs one's rights. This rule makes it advisable for a negotiable instrument to stipulate the place where it is drawn and where it is payable, but neither is essential for its negotiability.

Facts: By written agreement of May 6, David and Hazel Morrison loaned Shanwick International Corp. $25,000 for 60 days with $2,500 interest. On July 6, a written agreement extended the loan for 60 more days. Shanwick signed the agreement and attached a check for $27,500 postdated to September 6. The Morrisons also received a check for $2,500 postdated to July 12. Both checks were returned for insufficient funds and never paid. Morrison sued under the bad check statutes. Shanwick argued that the postdated checks were simply promises to pay and not negotiable instruments.

Outcome: The court held that postdated checks were fully negotiable instruments that had a demand date in the future.

Questions

1. State the seven requirements of negotiability.
2. Why must a signature be placed on a negotiable instrument?
3. Must the signature on a negotiable instrument be in the lower right-hand corner of the instrument?
4. Must a note contain the word *promise* in order to be negotiable?
5. The state signed a draft for $5,000 payable to Jenkins out of the Highway Trust Fund. Is the draft negotiable? Why or why not?

6 Must a negotiable instrument require payment in American dollars?
7 When the amount in words in an instrument conflicts with the amount in figures, is negotiability destroyed?
8 Must a negotiable instrument be dated and the location of payment be indicated?
9 What are the requirements for delivery of a negotiable instrument?
10 Explain the difference between negotiation of an instrument that is payable to order and one that is payable to bearer.

Case Problems

LO1 1 At his accountant's suggestion, Billy Huff invested in a limited partnership, Willow Creek Group, Ltd., as a tax shelter. Willow bought an apartment complex for $3.6 M by means of a $2.7 M mortgage and a $890,000 note. Willow then borrowed $1.05 M from Security Federal Savings & Loan which required all the partners to sign an agreement to pay the note and all future obligations of Willow if it defaulted. Willow defaulted and Security asked the partners to pay under the agreement. Huff refused to pay claiming he had been fraudulently induced to sign it. The other partners formed a new partnership called Guarantor Partners which bought the note and agreement from Security and sued Huff. He could raise the defense of fraudulent inducement if the agreement was not a negotiable instrument. Was it a negotiable instrument?

LO3 2 John Peragallo and his wife went to Vermont and bought a lot from Peter Sklat by executing two promissory notes. The Peragallos and Sklat were residents of Connecticut and the notes called for payment in Connecticut or "such other place as the holders hereof may direct." The notes specified 10.25 percent interest payable in advance, which was an effective rate of 12.11 percent. The Peragallos made no payments on the notes, so Sklat sued. In Connecticut the interest rate was usurious while in Vermont it was not. Thus the answer to which state's law applied to the notes determined whether they were enforceable. Did this problem destroy their negotiability?

LO2 3 On behalf of Nirmaco Corporation, Roger Khemlani ordered chemicals from Isaac Industries, Inc. to be shipped directly to a company in Jamaica. Khemlani gave Isaac two postdated checks in payment. Isaac shipped the chemicals and tried to cash the checks but payment had been stopped. Isaac discovered two other checks drawn on Florida National Bank payable to Isaac had been issued, but it never received them. Khemlani had had them and they had been deposited in Nirmaco's account at Southeast Bank. Isaac's indorsement had been forged. Isaac sued Florida National and Southeast claiming to be the payee of the checks. Did it have the rights of a payee?

LO1 4 Air Terminal Gifts, Inc. executed a $125,000 promissory note. The note stated it was secured by a separate agreement and, "Reference is made to the Purchase and Security Agreement for additional rights of the holder hereof." When sued for payment of the note, Air Terminal claimed the quoted language made it nonnegotiable. Decide this case.

LO2 5 Kathryn McCain was employed near a safety deposit box to which she and other employees had access at the front desk of a motel. Money ($110) was stolen from the safety deposit box, and McCain was investigated as a suspect. Following a polygraph test, McCain was fired. She went to the motel to pick up a payroll check due her and was told $110 was to be withheld from her wages, pending the results of the police investigation. While there, she saw her payroll check and refused a check for the amount of her wages less $110. After being refused a written demand for the payroll check, she filed suit, alleging wrongful conversion of her payroll check. Conversion requires the taking or a detention, interference, illegal assumption of ownership, or illegal use or misuse of property. Was there a wrongful conversion?

LO3 **6** S. Gentilotti wrote a check for $20,000 payable to the order of his son. It was postdated 15 years and delivered to the boy's mother. Before his death, Gentilotti frequently asked the mother if she had the check. After his death demand for payment was made and refused. The mother and son sued the executrix of Gentilotti's estate for payment of the check. Was it negotiable?

LO1 **7** All Ways, Inc. and its president, Gary Ross, purchased two motor vehicles from County Ford Lincoln Mercury by signing two installment contracts. County assigned the contracts to Ford Motor Credit Company. To pay for the vehicles, All Ways and Ross presented Ford with two "certified money orders." They stated that the sums of $20,500 and $25,200 were to be paid "On Demand, Money of Account of the United States, as required by law . . . of Coinage Act of 1792 . . . OR, in U.C.C.1-201(24) Credit Money." They further stated they were "REDEEMABLE AT FULL FACE VALUE WHEN PRESENTED To: O.M.B.; W.D. McCALL; P.O. Box 500-284; VICTORIA, TEXAS." Ford tried to deposit the documents in a bank, but they were returned as non-negotiable. Are they negotiable? Why or why not?

Internet Resources for Business Law

Name	Resources	Web Address
Uniform Commercial Code §3-103	The Legal Information Institute (LII), maintained by Cornell Law School, provides a hypertext and searchable version of UCC §3-103, Definitions.	http://www.law.cornell.edu/ucc/3/3-103.html
Uniform Commercial Code §3-108	LII provides a hypertext and searchable version of UCC §3-108, Payable on Demand or at Definite Time.	http://www.law.cornell.edu/ucc/3/3-108.html
Uniform Commercial Code §3-111	LII provides a hypertext and searchable version of UCC §3-111, Place of Payment.	http://www.law.cornell.edu/ucc/3/3-111.html
Uniform Commercial Code §3-105	The Legal Information Institute (LII), maintained by Cornell Law School, provides a hypertext and searchable version of §3-105, Issue of Instrument.	http://www.law.cornell.edu/ucc/3/3-105.html

22 Promissory Notes and Drafts

Learning Objectives

1. State the accountability of the maker and distinguish among the different types of notes.
2. Identify the two different kinds of drafts.
3. Explain how drafts are accepted and what admissions are made by acceptance.
4. Describe the characteristics of a check.

PREVIEW CASE

At about 3:30 Friday afternoon, Marcia Garcia purchased jewelry from Shaw's of San Antonio, Inc., by a check for $1,328.20 drawn on Groos National Bank. Before delivering the jewelry, Shaw's telephoned the bank and was told the check was good. On Saturday Garcia returned to Shaw's and tried to buy more jewelry. Finding out that the address Garcia used on her check was nonexistent, Shaw's became suspicious and sent an employee to the bank at 9 o'clock Monday when it opened for business. Garcia's account lacked enough money to pay the check. When Shaw's sued the bank for payment, the bank alleged it was not liable because it had not accepted the check. Had there been a proper acceptance? How must an acceptance be made?

Notes and drafts are negotiable instruments widely used in commercial and personal transactions. Each has unique features.

Notes

Any written promise to pay money at a specified time is a promissory note, but it may not be a negotiable instrument. To be negotiable, a note must contain the essential elements discussed in Chapter 21.

The two original parties to a promissory note are the maker, the one who signs the note and promises to pay, and the payee, the one to whom the promise is made.

ACCOUNTABILITY OF THE MAKER

The maker of a promissory note (1) expressly agrees to pay the note according to its terms, (2) admits the existence of the payee, and (3) warrants that the payee is competent to transfer the instrument by indorsement.

Facts: Thomas Sessions bought farm machinery from Charles McCarthy to use on the farms he owned and operated with his wife Dorothy. The Sessions signed a promissory note to McCarthy in the amount due on the machinery on February 8. Thomas Sessions died on March 31. McCarthy sued to collect on the note. Dorothy said she was not liable because Thomas purchased the machinery, not her, and Thomas was liable for the underlying debt.

Outcome: The court stated she was a maker of the note. As a maker, Dorothy contracted to pay the note according to its terms at the time she signed it and was liable to McCarthy.

TYPES OF NOTES

LO1 Types of notes

Many types of notes known by special names include:

1. Bonds
2. Collateral notes
3. Real estate mortgage notes
4. Debentures

Bond Sealed, written contract obligation with essentials of note

Bonds. A **bond** is a written contract obligation, usually under seal, generally issued by a corporation, a municipality, or a government, that contains a promise to pay a fixed amount of money at a set or determinable future time. In addition to the promise to pay, it will generally contain certain other conditions and stipulations. A bond issued by a corporation is generally secured by a deed of trust on the property of the corporation. A bond may be a coupon bond or a registered bond.

Coupon Bond Bond with detachable individual coupons representing interest payments

A **coupon bond** is so called because the interest payments that will become due on the bond are represented by detachable individual coupons to be presented for payment when due. Coupon bonds and the individual coupons are usually payable to the bearer; as a result, they can be negotiated by delivery. There is no registration of the original purchaser or any subsequent holder of the bond.

Registered Bond Bond payable to specific person, whose name is recorded by issuer

A **registered bond** is a bond payable to a named person. The bond is recorded under that name by the organization issuing it to guard against its loss or destruction. When a registered bond is sold, a record of the transfer to the new bondholder must be made under the name of the new holder of the bond.

Collateral Note Note secured by personal property

Collateral Notes. A **collateral note** is a note secured by personal property. The collateral usually consists of stock, bonds, or other written evidences of debt, or a security interest in tangible personal property given by the debtor to the payee-creditor.

The transaction may vary in terms of whether the creditor keeps possession of the property as long as the debt is unpaid or whether the debtor may keep possession of the property until default. When the creditor receives possession of collateral, reasonable care must be taken of it, and the creditor is liable to the debtor for any loss resulting from lack of reasonable care. If the creditor receives any interest, dividend, or other income from the property while it is held as collateral, such amount must be credited against the debt or returned to the debtor.

Regardless of the form of the transaction, the property is freed from the claim of the creditor if the debt is paid. If not paid, the creditor may sell the property in the manner prescribed by law. The creditor must return to the debtor any excess of the sale proceeds above the debt, interest, and costs. If the sale of the collateral does not provide sufficient proceeds to pay the debt, the debtor is liable for any deficiency.

Real Estate Mortgage Note
Note secured by mortgage on real estate

Real Estate Mortgage Notes. A **real estate mortgage note** is given to evidence a debt that the maker-debtor secures by giving to the payee a mortgage on real estate. As in the case of a real estate mortgage, generally the mortgagor-debtor retains possession of the property. If the real estate is not freed by payment of the debt, the holder may proceed on the mortgage or the mortgage note to enforce the maker-mortgagor's liability. Chapter 43 more thoroughly describes real estate mortgages.

Debenture
Unsecured bond issued by a business

Debentures. An unsecured bond or note issued by a business firm is called a **debenture**. A debenture, like any other bond, is nothing more or less than a promissory note, usually under seal. It may be embellished with gold-colored edges, but this does not in any way indicate its value. A debenture is usually negotiable in form.

Facts: Moxham National Bank loaned John and Anthony Horbal and Elaine Adams $120,000. The Horbals assigned a $25,000 CD to the bank. The assignment transferred all of the Horbals' right, title, and interest in the CD to the bank. The loan was not repaid, so the bank withdrew the CD and applied the proceeds to the loan balance. The Horbals assigned their causes of action against the bank to Highland Financial Limited and James Walsh, who sued the bank. The issue in the case was whether the CD was a negotiable instrument since if it was the bank was the holder and entitled to payment of it.

Outcome: The court held that the CD was a negotiable instrument since it was payable at an indefinite time and payable "to order."

Certificate of Deposit
Acknowledgment by bank of receipt of money with engagement to repay it

Certificates of Deposit. The UCC defines a **certificate of deposit** (CD) as "an acknowledgment by a bank that a sum of money has been received by the bank and a promise by the bank to repay the sum of money." The bank repays the sum to the person designated on the CD. Normally the money is repaid with interest. The UCC classifies a certificate of deposit as a note even though it does not contain the word *promise*. A CD is not a draft because it does not contain an order to pay.

Drafts

The drawer draws or executes a draft in favor of the payee, who has the drawer's authority to collect the amount indicated on the instrument. It must be clear that the signature is intended to be that of a drawer; otherwise the signature will be construed to be that of an indorser. A draft is addressed to the drawee, who is the person ordered by the drawer to pay the amount of the instrument. The drawee pays the amount to the payee or some other party to whom the payee has transferred the instrument by indorsement. The drawee, after accepting the instrument, that is, after agreeing to pay it, becomes the acceptor.

Inland Draft
Draft drawn and payable in the U.S.

An **inland**, or domestic, **draft** is one that shows on its face that it is both drawn and payable within the United States. A foreign draft shows on its face that it is drawn or payable outside the United States.

FORMS OF DRAFTS

LO2
Kinds of drafts

Two kinds of drafts exist to meet the different needs of business:

1 Sight drafts
2 Time drafts

Sight Draft
Draft payable upon presentation by holder

Sight Drafts. A **sight draft** is a draft payable at sight or upon presentation by the payee or holder. By it the drawer demands payment at once. Special types of sight drafts include money orders and checks.

Time Draft
Draft payable certain number of days or months after date or presentation

Time Drafts. A **time draft** has the same form as a sight draft except with respect to the date of payment. The drawer orders the drawee to pay the money a certain number of days or months after the date on the instrument or a certain number of days or months after presentation.

In the case of a time draft, the holder cannot require payment of the paper until it has matured. The holder normally presents the draft to the drawee for acceptance. However, whether or not the draft has been accepted does not affect the time when it matures if it is payable a certain length of time after its date.

A time draft payable a specified number of days after sight must be presented for acceptance. The due date is calculated from the date of the acceptance, not from the date of the draft.

TRADE ACCEPTANCE

Trade Acceptance
Draft drawn by seller on purchaser of goods

A **trade acceptance** is a type of draft used in the sale of goods. It is a draft drawn by the seller on the purchaser of goods sold and accepted by such purchaser. The drawer draws a trade acceptance at the time goods are sold. The seller is the drawer, and the purchaser is the drawee. A trade acceptance orders the purchaser to pay the face of the bill to the order of the named payee, who is frequently the seller.

PRESENTMENT FOR ACCEPTANCE

All trade acceptances and all time drafts payable a specified time after sight must be presented for acceptance by the payee to the drawee. In case of other kinds of drafts, presentment for acceptance is optional and is made merely to determine the intention of the drawee and to give the paper the additional credit strength of the acceptance. A qualified acceptance destroys the negotiability of the instrument. An acceptance could be qualified by adding additional terms such as "if presented for payment within 24 hours" or "in ten days from date."

Place. The instrument should be presented at the drawee's place of business. If there is no place of business, it may be presented at the drawee's home or wherever the drawee may be found.

Party. A draft must be presented to the drawee or to someone authorized either by law or by contract to accept it. If there are two or more drawees, the draft must be presented to all of them unless one has authority to act for them all.

PREVIEW CASE REVISITED

Facts: At about 3:30 Friday afternoon, Marcia Garcia purchased jewelry from Shaw's of San Antonio, Inc., by a check for $1,328.20 drawn on Groos National Bank. Before delivering the jewelry, Shaw's telephoned the bank and was told the check was good. On Saturday Garcia returned to Shaw's and tried to buy more jewelry. Finding out that the address Garcia used on her check was nonexistent, Shaw's became suspicious and sent an employee to the bank at 9 o'clock Monday when it opened for business. Garcia's account lacked enough money to pay the check. When Shaw's sued the bank for payment, the bank alleged it was not liable because it had not accepted the check.

Outcome: The court agreed, saying that an acceptance must be in writing and on the instrument.

FORM OF ACCEPTANCE

LO3 Acceptance procedure and admissions

The usual method of accepting a draft is to write on the face:

Accepted
Jane Roe.

The word *accepted* and the drawee's signature are all that are normally necessary to constitute a valid acceptance. If an acceptance on a sight draft does not include a date, the holder may supply the date. The drawee may use other words of acceptance, but the words used must indicate an intention to be bound by the terms of the instrument and must be written on the instrument.

If the drawee refuses to accept a draft or to accept it in a proper way, the holder of the draft has no claim against the drawee but can return the draft to the drawer. Any credit given the drawer by the delivery of the draft is thereby canceled. If the draft is a trade acceptance, the refusal of the drawee to accept means that the buyer refuses to go through with the financing terms of the transaction; unless some other means of financing or payment is agreed upon, the transaction falls through.

ADMISSIONS OF THE ACCEPTOR

A draft presented to a drawee for acceptance must be either accepted or returned. If not returned, the drawee is treated as having stolen the paper from the holder. By accepting the instrument, the drawee assumes liability for the payment of the paper. This liability of the acceptor runs from the due date of the paper until the statute of limitations bars the claim.

Facts: B. C. Dahl offered a check drawn on First State Bank of Rollingstone to Lou Hodnik, a supervisor of Greyhound Lines, in payment of a debt to Greyhound. Hodnik refused to take the check unless the bank confirmed that the funds were in the account. Dahl returned with the check signed by Duane Klein, vice president of the bank. Hodnik talked with Klein by phone. Klein assured him the money was in the bank. Hodnik took the check, which bounced. Greyhound sued First State.

Outcome: The court held that First State had accepted the check and had to pay it.

When the drawee accepts a draft, two admissions concerning the drawer are made:

1 That the signature of the drawer is genuine
2 That the drawer has both the capacity and the authority to draw the draft

The drawee, by accepting a draft, also admits the payee's capacity to indorse, but not the genuineness of the payee's indorsement.

Having made these admissions, the acceptor cannot later deny them against a holder of the instrument.

MONEY ORDERS

Money Order
Instrument issued by business indicating payee may receive indicated amount

A **money order** is an instrument issued by a bank, post office, or express company indicating that the payee may request and receive the amount indicated on the instrument. When paid for, issued, and delivered to the payee, the issuer has made a contract to pay.

Checks

LO4
Characteristics of checks

Check
Draft drawn on a bank and payable on demand

Chapter 20 mentioned that a **check** is a type of draft. To be a check, the draft must be drawn on a bank and payable on demand. It is a type of sight draft with the drawee, a bank, and the drawer, a depositor—a person who has funds deposited with a bank. Just like other drafts, a check is an order by the drawer, upon the drawee, to pay a sum of money to the order of another person, the payee.

The numbers at the bottom of a check (see Illustration 22-1) are printed in magnetic ink. The numbers identify the specific account and the bank that holds the account. Since the numbers are printed in magnetic ink, the check may be sorted by electronic data processing equipment. The Federal Reserve System requires that all checks passing through its clearinghouses be imprinted with such identifying magnetic ink. In most cases, however, the drawee bank will accept checks that do not carry the magnetic ink coding. In fact, the material upon which a check is written does not affect the validity of a check.

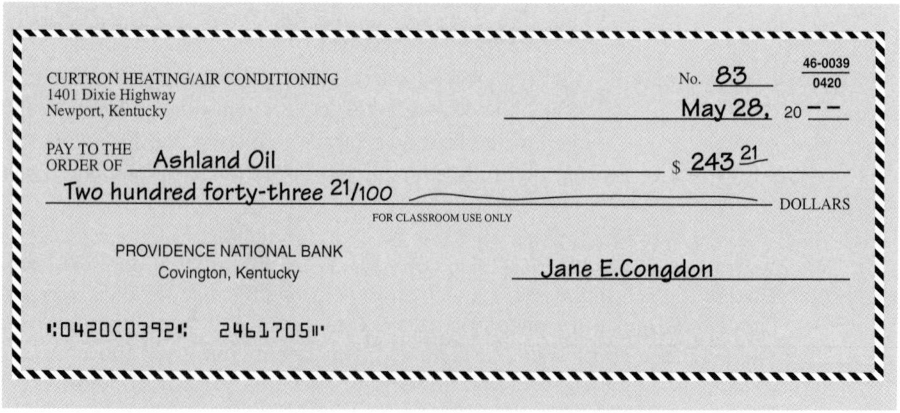

CURTRON HEATING/AIR CONDITIONING
1401 Dixie Highway
Newport, Kentucky

No. 83 46-0039/0420

May 28, 20--

PAY TO THE ORDER OF Ashland Oil $ 243 21

Two hundred forty-three 21/100 DOLLARS

FOR CLASSROOM USE ONLY

PROVIDENCE NATIONAL BANK
Covington, Kentucky

Jane E.Congdon

⑆0420C0392⑆ 24617O5⑈

Illustration 22-1
Check

SPECIAL KINDS OF CHECKS

Five special types of checks include:

1 Certified checks
2 Cashier's checks
3 Bank drafts
4 Voucher checks
5 Traveler's checks

Certified Check
Check accepted by bank's writing *certified* on it

Certified Checks. A **certified check** is an ordinary check accepted by an official of the drawee bank. The official accepts it by writing across the face of the check the word *certified*, or some similar word, and signing it. Either the drawer or the holder may have a check certified. The certification of the check by the bank has the same effect as an acceptance. It makes the bank liable for the payment of the check and binds it by the warranties made by an acceptor. A certification obtained by a holder releases the drawer from liability.

The drawer of a draft accepted by a bank is relieved of liability on the instrument. It does not matter when or by whom acceptance was obtained.

Facts: The Bank of New York certified a $60,000 check payable to Charles and Jean Thornton drawn by White Plains Hospital Medical Center. BNY later stopped payment on the check at the request of White Plains. The Thorntons then opened an account at Casco Bank and Trust Company using the check. BNY refused to pay the check because of the stop payment order. The Thorntons withdrew all the funds from the account at Casco, so Casco sued BNY.

Outcome: The court found that Casco was entitled to the $60,000 check amount.

Cashier's Check
Check drawn by bank on its own funds

Cashier's Checks. A check that a bank draws on its own funds and that the cashier or some other responsible official of the bank signs is called a **cashier's check**. It is accepted for payment when issued and delivered. A bank in paying its own obligations may use such a check, or it may be used by anyone else who wishes to remit money in some form other than cash or a personal check.

Bank Draft or Teller's Check
Check drawn by one bank on another

Bank Drafts. A **bank draft** or **teller's check** is a check drawn by one bank on another bank. Banks customarily keep a portion of their funds on deposit with other banks. A bank, then, may draw a check on these funds as freely as any corporation may draw checks. People purchase teller's checks because they rely on the bank's credit not an individual's. Also a purchaser of a teller's check has no right to insist that the issuing bank stop payment on a teller's check that is not payable to the purchaser. Thus, teller's checks are more readily accepted by payees than are personal checks.

Voucher Check
Check with voucher attached

Voucher Checks. A **voucher check** is a check with a voucher attached. The voucher lists the items of an invoice for which the check is the means of payment. In business the drawer of the check customarily writes on the check such words as *In full of account, For invoice No. 1622,* or similar notations. These notations make the checks excellent receipts when returned to the drawer. A check on which additional space is provided for the drawer to make a notation for which the check is issued is sometimes

Facts: Isabel Gonzales closed her accounts at New Haven Savings Bank and received two teller's checks payable to Isabel Rodriquez. The next day, New Haven received a notice of garnishment that the property of Isabel Gonzales was seized for collection of a debt. The notice did not mention anyone named Rodriquez. The Hospital of St. Raphael obtained a judgment against Gonzales and sued New Haven claiming that at the time of the notice the bank had owed Gonzales money. New Haven claimed it discharged its obligation to Gonzales when it issued the teller's checks, so when it received the notice it no longer owed her anything.

Outcome: The court agreed with New Haven saying that not only did it not owe Gonzales any money, but it could not have stopped payment on the teller's checks without being liable to the payee and possible future holders.

referred to as a voucher check. A payee who indorses a check on which a notation has been made agrees to the terms of the check, which include the terms written in the notation by the drawer.

Traveler's Checks. A traveler's check is an instrument much like a cashier's check of the issuer except that it requires signature and countersignature by its purchaser. Traveler's checks, sold by banks and express companies, are payable on demand. The purchaser of traveler's checks signs each check once at the time of purchase and then countersigns it and fills in the name of the payee when the check is to be used.

POSTDATED CHECKS

Postdated Check
Check drawn prior to its date

A check drawn prior to the time it is dated is a **postdated check**. If it is drawn on June 21, but dated July 1, it is, in effect, a 10-day draft. There is nothing unlawful about a postdated check as long as it was not postdated for an illegal or fraudulent purpose. A bank on which such a check is drawn may pay it before its date without liability unless the customer/drawer has properly notified the bank of the postdated check.

Facts: John McFadden presented a check for $395 drawn on United Bank and Trust to Midland Financial Services. McFadden had written his Midland savings account number on it and had crossed out the printed telephone number and written in a different number. Midland's teller did not notice the check was postdated and McFadden did not tell her it was postdated. The teller gave McFadden $395 for the check. After McFadden left, the teller checked his savings account and found it had $3 in it. She called United and found out McFadden's account had been closed five months before. Midland presented the check to United, which refused to pay it. The police arrested McFadden for theft for unlawfully giving a check in exchange for property while knowing the check would not be paid. McFadden argued the postdated check was not a check.

Outcome: The court held that a postdated check was a check and therefore McFadden had violated the theft law.

BAD CHECKS

www.state.ut.us

If a check is drawn with intent to defraud the payee, the drawer is civilly liable, as well as subject to criminal prosecution in most states under so-called bad check laws. A

Bad Check
Check the drawee bank refuses to pay

bad check is a check that the holder sends to the drawee bank and the bank refuses to pay, normally for insufficient funds. Usually these statutes state that if the check is not made good within a specific period, such as 10 days, a presumption arises that the drawer originally issued the check with the intent to defraud.

Facts: Alan Kolodkin leased real property to Amalgamated T-Shirts, Inc. As the president of Amalgamated, Stuart Cohen signed the lease. Kolodkin received a check signed by Cohen in the amount of $2,420 for the November rent on the 27th and he deposited it. The bank returned the check to Kolodkin for insufficient funds. Amalgamated's bank statements showed that at the end of October, the account had a balance of $690. No deposits were made in November or December.

Outcome: The court stated that Cohen's act of writing out a check for which Amalgamated's account did not have sufficient funds to cover made him liable.

DUTIES OF THE BANK

The bank owes several duties to its customer, the depositor-drawer. It must maintain secrecy regarding information acquired by it in connection with the depositor-bank relationship.

The bank also has the duty of comparing the signature on the depositor's checks with the signature of the depositor in the bank's files to make certain the signatures on the checks are valid. If the bank pays a check that does not have the drawer's signature, it is liable to the drawer for the loss.

Refusal of Bank to Pay. The bank is under a general contractual duty to its depositors to pay on demand all of their checks to the extent of the funds deposited to their credit. When the bank breaches this contract, it is liable to the drawer for damages. The bank must also pay checks that exceed the amount on deposit if there is an agreement that the bank will pay overdrafts. In the case of a draft other than a check, there is ordinarily no duty on the drawee to accept the draft or to make payment if it has not been accepted. Therefore, the drawee is not liable to the drawer when an unaccepted draft is not paid.

Even if the normal printed form supplied by the bank is not used, the bank must pay a proper order by a depositor. The bank must honor any written document that contains the substance of a normal printed check.

A divorced man making his last alimony payment wrote a check on a T-shirt to send a message to his ex-wife that she was taking "the shirt off his back." She did not care for the technique, but the T-shirt check was valid.

The liability of the drawee bank for improperly refusing to pay a check only runs in favor of the drawer. Even if the holder of the check or the payee may be harmed when the bank refuses to pay the check, a holder or payee has no right to sue the bank. However, the holder has a right of action against the person from whom the check was received. This right of action is based on the original obligation, which was not discharged because the check was not paid.

Stale Check
Check presented more than six months after its date

A check that is presented more than six months after its date is commonly called a **stale check**. A bank that acts in good faith may pay it. However, unless the check is certified, the bank is not required to pay it.

Stopping Payment. Drawers have the power of stopping payment of checks. After a check is issued, a drawer can notify the drawee bank not to pay it when presented for payment. This is a useful procedure when a check is lost or mislaid. A duplicate check can be written, and to make sure that the payee does not receive payment twice or that an improper person does not receive payment on the first check, payment on the first check can be stopped. Likewise, if payment is made by check and the payee defaults on the contract, payment on the check can be stopped, assuming that the payee has not cashed it.

A stop-payment order may be written or oral. The bank is bound by an oral stop-payment order only for 14 calendar days unless confirmed in writing within that time. A written order is effective for no more than six months unless renewed in writing (see Illustration 22-2 for a sample form).

Unless a valid limitation exists on its liability, the bank is liable for the loss the depositor sustains when the bank makes payment on a check after receiving proper notice to stop payment. However, the depositor has the burden of proving the loss sustained.

A depositor who stops payment without a valid reason may be liable to the payee. Also, the depositor is liable for stopping payment with respect to any holder in due course or other party having the rights of a holder in due course unless payment is stopped for a reason that may be asserted against such a holder as a defense. The fact that the bank refuses to make payment because of the drawer's instruction does not make the case any different from any other instance in which the drawee refuses to pay, and the legal consequences of imposing liability upon the drawer are the same.

When the depositor makes use of a means of communication such as the telegraph to give a stop-payment notice, the bank is not liable if the notice is delayed in reaching the bank and the bank makes payment before receiving the notice. The depositor can, however, sue the telegraph company if negligence on its part can be shown.

A payee who wants to avoid the potential of payment being stopped may require a certified check of the buyer or a cashier's check from the buyer's bank because neither the buyer nor the buyer's bank can stop payment to the payee on such checks.

Payment After Depositor's Death. Usually a check is ineffective after the drawer dies. However, until the bank knows of the death and has had a reasonable opportunity to act, the bank's agency is not revoked. A bank may even continue to pay or certify a depositor's checks for 10 days unless a person claiming an interest in the estate orders it to stop.

BANK CUSTOMER'S RESPONSIBILITY

While a bank has several duties to its customers, customers also have some important responsibilities. They must examine monthly bank statements and notify the bank "with reasonable promptness" of any forged signatures. If a customer fails to do this and the bank suffers loss as a result, the customer will be liable for the loss. "Reasonable promptness" is not defined, but the UCC provides that a customer who does not report an unauthorized signature or alteration within one year may not assert them against the bank. If there is a series of forgeries by the same person, the customer must discover and report the first forged check to the bank within the time prescribed by agreement between the customer and bank. If no such time is prescribed, it must be within 30 days of receiving the bank statement.

Using your Quicken Business Lawyer program, open this letter and complete it and the checklist that follows

Numerous Internet sites provide more information on stop-payment orders. Visit some of the following addresses, or look up the regulations in your own state.

http://www.state.me.us/ag/a_stop_pay_order.htm

http://www.courtinfo.ca.gov/courts/trial/smallclaims/stopchk.htm

http://www.law.cornell.edu/ucc/4/4-303.html

http://www.firstbankdecatur.com/legal/

SAMPLE

____

____

_______________, ___ _____

November 02, 2001

____

____

_______________, ___ _____

Dear Sir or Madam:

Please stop payment on the following check drawn on the account at _______________, account number _______________:

Check number: _______________
Payable to: _______________
Amount: $0.00
Signed by: _______________

This stop payment is being requested because the check is presumed lost and is being replaced.

I agree to pay your standard charge for this service. Please deduct the service charge from my account.

I agree that _______________ will not be liable if the information regarding the account number, amount, check number, or payee, as provided above, is incorrect.

I agree to hold _______________ harmless from any liability, costs, and expenses, arising from _______________'s refusal to pay this item.

I further agree to grant _______________ a reasonable time in which to act upon receipt of this stop-payment order. For the purpose of this letter, reasonable time is the next business day after the stop-payment order is received. If this check is paid on the banking day this order is received, the payment shall not constitute lack of good faith or failure to exercise ordinary care.

This written stop-payment order is effective for ___ month unless renewed.

Please contact me if you have any questions or need additional information.

Sincerely,

____

Illustration 22-2

Stop Payment on Check

Questions

1 Explain who the original parties to a promissory note are.
2 What is the difference among a bond, a collateral note, a real estate mortgage note, a debenture, and a certificate of deposit?
3 Who is the drawee of a draft and what is the drawee's responsibility?
4 What is the difference between sight drafts and time drafts?
5 Must all drafts be presented for acceptance?
6 How are drafts accepted?
7 When the drawee accepts a draft, what admissions are made concerning the drawer?
8 What is the difference between a check and a draft?
9 Why are bank drafts or teller's checks more readily accepted by payees than personal checks?
10 May a bank pay a postdated check before its date without incurring liability to the drawer?
11 What are three duties a bank owes its depositors?
12 How may a drawer stop payment on a check?

Case Problems

LO1 1 When Timothy Holloway was six years old, Rountree Crisp purchased a $20,000 certificate of deposit payable to "Timothy Holloway, by Rountree Crisp, Agent" from Wachovia Bank. After Crisp's death, Wachovia paid the proceeds of the CD to Marcia Coleman, Crisp's daughter and Timothy's mother, and Louise Crisp, Crisp's widow and Timothy's grandmother. They had indorsed the CD "Timothy Holloway by Estate of George Crisp, Marcia Coleman, Adminx., Louise Crisp, Adminx." Coleman put the proceeds into another CD in the name of "Timothy Holloway, by Marcia Coleman." Wachovia subsequently paid the check to Coleman. After Timothy became an adult he sued Wachovia. Should Wachovia be held liable?

LO4 2 Randall Stowell opened a checking account with Cloquet Co-op Credit Union, and he signed an agreement that required him to notify Cloquet of any errors in his account statement within 20 days of its mailing. Robert Nelson moved into a cabin the mailbox for which was next to Stowell's mailbox. The boxes were a half-mile from Stowell's house. For nine months after stealing some of Stowell's checks, Nelson forged Stowell's signature and cashed his checks. To hide the forgeries, Nelson also stole all the mail sent to Stowell from Cloquet. Stowell realized he had not received account statements from Cloquet, but when he called Cloquet and it sent duplicate statements, Nelson would steal them from the mailbox. Finally Stowell got a phone call from Finlayson State Bank at Barnum telling him a check written to Nelson had bounced and the thefts were discovered. Stowell sued Cloquet to recover the $22,000 paid on the forged checks. Should he recover? Explain.

LO2 3 National Bank of Austin sent North Valley Bank a letter authorizing North Valley to execute a sight draft on it for $75,000 within seven months. Based on that, North Valley loaned Donald Chambers $75,000 for six months. Chambers defaulted, so North Valley drew a draft on National for $75,000. The line for the signature of the drawer on the draft was blank; however, on the back was a stamp that said, "Pay to the Order of Any Bank, Banker or Trust Co. All Prior Endorsements Guaranteed. North Valley State Bank. . . ." Also on the back was the signature of the vice president of North Valley. National notified North Valley it would not honor the draft. North Valley sued. National alleged that the instrument was not a draft because it did not contain a proper signature of the drawer. Did it?

FOR VALUE AND IN GOOD FAITH

The law of negotiable instruments is concerned only with persons who give something for the paper. Thus, to attain the specially favored status of being a holder in due course, the holder must give value for the paper. Conversely, one who does not do so, such as a niece receiving a Christmas check from an uncle, cannot be a holder in due course. A mere promise does not constitute value.

The requirement that value be given in order to be a holder in due course does not mean that one must pay full value for a negotiable instrument. Thus, a person who purchases a negotiable contract at a discount can qualify as a holder in due course. The law states that it must be taken "for value and in good faith." If the instrument is offered at an exorbitant discount, that fact may be evidence that the purchaser did not buy it in good faith. It is the lack of good faith that destroys one's status as a holder in due course, not the amount of the discount.

If the payee of a negotiable instrument for $3,000 offered to transfer it for a consideration of $2,900, and the purchaser had no other reason to suspect any infirmity in the instrument, the purchaser can qualify as a holder in due course. The instrument was taken in good faith. If, on the other hand, the holder had offered to discount the note by $1,000, the purchaser could not take it in good faith because it should be suspected that there is some serious problem with the contract because of the large discount.

Often a purchaser pays for an instrument in cash and other property. An inflated value placed on the property taken in payment could conceal a discount large enough to destroy good faith. The test always is: Were there any circumstances that should have warned a prudent person that the instrument was not genuine and in all respects what it purported to be? If there were, the purchaser did not take it in good faith.

If the holder is notified of a problem with the instrument or a defect in the title of the transferor before the full purchase price has been paid, the holder will be a holder in due course to the extent of the amount paid before notification.

NO KNOWLEDGE THAT INSTRUMENT IS PAST DUE OR DISHONORED

One who takes an instrument known to be past due cannot be an innocent purchaser. However, a purchaser of demand paper on which demand for payment has been made and refused is still a holder in due course if the purchaser had no notice of the demand. A purchaser who has reason to know that any part of the principal is overdue, that an **uncured default** exists in payment of an instrument in the same series, or that acceleration of the instrument has been made has notice that the instrument is overdue. A note dated and payable in a fixed number of days or months shows on its face whether or not it is past due.

Uncured Default
Not all payments on instrument fully made and not all made by due date

Facts: Lionel and Maureen Bolduc executed notes to BankEast secured by a mortgage on condominiums. When the Bolducs had difficulty paying the notes, they executed an agreement with the bank which allowed them to put off paying the notes and granted BankEast "blanket" second mortgages on their home and other land. The Bolducs later defaulted on the notes and the holder foreclosed on the condominiums, but the sale did not pay off the notes. After the foreclosure the holder transferred the deficiency on the notes to Beal Bank. Beal tried to foreclose on the Bolduc's home and other land. The Bolducs raised a defense which could not be raised against a holder in due course.

Outcome: Since Beal Bank became a holder after foreclosure on the condominiums, it knew the notes had been dishonored and could not be a holder in due course.

An instrument transferred on the date of maturity is not past due but would be overdue on the next day. An instrument payable on demand is due within a reasonable time after issuance. For checks drawn and payable in the United States, 30 days is presumed to be a reasonable time.

NO KNOWLEDGE OF ANY DEFENSE OR CLAIM TO THE INSTRUMENT

Fiduciary
A person in relationship of trust and confidence

When one takes a negotiable instrument by negotiation, to obtain the rights of an innocent purchaser there must be no knowledge of any defense against or claim adverse to the instrument. Knowledge of a claim may be inferred if, for example, the holder knows that a **fiduciary** has negotiated an instrument in payment of a personal debt. As between the original parties to a negotiable instrument, any act, such as fraud, duress, mistake, or illegality, that would make a contract either void or voidable will have the same effect on a negotiable instrument. However, as will be seen in the next chapter, many of these defenses are not effective if the instrument is negotiated to an innocent purchaser.

Knowledge of other potential irregularities does not destroy holder in due course status. Knowing that an instrument has been antedated or postdated, was incomplete and has been completed, that default has been made in the payment of interest, or that it was issued or negotiated in return for an executory promise or accompanied by a separate agreement does not give a holder notice of a defense or claim.

Facts: Palmetto Leasing Company sued Winifred Crespo. Harry Chiles represented her and negotiated a settlement with Palmetto's attorney. The settlement required Crespo to pay Palmetto $9,000. Palmetto refused to accept an uncertified check or Crespo's check drawn on an out-of-state bank. The parties agreed that Chiles would write out a check from his trust account for $9,000, but that time would be needed to allow Crespo to get funds to Chiles to cover the check. Chiles wrote out the check and gave it to Palmetto, who held the check for six days. Palmetto then deposited the check, but the next day Chiles stopped payment on it because Crespo had not supplied the funds to cover it. Palmetto sued Chiles, alleging it was a holder in due course.

Outcome: The court held that Palmetto was not a holder in due course because it knew there was no consideration for the check when it took it.

Holder Through a Holder in Due Course

Holder Through a Holder in Due Course
Holder subsequent to holder in due course

The first holder in due course brings into operation all the protections that the law has placed around negotiable instruments. When these protections once accrue, they are not easily lost. Consequently, a subsequent holder, known as a **holder through a holder in due course**, may benefit from them even though not a holder in due course. For example, Doerhoff, without consideration, gives Bryce a negotiable note due in 60 days. Before maturity, Bryce indorses it to Cordell under conditions that make Cordell a holder in due course. Thereafter, Cordell transfers the note to Otke for no consideration. Otke is not a holder in due course, since she did not give any consideration for the note. But if Otke is not a party to any wrongdoing or illegality affecting this instrument, she acquires all the rights of a holder in due course. This is true because Cordell had these rights, and when Cordell transferred the note to Otke, he transferred all of his rights, which included his holder in due course rights.

Holders of Consumer Paper

LO4
Holders of consumer paper

Consumer Goods or Services
Goods or services primarily for personal, family, or household use

Setoff
A claim by the party being sued against the party suing

The UCC rules regarding the status of a holder in due course have been modified for holders of negotiable instruments given for consumer goods or services. **Consumer goods or services** are defined as goods or services for use primarily for personal, family, or household purposes. The changes resulted from both amendment to the UCC by the states—which means that the rules vary somewhat from state to state—and the adoption of an FTC rule.

Generally, the rights of the holder of consumer paper are subject to all defenses and setoffs of the original purchaser or debtor arising from the consumer transaction. A **setoff** is a claim a party being sued makes against the party suing. In the case of consumer sales, the FTC rule requires that consumer credit contracts contain specified language in bold print indicating that holders of the contracts are subject to all claims and defenses the debtor could assert against the seller. It means that no subsequent holder can be a holder in due course. The language is:

> NOTICE
>
> ANY HOLDER OF THIS CONSUMER CREDIT CONTRACT IS SUBJECT TO ALL CLAIMS AND DEFENSES WHICH THE DEBTOR COULD ASSERT AGAINST THE SELLER OF GOODS OR SERVICES OBTAINED PURSUANT HERETO OR WITH THE PROCEEDS HEREOF. RECOVERY HEREUNDER BY THE DEBTOR SHALL NOT EXCEED AMOUNTS PAID BY THE DEBTOR HEREUNDER.

The state laws generally make holder in due course rules inapplicable to consumer sales or limit the cutoff of consumer rights to a specified number of days after notification of assignment.

Normally these rights of the debtor are available only when the loan was arranged by the seller or lessor of the goods or was made directly by the seller or lessor. The state laws do not apply to credit card sales on a credit card issued by someone other than the seller. However, federal law allows a credit card holder to refuse to pay credit card issuers in some cases when an earnest effort at returning the goods is made or a chance to correct a problem is given the seller.

Modifying or abolishing the special status of a holder in due course for consumer goods prevents frauds frequently practiced upon consumers by unscrupulous businesspeople. Such individuals would sell shoddy merchandise on credit and immediately negotiate the instrument of credit to a bank or finance company. When the consumer discovered the defects in the goods, payment could not be avoided, because the new holder of the commercial paper had purchased it without knowledge of the potential defenses and was therefore a holder in due course. Further, the seller, who had frequently left the jurisdiction or gone bankrupt, was unavailable to be sued. Thus, the consumer would be unable to assert a defense or rescind the transaction against either the seller or the holder. The modifications based on changes to the UCC and adoption of the FTC rule have remedied this problem. A consumer who purchases goods that are not delivered or worthless can avoid paying more and recover what has been paid.

Allowing the consumer to have such rights against a holder who would otherwise be a holder in due course protects consumers who usually do not have knowledge of negotiable instrument laws. Normally a bank or finance company, which may buy many instruments from the seller, can more easily ascertain whether the seller is reliable than individual consumers can.

Facts: Rose and William Morgan bought a new car from Neponset Lincoln Mercury. To finance the car with Ford Credit, they signed a retail installment contract that contained the bold print language required by the FTC. The Morgans used the car for 18 months. They had such problems as water leaking into the trunk, a defective head gasket, rust, a misaligned hood, and when left unattended the transmission shifting into reverse from park so it would have to be shifted back to park to start it. They missed car payments. Ford got court approval to sell the car, but William delayed the sale for an inspection. By then the car had been vandalized and was worthless. Ford sued the Morgans for the amount due on the contract. They said the dealer had made false representations on which they had relied.

Outcome: The court agreed that the Morgans' defenses against the dealer could be raised against Ford.

Questions

1 On what basis does the UCC imposes liability on parties to negotiable instruments?
2 What constitutes a signature for purposes of liability for payment of a negotiable instrument?
3 What parties to commercial paper might be
   a. primarily liable?
   b. secondarily liable?
4 What conditions must be met in order for a party to be held secondarily liable?
5 When must presentment be made in order to be timely?
6 When does a dishonor occur?
7 When is notice of dishonor excused?
8 What two things must an agent do in order to escape personal liability?
9 What warranties are made by a transferor of commercial paper?
10 List the conditions that a person must meet to become a holder in due course.
11 What does it mean to take a negotiable instrument in good faith?
12 Is an instrument transferred on the date of maturity past due? Explain.
13 As between the original parties to a negotiable instrument, what is the effect of fraud, duress, mistake, or illegality?
14 What is the effect of the modification of UCC rules regarding the status of a holder in due course when a negotiable instrument has been given for consumer goods or services?

Case Problems

LO1 1 Laboratory Management, Inc. deposited a $150,000 check drawn on Texas American Bank/West Side (TAB/West Side) in its account at Pulaski Bank & Trust Company on February 5. Pulaski transmitted the check for collection. It was transferred through 2 banks and then to Texas American Bank/Fort Worth (TAB/Ft. Worth) which delivered it to a processing center on February 6. During processing the check was rejected and the center delivered notice of rejection to TAB/West Side. TAB/West Side gave TAB/Ft. Worth notice of dishonor on February 7. TAB/Ft. Worth misrouted the check and did not notify the prior holder of the dishonor until February 15. Pulaski did not receive notice of dishonor until February 22. By this time Laboratory had spent almost all the $150,000 from the check. Pulaski sued TAB/Ft. Worth and TAB/West Side. Should either bank be liable?

LO3 2 Janet Hollandsworth, an accountant for Dalton & Marberry, P.C., embezzled $130,000 by taking appropriately signed Dalton & Marberry checks payable to NationsBank and having the bank issue blank cashier's checks. Dalton & Marberry sued NationsBank for failing to inquire whether Hollandsworth was authorized to do this. The bank alleged it was a holder in due course and was therefore not liable for negligence. Was NationsBank a holder in due course?

LO4 3 Eugene Perez hired Perma-Stone to install siding, new windows, screen doors, and vents at his house. To finance the improvements, Perez signed a promissory note and retail improvement contract containing the FTC required language. Perma-Stone sold the note to Briercroft Service Corp. Several months later, the siding started to fall off the house, the new windows fell apart, the doors would not shut, and it was found the sewer vents stopped in the attic instead of going through the roof. Perez stopped paying on the note. In the resulting lawsuit, Briercroft said Perez was entitled only to a refund of the money he had paid but not to cancellation of the note. How should the court rule?

LO3 4 M-H Enterprises and Michael Holmes requested a loan from Brookwood National Bank to buy some real estate. To get the loan, Brookwood required M-H and Holmes to buy a title insurance policy on the property naming Brookwood as beneficiary. M-H and Holmes bought the property, signed a note to Brookwood, and gave it a mortgage. They also bought a title policy from American Title Insurance Co. with Brookwood as insured. A year later, a prior mortgage on the property, which American had failed to notice, was foreclosed. M-H and Holmes told Brookwood they would make no more payments on the note and asked it to file a claim with American. American learned this and paid the claim, so Brookwood assigned its note and mortgage to American. It sued M-H and Holmes for the balance on the note. To win, American had to be a holder in due course. Was it?

LO2 5 George Avery sent a letter to Jim Whitworth. Printed on the stationery was the name of Avery's employer, V & L Manufacturing Co., and the words *George Avery, President*. The letter stated, "This is your note for $45,000.00, secured individually and by our Company. . . ." Avery had signed the letter. V & L did not pay the entire $45,000, so Whitworth sued Avery. Avery said the stationery showed V & L was the debtor and he signed only in a representative capacity. Must Avery pay?

LO1 6 Eugene Weiss was an indorser on a promissory note for $20,000 made by a business associate. The terms of the note stated Weiss waived presentment, demand, notice, and all other demands related to performance, default, or enforcement of the note. After the note came due, the holder gave no notice to Weiss and spent several years trying to enforce payment against the maker. When that was unsuccessful, the holder finally sought payment from Weiss. Must Weiss pay?

LO4 7 Dan Lofing bought a grand piano from the Steinway dealer, Sherman Clay. Part of the purchase price was a note for $19,650, which included the FTC language limiting holder in due course rights. Music Acceptance Corp. (MAC) purchased the note from Clay. Lofing began to have serious problems with the piano, which Clay tried to fix many times, but after two years the piano was unplayable. Lofing stopped making payments on the note and MAC sued for the balance due. Lofing sued MAC and Clay. The jury awarded Lofing damages against Clay for breach of contract and MAC damages against Lofing on the note. Lofing appealed, saying that the FTC language meant that if he had a claim or defense against Clay, MAC would be subject to the same claim or defense. How should the case be decided?

LO2 8 Mestco Distributors sued Ralph Stamps for payment of four notes. The notes were signed as follows:

1. I.T.S. Inc.
   by Ralph W. Stamps
   Secty-Treas.
2. Ralph W. Stamps
   Secty-Treas. I.T.S. Inc.
3. Innovative Timber Specialties Inc.
   by Secty-Treas.
   Ralph W. Stamps
4. Ralph W. Stamps
   Innovative Timber Specialties, Inc.
   by: Secretary

Stamps argued that he executed the notes in a representative capacity. Decide whether Stamps executed each note as an agent or personally.

LO3 9 After making a loan, the Valley National Bank held an interest in all accounts, including checks, payable to Van Dyck Heating and Air Conditioning, Inc., but indorsed to a third party. Van Dyck was owned and operated by Shirley and Kenneth Horn. A loan was in default, but Valley allowed Van Dyck to operate for five months. Fred Couch, an IRS officer, contacted Kenneth Horn, because Van Dyck's federal tax payments were slow. Couch advised Horn to pay the taxes before other creditors to avoid civil and criminal penalties for delinquent tax payments. To avoid writing bad corporate checks to the IRS because of cash flow problems, Horn indorsed checks received from customers directly to the IRS. In accord with IRS policy, because Van Dyck's tax account was not classed as delinquent, no search for interests of others was made. Valley sued. Did the IRS take the checks in good faith?

LO1 10 Tours by Irene, Inc., signed a promissory note to Chemical Bank. Bernadetta Ciszewska signed a guaranty of the note, which stated, "[t]he undersigned hereby guarantees, absolutely and unconditionally, to the Bank the payment of all liabilities." Tours failed to pay the note, so Chemical sued Ciszewska. She claimed Chemical had to enforce the note against Tours first. Did Chemical have a valid suit against Ciszewska?

Internet Resources for Business Law

Name	Resources	Web Address
Uniform Commercial Code §3-302	LII provides UCC §3-302, Holder in Due Course.	http://www.law.cornell.edu/ucc/3/3-302.html
Uniform Commercial Code §3-501	LII provides a hypertext and searchable version of §3-501, Presentment.	http://www.law.cornell.edu/ucc/3/3-501.html
Uniform Commercial Code §3-503	LII provides a hypertext and searchable version of §3-503, Notice of Dishonor.	http://www.law.cornell.edu/ucc/3/3-503.html
Uniform Commercial Code §3-504	LII provides a hypertext and searchable version of §3-504, Excused Presentment and Notice of Dishonor.	http://www.law.cornell.edu/ucc/3/3-504.html

25 Defenses

Learning Objectives

1 State the chief advantage of being a holder in due course of a negotiable instrument.

2 Distinguish between limited and universal defenses to holders.

3 Explain the nature of hybrid defenses and list them.

PREVIEW CASE

James and Marie Estepp wanted to get a loan from United Bank and Trust Company of Maryland. United required an additional signature by an owner of real estate. Estepp brought Marvin Schaeffer to the bank, saying he needed Schaeffer, whose wife had died, to sign a character reference. Estepp supervised Schaeffer at work and had helped Schaeffer make funeral arrangements. Schaeffer had a learning disability and could not read or write. The bank officer handling the transaction did not explain to Schaeffer that he was assuming a financial responsibility. Schaeffer signed the note. The Estepps defaulted, so United sued Schaeffer. Did Schaeffer have an effective defense? What did the Estepps tell Schaeffer he needed to sign? Was this true?

When the holder of commercial paper is refused payment, a lawsuit may be brought. Chapter 24 discussed the parties liable for the payment of the face of the paper. What defenses can the defendant being sued raise? This question does not arise until it has first been determined that the plaintiff is the holder of the paper and that the defendant is a person who would ordinarily have liability for payment of the face of the paper. Assuming that those two questions have been decided in favor of the plaintiff, the remaining question concerns whether this defendant has a particular defense that may be raised.

Assume there are four successive indorsers and the holder who comes at the end of these four indorsers sues the first indorser. Can the first indorser raise against the holder a defense that the first indorser has against the second indorser? For example, can the defense be raised that the first indorser was induced by fraud to make the indorsement?

LO1

Advantage of being holder in due course

More commonly the situation will arise in which the remote holder sues the drawer of a check. The drawer then defends on the ground that the check had been given in payment for goods or services that the drawer never got, did not work, or were not satisfactory. Can the drawer now raise against the remote holder the defense that the drawer has against the payee of the check, namely, the defense of failure of consideration? The answer to this depends on the nature of the defendant's defense against the person with whom the dealings were made and the character of the holder. If the defense is a **limited defense** and the remote holder is a holder in due course, the defendant cannot raise such a defense. This is the chief advantage of being a holder in due course of a negotiable instrument. If the defense is a **universal defense** or the holder is an ordinary holder, the defendant may raise that defense.

Limited Defense
Defense that cannot be used against holder in due course

Universal Defense
Defense against any holder

Classification of Defenses

Certain defenses are limited to being raised against ordinary holders and cannot be raised against holders in due course. Limited defenses include:

1 Ordinary contract defenses
2 Fraud that induced the execution of the instrument
3 Conditional delivery
4 Improper completion
5 Payment or part payment
6 Nondelivery
7 Theft

LIMITED DEFENSES

LO2

Limited versus universal defenses

A significant number of defenses cannot be raised against a holder in due course or a holder through a holder in due course. Limited defenses, also called *personal defenses,* must be distinguished from universal ones.

Ordinary Contract Defenses. In general, the defenses available in a dispute over a contract may be raised only against holders who do not qualify as holders in due course. Accordingly, if a holder in due course holds the instrument, the defense of failure of consideration is not effective when raised by the maker who alleges that no consideration was received for the paper. In an action on an ordinary contract, the promisor may defend on the ground that no consideration existed for the promise; or that if consideration did exist in the form of a counterpromise, the promise was never performed; or that the consideration was illegal. Thus, if Smith agreed to paint Jones's house but did not do it properly, Jones would have a right of action against Smith for breach of contract, or Jones could refuse to pay Smith the price agreed upon. If Smith assigned the right to payment, Jones would be able to raise against the assignee the defenses available against Smith.

However, if Jones paid Smith by check before the work was completed, and the check was negotiated to a holder in due course, Jones could not defend on the ground of failure of consideration. The check would have to be paid. Jones's only right of action would be against Smith for the loss.

Facts: Louis Politis contracted to have Sverdrup Corp. build three buildings for him. After construction was completed and Politis had not paid, Politis signed a demand note for the amount owed Sverdrup. When Politis did not pay the note, Sverdrup sued. Politis alleged lack of consideration since he got nothing at the time he executed the note.

Outcome: The court pointed out that consideration for a negotiable instrument can be a previous debt. Sverdrup had given consideration.

Fraud That Induced the Execution of the Instrument. When a person knows a commercial paper is being executed and knows its essential terms but is persuaded or induced to execute it because of false representations or statements, this is not a defense against a holder in due course. For example, if Randolph persuades Drucker to buy a car because of false statements made by Randolph about the car, and Drucker gives Randolph a note for it that is later negotiated to a holder in due course, Drucker cannot defend on the ground that Randolph lied about the car. Drucker will have to pay the note and seek any recovery from Randolph.

Facts: Donald Mertens sold the personal property of a laundromat to Cliff Coffman, who sold it to Elna Phillips. The sale to Phillips was subject to a financing and security agreement between Mertens and Coffman that Phillips assumed and agreed to pay. Part of the security agreement included a promissory note. After Phillips went broke, Mertens sued for the balance on Coffman's note. Coffman had told Phillips that the business was profitable and the equipment in good working order, and Phillips relied on these representations. They were false. Phillips raised the defense of fraud in the inducement.

Outcome: The defense was good because Mertens was not a holder in due course. He was a creditor beneficiary of the Coffman-Phillips agreement.

Conditional Delivery. As against a holder in due course, an individual who would be liable on the instrument cannot show that the instrument, absolute on its face, was delivered subject to an unperformed condition or that it was delivered for a specific purpose but was not used for it. If Sims makes out a check for Byers and delivers it to Richter with instructions not to deliver it until Byers delivers certain goods, but Richter delivers it to Byers, who then negotiates it to a holder in due course, Sims will have to pay on the check.

Improper Completion. If any term in a negotiable instrument is left blank, for example, the payee or the amount, and the drawer then delivers the instrument to another to complete it, the drawer cannot raise the defense of improper completion against a holder in due course. In this case, the holder in due course may require payment from the drawer.

Payment or Part Payment. Upon payment of a negotiable instrument the party making the payment should demand the surrender of the instrument. If not surrendered, the instrument may be further negotiated, and a later holder in due course would be able to demand payment successfully. A receipt is not adequate as proof of payment, because the subsequent holder in due course would have no notice of the receipt, whereas surrender of the instrument would clearly prevent further negotiation.

If only partial payment is made, a holder would not and should not be expected to surrender the instrument. In such a case the person making the payment should note the payment on the instrument, thereby giving notice of the partial payment to any subsequent transferee.

Nondelivery. Normally, a negotiable instrument fully or partially completed but not delivered to the payee is not collectible by the payee. However, if a holder in due course holds the instrument, payment of it may be required. For example, if one person makes out a note to another person and that other person takes the note from the maker's desk without the maker's permission and negotiates the note to an innocent purchaser, or holder in due course, the holder in due course would be entitled to recover the amount of the note against the maker. This applies in spite of the nondelivery of the note.

Theft. A thief may not normally pass good title; however, an exception occurs when the thief conveys an instrument to a holder in due course. Such a purchaser will be able to enforce the obligation in spite of the previous theft of the paper. The thief or any ordinary holder cannot require payment of stolen paper.

UNIVERSAL DEFENSES

Those defenses thought to be so important that they are preserved even against a holder in due course are called universal or *real.* Universal defenses can be raised regardless of who is being sued or who is suing. Thus, they can be raised against the holder in due course as well as an ordinary holder. The more common universal defenses include:

1 Minority
2 Forgery
3 Fraud as to the nature of the instrument or its essential terms
4 Discharge in bankruptcy proceedings

Minority. The fact that the defendant is a minor capable of avoiding agreements under contract laws is a defense that may be raised against any holder.

Forgery. Except in cases where the defendant's negligence made the forgery possible, forgery may be raised successfully against any holder. However, a forged signature operates as the signature of the forger in favor of a holder in due course.

Fraud as to the Nature of the Instrument and Its Essential Terms. The defense that one was induced to sign an instrument when one did not know that it was in fact commercial paper is available against any holder. For example, an illiterate person told that a note is a receipt and thereby induced to sign it may successfully raise this defense against any holder. The defense is not available, however, to competent individuals who negligently fail to read or give reasonable attention to the details of the documents they sign.

Discharge in Bankruptcy Proceedings. Even holders in due course are subject to the defense that a discharge in bankruptcy has been granted.

PREVIEW CASE REVISITED

Facts: James and Marie Estepp wanted to get a loan from United Bank and Trust Company of Maryland. United required an additional signature by an owner of real estate. Estepp brought Marvin Schaeffer to the bank, saying he needed Schaeffer, whose wife had died, to sign a character reference. Estepp supervised Schaeffer at work and had helped Schaeffer make funeral arrangements. Schaeffer had a learning disability and could not read or write. The bank officer handling the transaction did not explain to Schaeffer that he was assuming a financial responsibility. Schaeffer signed the note. The Estepps defaulted, so United sued Schaeffer.

Outcome: The court found fraud existed as to the nature and essential terms of the note.

LO3 Hybrid defenses

HYBRID DEFENSES

Several defenses may be either universal or limited depending on the circumstances of a case. These include:

1 Duress
2 Incapacity other than minority
3 Illegality
4 Alteration

Duress. Whether or not duress is a valid defense against a holder in due course depends upon whether the effect of such duress under the state law makes a contract void or voidable. When the duress nullifies a contract, the defense is universal. When the duress merely makes the contract voidable at the option of the victim of the duress, the defense is limited.

Incapacity Other Than Minority. In cases of incapacity other than minority, if the effect of the incapacity makes the instrument void, a nullity, the defense is universal. If the effect of the incapacity does not make the instrument a nullity, the defense is limited.

Illegality. The fact that the law makes certain transactions illegal gives rise to a defense against an ordinary holder. Such a defense would be unavailable against a holder

Facts: William and Janet Westervelt executed a note to Gateway Financial Service for a loan secured by a mortgage on their house. Gateway required the Westervelts to obtain credit life insurance. The premium was deducted from the loan, but never sent to the insurance company. The state's Secondary Mortgage Loan Act (the act) governed the transaction. Gateway sold the note to Security Pacific Finance Corp. The Westervelts sued Gateway and Security to have the note declared void and unenforceable. The act prohibited requiring credit life insurance and provided that "any obligation . . . shall be void and unenforceable unless . . . executed in full compliance with the provisions of this act."

Outcome: The court held that the UCC provision subjecting a holder in due course to a defense of illegality that made the obligation a "nullity" applied here.

in due course unless the law making the transaction illegal also specifies that instruments based upon such transactions are unenforceable.

Alteration
Unauthorized change or completion of negotiable instrument to modify obligation of a party

Alteration. The UCC defines an **alteration** as "an unauthorized change in an instrument that purports to modify in any respect the obligation of a party, or . . . an unauthorized addition . . . to an incomplete instrument." When an alteration is fraudulently made, the party whose obligation is affected by the alteration is discharged. A payor bank or a drawee who pays a fraudulently altered instrument, or a person who takes it for value in good faith and with no notice of the alteration may enforce the instrument according to its original terms or to its terms as completed.

Facts: Milton Turner and his companies had executed promissory notes to United American Bank. Jacob Butcher, president of UAB, told Turner UAB was being audited and Turner needed to sign a guaranty for one of his company's files. Turner signed a guaranty form that had blanks for the name of the debtor and the amount of the guaranty. As part of Butcher's fraud, the name Lovell Road Properties Limited Partnership was put in as the debtor and the amount as $2 million. UAB's name, which was printed on the form, was erased with correction fluid and replaced with City and County Bank (CCB). Turner had no connection with Lovell or CCB and no knowledge of the improper completion or alteration. A holder in due course acquired Lovell's notes and the altered guaranty and sued Turner.

Outcome: The court said Turner was not liable.

Miscellaneous Matters

http://
www.allbusiness.com

In addition to the defenses described above, remember that every lawsuit presents certain standard problems. Any defendant may, under appropriate circumstances, raise the defense that the suit is not brought in the proper court, that no service of process existed, or that the statute of limitations has run and bars suit. Any defendant in a suit on a negotiable instrument can claim that the instrument is not negotiable; that the plaintiff is not the holder; and that the defendant is not a party liable for payment of the paper. If the holder claims that the defendant is secondarily liable for the payment of the face of the paper, the defendant may also show that the paper had not been properly presented to the primary party and that proper notice of default had not been given to the secondary party.

Questions

1 What is the difference between a limited defense and a universal defense?
2 When is there fraud in the execution of an instrument?
3 Why is it better to demand surrender of an instrument when paid rather than just give a receipt?
4 May a thief convey good title to an instrument?
5 Explain the circumstances under which forgery is a successful defense.
6 When does fraud as to the nature of the instrument and its essential terms occur?
7 Which defenses may be either universal or limited?
8 What is the effect upon a holder in due course if the instrument was not completed or delivered by the maker thereof but was subsequently filled in, naming an inappropriate party as payee and specifying an unduly large sum?

9 How can one know whether duress is a valid defense against a holder in due course?
10 What is the effect of an alteration on the rights of a holder in due course?

Case Problems

LO2 1 In order to pay for half the medical bill for alcohol and drug abuse treatment for David Thomas, Myles and Theresa Bryant executed a promissory note payable to Jerald Thomas. Theresa was David's mother, Myles his stepfather and Jerald Thomas was David's father. While Myles had no legal duty to pay for the treatment, he voluntarily signed the note because David was his friend. When sued for payment of the note, Myles alleged there was no consideration for the note. Was there consideration?

LO3 2 A group organized Evergreen Valley Nurseries Limited Partnership to acquire and raise nursery stock. One of the organizers purchased nursery stock for $4.2 M and two months later sold 91 percent of it to Evergreen for $10.4 M. Evergreen financed this purchase by offering limited partnership units which Roland Algrant and others purchased for $70,000 cash and $80,000 in promissory notes. After an IRS investigation Evergreen admitted in writing that it had overvalued the nursery stock. Algrant and the other limited partners obtained a copy of the writing on October 11. More than two years later, on November 16, they sued the organizers of Evergreen asking the court to declare that the promissory notes could not be enforced. The statute of limitations for an action based on fraud or deceit was two years. Can the notes be enforced?

LO1 3 Troy Garrison Sr. sued his son, Troy Jr., and daughter-in-law, Erika Garrison, on a note they had signed in the amount of $96,000. Erika alleged that she had never received any money from Troy Sr. She stated it had been given to Troy Jr. as a gift and they had only signed the note so Troy Sr. would have it for tax purposes. What defense did Erika allege? Discuss its effectiveness against various types of holders.

LO3 4 Marilyn Stephens signed a promissory note in favor of East Texas State Bank of Buna secured by a mortgage on the property on which she resided. When the bank failed, the Federal Deposit Insurance Corporation (FDIC) was appointed the receiver. FDIC tried to collect the note. Stephens argued that although FDIC was a holder in due course, it could not enforce the note because the mortgage violated the Texas constitution. Under Texas law the lien on the homestead was void. What should the court decide?

LO1 5 Raejean and Robert Stotler bought a lot from SilverCreek Development Company. They signed a promissory note in payment. SilverCreek assigned the note to Geibank Industrial Bank. SilverCreek went bankrupt, and the Stotlers defaulted on the note. In the ensuing lawsuit, the Stotlers alleged that they were induced to buy the lot and sign the note on the basis of false representations that SilverCreek would develop the surrounding property with condominiums, a golf course, and a Western theme park. The court said Geibank was a holder in due course. Are the Stotlers' allegations good against Geibank?

LO2 6 At a meeting with an old friend, Leroy Burch signed a promissory note in payment of an investment in a limited partnership. The partnership indorsed the note to Ingersoll-Rand Financial Corporation (IRFC), which became a holder in due course. Burch made only three payments on the note, so IRFC sued him. IRFC produced a note purportedly signed by Burch. The signature was not the same as Burch's signature. Burch claimed the note was not the one he signed and he had authorized no one else to sign for him. IRFC moved for judgment as a holder in due course based on the note it produced. Should the court grant its motion?

LO3 7 Iris Perry and her former husband executed two promissory notes to Norton Operating Services, Inc. for loans totaling $70,000. The loan money was deposited in the account of a liquor store owned by Perry's former husband. When sued for payment of the notes, Perry argued they were void as to her since her ex-husband had physically abused her and he had coerced her into signing the notes. She stated that Michael Klosk, the president of Norton, knew she had been beaten and threatened with further abuse if she did not sign the notes. Under state law duress made a contract void. Does Perry have a valid defense?

Internet Resources for Business Law

Name	Resources	Web Address
Legal Information Institute—Negotiable Instrument Law Materials	LII provides an overview of negotiable instruments law, federal and state statutes and regulations, and federal and state court decisions.	http://www.law.cornell.edu/topics/negotiable.html
Uniform Commercial Code §3-305	LII provides UCC §3-305, Defenses and Claims in Recoupment.	http://www.law.cornell.edu/ucc/3/3-305.html

Part 5 Summary Cases

Negotiable Instruments

1 Getty Petroleum Corporation sold gasoline and products through dealer-owner stations. When a station customer paid with a credit card, the credit card company paid Getty which then issued a check payable to the dealer for the sales. Getty did not intend many of the checks for the payees since it voided them and credited the amount toward the dealers' future gasoline purchases. Lorna Lewis had the job of voiding the checks. She stole 130 checks, forged indorsements of the dealers and sent the checks to American Express to pay her credit card debt. After Getty discovered Lewis' theft it sued American Express. Should American Express bear the loss as a result of the forged indorsements? [*Getty Petroleum Corp. v. American Exp.*, 660 N.Y.S.2d 689 (N.Y. Ct.App.)]

2 James Spolyar was a general partner of Plantation Oaks, a limited partnership. Spolyar met with Jerry Lutz and told him Plantation needed to sell one to three partnership units to purchase an apartment complex. He promised to buy back any units Lutz purchased. Four days later Lutz received documents including a note that recited that it constituted part of Lutz's purchase price of units in Plantation. Lutz signed the note, which stated a promise to pay and listed a schedule of payments totaling $69,308. Lutz returned the note to Spolyar, who indorsed it to European American Bank in return for a loan and a guarantee from Northwestern National Insurance Company. However, after the promise to pay $69,308 someone had handwritten a caret (^) and the words "per unit" and below the payment schedule "$69,308 x 3 units = $207,924." Lutz did not pay the note. Northwestern paid European the amount for 3 units and then sued Lutz. How much, if anything must Lutz pay? [*Northwestern Nat. Ins. Co. of Milwaukee v. Lutz*, 71 F. 3d 671 (7th Cir.)]

3 Dallas County State Bank sold a personal money order on a forged check. It then stopped payment on the money order and refused to accept and pay it when Northpark National Bank of Dallas presented it. The money order had a checkwriting imprint, "Dallas County State Bank," as well as the name of the bank printed on it. Northpark sued for payment. Dallas alleged it was not liable on the money order since its signature did not appear on it. Was it liable? [*Interfirst Bank Carrollton v. Northpark National Bank of Dallas*, 671 S.W.2d 100 (Tex. Ct. App.)]

4 George Weast borrowed $140,000 from State National Bank of Maryland (SNB), and his wife, Ruth, cosigned for him. This debt later was in default, so George indorsed and delivered some notes made by Francis and Josephine Arnold and Randall Co. to the order of SNB. Payments were made on these notes for several years before default. Ruth and George got divorced. When Ruth paid off the amount owed on their debt, SNB indorsed the notes of the Arnolds and Randall to Ruth. She sued them for payment on the notes. They alleged she was subject to a defense regarding the transaction that gave rise to the notes. Ruth claimed to be a holder through a holder in due course, so the defense would not be valid against her. Was Ruth a holder through a holder in due course when the notes had been indorsed to her after default? [*Weast v. Arnold*, 474 A.2d 904 (Md.)]

5 Public Relations Enterprises, Inc., paid Melco Products Corporation for goods by means of personal money orders purchased from Nassau Trust Company and Republic National Bank of New York. When Melco presented them for payment, the banks dishonored them on the ground that Public had stopped payment. Melco sued the banks for payment, alleging that the banks had no right to stop payment on the personal

money orders. Did they? [*Melco Products Corp. v. Public Relations Enterprises, Inc.*, 460 N.Y.S.2d 466 (N.Y. Sup. Ct.)]

6 Jacobson, Inc., sued Walter Burris personally on a charge account. The application for the charge account indicated Oak Tree Homes as the applicant, but at the end Walter Burris signed it with no indication that it was signed by other than him individually. At trial the judge entered judgment against Burris, relying on a law that referred to negotiable instruments. Was this the proper law to rely upon? [*Burris v. Jacobson, Inc.*, 417 So.2d 787 (Fla. Dist. Ct. App.)]

7 Berry executed a promissory note payable to William C. Stepp. The note was in perfect order. Stepp indorsed the note before maturity as follows: "I hereby transfer my right to this note over to W. E. McCullough. (signed) William C. Stepp." The maker failed to pay the note, and McCullough brought suit against Stepp, the indorser. Stepp's defense was that the indorsement was a qualified indorsement, and therefore he was not liable, since the maker's only reason for not paying was insolvency. Was this a qualified indorsement? [*McCullough v. Stepp*, 85 S.E.2d 159 (Ga. Ct. App.)]

8 Blas Garcia told Arthur and Lucy Casarez he was a representative of Albuquerque Fence Company, so they contracted with the company to build a home for them. Blas introduced them to Cecil Garcia, who said he would make a loan for the home. The Garcias were in no way affiliated with Albuquerque. Cecil got a $25,000 loan from Rio Grande Valley Bank in the form of a cashier's check. The Casarezes signed a note, and Cecil indorsed the check: "Pay to the order of Lucy N. Casarez, Cecil Garcia." Lucy indorsed it: "Pay to the order of Albuquerque Fence Co., Lucy N. Casarez." She handed the check to Blas, who indorsed the check: "Alb. Fence Co." Cecil signed his own name under that and presented the check to Rio Grande in return for $5,000 and four cashier's checks for $5,000. The Casarezes sued Rio Grande, alleging the words "Pay to the order of Albuquerque Fence Co." constituted a special indorsement and the check could be negotiated only by indorsement by an authorized official of the company. Was this a valid assertion? [*Casarez v. Garcia*, 660 P.2d 598 (N.M. Ct. App.)]

9 South Carolina Insurance Company issued a draft to Kevlin Owens drawn on the account of Seibels, Bruce Group at South Carolina National Bank. Owens negotiated the draft to First National Bank of Denham Springs, which paid him the entire amount and delivered it to South Carolina National Bank. The insurance company alleged fraud in Owens's claim and issued a stop-payment order. South Carolina National Bank did not honor the draft. The draft stated it was payable as follows: "Upon acceptance, pay to the order of Kevlin Owens." South Carolina Insurance Company was a wholly owned subsidiary of Seibels, Bruce Group. Therefore, South Carolina was both drawer and drawee. First National sued South Carolina for payment. South Carolina said the words upon acceptance made the draft conditional, therefore the draft was not negotiable; First National was not a holder in due course; and the defense of fraud could be raised. Was the draft conditional? [*First National Bank of Denham Springs v. South Carolina Insurance Company*, 432 So. 2d 417 (La. Ct. App.)]

10 Mr. Schafer, the chief operating officer of The Heights Bank, called Clifford Lee, told him he needed a favor, and asked him to come to the bank. Schafer asked Lee to cosign a note with Gordon, Lee's brother-in-law. Lee refused. Schafer told Lee the note was fully secured by a $10,000 bond and showed Lee a copy of the security agreement. Lee asked why he was needed if the loan was secured. Schafer said it would help him with the bank examiners. Schafer stated, "You've made a loan request and I am going to help you out, too." After deliberating, Lee agreed to cosign. Three months later Lee was told Gordon's note was in default. Lee told Schafer to sell the bond. Schafer told him there was none. The bank told Lee if he did not pay the Gordon note, it would ruin Lee's excellent credit rating. Lee paid the note and sued the

bank for reimbursement. Was the bank guilty of fraud in the inducement? [*Lee v. Heights Bank*, 446 N.E.2d 248 (Ill. App. Ct.)]

11 Omega Electronics, Inc., executed a promissory note to the order of State Bank of Fisk. Two officers of the corporation signed on the front and five individuals signed on the back. The note stated: "We, the makers, . . . endorsers and guarantors of this note, hereby severally waive presentment for payment, notice of nonpayment, protest and notice of protest." When the note was not paid, the bank sued the individuals. They alleged they were not liable because they had not been given notice of dishonor and protest. Were they liable? [*State Bank of Fisk v. Omega Electronics, Inc.*, 634 S.W.2d 234 (Mo. Ct. App.)]

Part 6 Agency and Employment

http://www.acinet.org

Employees and employers have rights and duties to each other. Many are covered in the chapters in this part. There are many sources of information on and assistance in maintaining employee/employer rights, including the Department of Labor, and the U.S. Equal Employment Opportunity Office. In addition to state employment offices, the DOL's *America's Career Infonet* is a resource for jobs, and their Web site is at http://www.acinet.org.

26 Nature and Creation of an Agency

Learning Objectives

1 Explain the nature of an agency and identify the parties involved.

2 Describe the different classifications of agents and the corresponding authority of each.

3 Discuss how an agency is usually created.

4 Distinguish between an agency and independent contractor or employer-employee relationships.

PREVIEW CASE

Because he did not want his daughter to inherit his home, George Pittman executed a power of attorney giving his wife, Rose, authority to make real property transactions "including the power to transfer the real estate known as the homeplace that I inherited from my mother." At George's directions, Rose executed a deed to the homeplace on behalf of George to Dessie Gaskill and Alice Durham. Gaskill and Durham paid George nothing. After George died, his daughter sued them claiming Rose did not have express authority to make a gift of the real estate since the law does not favor the power to make a gift. What does the word *transfer* mean? What was George's purpose in executing the power of attorney?

LO1
Nature of agency

Principal
Person who appoints another to contract with third parties

When one party, known as a **principal**, appoints another party, known as an **agent**, to enter into contracts with third parties in the name of the principal, a contract of agency is formed. By this definition every contract that an agent negotiates involves at least three parties, the principal, the agent, and the third party. It is this making of contracts with third persons on behalf of the principal that distinguishes an agency from other employment relationships. The principal, the agent, or the third party may be an individual, a partnership, or a corporation.

Importance of Agency

Agent
Person appointed to contract on behalf of another

Because of the magnitude and complexity of industries, many of the important details pertaining to business transactions must be delegated by the owners of businesses to agents. The general principles of law pertaining to contracts govern the relation creating this delegation of powers.

Even in the performance of routine matters by individuals, agents are necessary in order to bring one person into a business contractual relationship with other persons. Thus, a farmer who sends an employee to town to have a piece of machinery repaired gives the employee the authority to enter into a contract that binds the farmer to the agreement.

What Powers May Be Delegated to an Agent?

ETHICAL POINT
Would it be ethical for a person to try to do something that could not be done personally through an agent?

As a general rule, a person may do through an agent all of those things that could otherwise be done by the person. However, the courts will not permit certain acts of a personal nature to be delegated to others. Some of these acts that may not be performed by an agent include voting in a public election, executing a will, or serving on a jury.

What one may not lawfully do may not be done through another. Thus, no person can authorize an agent to commit a crime, to publish a libelous statement, to perpetrate a fraud, or to do any other act judged illegal, immoral, or opposed to the welfare of society.

Facts: Robert Miner, a prisoner serving a life sentence, applied to participate in a department of corrections family reunion program, claiming he was legally married. Under state law, a person serving a life sentence was considered civilly dead. Miner had executed a document appointing Michael Foster his agent for the purpose of entering into a proxy marriage, which Foster had done.

Outcome: The court held that Miner was not legally married. As a civilly dead person, he could not lawfully marry. Since he could not marry, Miner could not appoint an agent to enter into that relationship on his behalf.

Who May Appoint an Agent?

All people legally competent to act for themselves may act through an agent. This rule is based upon the principle that whatever a person may do may be done through another. Hence corporations and partnerships, as well as individuals, may appoint agents.

The contract by which a minor appoints an agent to act for the minor is normally voidable. Some states, however, find such contracts void, not voidable.

Who May Act as an Agent?

Ordinarily, any person who has sufficient intelligence to carry out a principal's orders may be appointed to act as an agent. The law does not impose this requirement. It arises from the practical consideration of whether the principal wants to have the particular person act as agent. Corporations and partnerships may act as agents.

An agent cannot perform some types of transactions without meeting certain requirements. For example, in many states a real estate agent must possess certain definite qualifications and must, in addition, secure a license to act in this capacity. Failure to do this disqualifies a person to act as an agent in performing the duties of a real estate agent.

Classification of Agents

LO2
Agent classification and authority

Agents may be classified as:

1 General agents
2 Special agents

GENERAL AGENTS

General Agent
Agent authorized to carry out particular kind of business or all business at a place

A **general agent** is one authorized to carry out the principal's business of a particular kind or all the principal's business at a particular place even though not all of one kind. Examples of general agents who perform all of the principal's business of a particular kind include a purchasing agent and a bank cashier. A general agent who transacts all of the principal's business at a particular place includes a manager in full charge of one branch of a chain of shoe stores. A general agent buys and sells merchandise, employs help, pays bills, collects accounts, and performs all other duties. Such an agent has a wide scope of authority and the power to act without express direction from the principal.

A general agent has considerable authority beyond that expressly stated in the contract of employment. In addition to express authority a general agent has that authority that one in such a position customarily has.

SPECIAL AGENTS

Special Agent
Agent authorized to transact specific act or acts

A **special agent** is one authorized by a principal to transact some specific act or acts. Such an agent has only limited powers that may be used only for a specific purpose. The authorization may cover just one act, such as buying a house; or it may cover a series of merely repetitious acts such as selling admission tickets to a movie.

Facts: Cecil and Linda Greer bought lot 5, adjacent to lot 1, from Placemaker, Inc. The plat of the subdivision containing the lots showed a small strip of land designated a street easement and on lot 1 was handwritten "common area" by Mike Day, a realtor marketing the lots. Day and Malinda Lenhart, a realtor with Day's firm, assumed that because of the location of a creek the lot could not be developed and told the Greers it would remain undeveloped. More than two years later, the strip designated as a street easement was no longer so needed. Placemaker filed a request to replat by combining the part of lot 1 adjacent to the Greers' lot with the strip. The Greers sued to prevent the replatting because of Day and Lenhart's representations.

Outcome: The court said a real estate agent is a special agent and has no power to bind the principal with unauthorized representations. Since Day and Lenhart were special agents, they had no authority to make representations binding on Placemaker.

Additional Types of Agents

There are several additional types of agents. Most of these are special agents, but because of the nature of their duties, their powers may exceed those of the ordinary special agent:

1. Factors
2. Factors del credere
3. Brokers
4. Attorneys in fact

FACTORS

Factor
Bailee seeking to sell property on commission

A **factor** is one who receives possession of another's property for the purpose of sale on commission. Factors, also called *commission merchants,* may sell in the name of the principal, but normally they sell in the merchant's own name. When factors collect the sale price, they deduct the commission, or factorage, and remit the balance to the principal. The third party, as a rule, is aware that the dealings are with an agent by the nature of the business or by the name of the business. The words *commission merchant* usually appear on all stationery. Commission merchants have the power to bind the principal for the customary terms of sale for the types of business they are doing. In this regard their powers are slightly greater than those of the ordinary special agent.

FACTORS DEL CREDERE

Factor del Credere
Factor who sells on credit and guarantees price will be paid

A **factor del credere** is a commission merchant who sells on credit and guarantees to the principal that the purchase price will be paid by the purchaser or by the factor. This is a form of contract of guaranty, but the contract need not be in writing as required by the Statute of Frauds, since the agreement is a primary obligation of the factor.

BROKERS

Broker
Agent with job of bringing two contracting parties together

A **broker** is a special agent whose task is to bring the two contracting parties together. Unlike a factor, a broker does not have possession of the merchandise. In real estate and insurance a broker normally acts as the agent of the buyer rather than the seller. If the job merely consists of finding a buyer or, sometimes, a seller, the broker has no authority to bind the principal on any contract.

ATTORNEYS IN FACT

Attorney in Fact
General agent appointed by written authorization

An **attorney in fact** is a general agent who has been appointed by a written authorization. The writing, intended to be shown to third persons, manifests that the agent has authority.

Extent of Authority

As a rule, a general agent has authority to transact several classes of acts: those clearly within the scope of the express authority, those customarily within such an agent's authority, and those outside of express authority but which appear to third parties to be within the scope of the agent's authority.

Express Authority
Authority of agent stated in agreement creating agency

Express authority is the authority specifically delegated to the agent by the agreement creating the agency. It amounts to the power to do whatever the agent is appointed to do.

PREVIEW CASE REVISITED

Facts: Because he did not want his daughter to inherit his home, George Pittman executed a power of attorney giving his wife, Rose, authority to make real property transactions "including the power to transfer the real estate known as the homeplace that I inherited from my mother." At George's directions, Rose executed a deed to the homeplace on behalf of George to Dessie Gaskill and Alice Durham. Gaskill and Durham paid George nothing. After George died, his daughter sued them claiming Rose did not have express authority to make a gift of the real estate since the law does not favor the power to make a gift.

Outcome: The court held that the word *transfer* included conveying by sale, gift, or other means, so Rose had the express authority to make the gift of the homeplace.

Frequently, in order to carry out the purposes of the agency, the agent must have the authority to do things not specifically enumerated in the agreement. This authority is called **implied authority**. An agent appointed to manage a retail shoe store has implied authority to purchase shoes from wholesalers in order to have a stock to sell.

Implied Authority
Agent's authority to do things in order to carry out express authority

Authority to act on behalf of another arises when by custom such agents ordinarily possess such powers. This is sometimes called **customary authority**.

Customary Authority
Authority agent possesses by custom

In addition, without regard to custom, the principal may have behaved in a way or made statements that caused the third person to believe that the agent has the authority. This is called **apparent authority**. For example, the Pardalos Insurance Company might advertise "For all your insurance problems see your local Pardalos Insurance agent." This would give the local Pardalos Insurance Company agent apparent authority to arrange any insurance matters even though the agents did not actually have such authority or had been told that certain kinds of cases had to be referred to the home office.

Apparent Authority
Authority agent believed to have because of principal's behavior

Facts: On the premises of a Mobil Mini Mart gas station leased under a franchise agreement to Alan Berman, an employee of Berman attacked and beat up Jeremy Bransford. Mobil owned the station and required Berman to use Mobil symbols and sell Mobil products. Bransford sued Mobil alleging it had an apparent agency relationship with Berman.

Outcome: The court held that mere use of franchise logos does not indicate Mobil has apparent control over the operation of Berman's business.

As to innocent third parties, the powers of a general agent may be far more extensive than those actually granted by the principal. Limitations upon an agent's authority do not bind a third party who has no knowledge of them; but they do bind a third party who knows of them.

In every case the person who would benefit by the existence of authority on the part of the alleged agent has the burden of proving the existence of authority. If a person appears to be the agent of another for the purpose of selling the car of that other person, for example, the prospective purchaser must seek assurance from the principal as to the agent's authority. Once the third party has learned the actual scope of an agent's express authority from the principal, the agent has no greater authority than the principal's actions and statements indicate, together with such customary authority as would attach.

Creation of an Agency

LO3

How agency is created

Usually any one of the following may create the relationship of **agency**:

Agency
Contract under which one party is authorized to contract for another

1 Appointment
2 Ratification
3 Estoppel
4 Necessity

APPOINTMENT

The usual way of creating an agency is by the statement of the principal to the agent. In most cases the contract may be either oral or written, formal or informal. In some instances, however, the appointment must be made in a particular form. The contract appointing an agent must be in writing if the agency is created to transfer title to real estate. Also, to extend an agent's authority beyond one year from the date of the contract, the Statute of Frauds requires the contract to be in writing. The appointment of an agent to execute a formal contract, such as a bond, requires a formal contract of appointment.

Power of Attorney
Writing appointing an agent

A written instrument indicating the appointment of an agent is known as a *warrant* or **power of attorney**. To record a power of attorney, it must also be acknowledged before a notary public or other officer authorized to take acknowledgments. Illustration 26-1 shows an ordinary form of power of attorney.

RATIFICATION

Ratification
Approval of unauthorized act

Ratification is the approval by one person of the unauthorized act of another done in the former's name. The unauthorized act may have been done by an assumed agent who purported to act as an agent without actual or apparent authority, or it may have been done by a real agent who exceeded actual and apparent authority. Such an act does not bind the supposed principal in such a case unless and until it is ratified. Ratification relates back to the date of the act done by the assumed agent. Hence, ratifying the act puts the assumed agent in the same position as if there had been authority to do the act at the time the act was done.

A valid ratification requires:

1 The one who assumed the authority of an agent must have made it known to the third person that he or she was acting on behalf of the party who attempts to ratify the act.
2 The one attempting to ratify must have been capable of authorizing the act at the time the act was done. Some jurisdictions apply this rule to corporations so that a corporation formed subsequent to the time of the act cannot ratify an act of a promoter. Other states have ignored this requirement in regard to ratification of the acts of corporate promoters.

Know All Men by These Presents:

That I, Amelia Clermont

of Portland

County of Multnomah *, State of* Oregon

have made, constituted and appointed, and by these presents do make, constitute and appoint James Turner

of Vancouver

County of Clark *, State of* Washington

my true and lawful attorney in fact, for me and in my name, place and stead,

to manage, operate, and let my rental properties in the City of Vancouver, County of Clark, State of Washington

giving and granting unto my said attorney full power and authority to do and perform all and every act and thing whatsoever requisite and necessary to be done in and about the premises, as fully to all intents and purposes as I might or could do, if personally present, with full power of substitution and revocation; hereby ratifying and confirming all that my said attorney —— or his *substitute —— shall lawfully do, or cause to be done, by virtue hereof.*

In Witness Whereof, I have hereunto set my hand this tenth *day of* July *, 20 --*

Amelia Clermont

Signed and acknowledged in presence of:

Samuel Adamick

Teresa Romano

Illustration 26-1
Power of Attorney

3 The one attempting to ratify must be capable of authorizing the act at the time approval of the act is given.
4 The one attempting to ratify must have knowledge of all material facts.
5 The one attempting to ratify must approve the entire act.
6 The ratified act must be legal, although a forgery on commercial paper may be ratified by the person whose name was forged.
7 The ratification must be made before the third party has withdrawn from the transaction.

ESTOPPEL

Agency by Estoppel
Agency arising when person leads another to believe third party is agent.

Agency by estoppel arises when a person by words or conduct leads another person to believe that a third party is an agent or has the authority to do particular acts. The principal who has made representations is bound to the extent of those representations for the purpose of preventing an injustice to parties who have been misled by the acts or the conduct of the principal.

NECESSITY

The relationship of agency may be created by necessity. Parents must support their minor children. If they fail to provide their children with necessaries, the parents' credit

Facts: Diamond Kamvakis & Co. had done business with Ace Fastener Company for many years. Paul Slepp, the salesman for Ace, offered to sell merchandise to Diamond at a substantial discount conditioned on immediate payment directly to Slepp. Diamond suspected a problem with this arrangement, so its president called Fred Riley, Ace's national sales manager. Riley had authority over making discounts and setting the terms of sale and method of payment. Riley okayed the arrangement, so Diamond bought the merchandise. It turned out that Slepp and Riley engaged in a criminal conspiracy to sell Ace merchandise and pocket the proceeds. When sued for payment for the merchandise, Diamond alleged Ace was estopped to deny Slepp's authority to make the deal because Riley, who had authority, said it was okay.

Outcome: The court agreed.

may be pledged for the children, even against the parents' will. Agency by necessity may also arise from some unforeseen emergency. Thus, the driver of a bus operating between distant cities may pledge the owner's credit in order to have needed repairs made and may have the cost charged to the owner.

Other Employment Relationships

LO4 Distinguish independent contractor

Two types of employment relationships differ from agency relationships:

1 Independent contractor
2 Employer and employee, originally referred to in law as master and servant

INDEPENDENT CONTRACTOR

Independent Contractor One who contracts to do jobs and is controlled only by contract as to how performed

An **independent contractor** is one who contracts to perform some tasks for a fixed fee. The other contracting party does not control an independent contractor as to the means by which the contractor performs except to the extent that the contract sets forth requirements to be followed. The independent contractor is merely held responsible for the proper performance of the contract. Because one who contracts with an independent contractor has much less control over the performance of the work, the contract does not create either a principal-agent relationship or an employer-employee relationship. The most usual type of independent contractor relationship is in the building trades.

EMPLOYER AND EMPLOYEE

An employee performs work for an employer. The employer controls the employee both as to the work to be done and the manner in which it is done. One contracting with an independent contractor does not have such control. The degree of control that the employer or principal exercises over the employee or **agent** and the authority the agent has to bind the principal to contracts constitute the main differences between an employee and an agent.

Agent Person appointed to contract on behalf of another

There are many reasons why a contract of employment must not be confused with a contract of an independent contractor. An employer may be held liable for any injuries employees negligently cause to third parties. This is not true for injuries caused by independent contractors. Second, employers must comply with laws relative to their employees. Employers must, for example, withhold social security taxes on employees' wages, pay a payroll tax for unemployment compensation, withhold federal income taxes, and, when properly demanded, bargain with their employees collectively. None of these laws apply when one contracts with independent contractors. Independent contractors are the employers of those employed by them to perform the contract.

Questions

1. What is a contract of agency?
2. What acts can be delegated to an agent?
3. Who is eligible to appoint an agent?
4. What are the two basic types of agents and their authority?
5. What is the difference between a factor and a broker?
6. Do limitations on an agent's authority bind a third party?
7. When must a contract creating an agency be in writing?
8. What information must persons who assume the authority of an agent give third parties in order to have their acts ratified by the purported principals?
9. How does an independent contractor relationship differ from an agent?
10. What control does an employer have over an employee which a person contracting with an independent contractor does not have?

Case Problems

LO2 1. George Tapp signed a durable power of attorney to Nancy Wabner. It granted Wabner the power "to cash any certificates of deposit which I own or to change and redesignate the ownership thereof." Tapp told her to collect the funds from his bank accounts and CD's and put them in a bank account with her as joint owner with right of survivorship. Wabner did as Tapp directed and Tapp died. Under Tapp's will two church organizations received one-quarter of his estate. If Wabner's actions were proper most of Tapp's estate remained in the joint account and passed automatically to her. The church organizations sued Wabner alleging she did not have the express authority to make gifts to herself. Did she have that authority?

LO3 2. Something bit Rhea Sampson on the arm. The arm got swollen so she went to the Southeast Baptist Hospital emergency room. Signs posted in the emergency room stated emergency room doctors were independent contractors. They, not the hospital, billed patients. Dr. Susan Howle, an emergency room physician, diagnosed the bite as an allergic reaction and prescribed accordingly. Sampson's arm got worse and she returned to the emergency room. Another emergency room physician, Dr. Mark Zakula, gave her pain medication and told her to continue Dr. Howle's treatment. Fourteen hours later she went to another hospital which admitted her in septic shock. The proper treatment was administered to save her life. Sampson sued the doctors and the hospital alleging the doctors were ostensible agents of the hospital. Were they?

LO1 3. Charged with a crime, Carl Rosati hired an attorney, John Cicilline. Before hiring Cicilline, Kenneth Kuzman, Rosati's former coach, volunteered his services to Rosati's parents. Cicilline asked Kuzman to help with the investigation. At Cicilline's request, Kuzman interviewed witnesses, discussed matters with Rosati at the prison, and helped a private investigator Cicilline hired. The indictment against Rosati was dismissed and two other people were indicted. Kuzman was told to appear for a deposition. Rosati sued to prevent Kuzman from disclosing information privileged under the attorney-client privilege. Was Kuzman acting as Cicilline's agent when he worked on Rosati's case?

LO3 4 Bob Dunn Ford, Inc. with Robert C. Dunn as the president leased Ford and Jaguar cars. Wachovia Bank would buy the leases from Bob Dunn. Occasionally Robert C. Dunn would personally guarantee payment of the leases. However he told two Wachovia vice presidents that he did not want to engage in any more transactions that allowed recourse against him and that only he personally could execute guarantees. He formed a new corporation, Bob Dunn Jaguar, to lease Jaguars. Mel Blackwell was the general manager of Dunn Jaguar. George and Lilly McKeathen leased a new Jaguar and the lease application was sent to Wachovia. A Wachovia employee, Charles Patterson, phoned Blackwell and said Dunn Jaguar would have to guarantee the lease payments. Joe Parker, vice president of Dunn Ford, signed the guaranty and indicated he was vice president of Dunn Jaguar. Wachovia paid Dunn Leasing $39,000 for the lease. Three years later the McKeathens defaulted on the lease and Robert C. Dunn was told Parker had executed the guaranty. Robert C. Dunn immediately repudiated the guaranty. The bank sued Dunn Jaguar on the guaranty. Can it recover on the basis of agency by ratification?

LO4 5 Lisa Millsap suffered injuries when a car driven by Christopher Pence hit her car. North County Express (NCE) paid Pence to deliver packages to its customers. In making deliveries, Pence used his own car, supplied his own gas, oil, and liability insurance, and paid for his car repairs. NCE paid him a lump sum based on distance for the deliveries. NCE would call when needing packages delivered or Pence would stop in. He received no employee benefits and had no taxes withheld from his paychecks. He would give NCE invoices when he wanted. Pence received no instruction from NCE about how to make the deliveries. It did require him to get a signed confirmation of them. Millsap sued Pence and NCE for her injuries. NCE incurred no liability if Pence contracted with it as an independent contractor. Decide the independent contractor issue.

LO2 6 Nelson, Hesse, Cyril, Weber & Sparrow hired Susan Blackmon as a secretary. She later inquired of Ms. Steeves, the office manager, about coverage under the firm's group health insurance plan. Blackmon stated she told Steeves she needed surgery but would wait until she had coverage. She further stated that Steeves told her upon completion of the application form that coverage began immediately, and Steeves made deductions from Blackmon's salary for premiums to start coverage that day. Eight days later, thinking she had coverage, Blackmon had the surgery. Steeves had just mailed the application, and the company did not approve it until five days after the surgery. Blackmon sued the firm, alleging Steeves was its agent and acted negligently in advising when the coverage took effect. Was Steeves the firm's agent?

LO2 7 William Savary, who operated an insurance agency, helped Rodney Carney fill out an application for "assigned risk" auto insurance through the Automotive Plan in New York. Neither knew which company would be assigned. Concord General Mutual Insurance Company sent a policy directly to Rodney, and the Plan notified Savary it had assigned Rodney to Concord. While driving Rodney's car, his brother, Brian, had an accident with Gilbert Libby. Libby's attorney tried to contact the Carneys and their insurers, but could not. Suit was filed against Rodney. Savary was not Concord's authorized agent, but Carney made the insurance payments to Savary, who received a commission on the insurance. At Rodney's request, Savary had sent statements and letters to Concord. Can Savary be held an express or implied agent of Concord?

LO3 8 Mr. and Mrs. Howard Anderson wanted to obtain a consolidation loan to reduce their monthly payments on their loans. They consulted First National Bank of Pine City. Mrs. Anderson went to First National and brought home papers for Mr. Anderson to sign. He refused because there were unfilled blanks on the papers. Mrs. Anderson signed his name as well as her own to a note and mortgage deed on their home and delivered them to First National. When the Andersons fell behind on their payments on the note, First National began foreclosure proceedings. The bank alleged that Mr. Anderson ratified his wife's forgery by being silent and failing to notify the bank. Mr. Anderson stated that he was silent because he feared his wife would be prosecuted for forgery. He had learned about her signing his name three months later and thought she had forged his name to a loan secured by personal property, not a mortgage. Had he ratified the forgery?

Internet Resources for Business Law

Name	Resources	Web Address
The Independent Contractor Report	*The Independent Contractor Report,* a monthly newsletter, has materials on employment tax cases, rulings, and issues for users of independent contractors.	http://www.webcom.com/ic_rep/
Nolo's Download Center—The Independent Contractor	The Independent Contractor law site, in Nolo's Legal Encyclopedia, provides articles, updates, and legislation for independent contractors and employers.	http://www.nolo.com/ic/
The Outsourcing Institute	The Outsourcing Institute provides general information on outsourcing, including the hiring of independent contractors.	http://www.outsourcing.com/
AHI's Employment Law Resource Center	The Alexander Hamilton Institute, Inc., provides newsletters, booklets, and looseleaf manuals, and discussion groups aimed at helping managers.	http://www.ahipubs.com/
EFF "Legal Issues and Policy: Cyberspace and the Law" Archive	The Electronic Frontier Foundation, a nonprofit civil liberties organization, provides articles and links to information regarding the use of technology and workplace privacy.	http://www.eff.org/pub/Legal/
Legal Information Institute (LII)—Workers Compensation Law Materials	LII, maintained by Cornell Law School, provides an overview of workers' compensation law.	http://www.law.cornell.edu/topics/workers_compensation.html

27 Operation and Termination of an Agency

Learning Objectives

1 Specify the duties an agent owes the principal and the principal owes the agent.

2 Describe the agent's and principal's liabilities to third parties.

3 State how an agency may be terminated, either by the parties or by operation of law.

PREVIEW CASE

John Kennon, doing business as Kennon Adjustment Company, was hired by Commercial Standard Insurance Company to investigate a workers' compensation claim. There was no agreement as to the amount to be paid Kennon. After an award was made to the claimant, Kennon submitted a bill for more than three times the amount of the award. Commercial refused to pay the bill, saying that it was too high. Kennon sued. In the absence of an agreement for compensation, how much, if anything, must be paid to an agent? Do you think Commercial expected such a high bill?

In a contract of agency, the law imposes upon the agent certain duties not set out in the contract. Likewise, the relationship of agency creates duties and obligations that the principal owes to an agent even though they are not specifically enumerated in the contract. In turn, the agency relationship imposes upon both principal and agent certain duties and obligations to third parties. An examination of these duties and obligations will reveal the importance of the relationship of agent and principal as well as the necessity for each party in the relationship to be fully cognizant of the rights and duties that exist.

Agent's Duties to Principal

LO1 Duties of agents and principals

An agent owes the following important duties to the principal:

1 Loyalty and good faith
2 Obedience

3 Reasonable skill and diligence
4 Accounting
5 Information

LOYALTY AND GOOD FAITH

The relationship of principal and agent is fiduciary in nature; thus, the principal must be able to trust the agent to perform the duties according to contract. The relationship of agent and principal calls for a higher degree of faith and trust than do most contractual relationships. For this reason the law imposes upon agents the duty of loyalty and good faith and deprives them of their right to compensation, reimbursement, and indemnification when they prove disloyal to their principal or act in bad faith. The interests of the principal must be promoted by agents to the utmost of their ability.

Loyalty and good faith are abstract terms. Thus, the courts have wide latitude in interpreting what acts constitute bad faith or a breach of loyalty. Such acts as secretly owning an interest in a firm that competes with the principal, disclosing confidential information, selling to or buying from the agent without the knowledge of the principal, and acting simultaneously as the agent of a competitor constitute acts that the courts have held to be breaches of good faith. An agent who acts in bad faith not only may be discharged but the principal may also recover any damages that have been sustained. Also, the principal may recover any profits the agent has made while acting in bad faith even though the act did not damage the principal.

Facts: Foster Winans and another journalist wrote a daily column, "Heard on the Street," for *The Wall Street Journal.* Because investors respected the column, it could potentially affect the price of stocks discussed. Winans knew that the *Journal's* practice and policy required that the columns were its confidential information before publication. He engaged in a plot with two brokers to give them advance information about the column so they could trade stock based on the expected impact of the column and all split the profits. In four months they made $690,000. Charged with fraud, Winans claimed he had really only violated a workplace rule.

Outcome: The court discussed Winans's obligation to the *Journal* as an agent to his principal. It said an employee has a fiduciary duty to protect confidential information obtained during the course of his employment.

OBEDIENCE

An agent may have two types of instructions from the principal: one routine and the other discretionary. The agent must carry out all routine instructions to the letter as long as compliance would not defeat the purpose of the agency, be illegal, or perpetrate a fraud on others. An instruction not to accept any payments made by check illustrates a routine instruction. The agent incurs liability for any losses caused by disobeying these instructions. There is no justification for disobeying such instructions under any conditions.

Agents must use the best judgment of which they are capable regarding discretionary instructions. For example, an agent instructed to accept checks incurs no liability for a bad check when in the agent's judgment the drawer of the check is solvent and reliable. If an agent accepts a check that the agent has reason to believe is bad, the agent incurs liability for any loss that the principal sustains by reason of this act.

REASONABLE SKILL AND DILIGENCE

One who acts as an agent must possess the skill required to perform the duties and must be diligent in performing the skill. An implied warranty exists that the agent has such skill and will exercise such diligence. Any breach of this warranty subjects the agent to a liability for damages for the loss by reason of the breach.

Because it is assumed that agents are appointed in reliance on their individual skills, talents, and judgment, agents may not generally appoint subagents. This, of course, is not true if the agency agreement provides for the appointment of subagents, if the work delegated is merely clerical, or if the type of agency is one in which it is customarily assumed that subagents would be appointed. Whenever appointing subagents, the agent must use skill and diligence in appointing competent subagents and remains liable to the principal for their breach of good faith or lack of skill.

ACCOUNTING

The duties of an agent include keeping a record of all money transactions pertaining to the agency. An accounting must be made to the principal for any of the principal's money and property that may come into the agent's possession. Money should be deposited in a bank in the name of the principal, preferably in a bank other than that in which the agent keeps personal funds. If the deposit is made in the name of the agent, any loss caused by the failure of the bank will fall on the agent. Personal property of the principal must be kept separate from property of the agent.

INFORMATION

Agents have a duty to keep principals informed of all facts pertinent to the agency that may enable the principals to protect their interests. In consequence, an agent cannot enforce a principal's promise to pay a bonus to the agent for information secured by the agent in the performance of agency duties because the principal was entitled to the information anyway. The promise was therefore not supported by consideration.

Principal's Duties to Agent

The principal has four important duties in respect to the agent:

1. Compensation
2. Reimbursement
3. Indemnification
4. Abidance by the terms of the contract

COMPENSATION

The contract of agency determines the compensation due an agent. As in most other contracts, this provision may be either express or implied. If the amount is clearly and expressly stated, disputes seldom arise. When an agency agreement does not state the amount of compensation, the agent may obtain reasonable or customary compensation for the services provided. In the absence of customary rates of compensation, the court will fix a reasonable rate according to the character of the services rendered. Frequently, the parties set the compensation on a contingent basis, such as a percentage of the selling price, provided a sale occurs. In such a case, the agent cannot collect compensation from the principal unless a sale actually occurs.

PREVIEW CASE REVISITED

Facts: Commercial Standard Insurance Company hired John Kennon, doing business as Kennon Adjustment Company, to investigate a workers' compensation claim. They made no agreement as to the amount to be paid Kennon. After the claimant received an award, Kennon submitted a bill for more than three times the amount of the award. Commercial refused to pay the bill, saying that it was too high. Kennon sued.

Outcome: The court held that in the absence of an agreement for compensation, an implied promise arises for a principal to pay a reasonable amount for such services rendered in the location where they were furnished.

REIMBURSEMENT

The principal must reimburse an agent for any expenses incurred or disbursements made by the agent from personal funds as a necessary part of the agency. If, for example, an agent had to pay from personal funds a $100 truck repair bill before a trip on behalf of the principal could be continued, the agent would be entitled to reimbursement. If, on the other hand, a $50 fine for speeding had to be paid, the principal would not be required to reimburse this expense. Any expense incurred as a result of an agent's unlawful act must be borne by the agent.

INDEMNIFICATION

A contractual payment made by the agent for the principal is an expense of the principal. If the agent makes the payment not by reason of a contract but as a result of a loss or damage due to an accident, the principal must indemnify the agent. The principal must reimburse expenses and indemnify for losses and damages. If the principal directs the agent to sell goods in the stockroom that already belong to the principal's customer, that customer can sue both the principal and the agent. If the agent must pay the customer damages, the agent can in turn sue the principal for giving the instructions that caused the loss.

ABIDANCE BY THE TERMS OF THE CONTRACT

The principal must abide by the terms of the contract in all respects including any implied compliance. Thus, the agent must be employed for the period stated in the contract unless justification exists for terminating the contract at an earlier date. If the cooperation or participation of the principal is required in order to enable the agent to perform duties under the agency agreement, the principal must cooperate or participate to the extent required by the contract. For example, if an agent sells by sample and receives a commission on all sales, the agent must be furnished samples, and the opportunity to earn the fee or commission must be given.

Agent's Liabilities to Third Parties

LO2
Agent's and principal's liabilities to third parties

Ordinarily, whenever an agent performs duties, the principal is bound but not the agent. In relations with third parties, however, an agent may be personally liable on contracts and for wrongs in several ways:

1 Agents who contract in their own names and do not disclose the names of the principals become liable to the same extent as though they were the principals. For this reason, agents who sign contracts in their own names will be held liable. The proper way for an agent to sign so as to bind only the principal is to sign "principal, by agent." A signing of the principal's name alone will likewise protect the agent, although the third person may require the placing of the agent's name under the name of the principal so that at a later date it can be determined which agent had obtained the contract.

2 Agents may make themselves personally liable to third parties by an express agreement to be responsible. This express agreement may be demonstrated if it is the only logical or legal interpretation of the contract.

Facts: An employee of Jay Duran Associates, Inc., Tim Redlinger expressed concern to Jay Duran, the majority stockholder, that he did not have a retirement plan. Duran signed a letter on company letterhead which stated: "I, Jay Duran, promise to purchase an insurance policy on myself for $50,000 with Tim Redlinger as sole beneficiary." Beneath the text of the letter appeared:

JAY DURAN ASSOCIATES INC.
[signed] Jay Duran
Jay Duran

Duran died without having set up a retirement plan or purchasing a life insurance policy. Redlinger made a claim against Duran's estate claiming since only Duran could take out insurance on his life and chose the beneficiary, he had obligated himself personally.

Outcome: The court said since Duran personally was the only person who could do what was promised in the letter, he, the agent of the company, had agreed to be personally bound for the insurance.

3 People who assume to act for others but actually have no authority, or who exceed or materially depart from the authority they were given, incur personal liability to those with whom they do business. The latter situation may arise when overzealous agents affect what they may think is a desirable contract.

4 An agent incurs personal liability for fraud or any other wrongdoing, whether caused by disobedience, carelessness, or malice, or whether committed on the order of the principal.

Principal's Duties and Liabilities to Third Parties

The principal ordinarily has liability to third parties for contracts made within the actual or the apparent scope of an agent's authority.

When the agent enters into an unauthorized contract not within the apparent scope of authority, the principal is not bound unless the contract is subsequently ratified. The test of when an agent has apparent authority is whether, on the basis of the conduct of the principal, a reasonable person would believe that the agent had the authority to make the particular contract. If such a person would, the contract binds the principal. For example, if the manager of a furniture store sells a suite of furniture on credit contrary to the authority granted, the principal must fulfill the contract with the third party, provided the third party did not know of the limitation upon the agent's authority. The agent has liability to the principal for any loss sustained.

The principal, as well as the agent, has liability for an injury to the person or the property of a third party caused by the negligence or the wrongful act of the agent in the course of employment. When the agent steps aside from the business of the principal and commits a wrong or injury to another, the principal is not liable for an unratified act.

Termination of an Agency by Acts of the Parties

LO3
How to terminate an agency

An agency may be terminated by acts of the parties by:

1 Original agreement
2 Subsequent agreement
3 Revocation
4 Renunciation by the agent

ORIGINAL AGREEMENT

The contract creating the agency may specify a date for the termination of the agency. In that event, the agency automatically terminates on that date. Most special agencies, such as a special agency to sell an automobile, terminate because their purpose has been accomplished.

SUBSEQUENT AGREEMENT

An agreement between the principal and the agent may terminate an agency at any time.

REVOCATION

The principal may revoke the agent's authority at any time, thereby terminating the agency. The principal may terminate the agency by notifying the agent of the termination or by taking actions that are inconsistent with the continuation of the agency.

Facts: Francis Gagnon executed a power of attorney in favor of his daughter, Joan Coombs. He specifically empowered Joan "to sell any of my real estate" and "to add property to . . . any trust of which I am the grantor or beneficiary." A few months later Gagnon executed a document revoking the power of attorney but did not tell Joan. Gagnon found someone who wanted to buy his house and they signed an agreement to sell. Gagnon told Joan about this sales agreement. Without telling Gagnon, Joan set up a trust with herself as trustee having total control of the trust without court approval and Gagnon as beneficiary. Under authority of the power of attorney, Joan conveyed Gagnon's house to herself as trustee. When Joan refused to return his house Gagnon sued her.

Outcome: The court found for Gagnon holding that Joan should have realized he had revoked her authority to sell the home when she found out he had contracted to sell it.

One must distinguish between the right to terminate the agency and the power to do so. The principal has the right to terminate the agency any time the agent breaches any material part of the contract of employment. If the agent, for example, fails to account for all money collected for the principal, the agent may be discharged, and the principal incurs no liability for breach of contract. The principal, on the other hand, has the power, with one exception, to revoke the agent's authority at any time. Under these circumstances, however, the principal becomes liable to the agent for any damage sustained by reason of an unjustifiable discharge. This is the agent's sole remedy. The agent cannot insist upon the right to continue to act as an agent even though nothing has been done to justify a termination before the end of the contract period.

Agency Coupled with an Interest
Agency in which agent has financial stake in performance of agency because of having given consideration to principal

The only exception to this rule that the principal has the power to terminate the agency occurs in the case of an **agency coupled with an interest**. Interest may take one of two forms: (1) interest in the authority and (2) interest in the subject matter. An agent has interest in the authority when authorized to act as an agent in collecting funds for the principal with an agreement not to remit the collections to the principal but to apply them on a debt owed to the agent by the principal. In the second case, the agent has a lien on the property of the principal as security for a debt and is appointed as agent to sell the property and apply the proceeds to the debt.

RENUNCIATION

Like the principal, the agent has the power to renounce the agency at any time. An agent who abandons the agency without cause before fulfillment of the contract incurs liability to the principal for all losses due to the unjustified abandonment.

Termination by Operation of Law

An agency may also be terminated by operation of law. This may occur because of:

1. Subsequent illegality
2. Death or incapacity
3. Destruction
4. Bankruptcy
5. Dissolution
6. War

SUBSEQUENT ILLEGALITY

Subsequent illegality of the subject matter of the agency terminates the agency.

DEATH OR INCAPACITY

Death or incapacity of either the principal or agent normally terminates the agency. For example, when the agent permanently loses the power of speech so that the principal's business cannot be performed, the agency automatically terminates.

An exception to the rule of termination by incapacity has been enacted by states that provide for durable powers of attorney. A **durable power of attorney** is a written appointment of agency designed to be effective even though the principal is incapacitated. Such a power of attorney may allow an agent to make health care decisions for the principal such as admission to a hospital or nursing home, authorization of a medical procedure, or insertion of a feeding tube. It may also direct the attorney in fact to withhold certain, specified medical treatments or procedures.

Durable Power of Attorney
Appointment of agency that survives incapacity of principal

DESTRUCTION

Destruction of the subject matter, such as the destruction by fire of a house to be sold by the agent, terminates the agency.

BANKRUPTCY

Bankruptcy of the principal terminates the agency. In most cases bankruptcy of the agent does not terminate the agency.

DISSOLUTION

Dissolution
Termination of corporation's operation except activities needed for liquidation

Dissolution of a corporation terminates an agency in which the corporation is a party. This is similar to death, since dissolution of a corporation is a complete termination of operation except for the activities necessary for liquidation.

WAR

When the country of the principal and that of the agent are at war against each other, the agent's authority usually terminates or at least lapses until peace occurs. A war that makes performance impossible terminates the agency.

Notice of Termination

When principals terminate agencies, they must give notice to third parties with whom the agents have previously transacted business and who would be likely to deal with them as an agent. If such notice is not given, the principal might still be bound on any future contracts negotiated by the agent. Notice can be given by sending written notice to the third parties in any way feasible. How the notice is given does not matter so long as the parties learn of the termination. Notice given to an agent constitutes notice to the principal.

Facts: Darrel Ireland bought a business known as George Pet Supply Shop and George Hall was the general manager. Hall was authorized to and did buy merchandise on credit from West Denver Feed Co. A year and a half later, Hall and his wife bought the shop from Ireland. They continued the business under the same name and the creditors continued their accounts with the shop without closing them out, although Hall told the salesmen for each creditor that he was then the owner of the business. About a year later Hall filed for bankruptcy. The creditors sued Ireland, claiming he was liable as the principal because no notice of termination of the agency was given them.

Outcome: The court held that notice of the termination of the agency to the agents of the creditors constituted notice to the creditors. Ireland was liable only for any amount owed when notice of termination was given the salesmen.

When operation of law terminates an agency, notice need not be given either to the agent or to third parties.

Questions

1. What are the legal consequences if an agent acts in bad faith or proves disloyal to the principal?
2. What is the difference between a routine instruction and a discretionary instruction from a principal to an agent?
3. What warranty regarding their skill and diligence do agents make?
4. Under what circumstances may an agent appoint subagents?
5. How should an agent handle deposits of the principal's money?
6. If the agent and the principal do not set the amount of the agent's compensation in the agency contract, on which basis is the amount determined if the agent and the principal cannot agree?

7 Under what circumstances must the principal cooperate with the agent?
8 When does a principal not have the power to terminate the agency?
9 For what reasons is an agency terminated by operation of law?
10 Why should notice of termination of an agency be given?

Case Problems

LO1 1 Needing money, Barbara Barlow "pawned" the title to her car with Quik Pawn Shop. EFS, Inc. owned Quik Pawn. Frank Evans was president and Charlotte Evans secretary of EFS. No advertisements or documents Barlow received disclosed EFS's existence or ownership of Quik Pawn. Barlow claimed the terms of the pawn violated the Truth in Lending Act and sued EFS and the Evanses. She claimed the Evanses conducted a business and acted as agents of Quik Pawn without disclosing their principal and therefore should be personally liable. Should the Evanses be liable as agents for an undisclosed principal?

LO1 2 Lerner Corporation had an agreement to act as the exclusive leasing and management agent for an apartment complex. Three Winthrop Properties, Inc. acted as the agent for the owners. The management agreement permitted the owner to terminate ". . . at anytime from and after the last day of the . . . month in which occurs the tenth anniversary of the date of this agreement [January 31]." The termination date could not be earlier than 90 days after written notice of termination. On October 17 Three Winthrop gave notice of termination as of January 31. Lerner claimed notice could not be given until January 31 and termination could not be until 90 days after that. Three Winthrop filed suit, but by the time the court tried the case Lerner had continued to manage and take management fees from rental proceeds for the 90 days after January 31. Had Lerner acted in good faith?

LO2 3 Nancy Imhof hired attorney Richard French to represent her in a lawsuit after her husband died in a plane crash. French contacted Donald Sommer by phone and hired him to investigate the crash and testify. Sommer sent French his fee schedule and French sent him a letter verifying their discussion and giving documents to review and a check as a retainer. French signed the letter. Sommer rendered services in excess of $18,000 but was not paid, so he sued French. French said he was only acting as an agent for Imhof. Should the court hold French personally liable?

LO3 4 Arthur Cloutier had an account with the Amesbury Franco-American Credit Union. Virginia Ploof opened an account at Amesbury. Two years later, Cloutier's account was closed and the funds transferred to Ploof's account, which was made a joint account, with Cloutier. A year later Ploof opened a new account with almost the entire balance in the joint account, and the joint account with a small balance remaining was changed to Cloutier's individual account. He told the bank president the account change was because he was to have serious surgery. The president convinced Cloutier to retain a power of attorney over Ploof's account. Two months later Ploof died and a week after that Cloutier used the power of attorney to withdraw the balance in Ploof's account. The administrator of Ploof's estate sued Cloutier for the amount withdrawn, alleging that the power of attorney was invalid. Was it? Why or why not?

LO1 5 Gerard Zell, a real estate agent, filed suit against his broker to recover commissions on sales. Zell had breached his fiduciary duty to his broker. The broker alleged Zell should lose the commission "earned" on a fraudulent transaction as well as all commissions earned thereafter. Should Zell receive any commissions for transactions unrelated to the fraudulent one and subsequent to it?

LO2 6 Robert Westlake and Glenn Shepherd, partners in real estate projects, had used the services of Dunn & Wendel Architects. Shepherd asked Wendel to visit apartment projects

Creation of Employer and Employee Relationship

LO1
Employer-employee relationship

The relationship of employer and employee arises only from a contract of employment, either express or implied (see Illustration 28-1 for a sample form). The common law allowed employers the right to hire whom they pleased and employees the right to freely choose their employers. The relationship of employer and employee could not be imposed upon either the purported employer or employee without consent. One who voluntarily performs the duties of an employee cannot by that act subject the employer to the liability of an employer. But the relationship may be implied by conduct that demonstrates that the parties agree that one is the employer and the other the employee.

LENGTH OF CONTRACT

An employee discharged without cause may recover wages due up to the end of the contract period from the employer. However, when creating an employer-employee relationship, seldom does either party mention the length of the contract period. In some jurisdictions, the terms of compensation determine the contract period. In such jurisdictions, the length of time used in specifying the compensation constitutes the employment period and an employee may be discharged at the end of that time without further liability. For example, an employee paid by the hour may be discharged without liability at the end of any hour. An employee paid by the week or by the month, as are many office employees, has a term of employment of one week or one month, as the case may be. For monthly paid employees, the term of employment may depend upon the way the employer specifies the compensation. A stated salary of $27,500 a year gives a one-year term of employment, even though the employer pays once a month. In other jurisdictions, employment at a set amount per week, month, or year does not constitute employment for any definite period but amounts to an indefinite hiring.

Employment at Will
Employment terminable by employer or employee for any reason

Many employer-employee situations have an indefinite length for the contract, and either the employer or the employee may terminate the employment for any reason or for no reason at any time. This situation is called **employment at will**.

Facts: Dan's Foods, Inc. distributed an employee handbook which stated, "Your employment at Dan's is at will and may be terminated without cause or prior notice by either you or Dan's." James Ryan, a pharmacist employed by Dan's, read the handbook and signed a form stating he had received and read it. Dan's received many customer complaints about Ryan and after the management repeatedly counseled and warned him about the complaints, Dan's fired him. Ryan sued.

Outcome: Ryan had an at will employment contract and could be fired at any time.

However, as a result of labor legislation, union or other employment contracts, employee handbooks, or other exceptions that have developed to employment at will, many employees have significant job security. They may not be discharged except for good cause. As in the case of an employee discharged without cause who is employed for a specified period, such an employee may sue the employer for money damages. In some cases the employee may also sue to be restored to the job.

DETERMINATION OF CONTRACT TERMS

Employer-employee contracts frequently do not state terms other than the compensation. Terms are determined by law, custom, employee handbooks, and possibly by

EMPLOYMENT AGREEMENT

This Employment Agreement (this "Agreement"), is made effective as of November 02, 2000, by and between ________________ ("________________"), of ________________, ________________, ________________ ________ and ________________ ("________________"), of ________________, ________________, ________________ ________.

1. EMPLOYMENT. ________________ shall employ ________________ as a ________________. ________________ accepts and agrees to such employment, subject to the general supervision, advice, and direction of ____________ and ____________'s supervisory personnel. ____________ agrees to perform faithfully, industriously, and to the best of ________________'s ability, experience, and talents, the services described on the attached Exhibit A, which is made part of this Agreement by reference. ________________ shall also perform (i) such other duties as are customarily performed by an employee in a similar position, and (ii) such other and unrelated services and duties as may be assigned to ________________ from time to time by ________________.

2. COMPENSATION. As compensation for the services provided by __________ under this Agreement, ________________ will pay ________________ an annual salary of $0.00 payable in accordance with ________________'s usual payroll procedures.

3. EXPENSE REIMBURSEMENT. ______________ will reimburse ______________ for "out-of-pocket" expenses incurred by ________________, in accordance with ________________'s policies in effect from time to time.

4. BENEFITS. ________________ shall be entitled to employment benefits, including _______ as provided by ________________'s policies in effect from time to time.

5. CONFIDENTIALITY. ______________ recognizes that ______________ has and will have information regarding matters such as trade secrets, customer lists, product design, and other vital information (collectively, "Information"), which are valuable, special, and unique assets of ____________. ______________ agrees that ______________ will not at any time or in any manner, either directly or indirectly, divulge, disclose, or communicate in any manner any Information to any third party without the prior written consent of ______________. ______________ will protect the Information and treat it as strictly confidential. A violation by ______________ of this paragraph shall be a material violation of this Agreement and will justify legal and/or equitable relief.

6. TERM/TERMINATION. ________________'s employment under this Agreement shall be for an unspecified term on an "at will" basis. Either ________________ or ________________ may terminate this Agreement at any time, with or without notice.

7. ENTIRE AGREEMENT. This Agreement contains the entire agreement of the parties and there are no other promises or conditions in any other agreement whether oral or written. This Agreement supersedes any prior written or oral agreements between the parties. Amendments to this Agreement must be made in writing and signed by both parties to be binding on either party.

EMPLOYER:

____

By: ________________________________ Date: ____________________

____

EMPLOYEE:

________________________________ Date: ____________________

____

Use the Quicken Business Lawyer to open this document. Complete it and the checklist at the end with a classmate, with one of you playing the role of the employer and the other the employee.

To what kinds of jobs do you think such an agreement would apply? Would you need to complete an employment agreement to work at a fast-food restaurant? How about a bank?

Visit the following Web sites for samples of different kinds of employment agreements:
http://www.cpsinc.com/consult/bonus.htm
http://lawsmart.com/documents/exec_agmt.shtml
http://www.housing.uiuc.edu/reslife/rajobs/page2.html
http://www.emory.edu/AGOATLANTA/newton1.htm

Illustration 28-1
Employment Agreement

union contracts. If the employer publishes a handbook stating contract terms, the employer will usually be bound by those terms as long as the employee had a reasonable opportunity to learn them. In some cases, courts have held that statements in the employer's written policy manual constitute terms of employer-employee contracts.

UNION CONTRACTS

Formerly the employer contracted individually with each employee. However, as the union movement developed and collective bargaining became commonplace, employers began agreeing with unions to provisions of employment that applied to large numbers of employees. The signed contract between them embodied this agreement between the employer and the union. An agent of the employees, the union, speaks and contracts for all the employees collectively. As a general rule, the employer still makes a contract individually with each employee, but the union contract binds the employer to recognize certain scales of union wages, hours of work, job classifications, and related matters.

Duties and Liabilities of the Employer

Under the common law the employer had five well-defined duties:

1. Duty to exercise care
2. Duty to provide a reasonably safe place to work
3. Duty to provide safe tools and appliances
4. Duty to provide competent and sufficient employees for the task
5. Duty to instruct employees with reference to the dangerous nature of employment

DUTY TO EXERCISE CARE

This rule imposes liability on employers if their negligence causes harm to an employee. Employers have exercised proper care when they have done what a reasonable person would have done under the circumstances to avoid harm.

DUTY TO PROVIDE A REASONABLY SAFE PLACE TO WORK

The employer must furnish every employee with a reasonably safe place to work. What constitutes a safe place depends upon the nature of the work. Most states have statutes modifying the common law for hazardous industries.

DUTY TO PROVIDE SAFE TOOLS AND APPLIANCES

The tools furnished employees by their employer must be safe. This rule applies also to machinery and appliances.

DUTY TO PROVIDE COMPETENT AND SUFFICIENT EMPLOYEES FOR THE TASK

Both the number of employees and their skill and experience affect the hazardous nature of many jobs. The employer has liability for all injuries to employees directly caused by either an insufficient number of workers or the lack of skill of some of the workers.

DUTY TO INSTRUCT EMPLOYEES

In all positions that use machinery, chemicals, electric appliances, and other production instruments, there are many hazards. The law requires the employer to give that degree of instruction to a new employee that a reasonable person would give under the circumstances to avoid reasonably foreseeable harm that could result from a failure to give such instructions.

Common-Law Defenses of the Employer

Under the common law, when an injured employee sues the employer, the employer could raise the following defenses:

1 The employee's contributory negligence
2 The act of a fellow servant
3 A risk assumed by the employee

CONTRIBUTORY NEGLIGENCE RULE

The contributory negligence rule states that an employer can escape liability for breach of duty if it can be established that the employee's own negligence contributed to the accident. An employee who could have avoided the injury by the exercise of due diligence has no right to collect damages from the employer.

THE FELLOW-SERVANT RULE

Fellow Servant Employee with same status and working with another worker

The fellow-servant rule allows an employer to avoid liability by providing that the injury was caused by a fellow servant. A **fellow servant** is an employee who has the same status as another worker and works with that employee. This rule has been abrogated or so severely limited that it very rarely has any significance now.

ASSUMPTION-OF-RISK RULE

Every type of employment in industry has some normal risks. The assumption-of-risk rule states that employees assume these normal risks by voluntarily accepting employment. Therefore, if the injury results from the hazardous nature of the job, the employer cannot be held liable.

Statutory Modification of Common Law

LO2 Statutory modification of employer's defenses

The rules of the common law have been greatly altered by the enactment of laws modifying an employer's defenses when sued by an employee, laws providing for workers' compensation, and the Occupational Safety and Health Act.

MODIFICATION OF COMMON-LAW DEFENSES

Statutes have modified the defenses an employer may use when sued for damages by an employee. For example, the Federal Employers' Liability Act and the Federal Safety Appliance Act apply to common carriers engaged in interstate commerce. A plaintiff suing under these laws must still bring an action in court and prove negligence by the employer or other employees. However, winning the case is easier because of limits on the employer's defenses. An employer has liability even if the employee is contributorily negligent. However, such negligence may reduce the amount of damages. Many states have also modified the common-law defenses of employers of employees engaged in hazardous types of work.

WORKERS' COMPENSATION

Every state has adopted workers' compensation statutes that apply to certain industries or businesses. These statutes allow an employee, or certain relatives of a deceased employee, to recover damages for injury to or death of the employee. They may recover whenever the injury arose within the course of the employee's work from a risk involved in that work. An injured party receives compensation without regard to whether the employer or the employee was negligent. Generally no compensation results for a willfully self-inflicted injury or a harm sustained while intoxicated. However, the employer has the burden of proving intentional self-inflicted injury. The law limits the amount of recovery and sets it in accordance with a prescribed schedule.

PREVIEW CASE REVISITED

Facts: As a busboy for Lori's Family Dining, one of Christopher Bingham's duties was emptying the trash into a dumpster. Bingham was carrying boxes to the dumpster when he started talking to and teasing a coworker. The teasing escalated to horseplay, resulting in Bingham falling and breaking his arm. Horseplay was customary at Lori's and while Lori's had a rule against it, that rule was not enforced. When Bingham claimed workers' compensation, Lori's objected, claiming that although the injury occurred in the course of employment, there was no causal connection between the work conditions and the injury—the risk of horseplay was not involved in the work.

Outcome: The court stated that since horseplay had become customary and was permitted by Lori's, it had become a regular part of the employment.

Workers' compensation laws generally allow recovery for accident-inflicted injuries and occupational diseases. Some states limit compensation for occupational diseases to those specified by name in the statute. These diseases include silicosis, lead poisoning, or injury to health from radioactivity. Other states compensate for any disease arising from the occupation.

Whether based on the common law or an employer's liability statute, damages actions are tried in court. Workers' compensation proceedings differ because a special administrative agency or workers' compensation board hears them. However, either party may appeal the agency or board decision to the appropriate court of law.

Workers' compensation statutes do not bar an employee from suing another employee for the injury.

OCCUPATIONAL SAFETY AND HEALTH ACT

In 1970, the federal government enacted the Williams-Steiger Occupational Safety and Health Act to ensure safe and healthful working conditions. This federal law applies to every employer engaged in a business affecting interstate commerce except governments. The Occupational Safety and Health Administration (OSHA) administers the act and issues standards that must be complied with by employers and employees. In order to ensure compliance with the standards, OSHA carries out job-site inspections. Employers must maintain detailed records of work-related deaths, injuries, and illnesses. The act provides fines for violations, including penalties of up to $1,000 per day for failure to correct violations within the allotted time.

Liabilities of the Employer to Third Parties

LO3 Employer's liability

Respondeat Superior Theory imposing liability on employers for torts of employees

An employer has liability under certain circumstances for injuries that are caused by employees to third parties. The theory of **respondeat superior** imposes liability on an employer for torts caused by employees. The employer is liable for personal injury as well as property damage.

To be liable, the employee must have committed the injury in the course of employment. An employee, who, without any direction from the employer, injures a third party and causes injury not as a result of the employment, has personal liability, but the employer does not. The employer has liability, however, if it ordered the act that caused the injury or had knowledge of the act and assented to it. Finally, the employer has liability for the torts of employees caused by the employer's negligence in not enforcing safe working procedures; not providing safe equipment, such as trucks; or not employing competent employees.

Facts: Nationwide Personal Security Corporation employed Arthur Hinton. While on the job at a supermarket, he got into an argument about the job with the supermarket manager. A cashier, Marta Rivas, screamed for help when Hinton started choking the manager. To silence Rivas, Hinton struck her. Rivas sued Nationwide for assault and battery, arguing that Hinton committed the attack in the course of his employment.

Outcome: The court agreed and ordered judgment for Rivas.

Employee's Duties to the Employer

The employee owes certain duties to the employer. Failure to comply with these duties may result in discharge. An employee's duties include:

LO4 Duties of employee

1. Job performance
2. Business confidentiality
3. Granting of right to use inventions

JOB PERFORMANCE

The duties required by the job must be performed faithfully and honestly and to advance the employer's interests. In skilled positions, the worker must perform the task with ordinary skill.

BUSINESS CONFIDENTIALITY

An employee has a duty of confidentiality regarding certain business matters. Trade secrets or other confidential business information must not be revealed.

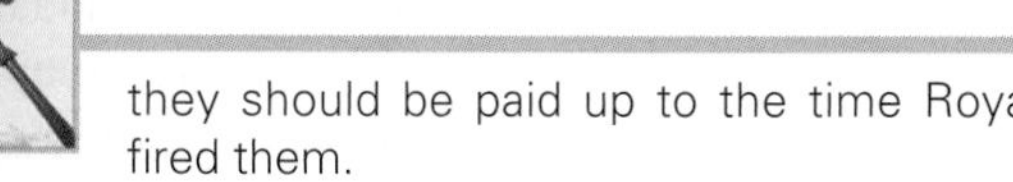

Facts: Royal Carbo Corp. employed Laurie McDonnell, Angel Ayala, and Anthony Lupo, Jr. While so employed, McDonnell, Ayala, and Lupo organized a competing corporation and used Royal's trade secrets to secretly undersell Royal's customers. Royal sued the three and they argued they should be paid up to the time Royal fired them.

Outcome: The court held that McDonnell, Ayala, and Lupo forfeited their right to compensation and Royal was entitled to recover damages from them.

INVENTIONS

In the absence of an express or implied agreement to the contrary, inventions belong to the employee who devised them, even though the time and property of the employer were used in their discovery, provided that the employee was not employed for the express purpose of inventing the things or the processes that were discovered.

If the invention is discovered during working hours and with the employer's material and equipment, the employer has the right to use the invention without charge in the operation of the business. If the employee has obtained a patent for the invention, the employer must be granted a nonexclusive license to use the invention without the payment of royalty. This **shop right** of the employer does not give the right to make and sell machines that embody the employee's invention; it only entitles the employer to use the invention in the operation of the plant.

Shop Right
Employer's right to use employee's invention without payment of royalty

When an employer employs a person to secure certain results from experiments to be conducted by that employee, the courts hold that the inventions equitably belong to the employer. Courts base this result on a trust relation or an implied agreement to make an assignment.

In any case, an employee may expressly agree that inventions made during employment will be the property of the employer. Such contracts must be clear and specific, or else courts normally rule against the employer. The employee may also agree to assign to the employer inventions made after the term of employment.

Federal Social Security Act

The federal Social Security Act has four major provisions:

1. Old-age and survivors' insurance
2. Assistance to persons in financial need
3. Unemployment compensation
4. Disability and Medicare benefits

OLD-AGE AND SURVIVORS' INSURANCE

The Social Security Act provides payments to the dependents of covered workers who die before the age of retirement. This part constitutes the survivors' benefits. If workers live to a specified age and retire, they and their spouses draw retirement benefits. This part constitutes the old-age benefits. Both parts are called insurance because they constitute risks that could be insured against by life insurance companies. The survivors' insurance covers the risk of the breadwinner's dying and leaving dependents without a source of income. Old-age benefits cover the risk of outliving one's savings after retirement.

Who Is Covered? The old-age and survivors insurance provisions of the Social Security Act cover practically everyone. Employees in state and local governments, including public school teachers, may be brought under the coverage of the act by means of agreements between the state and the federal government.

This provision of the act also covers farmers, professional people (such as lawyers), and self-employed businesspeople. The act does not cover certain types of work of close relatives, such as a parent for a child, work by a child under 21 for parents, and employment of a spouse by a spouse.

Eligibility for Retirement Benefits. To be eligible for retirement benefits, one must meet these requirements:

1. Be fully insured (40 quarters or the equivalent of 10 years) at the time of retirement.
2. Be 62 years of age or older.
3. Apply for retirement benefits after reaching the age of retirement. To be entitled to the maximum retirement benefits, one must wait until at least age 65 to apply for them.

Eligibility for Survivors' Benefits. The family of a worker who dies while fully insured or currently insured at the time of death has a right to survivors' benefits. Currently insured means the person had worked at least 6 quarters in the 13-quarter period ending with death.

ASSISTANCE TO PERSONS IN FINANCIAL NEED

People over 65 who have financial need may be eligible for federal supplemental security income payments. These monthly payments go to blind or disabled people in financial need. No one contributes specifically to this system based only on need.

UNEMPLOYMENT COMPENSATION

In handling unemployment compensation, the federal government cooperates with the states, which set up their own rules, approved by the federal government, for the payment of unemployment benefits. Payments of unemployment compensation are made by the states and not by the federal government.

The unemployment compensation laws of the various states differ, although they tend to follow a common pattern. They all provide for raising funds by levies upon employers. The federal government pays the cost of running the programs.

State unemployment compensation laws apply in general to workers in commerce and industry. Agricultural workers, domestic servants, government employees, and employees of nonprofit organizations formed and operated exclusively for religious, charitable, literary, educational, scientific, or humane purposes may not be included.

To be eligible for benefits, a worker generally must meet the following requirements:

1. Be available for work and registered at an unemployment office
2. Have been employed for a certain length of time within a specified period in an employment covered by the law
3. Be capable of working
4. Not have refused reasonably suitable employment

5 Not be self-employed
6 Not be out of work because of a strike or a lockout still in progress or because of voluntarily leaving a job without cause
7 Have served the required waiting period

DISABILITY AND MEDICARE BENEFITS

The government makes monthly cash benefits, called *disability insurance benefits*, to disabled persons under the age of 65 and their families. A disabled person is someone unable to engage in any substantial gainful activity because of a medically determinable physical or mental impairment expected to end in death or that has lasted or will last continually for 12 months.

Medicare is insurance designed to help pay a large portion of personal health care costs. Virtually everyone age 65 and over may be covered by this contributory hospital and medical insurance plan. The program covers only specified services.

TAXATION TO FINANCE THE PLAN

To pay the life insurance and the annuity insurance benefits of the Social Security Act, both the employer and the employee pay a payroll tax (FICA) of an equal percentage of all income earned in any one year up to a specified maximum. The maximum income and the rate may be changed at any session of Congress. A payroll tax finances the unemployment compensation part of the act. In most states the employer bears this entire tax. The assistance to persons in need is paid for by general taxation. No specific tax is levied to meet these payments. Disability and Medicare benefits are funded from a combination of four sources: FICA, a Medicare tax on people who are not covered by the old-age and survivors' insurance, premiums paid by the people covered, and the general federal revenue.

Questions

1 How does the relationship of employer and employee arise?
2 How may the terms of compensation determine the period of an employment contract and what does this mean to employers?
3 What does it mean for an employment contract to be at will?
4 How does the defense of contributory negligence help an employer?
5 How has the statutory modification of an employer's common-law defenses made it easier for an employee to win a case?
6 What are the basic provisions of workers' compensation statutes with regard to the injury or death of an employee?
7 What methods does OSHA use to try to ensure safe and healthful working conditions?
8 What is the doctrine of respondeat superior?
9 Explain the two types of payments under the Social Security Act.
10 For what Social Security programs are employees taxed?

Case Problems

LO1 1 Obstetricians & Gynecologists, P.C. offered Julie Goff-Hamel a full-time job, and Goff-Hamel accepted with employment starting October 4. Goff-Hamel resigned her current job. On October 3 Obstetricians' personnel consultant told Goff-Hamel not to report to work the next day. The wife of a part owner of Obstetricians opposed her employment. Goff-Hamel sued for breach of contract. Had Obstetricians breached the employment contract?

LO3 2 A tenant of the Kings Arms Apartments, Kimberly Jackman awoke to see a man standing in her hallway. He stated he was the maintenance man, sat down next to Jackman and started rubbing her thigh. She pleaded for him to leave and he did so. Jackman called the police and later sued the owner of the Kings Arms. Was the maintenance man's employer liable for his assault on Jackman?

LO4 3 J.B. Hunt Transport Services, Inc. hired Thomas Hostetler and Vincent McLoughlin to build a new division which turned out to be successful for the company. When hired, Hostetler and McLoughlin had signed an agreement stating that Hunt's methods, operations, marketing, and the like constituted confidential information. Several years later, they resigned to take jobs with Cardinal Freight Carriers. Hunt sued Hostetler and McLoughlin. Did they have a duty to keep Hunt's information confidential?

LO1 4 Arch of Wyoming, Inc. hired Gilbert Sisneros to work in its mine and gave him an employee handbook on the last page of which it stated that it was "not to be construed as a contract between Arch of Wyoming . . . and its employees." It included provisions relating to reductions in force and also indicated Arch had the right to change or cancel the handbook. Two years later Arch revised the handbook changing the reduction in force provision and moving the provision disclaiming a contract to the first page. Arch laid off Sisneros in a reduction of force. He sued for breach of contract created by the original handbook. Had the disclaimer of a contract in that handbook been adequate to prevent the creation of a contract?

LO4 5 For 24 years Kenneth Crisp ran a successful farm supply store and after Vigoro Industries, Inc. acquired the store, Crisp agreed to join Cleveland Chemical in operating a competitor store. Crisp offered his property as the location for the new store, gave Cleveland estimates of salaries and wages and asked his employees to join him at the new store. Crisp sent Vigoro a letter of resignation stating all his employees would leave with him. He also sent a letter to Vigoro's best customers asking for their business. Vigoro sued Crisp. Explain its best basis for the suit.

LO2 6 John Pappas and Joe Matthews, who worked for Marine Spill Response Corp., went to a work-related convention out of town. They encountered business prospects and indicated they would visit Bourbon Street in the evening after the convention. Pappas and Matthews went to a karaoke bar where they thought they might meet some business prospects. They befriended a Dutch couple. When the woman agreed to take the stage, Pappas knocked over another patron's beer bottle en route to the stage. Without notice, this patron kicked Pappas, causing $1,600 in medical expenses when Pappas returned home. Pappas sought workers' compensation and Marine opposed it. Was Pappas' injury work-related?

LO1 7 Marine Midland Bank recruited Patricia Feeney to work as a vice president. After a restructuring several years later, Marine fired her. She sued Marine, arguing that she had a contract of employment. Marine had sent a letter confirming the offer of employment. The letter mentioned a bonus payable the following January. Marine's two employee handbooks provided to Feeney stated Marine had no contractual arrangement with its employees and that employees were employed at will. Did the letter's reference to a January bonus set a guaranteed term of employment?

Internet Resources for Business Law

Name	Resources	Web Address
The Outsourcing Institute	The Outsourcing Institute provides general information on outsourcing, including the hiring of independent contractors.	http://www.outsourcing.com/
The Ultimate Employee Handbook—A Workshop	Court TV sponsored an online seminar, recorded here, in which lawyers from around the world offered advice on the "ultimate" employee handbooks.	http://www.courttv.com/legalhelp/business/seminars/handbook
Avoiding Booby Traps in Drafting Employee Manuals	*Avoiding Booby Traps in Drafting Employee Manuals*, by attorney James R. Macy, provides basic advice for drafting employment manuals.	http://www.abanet.org/genpractice/compleat/w96man.html
U.S. Department of Labor	The U.S. Department of Labor provides information and statistics, at the federal level, for workplace and agency issues.	http://www.dol.gov/
Getting Around Barriers to Non-compete Pacts	"Getting Around Barriers to Non-Compete Pacts," by James A. DiBoise and David J. Berger, originally published in *The National Law Journal*, discusses whether courts will consider trade secret confidentiality as covenants not to compete.	http://wsgrgate.wsgr.com/Resources/IntProp/Pubs/Articles/barriers.htm

29 Employees' Rights

Learning Objectives

1 List the bases in federal law upon which an employer may not discriminate against employees.

2 Explain the restrictions on employers in requiring invasive or offensive testing of employees and job applicants.

3 Discuss three significant protections given to employees by federal or state law, municipal ordinance, or employer regulation.

PREVIEW CASE

Wal-Mart employed Melanie Satterfield as a cashier. She had missed work without reason on May 28 and 29 and June 3. On June 16 she did not report to work and had her mother take a note to Wal-Mart saying she had pain in her side. Satterfield did not have a telephone, but drove to a pay phone to call her doctor. She did not call Wal-Mart and did not work on June 17–20. She contacted Wal-Mart on June 28 after she found out her health insurance had been canceled and the manager told her she had been fired. Satterfield sued Wal-Mart for violation of the FMLA. What is the purpose of the FMLA? Does saying a person has such pain give notice of a serious illness?

Many federal and state laws, municipal ordinances, and court decisions grant specific rights to employees. However, not all laws apply to all employees. State laws, court decisions, and ordinances vary. Some rights extend to all or almost all employees, while others may extend only to those in specified industries. The law is constantly extending rights to cover ever larger numbers of workers. Some of these rights include rights against discrimination on specified bases, the right not to be subjected to certain invasive or offensive tests, and various protections such as for taking leave, receiving notification of plant closing, and being protected from secondhand smoke.

Discrimination

LO1
Bases for protection from discrimination

Federal laws protect employees from discrimination on a number of grounds. Some laws prohibit discrimination on only one basis, while others protect on many bases. These laws include the Civil Rights Act of 1964, the Equal Pay Act, the Age Discrimination in Employment Act, and the Americans with Disabilities Act.

CIVIL RIGHTS ACT OF 1964

The most important law governing employment discrimination and also harassment on the basis of race, color, religion, sex, and national origin is Title VII of the federal Civil Rights Act of 1964. The act applies to every employer engaged in an industry affecting interstate commerce who has 15 or more employees and to labor unions with 15 or more members. It does not apply to the U.S. government (except the Congress) or certain private membership clubs exempt from federal taxation.

This law makes it an unlawful employment practice for an employer to fail to hire, to discharge, or to in any way discriminate against anyone with respect to the terms, conditions, or privileges of employment because of the individual's race, color, religion, sex, or national origin. (Discrimination because of sex includes discrimination because of pregnancy, childbirth, or related medical conditions.) The employer also may not adversely affect an employee's status because of one of these factors. In addition, it is an unlawful employment practice for an employment agency or a labor organization to discriminate, classify, limit, or segregate individuals in any way on any one of these bases. (See Illustration 29-1 for a sample employment application.)

When a person sues under Title VII, the discrimination is usually claimed on either of two theories. These theories are disparate treatment and disparate impact.

Facts: Community Bank hired Brenda Tatum, who was black, as a bookkeeper. Prior to her completing her probationary term she was fired. Her supervisor testified that Tatum sat with her back to her coworkers and rarely spoke to them. Tatum wore headphones while she worked and was given a written warning for attitude problems. She engaged in several angry outbursts, failed to cooperate with coworkers and was excessively absent, always on a Monday or Friday. The bank had fired white employees for inadequate job performance and absenteeism. Tatum sued for discrimination under Title VII alleging disparate treatment.

Outcome: The court pointed out that although Tatum proved all the elements of her case, the bank gave a nondiscriminatory reason for firing Tatum. Since white employees were treated similarly, there was no evidence of an intent to discriminate. Tatum could not recover.

Disparate Treatment
Intentional discrimination against a particular individual

Protected Class
Group protected by antidiscrimination laws

Disparate Treatment. In a discrimination case on the ground of **disparate treatment** in employment, the plaintiff alleges that the discrimination was against the plaintiff alone and was because of the plaintiff's membership in a protected class. A **protected class** is any group given protection by antidiscrimination laws, such as groups based on race, color, religion, sex, or national origin and protected by Title VII. Disparate treatment is basically intentionally different treatment. That is, women are treated differently than men, blacks are treated differently than whites, and people of one religion are treated differently than people of another religion, solely because of their sex, race, or religion, respectively. The plaintiff must show the employer acted

EMPLOYMENT APPLICATION

1.
Employer: ____________________
Address: ____________________
City/State/Zip: ____________, ____________ ______
Telephone: ________

It is the policy of ____________________ to provide equal employment opportunities to all applicants and employees without regard to any legally protected status such as race, color, religion, gender, national origin, age, disability, or veteran status.

2.
Applicant Name: ____________________
Address: ____________________
City/State/Zip: ____________________
Number of years at this address: ______
Daytime phone: __________ Evening phone: __________
Social Security Number: ______________

3.
Who should be contacted if you are involved in an emergency?
Contact Name: ____________________
Relationship to you: ____________________
Address: ____________________
City/State/Zip: ____________________
Daytime phone: __________ Evening phone: __________

4.
Job Position Applied For: ____________________

5.
Salary Desired: $ ________ per ________

6.
Referral Source: Who referred you to our company?
____

7.
Have you applied to our company previously? _____ Yes _____ No
If yes, when? ____________

(*continued*)

Use your Quicken Business Lawyer program to open this document on your computer. Read and complete the form and see the final checklist. Next visit the Web site of the Department of Labor's *Small Business Handbook* and read about what can and cannot be included on an employment application. If this application did *not* follow the law, what kinds of questions might be on it? http://www.dol.gov/dol/asp/public/programs/handbook/discrim.htm

Illustration 29-1
Employment Application

with the intention of discriminating. Plaintiffs make a case by showing direct evidence of discrimination or by showing:

1. They belong to one of the protected classes,
2. They were qualified for the job from which they were fired or for which they applied,
3. They were fired or not hired, and
4. The employer put a person in the job who was not in the protected class.

Once plaintiffs prove these four points, employers must offer a nondiscriminatory reason for their actions. If such reasons can be offered, plaintiffs must then show that the adverse treatment was because of their membership in one of the protected classes—that the employer intended to discriminate.

Disparate Impact
Fair policy disproportionately affecting protected class

Disparate Impact. To prove a discrimination claim based on **disparate impact**, an employee must show that an action taken by the employer that appears fair, nonetheless negatively and disproportionally affects a protected class of employees. An important difference between this theory and disparate treatment is that no intent to discriminate need be shown for disparate impact. The action complained of could be a testing policy, an application procedure, a job qualification, or any other employment practice whose adverse effect on employees is significantly greater on the members of a protected class than on employees that are not in that class.

Hostile Work Environment
Alteration of terms or conditions of employment by harassment

Sexual Harassment. Courts have held that the Title VII prohibition against discrimination on the basis of sex protects an employee against an employer who engages in or allows unwelcome sexual advances that create a **hostile work environment**. A hostile work environment exists when harassing conduct alters the terms or conditions of employment, creating an abusive work atmosphere, and it is based on the victim's membership in a protected class. Economic harm does not necessarily have to be proved. An employer can be liable for harassment by coworkers if it knows about the harassment and does not take prompt and appropriate corrective action.

Facts: Mechelle Vinson was employed by Meritor Savings Bank. She took indefinite sick leave and later was fired for excessive use of that leave. She sued the bank, claiming that while working at the bank she had constantly been subjected to sexual harassment by Sidney Taylor, her supervisor. She did not claim any economic damages, merely that there was a hostile work environment. The bank claimed that the Civil Rights Act was not concerned with the psychological aspects of the workplace environment.

Outcome: The court said the law was violated if sexual harassment altered the conditions of the victim's employment and created an abusive working environment. Vinson did not have to show economic loss.

In order to prove that the work environment was hostile, an alleged victim of sexual harassment must show that the environment was one that an objectively reasonable person would find abusive. This means that any reasonable employee would find the environment abusive. This requirement protects employers from overly sensitive employees who, for example, might feel that one isolated comment from a coworker created an abusive environment. In addition, victims themselves must find the environment abusive. Thus a victim who is less sensitive than reasonable employees would probably have to have a more abusive work environment before a claim of sexual harassment would be upheld. If both of these requirements are met, the victim need not show psychological injury—the hostile work environment alone is actionable.

Facts: Teresa Harris worked as a manager at Forklift Systems, Inc. and Charles Hardy was the president. Hardy often insulted Harris because of her gender, saying such things as, "You're a woman, what do you know." He often made her the target of unwanted sexual innuendos regarding her clothes, suggesting they go to a motel to negotiate her raise, and occasionally asked her to get coins from his front pants pocket. At one point Harris complained to him. He claimed he was only joking, apologized, and promised he would stop. A couple of weeks later he began making her the target of unwanted sexual innuendos again and Harris quit. She sued Forklift, claiming Hardy's behavior had created an abusive work environment because of her gender. Forklift claimed Hardy's behavior did not seriously affect Harris's psychological well-being or cause her to suffer injury.

Outcome: In a unanimous decision, the U.S. Supreme Court said that as long as the environment would reasonably be perceived and is perceived by the victim as hostile or abusive, Harris did not also have to show psychological injury.

Although many types of actions are prohibited under Title VII, to be actionable, the victim must be affected because of membership in a protected class. Behavior could discriminate or create an abusive work atmosphere, but only that behavior based on the victim's membership in a protected class is actionable. For example, a person could be teased about living in a highrise apartment, having short hair, long hair, a pierced nose, driving a particular type of car, having freckles, or being tall. Even if they are insensitive or designed to humiliate, as long as the comments are not found to be based on membership in a protected class, they are not actionable under Title VII.

Successful plaintiffs in Title VII cases are entitled to a remedy that would put them in the same position they would have been in if the discrimination had not occurred. This might include some kind of corrective action by employers, posting of notices about sensitivity training, reinstatement, promotion, payment of lost benefits, and attorneys' fees. If the discrimination is intentional, punitive damages may be recovered.

The act establishes the Equal Employment Opportunity Commission (EEOC), which hears complaints alleging violations of this and other laws. Individuals may file the complaints or the EEOC itself may issue charges. If the EEOC verifies the charge, it must seek by conference, conciliation, and persuasion to stop the violation. If this fails, the EEOC may bring an action in federal court. If the EEOC finds no basis for a violation, the employee may still sue the employer in court; however, the employee has the burden of hiring a lawyer and pursuing the case.

EQUAL PAY ACT

Recognizing that women were frequently discriminated against in the workplace by being paid less than men were paid for the same work, the federal government enacted the Equal Pay Act of 1963. As an amendment to the Fair Labor Standards Act (discussed in detail in Chapter 30), the law applies to employers covered by that act. The Equal Pay Act requires that employers pay men and women equal pay for equal work. The law prohibits employers from discriminating on the basis of sex by paying employees at a rate less than the rate at which employees of the opposite sex are paid for equal work. To be equal work, the jobs must be performed under similar working conditions and require equivalent skill, effort, and responsibility.

An employer is not required to pay employees at the same rate if the payments are made on the basis of:

1 a seniority system,
2 a merit system,
3 quantity or quality of production, or
4 a differential resulting from any factor other than sex.

Facts: Technical writers at Computer Associates, Jessica Meeks and Susan Cain were paid $24,500 each. The male technical writer with similar experience was paid $28,500. Meeks thought the salaries were discriminatory and complained to her supervisor, Laverne Peter. Meeks and Peter had a number of arguments about this and Meeks was put on probation. She sued Computer for discrimination and retaliation under the Equal Pay Act. Computer argued that the salaries of its 116 technical writers employed at offices around the country should be used in determining an equal pay claim.

Outcome: The court looked to the exact language of the act, which prohibits discrimination *within any establishment,* and said multiple offices were not a single establishment. Since no factor other than sex explained the pay differential, Computer was liable.

In addition to its application to employers, the equal pay act also prohibits labor unions from making or attempting to make employers discriminate against an employee on the basis of sex. Although the law was intended to help women, it is written in such a way that it requires equal pay for equal work and neither men nor women may be preferred.

AGE DISCRIMINATION IN EMPLOYMENT ACT

In order to protect persons age 40 or over from employment discrimination, the federal government enacted the Age Discrimination in Employment Act (ADEA). This statute prohibits arbitrary age discrimination by employment agencies, employers, or labor unions against persons age 40 or above. Employers are prohibited from firing or failing to hire persons in this age group, and they may not limit, segregate, or classify their employees so as to discriminate against persons in this age group solely because of their age. The firing can be an actual termination or a constructive discharge.

Facts: When 62 years old, Daniel Kirsch's employer, Fleet Street, Ltd., changed the compensation for his sales position from a commission which had given him $80,000–$100,000 a year to a salary of $60,000 plus 2 percent on sales over $2 M. Three years before, all the road sales representatives had been fired. They were all over 50. The sales manager who was a company officer told Kirsch he should watch out because all around him were young people. When a new employee inquired why the company did not expect Kirsch to be employed much longer, the sales manager said the company wanted "younger blood." Shortly thereafter Fleet reduced Kirsch's salary to $26,000. Kirsch sued Fleet alleging constructive termination based on his age in violation of the ADEA.

Outcome: The court said the reduction in compensation to $26,000 constituted a condition so grim it could have compelled Kirsch to resign thus constituting constructive discharge. The court further said age was a factor in the discharge in violation of the ADEA.

The ADEA does not prevent an employer from ever considering an employee's age or age-related criteria. It prohibits arbitrary discrimination, which occurs when age is considered despite its complete irrelevance to the decision being made. The law allows age discrimination when age is a true occupational qualification, such as the rule that commercial pilots cannot be more than 60 years old. In this case the age limit is related to very significant safety considerations affecting the lives of millions of people. Company seniority systems are also permitted even though they may have an impact on employees based on their ages.

An employee who wishes to pursue an ADEA claim must file a claim with the EEOC within 180 days of the occurrence of the adverse employer action. If the EEOC does not find the claim valid, the employee may bring a court action against the employer. A successful employee could recover back pay, lost benefits, future pay (called *front pay*), and, at the discretion of the court, attorney fees. In addition, the court could order reinstatement, promotion, or, for an individual denied a job, hiring. If violation of the ADEA was willful, liquidated damages equal to the back pay award is automatically awarded.

This law excludes from the definition of employee persons elected to state or local office and persons appointed at the policymaking level.

AMERICANS WITH DISABILITIES ACT

The Americans with Disabilities Act of 1990 (ADA), which applies to employers of 15 or more employees, prohibits employment discrimination against qualified people with disabilities. An employer may not discriminate because of the disability in job application, hiring, advancement, or firing. For the purposes of the ADA, a disability requires two elements:

1. a physical or mental impairment that
2. substantially limits one or more major life activities.

It is not enough simply to have an impairment and be unable to perform one specific job. The impairment must significantly limit a major life activity such as being unable to perform a class or broad range of jobs. A "major life activity" includes such actions as speaking, seeing, hearing, breathing, caring for oneself, walking, performing manual tasks, working, sitting, lifting, reaching, and standing.

Facts: Jamie Lowe worked for Angelo's Italian Foods and did purchasing and inventory control. She presented her supervisor with a letter from her doctor indicating Lowe had a neurological problem and could not carry anything heavier than 15 pounds and could only carry things up to 15 pounds occasionally. She was fired that day. Later diagnosed with multiple sclerosis, for which there is no known cure, she sued Angelo's, alleging the termination violated the ADA.

Outcome: The court said that lifting was a major life activity, so that if Lowe's impairment substantially limited her ability to lift, she was disabled under the ADA.

To determine whether other impairments constitute a major life activity, courts consider the type and severity of the impairment, the duration of the impairment, and any permanent or long-term impact of the impairment. Thus, temporary, short-term, or nonchronic impairments with no long-term impact are not *disabilities*. Such impairments include broken bones, flu, sprains, appendicitis, and concussions. In addition, specifically excluded from the definition of a disability is compulsive gambling, kleptomania, pyromania, sexual behavior disorders, and current illegal drug users and alcoholics.

Facts: Ingalls Shipbuilding hired Tamela Dutcher as a welder and assigned her to a job that required climbing 40 feet to reach her work. Dutcher had had a serious injury to her arm so she requested transfer to the fab shop because her bad arm made climbing difficult. Ingalls denied the transfer because of insufficient seniority. After a month of work, she obtained a transfer to the fab shop and worked until laid off. When recalled for a pre-employment physical, she told the doctor she needed a job that did not require climbing. The doctor gave her that job restriction and Ingalls told her it did not then have a job with no climbing. Shortly thereafter every welder in Dutcher's job classification was laid off. Dutcher sued Ingalls, asserting it violated the ADA by refusing to reinstate her in her job in the fab shop when called back.

Outcome: The court said her work in the fab shop showed she could work as a welder; she just could not work in a job requiring a lot of climbing. Therefore she was not significantly restricted in her ability to perform a class of jobs and did not have a disability protected by the ADA.

In addition, a person who has a history of an impairment that limits a major life activity, or is thought to have such an impairment is eligible for the benefits of the ADA. Thus an employee can obtain the benefits of the ADA not because of actual impairment, but because the employee is treated by the employer as having a limiting impairment.

Once a job applicant or employee has been identified as disabled according to the law, it must be determined if the individual with a disability is otherwise qualified for a particular job. If qualified, employers are required by the ADA to make "reasonable accommodations" to allow the disabled person to perform the essential functions of the job. The reasonable accommodation might include rescheduling employees, raising the height of desks to accommodate wheelchairs, acquiring equipment, or hiring a reader or sign language interpreter. An employer does not have to accommodate a disabled person if the accommodation would impose an undue hardship on the business. Violation of the ADA allows a qualified employee to recovery, such as reinstatement, back pay, compensatory damages, punitive damages, and attorneys' fees.

Testing

LO2 Restrictions on employee testing

In order to make sure businesses run properly, protect employees, protect company property from employee misuse, and weed out applicants for employment who might not be the best employees, many businesses have tried to institute various testing programs. These include polygraph testing, drug testing, and AIDS testing. The right of employers to use such tests either on a pre-employment basis or a random or mandatory basis after employment has been limited by statute as well as by the courts.

POLYGRAPH TESTING

As lie detector tests appeared to become more reliable, increasing numbers of employers began using them, both as a tool to find out which employees had violated workplace rules and to screen applicants for employment. As a result of perceived injustices, both because of an intrusion on employees' rights and because of the debate about the

Polygraph
Lie detector

reliability of such tests, the right to use these tests has been limited by statute. In 1988, the federal government enacted the Employee Polygraph Protection Act (EPPA). A **polygraph** is another word for a lie detector.

The EPPA limits the use of lie detector devices for pre-employment screening or random testing of employees by employers engaged in interstate commerce. An employer may not retaliate against an employee who refuses to take a polygraph test and may not use the test results as the exclusive basis for an employment decision adverse to an employee who took a test. Private employers may not use polygraphs unless:

1 they are investigating a specific incident of economic loss, such as theft or industrial espionage or sabotage,
2 the employer provides security services, or
3 the employer manufactures, distributes, or dispenses drugs.

An employer may use a polygraph as part of an ongoing investigation if the employee had access to the subject of the investigation and the employer has a reasonable suspicion of the employee's involvement. Before a polygraph test may be administered, the employee must be given written notice stating the specific economic loss, that the employee had access to the property that is the basis of the investigation, and giving a description of the employer's reasonable suspicion of the employee's involvement.

If an employer violates the EPPA, an employee or job applicant may sue the employer for the job, reinstatement, promotion, lost wages and benefits, or even punitive damages.

Except for the U.S. Congress, the law does not prohibit federal, state, and local governments from subjecting their employees to polygraphs.

AIDS TESTING

With the spread of the AIDS virus, employees have been concerned about contamination from afflicted coworkers. At the same time, workers with the virus have been concerned that they could be stigmatized and even lose their jobs. Since the test for AIDS is a blood test, the test is an invasive procedure and there are some limits to what an employer can require on constitutional grounds. The Fourth Amendment to the Constitution prohibits "unreasonable search and seizure" and courts have held that requiring a blood test for AIDS is a search and seizure; therefore, it must be reasonable. To determine whether a search is reasonable, the court balances the intrusion the testing would cause on the constitutional rights of the person to be tested with the interests said to justify the intrusion.

DRUG TESTING

There has been concern about the ability of employees in certain jobs to properly do their jobs while under the influence of drugs. This concern has resulted in private employers and several federal administrative agencies' requiring drug testing of employees or prospective employees. The Supreme Court has recognized three government interests that justify random drug testing. These are: (1) maintaining the integrity of employees in their essential mission, (2) promoting public safety, and (3) protecting sensitive information. For example, Customs Service employees seeking transfers or promotions to sensitive positions, and railroad workers involved in major railroad accidents or who violate certain safety rules are tested for drug use. Courts have upheld random drug testing for employees in order to promote safety.

Facts: The Federal Aviation Administration (FAA) issued a rule requiring random testing of airline employees for marijuana, cocaine, opiate, phencyclidine (PCP), and amphetamine use. The employees covered included flight crew members, attendants, instructors, and flight testing and maintenance personnel. Employees who tested positive and could not offer a satisfactory alternative explanation had to be removed from their positions. Employees subject to the FAA drug testing rules, labor organizations, and an organization of aviation employees and employers sued the FAA, arguing that the regulations were unreasonable searches in violation of the Constitution.

Outcome: The court held that the FAA's decision that safety concerns outweighed privacy concerns was reasonable and could not be overturned.

Protections

LO3 Protections for employees

In addition to rights against discrimination on various bases and against certain kinds of invasive or offensive testing, employees have been accorded a variety of protections. These include protection of their jobs when a family necessity or medical condition requires a leave, notification of plant closings, and protection from secondhand cigarette smoke.

FAMILY AND MEDICAL LEAVE

In order to allow employees the right to take leaves when family circumstances or illnesses require it, the federal government enacted the Family and Medical Leave Act (FMLA). This law allows an employee to take an unpaid leave of up to 12 workweeks in a 12-month period on the following occasions:

1. Because of the birth, adoption, or foster care of the employee's child
2. To care for the employee's spouse, child, or parent with a serious health condition
3. Because of a serious health condition that makes the employee unable to perform the job

The law applies to public and private employers who have 50 or more full- or part-time employees for 20 weeks during the year. It gives leave rights to employees who have worked for the employer for at least 12 months and a total of 1,250 hours.

While the FMLA gives workers the right to take leave, it is important to note that this leave is unpaid. Workers also may be required by their employers to use accrued paid vacation, personal, medical, or sick leave toward any part of the leave provided by the FMLA. If the leave is for the birth, adoption, or placement of a foster child, the leave must be taken within the first 12 months of the event. Unless the leave is not foreseeable, employees must give 30 days notice of a leave request.

A "serious health condition" for which leave may be requested is an illness, injury, impairment, or physical or mental condition that requires inpatient care or continuing medical treatment. Its purpose is to provide leave for the more exceptional and presumably time-consuming events. The care given to another includes psychological as well as physical care.

The benefit provided by the FMLA is that after taking the leave and returning to work, employees have to be given back their previous positions. If this is not possible, the employer must put them in an equivalent job in terms of pay, benefits, and the other terms and conditions of employment.

PREVIEW CASE REVISITED

Facts: Wal-Mart employed Melanie Satterfield as a cashier. She had missed work without reason on May 28 and 29 and June 3. On June 16 she did not report to work and had her mother take a note to Wal-Mart saying she had pain in her side. Satterfield did not have a telephone, but drove to a pay phone to call her doctor. She did not call Wal-Mart and did not work on June 17–20. She contacted Wal-Mart on June 28 after she found out her health insurance had been canceled and the manager told her she had been fired. Satterfield sued Wal-Mart for violation of the FMLA.

Outcome: The court held that telling her employer she had a pain in her side was "inconsistent with the purposes of the FMLA." It did not advise Wal-Mart that her condition might qualify for FMLA protection so the court held for Wal-Mart.

PLANT CLOSING NOTIFICATION

Under the provisions of the federal Worker Adjustment and Retraining Notification Act (WARN), a business that employs 100 or more employees must give 60 days' written notice of a plant closing or mass layoff. A mass layoff is defined by the Act as a decrease in the work force at a single site of employment that results in an "employment loss" during a 30-day period for:

1 33 percent of the full-time employees (at a minimum of 50 employees), or
2 at least 500 full-time employees.

An employment loss is a termination that is not a discharge for cause, a voluntary departure, or a retirement.

The written notice must be given to workers expected to experience some loss of employment, or their union representative, and to specified government officials. Workers in this instance include managers and supervisors. WARN does not require the full 60 days notice if the plant closing or mass layoff occurs as a result of an unforeseeable business event, a natural disaster, a labor dispute (a lockout or permanent replacement

Facts: AMR Services Corp. decided to eliminate its in-house security department at Kennedy Airport and notified its 91 security employees that they had been "surplussed." AMR's policy was to allow surplussed employees to fill job vacancies in the company. Of the 65 full-time employees surplussed, 18 were placed in other jobs and lost no pay, benefits, or work days. William Martin and others who were not placed in jobs sued under the WARN Act since AMR did not give the security workers 60 days' advance notice of the shutdown. They claimed that they had been terminated when they were notified they were surplussed. AMR claimed only 47 of the 65 full-time employees had been terminated since the 18 transferred to other jobs had suffered no "employment loss."

Outcome: The court agreed with AMR that the 18 transferred employees had suffered no "employment loss" since they missed no workdays.

of strikers), the completion of a project by employees who knew the employment was temporary, or certain relocations when employees are offered transfers.

In case of a violation of WARN, an employee may sue the employer for back pay for each day of violation as well as benefits under the employer's employee benefit plan. Courts have the discretion to allow the successful party in such lawsuits to recover their reasonable attorney's fees.

SMOKING

The disclosure of the damaging effects of breathing secondhand smoke has resulted in a desire by many nonsmoking employees to work in smoke-free environments. The right of employees to be protected from secondhand cigarette smoke is protected in a variety of ways.

Some employers have taken the initiative by prohibiting or restricting smoking at their workplaces. In addition, a number of states and municipalities have enacted restrictive smoking legislation. This legislation varies greatly. No state law totally bans smoking at all job sites. Some laws merely require employers to formulate and publicize a written policy about smoking in the workplace. Others require employers to designate smoking and nonsmoking areas. Nearly all the laws have exceptions to the smoking ban that allow smoking in private offices. In spite of these exceptions, a very large percentage of employers have some kind of smoking restrictions in effect.

Other Sources of Rights

There are many other rights granted to employees, particularly through federal laws, which apply to large numbers of workers. These laws include the Rehabilitation Act and the Pregnancy Discrimination Act. The rights granted by these two laws are similar to those granted by statutes mentioned in this chapter.

Questions

1. What employment practices are made unlawful for an employer under the Civil Rights Act of 1964?
2. What is a protected class?
3. What four things must a plaintiff show to prove an employer acted with the intention of discriminating when there is no direct evidence of discrimination?
4. What must the plaintiff in a sexual harassment case show in order to prove that the work environment was hostile?
5. Does the Equal Pay Act require that employees always be paid at the same rate for equal work?
6. Does the Age Discrimination in Employment Act prevent employers from ever considering an employee's age or age-related criteria?
7. Does the Americans with Disabilities Act protect all individuals with a physical or mental impairment?
8. Under the ADA, must an employer accommodate all disabled persons?
9. When may a private employer use a polygraph test?
10. What government interests justify random drug testing?
11. What type of leave and under what circumstances may an employee take leave under the Family and Medical Leave Act?
12. What type of notice of plant closing must employers give and to whom must the notice be given?

Case Problems

LO1 1 Albertson's, Inc. hired Hallie Kirkingburg as a truck driver. The doctor who examined his eyes erroneously certified that his eyesight met the Department of Transportation's (DOT) standards. A year later Kirkingburg took a leave of absence after an injury and Albertson's required a physical before he returned to work. This time the doctor told Kirkingburg his eyesight did not meet basic DOT standards. He applied for a waiver but Albertson's fired him since he did not meet the standard. Kirkingburg sued Albertson's alleging the firing violated the ADA. Albertson's alleged that if Kirkingburg was disabled he was not a "qualified" person with a disability because Albertson's only required the minimum eyesight standards. Was Kirkingburg "qualified?"

LO3 2 Paula Tardie worked for Braintree Hospital Rehabilitation Network (BHRN). After BHRN formed the Rehabilitation Hospital of R.I. (RHRI), Tardie became its director of human resources. The job required availability 24 hours a day and 50 to 70 hours of work a week. Six months later Tardie was having chest pains, numbness in her arms, and dizziness. Her doctor told her to take some time off. While on leave Tardie resigned her job. When contacted by her former supervisor at BHRN, he told Tardie he had no full-time job for her. The next day she called RHRI and said she wanted the human resources director's job but could not work more than 40 hours per week. The CEO told her she could not do the job in 40 hours per week and RHRI offered her a severance package. Tardie sued RHRI alleging that terminating her while she was on medical leave violated the FMLA. Did it?

LO1 3 Monica Kindred worked as a school bus driver for the Northome/Indus. School District No. 363. The district reconfigured some school bus routes to eliminate a 180 mile route, the East Route, and eliminate the need to pay the driver who had always been a male, a premium. The district assigned Kindred a 122 mile route that included part of the former East Route. Kindred asked for premium pay, but since she could complete the route in the time limit specified by a union/district agreement the district denied her request. Another female driver asked for premium pay and the district granted her request because her route exceeded the time limit. Kindred sued the district for violation of the Equal Pay Act. Did the refusal to pay Kindred premium pay violate the act?

LO2 4 After he refused to take a polygraph test, Citibank fired Dennis Wiltshire, a manager in the Global Custody Department. Citibank had learned that a debit ticket date stamped in that department had been used to make a fraudulent wire transfer of $1.5 million. Citibank got the money back after paying $7,500 in fees. A date stamp on debit slips was not required or customary. Citibank learned a person from Brooklyn who described himself as a Citibank manager of Guyanese descent was involved. Wiltshire was the only employee with the requisite access and knowledge to be involved who fit that description, and he stated that a date stamp on a debit ticket was needed for a wire transfer. Wiltshire sued Citibank for violation of the EPPA alleging that the bank suffered no economic loss since it got the $1.5 million back and the bank had no reasonable suspicion to believe he was involved. Did it?

LO1 5 Governor John Ashcroft appointed Judge Ellis Gregory to office. The Missouri constitution made retirement mandatory for judges at age 70. When he reached 70, he sued alleging that mandatory retirement violated the Age Discrimination in Employment Act. Gregory argued that, as a judge he only resolved factual issues and decided legal questions, therefore the exception for persons appointed at the policymaking level did not apply to him. Ashcroft argued that judges made policy by applying the common law to cases. They also had supervisory authority over inferior courts and the state bar. Does the ADEA apply to judges?

LO2 6 The U.S. Customs Service, which interdicts and seizes illegal drugs, announced that drug tests would be a condition of employment in positions that directly involved illegal drug interdiction or required the employee to carry a firearm. The National Treasury Employees Union sued the Service, alleging the policy violated the Fourth Amendment as an unreasonable search and seizure. The Customs Service is the first line of defense against illegal drug trafficking; employees involved in interdiction have access to vast sources of seized drugs and have been the targets of violence and bribery by drug smugglers. Does the government have a sufficient compelling interest in ensuring these employees are physically fit, honest, and have good judgment to warrant the drug tests?

LO3 7 Jane Doe, who worked at R.R. Donnelley & Sons Co., told her supervisor, Anthony Malandro, that coworker Curt Buethe had left simulated heavy breathing on her voicemail. Buethe denied it, but Malandro put an adverse notation in Buethe's personnel file and told him sexual harassment was against company policy. Other incidents of sexual harassment involving coworkers occurred, including inquiry about her lingerie and size, asking her repeatedly for a date, asking her to have a drink and go to a motel, and repeated hugs and attempts to kiss her. Doe never reported these incidents. Then an unknown assailant raped Doe on Donnelley's premises. This was not reported to the local authorities or Donnelley until three months later. Doe sued Donnelley, alleging sexual harassment based on a hostile work environment. Should Donnelley be liable for sexual harassment?

LO3 8 A customer service supervisor at J.C. Penney, Ross Brown received a leave of absence under the FMLA to care for his terminally sick father. Brown's last day of work was July 24 and his father died on September 23. Brown did not report his father's death or return to work until October 22, a month after his father's death. Penney had assigned someone else to Brown's position and assigned him to be a sales associate in men's wear at his previous pay rate. Brown refused this position and Penney fired him. Brown sued, alleging a violation of the FMLA and arguing that Penney had to give him his old job back or a job of comparable stature. Penney argued that Brown had relinquished any rights under the FMLA by failing to return promptly after his father's death. Had he?

LO1 9 Employed by Olsten Corporation, Mary Ann Luciano had had consistently excellent performance reviews. Olsten's CEO offered to match the salary another company offered her and give her a written promise to review her performance in a year, promoting her to vice president if her performance was acceptable. Several male Olsten vice presidents and Luciano's supervisor formulated a new job description for Luciano, which would be the basis of that performance review. They designed a job description to ensure unsatisfactory performance. Nine months later, the CEO left. Luciano got a new supervisor, Gordon Bingham, and increased job responsibilities. Luciano never got the promised review. Two years later Bingham said her position was being eliminated and she was fired. Luciano's responsibilities were given to two males, one currently employed and the other newly hired. Luciano was not given an opportunity to apply for either position or any other Olsten position. Olsten had promoted male employees with poor performance records to senior management and created new positions for male employees whose positions were eliminated. Luciano sued, alleging gender discrimination. Is Olsten liable?

LO3 10 In a three-month period, 562 employees of McDonnell Douglas Corp. were laid off. None of them received the 60-day notice provided by the WARN Act. Of the 562, 50 were part-time employees, 32 were rehired within six months, and 31 elected early retirement instead of being laid off. Leonard Rifkin and others sued the company, alleging a violation of the WARN Act. McDonnell Douglas argued that both the employees rehired within six months and those who chose early retirement did not experience an employment loss as defined by WARN. One-third of the total employees was much more than 562. Did McDonnell Douglas violate the WARN Act?

LO1 11 Dover Elevator Systems, Inc. employed Michael Taylor, who had epilepsy, but it did not affect his ability to perform his job. Taylor's doctor put him on Felbatol on June 22 and took him off it on August 4. On August 31, a coworker, Rodney Bennett, asked Taylor to fix a broken air line. Taylor examined the line and decided it did not need fixing. Bennett then cut the line in two and yelled profanity at Taylor to fix it. The two got into a fight and at one point Taylor grabbed Bennett and said he was going to kill him. The two had a history of problems with each other. Dover had a rule against fighting, a violation of which could result in discharge. On three previous occasions, employee fights had resulted in resignation or discharge of the violators. Bennett and Taylor were both fired and Taylor sued Dover under the ADA, alleging the Felbatol caused him to have difficulty getting along with others. Did the discharge of Taylor violate the ADA on any basis?

Internet Resources for Business Law

Name	Resources	Web Address
Civil Rights Act of 1964, Definitions	LII provides 42 USC §2000e, the Civil Rights Act of 1964.	http://www.law.cornell.edu/uscode/42/2000e.html
Equal Pay Act of 1963	LII provides 29 USC §206, the Equal Pay Act of 1963.	http://www.law.cornell.edu/uscode/29/206.shtml
Age Discrimination in Employment Act of 1967	LII provides 29 USC §621, the Age Discrimination in Employment Act of 1967.	http://www.law.cornell.edu/uscode/29/621.shtml
Rehabilitation Act of 1973	LII provides 29 USC §701, the Rehabilitation Act of 1973.	http://www.law.cornell.edu/uscode/29/701.shtml
Occupational Safety and Health Act of 1970	LII provides 29 USC §651, the Occupational Safety and Health Act.	http://www.law.cornell.edu/uscode/29/651.shtml
Americans with Disabilities Act (ADA) Document Center	The ADA Document Center, maintained by attorney Duncan C. Kinder, provides the full ADA and relevant regulations and guidelines.	http://janweb.icdi.wvu.edu/kinder/
Family and Medical Leave Act (FMLA) of 1993	The Department of Labor (DOL) Employment Standards Administration provides the full text of the FMLA, fact sheets, compliance guides, and DOL regulations.	http://www.dol.gov/dol/esa/
U.S. Equal Employment Opportunity Commission (EEOC)	The EEOC provides publications and media releases, fact sheets, and information on the laws enforced by the EEOC.	http://www.eeoc.gov/
Occupational Safety and Health Administration (OSHA)	OSHA provides publications and media releases, program information, software, and data, among other services.	http://www.osha.gov/index.html
Social Security Administration (SSA)	The SSA maintains publications, information, and forms.	http://www.ssa.gov/

30 Labor Legislation

Learning Objectives

1 Discuss the objectives and coverage of the Fair Labor Standards Act.

2 State the five major provisions of the Labor Management Relations Act.

3 Name the three major provisions of the Labor-Management Reporting and Disclosure Act.

PREVIEW CASE

Tim Schermerhorn and other members of Local 100, Transport Workers Union of America tried to enter meetings of groups of members of the local in order to hand out flyers or raise issues of concern to the union. Local 100's executive committee enacted a policy limiting attendance at meetings only to members of the particular smaller group of the union that was meeting unless the meeting participants voted to invite another member to speak on a specified subject at a subsequent meeting (the attendance policy). The executive committee also enacted a policy that distribution of flyers was to be by placing them on a table outside a meeting; members had to request that an officer place the flyers on the table; and a union officer could refuse to place flyers unrelated to operation of the local (the flyer distribution policy). Schermerhorn and others sued the union, claiming that the attendance and flyer distribution policies violated the Labor-Management Reporting and Disclosure Act. Did it? What was the real purpose behind the policies?

Since 1930, the federal government has enacted more laws dealing with industrial relations than had been enacted during the prior history of the republic. Although the scope of a course in business law does not include all of these laws together with court interpretations, some basic knowledge of them is valuable. This chapter covers the Fair Labor Standards Act, the Labor Management Relations Act, and the Labor-Management Reporting and Disclosure Act.

The Fair Labor Standards Act

LO1
Objectives and coverage of FLSA

The federal Fair Labor Standards Act (FLSA) had two major objectives. The first objective placed a floor, regardless of economic conditions, under wages of employees engaged in interstate commerce (trade among or between states). The second objective discouraged a long workweek and thus spread employment. Setting a minimum wage accomplished the first objective. By successive amendments, this wage increased to a rate of $5.15 per hour. Employers are allowed to pay new employees under age 20 a lower hourly wage during the first 90 days of employment. Requiring employers to pay time and a half for all hours over 40 achieved the second objective. An employer may work employees, other than children, any number of hours a week if the employer pays the overtime wage.

EXCLUSIONS FROM THE ACT

The FLSA does not cover the following:

1 Employees working for firms engaged in intrastate commerce (trade within a state). This results from the constitutional provision giving Congress power to regulate interstate, not intrastate, commerce.
2 Employees working for firms engaged in interstate commerce but in a business excluded from the act, such as agriculture.
3 Employees in certain positions such as executives, administrators, and outside salespeople.
4 The workweek provisions do not apply to employees in that part of the transportation industry over which the Interstate Commerce Commission has control, to any employee engaged in the canning of fish, and to persons who are employed as outside buyers of poultry, eggs, cream, or milk in their natural state.

CHILD LABOR PROVISIONS

The FLSA forbids "oppressive child labor." It prohibits or severely limits the employment of children less than 16 years of age. This rule does not apply to certain agricultural employment, to parents or guardians employing their children or wards, to children employed as actors, or to certain types of employment specified by the Secretary of Labor as being exempted by the regulations. Youth between the ages of 16 and 18 are not permitted to work in industries declared by the Secretary of Labor to be particularly hazardous to health.

Facts: The Fair Labor Standards Act permits employers to ask the Secretary of Labor for a waiver of child labor laws so 10- and 11-year-olds may harvest certain crops. The secretary must grant the waivers if: "the employment . . . would not be deleterious to their health or well-being" and "the level and type of pesticides and other chemicals used would not have an adverse effect on the health or well-being of" the children. After reviewing existing scientific literature, the Department of Labor issued regulations. They allowed the use of certain pesticides a set time before harvesting by 10- and 11-year-olds. Two private, nonprofit organizations representing farm worker families asked the court to rule that the approval of pesticide use violated the statutory waiver provision. None of the scientific literature had addressed the risk to children.

Outcome: The court ruled that because there was no objective proof of the safety of the regulations, they were invalid.

CONTINGENT WAGES

Many types of employment call for the payment of wages on a commission basis or on a piece-rate basis. Many salespeople receive a commission on their sales rather than a salary. For employees covered by the act, if commissions earned in any one week are less than the minimum wages for the hours worked, the employer must add to the commission enough to bring the total earnings to the minimum wage. The same applies to employees being paid on a piece-rate basis. The act allows these types of incentive wages, but they cannot be used to evade the minimum-wage provisions of the act.

The National Labor Relations Act and the Labor Management Relations Act

Collective Bargaining Process by which employer and union negotiate and agree on terms of employment

The National Labor Relations Act of 1935 (NLRA known as the *Wagner Act*), expanded by the federal Labor Management Relations Act of 1947 (LMRA), also known as the *Taft-Hartley Act,* sought to create bargaining equality between employers and employees by permitting union activity. Specifically, it did this by attacking the denial of some employers of the right of employees to organize and the refusal to accept collective bargaining. **Collective bargaining** is the process by which employers and unions negotiate and agree on the terms of employment for the employees, which are then spelled out in a written contract. It requires that the employer recognize and bargain with the representative selected by the employees. The employees' representative is typically a union. The act also sought to eliminate certain forms of conduct from the scene of labor negotiations and employment by condemning them as unfair practices.

The NLRA excludes agricultural laborers and domestic servants, individuals employed by a parent or spouse, and independent contractors from its definition of *employees.* Thus they are not covered by the act. Included are all employers engaged in interstate commerce except:

1. The railroad industry, covered by the Railway Labor Act of 1947
2. Supervisory employees, who are considered part of management
3. Governments or political subdivisions of governments

Facts: The Hardin County Board of Education hired Charles Strasburger as an industrial arts teacher, athletic director, and basketball coach. After Strasburger disciplined a basketball player the player's father won a seat on the school board. The school board learned that Strasburger had been convicted of criminal trespass and disorderly conduct. It suspended him with pay from coaching and as athletic director without giving him notice or a hearing. After an investigation the board reinstated Strasburger. At the end of the year the board terminated him saying it needed to save money and he did not have enough students to justify his teaching position. Strasburger sued the union under the LMRA for inadequate representation in his grievance against the board.

Outcome: The court stated that the act excluded political subdivisions from the definition of *employer.* Since the school board was a political subdivision it was not an employer and Strasburger was not covered by the act.

LO2
Provisions of LMRA

The Labor Management Relations Act has the following five major provisions:

1. Continuation of the National Labor Relations Board (NLRB) created by the National Labor Relations Act
2. A declaration as to the rights of employees
3. A declaration as to the rights of employers
4. A prohibition of employers' unfair labor practices
5. A prohibition of unfair union practices

THE NATIONAL LABOR RELATIONS BOARD

The Labor Management Relations Act provides a continuation of the National Labor Relations Board (NLRB) of five members appointed by the president and confirmed by the Senate. This board hears and conducts investigations of complaints of employer and union unfair labor practices. If the board finds that an unfair practice exists, it has the power to seek an injunction to stop the practice. When a strike threatens national health or safety, the president may appoint a five-person board of inquiry and upon the basis of their findings may apply to the federal court for an injunction that will postpone the strike for 80 days. The NLRB supervises elections to determine the bargaining representative for the employees within each bargaining unit. In case of dispute, the NLRB determines the size and nature of the bargaining unit.

In addition to appointing the NLRB, the president appoints and the Senate confirms a general counsel. This general counsel has complete independence from the board in prosecuting complaint cases but in most other matters acts as the chief legal advisor to the board.

DECLARATION AS TO THE RIGHTS OF EMPLOYEES

The Labor Management Relations Act sets forth the following rights of employees:

1. To organize
2. To bargain collectively through their own chosen agents
3. To engage in concerted action; that is, **strike**, for their mutual aid and protection
4. To join or not to join a union unless a majority of all workers vote for a **union shop** and the employer agrees thereto

Strike
Temporary, concerted action of workers to withhold their services from employer

Union Shop
Work setting in which all employees must be union members

DECLARATION AS TO THE RIGHTS OF EMPLOYERS

The Labor Management Relations Act gives the employer many important rights:

1. To petition for an investigation when questioning the union's right to speak for the employees
2. To refuse to bargain collectively with supervisory employees
3. To institute charges of unfair labor practices by the unions before the board
4. To sue unions for breaches of the union contract whether the breach is done in the name of the union or as an individual union member
5. To plead with workers to refrain from joining the union provided the employer uses no threats of reprisal or promises of benefits

PROHIBITION OF EMPLOYERS' UNFAIR LABOR PRACTICES

The chief acts prohibited as unfair practices by employers comprise:

1 Interfering in the employees' exercise of the rights granted by the act.
2 Refusing to bargain collectively with employees when they have legally selected a representative.
3 Dominating or interfering with the formation or administration of any labor organization or contributing financial support to it.
4 Discriminating against or favoring an employee in any way because of membership or lack of membership in the union. An employee may be fired for nonmembership in a union when the union has a valid union shop contract.

Facts: An electrical contractor, 3-E Company, hired Charles Campbell and then Elliot Tonken, a union member, to work full-time on a project. The foreman, Paul Werner, noticed Campbell talking to Tonken during a break. Werner asked Campbell if Tonken was talking about the union and Campbell said he was. Werner said he did not like Tonken talking about the union at the project and that Tonken would be one of the first laid off when there was a layoff. Werner showed Campbell a notebook with the names of the first employees who would be laid off. Tonken's name was first. Werner also asked Tonken if he belonged to the union and if he was there to cause trouble. A month later Tonken was laid off. The International Brotherhood of Electrical Workers alleged an unfair labor practice.

Outcome: The court held that Werner's actions interfered with and coerced employees in the exercise of the right to organize.

5 Discriminating against an employee who has filed charges against the employer under the act.

When the National Labor Relations Board finds the employer guilty of any of these acts, it usually issues a "cease and desist order." If the cease and desist order does not prove effective, an injunction may be obtained.

PROHIBITION OF UNFAIR UNION PRACTICES

The Labor Management Relations Act lists seven specific acts that unions and their leaders may not engage in:

1 Coercion or restraint of workers in the exercise of their rights under the act.
2 Picketing an employer to force bargaining with an uncertified union (one that has not been elected to represent the employees).
3 Refusal to bargain collectively with the employer.
4 Charging excessive initiation fees and discriminatory dues and fees of any kind.
5 Barring a worker from the union for any reason except the nonpayment of dues.
6 Secondary boycotts or strikes in violation of law or the contract, although certain exceptions are made in the construction and garment industries. A **secondary boycott** is an attempt by employees to cause a third party to stop dealing with the employer. The third party would normally be a customer or supplier of the employer. The most common ways the boycott is carried out are by a strike or by picketing.
7 Attempts to exact payment from employers for services not rendered.

Secondary Boycott
Attempt by employees to stop third party dealing with employer

The Labor-Management Reporting and Disclosure Act

LO3
Provisions of LMRDA

In 1959, Congress passed the Labor-Management Reporting and Disclosure Act (LM-RDA), also called the *Landrum-Griffin Act.* The purpose of this act was to protect union members from improper conduct by union officials. The act contains a bill of rights for union members, it classifies additional actions as unfair labor practices, and it requires unions operating in interstate commerce and their officers and employers to file detailed public reports.

BILL OF RIGHTS

The bill of rights provisions of the Labor-Management Reporting and Disclosure Act guarantee union members the right to meet with other union members, to express any views or opinions at the union meetings, and to express views on candidates for union office or business before the meeting.

PREVIEW CASE REVISITED

Facts: Tim Schermerhorn and other members of Local 100, Transport Workers Union of America tried to enter meetings of groups of members of the local in order to hand out flyers or raise issues of concern to the union. Local 100's executive committee enacted a policy limiting attendance at meetings only to members of the particular smaller group of the union that was meeting unless the meeting participants voted to invite another member to speak on a specified subject at a subsequent meeting (the attendance policy). The executive committee also enacted a policy that distribution of flyers was to be by placing them on a table outside a meeting; members had to request that an officer place the flyers on the table; and a union officer could refuse to place flyers unrelated to operation of the local (the flyer distribution policy). Schermerhorn and others sued the union, claiming that the attendance and flyer distribution policies violated the Labor-Management Reporting and Disclosure Act.

Outcome: The court held that the policies violated the law and issued an injunction prohibiting the union from enforcing them.

ADDITIONAL UNFAIR LABOR PRACTICES

In addition to the unfair labor practices outlawed by the Labor Management Relations Act, the Labor-Management Reporting and Disclosure Act declares the following acts unfair labor practices:

1. Picketing by employees in order to extort money and for recognition when another union is the legally recognized bargaining agent, and there is no question regarding union representation.
2. To close loopholes, an expanded range of activities defined as secondary boycotts, except in the garment industry.
3. "Hot cargo agreements," except in the construction and garment industries. A **hot cargo agreement** is an agreement between a union and an employer that the employer will not use nonunion materials.

Hot Cargo Agreement
Agreement employer will not use nonunion materials

REPORTING REQUIREMENTS

The very detailed reporting requirements of the act require unions to file copies of their bylaws and constitutions in addition to reports listing the name and title of each officer; the fees and dues required of members; and the membership qualifications, restrictions, benefits, and the like. Financial information required to be reported includes a complete listing of assets and liabilities, receipts, and disbursements. Officials of the union must sign the union reports and the information contained in them must be made available to the union members.

The officials of the union must each file a report indicating any financial interest in or benefit they have received from any employer whose employees the union represents. They must also report whether they have received any object of value from an employer.

In addition to the requirement of annual reports by the union and its officials, employers must file annual reports listing any expenditures made to influence anyone regarding union organizational or bargaining activities. Everyone involved in labor persuader activities must disclose certain information. As public information, these reports must be available to anyone who requests them.

Facts: The law firm of Humphreys, Hutcheson & Moseley represented Southern Silk Mills, Inc., which was facing an election to be conducted by the NLRB to determine whether its employees would be represented by the Amalgamated Clothing and Textile Workers Union. Before the election, two attorneys from the firm made speeches to groups of Southern's employees to persuade them to vote against the union in the election. They were introduced as attorneys in the law firm representing Southern. The law firm refused to comply with the disclosure requirements of the Labor-Management Reporting and Disclosure Act. It alleged that the requirements did not apply because the intent of the law was to discourage secret persuader activities and that its relationship to Southern was announced before the presentation.

Outcome: The court held that the goal of the law was disclosure, and since the activities of the law firm were persuader activities, it must comply with the disclosure requirements.

The act also contains a number of additional provisions aimed at making unions more democratic and at protecting union funds from embezzlement and misappropriation.

Questions

1 Name two groups of employees who are not covered by the Fair Labor Standards Act.

2 May an employer use incentive wages and still comply with the Fair Labor Standards Act? Explain.

3 What was the purpose of the National Labor Relations Act of 1935?

4 What was the chief purpose of the Labor Management Relations Act?

5 What does the National Labor Relations Board do?

6 What are the rights of employees set forth in the Labor Management Relations Act?

7 a. If an employer refuses to bargain collectively with employees, is this an unfair labor practice?
b. Name some unfair labor practices by employers.

8 What is a secondary boycott and how is one usually carried out?

9 What rights do the bill of rights provisions of the Labor-Management Reporting and Disclosure Act guarantee?

10 Who is required by the Labor-Management Reporting and Disclosure Act to make financial reports?

Case Problems

LO3 1 Eugene Ruocchio served as treasurer of Local 60 of the United Transportation Union (UTU). In a letter to the union vice chairperson, Ruocchio mistakenly stated that a check received to replace one incorrectly made out to the secretary instead of the local had been for a "drastically reduced" amount. The secretary was the wife of the local's general chairperson and after the letter was read at a union meeting Ruocchio was removed from office. Ruocchio sued for money damages alleging the local and its general chairperson violated his free speech rights under the LMRDA. Before the case was tried the international president reinstated Ruocchio. The trial court dismissed Ruocchio's suit because of his reinstatement. Should he be able to pursue his suit?

LO1 2 Pine Lodge Nursing and Rehabilitation Center sent a letter addressed to the union representing its employees offering a wage increase. Shortly after sending the letter Pine Lodge posted a copy of it near the employee time clock so employees could read it. The union allowed the offer to expire and Pine Lodge sent another offer to the union. Pine Lodge copied this offer to its employees after sending it to the union. The union charged Pine Lodge had violated the NLRA by dealing directly with its employees thus refusing "to bargain collectively with the representatives" of the employees. Was the publication of the letters to the employees after sending them to the union a refusal to bargain with the union?

LO2 3 Limbach Constructors, Inc. (LCI) had wholly owned subsidiaries Limbach Company, a union contractor, and Jovis Construction. Jovis bought Harper Plumbing and Heating, Inc., a nonunion contractor. Union employees warned LCI that labor troubles would ensue for Limbach if it did not make Harper sign a collective bargaining agreement with the union. After more of such threats, the union terminated its collective bargaining agreement with Limbach. All Limbach's employees left their job sites and quit. Limbach filed unfair labor practice charges, alleging that the union had engaged in secondary boycott activity because it and Harper constituted separate employers; thus, a labor dispute between Harper and the union did not involve Limbach. Did the union's activity amount to coercion to get a secondary objective?

LO3 4 Ervin Shimman was a member of Local 18 of the International Union of Operating Engineers. When the U.S. Senate Labor Committee held hearings, Shimman testified about alleged manipulation of the hiring hall by the local so it could discriminate against those who disagreed with the current leadership. Frank Miller, editor of the local's newsletter, published an article attacking the hearings. The article stated that two members of the local testified and their allegations were false or misleading. Shimman responded by writing a letter to the editor of the newsletter and asked that it be published. Miller refused to print the letter because he disagreed with its content. The newsletter was the only means a local member had to present a differing point of view to other members and member dues alone financed it. The newsletter had been used to defend attacks by critics of the local, to run articles by the Ohio governor similar to advertisements by candidates for political office, and to denounce reform efforts of union members. Did Miller's failure to print Shimman's letter violate the free speech provisions of the Labor-Management Reporting and Disclosure Act?

LO2 5 The Greater Cleveland Regional Transit Authority (GCRTA) was formed under authority of state law, which allowed counties to create transit authorities. It was administered by a board appointed and removable by various municipal and county officials. GCRTA employed Michael Moir. He was notified that pursuant to merit system rules and the collective bargaining agreement, he had been promoted to equipment electrician, grade 5 because he got the highest rating on a promotion exam. Two months later Moir was notified that because of seniority, another GCRTA employee was being transferred to replace him and he could not keep his position. He sued GCRTA under the NLRA alleging that rescission of his promotion violated his rights under the collective bargaining agreement. GCRTA argued that it was a political subdivision and therefore exempt from the NLRA. Is it?

LO1 6 Scott Hageman worked for several years as a maintenance person for Park West Gardens apartments. He had no other employment. He performed various jobs including electrical, plumbing, heating, and air conditioning repairs. The apartment management gave Hageman a check for $100 or $150 each month for supplies. It paid him $7 an hour, $10 a week for gas, and reduced his rent $125 a month. Hageman had no set hours, but went to the office daily at 10 A.M. for work orders. He had a voice pager so the management could page him in emergencies. He sued Park West Gardens for overtime compensation, alleging that he was an employee, subject to the Fair Labor Standards Act. The trial court found that as an independent contractor, Hageman was not covered by the act. Should Hageman get overtime compensation?

Internet Resources for Business Law

Name	Resources	Web Address
Norris-LaGuardia Act—29 USC §101	Legal Information Institute (LII), maintained by Cornell Law School, provides 29 USC §101, the Norris-LaGuardia Act.	http://www.law.cornell.edu/uscode/29/101.shtml
Wagner Act—29 USC §151	LII provides 29 USC §151, the Wagner Act.	http://www.law.cornell.edu/uscode/29/151.shtml
Taft-Hartley Act—29 USC §171	LII provides 29 USC §171, The Taft-Hartley Act.	http://www.law.cornell.edu/uscode/29/171.shtml
Landrum-Griffin Act—29 USC §185	LII provides 29 USC §185, the Landrum-Griffin Act.	http://www.law.cornell.edu/uscode/29/185.shtml
National Labor Relations Board	The National Labor Relations Board provides speeches, publications, board decisions, and other materials.	http://www.nlrb.gov

Part 6 Summary Cases

Agency and Employment

1 Willie Ray Burwell browsed throught the Giant Genie food store; went to the checkout line and paid the cashier the total for his groceries. When Burwell picked up his bags of groceries and started to leave the store, the manager blocked his path and accused him of stealing two cartons of cigarettes. The manager grabbed Burwell's arm and pulled him toward the store office. After searching Burwell's bags and patting him down the manager found no cigarettes. Burwell sued Giant Genie for false imprisonment and assault and battery. Should the actions of the manager be imputed to Giant Genie? [*Burwell v. Giant Genie Corp.*, 446 S.E.2d 126 (N.C. App.)]

2 Cathy Jackson consented to sell 5 lots and to have her husband, Mark, show the property. Mark met with Larry McSweeney to look at the property. The next day Mark was showing the property to someone else and McSweeney appeared at the property. After Mark came over to him, McSweeney tried to give him a check for $4,000. Mark told McSweeney he could not take the check because he was showing the property to someone else. McSweeney folded the check and stuck it in Mark's shirt pocket. McSweeney left and returned with a friend. Mark asked if McSweeney had already contracted to resell the property and told him he wanted McSweeney to take the check back. Mark said they did not have a deal and gave back the check. When sued by McSweeney, the Jacksons alleged Mark was not the agent of Cathy simply because they were married so he could not have made a binding agreement to sell without her. Was Mark Cathy's agent? [*McSweeney v. Jackson*, 691 N.E.2d 303 (Ohio App.)]

3 Someone stole a guitar, two drum machines and a receiver from Thomas Martin's home. Martin suspected Christopher DiGiulio who repaired electronic equipment at the house and two days prior to the burglary had asked for more work. Eager to recover his guitar, Martin asked DiGiulio to help him find it and said he would pay for its return. The next day DiGiulio told Martin he had found it and could get it for $350, but asked Martin to write a note authorizing him to get it. The note Martin signed said, "I have empowered Chris DiGiulio to recover . . . [the guitar] . . . he is not to be held responsible or liable to prosecution in the theft." Martin gave him the money. DiGiulio went to an electronics business where he got the guitar. He had sold it to the owner for $65. When he returned the guitar the police arrested him for trafficking in stolen property. DiGiulio claimed he was merely acting as Martin's agent. Was there a valid agency? [*State v. DiGiulio*, 835 P.2d 488 (Ariz. App. Div.)]

4 Joseph and Frida Friedman owned adjoining lots, No. 3 and No. 5, with Leonard and Bernice Feldman. They retained Lam and Buchsbaum as their agent to sell the lots. Charles Samter, a salesman for Lam and Buchsbaum, showed Lot No. 3 to Victor and Barbara Kasser. The Friedmans had left the sale of the lots to Leonard Feldman, so Samter told Feldman the Kassers liked Lot No. 3. He asked Feldman to meet them at the lot to show them its dimensions. The meeting could not be arranged, but Feldman met Samter, gave him a plot plan, and paced off the lot's boundaries, which they staked off. Feldman told Samter the staking was probably a bit off, and any purchaser should have the lot surveyed. Samter showed the lot to the Kassers, pointed out the stakes, and gave them a copy of the plot plan. They bought the lot and built a house. The Friedmans got full title to adjoining Lot No. 5 and moved into the house there. They had parking pads built within the area designated by the stakes. A survey showed the Kassers' carport was

5.8 feet on Lot No. 5, and their driveway was up to 45 feet on the lot. The Friedmans sued to have the Kassers' carport, driveway, and so much of their house as was within 15 feet of Lot No. 5 removed because they were in violation of the zoning ordinance. Does the property line as demonstrated by Samter bind the Friedmans? [*Friedman v. Kasser*, 481 A.2d 886 (Pa. Super. Ct.)]

5 Fluor Corporation employed John Leffler in Iran. The employment agreement stated Fluor would provide housing and utilities. Leffler and his wife lived on the third floor of an apartment complex occupied by Fluor employees. There was a swimming pool beneath the balcony of their apartment. At a party, Leffler made a $20 bet with his new boss that he could dive off the balcony of the apartment into the pool. Leffler was a skilled high diver, but the balcony was 10 to 20 feet higher than any dive he had made. The next day Leffler dove from his balcony into the pool. He returned to the building, announcing he was the first person to dive from the third floor. At his apartment he complained of back and chest pain. He collapsed and was taken to the hospital, where he died. Death was due to a ruptured aorta as a result of the dive. Leffler's widow sought workers' compensation benefits. Should they be awarded? [*Leffler v. Workers' Compensation Appeals Bd.*, 177 Cal. Rptr. 552 (Cal. Ct. App.)]

6 Employed by Arneson Products, Inc., Sidney Sanders was diagnosed with cancer. He had surgery during a leave from October 26 to December 2. He then worked part-time but on December 18 he was diagnosed as suffering a psychological reaction to the cancer. His doctor told him to take time off and estimated he could return to work on March 1. In March, Sanders's doctor said he could return to work on April 5. Arneson paid Sanders's full salary until April 5, but refused to allow him to return to work. Sanders sued Arneson, alleging a violation of the ADA. Arneson claimed Sanders's temporary psychologial impairment was not a disability under the ADA. Was it an ADA disability? [*Sanders v. Arneson Products, Inc.*, 91 F.3d 1351 (9th Cir.)]

7 The Aroostook County Regional Ophthalmology Center (ACROC) had an office policy manual, which at the end of a discussion of patient confidentiality stated, "No office business is a matter for discussion with spouses, families or friends." It also stated, "It is totally unacceptable for an employee to discuss any grievances within earshot of patients." Four ACROC employees, within earshot of patients, expressed dissatisfaction and exasperation over the inconvenience caused by sudden changes in work schedules and complained that work schedules were often changed. They were fired. They filed a complaint alleging that enforcing the policies was an unfair labor practice. Was it? [*Aroostook County v. N.L.R.B.*, 81 F.3d 209 (D.C. Cir.)]

8 While employed as a professor of food science and microbiology at the University of North Carolina, Marvin Speck, with the assistance of Stanley Gilliland, professor of food science, developed a new procedure by which lactobacillus acidophilus could be added to milk without causing a sour taste. Both were employed to teach and do research on the use of high temperature for pasteurization and sterilization of foods. It was in the course of this research that the new procedure was developed. The process was discovered at the university, and resources provided for their research by the university made it possible for them to discover it. They sued the university to share in the royalties from the commercial use of the process. Are they entitled to payment? [*Speck v. North Carolina Dairy Foundation*, 319 S.E.2d 139 (N.C.)]

9 In response to a newspaper ad, Helen Campbell looked at a car at Al Duncan's residence. She believed he was the only person who had owned the car and that although the right door had been dented it had been fixed and was all right. She purchased the car, believing it was nearly brand new. After receiving her title and finding out the transferor was Hamilton Auto Company, she learned the car had not been a one-owner car owned by Duncan. The car had been totaled, sold as salvage, and transferred

through a series of dealers. It was worth $3,000 less than she had paid, considering its actual condition. Had she known all this, she would not have bought it. Gordon Hamilton authorized Duncan to buy cars with drafts drawn on Hamilton Auto Company. The purchase was financed at a bank with Hamilton's credit. Hamilton held title to the cars and he limited Duncan to buying three cars at any time. Hamilton required him to dispose of them within 30 days. Campbell sued Hamilton, alleging that his agent, Duncan, committed fraud. Should she recover? [*Campbell v. Hamilton*, 632 S.W.2d 633 (Tex. Ct. App.)]

10 Police officer Lori Ann Molloy heard an officer, Robert Sabetta, complain about being suspended for improper use of force. He said he should have killed, or should kill the people who had complained. A month later he shot and killed three teenage boys and wounded another. Some of the victims had filed the brutality complaints. The RI state police asked Molloy some general questions about Sabetta and she did not volunteer what he had said. During his murder trial the state police received a "tip" that Molloy had relevant information. When questioned she disclosed his comments but the police believed she knew more. They told Molloy's chief, Wesley Blanchard, she was refusing to cooperate. She insisted she had disclosed everything but Blanchard suspended her. He did not give her the hearing she requested under the Officers' Bill of Rights. In about 12 cases against male officers Blanchard had granted such rights. He did not even suspend some of the male officers suspected of highly questionable behavior. Molloy sued Blanchard and the town for sex discrimination. Who should win and why? [*Molloy v. Blanchard*, 115 F.3d 86 (1st Cir.)

Part 7 Business Organization

The Department of Business Services

Limited Liability Company Forms and Fees

Forms are provided in PDF (Portable Document Format) files, which can be viewed or printed using your Web browser and Adobe's Acrobat Reader software. Macintosh and Windows versions of Acrobat Reader may be downloaded free of charge from Adobe.

Get Acrobat Reader Click here to find out how to obtain the Adobe Acrobat Reader.

Form No.	Type of Form	Filing Fee
LLC-1.15	Application to Reserve a Name	$300.00
LLC-1.15	Renewal of Reserved Name	$100.00
LLC-1.15	Transfer of Reserved Name	$100.00
LLC-1.20	Application to adopt Assumed Name	$ 20.00+ $5.00 per month
LLC-1.20	Application to change Assumed Name	$100.00
LLC-1.20	Application to cancel Assumed Name	$100.00
LLC-1.20d	Assumed Name Renewal Application	$300.00
LLC-2.56	Assumed Name Fee Schedule	Effective January 1, 2000
LLC-1.35	Resignation of Registered Agent	$100.00
LLC-1.50	Affidavit of Compliance	$100.00
LLC-5.5	Articles of Organization	$400.00
LLC-5.25	Articles of Amendment	$25.00, $100.00
LLC-5.30	Restated Articles of Organization	$400.00
LLC-5.40	Application for Withdrawal-Domestic	$100.00
LLC-35.15	Articles of Dissolution	$100.00
LLC-35.40/ 45.65	Reinstatement following Administrative Dissolution	$500.00
LLC-37.10	Conversion Requirements	$100.00

http://www.sos.state.il.us/depts/bus_serv/llc.html

Businesses come in all sizes, from small businesses like local restaurants, hair salons, dry cleaners, and others, to franchises and corporations. These types of businesses and the legal details of their organizational structures are covered in this part. You can also find more information on the Web sites of your state governments. The screen above is from the State of Illinois and provides information on necessary forms and fees for LLCs. http://www.sos.state.il.us/depts/bus_serv/llc.html

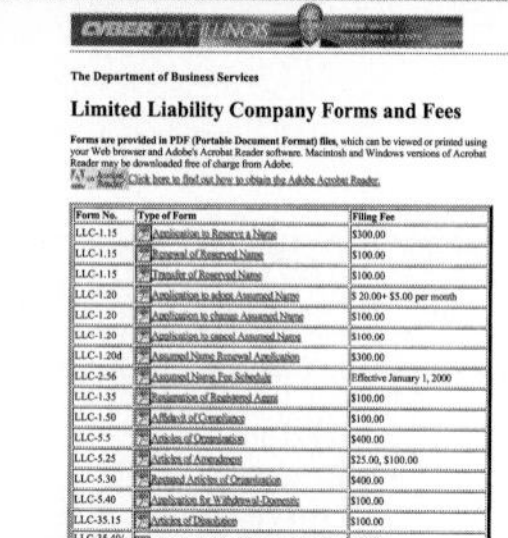

CYBERDRIVEILLINOIS

The Department of Business Services

Limited Liability Company Forms and Fees

Forms are provided in PDF (Portable Document Format) files, which can be viewed or printed using your Web browser and Adobe's Acrobat Reader software. Macintosh and Windows versions of Acrobat Reader may be downloaded free of charge from Adobe.

Click here to find out how to obtain the Adobe Acrobat Reader.

Form No.	Type of Form	Filing Fee
LLC-1.15	Application to Reserve a Name	$300.00
LLC-1.15	Renewal of Reserved Name	$100.00
LLC-1.15	Transfer of Reserved Name	$100.00
LLC-1.20	Application to adopt Assumed Name	$ 20.00+ $5.00 per month
LLC-1.20	Application to change Assumed Name	$100.00
LLC-1.20	Application to cancel Assumed Name	$100.00
LLC-1.20d	Assumed Name Renewal Application	$300.00
LLC-2.56	Assumed Name Fee Schedule	Effective January 1, 2000
LLC-1.35	Resignation of Registered Agent	$100.00
LLC-1.50	Affidavit of Compliance	$100.00
LLC-5.5	Articles of Organization	$400.00
LLC-5.25	Articles of Amendment	$25.00, $100.00
LLC-5.30	Restated Articles of Organization	$400.00
LLC-5.40	Application for Withdrawal-Domestic	$100.00
LLC-35.15	Articles of Dissolution	$100.00
LLC-35.40/ 45.65	Reinstatement following Administrative Dissolution	$500.00
LLC-37.10	Conversion Requirements	$100.00

31 Introduction to Business Organization

Learning Objectives

1 Discuss the differences in setting up a sole proprietorship, a partnership, and a corporation.

2 Explain the most important disadvantages of sole proprietorships and partnerships.

3 Give two reasons why the corporate form of business organization is important.

PREVIEW CASE

J. David Cassilly was a partner in Glen Park Properties, a general partnership for real estate development. He entered into an agreement with Schnuck Markets, Inc., to share the cost of extending a sewer line to certain property. Glen Park did not pay its share of the construction costs. Schnuck sued Glen Park for damages. Glen Park defended by saying that Cassilly did not have the authority to contract for Glen Park. Did Cassilly have such authority? Was the agreement part of the business of developing real estate? What powers do partners have?

An individual who is contemplating starting a business has a choice of several common types of business organizations. The number of owners, the formality in setting up the business, and the potential for personal liability are some of the factors that help distinguish the three most widely used types of business organization: sole proprietorship, partnership, and corporation.

Sole Proprietorship

Sole Proprietorship Business owned and carried on by one person

Proprietor Owner of sole proprietorship

A **sole proprietorship** is a business owned and carried on by one person called the **proprietor**. A sole proprietorship, the simplest and most common form of business, has a unique nature different from other businesses. It also has significant advantages and disadvantages as a result of the fact that one individual owns and runs it.

NATURE

LO1
Differences setting up businesses

The proprietor directly owns the business. This means that the proprietor owns every asset of the business including the equipment, inventory, and real estate just as personal assets are owned. Although owned and run by one person, the business may have any number of employees and agents. However, the proprietor has ultimate responsibility for business decisions.

To start a sole proprietorship, an individual need only begin doing business. The law does not require any formalities to begin and operate this form of business. A license may be needed for the particular type of business undertaken. However, the type of business imposes this requirement, not the form of business organization. (See Illustration 31-1 for a sample Application for Employer Identification Number form.)

It is equally easy to end a sole proprietorship. The proprietor simply stops doing business. Because the proprietor directly owns all the business assets, the proprietor need not dispose of them in order to go out of business. A sole proprietorship normally ends at the death of the proprietor. Such a business may be willed to another, but the proprietor has no assurance the business will be continued.

ADVANTAGES

The sole proprietorship form of business has two major advantages.

1 Flexible management
2 Ease of organization

Flexible Management. As the sole owner, the proprietor has significant flexibility in managing the business. Other people do not have to be consulted before business decisions may be made. The proprietor has full control and has the freedom to operate the business in any way desired.

Fictitious Name Registration Statute
Law requiring operator of business under assumed name to register with state

Ease of Organization. Since an individual need do nothing but start doing business, the sole proprietorship is the simplest type of business to organize. The law imposes no notice, permission, agreement, or understanding for its existence. If the proprietor intends to operate the business under an assumed name, a state law will normally require registration of the name with the appropriate state official. These laws are called **fictitious name registration statutes**. In registering a fictitious name, the business must disclose the names and addresses of the owners of the business and the business' purpose. This allows anyone who wishes to sue the business to know whom to sue. A business operated under the proprietor's name and that does not imply additional owners does not have to be registered.

DISADVANTAGES

LO2
Disadvantages of proprietorships and partnerships

Unlimited Liability
Business debts payable from personal assets

The most significant disadvantage of the sole proprietorship form of business is the **unlimited liability** of the owner for the debts of the business. Unlimited liability means that business debts are payable from personal, as well as business, assets. If the business does not have enough assets to pay business debts, the proprietor's personal assets may also be taken by business creditors. The sole proprietor's financial risk cannot be limited to the investment in the business.

In addition to unlimited liability, a sole proprietorship has additional disadvantages of limited management ability and capital. Since only one person runs a sole proprietorship,

Form **SS-4** (Rev. April 2000) Department of the Treasury Internal Revenue Service

Application for Employer Identification Number

(For use by employers, corporations, partnerships, trusts, estates, churches, government agencies, certain individuals, and others. See instructions.)

► **Keep a copy for your records.**

EIN

OMB No. 1545-0003

SAMPLE

Please type or print clearly.

1 Name of applicant (legal name) (see instructions)

2 Trade name of business (if different from name on line 1) | 3 Executor, trustee, "care of" name

4a Mailing address (street address) (room, apt., or suite no.) | 5a Business address (if different from address on lines 4a and 4b)

4b City, state, and ZIP code | 5b City, state, and ZIP code

6 County and state where principal business is located

7 Name of principal officer, general partner, grantor, owner, or trustor—SSN or ITIN may be required (see instructions) ►

8a Type of entity (Check only one box.) (see instructions)
Caution: *If applicant is a limited liability company, see the instructions for line 8a.*

☐ Sole proprietor (SSN) ______ ☐ Estate (SSN of decedent) ______
☐ Partnership ☐ Personal service corp. ☐ Plan administrator (SSN) ______
☐ REMIC ☐ National Guard ☐ Other corporation (specify) ► ______
☐ State/local government ☐ Farmers' cooperative ☐ Trust
☐ Church or church-controlled organization ☐ Federal government/military
☐ Other nonprofit organization (specify) ► ______ (enter GEN if applicable) ______
☐ Other (specify) ►

8b If a corporation, name the state or foreign country (if applicable) where incorporated | State | Foreign country

9 Reason for applying (Check only one box.) (see instructions) ☐ Banking purpose (specify purpose) ► ______
☐ Started new business (specify type) ► ______ ☐ Changed type of organization (specify new type) ► ______
☐ Purchased going business
☐ Hired employees (Check the box and see line 12.) ☐ Created a trust (specify type) ► ______
☐ Created a pension plan (specify type) ► ☐ Other (specify) ►

10 Date business started or acquired (month, day, year) (see instructions) | 11 Closing month of accounting year (see instructions)

12 First date wages or annuities were paid or will be paid (month, day, year). **Note:** *If applicant is a withholding agent, enter date income will first be paid to nonresident alien. (month, day, year)* . . . . ►

13 Highest number of employees expected in the next 12 months. **Note:** *If the applicant does not expect to have any employees during the period, enter -0-. (see instructions)* . . . . ►	Nonagricultural	Agricultural	Household

14 Principal activity (see instructions) ►

15 Is the principal business activity manufacturing? . . . . ☐ Yes ☐ No
If "Yes," principal product and raw material used ►

16 To whom are most of the products or services sold? Please check one box. ☐ Business (wholesale)
☐ Public (retail) ☐ Other (specify) ► ☐ N/A

17a Has the applicant ever applied for an employer identification number for this or any other business? . . . . . ☐ Yes ☐ No
Note: *If "Yes," please complete lines 17b and 17c.*

17b If you checked "Yes" on line 17a, give applicant's legal name and trade name shown on prior application, if different from line 1 or 2 above.
Legal name ► Trade name ►

7c Approximate date when and city and state where the application was filed. Enter previous employer identification number if known.
Approximate date when filed (mo., day, year) | City and state where filed | Previous EIN

r penalties of perjury, I declare that I have examined this application, and to the best of my knowledge and belief, it is true, correct, and complete. | Business telephone number (include area code) ( )
Fax telephone number (include area code) ( )

and title (Please type or print clearly.) ►

Signature ► Date ►

Note: *Do not write below this line. For official use only.*

Please leave blank ►	Geo.	Ind.	Class	Size	Reason for applying

For Privacy Act and Paperwork Reduction Act Notice, see page 4. Cat. No. 16055N Form **SS-4** (Rev. 4-2000)

Use your Business Lawyer program to open this document. Complete it as if you were applying for an EIN for your own business.

As you see in the upper left corner, this is Form SS-4; you can find the most recent version on the Web site of the IRS, where you will need to select it from a list of forms. You can also find several pages of detailed instruction and information on this and other corporate forms.

http://www.irs.gov/forms_pubs/forms.html

Illustration 31-1

Application for Employer Identification Number

U.S. Internal Revenue Service (http://www.irs.gov)

the management ability of the proprietor limits the business. The business also has only whatever capital the proprietor has or can raise. This may limit the size of the business.

A sole proprietor has liability for the activities of the business because the proprietor is the sole manager of the business. The proprietor is in a sense the business. The responsibility for all business decisions rests with the proprietor. A sole proprietor may not only be liable in damages for torts committed by the business, but also criminally liable for crimes.

Partnership

Partnership
Association of two or more people to carry on business for profit

Partner
Member of a partnership

A **partnership** is a voluntary association of two or more people who have combined their money, property, or labor and skill, or a combination of these, for the purpose of carrying on as coowners some lawful business for profit. The agreement of individuals to organize a partnership and run a business forms this type of organization. The individuals who have formed a partnership and constitute its members are called **partners**. They act as agents for the partnership.

The partnership must be formed for the purpose of operating a lawful business. The attempt to form a partnership to operate an unlawful business does not result in a partnership. Furthermore, a partnership may not be formed for the purpose of conducting a lawful business in an illegal manner.

A hunting club, a sewing circle, a trade union, a chamber of commerce, or any other nonprofit association cannot be treated as a partnership because the purpose of a partnership must be to conduct a trade, business, or profession for profit.

CLASSIFICATION

Several different kinds of partnerships exist depending on the liabilities of the partners and the business carried out. Partnerships may be classified as follows:

1. Ordinary, or general, partnerships
2. Limited partnerships
3. Trading and nontrading partnerships

Ordinary or General Partnership
Partnership with no limitation on rights and duties of partners

Ordinary, or General, Partnerships. An **ordinary or general partnership** forms when two or more people voluntarily contract to pool their capital and

PREVIEW CASE REVISITED

Facts: J. David Cassilly was a partner in Glen Park Properties, a general partnership for real estate development. He entered into an agreement with Schnuck Markets, Inc., to share the cost of extending a sewer line to certain property. Glen Park did not pay its share of the construction costs. Schnuck sued Glen Park for damages. Glen Park defended by saying that Cassilly did not have the authority to contract for Glen Park.

Outcome: The court said that every partner of a general partnership is an agent of the partnership and binds the partnership when carrying on in the usual way the business of the partnership. Glen Park had to pay.

skill to conduct some business undertaking for profit. An ordinary partnership results in no limitations upon a partner's rights, duties, or liabilities. The Uniform Partnership Act governs this type of business organization in most states.[1] This act aims to bring about uniformity in the partnership laws of the states.

Limited Partnership
Partnership with partner whose liability is limited to capital contribution

Limited Partnerships. A **limited partnership** is one in which one or more partners have their liability for the firm's debts limited to the amount of their investment. This type of partnership cannot operate under either the common law or the Uniform Partnership Act. However, all states now permit limited partnerships. Most do so because of passage of the Uniform Limited Partnership Act or the Revised Uniform Limited Partnership Act. A limited partnership cannot be formed without a specific state statute prescribing the conditions under which it can operate. If the limited partnership does not comply strictly with the enabling statute, courts hold it to be an ordinary partnership.

Trading Partnership
One engaged in buying and selling

Nontrading Partnership
One devoted to professional services

Trading and Nontrading Partnerships. A **trading partnership** is one engaged in buying and selling merchandise. A **nontrading partnership** is one devoted to providing services, such as accounting, medicine, law, and similar professional services. The distinction matters because the members of a nontrading partnership usually have considerably less apparent authority than the partners in a trading partnership. For example, one partner in a nontrading partnership cannot borrow money in the name of the firm and bind the firm. One dealing with a nontrading partnership must exercise more responsibility in ascertaining the actual authority of the partners to bind the firm than a person dealing with a trading partnership.

WHO MAY BE PARTNERS?

ETHICAL POINT
Do you think it would be ethical for a minor to be able to withdraw the entire contribution orginally made or should losses first be deducted?

As a contractually based entity, any person competent to make a contract has the competence to be a partner. A minor may become a partner to the same extent to which the minor may make a contract about any other matter. The law holds such contracts voidable, but a minor acting as the agent of the other partner or partners can bind the partnership on contracts within the scope of the partnership business. A minor partner also incurs the liabilities of the partnership. The states disagree as to whether a minor who withdraws from a partnership can withdraw the entire contribution originally made or whether a proportion of any losses must first be deducted.

KINDS OF PARTNERS

The members of a partnership may be classified as follows:

1. General partner
2. Silent partner
3. Secret partner
4. Dormant partner
5. Nominal partner

General Partner
One actively and openly engaged in business

General Partner. A **general partner** is one actively and openly engaged in the business and held out to everyone as a partner. Such a partner has unlimited liability in respect to the partnership debts. A general partner appears to the public as a full-fledged partner, assumes all the risks of the partnership, and does not have any limitations of rights. This is the usual type of partner.

[1] The Uniform Partnership Act has been adopted in all states except Louisiana.

Facts: A limited partnership, the Quinn-L Baton Rouge Partnership, was formed to build an apartment complex. The Quinn-L Corporation was a general partner. Thomas R. Elkins was a limited partner. The corporation became the managing general partner. When the project proved to be more expensive than anticipated, the corporation loaned substantial money to the partnership. After construction was completed, the corporation was removed as managing general partner and replaced by Elkins. Three years later the corporation had received no payments on its loan. It sued the partnership and the partners.

Outcome: The court said that, having become the managing general partner, Elkins had the unlimited liability of a general partner.

Silent Partner
Partner who takes no part in firm

Silent Partner. A **silent partner** is one who, though possibly known to the public as a partner, takes no active part in the management of the business. In return for investing in the partnership capital, such a partner has a right as a partner only to share in the profits in the ratio agreed upon. Why would a person invest money but take no active part in the management? Because such a partner gains limited liability and no share of the losses beyond the capital contribution. People frequently refer to this type of partner as a **limited partner** when known to the public as a partner.

Limited Partner
Partner who takes no active part in management and who the public knows as a partner

Secret Partner
Partner active but unknown to public

Secret Partner. An active partner who attempts to conceal that fact from the public is a **secret partner**. Such a partner tries to escape the unlimited liability of a general partner but at the same time takes an active part in the management of the business. Should the public learn of such a partner's relationship to the firm, however, unlimited liability cannot be escaped. Secret partners differ from silent partners in that secret partners: (1) are unknown to the public and (2) take an active part in the management of the business. Secret partners may feign the status of employees or may work elsewhere, but they meet frequently with the other partners to discuss management problems.

Dormant or Sleeping Partner
Partner unknown to public with no part in management

Dormant Partner. A **dormant partner** (sometimes referred to as a **sleeping partner**) usually combines the characteristics of both the secret and the silent partner. A dormant partner is usually unknown to the public as a partner and takes no part in the management of the business of the firm. When known to the public as a partner, a dormant partner has liability for the debts of the firm to the same extent as a general partner. In return for limited liability so far as the other partners can effect it, a dormant partner foregoes the right to participate in the management of the firm. In addition, such a partner may agree to limit income to a reasonable return on investment, since no services are contributed.

Nominal Partner
Person who pretends to be a partner

Nominal Partner. **Nominal partners** hold themselves out as partners or permit others to do so. In fact, however, they are not partners, since they do not share in the management of the business nor in the profits; but in some instances they may be held liable as a partner.

ADVANTAGES OF THE PARTNERSHIP

By the operation of a partnership instead of a proprietorship, capital and skill may be increased, labor may be made more efficient, the ratio of expenses per dollar of business may be reduced, and management may be improved. Not all of these advantages will accrue to every partnership, but the prospect of greater profits by reason of them leads to the formation of a partnership.

DISADVANTAGES OF THE PARTNERSHIP

A partnership has the following disadvantages:

1. The unlimited personal liability of each partner for the debts of the partnership
2. The relative instability of the business because of the danger of dissolution by reason of the death or withdrawal of one of the partners
3. The divided authority among the partners, which may lead to disharmony

ORGANIZATIONS SIMILAR TO PARTNERSHIPS

Some business organizations resemble partnerships. However, they differ from them. These include joint-stock companies, joint ventures, and limited liability companies.

Joint-Stock Company
Entity that issues shares of stock, but investors have unlimited liability

Joint-Stock Companies. A **joint-stock company** resembles a partnership, but shares of stock, as in a corporation, indicate ownership. The ownership of these shares may be transferred without dissolving the association. Thus, one of the chief disadvantages of the general partnership is overcome. Shareholders in a joint-stock company do not have the authority to act for the firm. The joint stockholders have liability, jointly and severally, for the debts of the firm while members. For this reason, joint-stock companies do not offer the safeguards of a corporation. Some states permit joint-stock companies to operate by special statutes authorizing them, or in some states, without statute, as common-law associations.

Joint Venture
Business relationship similar to partnership, except existing for single transaction only

Joint Ventures. A **joint venture** is a business relationship in which two or more persons combine their labor or property for a single undertaking and share profits and losses equally or as otherwise agreed. For example, two friends enter into an agreement to get the rights to cut timber from a certain area and market the lumber. A joint venture resembles a partnership in many respects, the primary difference being that a joint venture exists for a single transaction, though its completion may take several years. A partnership generally constitutes a continuing business.

Facts: After Eileen LeFlore won a beauty contest, KRAV radio station hosted a party at Reflections, a restaurant and nightclub. Reflections provided the establishment, personnel, wine and cheese and sold drinks and club memberships to attendees. KRAV hosted the party and advertised it to promote its station. LeFlore felt the advertising about the party invaded her privacy and sued Reflections. Since KRAV did all the advertising about the party LeFlore had to establish a joint venture by KRAV and Reflections.

Outcome: The court held that since Reflections supplied the location, refreshments, and personnel for the party and KRAV hosted and advertised it, they clearly had combined labor and property for the undertaking—the party. They had also shared profits and expenses since neither received reimbursement for what they contributed to the party and Reflections received payment for drinks and memberships it sold. KRAV received publicity and promoted its station so the court said there was a joint venture.

Limited Liability Companies. Some states have enacted statutes providing for the formation of a business organization similar to a partnership but without the disad-

http://
www.sos.state.il.us/depts/bus_serv/llc.html

vantage of unlimited liability. This is a **limited liability company** or LLC. The owners, who also run an LLC, are called members. The initial members sign an operating agreement or articles of organization, the contract that governs the operations of the LLC. This contract must be filed with the appropriate state office. Most states require two members for an LLC, which may be formed for any legal business purpose.

Corporations

LO3
Importance of corporate form

Limited Liability Company
Partnership-type organization but with limited liability

Corporation
Association of people created by law into an entity

The Supreme Court described a **corporation** as "an association of individuals united for some common purpose, and permitted by law to use a common name and to change its members without dissolution of the association." The law creates a corporation—it does not exist merely by agreement of private individuals. It comes into existence by the state's issuing a charter. A corporation may be organized for any lawful purpose, whether pleasure or profit.

The law recognizes a corporation as an *entity,* something that has a distinct existence separate and apart from the existence of its individual members. The law views a corporation as an artificial person substituted for the natural persons responsible for its formation who manage and control its affairs. When a corporation makes a contract, the contract is made by and in the name of this legal entity, the corporation, and not by and in the name of the individual members. It has almost all the rights and powers of an individual. It can sue and be sued, it can be fined for violating the law, and it has recourse to the Constitution to protect its liberties.

IMPORTANCE OF CORPORATIONS

There are two major reasons why the corporation has such importance as a form of business organization. Corporations allow:

1 Pooling of capital from many investors
2 Limited liability

Pooling of Capital. The rapid expansion of industry from small shops to giant enterprises required large amounts of capital. Few people had enough money of their own to build a railroad or a great steel mill, and people hesitated to form partnerships with any but trusted acquaintances. In addition, even though four or five people did form a partnership, insufficient capital was still a major problem. Such a business needed hundreds or even thousands of people, each with a few hundred or a few thousand dollars, to pool their capital for concerted undertakings. The corporate form of business provided the necessary capital from any number of investors.

Limited Liability
Capital contribution is maximum loss

Limited Liability. Incorporation is attractive to businesspersons as a means of obtaining **limited liability**. Limited liability means that the maximum amount an investor can lose equals that person's actual investment in the business. Suppose three people with $20,000 each form a partnership with capital of $60,000. Each partner risks losing not only this $20,000 but also almost everything else owned, because of personal liability for all partnership debts. If a corporation is formed and each investor contributes $20,000, this amount is the maximum that can be lost, since an investor has no liability for corporate debts beyond the investment. Many businesses that formerly would have been organized as either a partnership or a sole proprietorship are today corporations in order to have the benefit of limited liability. The partners or the sole proprietor simply owns all, or virtually all, the stock of the corporation.

Facts: As the president of Laurence J. Rice, Inc., Laurence Rice signed a contract by which Rice, Inc. was to construct a building for JoAnne Von Zwehl. Laurence Rice was a stockholder in Rice, Inc. Von Zwehl later sued for breach of the contract and sued Laurence Rice personally. He asked the court to dismiss the suit because he had never acted or implied that he acted in his individual capacity.

Outcome: The court said that as a stockholder Rice could not be personally liable for the actions of the corporation.

Piercing the Corporate Veil
Ignoring the corporate entity

Piercing the Corporate Veil. Courts will, however, ignore the corporate entity under exceptional circumstances. When courts do, they say they are **piercing the corporate veil**. This can occur if one individual or a few individuals own all the stock of a corporation and ignore the corporate entity. Instead of avoiding the disadvantage of unlimited liability of a sole proprietorship and a partnership, a corporate investor can thus be held personally liable.

Facts: Allen and Sandra Lorenz leased land to David Read. The lease stated that if Read defaulted the Lorenzes could give notice to cure the default within 30 days. If the default was not cured the Lorenzes could enter the property and terminate the lease. On December 23, the Lorenzes served Read a notice of default for unpaid rent and profits. On January 17, Read orally assigned the lease to Beltio, Ltd., a corporation owned by Arthur and Barbara Struble and they signed a written assignment on January 20. On January 23, 31 days after serving notice of default the Lorenzes entered the property and declared the lease terminated. The secretary of state issued the certificate of incorporation for Beltio on January 30. Arthur conducted Beltio's business through his sole proprietorship and mingled corporate and noncorporate funds. Barbara was secretary of Beltio, but knew and did basically nothing with respect to Beltio's business affairs. The Lorenzes sued Arthur personally.

Outcome: The court found that since Arthur ran the corporation as his sole proprietorship, comingled funds, and had no functional corporate secretary, he had personal liability on the lease.

DISADVANTAGE OF CORPORATIONS

In a sole proprietorship, the investor completely manages the business. In a partnership, each investor has an equal voice in the management of the business. The main disadvantage of a corporation is that the people who own or control a majority of the voting stock have not merely a dominant voice in management but the sole voice. If there are 15 stockholders, but one owns 51 percent of the voting stock, this stockholder is free to run the corporation as desired. The stockholder who owns the majority of the voting stock has the ability to dominate the board of directors and therefore the corporate officers. People who invest their savings in a business in the hope of becoming "their own boss" will not find the corporate type of business organization the most desirable unless they can control a majority of the voting stock.

Questions

1. What are some of the factors that help distinguish the three most widely used types of business organization?
2. What formalities must a person go through in order to set up a sole proprietorship?
3. What are the advantages and the most serious disadvantage of a sole proprietorship?
4. What is a partnership?
5. What is the difference between an ordinary partnership and a limited partnership?
6. Why is it important to distinguish between a trading and a nontrading partnership?
7. May anyone be a partner?
8. What is the main difference between a partnership and a joint venture?
9. Explain the two reasons for the importance of the corporate form of business organization.
10. What is the main disadvantage of the corporate form of business organization?

Case Problems

LO2 1. The original limited partners of Kanawha Trace Development Partners (KTDP) consisted of Jeffrey Rawn and John Thornton. Thornton withdrew as a limited partner but returned three years later. While Thornton was not a limited partner, KTDP contracted with William Sloan to do some construction work on KTDP's condominium project. KTDP did not pay Sloan and he sued Thornton alleging Thornton had signed a guaranty contract on behalf of KTDP and therefore had personal liability for KTDP's debt as a limited partner in control of KTDP. Prior to the lawsuit Sloan had never met or dealt with Thornton. Should Thornton be personally liable?

LO1 2. The partnership agreement for Antiques Etc., a general partnership, stated, "Each partner hereto shall be a general partner . . . and may bind the other partner only as to the partnership business and assets." It stated that neither partner could bind the other as to the partners' personal assets. The partners were Raymond L. Gugelman and Marian E. McCoy. McCoy executed a number of promissory notes to obtain funds used in the operation of the partnership. The bank sued Gugelman for payment of the notes. Was he liable?

LO2 3. A general partnership, Bamco 18, guaranteed payment of a $4.5 million note by Hospitality Associates payable to United States Trust Co. When Hospitality defaulted on the note, U.S. Trust sued Bamco and all its individual partners to recover on the guarantee. Are the individual partners liable on Bamco's debt?

LO1 4. John Hackney owned a building that housed Johnny's Barbeque. He leased the building and equipment to Luther Massengil, Sammie Hunt, and Doris Johnson for five years. Massengil, Hunt, and Johnson operated the restaurant and occupied the premises for a short time, but trouble occurred. Hackney, Massengil, and Hunt executed a release of each other from the lease. Johnson refused to sign and sued Hackney for eviction. Hackney argued that the business arrangement among Massengil, Hunt, and Johnson constituted a partnership and as agents of a trading partnership, Massengil and Hunt bound the partnership by the release. Johnson said giving the release did not constitute a transaction in the ordinary course of the business because without the lease there could be no business. Did the release bind Johnson?

LO3 5. A corporation, Unlimited Business Exchange of North Dakota, Inc. (UBE), was formed by Richard Collins and other investors. Collins later bought out the interests of the other investors. As the sole owner and the only person receiving benefit from UBE, Collins considered the corporation to be a sole proprietorship. He conducted the business as a sole proprietorship called UBE. UBE leased office space for 24 months from

John A. Larson. Less than a year later, UBE informed Larson that it would be moving out at the end of only 12 months. Larson sued UBE and Collins for unpaid rent. Do the facts warrant the decision that the corporation was in fact a sole proprietorship?

LO2 6 Jerome Micco and R. R. Buescher were major shareholders in two corporations that formed a general partnership, Harbor Creek Company. Harbor was the general partner in a limited partnership, Harbor Creek Limited (Limited). Micco and Buescher were limited partners in Limited which was constructing a condominum project. Limited hired a construction supervisor who supervised day-to-day construction site decisions and consulted with Buescher and Micco who had the final "say so" on all major decisions on the project. Limited had financial difficulty and Micco took over construction supervision. Frederick Hommel, an electrical contractor, did work for Limited. In bidding and performing his work Hommel had dealings with Micco and Buescher. Limited did not pay Hommel so he sued Micco and Buescher. Should they be liable?

Internet Resources for Business Law

Name	Resources	Web Address
Smart Business Supersite (SBS)—Company Structure	SBS, a distributor of "how-to" business information, provides publications on sole proprietorships, partnerships, corporations, limited liability companies, agreements, forms, and similar topics.	http://www.smartbiz.com/sbs/cats/struct.htm
U.S. Business Advisor	The U.S. Business Advisor, a federal government program, provides businesses with access to government information and services.	http://www.business.gov/
U.S. Small Business Administration (SBA)	The SBA provides information and materials, such as forms, software, and publications, to help start, finance, and expand a business.	http://www.sba.gov/
Legal Information Institute (LII)—Enterprise Law Materials	LII, maintained by Cornell Law School, provides an overview of corporation and partnership law, including links to state statutes and recent relevant Supreme Court decisions.	http://www.law.cornell.edu/topics/topic2.html# enterprise law
Internal Revenue Service	The Internal Revenue Service and its publication, the *Digital Daily,* provide tax advice and information on a variety of issues, including business formation issues.	http://www.irs.ustreas.gov/
U.S. Internal Revenue Code—26 USC	LII maintains the U.S. Internal Revenue Code, 26 USC, in a hypertext and searchable format.	http://www.law.cornell.edu/uscode/26/
The National Conference of Commissioners on Uniform State Laws	The National Conference of Commissioners on Uniform State Laws (NCCUSL), the drafters of the UCC, provides drafts and revisions of its uniform and model acts.	http://www.law.upenn.edu/library/ulc/ulc.htm
State of Indiana's Uniform Partnership Act	The State of Indiana maintains its adopted version of the Uniform Partnership Act.	http://www.state.in.us/legislative/ic/code/title23/ar4/
Code of Hammurabi	The Yale Law School maintains a hypertext version of the legal Code of Hammurabi.	http://www.yale.edu/lawweb/avalon/hamframe.htm

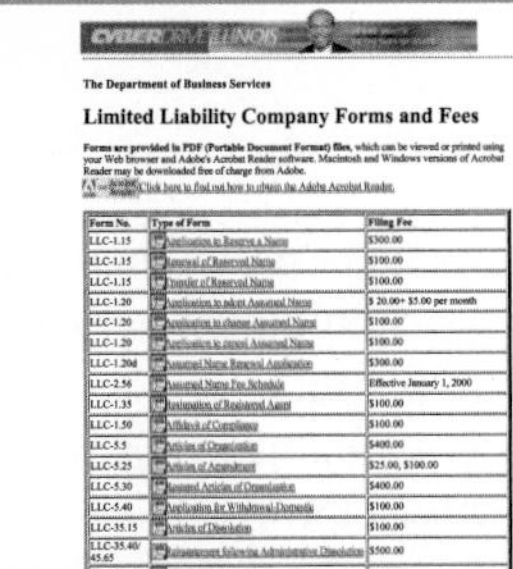

The Department of Business Services

Limited Liability Company Forms and Fees

Forms are provided in PDF (Portable Document Format) files, which can be viewed or printed using your Web browser and Adobe's Acrobat Reader software. Macintosh and Windows versions of Acrobat Reader may be downloaded free of charge from Adobe.

Click here to find out how to obtain the Adobe Acrobat Reader.

Form No.	Type of Form	Filing Fee
LLC-1.15	Application to Reserve a Name	$300.00
LLC-1.15	Renewal of Reserved Name	$100.00
LLC-1.15	Transfer of Reserved Name	$100.00
LLC-1.20	Application to adopt Assumed Name	$ 20.00+ $5.00 per month
LLC-1.20	Application to change Assumed Name	$100.00
LLC-1.20	Application to cancel Assumed Name	$100.00
LLC-1.20d	Assumed Name Renewal Application	$300.00
LLC-2.56	Assumed Name Fee Schedule	Effective January 1, 2000
LLC-1.35	Designation of Registered Agent	$100.00
LLC-1.50	Affidavit of Compliance	$100.00
LLC-5.5	Articles of Organization	$400.00
LLC-5.25	Articles of Amendment	$25.00, $100.00
LLC-5.30	Restated Articles of Organization	$400.00
LLC-5.40	Application for Withdrawal-Domestic	$100.00
LLC-35.15	Articles of Dissolution	$100.00
LLC-35.40/ 45.65	Reinstatement following Administrative Dissolution	$500.00
LLC-37.10	Conversion Requirements	$100.00

32
Creation and Operation of a Partnership

Learning Objectives

1. Describe how a partnership is created.
2. Specify the duties the law imposes upon partners.
3. Identify the rights and liabilities every partner has.
4. Explain how partnership profits and losses are shared.

PREVIEW CASE

Without having a mine drainage permit, the King Coal Company, a partnership, conducted mining operations. Robert Woods, the managing partner who directed the mining, and the company were both charged with operating a surface mine without a mine drainage permit. Were the partnership and/or Woods guilty of the charge? On whose behalf was Woods acting? Was he acting in the scope of his employment?

A partnership is formed as a result of a contract, written or oral, express or implied, just as all other business commitments result from a contract. The parties to the contract must give the utmost fidelity in all relationships with the other partners. If any partner fails in this duty, the other partners have several legal remedies to redress the wrong.

Partnership Agreements

The partnership agreement must meet the five tests of a valid contract as set out in Chapter 5. A partnership may also be created when two or more parties who do not have a written agreement act in such a way as to lead third parties to believe that a partnership exists.

WRITTEN AGREEMENT

LO1
How partnership is created

Articles of Partnership
Written partnership agreement

The partners ordinarily need not have a written agreement providing for the formation of a partnership. However, having an agreement in writing might help avoid some disputes over rights and duties. If the parties choose to put their agreement in writing, in the absence of a statute to the contrary, the writing need not be in a particular form. The written partnership agreement is commonly known as the **articles of partnership**. Articles of partnership vary according to the needs of the particular situation, but ordinarily they should contain the following:

1 Date
2 Names of the partners
3 Nature and duration of the business
4 Name and location of the business
5 Individual contributions of the partners
6 Sharing of profits, losses, and responsibilities
7 Keeping of accounts
8 Duties of the partners
9 Amounts of withdrawals of money
10 Unusual restraints upon the partners
11 Provisions for dissolution and division of assets
12 Signatures of partners

IMPLIED AGREEMENT

A partnership arises whenever the persons in question enter into an agreement that satisfies the definition of a partnership. Thus, three persons who agree to contribute property and money to the running of a business as coowners for the purpose of making a profit, even though they do not in fact call themselves partners, have formed a partnership. Conversely, the mere fact that persons say, "we are partners now" does not establish a partnership if the elements of the definition of a partnership are not satisfied.

Prima Facie
On the face of it

Prima Facie Evidence
Evidence sufficient on its face, if uncontradicted

In many instances, the death of witnesses or the destruction of records makes proof of exactly what happened impossible. Because of this, the Uniform Partnership Act provides that proof that a person received a share of profits is **prima facie** evidence of a partnership. This means that in the absence of other evidence, it should be held that a partnership existed. This **prima facie evidence** can be overcome, and the conclusion then reached that no partnership existed, by showing that the share of profits received represented wages or payment of a debt, interest on a loan, rent, or the purchase price of a business or goods.

Facts: Brothers George and Clarence Simandl owned 6.638 acres of land on which they operated a gas station, delicatessen, and magazine stand. Clarence conveyed his share of the land to George, and a year later George reconveyed the property to Clarence. The conveyances were to aid the brothers' ability to get credit. When Clarence sold 5.5 acres of the land to nonfamily members, George and Clarence divided the proceeds equally. They shared in the receipts of the businesses, and both signed contracts for the purchase of goods sold. The brothers made business decisions only after consulting each other, and each bound the other. After they both died, George's widow sued for half the real property and business.

Outcome: The court said a partnership can be found when there was a sharing of net profits from a continuing business and each person is able to bind the business. This was a partnership.

PARTNERSHIP BY ESTOPPEL

The conduct of persons who in fact are not partners could be such as to mislead other persons into thinking they are partners. The situation resembles that in which a person misleads others into thinking that someone is an authorized agent. In a case of a false impression of a partnership, the law will frequently hold that the apparent partners are estopped from denying that a partnership exists; otherwise, third persons will be harmed by their conduct.

Facts: Under a written agreement, Carmen Allen and Sandy Newsome engaged in business using the name Newsome Carpets. Allen agreed to invest $5,000 and Newsome agreed to invest an equal value of carpet stock, fixtures, and equipment. Newsome also agreed to supply purchasing power and John Robertson agreed to supply credit backing. The parties agreed to divide profits 50 percent to Newsome, 40 percent to Allen, and 10 percent to Robertson. Eight months later Allen and Newsome signed a partnership agreement that referred to each as *partners* with a 50 percent interest. Allen did share in profits from the business, gave business advice, and signed documents as a general partner of Newsome Carpets. Orders Distributing Company sued Allen and Newsome as partners for carpet stock delivered to Newsome Carpets. Allen claimed she was not a partner.

Outcome: The court found Allen and Newsome acted like partners so even if they were not, Allen was estopped to deny it.

Partnership Firm Name

The law does not require a firm name for a partnership, but it makes identification convenient. The firm may adopt any name that does not violate the rights of others or the law. The partnership name may be changed at will by agreement. In some states the name of a person not a member of the firm or the words *and Company*, unless the term indicates an additional partner(s), may not be used. Many of the states permit the use of fictitious or trade names but require the firm to register under the fictitious name registration statutes (see Chapter 31).

A partnership may sue or be sued either in the firm name or in the names of the partners. Under the Uniform Partnership Act any partnership property, whether real or personal, may be owned either in the names of the partners or in the name of the firm. To hold partnership property in the names of the partners, the owner should convey the property to the partners d/b/a (doing business as) the partnership.

Partner's Interest in Partnership Property

Tenancy in Partnership
Ownership of partner in partnership property

In a **tenancy in partnership** (also called *owner in partnership*), each partner owns and can sell only a pro rata interest in the partnership as an entity. The purchaser of one partner's share cannot demand acceptance as a partner by the other partners. The purchaser acquires only the right to receive the share of profits the partner would have received. A surviving partner does not get full ownership upon the death of the other partner, as is the case in joint tenancy. One partner may not freely sell an interest in partnership property. The personal creditors of one partner cannot force the sale of specific pieces of property of the partnership to satisfy personal debts, nor can they force the sale of a fractional part of specific assets. The personal creditors of one partner can ask a court to order that payments due the debtor partner from the partnership be made to the creditors. They also can force the sale of a debtor partner's interest in the partnership.

Duties of Partners

LO2
Partner's duties

Five common duties that one partner owes to the others include:

1 Duty to exercise loyalty and good faith
2 Duty to work for the partnership
3 Duty to abide by majority vote
4 Duty to keep records
5 Duty to inform

EXERCISE LOYALTY AND GOOD FAITH

Partners owe each other and the firm the utmost loyalty and good faith. As an agent of the firm, each partner has a fiduciary duty to the firm, so strict fidelity to the interests of the firm must be observed at all times. No partner may take advantage of the copartners. Any personal profits earned directly as a result of one's connection with the partnership must be considered profits of the firm. If the personal interest or advantage of the partner conflicts with the advantage of the partnership, the partner has a duty to put the firm's interest above personal advantage. This duty lasts as long as the enterprise exists.

Facts: Philip Zinke was the general partner of a limited partnership in which he had made an investment and had total control of the running of the partnership. When Zinke needed money urgently for the purchase of a building in his own name he used $1,050,000 of partnership funds for the purchase. Zinke sold the building after owning it seven months and made a $2M profit yet he did not repay the money taken from the partnership. When charged with grand larceny Zinke claimed he was a joint or common owner of partnership assets and therefore could not be prosecuted even for misappropriation of partnership assets.

Outcome: The court held that as a general partner he had an obligation to handle the partnership property for the benefit of the limited partners. He owed the other partners the duty of loyalty and good faith and he had breached this duty.

The partnership contract must be observed scrupulously. Each partner has the power to do irreparable damage to the copartners by betraying their trust. For this reason, the law holds each partner to the utmost fidelity to the partnership agreement. Any violation of this agreement gives the other partners at least two rights: First, they can sue the offending partner for any loss resulting from the failure to abide by the partnership agreement; second, they may elect also to ask a court to decree a dissolution of the partnership. A trivial breach of the partnership agreement will not justify a dissolution, however.

WORK FOR THE PARTNERSHIP

Unless provided otherwise in the partnership agreement, each partner has a duty to work on behalf of the partnership. In working for the partnership, partners must use reasonable care and skill in conducting the firm's business. Each partner has liability for partnership debts, but any loss resulting to the firm because of a partner's failure to use adequate care and skill in transacting business must be reimbursed by that partner. If the partnership supplies expert services, such as accounting services or engineering services, then each partner must perform these services in a manner that will free the firm from liability for damages for improper services. However, honest mistakes and errors of judgment do not render a partner liable individually nor the partnership liable collectively.

Facts: Dr. Donald Schwartz prescribed Poly-vi-flor for a child, Daniel Keech. The doctor instructed the parents to use the tablet form of Poly-vi-flor. When Keech tried to swallow a tablet, he suddenly choked on it and could not breathe. He suffered massive brain damage. The parents sued Schwartz, his medical partnership, and his partner, Joan Magee, for failure to use adequate care and skill as physicians.

Outcome: The court removed Magee as a party, saying that she did not have personal liability. Any liability Magee had resulted from her participation in the partnership.

ABIDE BY MAJORITY VOTE

A partnership operates on the basis of a majority vote. Unless the partnership agreement provides otherwise, the majority of the partners bind the firm on any ordinary matters in the scope of the partnership business. A decision involving a basic change in the character of the enterprise or the partnership agreement requires the unanimous consent of the partners. Therefore, the majority rule does not apply to such actions as an assignment for the benefit of creditors, disposition of the firm's goodwill, actions that would make carrying on the firm's business impossible, confession of a judgment, or submitting a firm claim to arbitration.

KEEP RECORDS

Each partner must keep such records of partnership transactions as required for an adequate accounting. If the partnership agreement provides for the type of records to be kept, a partner fulfills this duty when such records are kept, even though they may not be fully adequate. Since each partner must account to the partnership for all business transactions including purchases, sales, commission payments, and receipts, this accounting should be based upon written records.

INFORM

Each partner has the duty to inform the other partners about matters relating to the partnership. On demand, true and full information of all things affecting the partnership

Facts: For $260,500, Al Shacket and Leroy Helfman purchased options to buy land. They assigned the options to Hulett, Inc. Before Hulett closed the purchase of the land, Shacket and Helfman offered to buy the land for $525,000. After this offer was accepted, Shacket and Helfman assigned their purchase rights to a partnership they had with Harold Jaffa and Irving Taran, and the partnership bought the property from Hulett. The partnership agreement required Shacket and Helfman to transfer the property "at their cost." Jaffa and Taran sued, alleging Shacket and Helfman violated their duty to give to the other partners full and true information of all things affecting the partnership, because they failed to disclose that they had purchased the options for only $260,500. Shacket and Helfman alleged there is no violation of the duty to disclose information so long as there is no concealment of profit.

Outcome: The court held that *information* means all relevant information regardless of whether it relates to profit.

must be rendered to any partner or the legal representative of any deceased partner or partner under legal disability.

Rights of Partners

LO3 Rights and liabilities of partners

Every partner, in the absence of an agreement to the contrary, has five well-defined rights:

1. Right to participate in management
2. Right to inspect the books at all times
3. Right of contribution
4. Right to withdraw advances
5. Right to withdraw profits

PARTICIPATE IN MANAGEMENT

In the absence of a contract limiting these rights, each partner has the right by law to participate equally with the others in the management of the partnership business. The exercise of this right often leads to disharmony. It is a prime advantage, however, because the investor maintains control over the investment. The right of each partner to a voice in management does not mean a dominant voice. With respect to most management decisions, regardless of importance, the majority vote of the individual partners is controlling.

Facts: Rex Hammons and Donald Ball began a business, Hammons Heating and Air Conditioning, in which Ball was not active. A few years later, Hammons and Ball moved their business from Raleigh to Laurel and adopted a new name, Shady Grove TV and Appliance. When they got into severe financial difficulties, they petitioned to have their debts discharged in bankruptcy. The Bankruptcy Court found that Hammons and Ball had established a new business under a new name at Laurel, with both serving as active partners.

Outcome: The appellate court, however, held that Ball's becoming active in the business did not mean that they formed a new business. Every partner has a right to participate in the management and conduct of the business.

INSPECT THE BOOKS

Each partner must keep a clear record of all transactions performed for the firm. The firm's books must be available to all partners, and each partner must explain on request the significance of any record made that is not clear. All checks written must show the purpose for which they are written. There may be no business secrets among the partners.

CONTRIBUTION

A partner who pays a firm debt or liability from personal funds has a right to contribution from each of the other partners.

The Uniform Partnership Act states that "the partnership must indemnify every partner in respect of payments made and personal liabilities reasonably incurred by him in the ordinary and proper conduct of its business or for the preservation of its business or property." The partner has no right, however, to indemnity or reimbursement when (1) acting in bad faith, (2) negligently causing the necessity for payment, or (3) previously agreeing to bear the expense alone.

Facts: After David Rosenbaum bought some real estate, he and Steve Beilgard executed a partnership agreement to improve and develop the property. They began building a house and took out a loan to complete it. When they finished the house Beilgard wanted to buy it. While waiting for a loan to finance the purchase Beilgard and his wife moved in to the house. Beilgard made the loan payments. Several months later Beilgard had not concluded the purchase and without telling him, Rosenbaum sold the house to another couple. While living in the house Beilgard had upgraded the appliances. He sued for reimbursement of the appliance upgrades.

Outcome: The court stated that a partner is entitled to reimbursement for money advanced to the partnership which were within the scope of the partnership.

WITHDRAW ADVANCES

A partner has no right to withdraw any part of the original investment without the consent of the other partners. One partner, however, who makes additional advances in the form of a loan, has a right to withdraw this loan at any time after the due date. Also, a partner has a right to interest on a loan unless there is an agreement to the contrary. A partner has no right to interest on the capital account. Therefore, the firm should keep each partner's capital account separate from that partner's loan account.

WITHDRAW PROFITS

Each partner has the right to withdraw a share of the profits from the partnership at such time as specified by the partnership agreement. Withdrawal of profits could be by express authorization by vote of the majority of the partners in the absence of a controlling provision in the partnership agreement.

Liabilities of Partners

A partner's liabilities include the following:

1 Liability for contracts
2 Liability for torts
3 Liability for crimes

CONTRACTS

Every member of a general partnership has individual personal liability for all the enforceable debts of the firm. A partner who incurs a liability in the name of the firm but acted beyond both actual and apparent authority has personal liability. The firm has no liability for such unauthorized acts. The firm also has no liability for illegal contracts made by any member of the firm, since everyone is charged with knowledge of what is illegal. Thus, if a partner in a wholesale liquor firm contracted to sell an individual a case of whiskey, the contract would not be binding on the firm in a state where individual sales are illegal for wholesalers.

TORTS

A partnership has liability for the torts committed by a partner in the course of partnership business and in furtherance of partnership interests. When such liability occurs, the responsible partner has liability for indemnifying the partnership for any loss it sustains. The partnership does not have liability for deeds committed by one partner outside the course of partnership business and for the acting partner's own purposes, unless the deeds have been authorized or ratified by the partnership.

In addition to the partnership's liability, a partner has liability for the torts of another partner committed in the course of partnership business. This rule applies to negligent as well as intentional acts, such as embezzlement of funds, even if the innocent partner has no knowledge of the acts.

CRIMES

Courts will not imply criminal liability. In order to be liable for a crime, an individual partner must somehow have agreed to or participated in the crime. The individual partners could not be punished if they are free of personal guilt. However, the partnership has liability for any penalty incurred by the act of a partner in the ordinary course of business. *In the ordinary course of business* means while the partner acts as a partner in the business and in the promotion of partnership interests. The partnership has liability to the same extent as the acting partner. Thus, the criminal acts of one partner can justify a fine levied on partnership assets.

PREVIEW CASE REVISITED

Facts: Without having a mine drainage permit, the King Coal Company, a partnership, conducted mining operations. Robert Woods, the managing partner who directed the mining, and the company were both charged with operating a surface mine without a mine drainage permit.

Outcome: The partnership was guilty because the conduct was performed by its agent in the scope of employment and acting in its behalf. Woods was guilty because he was a partner who caused unlawful conduct to be performed on the partnership's behalf.

Nature of Partnership Liabilities

The partners have joint liability on all partnership contractual liabilities unless the contract stipulates otherwise. They have joint and several liability on all tort liabilities. For joint liabilities, the partners must be sued jointly. If the firm does not have adequate assets to pay the debts or liabilities of the firm, the general partners, of course, have individual liability for the full amount of debts or liabilities. If all the partners but one are insolvent, the remaining solvent partner must pay all the debts even though the judgment is against all of them. The partner who pays the debt has a right of contribution from the other partners but as a practical matter, may be unable to collect from the other partners.

Withdrawing partners have liability for all partnership debts incurred up to the time they withdraw unless the creditors expressly release these partners from liability. Under the Uniform Partnership Act, incoming partners have liability for all debts as fully as if they had been partners when the debt was incurred, except that this liability for old debts is limited to their investment in the partnership. Withdrawing partners may contract with incoming partners to pay all old debts, but this does not bind creditors.

Authority of a Partner

A partner has authority expressly given by the partnership agreement, by the partnership, and by law. By virtue of the existence of the partnership, each partner has the authority to enter into binding contracts on behalf of the partnership, as long as they are within the scope of the partnership business. Thus, each partner can, and often does, act as an agent of the partnership. This right can be limited by agreement as long as there is notice given of the limitation.

In addition, a partner has all powers that it is customary for partners to exercise in that kind of business in that particular community. As in the case of an agent, any limitation on the authority the partner would customarily possess does not bind a third person unless made known. The firm, however, has a right to indemnity from the partner who causes the firm loss through violation of the limitation placed on the authority.

Facts: Organized to buy and sell real estate, The Rittenhouse Investors was a partnership composed of Robert Durkin and James Cazanas. As trustee for Rittenhouse, Cazanas contracted to buy the Rice Hotel. Durkin and Cazanas signed an agreement stating that the hotel was purchased by Cazanas for Rittenhouse, and Durkin stated that to the extent there was any personal liability as a result of the purchase, he would be responsible for 50 percent of it. Cazanas contracted for renovation of the hotel and failed to pay some of the workers on the project. They filed liens against the property to secure payment. To get the liens released, Cazanas, as trustee, obtained release of lien bonds from American General Fire & Casualty Company (AGF & C). By these bonds, AGF & C agreed to pay the workers if they released their liens and Cazanas, as trustee, did not pay them. Cazanas also agreed to indemnify AGF & C if it had to pay. Cazanas did not pay the workers, so AGF & C did. AGF & C then sued Durkin and Cazanas as partners of Rittenhouse. Durkin argued that Cazanas's executing the agreement to repay AGF & C if it had to pay the workers was not within the scope of the partnership business and therefore he should not be liable on it.

Outcome: The court stated that Cazanas had to sign the agreement to repay AGF & C in order to get the release of lien bonds and therefore the business purposes of the partnership were directly served. Durkin was liable.

CUSTOMARY OR IMPLIED AUTHORITY

Each partner in an ordinary trading partnership has the following customary or implied authority:

1 To compromise and release a claim against a third party
2 To receive payments and give receipts in the name of the firm
3 To employ or to discharge agents and employees whose services are needed in the transaction of the partnership business
4 To draw and indorse checks, to make notes, and to accept drafts
5 To insure the property of the partnership, to cancel insurance policies, or to give proof of loss and to collect the proceeds
6 To buy goods on credit or to sell goods in the regular course of business

Sharing of Profits and Losses

LO4 Partnership profits and losses

The partnership agreement usually specifies the basis upon which the profits and the losses are to be shared. This proportion cannot be changed by a majority of the members of the firm. If the partnership agreement does not fix the ratio of sharing the profits and the losses, they will be shared equally and not in proportion to the contribution to the capital. If designated partners fix the ratio, it must be done fairly and in good faith. In the absence of a provision in the partnership agreement to the contrary, the majority of the partners may order a division of the profits at any time.

Questions

1. Must a partnership agreement be in writing? Discuss.
2. Does the fact that two people say they are partners establish the existence of a partnership?
3. Is the purchaser of one partner's share of a partnership a new partner? Explain.
4. If one partner is able to make a personal profit as a result of membership in the firm, must this profit be shared with the other partners?
5. What level of skill is required of partners and what is a partner's liability for failure to exercise that level of skill?
6. How many partners are required to agree on a matter in order to bind the firm on ordinary matters?
7. Under what circumstances does a partner not have a right to indemnity or reimbursement from the firm?
8. When the partnership agreement does not authorize withdrawal of profits from the partnership how can such authorization be obtained?
9. What is a partner's potential liability for the torts of another partner?
10. How are profits and losses shared among partners?

Case Problems

LO3 1. Stephen Jones, Daniel Fern, and three others were partners in a law firm. Kansallis Finance Ltd. obtained an opinion letter from Jones issued on the law firm's letterhead. It contained several intentional misrepresentations concerning a proposed transaction and was part of a conspiracy by Jones and others (but not any of his law partners) to defraud Kansallis. Jones was convicted of fraud, but Kansallis was unable to recover its loss from Jones or the other conspirators. Kansallis sued Jones' law partners alleging Jones had authority to issue the letter, thus they were liable for the damage caused by it when issued on the partnership letterhead and within the scope of its business. How should the court rule on the liability of Jones' partners?

LO1 2. Wilton and Janet Jackson, husband and wife, and their adult son, Walter Jackson, filed a voluntary petition under the Bankruptcy Code. The petition purported to be a partnership filing. They operated a hog farm. Wilton and Janet, on the one hand, and Walter, on the other, were to share profits and losses equally. However, all the losses were absorbed by Wilton and Janet, and there never were any profits. Walter testified that his wife, Carol, was a member of the partnership, while his parents said she was not. The three could not agree on when the alleged partnership was formed. Was there a partnership?

LO3 3. Larry West and Alan Falconer were the partners in A & L Farms which purchased farms, cleaned them up, farmed them for a time, and then sold them. Falconer was the general manager, responsible for the day-to-day activity of the farms. He contracted to have Eugene Stratemeyer construct grain bins on farms owned by A & L. Stratemeyer had previously constructed a bin for the partnership at Falconer's request, so he assumed this transaction was the same. Falconer went bankrupt and did not pay Statemeyer for the bins, so he sued West. West argued that contracting for the bins was outside Falconer's authority as a partner since he had no authority to incur major expenses. Was it?

LO2 4 Bernard Peskin and Earl Deutsch were partners in a law firm until Peskin withdrew. The partnership agreement obligated each partner to "devote his entire time" to the partnership business. Each accounted to the partnership for earnings not specifically related to legal work, such as fees for serving as a master in chancery and salary as a state legislator. After his withdrawal, Peskin happened to find out that Deutsch had filed income tax returns showing income from "legal fees," which had not been reported to the partnership. Peskin sued Deutsch to require him to account for sums received during the partnership existence that had not been reported. Should Deutsch be required to account for these sums?

LO2 5 Linda Crouse hired the law firm of Brobeck, Phleger & Harrison to represent her in selling a partnership interest. David Boatright was the BPH attorney responsible. She sold her interest for a promissory note of $7.25 M. Boatright did not deliver the note to Crouse. Boatright left BPH and became a partner at Page, Polin, Busch & Boatwright. More than a year after the sale Crouse told Boatwright that she did not have the note. When BPH transferred Crouse's file to Boatwright at PPB&B it did not include the note. Boatwright negotiated a restructuring of the note by which Crouse would receive $6.25M cash and a $1M note for the $7.25M note. The parties scheduled this restructuring to take place in six months. During this time Boatwright made no effort to find the $7.25M note. The restructuring did not go through as scheduled because Boatwright could not produce the note. When Crouse sued Boatwright and the two law firms, BPH sued Boatwright for indemnity. Boatwright claimed that BPH's suit violated its duty of loyalty and good faith. Did it?

LO4 6 A partner in the law firm Fordham & Starrett, Ian Starr withdrew from the partnership at the end of his second year. The partnership agreement provided that the founding partners had the authority to determine each partner's share of the firm's profits. Starr had been hesitant to join the firm because he did not expect to be able to get a lot of clients for the firm, but one of the founding partners had assured him that business origination would not be significant in allocating profits. The first year in business, the founding partners had divided the profits equally among the partners. After Starr's withdrawal, the founding partners allocated 6.3 percent of the profits to him. The other four partners divided the remainder. In making the allocation, the founding partners did not take into consideration any of the firm's accounts receivable or work in process even though Starr had produced billable dollar amounts of 15 percent of the total for all partners. Was the profit allocation proper?

LO1,4 7 Ronald Dreier withdrew from the law partnership of which he had been a member. The oral partnership agreement made no provision for withdrawal of a partner. Dreier sued his former partners for his share of the firm's earnings during the term of his membership. What should happen to fees that were unpaid or unbilled when Dreier withdrew?

LO1 8 Richard Missan was hired as a lawyer by the law firm of Gerald Schoenfeld and Bernard B. Jacobs. The firm received a large fee for work on an estate, and Missan sued, claiming a right to share in the fee as a partner. He alleged he was represented as a partner on the firm's letterhead, opinion letters, tax returns, professional directories, pension plan, and professional liability insurance policy. He also alleged that the parties had entered into an agreement admitting him as a member of the firm to receive a percentage of the profits. Schoenfeld and Jacobs submitted a written agreement that provided they would practice law as partners for one year. It also stated: "[U]nless this agreement is extended by an agreement in writing . . . it shall terminate in all respects" and "This agreement constitutes the entire understanding among the parties." The agreement was executed many years before the suit and was not extended in writing. Schoenfeld and Jacobs contended Missan was barred from alleging an oral partnership agreement. Was he?

Internet Resources for Business Law

Name	Resources	Web Address
Fambiz.com	Fambiz.com, a legal resource for family-owned businesses, provides news, events, and services	http://www.fambiz.com/
American Success Institute	American Success Institute promises a "free business education on the Web," and provides tips on operating small businesses.	http://www.success.org/
The Limited Liability Company	Attorney Steven E. Davidson provides basic information on limited liability companies, including a state-by-state comparison chart.	http://www.llcweb.com/
State of Indiana's Uniform Partnership Act	The state of Indiana maintains its adopted version of the Uniform Partnership Act.	http://www.ai.org/legislative/ic/code/title23/ar4/ch1.html
General Business Forms	The 'Lectric Law Library's™ business forms include a variety of sample partnership and corporation documents.	http://www.lectlaw.com/formb.htm

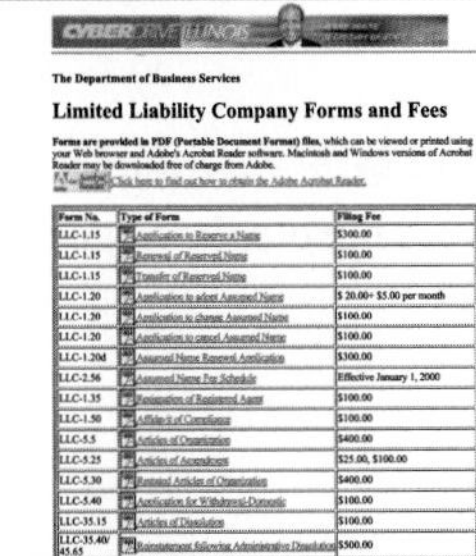

CYBERDRIVEILLINOIS

The Department of Business Services

Limited Liability Company Forms and Fees

Forms are provided in PDF (Portable Document Format) files, which can be viewed or printed using your Web browser and Adobe's Acrobat Reader software. Macintosh and Windows versions of Acrobat Reader may be downloaded free of charge from Adobe.

Click here to find out how to obtain the Adobe Acrobat Reader.

Form No.	Type of Form	Filing Fee
LLC-1.15	Application to Reserve a Name	$300.00
LLC-1.15	Renewal of Reserved Name	$100.00
LLC-1.15	Transfer of Reserved Name	$100.00
LLC-1.20	Application to adopt Assumed Name	$ 20.00+ $5.00 per month
LLC-1.20	Application to change Assumed Name	$100.00
LLC-1.20	Application to cancel Assumed Name	$100.00
LLC-1.20d	Assumed Name Renewal Application	$300.00
LLC-2.56	Assumed Name Fee Schedule	Effective January 1, 2000
LLC-1.35	Resignation of Registered Agent	$100.00
LLC-1.50	Affidavit of Compliance	$100.00
LLC-5.5	Articles of Organization	$400.00
LLC-5.25	Articles of Amendment	$25.00, $100.00
LLC-5.30	Restated Articles of Organization	$400.00
LLC-5.40	Application for Withdrawal-Domestic	$100.00
LLC-35.15	Articles of Dissolution	$100.00
LLC-35.40/ 45.65	Reinstatement following Administrative Dissolution	$500.00
LLC-37.10	Conversion Requirements	$100.00

33

Dissolution of a Partnership

Learning Objectives

1. List the methods the partners may use to dissolve a partnership.
2. Discuss the reasons why a court may order dissolution of a partnership.
3. Identify those events that result in dissolution of a partnership by operation of law.
4. Explain who should be notified of a partnership dissolution.

PREVIEW CASE

Gerald Olivet, Bennett Marcus, and Edgar Lucidi were members of Whittier Leasing Company, a partnership that engaged in sale–lease-back transactions with Whittier Hospital. The partnership would purchase equipment from the hospital and lease it back at favorable rates. The partnership was successful because seven of the partners (other than Olivet, Marcus, and Lucidi) were members of the board of directors of Whittier Hospital. These seven, together with the other two directors of the hospital, formed a competing partnership, named Friendly Hills Leasing Company, which then got all the lease-back business of the hospital. Olivet, Marcus, and Lucidi sued for dissolution of the Whittier partnership, alleging misconduct on the part of the other seven partners. Was this misconduct? Was the action harmful to Whittier Leasing? Is it appropriate for a partner or partners to engage in conduct detrimental to the partnership?

Dissolution of a Partnership
Change in relation of partners by elimination of one

Winding Up
Taking care of outstanding obligations and distributing remaining assets

The change in the relation of the partners caused by any partner's ceasing to be associated in the carrying on of the business is called **dissolution of a partnership**. The withdrawal of one member of a going partnership historically dissolved the partnership relation, and the partnership could not thereafter do any new business. The partnership continued to exist for the limited purpose of **winding up** or cleaning up its outstanding obligations and business affairs and distributing its remaining assets to creditors and partners. After the partnership completed this process, it was deemed terminated and went out of existence. However, if a partner wrongfully withdrew, the remaining partners could continue the business. These rule have been somewhat modified by the Revised Uniform Partnership Act.

Dissolution by Acts of the Parties

LO1
Dissolution by partners

Acts of the partners that dissolve a partnership include:

1. Agreement
2. Withdrawal or alienation
3. Expulsion

AGREEMENT

At the time they form the partnership agreement, the partners may fix the time when the partnership relation will cease. Unless they renew or amend the agreement, the partnership is dissolved on the agreed date. If no date for the dissolution is fixed at the time the partnership is formed, the partners may by mutual agreement dissolve the partnership at any time. Even when a definite date is fixed in the original agreement, the partners may dissolve the partnership prior to that time. In this case the subsequent decision to dissolve the partnership does not bind the partnership unless all the partners consent to the dissolution.

Sometimes the parties do not fix a date for dissolving the partnership, but the agreement sets forth the purpose of the partnership, such as the construction of a building. In this event the partnership is dissolved as soon as the purpose has been achieved.

WITHDRAWAL OR ALIENATION

The withdrawal of one partner at any time and for any reason unless wrongful historically dissolved the partnership. In a partnership for a definite term, any partner has the power, but not the right, to withdraw at any time. A withdrawing partner has liability for any loss sustained by the other partners because of the withdrawal. If the partnership agreement does not set a dissolution date, a partner may withdraw at will without liability. After creditors are paid, the withdrawing partner is entitled to receive capital, undistributed profits, and repayment of any loans to the partnership.

If the partnership agreement or a subsequent agreement sets a dissolution date, the withdrawing partner breaches the contract by withdrawing prior to the agreed date. When a partner withdraws in violation of agreement, the withdrawal is wrongful and damages suffered by the firm may be deducted from that partner's distributive share of the assets of the partnership.

Similar to withdrawal, the sale of a partner's interest either by a voluntary sale or an involuntary sale to satisfy personal creditors does not of itself dissolve the partnership. But the purchaser does not become a partner by purchase, since the remaining partners cannot be compelled to accept as a partner anyone who might be persona non grata to them. The buying partner has a right to the capital and profits of the withdrawing partner but not a right to participate in the management.

EXPULSION

The partnership agreement may, and should, contain a clause providing for the expulsion of a member, especially if the partnership has more than two members. This clause should spell out clearly the acts for which a member may be expelled and the method of settlement for such a partner's interest. A partnership may not expell a partner for self-gain. The partnership agreement should also set forth that the remaining partners agree to continue the business upon expulsion of a partner; otherwise, it might be necessary to wind up the partnership business and distribute all the assets to the creditors and partners, thereby terminating the partnership's existence.

Facts: In accordance with a clause in the partnership agreement, the executive committee of a large law firm expelled a partner, Philip Heller. Heller had produced little more than half the expected billable hours a year for the firm. The firm lost a potential client because Heller made a proposal to it which differed from a proposal made by another partner Heller knew was working with the prospective client. Heller also wrote an off-color letter to the executive vice president of Bank of America, one of the firm's most important clients. A few days later Heller sent an off-color story to him. The bank called the firm to indicate it would use another firm if such mailings did not stop. A member of the firm's executive committee told Heller not to send anything more to the bank, not even an apology. Heller sent an apology and the firm expelled him. Heller sued the firm.

Outcome: The court held that Heller's expulsion was not for self-gain and therefore was valid.

Dissolution by Court Decree

LO2 Court-ordered dissolution

Under certain circumstances a court may issue a decree dissolving a partnership. The chief reasons justifying such a decree include:

1. Insanity of a partner
2. Incapacity
3. Misconduct
4. Futility

INSANITY OF A PARTNER

A partner may obtain a decree of dissolution when a court declares another partner insane or of unsound mind.

INCAPACITY OF A PARTNER

If a partner develops an incapacity that makes it impossible for the partner to perform the services to the partnership that the partnership agreement contemplated, a petition may be filed to terminate the partnership on that ground. A member of an accounting firm who goes blind would probably be incapacitated to the extent of justifying a dissolution. The court, not the partners, must be the judge in each case as to whether or not the partnership should be dissolved. As a rule, the incapacity must be permanent, not temporary, to justify a court decree dissolving the partnership. A temporary inability of one partner to perform duties constitutes one of the risks that the other partners assumed when they formed the partnership.

A question may arise as to whether an illness or other condition causing a partner's inability to perform duties is temporary or not. The safest procedure is for the remaining partners to seek a court order determining the matter.

MISCONDUCT

If one member of a partnership engages in misconduct prejudicial to the successful continuance of the business, the court may, upon proper application, decree a dissolution of the partnership. Such misconduct includes habitual drunkenness, dishonesty, persistent violation of the partnership agreement, irreconcilable discord among the partners as to major matters, and abandonment of the business by a partner.

PREVIEW CASE REVISITED

Facts: Gerald Olivet, Bennett Marcus, and Edgar Lucidi were members of Whittier Leasing Company, a partnership that engaged in sale–lease-back transactions with Whittier Hospital. The partnership would purchase equipment from the hospital and lease it back at favorable rates. The partnership was successful because seven of the partners (other than Olivet, Marcus, and Lucidi) were members of the board of directors of Whittier Hospital. These seven, together with the other two directors of the hospital, formed a competing partnership, named Friendly Hills Leasing Company, which then got all the lease-back business of the hospital. Olivet, Marcus, and Lucidi sued for dissolution of the Whittier partnership, alleging misconduct on the part of the other seven members.

Outcome: The court held that if partners elect to compete with the partnership, the remaining partners are entitled to a court-ordered dissolution.

FUTILITY

All business partnerships are conducted for the purpose of making a profit. If this objective clearly cannot be achieved, the court may decree a dissolution. One partner cannot compel the other members to assume continued losses after the success of the business becomes highly improbable and further operation appears futile. A temporarily unprofitable operation does not justify a dissolution. A court will issue a decree of dissolution only when the objective reasonably appears impossible to attain.

Dissolution by Operation of Law

LO3 Events resulting in dissolution by operation of law

Under certain well-defined circumstances, a partnership will be dissolved by operation of law; that is to say, it will be dissolved immediately upon the happening of the specified event. No decree of the court is necessary to dissolve the partnership. The most common examples include:

1. Death
2. Bankruptcy
3. Illegality

DEATH

The death of one member of a partnership automatically dissolves the partnership unless the agreement provides it shall not be dissolved. A representative of the deceased may act to protect the interest of the heirs but cannot act as a partner. This is true even

Internet Resources for Business Law

Name	Resources	Web Address
U.S. Chamber of Commerce	U.S. Chamber of Commerce provides news, information, services, and products to assist small business owners.	http://www.uschamber.org/
Law Journal EXTRA! (LJX!)—Corporate Law	LJX!, sponsored by the New York Law Publishing Company, provides daily corporate law news, case law, and legal analysis.	http://www.ljx.com/practice/corporate/index.html
CNNfn: The Financial Network	CNNfn, Turner Broadcasting's financial news complement to CNN, provides reports on mergers and takeovers. CNNfn is interactive, allowing visitors to "ask the experts" or respond to the day's programs.	http://www.cnnfn.com/
Business and General Forms	The 'Lectric Law Library's business forms include a variety of sample partnership and corporation documents.	http://www.lectlaw.com/formb.htm

CYBERDRIVEILLINOIS

The Department of Business Services

Limited Liability Company Forms and Fees

Forms are provided in PDF (Portable Document Format) files, which can be viewed or printed using your Web browser and Adobe's Acrobat Reader software. Macintosh and Windows versions of Acrobat Reader may be downloaded free of charge from Adobe.

Click here to find out how to obtain the Adobe Acrobat Reader.

Form No.	Type of Form	Filing Fee
LLC-1.15	Application to Reserve a Name	$300.00
LLC-1.15	Renewal of Reserved Name	$100.00
LLC-1.15	Transfer of Reserved Name	$100.00
LLC-1.20	Application to adopt Assumed Name	$ 20.00+ $5.00 per month
LLC-1.20	Application to change Assumed Name	$100.00
LLC-1.20	Application to cancel Assumed Name	$100.00
LLC-1.20d	Assumed Name Renewal Application	$300.00
LLC-2.56	Assumed Name Fee Schedule	Effective January 1, 2000
LLC-1.35	Resignation of Registered Agent	$100.00
LLC-1.50	Affidavit of Compliance	$100.00
LLC-5.5	Articles of Organization	$400.00
LLC-5.25	Articles of Amendment	$25.00, $100.00
LLC-5.30	Restated Articles of Organization	$400.00
LLC-5.40	Application for Withdrawal-Domestic	$100.00
LLC-35.15	Articles of Dissolution	$100.00
LLC-35.40/ 45.65	Reinstatement following Administrative Dissolution	$500.00
LLC-37.10	Conversion Requirements	$100.00

34 Nature of a Corporation

Learning Objectives

1. List the different classifications and kinds of corporations.
2. Discuss how a corporation is formed and potential promoter liability.
3. Name the types of powers a corporation has and the significance of ultra vires contracts.

PREVIEW CASE

Coosa Valley Electric Cooperative, Inc., a not-for-profit corporation formed to provide electric service to its members, incorporated Coosa Valley Propane Services, Inc. Coosa Propane bought all the stock of DeKalb Co. LP Gas Co., Inc. Coosa Electric, Coosa Propane, and DeKalb then chose the same officers and directors. A group of propane dealers sued the companies alleging Coosa Electric did not have the authority to operate a propane business. Coosa Electric argued the propane dealers had no right to contest the power of Coosa Electric to acquire Dekalb's stock. One of the propane dealers, Suburban Gas, was a member of Coosa Electric. What does it mean to be a *member* of a not-for-profit corporation? What powers does a member have?

Corporations have become a widely used form of business organization. No matter what the size of a business, a corporation may be formed to run it. Because of the variety of uses to which corporations may be put, there are different types of corporations. They are also classified by the state of incorporation because, as an entity of the state, its laws of incorporation govern them.

Classification by Purpose

LO1 Types of corporations

Corporations may be classified according to their purpose or function as public or private.

PUBLIC CORPORATIONS

Public Corporation
One formed for governmental function

A **public corporation** is one formed to carry out some governmental function. Examples of public corporations include a city, a state university, and a public hospital. The powers and functions of public corporations may be much greater than those of private corporations conducted for profit. Public corporations may, for example, have the power to levy taxes, impose fines, and condemn property. Public corporations are created by the state primarily for the purpose of facilitating the administration of governmental functions.

Some public bodies, such as school boards, boards of county commissioners, and similar bodies, are not true public corporations but have many similar powers. Such powers include the right to sue and be sued; the power to own, buy, and sell property; and the power to sign other contracts as an entity. These bodies are called **quasi public corporations**, quasi meaning "as if" or "in the nature of."

Quasi Public Corporation
Public body with powers similar to corporations

PRIVATE CORPORATIONS

Private Corporation
One formed to do nongovernmental function

Private corporations are those formed by private individuals to perform some nongovernmental function. They in turn include:

1 Not-for-profit corporations
2 Profit corporations

Not-for-Profit Corporation
One formed by private individuals for charitable, educational, religious, social, or fraternal purpose

Not-for-Profit Corporations. A **not-for-profit corporation** is one formed by private individuals for some charitable, educational, religious, social, or fraternal purpose. This corporation is not organized for profit, does not distribute income or profits to members, officers, or directors, and usually does not issue stock. As a legal entity like any other corporation, it can sue and be sued as a corporation, can buy and sell property, and can otherwise operate as any other corporation. A person acquires membership in a not-for-profit corporation by agreement between the charter members in the beginning and between the present members and new members thereafter.

PREVIEW CASE REVISITED

Facts: Coosa Valley Electric Cooperative, Inc., a not-for-profit corporation formed to provide electric service to its members, incorporated Coosa Valley Propane Services, Inc. Coosa Propane bought all the stock of DeKalb Co. LP Gas Co., Inc. Coosa Electric, Coosa Propane, and DeKalb then chose the same officers and directors. A group of propane dealers sued the companies alleging Coosa Electric did not have the authority to operate a propane business. Coosa Electric argued the propane dealers had no right to contest the power of Coosa Electric to acquire Dekalb's stock. One of the propane dealers, Suburban Gas, was a member of Coosa Electric.

Outcome: The court held that as a member of the not-for-profit corporation, Suburban Gas had the right to challenge Coosa's acts as illegal.

Profit Corporation
One organized to run a business and earn money

Profit Corporations. A **profit corporation** is one organized to run a business and earn money. In terms of number and importance, **stock corporations** organized for profit constitute the chief type. Certificates called *shares of stock*

Stock Corporation
One in which ownership is represented by stock

represent ownership in a stock corporation. The number of shares of stock owned and the charter and the bylaws of the corporation determine the extent of one's rights and liabilities.

Close or Closely Held Corporation
One with very small number of shareholders

A profit corporation that has a very small number of people who own stock in it is called a **close corporation** or a **closely held corporation**. Because of the small number of stockholders, they normally expect to be and are active in the management of the business.

Many close corporations choose to be designated Subchapter S corporations for federal income tax purposes. Unlike other corporations, a Subchapter S corporation files only an information tax return. It does not pay corporate income tax. The owners report the profit of the corporation as income on their personal income tax returns. This results in tax savings. The corporation's profits are not taxed twice—once when shown on a corporate tax return and second when shown as income from the corporation to the owners on their personal tax returns.

Classification by State of Incorporation

Domestic Corporation
One chartered in the state

Foreign Corporation
One chartered in another state

Alien Corporation
One chartered in another country

Corporations may be classified depending on where they were incorporated. A corporation is a **domestic corporation** in the state where it received its initial charter; it is a **foreign corporation** in all other states. If incorporated in another country, a corporation may be referred to as an **alien corporation**. The corporation can operate as a foreign corporation in any other state it chooses as long as it complies with the registration or other requirements of the other state.

Formation of a Corporation

LO2
Formation of corporation and liability

Promoter
One who takes initial steps to form corporation

One who acts as the **promoter** usually takes the initial steps of forming a corporation. A corporation can be organized in any state the promoter chooses. A lot of preliminary work must be done before the corporation comes into existence. The incorporation papers must be prepared, a registration statement may need to be drawn up and filed with the Securities and Exchange Commission (SEC) and the appropriate state officials, the stock must be sold, and many contracts must be entered into for the benefit of the proposed corporation. Filing with the SEC is not required in the case of smaller corporations.

Minor defects in the formation of a corporation may generally be ignored. In some instances the defect is of a sufficiently serious character that the attorney general of the state that approved the articles of incorporation of the corporation may obtain the cancellation or revocation of such articles. In other cases, the formation of the corporation is so defective that the existence of a corporation is ignored, and the persons organizing the corporation are held liable as partners or joint venturers.

Liability on Promoter's Contracts and Expenses

The corporation does not automatically become a party to contracts made by the promoter. After the corporation is organized, it will ordinarily approve or adopt the contracts made by the promoter. The approval may be either express or by the corporation's conduct. Once approved, such contracts bind the corporation, and it may sue on them.

ETHICAL POINT
Regardless of the law on the subject, do you think it is ethical for a promoter to be able to be relieved of liability on contracts made for the benefit of the corporation?

The promoter may avoid personal liability on contracts made for the benefit of the corporation by including a provision in the contract that the promoter incurs no personal liability if the corporation does or does not adopt the contract. In the absence of such a provision, the promoter may have liability. Courts look at whether the other contracting party knew the corporation was not yet in existence. The wording of the contract is also very significant in determining whether it binds the promoter either pending the formation of the corporation or after it has come into existence.

Facts: Clinton Investors Company owned property it leased for three years to the Clifton Park Learning Center, Inc. Berne Watkins executed the lease on behalf of the Learning Center and represented himself as its treasurer. The state did not issue a certificate of incorporation for the Learning Center until eight months later. A year later the Learning Center had failed to pay all the rent due. Clinton sued Watkins.

Outcome: The court found that because no corporation existed when Watkins executed the lease on behalf of the Learning Center, he signed as a promoter. Since the parties did not agree that Watkins should not be bound by the contract, the court held him liable on it.

Along with the adoption of the promoter's contracts, the corporation may or may not pay the expenses of the promoter in organization of the corporation. After the corporation comes into existence, it customarily reimburses the promoter for all necessary expenses in forming the corporation. This may be done by a resolution passed by the board of directors.

Issuance of Stock

Subscriber
One who agrees to buy stock in proposed corporation

When a new corporation is about to be formed, agreements to buy its stock will generally be made in advance of actual incorporation. In such a case the purchase agreement or subscription to stock by a prospective stockholder or investor, called a **subscriber**, constitutes merely an offer to buy. In most jurisdictions this offer may be revoked any time prior to acceptance. As the offeree, the corporation cannot accept the subscription until the state issues its charter. If an existing corporation sells stock, it

Facts: Richard Bielinski and Richard Miller prepared a written agreement for a corporation they were organizing. At a meeting of incorporators it was voted that the capital stock of the corporation would be 500 shares and that 100 shares each to Bielinski and Miller were to be issued for $1,000 cash. The corporation was formed, but at a board meeting Bielinski resigned from the board and presidency because of illness. Pursuant to a law allowing a shareholder in a closely held corporation to seek judicial relief, Bielinski later filed suit to again have a say in running the corporation.

Outcome: The court found he was eligible to file suit because he was a subscriber to 50 percent of the stock. When he and Miller agreed to take and pay for 100 shares of stock, they clearly expressed an intention to become subscribers. Acceptance by the corporation of this subscription offer was implied. A valid subscription gives a subscriber the rights of a stockholder.

can accept all subscriptions immediately and make them binding contracts. If the promoter is to be paid by means of a stock option, the corporation can make such a contract with the promoter before any services are performed. Most state laws provide that a minimum amount of stock must be sold and paid for before the corporation can begin operations.

Once a valid subscription agreement is signed, the subscriber has rights in the corporation even if the stock certificates have not been received or issued.

Articles of Incorporation

Articles of Incorporation Document stating facts about corporation required by law

Incorporators People initially forming a corporation

The written document setting forth the facts prescribed by law for issuance of a certificate of incorporation or a charter and asserting that the corporation has complied with legal requirements is the **articles of incorporation** (see Illustration 34-1 for a sample form). Once approved by the state, the articles determine the authority of the corporation. This document constitutes a contract between the corporation and the state. So long as the corporation complies with the terms of the contract, the state cannot alter the articles in any material way without obtaining the consent of the stockholders. The articles include such information as the name of the corporation, the names of the people forming the corporation (the **incorporators**), and the amount and types of stock the corporation has authorization to issue. The incorporators elect a board of directors and begin business, which constitutes acceptance of the charter and binds all parties.

Powers of a Corporation

LO3 Types of powers

A corporation has three types of powers: express, incidental, and implied.

EXPRESS POWERS

The statute or code under which the corporation is formed and to a lesser degree the corporation's articles of incorporation determine its express powers. In a few instances, the state constitution sets forth the powers of a corporation. The statutes limit a corporation's powers to what they grant and a corporation may not do what statutes prohibit.

INCIDENTAL POWERS

Certain powers always incidental to a corporation's express powers or essential to its existence as a corporation include:

1. To have a corporate name
2. To have a continuous existence
3. To have property rights
4. To make bylaws and regulations
5. To engage in legal actions
6. To have a corporate seal

Corporate Name. A corporation must have a corporate name. The members may select any name they wish, provided that it does not violate the statutes or that another firm or corporation within the state does not use it. Many of the states have statutes

ARTICLES OF INCORPORATION
of
____

The undersigned person(s), acting as incorporator(s) of a corporation organized under the laws of Delaware, hereby adopt(s) the following Articles of Incorporation:

ARTICLE I
CORPORATE NAME

The name of this corporation is____.

ARTICLE II
INITIAL PRINCIPAL OFFICE

The mailing address of the corporation's initial principal office is:

____
______________________, _______ __________

ARTICLE III
SHARES

The total number of shares which the corporation shall have authority to issue is _____ shares of no par value stock.

ARTICLE IV
REGISTERED OFFICE AND AGENT

The street address of the corporation's initial registered office and the name of its initial registered agent at such address is:

____
____
______________________County
______________________, _______ _________

ARTICLE V
PURPOSE

The purpose of the corporation is to engage in any lawful activity permitted by the laws of this state.

ARTICLE VI
DIRECTORS

The names and residence addresses of the persons constituting the initial board of directors are:

____
____
______________________, _______ _________

After the initial board of directors, the board shall consist of such number of directors as shall be determined by the shareholders from time to time at each annual meeting at which directors are to be elected.

The directors shall be divided into________classes, the number of directors to be allocated to each class to be as nearly equal as possible and with the term of office in one class expiring each year after the initial annual meeting of shareholders.

ARTICLE VII
LIABILITY OF DIRECTORS

To the fullest extent permitted by law, no director of this corporation shall be personally liable to the corporation or its shareholders for monetary damages for breach of any duty owed to the corporation or its shareholders, except that a director may be held personally liable for (i) breaches of the duty of loyalty, (ii) acts or omissions not in good faith or which involve intentional misconduct or a knowing violation of law, (iii) declaration of unlawful dividends or unlawful stock repurchases or redemptions, or (iv) a transaction for which the director derives an improper personal benefit.

(continued)

Illustration 34-1
Articles of Incorporation for Delaware

Any director or officer who is involved in litigation or other proceeding by reason of his or her position as a director or officer of this corporation shall be indemnified and held harmless by the corporation to the fullest extent permitted by law.

ARTICLE VIII
OTHER PROVISIONS

Preemptive Rights. The corporation elects to have preemptive rights so that each shareholder has the right to acquire a proportional amount of any shares that are issued.

Director or Officer Interest. In the absence of fraud, no transaction between (a) this corporation and (b) any other association, corporation or any director or officer of this corporation individually, shall be affected by the fact that any director or officer of this corporation is individually a party to the transaction or is interested in or is a director or officer of such other association or corporation.

Stock Transfer Restriction. No shareholder of this corporation shall sell any shares of stock held by him or her in this corporation without first offering to sell such stock to the corporation on the same terms and conditions and at the price offered in good faith and in writing, by any proposed purchaser. The written offer by such proposed purchaser shall be delivered to the corporation at the time the stock is offered to the corporation for sale. The corporation shall have the right to accept the offer any time within thirty (30) days from and after the date on which the offer is made to the shareholder and shall exercise the option to purchase by notifying the shareholder in writing. If the corporation shall not exercise its option to purchase the shares of stock, it shall notify the shareholder in writing within the thirty (30) day period and the shares may then be sold by the shareholder, but only to the proposed purchaser on the same terms and conditions as offered to the corporation, and only within thirty (30) days from and after the date on which the corporation declines to exercise its option.

Corporate Seal. The corporation shall have no corporate seal.

Execution of Written Instruments. All instruments that are executed on behalf of the corporation which are acknowledged and which affect an interest in real estate shall be executed by the President or any Vice-President and the Secretary or Treasurer. All other instruments executed by the corporation, including a release of mortgage or lien, may be executed by the President or Vice-President. Notwithstanding the preceding provisions of this section, any written instrument may be executed by any officer(s) or agents(s) that are specifically designated by resolution of the board of directors.

Certification

I certify that I have read the above Articles of Incorporation and that they are true and correct to the best of my knowledge.

____

____

______________________________, Incorporator

____________________, ________ ________

State of ____________________, County of ______________________________,ss:

Subscribed and sworn to (or affirmed) before me this ______ day of ______________, ______.

____
Notary Public

Illustration 34-1
Articles of Incorporation for Delaware *(continued)*

regulating corporate names. For example, statutes may require the name to end with *Corporation* or to be followed by the word *Incorporated,* an abbreviation thereof, or other indication of corporate status.

Continuous Existence. The existence of the corporation continues for the period for which the state grants the charter. This feature of a corporation makes this form of organization valuable. The death of a stockholder does not dissolve the organization. Sometimes people refer to this characteristic as *perpetual,* or *continuous, succession.*

Property Rights. A corporation has the right to buy, sell, and hold property necessary in its functioning as a corporation and not foreign to its purpose.

Bylaws and Regulations. The organization needs rules and regulations to govern it and to determine its future conduct. They must conform to the statutes and must not be contrary to public policy. The corporation's board of directors adopts these rules, called the corporation **bylaws**.

Bylaws
Rules enacted by directors to govern corporation's conduct

Legal Actions. Long considered incidental to corporate existence is the corporation's power to sue in its own name. Since a corporation may be composed of hundreds or thousands of stockholders, it would be a cumbersome, if not impossible, task to secure the consent of all the stockholders each time a suit needed to be brought by a corporation. A corporation may likewise be sued in the corporate name. In some states a corporation may represent itself in low-level trial courts by an officer/shareholder who is not an attorney just as a human being who is not an attorney may represent himself.

Corporate Seal. A corporation has the incidental power to have and to own a seal. Normally a corporation need not use a seal except (1) in executing written instruments that require the use of a seal when executed by natural individuals, or (2) in carrying out transactions where special statutory requirements require the use of the seal.

IMPLIED POWERS

In addition to incidental or express powers conferred upon all corporations, a corporation has the implied power to do all acts reasonably necessary for carrying out the purpose for which the corporation was formed. A corporation may borrow money and contract debts if such acts are necessary for the transaction of the corporate business. It may make, indorse, and accept negotiable instruments. It has the power to acquire and convey property and to mortgage or lease its property in case such transactions are necessary for carrying on its business. Corporation codes as a rule expressly list the various implied powers described above so that they constitute express powers.

Ultra Vires Contracts

Ultra Vires Contract
Contract exceeding corporation's powers

Any contract entered into by a corporation that goes beyond its powers is called an **ultra vires contract**. As between the parties to the contract, the corporation and the third person, the contract generally binds them. However, a stockholder may bring an action to prevent the corporation from entering into such a contract or to recover damages from the directors or officers who have caused loss to the corporation by such contracts. In extreme cases, the attorney general of a state may obtain a court order revoking the articles of incorporation of the corporation for frequent or serious improper acts that make it proper to impose such an extreme penalty.

Facts: Billy Mansell organized J.F.K. Carwash, Inc. He sold a one-third interest in it to Charles James and to David Grubbs. James later wanted to get out of the business, so the three agreed to have the corporation repurchase James's stock. The corporation executed a note for the repurchase, which note Mansell and Grubbs guaranteed. On the day of the execution, the corporation had a deficit and no unrestricted earned surplus, so the repurchase violated state law. When the corporation failed to make the note payments, James sued J.F.K., Mansell, and Grubbs. They contended the note was void since it was ultra vires.

Outcome: The court stated the note was not void and held it binding between the corporation and James.

Questions

1 What is the purpose of public corporations?
2 What powers does a not-for-profit corporation have?
3 How does a Subchapter S corporation differ from other corporations?
4 How is a corporation formed, and for what is the promoter potentially personally liable?
5 Does a subscriber have any rights in a corporation?
6 What is a corporation's articles of incorporation and what is their importance?
7 List and explain two incidental powers of a corporation.
8 What action may the state take if a corporation engages in an ultra vires act?

Case Problems

LO2 1 Lennox Hill Hospital employed radiologists Frank Purnell and Carmel Donovan along with 10 others. The 12 doctors agreed to form a corporation to employ them to provide radiology services at the hospital. They were to be equal shareholders of the corporation and 10 of them contributed $3,000 to start it. Lewis Rothman who paid only $100 signed the certificate of incorporation which listed each of the 12 doctors as shareholders. He had all the corporation's stock issued to him. Purnell and Donovan demanded the right to inspect the corporation's records but Rothman refused saying they were not shareholders. Were they shareholders?

LO1 2 Consolidated Mutual Water Company (CMWC) was organized as a nonprofit corporation but authorized to issue stock. Joseph Meiresonne and others were unsuccessful candidates for the board of directors of CMWC. They sought to oust Leslie Arnold and others as directors of CMWC, alleging that a corporate bylaw authorizing six-year terms for directors was illegal. If CMWC was a nonprofit corporation the term was valid. If it was for-profit the term was invalid. Meiresonne alleged that corporate acts such as issuing stock, repurchasing its stock, and competing against other water organizations for the sale of water destroyed the nonprofit aspects of CMWC. No income or profit of CMWC was distributed to its members or directors. Is CMWC a for-profit or nonprofit corporation?

LO3 3 Renaissance Enterprises, Inc., a corporation with only Mr. and Mrs. Malcolm Babb as shareholders, was a party to a lawsuit in an appellate court. Babb who was not an attorney had represented Renaissance. Does a corporation have the power to represent itself in court by a shareholder/officer who is not an attorney?

LO2 4 Roy Lathan signed a contract on behalf of Royal Development and Management Corp. with Guardian 50/50 Fund V Ltd. By the contract, Guardian agreed to sell Royal 23 lots on a closing date set by North Carolina National Bank (NCNB). NCNB set the date, but Guardian had not removed construction debris as required, so Royal refused to close. Guardian sued Royal and Lathan for breach of contract. Lathan contended he should not be personally liable because he did not know when he signed the contract that Royal had not been incorporated. Lathan signed the articles of incorporation three days after executing the contract. Should Lathan have personal liability on the contract?

LO2 5 William Putnam approached Robert Williams about starting a franchise of a soccer league. Williams orally agreed to put up $75,000 "seed money" in return for 50 percent of the stock of a future corporation, Georgia Soccer, Inc. Neither the franchise nor Georgia Soccer, Inc., materialized, and Williams's only investment amounted to an advance of $2,500. Putnam sued Williams, alleging breach of a stock subscription agreement. Does Williams have any liability on this agreement?

LO2 6 Bill Weiss orally agreed to give Clifford Anderson temporary possession of a lot and building in exchange for monthly rental payments. For two years Anderson sent checks payable to and accepted by Weiss. These checks constituted rental payments while Anderson was in possession. The first two checks were drawn on Capital Rentals & Import Repair and subsequent ones on Import Repair Self Service, Inc. Anderson's business, Import Repair & Body Shop, Inc., was not incorporated until five months after the lease began. Weiss alleged that Anderson had not paid enough rent and sued him. Anderson alleged that Import Repair Self Services, Inc., not he personally, should be liable for any rent due. Is Anderson liable?

LO3 7 The state Blue Cross and Blue Shield corporation requested approval from the commissioner of insurance to buy a life insurance company, United Trust Life Insurance Company. Several competing insurance companies opposed the purchase. The single purpose for which Blue Cross was organized was to establish, maintain, and operate "a health-care service plan" for subscribers. Is the selling of life insurance beyond the powers of Blue Cross?

LO2 8 Claud Koch and Don Czeschin resolved to form a corporation called Quality Aloe Vera Labs, Inc. and it was incorporated on June 3. However, on April 25, knowing Quality was not yet incorporated, Thoeni Aloe Vera agreed to sell aloe vera leaves to Quality. The agreement recited it was between Quality and Thoeni and Czeschin signed it, "Quality Aloe Vera Labs, Inc. by Don Czeschin." Quality ordered and paid for 10 shipments of leaves through August. Then Quality ordered 10 more shipments but did not pay for them and went into bankruptcy. Thoeni sued Koch and Czeschin alleging they were liable as promoters because the contract was signed before the corporation was incorporated. Should Koch and Czeschin be personally liable?

Internet Resources for Business Law

Name	Resources	Web Address
Business and General Forms	The 'Lectric Law Library's business forms include a variety of sample partnership and corporation documents.	http://www.lectlaw.com/formb.htm
Limited Liability Companies—USA	Limited Liability Companies—USA, sponsored by The Limited Liability Company Reporter, provides articles, documents, and links relevant to limited liability companies.	http://www.llc-usa.com/
Educause	EDUCAUSE, an international, nonprofit association specializing in the use of information resources and technologies in higher education, maintains its bylaws, and lists of board members, staff, and membership, on its Web site.	http://www.educause.edu
State of Arizona's Corporation Laws	The state of Arizona maintains its corporation laws.	http://www.azleg.state.az.us/ars/10/title10.htm
State of New York's Corporation Laws	The state of New York maintains its corporation laws.	http://www.law.cornell.edu/ny/statutes/buscorp.htm

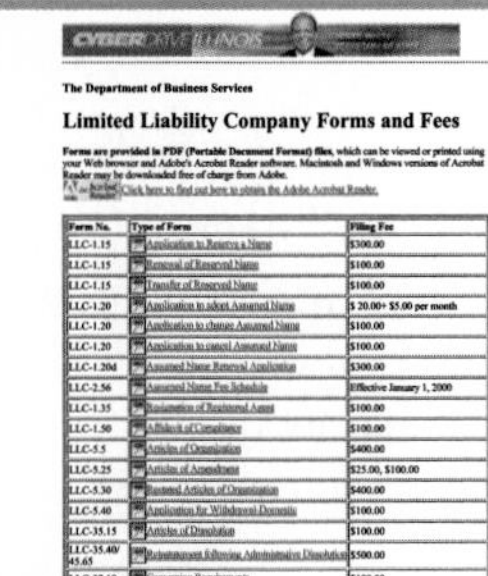

CYBERDRIVEILLINOIS

The Department of Business Services

Limited Liability Company Forms and Fees

Forms are provided in PDF (Portable Document Format) files, which can be viewed or printed using your Web browser and Adobe's Acrobat Reader software. Macintosh and Windows versions of Acrobat Reader may be downloaded free of charge from Adobe.
Click here to find out how to obtain the Adobe Acrobat Reader.

Form No.	Type of Form	Filing Fee
LLC-1.15	Application to Reserve a Name	$300.00
LLC-1.15	Renewal of Reserved Name	$100.00
LLC-1.15	Transfer of Reserved Name	$100.00
LLC-1.20	Application to adopt Assumed Name	$ 20.00+ $5.00 per month
LLC-1.20	Application to change Assumed Name	$100.00
LLC-1.20	Application to cancel Assumed Name	$100.00
LLC-1.20d	Assumed Name Renewal Application	$300.00
LLC-2.56	Assumed Name Fee Schedule	Effective January 1, 2000
LLC-1.35	Resignation of Registered Agent	$100.00
LLC-1.50	Affidavit of Compliance	$100.00
LLC-5.5	Articles of Organization	$400.00
LLC-5.25	Articles of Amendment	$25.00, $100.00
LLC-5.30	Restated Articles of Organization	$400.00
LLC-5.40	Application for Withdrawal Domestic	$100.00
LLC-35.15	Articles of Dissolution	$100.00
LLC-35.40/ 45.65	Reinstatement following Administrative Dissolution	$500.00
LLC-37.10	Conversion Requirements	$100.00

35

Ownership of a Corporation

Learning Objectives

1 Define capital stock.

2 List the various types of stock and stock rights.

3 Explain what dividends are and how they may be paid.

4 Name the various laws regulating the sale of securities, exchanges, and brokers.

PREVIEW CASE

James Junker owned stock in Reco Investment Corporation. At a stockholders' meeting, Frederick Heisler, the attorney for Reco and Road Equipment Company, Inc., suggested that since Reco could not pay a debt it owed to Road, the solution was to merge Reco into another company such as Road. The merger passed. The merger formula for exchanging Reco stock for Road stock used book values despite the fact that Reco's property was located in an area where real estate values and the cost of building had greatly increased. Two months after the merger, Junker was notified that Road's annual report would show a loss. This had not been mentioned at the stockholders' meeting. Junker sued, alleging violation of the federal Securities Act. This act establishes a cause of action for a purchaser of securities against a person who sold the securities by means of oral communication that includes an untrue statement of material fact or omits a material fact required to render the statements not misleading. Did Heisler violate the act? What part did Heisler play in the transaction?

LO1

Capital stock

Capital Stock
Declared value of outstanding stocks

Share
Unit of stock

The **capital stock** of the corporation is the declared money value of its outstanding stock. The owners subscribe and pay for this stock. Generally, not all the stock a corporation may issue need be subscribed and paid for before the corporation begins operation. The amount of capital stock authorized in the charter cannot be altered without the consent of the state and a majority of the stockholders. The capital stock is divided into units called **shares**.

Ownership

Shareholder or Stockholder
Person who owns stock

A person achieves ownership in a stock corporation by acquiring title to one or more shares of stock. Owners are known as **shareholders** or **stockholders**. A person may obtain shares of stock by subscription either before or after organization of the corporation, or shares may be obtained in other ways, such as by gift or purchase from another shareholder.

Stock Certificate

The amount of ownership (the number of shares owned) may be evidenced by a stock certificate. It is not the actual stock, just written evidence of ownership of stock. The certificate shows on its face the number of shares represented, the par value of each share if the stock has a par value, and the signatures of the officers.

Facts: General Export Iron and Metal Company of Louisiana authorized the issuance to Sam Goltzman of 12 shares of stock. Sam paid for the stock, and General issued and delivered certificate number 004 for 12 shares in Sam's name. Ronald Goltzman, the president, and Grace Kennedy, the secretary-treasurer, had not signed the certificate. Sam endorsed the certificate and transferred the 12 shares to Ronald, his son. Sam delivered the certificate to Ronald who signed it as president and had Kennedy sign it. Sam later filed suit to compel General to issue 12 shares of stock. He alleged that the defectiveness of the first certificate meant he had not owned the 12 shares and could not have transferred them to Ronald.

Outcome: The court held that the certificate was not the actual shares of stock. It was simply evidence of ownership of stock. Sam owned 12 shares when he endorsed and transferred the certificate to Ronald.

Classes of Stock

LO2
Types of stock and rights

Stock is divided into many classes. The laws under which the corporation is organized and the articles of incorporation determine the classes. The two principal classes of stock are:

1. Common stock
2. Preferred stock

COMMON STOCK

Common Stock
Stock that entitles owner to vote

Common stock is the simplest form of stock and the normal type of stock issued. The owners of common stock control the corporation because they may vote for members of the board of directors. The board in turn hires the individuals who manage and operate the corporation. Unless selected as a director or appointed as an officer, a stockholder has no voice in the running of the corporation beyond the annual vote for the board of directors.

Common stockholders have the right to a share of the assets of a corporation upon dissolution.

PREFERRED STOCK

Preferred Stock
Stock giving special advantage

Preferred stock differs from common stock in that the holder of this stock has some sort of special advantage or preference. In return for a preference, the preferred stockholders usually give up two rights common stockholders retain—the right to vote in stockholders' meetings and the right to participate in profits beyond the percentage fixed in the stock certificate.

The preference granted may pertain to the division of dividends, to the division of assets upon dissolution, or to both of these. Most often, the preference relates both to dividends and assets. Calling particular stock preferred does not tell what preference the holder has. The stock certificate will indicate the type of preference, although the certificate of incorporation governs the exact rights of preferred shareholders. Preferred stock may be

1 preferred as to assets
2 preferred as to dividends
3 participating
4 nonparticipating

Preferred as to Assets. Stock preferred as to assets gives the holder an advantage only in the event of liquidation. Preferred stockholders receive their proportionate share of the corporation's assets prior to any share going to common shareholders.

Preferred as to Dividends. Stock preferred as to dividends means the preferred stockholders receive a dividend before any common stockholders do. Preferred stock usually states the percentage it receives. Once this percentage has been paid to preferred stockholders, any money remaining may be paid as a dividend to holders of common stock. This right to preference as to dividends may be cumulative or noncumulative.

Cumulative Preferred Stock
Stock on which all dividends must be paid before common dividends

Noncumulative Preferred Stock
Stock on which current dividends must be paid before common dividends

Cumulative preferred stock is preferred stock on which all dividends must be paid before the common stock receives any dividend. These dividends on cumulative preferred stock must be paid even for years in which the corporation did not earn an adequate profit to pay the stated dividend.

Noncumulative preferred stock is preferred stock on which dividends have to be paid only for the current year before common stock dividends are paid. Thus, dividends do not have to be paid for years in which the corporation does not make a profit or even for years in which the directors simply do not declare a dividend.

The difference between cumulative and noncumulative preferred stock can be significant if the corporation operates at a loss in any given year or group of years. For example, a corporation that has $1 million outstanding common stock and $1 million outstanding 7 percent preferred stock operates at a loss for two years and then earns 21 percent net profit the third year. Noncumulative preferred stock would be entitled to only one dividend of 7 percent. The common stock is entitled to the remaining 14 percent. Cumulative preferred stock would be entitled to three preferences of 7 percent, or 21 percent in all, before the common stock is entitled to any dividend. If the company earned a net profit each year equal to only 7 percent on the preferred stock, and the preferred stock was noncumulative, the directors could pass the dividend the first year and declare a 7 percent dividend on both the common and the preferred stocks for the second year. Since the common stockholders elect the directors, the common stockholders could easily elect directors who would act in ways to help them as much as possible. For that reason, the law provides that preferred stock be cumulative unless specifically stated to be noncumulative. All this can occur, however, only when the corporation earns a profit but fails to declare a dividend. Unless the stock certificate expressly states that it is cumulative, the preference does not cumulate in the years during which the corporation operated at a loss.

Participating Preferred Stock
Stock that shares with common stock in extra dividends

Participating. Shareholders with **participating preferred stock** are entitled to share equally with the common shareholders in any further distribution of dividends made after the common shareholders have received dividends equal to those that the preferred shareholders have received by virtue of their stated preference. Thus, 7 percent participating preferred stock may pay considerably more than 7 percent annually. If the preferred stock is to participate, this right must be expressly stated on the stock certificate and in the articles of incorporation. It can participate only according to the terms of the articles of incorporation. The articles may provide that the preferred stock shall participate equally with the common stock. On the other hand the articles may provide, for example, that the preferred stock is entitled to an additional 1 percent for each additional 5 percent the common stock receives.

Nonparticipating Preferred Stock
Stock on which maximum dividend is stated percentage

Nonparticipating. **Nonparticipating preferred stock** is stock on which the maximum dividend is the percentage stated on the stock. If it is 7 percent nonparticipating preferred, for example, 7 percent annually would be the maximum to which the preferred stockholders would be entitled no matter how much the corporation earned. The law presumes stock is nonparticipating in the absence of a provision to the contrary in the articles of incorporation.

Kinds of Stock

In addition to the two classes of stock, stock comes in several different kinds. These include par-value stock, no-par-value stock, treasury stock, and watered stock.

PAR-VALUE STOCK

Par-Value Stock
Stock with assigned face value

Stock to which a face value, such as $25, $50, or $100, has been assigned and that has this value printed on the stock is **par-value stock**. Preferred stock usually has a par value. The law requires that when a corporation issues par-value stock in return for payment in money, property, or services, the par value of the stock must be equal in value to the money, property, or services. This relates only to the price at which the corporation may issue the stock to an original subscriber. It has no effect upon the price paid between a shareholder and a buyer thereafter. The price a buyer pays a shareholder ordinarily equals the market price, which may be more or less than the par value. If a corporation sells par-value stock at a discount, the purchaser incurs liability to subsequent creditors of the corporation for the discount.

NO-PAR-VALUE STOCK

No-Par-Value Stock
Stock without face value

Stock to which no face value has been assigned is **no-par-value stock**. A corporation may issue no-par-value stock at any price, although some states do set a minimum price, such as $5, for which it can be issued. Common stock may be either par-value or no-par-value stock.

TREASURY STOCK

Treasury Stock
Stock reacquired by a corporation

If a corporation purchases stock that it has sold, this reacquired stock is referred to as **treasury stock**. When a corporation first offers stock for sale, less sales resistance may be encountered if the prospective purchaser can be assured that the corporation will repurchase the stock upon request. Treasury stock may also be reacquired by gift. The reacquired stock may be sold at any price fixed by the directors. Until the corporation resells it, no dividends can be paid on it nor can it be voted.

Facts: Ampco-Pittsburgh Corp. attempted to buy all Buffalo Forge Company stock at $25 a share. Buffalo resisted the acquisition and contracted to merge with Ogden Corporation. By the contract, Ogden bought 425,000 shares of Buffalo treasury stock for $32.75 per share. Ogden also obtained an option to buy 143,400 more treasury shares. A bidding war between Ampco and Ogden ended with Ampco offering $37.50 per share. Ogden tendered its 425,000 shares of Buffalo stock, but Ampco refused to buy them. Ampco also refused to allow Ogden to exercise its option to buy the additional 143,400 treasury shares. Ampco sued for rescission of the treasury stock sale and option, claiming Buffalo's directors had breached their duty by selling the treasury stock at too low a price.

Outcome: The court held that Buffalo could sell the treasury shares at any price it wanted.

WATERED STOCK

Watered Stock
Stock paid for with property of inflated value

Stock issued as fully paid up, but paid with property of inflated values, is said to be **watered stock**. If someone conveys real estate actually worth $40,000 for stock having a par value of $100,000, the stock is watered to the extent of $60,000. Watering stock may be prohibited outright, but in any case it cannot be used to defraud creditors. In the event of insolvency, the creditors may sue the original recipients of watered stock for the difference between the par value and the actual purchase price. This may not be true, of course, if the creditors knew the stock was watered. Although creditors are allowed these rights, most state statutes do not prohibit the watering of stock by corporations other than public utility companies.

If a person pays for stock with overvalued real estate, the extent of the watering can be determined with reasonable accuracy. If a person pays in the form of patents, trademarks, blueprints, or other similar assets, the extent of the watering may be difficult to determine.

Transfer of Stock

A stock certificate indicates the manner in which the stock may be transferred to another party. The owner may use a blank form on the back of the certificate in making a transfer. The signature of the previous owner gives the new holder full possession and the right to exchange the certificate for another made out by the corporation to the new owner. Whenever an owner transfers stock, the new owner should have the certificate exchanged for a new one showing the correct name so that the corporation's books will show the correct stockholders' names. Stockholders who are not registered do not have the rights and privileges of a stockholder and will not receive any declared dividends.

If a broker holds the stock and certificates have not been issued, the broker can transfer the stock at the written direction of the owner. Under the Uniform Stock Transfer Act, the unregistered holder of stock has a right to the distribution that represents a return of capital. As under common law, the unregistered holder has no right to any distribution that represents a share of the profits.

Stock Options

Stock Option
Right to purchase shares at set price

A **stock option** is a contract entered into between a corporation and an individual. The contract gives the individual the option for a stated period of time to purchase a prescribed number of shares of stock in the corporation at a given price. If a new corporation sells stock to the public at $2 a share, the individual having the option must also pay $2 but may be given 2, 5, or even 10 years in which to exercise the option. If the corporation succeeds, and the price of the stock goes up, the individual will of course want to exercise the option and buy at the low option price and then resell at the higher market price. If the corporation fails, the option does not have to be exercised. Existing corporations may give officials of the corporation an option to purchase a given number of shares of stock in lieu of a salary increase. If the market price of the stock rises, an official may make a capital gain by buying the stock, holding it for the required time, and selling it. The income tax on a capital gain may be considerably less than that on other income. This type of compensation may be more attractive to top management officials than a straight increase in salary, enabling a corporation to retain their services at a lower cost than with a salary increase. If the corporation makes stock available to all the corporation's employees, the option price may be less than the fair market value.

Dividends

LO3
Dividends and how paid

The profits of a corporation belong to the corporation until the directors set them aside for distribution by declaring a dividend. Dividends may be paid in cash, stock, or other property.

A cash dividend usually can be paid only out of retained earnings with two exceptions. A cash dividend may be paid out of donated or paid-in surplus. Also, for corporations with depleting assets, such as coal mines, oil companies, lumber companies, and similar industries, cash dividends may be paid out of capital.

Stock dividends may be in the corporation's own stock or in stock the corporation owns in another corporation. When in the corporation's own stock, they are usually declared out of retained earnings, but they can be paid out of other surplus accounts. A stock dividend of the corporation's own stock cannot be declared if the corporation has no surplus of any kind. Dividends also may be paid in the form of property that the corporation manufactures, but this seldom happens.

The declaration of a dividend on either common or preferred stock depends almost entirely upon the discretion of the directors. The directors, however, must act reasonably and in good faith. This means minority stockholders can ask the court to require a corporation to declare a dividend out of surplus profits only when they clearly have a right to a dividend.

Facts: GM Sub Corporation bought up 87.4 percent of Liggett Group, Inc.'s common stock. Gabelli and Company, Inc. Profit Sharing Plan, which owned 800 shares of Liggett, did not sell its shares to GM. The majority of Liggett stockholders approved a merger of GM and Liggett. The merger became effective on August 7 and the Liggett stock was bought out. Liggett had historically paid quarterly dividends. That year the March and June dividends were paid, but no dividend was declared or paid Liggett stockholders for the third quarter, which in the past had been declared in July with an August record date and September payment. Gabelli sued Liggett and GM to compel the declaration and payment of a third-quarter dividend.

Outcome: The court said a minority shareholder (Gabelli) could not force the payment of a dividend without a showing of fraud or gross abuse of discretion by the board of directors. Since there was no such showing, no dividend could be compelled.

Once the directors declare a cash dividend, it cannot later be rescinded. It becomes a liability of the corporation the minute the directors declare it. A stock dividend, on the other hand, may be rescinded at any time prior to the issuance and delivery of the stock.

Laws Regulating Stock Sales

LO4 Laws regulating securities sales, exchanges, brokers

In order to protect investors in corporations, a number of laws have been enacted. These laws seek to prevent fraudulent activities and protect investors from loss as a result of stockbrokers becoming insolvent.

BLUE-SKY LAWS

Blue-Sky Laws State laws to prevent sale of worthless stock

The purpose of so-called **blue-sky laws** is to prevent fraud through the sale of worthless stocks and bonds. State blue-sky laws apply only to intrastate transactions.

These security laws vary from state to state. Some prescribe criminal penalties for engaging in prohibited transactions. Others require that dealers be licensed and that a state commission approve sales of securities before a corporation offers them to the public.

SECURITIES ACT, 1933

Prospectus Document giving specified information about a corporation

Because the state blue-sky laws apply only to intrastate sales of securities, in 1933 Congress passed the federal Securities Act to regulate the sale of securities in interstate commerce. Any corporation offering a new issue of securities for sale to the public must register it with the SEC and issue a **prospectus**, which is a document containing specified information about the stock offering and the corporation, including the information contained in the registration statement. This act does not apply to the issuance of securities under $5 million nor does the act regulate the sale or purchase of securities after they have been issued by the corporation.

PREVIEW CASE REVISITED

Facts: James Junker owned stock in Reco Investment Corporation. At a stockholders' meeting, Frederick Heisler, the attorney for Reco and Road Equipment Company, Inc., suggested that since Reco could not pay a debt it owed to Road, the solution was to merge Reco into another company such as Road. The merger passed. The merger formula for exchanging Reco stock for Road stock used book value despite the fact that Reco's property was located in an area where real estate values and the cost of building had greatly increased. Two months after the merger Junker was notified that Road's annual report would show a loss. This had not been mentioned at the stockholders' meeting. Junker sued, alleging violation of the federal Securities Act. This act establishes a cause of action for a purchaser of securities against a person who sold the securities by means of oral communication that includes an untrue statement of material fact or omits a material fact required to render the statements not misleading.

Outcome: The court held that the exchange of Reco stock for Road stock by the merger made Junker a purchaser. Heisler's participation in the sales transaction was a substantial factor in causing the transaction to take place, so he was a seller, and he did violate the act.

In addition to filing the registration statement with the SEC, a corporation must furnish a prospectus to each purchaser of the securities. Full information must be given relative to the financial structure of the corporation. This information must include the types of stock to be issued; types of securities outstanding, if any; the terms of the sale; bonus and profit-sharing arrangements; options to be created in regard to the securities; and any other data the SEC may require.

The company, its principal officers, and a majority of the board of directors must sign the registration statement. If either the registration statement or the prospectus contains misstatements or omissions, the SEC will not permit the corporation to offer the securities for sale. If the corporation sells them before the SEC ascertains the falsity of the information, an investor may rescind the contract and sue for damages any individual who signed the registration statement. Any failure to comply with the law also subjects the responsible corporate officials to criminal prosecution.

SECURITIES EXCHANGE ACT, 1934

The security exchanges and over-the-counter markets constitute the chief markets for the sale of securities after the initial offerings. In 1934 Congress passed the Securities Exchange Act to regulate such transactions. The act requires the registration of stock exchanges, brokers, and dealers of securities traded in interstate commerce and SEC-regulated, publicly held corporations. The law also requires regulated corporations to make periodic disclosure statements regarding corporate organization and financial structure.

Under rule-making authority of the Securities Exchange Act, the SEC has declared it unlawful for any broker, dealer, or exchange to use the mails, interstate commerce, or any exchange facility to knowingly make an untrue statement of a material fact or engage in any other act that would defraud or deceive a person in the purchase or sale of any security. This provision applies to sellers as well as buyers.

Insider
Officer, director, or owner of more than 10 percent of stock

Short-Swing Profits
Profits made by insider buying and selling corporation's stock in six months

The act requires certain disclosures of trading by **insiders**—officers, directors, and owners of more than 10 percent of any class of securities of the corporation. The corporation or its stockholders suing on behalf of the corporation may recover any profits made by an insider in connection with the purchase and sale of the corporation's securities within a six-month period. Such profits are called **short-swing profits**.

A 1975 amendment to this act attempts to foster competition among securities brokers by reducing regulation of the brokerage industry.

SECURITIES INVESTOR PROTECTION ACT OF 1970

In order to protect investors when the stockbroker or investment house with which they did business had severe financial difficulty that threatened financial loss to the customers, Congress passed the Securities Investor Protection Act. This federal law requires generally that all registered brokers and dealers and the members of a national securities exchange contribute a portion of their gross revenue from the securities business to a fund regulated by the Securities Investor Protection Corporation (SIPC).

The SIPC is a not-for-profit corporation whose members are the contributors to the fund. If the SIPC determines that any of its members has failed or is in danger of failing to meet its obligations to its customers and finds any one of five other specified indications of its being in financial difficulty, the SIPC may apply to the appropriate court for a decree adjudicating the customers of such member in need of the protection provided by the act. If the court finds the requisite financial problems, it will appoint a trustee for liquidation of the SIPC member. The SIPC fund may be used to pay certain customers' claims, up to $500,000 for each customer.

Questions

1 How can the amount of capital stock authorized in the charter be altered?
2 How may a person obtain shares of stock?
3 What voice does a stockholder have in the running of a corporation?
4 What rights does a preferred stockholder normally give up in return for a preference?
5 How can one know if preferred stock is participating and on what terms it participates?
6 a. At what price must a corporation issue par-value stock?
  b. What liability can a purchaser of par-value stock at a discount from a corporation incur?
7 Who exercises voting rights and receives dividends on treasury stock?
8 Why should the new owner of stock have the certificate exchanged for a new one showing the correct name?
9 Discuss the difference in the ability of a corporation to rescind a cash dividend and a stock dividend.
10 Why should insiders be careful about buying and then selling the corporation's stock within a six-month period?

Case Problems

LO2 1 Drever Partners Inc. employed Allen Stephenson. The two executed an agreement with Maxwell Drever, the majority shareholder, by which Drever Partners sold Stephenson 500 shares of its stock. The agreement provided that if Stephenson left Drever's employ then within 90 days Drever had the right and duty to repurchase the shares at their fair market value. Later the parties agreed to terminate Stephenson's employment and value the shares as of May 1 of that year. They could not agree on the shares' value by May 1 and Stephenson filed suit. Drever alleged that Stephenson had ceased to be a shareholder. Was Stephenson a shareholder or were the 500 shares treasury stock?

LO3 2 Charles Naekel, president of a corporation, Arkota Industries, did not invest in Arkota, but received 450 shares of its par-value stock, and his sons received 250 shares. Several years later the directors fired Naekel and canceled the stock because of questions about whether he had paid adequate consideration for it. The parties reached a settlement by which Naekel received cash and 50 shares of stock. Two years later, Naekel sued Arkota for wrongfully canceling most of the stock. In the suit, a question arose as to the value of the sons' stock. Since it was par-value stock, the trial court stated that the market value equaled the par value. Does the market value of stock equal its par value?

LO1 3 Kirk's Auto Electric, Inc., issued shares of stock to Billy Bone, Andre Bone, and Joe Bone. In return, the Bones executed unsecured, interest-bearing, demand promissory notes, which they delivered to the corporation. They had made no payment on the notes. Clarence Kirk, a shareholder, sued the corporation and the Bones, alleging that the shares were void for nonpayment. Are the shares void, outstanding shares of the corporation?

LO4 4 Arthur Gustafson contracted to sell his stock in Alloyd, Inc. to Wind Point Partners II, LP through Alloyd Holdings, a corporation Wind Point owned. Holdings was to pay $18,709,000 for the stock plus $2 million to reflect the estimated increase in Alloyd's net worth since its most recent financial statements. The agreement recited assurances by Gustafson that the financial statements "present fairly . . . the Company's financial condition" and provided for adjustment of the $2 million figure if the end of the year audit showed a difference between actual and estimated increase in net worth. The audit showed the increase was less than estimated and the buyer was entitled to recover $815,000. However, Wind Point sued for rescission of the contract, alleging that the assurances in the contract were false, the contract was a prospectus, and therefore under the Securities Act of 1933, Wind Point was allowed to rescind the contract. Gustafson alleged that a prospectus was a solicitation to the public to purchase stock from the issuer. Was the contract a prospectus?

LO4 5 Prince Alwaleed Bin Talal Bin Abdulaziz Al Saud entered into an agreement with Citicorp by which Alwaleed became the owner of 5,900 shares of Citicorp nonvoting convertible preferred stock. Under the agreement, Alwaleed promised he would not become the owner of more than 10 percent of Citicorp common stock for five years. Before five years had passed, Lawrence Levner, a stockholder of Citicorp, sued Alwaleed, alleging that he had violated the Securities Exchange Act of 1934 by engaging in a short-swing purchase and sale while he owned more than 10 percent of Citicorp's common stock. In order to have owned more than 10 percent of the common stock, Alwaleed would have to have been considered as owning the common stock into which his preferred stock could be converted. Was the law violated?

LO3 6 Rose Udoff was a stockholder in a corporation that had granted stock options to officers and employees. The directors of the corporation lowered the exercise price of the stock to the market price under the authority of and in accordance with the option plan. Udoff filed suit. Was the reduction in the price actionable as detrimental to the corporation?

Internet Resources for Business Law

Name	Resources	Web Address
State of Arizona's Corporation Laws	The state of Arizona maintains its corporation laws.	http://www.azleg.state.az.us/ars/10/title10.htm
State of New York's Corporation Laws	The state of New York maintains its corporation laws.	http://www.law.cornell.edu/ny/statutes/buscorp.htm
U.S. Business Advisor	The U.S. Business Advisor, a federal government program, provides businesses with access to government information and services.	http://www.business.gov/
Internal Revenue Service	The Internal Revenue Service and its publication, the *Digital Daily*, provide tax advice and information on a variety of issues, including business formation issues.	http://www.irs.ustreas.gov/
The Center for Corporate Law at the University of Cincinnati College of Law	The Center for Corporate Law at the University of Cincinnati College of Law maintains rules and forms associated with the 1933 and 1934 acts and various SEC regulations.	http://www.law.uc.edu/CCL/

CYBERDRIVEILLINOIS

The Department of Business Services

Limited Liability Company Forms and Fees

Forms are provided in PDF (Portable Document Format) files, which can be viewed or printed using your Web browser and Adobe's Acrobat Reader software. Macintosh and Windows versions of Acrobat Reader may be downloaded free of charge from Adobe.

Click here to find out how to obtain the Adobe Acrobat Reader.

Form No.	Type of Form	Filing Fee
LLC-1.15	Application to Reserve a Name	$300.00
LLC-1.15	Renewal of Reserved Name	$100.00
LLC-1.15	Transfer of Reserved Name	$100.00
LLC-1.20	Application to adopt Assumed Name	$ 20.00+ $5.00 per month
LLC-1.20	Application to change Assumed Name	$100.00
LLC-1.20	Application to cancel Assumed Name	$100.00
LLC-1.20d	Assumed Name Renewal Application	$300.00
LLC-2.56	Assumed Name Fee Schedule	Effective January 1, 2000
LLC-1.35	Resignation of Registered Agent	$100.00
LLC-1.50	Affidavit of Compliance	$100.00
LLC-5.5	Articles of Organization	$400.00
LLC-5.25	Articles of Amendment	$25.00, $100.00
LLC-5.30	Restated Articles of Organization	$400.00
LLC-5.40	Application for Withdrawal-Domestic	$100.00
LLC-35.15	Articles of Dissolution	$100.00
LLC-35.40/ 45.65	Reinstatement following Administrative Dissolution	$500.00
LLC-37.10	Conversion Requirements	$100.00

36

Management and Dissolution of a Corporation

Learning Objectives

1. Discuss how a corporation is managed and controlled by the stockholders.
2. Identify the rights of stockholders.
3. Specify the responsibilities and powers of directors and officers.
4. Describe how a corporation is combined or dissolved.

PREVIEW CASE

Washington Preferred Life Insurance Company called a stockholders' meeting to vote on a proposed merger. Washington mailed notice of the meeting to stockholders of record and published it in two legal newspapers. The published notice indicated that the meeting was for the purpose of voting on the merger; that proxies, proxy statements, and notices were mailed to stockholders at their last known addresses; and that if anyone was a stockholder of record and had not received the material, inquiry should be made to the company at the address given. A week later Washington asked a court to appoint a representative for missing shareholders in accordance with state law. This law allowed for such appointment if addresses of the shareholders were lost or inadequate and if the purpose of the meeting required a two-thirds vote. The law stated that approval by the court of the representative's findings acted as an affirmative vote at the stockholders' meeting by the missing shareholders. The court appointed a representative, who approved the merger. James Watson, a Washington stockholder, asked the court to vacate the order of appointment because the notice to the allegedly missing stockholders was insufficient. The notice did not inform stockholders that if they did not attend the meeting, a person would be appointed to vote their shares. Was the notice inadequate? What is normally the result if a stockholder does not attend a stockholders' meeting?

As an artificial being, existing only in contemplation of law, a corporation can perform business transactions only through actual persons, acting as agents. The directors as a group act as both fiduciaries and agents. To the corporation, they are trustees and have responsibility for breaches of trust. To third parties, directors as a group constitute agents of the corporation.

LO1
Management and control of corporations

The board of directors selects the chief agents of the corporation, such as the president, the vice president, the treasurer, and other officers, who perform the managerial functions. The board of directors is primarily a policy-making body. The chief executives in turn appoint subagents for all the administrative functions of the corporation. These subagents constitute agents of the corporation, however, not of the appointing executives.

The directors and officers manage the corporation. Since the stockholders elect the board of directors, they indirectly control it. However, neither the individual directors nor a stockholder, merely by reason of membership in the corporation, can act as an agent or exercise any managerial function.

Even a stockholder who owns 49 percent of the common stock of a corporation has no more right to work or take a direct part in running the corporation than another stockholder or even a stranger would have. In contrast, a person who owns even 1 percent of a partnership has just as much right to work for the partnership and to participate in its management as any other partner.

Stockholders' Meetings

In order to make the will of the majority binding, the stockholders must act at a duly convened and properly conducted stockholders' meeting.

A corporation usually holds a regular meeting such as its annual meeting at the place and time specified in the articles of incorporation or in the bylaws; notice of the meeting is ordinarily not required (see Illustration 36-1). The directors of the corporation or, in some instances, a particular officer or a specified number of stockholders, may call a special meeting. The corporation must give notice specifying the subjects to be discussed for a special meeting.

PREVIEW CASE REVISITED

Facts: Washington Preferred Life Insurance Company called a stockholders' meeting to vote on a proposed merger. It mailed notice of the meeting to stockholders of record and published it in two legal newspapers. The published notice indicated that the meeting was for the purpose of voting on the merger; that proxies, proxy statements, and notices were mailed to stockholders at their last known addresses; and that if anyone was a stockholder of record and had not received the material, inquiry should be made to the company at the address given. A week later Washington asked a court to appoint a representative for missing shareholders in accordance with state law. This law allowed for such appointment if addresses of shareholders were lost or inadequate and if the purpose of the meeting required a two-thirds vote. The law stated that approval by the court of the representative's findings acted as an affirmative vote at the stockholders' meeting by the missing shareholders. The court appointed a representative who approved the merger. James Watson, a Washington stockholder, asked the court to vacate the order of appointment because the notice to the allegedly missing stockholders was insufficient.

Outcome: The court found that the notice did not inform stockholders that if they did not attend the meeting, a person would be appointed to vote their shares. Normally, absence from a stockholders' meeting constitutes a negative vote, so the notice was inadequate.

WATERS, MELLEN AND COMPANY
900 West Lake Avenue
Cincinnati, Ohio 45227

NOTICE OF ANNUAL MEETING OF STOCKHOLDERS
August 22, 20–

The Annual Meeting of Stockholders of Waters, Mellen and Company, a Delaware corporation, will be held in the Auditorium, Building C, at the headquarters of the Company, 900 West Lake Avenue, Cincinnati, Ohio, on Wednesday, August 22, 20– at 10:00 A.M. for the following purposes:

1. To elect a Board of thirteen Directors of the Company;
2. To consider and vote upon the ratification of the appointment of Arthur Andrews & Co. as independent public accountants for the Company for the fiscal year May 1, 20– through April 30, 20– and
3. To transact such other business as may properly come before the meeting or any adjournment thereof.

The Accompanying Proxy Statement provides additional information relating to the above matters.

The Board of Directors has fixed the close of business on Friday, July 6, 20– as the record date for the determination of stockholders entitled to notice of and to vote at this meeting or any adjournment thereof. The stock transfer books will not be closed.

Please sign and mail the accompanying proxy in the envelope provided. If you attend this meeting and vote in person, the proxy will not be used.

By order of the Board of Directors.

RICHARD P. ROBERTS

Secretary

July 18, 20–

IMPORTANT—You can help in the preparation for the meeting by mailing your proxy promptly.

Illustration 36-1
Notice of a Stockholders' Meeting

Meetings of the stockholders theoretically act as a check upon the board of directors. Corporations must have one annually. If the directors do not carry out the will of the stockholders, they can elect a new board that will carry out the stockholders' wishes. In the absence of fraud or bad faith on the part of the directors, this procedure constitutes the only legal means by which the investors can exercise any control over their investment.

QUORUM

Quorum
Minimum number of shares required to be represented to transact business

A stockholders' meeting, in order to be valid, requires the presence of a **quorum**, or a minimum number of shares that must be represented in order that business may be lawfully transacted. At common law a quorum consisted of the stockholders actually assembled at a properly convened meeting. A majority of the votes cast by those present expressed the will of the stockholders. Statutes, bylaws, or the articles of incorporation now ordinarily require that a majority of the outstanding stock be represented at the stockholders' meeting in order to constitute a quorum. This representation may be either in person or by proxy.

VOTING

LO2 Stockholders' rights

The right of a stockholder to vote is the most important right, because only in this way can the stockholder exercise any control over investment in the corporation. Only stockholders shown by the stockholders' record book have a right to vote. A person who purchases stock from an individual does not have the right to vote until the corporation makes the transfer on its books. Subscribers who have not fully paid for their stock, as a rule, may not vote. State corporation laws control the right to vote. Voting and nonvoting common stock may be issued if the law permits.

Two major classes of elections are held during stockholders' meetings in which the stockholders vote. They include the annual election of directors and the elections to approve or disapprove some corporate acts that only the stockholders can authorize. Examples of some of these acts are consolidating with another corporation, dissolving, increasing the capital stock, and changing the number of directors.

Giving Minority Stockholders a Voice. Each stockholder normally has one vote for each share of common stock owned. In the election of a board of directors, the candidates receiving a majority of the votes of stock actually voting win. In corporations with 500,000 stockholders, control of 10 percent of the stock often suffices to control the election. In all cases the owners of 51 percent of the stock can elect all the directors. This leaves the minority stockholders without any representation on the board of directors. To alleviate this situation, two legal devices exist that may give the minority stockholders a voice, but not a controlling voice, on the board of directors. These devices are:

1 Cumulative voting
2 Voting trusts

Cumulative Voting Stockholder has votes equal to shares owned times number of directors to be elected

Some state statutes provide that in the election of directors, a stockholder may cast as many votes in the aggregate equal to the number of shares owned multiplied by the number of directors to be elected. This method of voting is called **cumulative voting**. Thus, if a stockholder owns 10 shares and 10 directors are to be elected, 100 votes may be cast. All 100 votes may be cast for one director. As a result, under this plan of voting the minority stockholders may have some representation on the board of directors, although still a minority.

Voting Trust Device whereby stock is transferred to trustee to vote it

Under a voting trust, stockholders give up their voting privileges by transferring their stock to a trustee and receiving in return **voting trust** certificates. This is not primarily a device to give the minority stockholders a voice on the board of directors; but it does do that, and often in large corporations it gives them a controlling voice. Twenty percent of the stock always voted as a unit has more effect than individual voting. State laws frequently impose limitations on voting trusts, as by limiting the number of years that they may run.

Absentee Voting. Under the common law only stockholders who were present in person were permitted to vote. Under the statutory law, the articles of incorporation, or the bylaws, stockholders who do not wish to attend a meeting and vote in person may authorize another to vote their stock for them. The person authorized to vote for another is known as a **proxy**. The written authorization to vote is also called a proxy (see Illustration 36-2). Corporations send proxy forms to shareholders; the law does not require any special form for a proxy (see Illustration 36-3 for a sample form).

Proxy Person authorized to vote for another; written authorization to vote for another

As a rule, a stockholder may revoke a proxy at any time. If a stockholder should sign more than one proxy for the same stockholders' meeting, the proxy having the

WATERS, MELLEN AND COMPANY

PROXY
ANNUAL MEETING AUGUST 22, 20–

KNOW ALL MEN BY THESE PRESENTS, That the undersigned shareholder of WATERS, MELLEN AND COMPANY hereby constitutes and appoints O. W. PRESCOTT, A. B. BROWN, and GEORGE CONNARS, and each of them, the true and lawful proxies of the undersigned, with several power of substitution and revocation, for and in the name of the undersigned, to attend the annual meeting of shareholders of said Company, to be held at the Main Office of the Company, 900 West Lake Avenue, Cincinnati, Ohio, on Thursday, August 22, 20–, at 10:00 o'clock A.M., Standard Time, and any and all adjournments of said meeting, receipt of the notice of which meeting, stating the purposes thereof, together with Proxy Statement, being hereby acknowledged by the undersigned, and to vote for the election of a Board of thirteen directors for the Company, to vote upon the ratification of the appointment of Arthur Andrews & Co. as independent public accountants for the fiscal year May 1, 20– through April 30, 20– and to vote as they or he may deem proper upon all other matters that may lawfully come before said meeting or any adjournment thereof.

Signed the 1st day of March, 20–

Wanda Klimecki

Illustration 36-2
Proxy

later date would be effective. A proxy may be good in some states for only a limited period of time. If the stockholder attends the stockholders' meeting in person, this acts as a revocation of the proxy.

Facts: A property settlement agreement signed by Jack Lewis and Cecilia, his former wife, granted Cecilia 175,000 shares of Health Concepts IV, Inc., titled in her name and 175,000 shares titled in Jack's name. However, the agreement granted Jack the voting rights to all those shares. The agreement required Cecilia to execute a proxy designating Jack as the person authorized to vote the stock. At a stockholders' meeting, Jack voted Cecilia's 175,000 shares under the authority of the settlement agreement since she had not executed a formal proxy. A stockholder sued for a determination of whether Jack could validly vote Cecilia's shares.

Outcome: The court said he could since a proxy need only appoint someone to vote the shares and have the signature of the stockholder.

The management of a corporation may legally solicit proxies for candidates selected by the board of directors. However, proxies secured by means of fraudulent representations to stockholders may not be voted.

PROXY WARS

Stockholders dissatisfied with the policies of the present board of directors can try to elect a new board. Electing a new board is often a difficult or impossible task. If one or even several people own a majority of the voting stock, the objecting stockholders cannot obtain a majority of the voting stock to ensure success. If the voting stock is widely held and no group owns a majority of the voting stock, then the objecting stockholders at least have a chance to elect

CORPORATE PROXY

________________________, the undersigned stockholder(s) (the "Stockholder"),
________________________, ________________________,
________________________, hereby designate(s)
________________________, (the "Proxy") as the proxy for the Stockholder, with respect to the Stockholder's shares of stock (the "Stock") in ____________________ (the "Corporation").

By this designation of proxy, the Stockholder hereby revokes any prior designation of proxy that the Stockholder may have previously given with respect to the Stock.

This designation of proxy shall be effective for the Annual Meeting of the Stockholders of the Corporation to be held on _______________, at ____________________, and at all adjournments of such meeting.

The Proxy shall have the full power, as the Stockholder's substitute, to represent the Stockholder and vote the Stock on all issues and motions that are properly presented at the meeting(s) for which this designation of proxy is effective. The Proxy shall have the authority to vote entirely in the discretion of the Proxy.

Provided, however, with respect to the following issue(s) the Proxy shall vote as follows:

____

Date of Signing: ________________________

STOCKHOLDER:

____
____

WITNESS:

____
____

Illustration 36-3
Corporate Proxy

a new board. To do this a majority of the stock represented at a stockholders' meeting must be controlled by this dissatisfied group. To ensure success, the leaders of the group will obtain proxies from stockholders who cannot attend the stockholders' meeting in person. The current board members will also attempt to secure proxies. This is known as a **proxy war**. The present board of directors may in most instances pay the cost of this solicitation from corporate funds. The "outsiders" generally must bear the cost of the proxy war out of their personal funds. If there are one million shareholders, the cost of soliciting their proxies is enormous. For this reason proxy wars seldom happen.

Proxy War
Attempt by competing sides to secure majority of stockholders' votes

Rights of Stockholders

The stockholders of a corporation enjoy several important rights and privileges. Three of these rights that have already been discussed include the following:

1. A stockholder has the right to receive a properly executed certificate as evidence of ownership of shares of stock.
2. A stockholder has the right to attend corporate meetings and to vote unless this right is denied by express agreement, the articles of incorporation, or statutory provisions.
3. A stockholder has the right to receive a proportionate share of the profits when profits are distributed as dividends.

In addition, each stockholder has the following rights:

4. The right to sell and transfer shares of stock.
5. The right, when new stock is issued by the corporation, to subscribe for new shares in proportion to the shares the stockholder owns. For example, a stockholder who owns 10 percent of the original capital stock has a right to buy 10 percent of the shares added to the stock. If this were not true, stockholders could be deprived of their proportionate share in the accumulated surplus of the company. This is known as a **preemptive right**. Only stockholders have the right to vote to increase the capital stock.
6. The right to inspect the corporate books and to have the corporate books inspected by an attorney or an accountant. This right is not absolute, since most states have laws restricting the right. These laws tend to be drawn to protect the corporation from indiscriminate inspection, not to hamper a stockholder who has a proper purpose for the inspection.

Preemptive Right
Right to purchase new shares in proportion to shares owned

Facts: Rick Bostic became the director of one of the schools of Wrights Beauty College, Inc. A few years later he and his wife, Kathy, acquired stock in Wrights making them and Martin and Vicky Wagoner the only shareholders. Several years later Bostic was terminated and he requested that Wrights allow him to inspect and copy specified corporate documents. Whenever a shareholder wanted to sell Wrights' stock, the corporation had the right to offer to buy it first. The shareholder could refuse to accept the corporation's offer and then the case went to arbitration. The stock was closely held and not publicly traded. Wrights allowed him to see a few but not most of the documents. Bostic sued for an order compelling Wrights to allow him to inspect and copy the documents. He alleged that he needed to see the documents to evaluate his holdings in Wrights.

Outcome: The court found that the documents requested were necessary to value Bostic's stock in order to sell it and ordered Wrights to allow inspection and copying.

7 The right, when the corporation is dissolved, to share pro rata in the assets that remain after all the obligations of the company have been paid. In the case of certain preferred stock, the shareholders may have a preference in the distribution of the corporate assets upon liquidation.

Directors

LO3
Responsibilities and powers of directors and officers

A board of directors elected by the stockholders manages every corporation. Laws normally require every board to consist of at least three members; but if the number exceeds three, the articles of incorporation and the bylaws of the corporation fix the number, together with qualifications and manner of election.

The directors, unlike the stockholders, cannot vote by proxy, nor can they make corporate decisions as individual directors. All decisions must be made collectively and in a called meeting of the board.

The functions of the directors can be classified as:

1 Powers
2 Duties
3 Liabilities

POWERS

Law, the articles of incorporation, and the bylaws limit the powers of the board of directors. The directors have the power to manage and direct the corporation. They may do any legal act reasonably necessary to achieve the purpose of the corporation so long as this power is not expressly limited. They may elect and appoint officers and agents to act for the corporation, or they may delegate authority to any number of its members to so act. If a director obtains knowledge of something while acting in the course of employment and in the scope of authority with the corporation, the corporation is charged with this knowledge.

DUTIES

The directors have the duty of establishing policies that will achieve the purpose of the corporation, selecting executives to carry out these policies and supervising these executives to see that they efficiently execute the policies. They must act in person in exercising all discretionary power. The directors may delegate ministerial and routine duties to subagents, but the duty of determining all major corporate policies, except those reserved to the stockholders, must be assumed by the board of directors.

LIABILITIES

As fiduciaries of the corporation, the directors incur liability for bad faith and for negligence. They do not incur liability for losses when they act with due diligence and reasonably sound judgment. Directors make countless errors of judgment annually in operating a complex business organization. Only when these errors result from negligence or a breach of good faith can a director be held personally liable.

The test of whether the directors failed to exercise due care depends upon whether they exercised the care that a reasonably prudent person would have exercised under the circumstances. If they did that, they were not negligent and do not incur liability for the loss that follows. The test of whether they acted in bad faith is whether they acted in a way that conflicted with the interests of the corporation. The corporate directors have a duty of loyalty to the corporation similar to the duty of loyalty an agent has to a principal or a partner has to the partnership and the other partners.

Directors may be held liable for some acts without evidence of negligence or bad faith either because the act is illegal or bad faith is presumed. Paying dividends out of capital and ultra vires acts constitute illegal acts. Loaning corporate funds to officers and directors constitutes an act to which the court will impute bad faith.

The members of the board of directors incur civil and criminal liability for their corporate actions. This means a director does not get any immunity or protection from the legal consequences of actions taken. Because of this, individual directors who do not agree with action taken by the other directors must be careful to protect themselves by having the minutes of the meeting of the directors show that they dissented from the board's action. Otherwise stated, every director present at a board meeting is conclusively presumed to have assented to the action taken unless the director takes positive action to overcome this presumption. If the directors present who dissent have a record of their dissent entered in the minutes of the meeting, then they cannot be held liable for the acts of the majority.

Officers

In addition to selecting and removing the officers of a corporation, the board of directors authorizes them to act on behalf of the corporation in carrying out the board's policies. As agents of the corporation, the principles of agency apply to the officers' relationship with the corporation and define many of their rights and obligations.

Facts: Independent of her position as the president of Northeast Harbor Golf Club, a corporation, Nancy Harris learned that real estate surrounded on three sides by the club was for sale. The land was adjacent to three of the club's golf holes. The club's board of directors had discussed the possibility of buying and developing land adjacent to the club, but did not have the money to do so. Harris bought the property and disclosed her purchase to the club's board of directors. The club later sued Harris for usurping an opportunity that belonged to the club.

Outcome: The court said that since the club was interested in purchasing land adjacent to it and developing it, Harris' purchase of such land did constitute usurping a corporate opportunity. Harris would be liable for breaching her fiduciary duty to the club.

State statutes may specify a few of the officers that corporations must have. The corporation's bylaws will specify what additional officers the corporation must have and the duties of each officer. A corporation commonly has a president, vice president, secretary, and treasurer. In small corporations, some of these offices may be combined. Additional officers may be assistant secretaries or treasurers, additional vice presidents, and a chief executive officer. The chief executive officer is frequently the president or the chairman of the board of directors. The board of directors creates or deletes some positions.

A corporate officer or agent who commits a tort or crime incurs personal liability even when the act was done for the corporation in a corporate capacity. In this case, both the corporation and the individual could be jointly liable. Only personal liability is imposed when the acts are detrimental to the corporation and outside the scope of the officer's authority. Thus, an officer has liability when actions are improper or unjustified such as when based on spite toward the injured party. Federal law even imposes liability on officers and agents for aiding and abetting lower-ranking employees in the commission of crimes. Specific statutes may impose liability on officers if they have a duty to ensure violations do not occur and to seek out and remedy violations that do occur. Corporate officers and agents are not personally liable for acts in which they do not participate, authorize, consent to, or direct.

Corporate Combinations

LO4
Combination and dissolution

Merger
One corporation absorbed by another

Consolidation
Combining two corporations to form a new one

When two corporations wish to combine, they frequently do so by means of a **merger** or a **consolidation**. A merger of two corporations occurs when they combine so that one survives and the other ceases to exist. One absorbs the other. A consolidation occurs when two corporations combine to form a new corporation. Both of the two previous corporations disappear.

It has become a rather common practice recently for a corporation to try to take over another corporation. The acquiring corporation can do this by making a formal tender offer, an offer to buy stock in the target corporation at a set price. Since attempts at takeovers usually cause the price of the stock of the target company to rise, the acquiring corporation may try to obtain the amount of stock it wants in its target through the purchase of large blocks of the target's stock. The purchase of a large amount of stock cannot be kept quiet for long, however, because the Securities Exchange Act requires any person who acquires 5 percent of any class of stock to file a schedule reporting the acquisition within 10 days.

Dissolution

A corporation may terminate its existence by paying all its debts, distributing all remaining assets to the stockholders, and surrendering its articles of incorporation. The corporation then ceases to exist and completes its dissolution. This action may be voluntary on the part of the stockholders, or it may be involuntary by action of the court or state. The state may ask for a dissolution for any one of the following reasons:

1. Forfeiture or abuse of the corporate charter
2. Violation of the state laws
3. Fraud in the procurement of the charter
4. In some states, failure to pay specified taxes for a specified number of years

A foreign corporation that has been granted authority to do business in a state may have its authority revoked for similar reasons.

When a corporation dissolves, its existence is terminated for all purposes except to wind up its business. It cannot sue, transfer property, or form contracts except for the purpose of converting its assets into cash and distributing the cash to creditors and stockholders. Similarly, a foreign corporation whose authority to do business in the state has been revoked may not sue, transfer property, or form contracts until its authority has been reinstated.

In the event that assets cannot cover the corporation's debts, the stockholders do not incur personal liability. This is one of the chief advantages to business owners of a corporation over a sole proprietorship or partnership. It is an advantage from the stockholders' standpoint, but a disadvantage from the creditors' standpoint.

Questions

1 Explain the function of the board of directors of a corporation.
2 What is the only legal means by which investors in a corporation can exercise control over their investment?
3 What is normally a quorum and how is it determined?
4 Explain how a shareholder who cannot attend a stockholders' meeting can vote at it.
5 Explain the two legal devices that may give minority stockholders a voice on the board of directors.
6 What is the purpose of giving stockholders a preemptive right?
7 What limits the powers of the board of directors?
8 What is the test of whether directors exercised due care when making corporate decisions?
9 When does a corporate officer alone have liability for a tort or a crime?
10 What is the difference between a merger and a consolidation?

Case Problems

LO4 1 Health Care Facilities, Inc. (HCF) bought the real estate, nursing home license, all the equipment, patient medical records, and facility name of Crestview Manor Nursing Home II, Inc. All other assets of Crestview were expressly excluded from the purchase. HCF was a self-insured employer for workers' compensation purposes. HCF notified the state Bureau of Workers' Compensation (BWC) of the purchase and asked it to add Crestview to its self-insurance coverage. The BWC refused saying that HCF had merged with Crestview by buying so much of its business. Had HCF merged with Crestview?

LO1 2 A corporation was formed from the merger of two companies. Martin and Leonard Lewis owned one company and Messers Steinhart and Simon the other. They were the directors and stockholders of the new corporation. The bylaws required three directors for a quorum and the affirmative vote of three to transact any business. A stockholder who wanted to sell stock had to offer to sell the stock proportionately to the other three and if they did not purchase it, to the corporation. The Lewises, on one side, and Steinhart and Simon on the other, had a major disagreement. Martin Lewis offered to sell his stock proportionately to the other three. Leonard refused to purchase his share, so Martin offered it to the corporation. A meeting was called to accept that offer. Neither of the Lewises attended. Steinhart and Simon voted to accept Martin's offer. Was their action a valid acceptance of the offer?

LO4 3 In Mississippi, Sally Southland, Inc. and Frank Malta, Southland's shareholder, entered into a 60-month lease of security cameras and equipment from Capital Associates, Inc. The equipment was supplied by Stanco Communications. Malta acknowledged delivery and acceptance of the equipment and made the monthly lease payments for 20 months; however, when Capital and Stanco did not upgrade the equipment as requested by Malta, he stopped making the payments. Capital, a foreign corporation authorized to do business in Mississippi, sued Southland and Malta for the rent. More than a year after the suit was filed, Capital's certificate of authority to do business in Mississippi was suspended for failure to pay franchise tax. Southland and Malta argued that the suit had to be dismissed. Does it?

LO2 4 Dynamics Corporation of America (DCA) began to acquire stock in CTS Corporation (CTS) and later filed a lawsuit against CTS. CTS counterclaimed and sought an injunction against DCA's acquisition of CTS stock. CTS received a letter from DCA's general counsel demanding inspection by DCA of records of CTS research and development expenditures. The letter stated no purpose for the inspection. DCA had questioned CTS management at a shareholders' meeting about research and development expenditures and praised the way CTS had answered the questions. The information on research and development expenditures was found only in work papers prepared by CTS accountants, and the work papers contained the names of employees engaged in research, their salaries, and the activities being researched. CTS and DCA were in direct and substantial competition in some products and potentially in others. Should DCA be allowed to inspect the books?

LO3 **5** Crawford and Thibaut, Inc. held its annual meeting at which John Thibaut held a proxy for two-thirds of a share owned by Jerry Boyce. However, Boyce had not signed the proxy, so the chairman of the meeting did not allow John Thibaut to vote the two-thirds share. The stockholders elected three directors by a vote of 60 to 59⅓. John Thibaut sued the elected directors challenging the election. How should the court rule regarding the validity of the proxy?

LO2 **6** James Tooley was a shareholder of Robinson Springs Corp. (RSC). When Tooley asked to examine RSC's books and records to value his share and determine the financial status and health of the corporation RSC denied the request. Tooley sued to require RSC to make the records available for his inspection. Did Tooley have a proper purpose for inspection so that the records had to be made available?

LO3 **7** Angelique Stahl was chairman of the board and later chief executive officer and W. George Allen and Ross Beckerman were directors of Broward Federal Savings and Loan Association. Broward had a growth strategy of paying high interest rates to attract depositors. To do so it had to reinvest the deposits in high-yield assets like commercial real estate loans. It made a large number of risky loans. Federal regulators found deficiencies in its loan underwriting and made Broward execute an agreement promising to take steps to eliminate the weaknesses. Broward made six loans that violated the agreement; it became insolvent and lost about $30 million on the six loans. The federal agency that insured Broward sued Allen, Beckerman, and Stahl. What standard of liability was applicable to the directors in this case?

Internet Resources for Business Law

Name	Resources	Web Address
Business and General Forms	The 'Lectric Law Library's business forms include a variety of sample partnership and corporation documents.	http://www.lectlaw.com/formb.htm
Limited Liability Companies—USA	Limited Liability Companies—USA, sponsored by The Limited Liability Company Reporter, provides articles, documents, and links relevant to limited liability companies.	http://www.llc-usa.com/
U.S. Chamber of Commerce	The U.S. Chamber of Commerce provides news, information, services, and products to assist small business owners.	http://www.uschamber.org/
Law Journal EXTRA! (LJX!)—Corporate Law	LJX!, sponsored by The New York Law Publishing Company, provides daily corporate law news, case law, and legal analysis.	http://www.ljx.com/practice/corporate/index.html
CNNfn: The Financial Network	CNNfn, Turner Broadcasting's financial news complement to CNN, provides reports on mergers and takeovers. CNNfn is interactive, allowing visitors to "ask the experts" or respond to the day's programs.	http://www.cnnfn.com/

Part 7 Summary Cases

Business Organization

1 Amos Welder purchased, as an equal partner, an interest in an accounting firm. His partner, William Green, was the accountant and trustee for a major client who paid the firm about $80,000 in fees annually. Unknown to Welder, from those fees Green annually received $5,000 as a trust management fee. Green increased this fee to $45,000; Welder found out and objected. Green paid all the fees back to the firm, gave Welder a $27,500 check and told him the partnership was over. Welder sued. Had Green breached his duty of good faith to Welder? [*Welder v. Green*, 985 S.W.2d 170 (Tex. App.)]

2 Black and Graham each owned fifty percent of an incorporated building supply business. They could not agree on how to manage the business. Since each owned 50 percent of the corporation neither had the power to prevail in his view on how to run the business. Graham sued to dissolve the corporation. Was a dissolution warranted? [*Black v. Graham*, 464 S.W.2d 814 (Ga.)]

3 Darden, Doman & Stafford Associates (DDS), a partnership, executed a renovation contract with "Building Design and Development Inc. (in formation) John A. Goodman, President." DDS knew the corporation was not in existence, but Goodman had told them he would form a corporation to limit his personal liability. The work was to be completed by October 15, and disputes were to be settled by arbitration. The first check in payment for the work was made out to "Building Design and Development Inc.—John Goodman." Goodman crossed out his name and indorsed it "Bldg. Design & Dev. Inc., John A. Goodman, Pres." and told DDS to make payments only to the corporation. The work was not finished by October 15 and DDS claimed it was of poor quality. A corporate license for Building Design and Development Inc. was issued on November 2. DDS served a demand for arbitration and named the corporation and Goodman. DDS testified it never agreed to make the contract only with the corporation; therefore, Goodman should be a party to the arbitration. Should he? [*Goodman v. Darden, Doman & Stafford Associates*, 670 P. 2d 648 (Wash.)]

4 The Timely Investment Club (TIC), a partnership, was formed to educate the partners in investing and allow them to invest on a regular basis. The partnership agreement provided that when partners withdrew, TIC was required to redeem units of ownership of the withdrawing partners from the funds available. Eight partners withdrew. Was the partnership dissolved by their withdrawal? [*Cagnolatti v. Guinn*, 189 Cal. Rptr. 151 (Cal. Ct. App.)]

5 Jerold Murphy and three others were the incorporators and original stockholders of Country House, Inc. For nine years they all worked as full-time employees of Country House and were paid wages. Twice they were paid "bonuses" which were authorized when fiscal reports indicated sufficient corporate earnings. Murphy terminated his employment but kept his stock. Then Country House paid stockholder-employee bonuses in addition to their wages. No dividends were ever paid. Murphy brought suit, alleging the bonuses were really dividends and, as a stockholder, money was due him, too. Were the payments dividends? [*Murphy v. Country House, Inc.*, 349 N.W. 2d 289 (Minn. Ct. App.)]

6 Paul Wright and John Termeer were partners in an auto repair business. Interstate Motors, Inc. brought in a car for repairs. The car was accepted by Wright, who then drove it to Houston and into a lake, causing significant damage. Is Termeer liable for Wright's negligence? [*Termeer v. Interstate Motors, Inc.*, 634 S.W. 2d 12 (Tex. Ct. App.)]

7 United Electronics Co. (UE) borrowed money from Factors and Note Buyers and pledged stock it owned in Frost Controls Corp. UE defaulted on the loan, so Factors foreclosed. Factors offered the stock for sale publicly and then bought it itself. Frost's president, Arthur Thomson, started a new company, which bought Frost's assets. UE sued Thomson and his new company. To win the lawsuit UE had to have owned the Frost stock when Frost's assets were sold. To establish that it owned the stock at that time, UE tried to show the foreclosure sale was invalid because Factors, trying to sell the Frost stock, was an "underwriter" as defined in the Securities Act. UE alleged that Factors, with a view to the distribution of the securities, sold the stock for UE, which controlled Frost. Since the Frost stock was unregistered, it alleged the public foreclosure sale violated the Securities Act. Did the sale violate the Securities Act? [*A.D.M. Corp. v. Thomson*, 707 F. 2d 25 (1st Cir.)]

8 Chet Ellingson, a licensed real estate broker, told Gregory Walsh that he owned real estate with "some partners" and that it was for sale. A buy-sell agreement was executed by Walsh and Ellingson, and Walsh gave Ellingson $1,000 in earnest money. The closing was set for April 5. Four Seasons Motor Inn owned the real estate with Ellingson as tenants in common. On April 5, Walsh told Ellingson he was ready to close, but Ellingson told Walsh he could not get his partners to sell. The real estate had a building on it that Ellingson managed. There had been a prior land holding between Ellingson and Four Seasons by which they had owned property as tenants in common and then sold it and divided the profits equally. Walsh sued for specific performance of the buy-sell agreement, alleging Ellingson had a partnership with Four Seasons and as an agent of the partnership bound it to sell. Was there a partnership? [*Walsh v. Ellingson Agency*, 613 P. 2d 1381 (Mont.)]

9 Bernard Susman and members of the Asher family were partners in a real estate business. They had a dispute concerning whether the partnership was to develop a portion of the property or whether it was to be sold to a developer. Their dispute became so heated the Ashers told Susman he was no longer a partner, changed the partnership tax returns to show Susman's interest was zero, kept him out of partnership business, refused to give him information concerning the business, and refused to account for expenses of the partnership. Susman sued for breach of the partnership agreement. Were the breaches serious enough to order dissolution? [*Susman v. Venture,* 449 N.E. 2d 143 (Ill. App. Ct.)]

10 W. E. Groves and Lloyd Lindsey signed an act of exchange. One of the provisions was that Groves transfer his "ownership in Rosemound Improvement Association, Inc., represented by the following stock certificates" to Lindsey. No certificates were described and none were signed over by Groves. Rosemound's charter provided: "Stock certificates herein shall not be transferable except back to the corporation." After the act of exchange was signed, the parties became dissatisfied, and the provisions were not all fulfilled. Groves sued to require Rosemound to recognize his right to vote at shareholders' meetings. Is Groves entitled to vote? [*Groves v. Rosemound Improvement Association, Inc.*, 413 So. 2d 925 (La. Ct. App.)]

11 Jack Alpert and others owned 26 percent of the stock of 79 Realty Corp., which had an office building as its principal asset. Another corporation, 28 William St. Corp., purchased more than two-thirds of 79 Realty's stock. The board of directors of 79 Realty was replaced, and the new board approved a merger of 28 William St. into 79 Realty. The minority shares would be canceled, and title to the office building would end up in Madison 28 Associates, a partnership. The minority shareholders were to be paid the same price per share as had been paid to acquire the majority interest. The merger was to get more capital for necessary renovation and realize tax savings by owning as a partnership rather than as a corporation. The minority shareholders sued to rescind the merger. There was no showing of fraud, illegality, or self-dealing. Should the merger be rescinded? [*Alpert v. 28 Williams St. Corp.*, 457 N.Y.S. 2d 4 (N.Y. App. Div.)]

Part 8 Risk-Bearing Devices

Department of Commerce and Insurance

More than a century ago, the state Legislature realized the need for consumer protection and insurance company regulation. The General Assembly created the Bureau of Insurance in 1873, and the state treasurer acted as insurance commissioner. In 1913, a separate Department of Insurance was formed and put under the direction of a commissioner, who became an officer in the governor's Cabinet. To reflect its expanded role in business regulation and consumer protection, the State Insurance Department became the Department of Commerce and Insurance in 1983.

Today the department is close to becoming state government's "one stop" consumer center along with fulfilling its traditional role in business regulations. Nearly every office in this diverse agency has a duty, within its scope of operations, to consumers.

In addition to its regulation of the insurance industry, a separate division regulates securities and another division carries out the responsibility of lending administrative support to 26 regulatory boards and commissions. These divisions also process consumer complaints and take disciplinary action against license holders found guilty of breaking the state laws governing their profession.

The state's Division of Fire Prevention is yet another part of the Department of Commerce and Insurance. Among its other duties in arson investigation and codes enforcement, this division inspects schools, mobile homes, and electrical installations and reviews plans of certain buildings.

The impact of the Department of Commerce and Insurance is felt throughout the state through its wide range of activities and because of its revenue collecting authority. In 1995-96, the department took approximately $289,089,874 in taxes and fees. The total ranked the department second only to the Department of Revenue as a collector of funds to operate state government.

Divisions within the Department of Commerce and Insurance

At This Site

- Departmental Directory
- Consumer Insurance Information
- About the Department
- Licensee Roster Search
- Press Releases & Publications
- Online Resources List
- Related Web Links
- Fire Marshal Kids' Page
- Tennessee Laws
- Employee Appreciation

http://www.state.tn.us/commerce/

Insurance companies are regulated by both the federal and state governments. Bankruptcy laws are also both state and federal. All of these issues are covered in the following chapters.

An excellent resource for specific information on state insurance, bankruptcy and other related laws are state Web sites. Some state sites, such as Tennessee's, have easy ways to get to insurance information, while others will require a search through a list of state agencies. Try out Tennessee's Web site at http://www.state.tn.us/commerce.

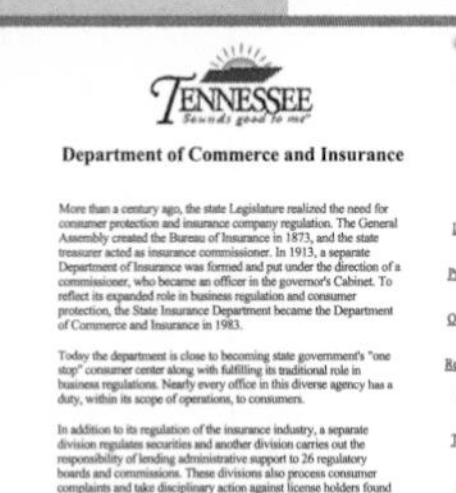

Tennessee
Sounds good to me

Department of Commerce and Insurance

More than a century ago, the state Legislature realized the need for consumer protection and insurance company regulation. The General Assembly created the Bureau of Insurance in 1873, and the state treasurer acted as insurance commissioner. In 1913, a separate Department of Insurance was formed and put under the direction of a commissioner, who became an officer in the governor's Cabinet. To reflect its expanded role in business regulation and consumer protection, the State Insurance Department became the Department of Commerce and Insurance in 1983.

Today the department is close to becoming state government's "one stop" consumer center along with fulfilling its traditional role in business regulations. Nearly every office in this diverse agency has a duty, within its scope of operations, to consumers.

In addition to its regulation of the insurance industry, a separate division regulates securities and another division carries out the responsibility of lending administrative support to 26 regulatory boards and commissions. These divisions also process consumer complaints and take disciplinary action against license holders found guilty of breaking the state laws governing their profession.

The state's Division of Fire Prevention is yet another part of the Department of Commerce and Insurance. Among its other duties in arson investigation and codes enforcement, this division inspects schools, mobile homes, and electrical installations and reviews plans of certain buildings.

Departmental Directory
Consumer Insurance Information
About the Department
Licensee Roster Search
Press Releases & Publications
Online Resources List
Related Web Links
Fire Marshal Kids' Page
Tennessee Laws
Employee Appreciation

37 Principles of Insurance

Learning Objectives

1. Identify important terms used in insurance.
2. Explain who may obtain insurance.
3. List the five aspects of the law of contracts that have special significance for insurance contracts.

PREVIEW CASE

Freddie Long obtained a life insurance policy from Mutual Benefit Life Insurance Company of New Jersey. Richard Chisholm was the beneficiary. Question 15 in the application for the insurance asked if the applicant "had any surgery, treatment, observation, or routine examination in doctor's office, hospital, clinic . . . ?" It instructed, "For routine physical examinations indicating only good health . . . state 'routine exams' beside your 'yes' answer." Long marked "yes" and stated "routine exams." Long died five months later in a car accident. Mutual denied Chisholm's claim for payment, stating that in answering Question 15 Long had failed to disclose that after an auto accident he had received hospital treatment for minor injuries for which the prognosis was good. Mutual's underwriting department indicated the injuries were of no underwriting concern. Was there concealment? What type of information must be withheld to constitute concealment?

Insurance
Contract that transfers risk of financial loss for a fee

Insurance provides a fund of money when a loss covered by the policy occurs. Life is full of unfavorable financial contingencies. Not every financial peril in life can be shifted by insurance, but many of the most common perils can. **Insurance** is a contract whereby a party transfers a risk of financial loss to the risk bearer, the insurance company, for a fee.

Every insurance contract specifies the particular risk being transferred. The name that identifies the policy does not control either the coverage or protection of the policy. For example, a particular contract may carry the name "Personal Accident Insurance Policy," but this name may not clearly indicate the risk being assumed by the insurance company. A reading of the contract may reveal that the company will pay only if an accident occurs while the insured is actually attending a public school. In such a case, in spite of the broad title of the policy, the premium paid covers only the described protection against a financial loss due to an accident, not the loss due to any accident. The contract determines the risk covered, and it binds the parties.

Terms Used in Insurance

LO1
Important terms

Insurer
Company writing insurance

Insured
Person protected against loss

Beneficiary
Person who receives proceeds of life insurance

Policy
Written contract of insurance

Face
Maximum insurer pays for loss

Premium
Consideration paid by insured

Risk or Peril
Danger of loss

Hazards
Factors that contribute to uncertainty

The company agreeing to compensate a person for a certain loss is known as the **insurer**, or sometimes as the underwriter. The person protected against the loss is known as the **insured**, or the policyholder. In life insurance the person who will receive the benefits or the proceeds of the policy is known as the **beneficiary**. In most states the insured may make anyone the beneficiary.

Whenever a person purchases any kind of insurance, a contract is formed with the insurance company. The written contract is commonly called a **policy**. The maximum amount that the insurer agrees to pay in case of a loss is known as the **face** of the policy, and the consideration the insured pays for the protection is called the **premium**.

The danger of a loss of, or injury to, property, life, or anything else, is called a **risk** or **peril**; when the danger may be covered by insurance, it is known as the insurable risk. Factors, such as fire, floods, and sleet, which contribute to the uncertainty, are called **hazards**.

An insurance company assumes the risks caused by normal hazards. The insured must not do anything to increase the risk. Negligence by the insured constitutes a normal hazard. Gross negligence indicating a criminal intent does not. With regard to the risk, when a loss occurs, the insured must use all due diligence to minimize it. However, the insured has no responsibility for an increased risk over which the insured has no control or knowledge. For example, the insured must remove household effects from a burning building or keep a car involved in an accident from being vandalized if it can be done safely.

Facts: Kevin Cumiskey leased property for a restaurant and insured the property in his name, d/b/a "Chiripa's." Later the insurance lapsed and the business was incorporated as K.S.J., Inc., with Kevin and his parents, Stephanie and John, as stockholders and officers. One summer Stephanie and John were to run the restaurant. They insured the property with St. Paul Fire and Marine Insurance Co. in the same name as previously, Kevin Cumiskey, d/b/a "Chiripa's." The restaurant consistently lost money, and a series of explosions and fire damaged the property. Circumstantial evidence indicated John had set the fire. St. Paul's filed for a declaratory judgment, an action asking the court to decide the rights of the parties. The Cumiskeys claimed St. Paul wrongfully refused to pay the claim.

Outcome: The court found St. Paul did not act in bad faith in failing to pay the claim. Where an officer, director, stockholder, or managing agent deliberately sets a fire, the insurer has a good defense to a claim on the policy.

Rider
Addition to insurance policy to modify, extend, or limit base contract

A **rider** on an insurance policy is a clause or even a whole contract added to another contract to modify, extend, or limit the base contract. A rider must be clearly incorporated in, attached to, or referred to in the policy so that there is no doubt the parties wanted it to become a part of the policy.

Facts: Eza Rozas had hospital and medical insurance with Louisiana Hospital Service, Inc. She had a severe headache and dizziness, was hospitalized, and was found to have two aneurysms and a large blood clot in her brain. Louisiana refused to pay her hospital bill because riders to her policy excluded coverage. The riders were stapled to her application for insurance, which had been put inside the policy and given to her. Rozas alleged the riders were not effective because they were not physically attached to the policy.

Outcome: The court held that Rozas had the entire contract in her possession at all times, and to require the riders to have been attached by staples, paper clips, or glue would be an absurd and unintended result.

Types of Insurance Companies

There are two major types of insurance companies:

1 Stock companies
2 Mutual companies

STOCK COMPANIES

Stock Insurance Company
Corporation of stockholder-investors

A **stock insurance company** is a corporation for which the original investment was made by stockholders and whose board of directors conducts its business. As in all other corporations, the stockholders elect the board of directors and receive the profits as dividends. Unlike other corporations, insurance companies must place a major portion of their original capital in a reserve account so claims can be paid. As business volume increases, the reserve must be increased by setting aside part of the premiums into this account.

MUTUAL COMPANIES

Mutual Insurance Company
Company of policyholder-investors

Assessment Mutual Company
Mutual insurance company in which losses are shared by policyholders

In a **mutual insurance company** the policyholders are the members and owners and correspond to the stockholders in a stock company. In these companies the policyholders are both the insurer and the insured, but the corporation constitutes a separate legal entity. A person who purchases a $10,000 fire insurance policy in a mutual company that has $10 million of insurance in force owns 1/1000 of the company and is entitled to share the profits in this ratio. Losses may also have to be shared in the same ratio in an **assessment mutual company**. A policyholder is not subject to assessment where the policy makes no provision for it. In a stock company, policyholders never share the losses.

Who May Be Insured

LO2
Insureds

To contract for a policy of insurance, an individual must be competent to contract. Insurance does not constitute a necessary; thus, a minor who wishes to disaffirm is not bound on insurance contracts. A minor who disaffirms a contract may demand the return of any money. Since insurance contracts provide protection only, this cannot be returned. Some states hold that because of this a minor can demand only the unearned premium for the unexpired portion of the policy. A few states have passed laws preventing minors from disaffirming some insurance contracts by reason of minority.

Insurable Interest
Interest in nonoccurrence of risk insured against

To become a policyholder, one must have an insurable interest. An **insurable interest** means that the policyholder has an interest in the nonoccurrence of the risk insured against, usually because there would be financial loss. The insurance contract is in its entirety an agreement to assume a specified risk. If the insured has no interest to protect, there can be no assumption of risk, and hence no insurance. The law covering insurable interest is different for life insurance and for property insurance.

LIFE INSURANCE

The insured has an insurable interest in his or her own life. When people insure another's life, however, and make themselves or someone else the beneficiary, they must have an insurable interest in the life of the insured at the time the policy is taken out. That interest does not need to exist at the time of the death of the insured.

A person has an insurable interest in the life of another when such a relationship exists between them that a reasonable expectation of benefit will be derived from the continued existence of the other person. The relationships most frequently giving rise to an insurable interest are those between parents and children, husband and wife, partner and copartner, and a creditor in the life of the debtor to the extent of the debt. There are numerous other relationships that give rise to an insurable interest. With the exception of a creditor, if the insurable interest exists, the amount of insurance is irrelevant.

PROPERTY INSURANCE

One must have an insurable interest in the property at the time the policy is issued and at the time of the loss to be able to collect on a property insurance policy. Ownership is, of course, the clearest type of insurable interest; but there are many other types of insurable interest. Insurable interest occurs when the insured would suffer a monetary loss by the destruction of the property. Common types of insurable interest other than ownership include:

1. The mortgagee has an insurable interest in the property mortgaged to the extent of the mortgage.
2. The seller has an insurable interest in property sold on the installment plan when the seller retains a security interest in it as security for the unpaid purchase price.
3. A bailee has an insurable interest in the property bailed to the extent of possible loss. The bailee has a potential loss from two sources. Compensation as provided for in the contract of bailment might be lost. Secondly, the bailee may be held legally liable to the owner if the bailee's negligence or the negligence of the bailee's employees causes the loss.
4. A partner has an insurable interest in the property owned by the firm to the extent of the possible loss.
5. A tenant has an insurable interest in property to the extent of the loss that would be suffered by damage to or destruction of the property.

A change in title or possession of the insured property may destroy the insurable interest, which in turn may void the contract, because insurable interest must exist at the time of the loss.

Facts: Fire totally destroyed Gaylon and Tammy Foote's home which Farm Bureau Mutual Insurance Company insured. The Foots sued Farm Bureau which claimed they did not have an insurable interest in the home. Title to the home was in Gaylon's parents' names because when purchased, Gaylon and Tammy were divorced and trying to reconcile. Gaylon and Tammy had lived in the home several years and built a garage and a two-story addition. They had made all mortgage, insurance, and tax payments.

Outcome: The court said Gaylon and Tammy had a substantial economic interest in safeguarding the home and would definitely endure loss as a result of its destruction. Thus, they had an insurable interest.

Some Legal Aspects of the Insurance Contract

LO3 Contract law specially applicable to insurance

The laws applicable to contracts in general apply to insurance contracts. Five aspects of the law, however, have special significance for insurance contracts:

1 Concealment
2 Representation
3 Warranty
4 Subrogation
5 Estoppel

CONCEALMENT

Concealment Willful failure to disclose pertinent information

An insurer must rely upon the information supplied by the insured. This places the responsibility of supplying all information pertinent to the risk upon the insured. A willful failure to disclose this pertinent information is known as **concealment**. To affect the contract the concealed facts must be material; this means they must relate to matters that would affect the insurer's decision to insure the insured and the determination of the premium rate. Also, the concealment must be willful. The willful concealment of a material fact in most states renders the contract voidable.

PREVIEW CASE REVISITED

Facts: Freddie Long obtained a life insurance policy from Mutual Benefit Life Insurance Company of New Jersey. Richard Chisholm was the beneficiary. Question 15 in the application for the insurance asked if the applicant "had any surgery, treatment, observation, or routine examination in doctor's office, hospital, clinic . . . ?" It instructed, "For routine physical examinations indicating only good health . . . state 'routine exams' beside your 'yes' answer." Long marked "yes" and stated "routine exams." Long died five months later in a car accident. Mutual denied Chisholm's claim for payment, stating that in answering Question 15 Long had failed to disclose that after an auto accident he had received hospital treatment for minor injuries for which the prognosis was good. Mutual's underwriting department indicated the injuries were of no underwriting concern.

Outcome: The court held that there was no concealment.

The rule of concealment does not apply with equal stringency to all types of insurance contracts. In the case of property insurance, where the agent has an opportunity to inspect the property, the insurance company waives the right to void the contract. Concealment arises in ocean marine insurance whenever the insured withholds pertinent information, even if there is no intent to defraud.

REPRESENTATION

False Representation
Misstatement of material fact

An oral or written misstatement of a material fact by the insured prior to the finalization of the contract is called a **false representation**. If the insured makes a false representation, the insurer may avoid the contract of insurance. This results whether or not the insured made the misstatement purposely.

Insurance policies now usually provide that if the age of the insured is misstated, the policy will not be voided; however, the face amount paid on the policy "shall be that sum which the premium paid would have provided for had the age been correctly stated."

Facts: Thomas Foster obtained a fire insurance policy from Auto-Owners Insurance Company on a house. Fire later damaged the house. The application of the insurance included a request to "List all losses for past 5 years at this . . . location." Although Foster had incurred several fire losses the box "None" was checked. If Auto-Owners had known about the previous losses it would not have issued the policy. Foster claimed he had supplied the insurance agent who filled out the application with the truth and therefore although he had signed the application he had made no misrepresentation.

Outcome: The court stated that since he had signed the application Foster was responsible for the misrepresentation.

WARRANTY

Warranty
Statement of insured that relates to risk and appears in contract

A **warranty** is a statement or promise of the insured that relates to the risk and appears in the contract or another document incorporated in the contract. Untrue statements or unfulfilled promises permit the insurer to declare the policy void.

Warranties differ from representations in several ways. The insurance company includes warranties in the actual contract of insurance or incorporates them in it by reference. Representations are merely collateral or independent, such as oral statements or written statements appearing in the application for insurance or other writing separate from the actual contract of insurance.

Also, in order to void the contract of insurance, the false representations must concern a material fact, whereas the warranties may concern any fact or be any promise. A representation need only be substantially correct, whereas a warranty must be absolutely true or strictly performed.

Several states have enacted legislation that eliminates any distinction between warranties and representations and does not require a showing of materiality for a warranty or that the insured intended to defraud. In these states, a breached warranty does not void the policy. Even in states without such statutes, courts are reluctant to find policies invalid and will construe warranties as representations whenever possible and interpret warranties strictly against the insurer so as to favor the insured.

SUBROGATION

Subrogation
Right of insurer to assume rights of insured

In insurance, **subrogation** is the right of the insurer under certain circumstances to assume the legal rights of, or to "step into the shoes" of, the insured. Subrogation particularly applies to some types of automobile insurance. If the insurer pays a claim to the insured, under the law of subrogation the insurer has a right to any claims that the insured had because of the loss. For example, A has a collision insurance policy on a car. B negligently damages the car. The insurance company will pay A but then has the right to sue B to be repaid.

ESTOPPEL

Estoppel
One party leads the second to a false conclusion the second party relies on. The second party would be harmed if the first party were later allowed to show the conclusion was false.

Neither party to an insurance contract may claim the benefit of a violation of the contract by the other party. Each party is said to be **estopped**, or prevented, from claiming the benefit of such violation. An estoppel can arise whenever a party, by statements or actions, leads the second party to a conclusion, even if false, that the second party relies upon. If the second party would be harmed if the first party were later allowed to show that the conclusion was not true, there is an estoppel. For example, if an insurer gives the insured a premium receipt, the insurance company would lead the insured to the conclusion that the premium had been paid. The insurer would be estopped from later asserting that the insured had not paid the premium in accordance with the terms of the policy.

Facts: Jack McGeehee called a Farmers Insurance Co. agent and told him he wanted to get insurance on a house he owned. McGeehee told the agent his son, Howard McGeehee, lived in the house and Jack also wanted to get insurance on Howard's furniture. The agent had a homeowner's insurance policy issued, which covered the house and its contents, showing Howard as the insured (owner) and Jack as the mortgagee. Jack paid the premiums. Four years later, fire destroyed the house. Farmers paid for the destroyed contents, but refused to pay for the destruction of the house since the policy showed Howard as the insured and he did not own the house.

Outcome: The court held that since the Farmers agent made the choice as to how to insure the property and thus as to "insurable interest," Farmers was estopped to deny liability on its policy.

Questions

1. Does the name that identifies an insurance policy control the coverage and protection of the policy? Explain.
2. Identify the parties to a contract of insurance.
3. What is the responsibility of the insured with regard to risk when a loss occurs?
4. How do stock insurance companies differ from other types of corporations?
5. a. When must a person have an insurable interest for life insurance purposes?
   b. Give three examples of relationships giving rise to an insurable interest for life insurance.
6. a. When must a person have an insurable interest for property insurance purposes?
   b. Give three examples of persons who have an insurable interest in property.
7. Under what circumstances does an insurance company waive its right to avoid an insurance contract for concealment?
8. What is the difference between a warranty and a representation?
9. What is subrogation in insurance law?
10. When can an estoppel arise?

Case Problems

LO3 **1** The application for a home health care benefits policy with Life & Health Insurance Company of America listed nine medical conditions and asked "Have you or your spouse within the past 5 years had or been told you have the following." Next to "kidney failure" and "chronic obstructive lung disease" Harold Green checked the "no" box. Green signed the application and Life issued the policy. A year later Green made a claim. In checking with Green's physician Life discovered Green suffered from chronic renal failure and chronic obstructive pulmonary disease, although the physician had merely told Green he had "some sluggish kidneys" and "a little bronchitis." Life rescinded the policy based on material misrepresentations in the application and Green sued alleging the misrepresentations were made unknowingly. May Life rescind the policy?

LO2 **2** Federal Home Loan Mortgage held a mortgage on a home owned by Bobby and Josie Wright. The Wrights put a second mortage on the home in favor of Citizens Bank and Trust. Assurance Company of America issued a property insurance policy on the home. Federal foreclosed on the home and the sheriff sold it at auction to Citizens. Citizens sent a check for its bid to the sheriff's department but the sheriff's department did not immediately complete processing the sheriff's sale and held Citizens' check until after fire destroyed the home. When asked to pay for the destruction of the home, Assurance claimed the Wrights did not have an insurable interest. Did they?

LO3 **3** Barbara Garnes had two Bose speakers stolen from her. Her insurance company paid her for the loss. The thief pawned the speakers at King's Pawn Shop, owned by Jerry King. The police seized them as evidence. In court proceedings to determine to whom the speakers should go, King argued he purchased them in good faith and had a right to them against everyone but the true owner—Garnes. Having paid Garnes, the insurance company claimed it was entitled to subrogation and could assert Garnes's superior rights to the speakers. Who should get the speakers?

LO2 **4** Hazel loaned Bean $120,000 and the note required Bean to maintain a life insurance policy on his life with Hazel the beneficiary in an amount not less than the remaining balance due on the note. Bean changed the beneficiary on a $200,000 life insurance policy he owned naming Hazel the beneficiary of $120,000. Bean made payments on the note and paid all the premiums on the life insurance policy. Bean died owing $80,000 on the note. When the insurance company paid Hazel $120,000 Bean's estate sued for the $40,000 which exceeded the balance due on the note. Since a creditor has an insurable interest in the life of the debtor only to the amount of the debt, the estate argued Hazel could only be paid $80,000. Whose insurable interest is relevant here and what impact does that have on naming Hazel the beneficiary of $120,000?

LO3 **5** Kimberly and Walter Goodwin applied for a life insurance policy on Walter from Investors Life Insurance Co. through its agent, Charles Toomey. Toomey asked the Goodwins questions from the application and filled out the form. One question asked, "Within the past two years have you had your driver's license suspended or had two or more moving violations or accidents?" Toomey checked the box indicating "no." Kimberly knew Walter's license had been suspended three months previously and that he had two moving violations as well as two accidents within two years. The Goodwins signed the application, which stated they had read it and given complete and true answers. Investors issued the policy. Eight months later Walter died from massive head trauma received in an accident while racing at 70 mph in a 35 mph zone. Investors found out about Walter's driving record and refused to pay, claiming false representation. Should Investors have to pay?

LO3 **6** Steven and Annette Ramon owned a barn insured by Farm Bureau Insurance Co. against damage by fire. A fire damaged the barn and personal property inside it. The

Ramons made a claim for their loss that was denied by Farm Bureau because of allegations of arson and fraud on the part of Steven Ramon. No charges were alleged against Annette. The policy limited an insured's recovery to an amount not "more than the interest of the insured." The Ramons sued Farm Bureau under the fire policy. The trial court held that as an innocent insured who owned a half interest in the property, Annette's recovery was limited to half of the proceeds under the policy. The Ramons appealed. Decide the case.

LO2 **7** While married to James, Dorothy Morgan bought insurance on the home they shared from American Security Insurance Co. The policy listed the named insured as Dorothy and any relative living in the home. The Morgans divorced and Dorothy deeded James her interest in the house. He bought insurance on the house from another company. A month later, fire destroyed the house. James' insurance company paid the limits of its policy. The Morgans also sought recovery from American on Dorothy's policy. American refused claiming no insurable interest existed on the policy at the time of the fire. Did either Morgan have an insurable interest?

LO3 **8** Gary and Patricia Lighton insured their house with Madison-Onondaga Mutual Fire Insurance Co. A fire damaged the house and Madison-Onondaga refused to pay under the policy. It asserted the Lightons had concealed the fact that a few months before applying for the policy a fire had occurred in their basement. The fire investigator had called that fire suspicious and told the Lightons. Madison-Onondaga said it would not have issued the policy if it had known about the previous, suspicious fire. The company had not asked the Lightons about any prior fires. Should the court find concealment?

Internet Resources for Business Law

Name	Resources	Web Address
The National Association of Insurance Commissioners	The NAIC maintains a site with links to news, updates, related sources, and other information.	http://www.naic.org/
Federal Emergency Management Agency	The FEMA site contains news and links to sites on emergency relief procedures, weather warnings and related information, flood insurance, U.S. Fire Administration, and other related sites.	http://www.fema.gov/

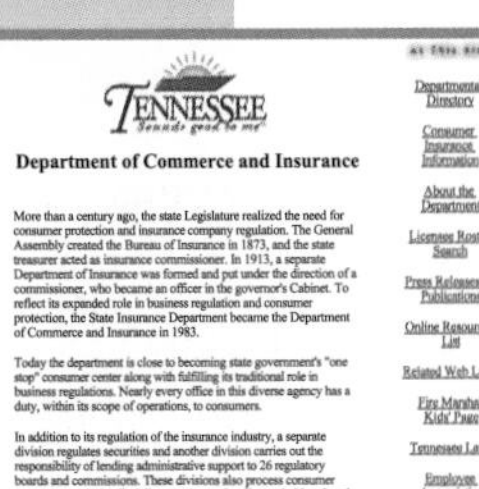

TENNESSEE
Sounds good to me

Department of Commerce and Insurance

More than a century ago, the state Legislature realized the need for consumer protection and insurance company regulation. The General Assembly created the Bureau of Insurance in 1873, and the state treasurer acted as insurance commissioner. In 1913, a separate Department of Insurance was formed and put under the direction of a commissioner, who became an officer in the governor's Cabinet. To reflect its expanded role in business regulation and consumer protection, the State Insurance Department became the Department of Commerce and Insurance in 1983.

Today the department is close to becoming state government's "one stop" consumer center along with fulfilling its traditional role in business regulations. Nearly every office in this diverse agency has a duty, within its scope of operations, to consumers.

In addition to its regulation of the insurance industry, a separate division regulates securities and another division carries out the responsibility of lending administrative support to 26 regulatory boards and commissions. These divisions also process consumer complaints and take disciplinary action against license holders found guilty of breaking the state laws governing their profession.

The state's Division of Fire Prevention is yet another part of the Department of Commerce and Insurance. Among its other duties in arson investigation and codes enforcement, this division inspects schools, mobile homes, and electrical installations and reviews plans of certain buildings.

At This Site

Departmental Directory

Consumer Insurance Information

About the Department

Licensee Roster Search

Press Releases & Publications

Online Resources List

Related Web Links

Fire Marshal Kids' Page

Tennessee Laws

Employee Appreciation

38
Types of Insurance

Learning Objectives

1 Explain the nature of life insurance and its normal limitations.

2 Define property insurance.

3 Identify the types of coverage afforded by automobile insurance.

PREVIEW CASE

After the court entered a decree of divorce for Joseph and Marcia Hortega, it ordered Joseph to keep Lonna and Josiah Hortega as the primary beneficiaries of his life insurance through Northern Illinois Gas Co. until they reached 21. However, six months later, Joseph completed a new beneficiary card naming his new wife, Mary Hortega, as primary beneficiary. Joseph died, and the insurance company, Aetna Life Insurance Co., asked the court to determine who should receive the insurance proceeds. What should the court order? Was Joseph required to obey a court order?

Insurance companies provide many types of policies to help people protect against financial loss. Three types of policies that most people purchase include:

1 Life insurance
2 Property insurance
3 Automobile insurance

Life Insurance

LO1
Nature of life insurance

Life Insurance
Contract of insurer to pay money on death of insured

Life insurance is a contract by which the insurer agrees to pay a specified sum or sums of money to a beneficiary upon the death of the insured. An insured generally obtains life insurance to protect the beneficiary from financial hardship resulting from the death of the insured.

TYPES OF LIFE INSURANCE CONTRACTS

The most important types of life insurance policies include:

1 Term insurance
2 Endowment insurance
3 Whole life insurance
4 Combinations

TERM INSURANCE

Term Insurance
Contract whereby insurer assumes risk of death of insured for specified time

Renewable Term Insurance
Term insurance renewable without physical examination

Term insurance contracts are those whereby the company assumes for a specified period of time the risk of the death of the insured. The term may be for only 1 year; or it may be for 5, 10, or even 50 years. The term must be stated in the policy.

Many variations of term policies exist. In short-term policies, such as five years, the insured might have the option of renewing it for another equal term without a physical examination. This is called **renewable term insurance**. The cost is higher for each renewal period. In nonrenewable term insurance the insured does not have the right to renew unless the company consents.

Term policies also may be either level term or decreasing term. In level term, the face of the policy is written in units of $1,000. The face amount remains the same during the entire term of the policy. In decreasing term contracts, the length of time the proceeds are collected or the face amount decreases over the life of the policy. The policy may be written in multiples of an amount of monthly income. For example, a person age twenty could purchase a decreasing term policy of 50 units, or $500 a month, covering a period of 600 months, or 50 years. If the insured dies the first month after purchasing the policy, the beneficiary would draw $500 a month for 600 months or $300,000 ultimately. If the insured dies at the end of 25 years, the beneficiary would draw $500 a month for 300 months or $150,000 ultimately. Some decreasing term insurance is paid in a lump sum rather than periodically.

All term policies have one thing in common—they are pure life insurance. They shift the specific risk of loss as a result of death and nothing more.

ENDOWMENT INSURANCE

Endowment Insurance
Decreasing term insurance plus savings account

An **endowment insurance** policy is decreasing term insurance plus a savings account. Part of the premium pays for the insurance, and the remainder earns interest so that at the end of the term the savings will equal the face amount of the policy. If the insured dies during the term of the policy, the beneficiary will collect the face. If the insured is still living at the end of the term, the insurance company pays the face to the insured or a designated beneficiary.

WHOLE LIFE INSURANCE

All life insurance contracts are either term insurance or endowment insurance. A whole life insurance policy is one that continues, assuming the premium is paid, until age 100 or death, whichever occurs first. If the insured is still living at age 100, the face of the policy is collected as an endowment. A whole life policy might correctly be defined as endowment insurance at age 100.

COMBINATIONS

The three basic life insurance contracts—term, endowment, and whole life—can be combined in an almost endless variety of combinations to create slightly different contracts. In the case of universal life insurance, any premiums paid that exceed the current cost of term insurance are put into a fund and earn interest. The fund can be withdrawn by the owner or paid to the beneficiary at the death of the insured. The Family Income Policy, for example, is merely a straight life policy with a 20-year decreasing term policy attached as a rider.

Insurors frequently add several other riders to life insurance policies for an added premium. The disability income rider may be attached to any policy and pays an income to an insured who becomes disabled. A rider requiring the insurer to make a greater payment, customarily twice the ordinary amount when death is caused by accidental means, is called a **double indemnity rider**.

Double Indemnity Rider
Policy requiring insurer to pay twice ordinary face amount if death is accidental

LIMITATION ON RISKS IN LIFE INSURANCE CONTRACTS

Two common limitations upon the risk covered by life insurance include: (1) suicide and (2) death from war activity.

SUICIDE

Life insurance policies commonly refuse payment when death occurs from suicide. Other suicide clauses stipulate that the company will not pay if the suicide occurs within two years from the date of the policy.

Facts: Farmers New World Life Insurance Co. issued two policies on the life of Lawrence Malcom. They each contained the following clause: "Suicide, whether sane or insane, will not be a risk assumed during the first two policy years. In such a case we will refund the premiums paid." Within two years of the issuance, Lawrence committed suicide. Farmers refused to pay the face of the policies. The beneficiaries sued, alleging the suicide provision was not plain and clear.

Outcome: The court found the words of the clause understandable, and Farmers did not have to pay the face of the policies.

DEATH FROM WAR ACTIVITY

A so-called war clause provides that if the insured dies as a consequence of war activity the company will not pay. If a member of the armed forces dies a natural death, the company must pay. In order to refuse payment, the insurance company has the burden of proving war activity caused the death.

PAYMENT OF PREMIUMS

If the premiums are not paid when due, and the policy so provides, it either will lapse automatically or may be declared forfeited at the option of the insurer. The policy or a statute of the state may provide that after a certain number of premiums have been paid, an unpaid premium results in the issuance of a smaller, paid-up policy for the same term. By the payment of an additional premium the insured may generally obtain a policy containing a waiver of premiums that becomes effective if the insured becomes disabled. When disability occurs, the insured does not have to pay premiums for the period of time during which the disability exists.

GRACE PERIOD

Grace Period
30- or 31-day period in which late premium may be paid without policy lapsing

The law requires life insurance companies to provide a **grace period** of 30 or 31 days in every life insurance policy. This grace period gives the insured 30 or 31 days from the due date of the premium in which to pay it without the policy's lapsing. Without this provision, if the insured paid the premium one day late, the policy either might lapse or be forfeited by the insured. The insured might be able to obtain a reinstatement of the policy but might be required to pass a new physical examination. To buy a new policy, the insured might have to pass a physical examination and would have to pay a higher rate for the current age.

INCONTESTABILITY

Life insurance policies are incontestable after a certain period of time, usually one or two years. After that time, the insurance company usually cannot contest the validity of a claim on any ground except nonpayment of premiums.

CHANGE OF BENEFICIARY

Life insurance policies ordinarily reserve to the insured the right to change the beneficiary at will. Policies also permit the insured to name successive beneficiaries so that if the first beneficiary should die before the insured, the proceeds would pass to the second named or contingent beneficiary.

Courts uphold divorce decrees or separation agreements fixing beneficiaries of insurance policies. Later attempts by the insured to change a beneficiary required by a court order do not succeed.

PREVIEW CASE REVISITED

Facts: After the court entered a decree of divorce for Joseph and Marcia Hortega, it ordered Joseph to keep Lonna and Josiah Hortega as the primary beneficiaries of his life insurance through Northern Illinois Gas Co. until they reached 21. However, six months later, Joseph completed a new beneficiary card naming his new wife, Mary Hortega, as primary beneficiary. Joseph died, and the insurance company, Aetna Life Insurance Co., asked a court to determine who should receive the insurance proceeds.

Outcome: The court held that the proceeds should go to Lonna and Josiah as the divorce decree required.

ASSIGNMENT OF THE POLICY

The policy of insurance may be assigned (or the rights in the policy may be transferred to another) by the insured. The assignment may be either absolute or as collateral security for a loan that the insured obtains from the assignee, such as a bank.

A beneficiary may also make an assignment; however, the assignee of the beneficiary is subject to the disadvantage that the insured may change beneficiaries. If the assignment is made after the insured has died, the assignment is an ordinary assignment of an existing money claim.

ANNUITY INSURANCE

Annuity Insurance
Contract that pays monthly income to insured while alive

Joint and Survivor Annuity
Annuity paid until second of two people die

An **annuity insurance** contract pays the insured a monthly income from a specified age, generally age 65, until death. It is a risk entirely unrelated to the risk assumed in a life insurance contract, even though life insurance companies sell both contracts. Someone has defined life insurance as shifting the risk of dying too soon and annuity insurance as shifting the risk of living too long, or outliving one's savings. An individual age 65 who has $50,000 and a life expectancy of 72 years could use up the $50,000 over the expected 7 additional years of life by using approximately $600 a month for living expenses. However, if the individual lives for more than 7 years, there would be no money left. An annuity insurance policy could be purchased for $50,000, and the monthly income would be guaranteed no matter how long the insured lives. If the annuity contract calls for the monthly payments to continue until the second of two insureds dies, it is called a **joint** and **survivor annuity**. Couples who wish to extend their savings as long as either one is still living frequently use this type of annuity.

Property Insurance

LO2
Property insurance

Property Insurance
Contract by which insurer pays for damage to property

Property insurance is a contract whereby the insurer, in return for a premium, agrees to reimburse the insured for loss or damage to specified property caused by the hazard covered. A contract of property insurance is one of indemnity or compensation for loss that protects the policyholder from actual loss.

If a building actually worth $40,000 is insured for $45,000, the extra premiums that were paid for the last $5,000 worth of coverage do not provide any benefit for the insured. The actual value, $40,000, is the maximum that can be collected in case of total loss. On the other hand, if a building is insured for only $20,000 and is totally destroyed, the insurance company has to pay only $20,000. The maximum amount paid for total loss of property is the lesser of the face of the policy or the value of the property.

LOSSES RELATED TO FIRE

Hostile Fire
Fire out of its normal place

Friendly Fire
Fire contained where intended

Normally, fire insurance covers damage to property caused only by hostile fires. A **hostile fire** is defined as one out of its normal place, whereas a **friendly fire** is one contained in the place where it is intended to be. Scorching, searing, singeing, smoke, and similar damages from a friendly fire are not covered under a fire policy. For a fire policy to cover damage, an actual fire must occur. The policy does not cover loss caused by heat without fire. In one case several thousand bales of cotton were under water during a flood. After the flood receded, heat in the bales of cotton was so intense smoke poured forth for days, but no flame was ever detected. The court held there was no fire.

Facts: Washington State Hop Producers, Inc. carried fire insurance with Harbor Insurance Company. Hop Producers discovered that "browning" damaged 253 bales of hops in its warehouse. Heat generated by chemical oxidation causes browning. It may happen without flame, glow, or light, and none of those things were observed. The policy insured "against all direct loss by fire. . . ." When Harbor refused coverage, Hop Producers sued, alleging that fire damaged the hops.

Outcome: The court held that since the damage can occur without flame and no evidence of flame existed, no fire damage occurred.

ETHICAL POINT
Do you think the behavior of the insurance company was ethical in this case?

Business Interruption Insurance
Insurance covering loss of profits while business building is repaired

Leasehold Interest Insurance
Covers cost of higher rent when leased building is damaged

Fire insurance also does not cover economic loss that results from a fire. A hostile fire may cause many losses other than to the property insured, yet the fire policy on the building and contents alone will not cover these losses. An example is the loss of profits while the building is being restored. This loss can be covered by a special policy called **business interruption insurance**. If one leases property on a long-term, favorable lease and the lease is canceled because of fire damage to the building, the tenant may have to pay a higher rent in new quarters. This increased rent loss can be covered by a **leasehold interest insurance** policy but not by a fire policy.

The typical fire policy may also cover the risks of loss by windstorm, explosion, smoke damage from a friendly fire, falling aircraft, water damage, riot and civil commotion, and many others. Each of these additional risks must be added to the fire policy by means of riders. This is commonly known as **extended coverage**.

THE PROPERTY INSURANCE POLICY

Open Policy
Policy that requires insured to prove loss sustained

Valued Policy
Policy that fixes values for insured items

The property insurance policy will state a maximum amount that will be paid by the insurer. When only a maximum is stated, the policy is called an **open policy**, and in the event of partial or total loss, the insured must prove the actual loss that has been sustained. The policy may be a **valued policy**, in which case, instead of stating a maximum amount, it fixes values for the insured items of property. Once a policyholder shows a covered total destruction of the property, the insurer pays the total value. If only a partial loss occurs, the insured under a valued policy must still prove the amount of loss, which amount cannot exceed the stated value of the property.

Floating Policy
Coverage no matter where property is located

Insurance policies also may be specific, blanket, or floating. A **specific policy** applies to one item only, such as one house. A **blanket policy** covers many items of the same kind in different places or different kinds of property in the same place, such as a building, fixtures, and merchandise in a single location. **Floating policies** are used for trucks, theatrical costumes, circus paraphernalia, and similar items that are not kept in a fixed location. A floating policy is also desirable for items that may be sent out for cleaning, such as rugs or clothes, and articles of jewelry and clothes that may be worn while traveling. An insurance policy on household effects covers for loss only at the named location. The purpose of the floating policy is to cover the loss no matter where the property is located at the time of the loss.

Homeowners' Policy
Coverage of many perils plus liability for owners living in their houses

Most people who own their homes obtain homeowners' insurance. A **homeowners' policy** protects the house and also its contents from almost every peril. It covers damage from such perils as fire, wind, lightning, hail, and theft. It also covers liability of the homeowner in case someone suffers injury on the property. A tenant can obtain similar insurance that protects the tenant's personal property but not the building itself.

Reporting Form for Merchandise Inventory
Policy allowing periodic reporting of inventory on hand to vary coverage amount

Another type of insurance policy of particular interest to merchants is the **Reporting Form for Merchandise Inventory**. This policy permits the merchant to report periodically, usually once a month, the amount of inventory on hand. This enables the merchant to carry full coverage at all times and still not be grossly overinsured during periods when inventory is low.

Description of the Property

All property and its location must be described with reasonable accuracy in order to identify the property and to inform the insurer of the nature of the risk involved. It is not accurate to describe a house with asphalt brick siding as brick. Personal property should be so described that in the event of loss, its value can be determined. The general description "living room furniture" may make it difficult to establish the value and the number of items. A complete inventory should be kept. If this is done, such description as "household furniture" in the policy is adequate.

Since the location of the property affects the risk, it must be specified. If personal property used in a brick house on a broad paved street is moved to a frame house on an out-of-the-way dirt road, the risk from fire may be increased considerably. To retain coverage, express permission must always be obtained from the insurer when property is moved except under a floating policy. Most homeowners' policies sold today continue coverage at a new location for several days together with coverage during the moving trip. If a loss occurs during the specified period, the company must pay, even though it received no notice of the changed location.

Coinsurance

Coinsurance
Insured recovers in ratio of insurance to amount of insurance required

Under the principle of **coinsurance**, the insured recovers on a loss in the same ratio as the insurance bears to the amount of insurance that the company requires. Many policies contain an 80 percent coinsurance clause. This clause means the insured may carry any amount of insurance up to the value of the property, but the company will not pay the full amount of a partial loss unless insurance is carried for at least 80 percent of the value of the property. If a building is worth $50,000 and the insured buys a policy for $20,000, the company under the 80 percent coinsurance clause will pay only half of the damage and never more than $20,000. The 80 percent clause requires the insured to carry $40,000, or 80 percent of $50,000, to be fully protected from a partial loss. Since only half of this amount is carried, only half of the damage can be collected.

The coinsurance clause may be some percentage other than 80 percent. In burglary insurance it may be as low as 5 or 10 percent. On rare occasions it is as high as 100 percent in fire insurance.

Repairs and Replacements

Most insurance contracts give the insurer the option of paying the amount of loss or repairing or replacing the property. The amount the insurance company will pay for a loss will vary depending on whether market value or replacement cost is used to measure the amount of loss. If market value is used, the insurance company will pay whatever the value of the property was immediately before the loss. If the property has been used for several years, the market value could be much less than the cost to replace the property. If replacement value is used, the insurance company will pay what the cost is to procure another item as identical to the insured item as possible. Even if the item is older and shows wear and tear, it will be replaced with a new one. For example, suppose fire damages Alphonse's 15-year-old furniture for which he paid $5,000. Alphonse has raised four children, so the furniture has seen a lot of use and not always had the best treatment. The market value of his much used, 15-year-old furniture would probably be very little, say $500. If Alphonse has an insurance policy that pays only market value, he would recover only $500. If the policy pays replacement cost it could easily cost $5,000 or more to replace the furniture. The amount paid by the insurance company can thus vary dramatically depending on whether market value or replacement cost is the measure. Which measure is used will depend on the policy.

When the property is repaired or replaced, materials of like kind and quality must be used. The work must be completed within a reasonable time. When the insurance company has the choice of repair or replacement, the option to replace is seldom exercised by the insurer. The insurer also may have the option of taking the property at an agreed valuation and then paying the insured the full value of the damaged property.

Defense and Notice of Lawsuits

Defense Clause
Policy clause in which insurer agrees to defend insured against damage claims

Under a **defense clause** found in property insurance policies that protect the insured from liability to others injured on the property or by the property, the insurer agrees to defend the insured against any claim for damages. This means that if the insured is sued, the insurance company supplies a lawyer to defend the suit. For example, under a normal homeowners' policy, the homeowner is protected not only against damage to the property but also from liability to anyone injured on the property. If the homeowner is sued by someone who slips on ice at the door, the insurance company will supply a lawyer to defend the suit. This saves the insured the cost of hiring an attorney.

In the event of an injury to a third party or an accident in the case of automobile insurance, the policyholder has the duty to give the insurer written notice and proof of loss regarding the damages. The notice must identify the insured and give such information as the names and address of injured persons, the owner of any damaged property, witnesses, and the time, place, and detailed circumstances of the incident. This notice must be given within a reasonable time.

Facts: Arc Electrical Construction Co. employed Edward Holmes on a construction project for which Arc was a subcontractor for Tishman Construction Corp. Holmes was injured on the job and sued Tishman and Morgan Guaranty and Trust Company, the owner of the property. Tishman and Morgan sued Northbrook Property and Casualty Company which had issued an insurance policy, claiming Northbrook was obligated to defend them. Once Holmes sued Tishman and Morgan, they did not notify Northbrook of the suit for 10 months.

Outcome: The court held that the unexcused delay of 10 months in notifying Northbrook of Holmes' suit released Northbrook from its duty to defend the suit.

If a claim or a suit is brought against the insured, every demand, notice, or summons received must immediately be forwarded to the insurance company. The insured must give the fullest cooperation to the insurer, who normally has the right to settle out of court any claims or lawsuits as it deems best.

Automobile Insurance

LO3
Auto insurance coverage

Automobile insurance is a special type of property insurance and includes two major classes of insurance: physical damage insurance (including fire, theft, and collision) and public liability insurance (including bodily injury and property damage). To understand the law one must know what specific risk the insurance carrier assumes and the terms of the policy covering that specific risk. The term *automobile insurance* refers to insurance that the insured obtains to cover a car and the injuries that the insured and other members of the family may sustain. The term also refers to liability insurance, which protects the insured from claims that third persons may make for injuries to them or damage to their property caused by the insured.

PHYSICAL DAMAGE INSURANCE

Physical Damage Insurance
Insurance for damage to car itself

As the name implies, **physical damage insurance** covers the risks of injury or damage to the car itself. It includes:

1 Fire insurance
2 Theft insurance
3 Collision insurance
4 Comprehensive coverage

FIRE INSURANCE

Much of the law of property insurance discussed in the preceding pages applies to automobile insurance. The fire policy covers loss to a car damaged or destroyed by the burning of any conveyance upon which the car is being transported, such as a barge, boat, or train. Fire insurance can be obtained separately but is normally included in comprehensive coverage.

THEFT INSURANCE

Theft
Taking another's property without consent

Conversion
Obtaining possession of property and converting it to own use

Robbery
Taking property by force

Theft is taking another's property without the owner's consent with the intent to wrongfully deprive the owner of the property. Automobile theft insurance either by law or by contract normally covers a wide range of losses. Obtaining possession of a car and converting it to one's own use to the exclusion of or inconsistent with the rights of the owner is known as **conversion**. Taking another's car by force or threat of force is known as **robbery**. In some states the automobile theft policy must cover all these losses. The policy itself may define theft broadly enough to cover theft, conversion, and robbery. Unless the policy is broadened either by law or by the wording of the policy, a theft policy covers only the wrongful deprivation of the car without claim of right.

Automobile theft insurance usually covers pilferage of any parts of the car but not articles or clothes left in the car. It also covers any damage done to the car either by theft or attempted theft. It does not cover loss of use of the car unless the policy specifically provides for this loss.

Facts: Cyrus See had an auto insurance policy with St. Paul Insurance Company. The policy covered theft of equipment from his vehicle "only if the equipment at the time of the loss . . . was permanently installed in or upon" the vehicle. See had removed a citizens band radio and microphone from the mounting bracket on the dashboard of his truck and put them out of sight on the floor behind the driver's seat. To do this he had disconnected the electrical and aerial wires before leaving the truck. When he returned, the truck had been broken into, and the radio and microphone were missing. He sued St. Paul for the value of them.

Outcome: The court held that they were not permanently installed in the truck at the time of the theft, so St. Paul was not liable.

COLLISION INSURANCE

The standard collision policy covers all damage to the car caused by a collision or upset. A collision occurs whenever an object strikes the insured car or the car strikes an object. Both objects need not be automobiles nor be moving. Frequently collision policies require the collision to be "accidental." A court held that a rolling rock that crashed into a parked car constituted a collision. Likewise, there was a collision when a horse kicked the door of the insured automobile. However, no collision occurs when the colliding object consists of a natural phenomenon, such as rain or hail. If the language of an insurance policy can be given two different, reasonable interpretations, the interpretation most helpful to the insured is used.

Practically all collision policies void or suspend coverage if a car hauls a trailer unless insurance of the same kind carried on the car is placed on the trailer. The question of interpretation then arises as to what constitutes a "trailer." A small boat trailer and a small two-wheel trailer generally are not considered trailers but horse or cattle trailers are.

If a car has collision insurance but not fire insurance, the policy will, in most states, pay both the fire loss and the collision loss occurring in the same wreck so long as the fire ensues after collision and is a direct result of it.

Deductible Clause
Insurance provision whereby insured pays damage up to specified amount; company pays excess up to policy limits

Most collision insurance policies have a **deductible clause**. A deductible clause provides that the insurance company will pay for damages to the car in excess of a specified amount. The specified amount, called the *deductible,* is usually $100 to $250. The insured must pay this amount. Suppose a collision results in $850 in damages to a car covered by $250 deductible collision insurance. The insured must pay the first $250 and the insurance company pays the remainder—$600. Policies without any deductible clause have extremely high rates. It is much cheaper for the insured to assume some of the risk.

An insurance company may pay the insured a claim for collision damage caused by someone else's negligence. If so, under the law of subrogation the company has the right to sue this other party to the collision for the damages.

COMPREHENSIVE COVERAGE

Comprehensive Policy
Insurance covering large number of miscellaneous risks

Insurance companies will write automobile insurance covering almost every conceivable risk to a car, such as windstorm, earthquake, flood, strike, spray from trees, malicious mischief, submersion in water, acid from the battery, riot, glass breakage, hail, and falling aircraft. A **comprehensive policy** may include all of these risks plus fire and theft. A comprehensive policy covers only the hazards enumerated in the policy, and collision is normally excluded.

PUBLIC LIABILITY INSURANCE

Public Liability Insurance
Insurance designed to protect third persons from bodily injury and property damage

The second major division of automobile insurance, **public liability insurance**, protects third persons from bodily injury and property damage.

BODILY INJURY INSURANCE

Bodily injury insurance covers the risk of bodily injury to the insured's passengers, pedestrians, or the occupants of another car. The insurance company obligates itself to pay any sum not exceeding the limit fixed in the policy for which the insured may be personally liable. If the insured has no liability for damages, the insurance company has no liability except the duty of defending the insured in court actions brought by injured persons. This type of insurance does not cover any injury to the person or the property of the insured.

Coverage under an automobile liability policy is usually written as 10/20/5, 25/50/10, 100/300/15, or similar combinations. The first number indicates that the company will pay $10,000, $25,000, or $100,000, respectively, to any one person for bodily injury in any one accident. The middle number fixes the maximum amount the company will pay for bodily injury to more than one person in any one accident. The third figure sets the limit the company will pay for property damage. This usually is the damage to the other person's car but may include damage to any property belonging to someone other than the insured.

A bodily injury insurance policy does not cover accidents occurring while an underage person drives the car. It may not cover accidents occurring while the car is rented or leased unless specifically covered, while the car is used to carry passengers for a consideration, while the car is used for any purpose other than that named in the policy, or while it is used outside the United States and Canada. Some policies exclude accidents while the car is being used for towing a trailer or any other vehicle used as a trailer. These are the ordinary exclusions. Policies may have additional exclusions of various kinds.

The insured may not settle claims or incur expenses other than those for immediate medical help. As in the case of property insurance the insurer has a duty to defend any lawsuits and the insured must give prompt notice of any claims or suits. In the event that the insurance company pays a loss, it is subrogated to any rights that the insured has against others because of such losses.

Facts: Continental Western Insurance Co. insured Deprez' car. Deprez was seriously injured when an oncoming car driven by Susan Sedelmeier spun out of control and hit his car. He sued Sedelmeier but later dismissed the suit. Deprez did not notify Continental of the suit or the accident until four years later when he sought payment under one of the provisions of his policy. The statute of limitations had run on any claims against Sedelmeier. Continental refused to pay on the ground he had breached the contract provisions which required him to promptly notify it of an accident or any lawsuit. Deprez sued Continental.

Outcome: The court pointed out that the policy required prompt notice of any accident or lawsuit. Deprez failed to notify Continental of either and it could otherwise have intervened in the lawsuit to protect its interests. Judgment was for Continental.

PROPERTY DAMAGE INSURANCE

In automobile property damage insurance the insurer agrees to pay, on behalf of the insured, all sums the insured may be legally obligated to pay for damages arising out of the ownership, maintenance, or use of the automobile. The liability of the insurer, however, is limited as stated in the policy.

The policy usually provides that the insurer will not be liable in the event that the car is being operated, maintained, or used by any person in violation of any state or federal law as to age or occupation. The insurer has no liability for damage to property owned by, leased to, transported by, or in charge of the insured.

MEDICAL PAYMENTS AND UNINSURED MOTORIST INSURANCE

In addition to physical damage and public liability insurance, there is insurance that covers injury to the insured or passengers in the insured's car. Medical payments cover bodily injury and are paid regardless of other insurance. Uninsured motorist coverage protects the insured when injury results from the negligence of another driver who does not have liability insurance.

RECOVERY EVEN WHEN AT FAULT

Last Clear Chance
Negligent driver recovers if other driver had one last clear chance to avoid injury

Comparative Negligence
Contributory negligence reduces but does not bar recovery

No-Fault Insurance
Insurance companies pay for their insureds' injuries regardless of fault

Normally the injured party must prove the driver of the insured car was negligent or at fault before the insurer becomes liable. Frequently, both drivers are negligent. Formerly, if the driver bringing suit negligently contributed even slightly to the accident, no recovery could be had. This harsh rule has been replaced in most states by the **last clear chance** rule. This rule states that if one driver is negligent but the other driver had one last clear chance to avoid hitting the negligent driver and did not take it, then the driver who had the last clear chance is liable.

In a number of states **comparative negligence** statutes have also modified the harshness of the common-law rule as to contributory negligence. These statutes provide that the contributory negligence of the plaintiff reduces the recovery but does not completely bar recovery from a negligent defendant. That means the court balances the negligence of each party against that of the other. Suppose Roemer and Griffero have an automobile accident. Both were negligent. It is determined that the damage to Roemer's car was caused 60 percent by Griffero and 40 percent by Roemer's own negligence. If the total damage to Roemer's car is $2,500, Griffero will have to pay 60 percent or $1,500.

Some states have established **no-fault insurance**. Under this plan, insurance companies pay for injuries suffered by their insureds no matter who has responsibility for negligence. States use this no-fault plan for a limited amount of damages. Above this amount, the fault rules apply. The purpose of no fault insurance is to make sure that injured parties are compensated promptly and reduce the number of lawsuits. It is assumed that it is faster and easier to collect from your own insurance company than from the insurance company of the other driver.

REQUIRED INSURANCE

People with poor driving records might find it difficult or impossible to obtain mandatory automobile insurance. When the law requires a person to carry insurance in order to be permitted to drive but no insurance company will sell a policy, a state agency will assign this driver to an insurance company. The company must issue the policy under the "assigned risk" rule. States require all insurance companies to accept the drivers assigned in this manner.

Questions

1. What is it that all term life insurance policies have in common?
2. What is a double indemnity rider?
3. When may the insured change the beneficiary of a life insurance policy?
4. What is the difference between a hostile fire and a friendly fire?
5. What is the purpose of a floating policy of property insurance?
6. Why must the property and its location be described accurately when obtaining insurance on it?
7. What losses does automobile theft insurance usually cover as well as wrongful deprivation of the car without claim of right?
8. Why do most automobile collision insurance policies have a deductible clause?
9. If an insured has no liability for damages after an auto accident, does this mean the insurance company has no responsibility under the insured's bodily injury insurance coverage?
10. Under what theories or programs may the injured party recover even when at fault?

Case Problems

LO1 1 Standard Life Insurance Company of Indiana insured Michael Tedrow's life. He became despondent when his marriage broke up and left a suicide note. Then he started his pickup's engine in his enclosed garage. He apparently changed his mind about committing suicide because he was found overcome by carbon monoxide in the house near the front door. The medical examiner ruled Tedrow's death a suicide so Standard denied the beneficiary's claim for death benefits since the policy excluded suicide within two years from issue. Did Tedrow die by suicide?

LO3 2 Kelly Strode ran over Dianna Silcox while driving a pickup truck and fled the scene of the accident. The police were able to identify Strode as the driver and Silcox learned his identity also. She notified Strode's insurer, Utica Mutual Insurance Company, a year after the accident. She then sued Strode and obtained a $60,000 default judgment. Again, she informed Utica of the judgment. The insurer sued Silcox and Strode asking the court to order that it had no duty under the insurance policy because the policy required prompt notice of accidents. Did the insurer have any responsibility under the policy?

LO2 3 Guardian Pearl Street Garage Corp. leased a portion of a building from ZKZ Associates LP. Guardian carried a liability insurance policy with CNA Insurance Company, which also covered ZKZ for liability "arising out of the ownership, maintenance and use of that part of the described premises which is leased" to Guardian. A pedestrian tripped and fell on the sidewalk used for access in and out of Guardian's garage and sued ZKZ. Did CNA have a duty to defend the suit?

LO2 4 Edwin Fowler carried collision insurance with Canal Insurance Company on a tandem dump truck. The policy definition of collision included an "upset of the covered" vehicle. Fowler was unloading sand when he was told that the trailer was about to tip over. Both the tractor and trailer were leaning to the left and the two right tandems were partially off the ground, badly damaging the vehicle. Fowler set a front end loader against the side of the trailer to keep it from going over completely while another front end loader scooped out the sand. Canal refused to pay for the damage, claiming there was no collision under the policy since the truck did not completely overturn. Was there a collision under the policy?

LO2 5 Ernest Robinson stored a disassembled 1957 Gull Wing Mercedes he owned in his garage. He, Herman Quint, and others had an antique car restoration business and agreed to restore and show the Mercedes. After the business failed, Quint allegedly took the Mercedes and Robinson claimed it as a loss under his homeowners' insurance with Nationwide Mutual Insurance Company. The policy covered loss of personal property, but excluded from coverage "motorized land vehicles . . . designed for travel on public roads as subject to motor vehicle registration." Did the policy cover the disassembled Mercedes?

LO1 6 On March 21, John D'Allessandro applied for life insurance with Durham Life Insurance Co. He signed an application, a copy of which was given to him, indicating that he had not consulted a doctor or been hospitalized within five years and had no heart trouble, chest pains, or other health problems. He actually had been treated and hospitalized within five years for heart and kidney problems. The policy was issued July 1, and D'Allessandro died of coronary artery disease on October 14. The incontestability clause in the policy stated: "no . . . statement shall be used in defense of a claim hereunder unless a copy of the instrument containing the statement has been furnished to the person making the claim." Durham furnished the beneficiary, Barbara D'Allessandro, with a copy of the instrument after John died. She claimed Durham could not raise the misrepresentations because she had not been given a copy of the instrument before D'Allessandro died. Did the incontestability clause apply?

LO3 7 Sheila Blaylock bought a car for $8,500. Three months later the police informed her that the car had been stolen from its owner. They took the car and it was never returned. She filed suit against her insurance company, alleging it was liable on her comprehensive auto insurance. The policy stated it did "not apply to loss or damage . . . which may be caused by war, declared or undeclared, invasion, directly or indirectly, insurrection, civil war, military or usurped power, or to confiscation by duly constituted governmental or civil authority." Is the company liable?

Internet Resources for Business Law

Name	Resources	Web Address
Highway Loss Data Institute	The Highway Loss Data Institute contains news and links to injury, collision, theft loss, state laws, and other related sites.	http://www.carsafety.org/
National Association of Insurance Commissioners	The NAIC lists links to some state workers' insurance sites.	http://www.naic.org/
A.M. Best Company	The A.M. Best Company site provides insurance information and company ratings.	http://www.ambest.com/
Better Business Bureaus	Both national and regional Better Business Bureaus offer information on understanding insurance, including homeowners'.	http://www.bbb.org/ http://www.bosbbb.org/

TENNESSEE
Sounds good to me

Department of Commerce and Insurance

More than a century ago, the state Legislature realized the need for consumer protection and insurance company regulation. The General Assembly created the Bureau of Insurance in 1873, and the state treasurer acted as insurance commissioner. In 1913, a separate Department of Insurance was formed and put under the direction of a commissioner, who became an officer in the governor's Cabinet. To reflect its expanded role in business regulation and consumer protection, the State Insurance Department became the Department of Commerce and Insurance in 1983.

Today the department is close to becoming state government's "one stop" consumer center along with fulfilling its traditional role in business regulations. Nearly every office in this diverse agency has a duty, within its scope of operations, to consumers.

In addition to its regulation of the insurance industry, a separate division regulates securities and another division carries out the responsibility of lending administrative support to 26 regulatory boards and commissions. These divisions also process consumer complaints and take disciplinary action against license holders found guilty of breaking the state laws governing their profession.

The state's Division of Fire Prevention is yet another part of the Department of Commerce and Insurance. Among its other duties in arson investigation and codes enforcement, this division inspects schools, mobile homes, and electrical installations and reviews plans of certain buildings.

Departmental Directory
Consumer Insurance Information
About the Department
Licensee Roster Search
Press Releases & Publications
Online Resources List
Related Web Links
Fire Marshal Kids' Page
Tennessee Laws
Employee Appreciation

39 Security Devices

Learning Objectives

1. State the general nature of contracts of guaranty or suretyship.
2. Identify ways contracts of guaranty and suretyship are discharged.
3. Discuss the rights of the parties in a secured credit sale.
4. Discuss the rights of the seller and buyer in a secured credit sale.

PREVIEW CASE

Yvonne Sanchez defaulted on her auto payments to MBank El Paso. MBank hired two men to repossess the car. They found the car in Sanchez' driveway and hooked it to a tow truck. Sanchez ordered them to leave. When they did not, she jumped into the car, locked the doors, and refused to get out. The men towed the car at high speed to a repossession yard, parked the car, and padlocked the gate to the yard. A Doberman pinscher guard dog roamed loose in the yard. Sanchez remained in the car until rescued by her husband and the police. Did the bank properly repossess the car? How quietly was the repossession made?

This chapter discusses two types of security devices: (1) guaranty and suretyship contracts and (2) secured credit sales.

Guaranty and Suretyship

LO1 Nature of guaranty and suretyship

A contract of guaranty or suretyship is an agreement whereby one party promises to be responsible for the debt, default, or obligation of another. Such contracts generally arise when one person assumes responsibility for the extension of credit to another, as in buying merchandise on credit or in borrowing money from a bank.

A person entrusted with the money of another, such as a cashier, a bank teller, or a county treasurer, may be required to have someone guarantee the faithful performance of the duties. This contract of suretyship is commonly referred to as a **fidelity bond**.

Fidelity Bond
Suretyship for someone who handles another's money

Bonding Company
Paid surety

In recent years **bonding companies** have taken over most of the business of guaranteeing the employer against losses caused by the dishonesty of employees. These bonding companies are paid sureties, which means they receive money for entering into the suretyship. The bonding company's obligation arises from its written contract with the employer. This contract of indemnity sets out in detail the conditions under which the surety will be liable.

PARTIES

Guarantor or Surety
Party who agrees to be responsible for obligation of another

Creditor
Party who receives guaranty

Principal
Party primarily liable

A contract of guaranty or of suretyship involves three parties. The party who undertakes to be responsible for another is the **guarantor**, or the **surety**; the party to whom the guaranty is given is the **creditor**; and the party who has primary liability is the principal debtor, or simply the **principal**. Because these three parties are distinct and have differing rights and obligations it is important to identify exactly what role a party has in a guaranty or suretyship arrangement.

Facts: As the trustees of Hopping Brook Trust, James Flett and John Arno signed a promissory note for $4 million. A mortgage on land owned by the trust secured payment of the note. Flett and Arno each also signed a personal guaranty of the trust's debt up to $1 million. The guaranties included a clear waiver of "presentment and demand for payment and protest of nonpayment." The trust defaulted on the note and it was taken over by the FDIC. The FDIC foreclosed on the mortgage without any notice to Flett and Arno. When the mortgage sale did not pay off the note, the FDIC sued Flett and Arno for the deficiency. They alleged that they were not really guarantors but the primary obligors or principals and as such the FDIC had to give them notice of the foreclosure.

Outcome: The court stated that the waivers in the guaranties would be unnecessary if Flett and Arno were the principals instead of guarantors; therefore, they were guarantors not principals and the FDIC did not have to give them notice of foreclosure.

DISTINCTIONS

The words *surety* and *guarantor* are often used interchangeably, and they have many similarities. Some states have abolished any distinction between them. However, in other states their legal usages differ. In a contract of suretyship, the surety has liability coextensive with that of the principal debtor. The surety has direct and primary responsibility for the debt or obligation just like the primary debtor. The surety's obligation, then, is identical with the debtor's.

A guarantor's obligation is secondary to that of the principal debtor. As a secondary obligation, the guaranty agreement may not even be executed at the same time or in the same instrument as the principal obligation. The guarantor's promise to pay comes into effect only in the event the principal defaults. The guarantor's obligation does not arise simultaneously with the principal's. The obligation depends upon the happening of another event, namely, the failure of the principal to pay.

For the most part, the law of suretyship applies with equal force to both paid sureties and accommodation sureties. A bail bondsman is a paid surety. An accommodation surety agrees to be a surety as a favor to the principal. A parent who cosigns a note for a teenager constitutes an accommodation surety. In some instances the contract of a paid surety will be interpreted strictly. Thus, in the case of acts claimed to discharge the surety, courts sometimes require paid sureties to prove that they have actually been harmed by the conduct of the principal before allowing recovery.

IMPORTANCE OF MAKING A DISTINCTION

In states that recognize a difference between guarantors and sureties, the distinctions involve three aspects:

1 Form
2 Notice of default
3 Remedy

Form. All the essential elements of a contract must be present in both contracts of guaranty and contracts of suretyship. However, a contract of guaranty must be in writing (see Illustration 39-1), whereas most contracts of suretyship may normally be oral.

The Uniform Commercial Code provides: "The promise to answer for the debt, default, or obligation of another must be in writing and be signed by the party to be charged or by his authorized agent." This provision should apply to a promise that creates a secondary obligation, which means an obligation of guaranty, not to a promise that creates a primary obligation or suretyship.

WATERS, MELLEN AND COMPANY
900 West Lake Avenue
Cincinnati, Ohio 45227

May 16, 20-

Ms. Norma Rae
201 E. Fifth Street
Campton, KY 41301

Dear Ms. Rae

In consideration of the letting of the premises located at 861 South Street, this city, to Mr. William H. Prost for a period of two years from date, I hereby guarantee the punctual payment of the rent and the faithful performance of the covenants of the lease.

Very truly yours

Orvinne L. Meyer
Vice-President, Personnel

Illustration 39-1
A Letter of Guaranty

Notice of Default. As parties primarily liable for the debt, a creditor need not notify sureties if the principal defaults. On the other hand, the creditor must notifiy guarantors. In some states, failure to give notice does not of itself discharge the guarantyship. A guarantor damaged by the failure to receive notice may offset the amount of the damage against the claim of the creditor.

Remedy. In the case of suretyship, the surety assumes an original obligation. The surety must pay. Sureties have liability as fully and under the same conditions as if the debt were theirs from the beginning. The rule is different in many contracts of guaranty. In a conditional guaranty, the guarantor has liability only if the other party cannot pay.

Arnold writes, "Let Brewer have a suit; if he cannot pay you, I will." This guaranty depends upon Brewer's ability to pay. Therefore, the seller must make all reasonable efforts to collect from Brewer before collecting from Arnold. If Arnold had written, "Let Brewer have this suit, and I will pay you," an original obligation would have been created for which Arnold would have been personally liable. Therefore, Arnold would be deemed a surety if the understanding was that Arnold was to pay for the suit.

RIGHTS OF THE SURETY AND THE GUARANTOR

A guarantor and a surety have the following rights:

1. Indemnity
2. Subrogation
3. Contribution
4. Exoneration

Indemnity
Right of guarantor to be reimbursed by principal

Indemnity. A guarantor or surety who pays the debt or the obligation of the principal has the right to be reimbursed by the principal, known as the right of **indemnity**. The guarantor or the surety may be induced to pay the debt when it becomes due to avoid the accumulation of interest and other costs on the debt.

Subrogation. When the guarantor or the surety pays the debt of the principal, the law automatically assigns the claim of the creditor to the guarantor or surety. The payment also entitles the guarantor or surety to all property, liens, or securities that were held by the creditor to secure the payment of the debt. This right of subrogation does not arise until the creditor has been paid in full, but it does arise if the surety or the guarantor has paid a part of the debt and the principal has paid the remainder.

Facts: Raymond Fulton guaranteed a lease of J. D. Edge's to South Oak Cliff State Bank. When Edge defaulted on the lease, the bank sued Edge. Fulton gave the bank his note in payment of his guaranty. Without Fulton's knowledge, the bank dismissed its suit against Edge with prejudice (meaning the same suit could not be refiled). The bank sued Fulton on his note. Fulton said he should not have to pay because when the bank dismissed the suit against Edge with prejudice, it made it impossible for Fulton to sue Edge on the transaction.

Outcome: The court held that once Fulton paid his guaranty, he acquired subrogation rights. The subrogation rights arose from payment of the guaranty, not from the lease on which the bank had sued Edge. Fulton could still sue Edge.

Coguarantors or Cosureties
Two or more people jointly liable for another's obligation

Contribution
Right of coguarantor to recover excess of proportionate share of debt from other coguarantor(s)

Exoneration
Guarantor's right to have creditor compel payment of debt

Contribution. Two or more persons jointly liable for the debt, default, or obligation of a certain person are **coguarantors** or **cosureties**. Guarantors or sureties who have paid more than their proportionate share of the debt are entitled to recover from the other guarantors or sureties the amount in excess of their pro rata share of the loss. This is the right of **contribution**. It does not arise until the surety or the guarantor has paid the debts of the principal in full or has otherwise settled the debt.

Exoneration. A surety or guarantor may call upon the creditor to proceed to compel the payment of the debt; otherwise the surety or guarantor will be released. This is the right of **exoneration**. The creditor may delay in pressing the debtor to pay because of the security of the suretyship. In cases where the debtor can pay, failure of the creditor to compel payment when due releases the surety. The surety then has no uncertainty concerning potential liability.

DISCHARGE OF A SURETY OR A GUARANTOR

LO2
Discharge of guaranty or suretyship

The usual methods of discharging any obligation, including performance, voluntary agreement, and bankruptcy of the surety or guarantor, discharge both a surety and a guarantor. However, some additional acts that will discharge the surety or the guarantor include:

1 Extension of time
2 Alteration of the terms of the contract
3 Loss or return of collateral by the creditor

Extension of Time. If the creditor extends the time of the debt without the consent of the surety or the guarantor and for a consideration, the surety or the guarantor is discharged from further liability.

Alteration of the Terms of the Contract. A material alteration of the contract by the creditor without the surety's or guarantor's consent discharges the surety or guarantor. In most states the change must be prejudicial to the surety or the guarantor. A reduction in the interest rate has been held not to discharge the surety, whereas a change in the place of payment has been held to be an act justifying a discharge of the surety. A material change in a contract constitutes substituting a new contract for the old. The surety guaranteed the payment of the old contract, not the new one.

Facts: Dee Keip and Fina Shubert guaranteed a lease entered into by their closely held corporation with Elva Mangold, the owner of the leased property. The corporation and Mangold renewed the lease and added a provision that gave Mangold an unqualified right to end the lease if the corporation-tenant made an unauthorized commercial use of the property. When the corporation defaulted on the renewed lease Mangold sued Keip and Shubert under their guaranty.

Outcome: The court said that adding the provision in the renewed lease was a material change and released the guarantors.

Loss or Return of Collateral by the Creditor. If the creditor through negligence loses or damages collateral security given to secure the debt, a surety or a guarantor is discharged. The return of any collateral security to the debtor also discharges a surety or guarantor. Collateral must be held for the benefit of the surety until the debtor pays the debt in full.

Secured Credit Sales

LO3

Rights in secured credit sales

Secured Credit Sale
Sale in which seller retains right to repossess goods upon default

When someone other than the buyer finances goods (they purchase on credit), a convenient way to protect creditors from loss is to allow them to have an interest in the goods. When sellers retain the right to repossess the items sold if the buyers breach the sales contracts, the transactions are **secured credit sales**. In such cases, the buyers obtain possession of the items, and the risk of loss passes to them. Article 9 of the UCC governs secured credit sales. A security interest cannot attach or become enforceable until the buyer and seller agree it shall attach, the seller gives value, and the buyer has the right to possess or use the item.

SECURITY AGREEMENT

Security Agreement
Written agreement signed by buyer that creditor has a security interest in collateral

A creditor may not enforce a security interest unless the buyer has signed a security agreement. The **security agreement** is a written agreement, signed by the buyer, that describes the collateral, or the item sold, and usually contains the terms of payment and names of the parties.

RIGHTS OF THE SELLER

LO4

Rights of buyer and seller

The rights of the seller, referred to as the secured party under the security agreement, may be transferred to a third person by assignment. In any sale, the buyer may have claims or defenses against the seller. In the case of consumer sales, the Federal Trade Commission requires the seller to include in the agreement a notice that any holder of the agreement is subject to all claims and defenses that the buyer could assert against the seller. Thus, an assignee would be subject to any claims or defenses. This protection for the buyer applies only to consumer transactions.

Facts: David Ziluck filled out and signed a Radio Shack credit card application. The space for his signature appeared on the front below the statement: "I have read the Radio Shack Credit Account and Security Agreement. . . . I agree to the terms of the Agreement and acknowledge receipt of a copy. . . ." The back of the application had the title, "Radio Shack Credit Account and Security Agreement." Radio Shack issued Ziluck a credit card, which he used to buy several items. Ziluck later filed for bankruptcy and Radio Shack asked for possession of these items claiming a security interest in them. The bankruptcy court found that Ziluck had not "signed" the security agreement.

Outcome: The appellate court said signing the front underneath language indicating agreement to the terms of the security agreement constituted a signature by Ziluck.

RIGHTS OF THE BUYER

The buyer, also called the debtor, has the right to transfer the collateral and require a determination of the amount owed.

Transfer of Collateral. Even though there is a security interest in the collateral, the debtor may transfer the collateral to others. Such a transfer will usually be subject to the security interest.

Determination of Amount Owed. A buyer who wishes may sign a statement indicating the amount of unpaid indebtedness believed to be owed as of a specified date and send it to the seller with the request that the statement be approved or corrected and returned.

PERFECTION OF SECURITY INTEREST

Perfected Security Interest
Seller's right to collateral that is superior to third party's right

When the rights of the seller to the collateral are superior to those of third persons, the seller has a **perfected security interest**. The use to which the buyer puts collateral at the time of perfection of the security interest determines how the creditor perfects a security interest.

Inventory
Articles purchased with intention of reselling or leasing

Equipment
Goods for use in business

Inventory and Equipment. Articles purchased with the intention of reselling or leasing them are called **inventory**. **Equipment** consists of goods used or purchased for use in a business, including farming or a profession. In order to have a perfected security interest in inventory or equipment, the seller must usually file a financing statement in the appropriate public office. However, filing need not be made when the law requires a security interest to be noted on the document of title to the goods, such as in the case of noting a lien on a title to a motor vehicle. Buyers of inventory sold in the regular course of business and for value acquire title free of the security interest. For example, any time a customer goes into a store, buys, and pays for a TV, the customer obtains the TV free of any security interest. Any time an item subject to a security interest is sold at the direction of the secured party, the buyer takes it free of the security interest.

Financing Statement
Writing with signatures and addresses of debtor and secured party and description of collateral

A **financing statement** is a writing signed by the debtor and the secured party that contains the address of the secured party, the mailing address of the debtor, and a statement indicating the types of or describing the collateral. A copy of the security agreement may serve as a financing statement if it contains the required items.

Fixtures
Personal property attached to real estate

Fixtures. Personal property attached to buildings or real estate is called a **fixture**. A creditor perfects a security interest in fixtures by filing the financing statement in the office where a mortgage on the real estate involved would be filed or recorded.

Facts: Pauline Fink bought a mobile home from Palmer Mobile Homes, Inc. Palmer retained a security interest that was assigned to Endicott Trust Company. Endicott filed a financing statement as if the mobile home were personal property. Fink bought real property from Wemco Corp. and gave Wemco a mortgage on the property. A crawl space was dug on the property, footings were installed, a cinder block pillar was cemented to the footings to support the home, a septic tank system was installed, and water and electricity were run to it. The mobile home was delivered in two sections that were then bolted together. A roof cap was put over the joint and was cemented and nailed down. Siding was installed on the ends of the house and nailed over the joint in the two sections. Fink went bankrupt. Endicott claimed a security interest in the home.

Outcome: The court held the home was so annexed to the realty as to become a part of it; therefore the mobile home was a fixture. The financing statement should have been filed in the office where real estate mortgages would be recorded. Endicott's filing was improper, which meant that the security interest was not perfected. Because of this, the rights of Endicott to the collateral were not superior to the rights of third persons.

Consumer Goods
Items purchased for personal, family, or household purposes

Consumer Goods. **Consumer goods** are items used or bought primarily for personal, family, or household purposes. A security interest in consumer goods is perfected as soon as it attaches and without filing in most cases. It is not perfected, however, against a buyer who purchases the item without knowledge of the security interest for value and for the buyer's own personal, family, or household use. The secured party can be protected against such a buyer only by filing a financing statement.

Duration of Filing. Filed financing statements last for five years from their date. However, creditors may file a continuation statement that continues the effectiveness of the filing for five more years. Succeeding continuation statements may be filed, each of which lasts five years.

If a continuation statement is not filed, the effectiveness of a filing statement lapses at the end of five years. The security interest is then unperfected even against a purchaser of the goods before the lapse.

Effect of Default

Under the UCC, the seller has certain rights if the buyer fails to pay according to the terms of the security agreement or otherwise breaches the contract. These rights include repossession and resale. The buyer has the rights to redemption and an accounting.

Repossession. When the buyer has the right to possession of the collateral before making full payment and the buyer breaches the purchase contract, the seller may repossess, or take back, the collateral. If it can be done without a breach of the peace, the repossession may be made without any judicial proceedings. In any case, judicial action may be sought. The seller may retain the collateral in satisfaction of the debt unless the debtor, after being notified, objects.

PREVIEW CASE REVISITED

Facts: Yvonne Sanchez defaulted on her auto payments to MBank El Paso. MBank hired two men to repossess the car. They found the car in Sanchez' driveway and hooked it to a tow truck. Sanchez ordered them to leave. When they did not, she jumped into the car, locked the doors, and refused to get out. The men towed the car at high speed to a repossession yard, parked the car, and padlocked the gate to the yard. A Doberman pinscher guard dog roamed loose in the yard. Sanchez remained in the car until rescued by her husband and the police. Sanchez sued MBank for damages alleging it had not repossessed the car without a breach of the peace.

Outcome: The court agreed.

Resale. After default, the seller may sell the collateral. A public or private sale may be used, and any manner, time, place, and terms may be used as long as the disposition is commercially reasonable and done in good faith. Advance notice of the sale must be given to the debtor unless the goods are perishable. If the buyer has paid 60 percent or more of the cash price of the goods, the seller must resell the goods within 90 days after possession of them unless the buyer, after default, has signed a statement waiving the right to require resale. The purpose of this requirement is to cause a sale before the goods decline in value.

Redemption. At any time prior to the sale or the contracting to sell of the collateral, the buyer may redeem it by paying the amount owed and the expenses reasonably incurred by the seller in retaking and holding the collateral and preparing for the sale. This includes, if provided in the agreement, reasonable attorney's fees and legal expenses.

Accounting. After the sale of the collateral, the creditor must apply payments in the following order: the expenses of retaking and selling the collateral, the amount owed on the security interest, and all amounts owed on any subordinate security interests. The seller must pay any surplus remaining to the buyer. The buyer has liability for any deficiency.

Questions

1 Who are the parties to a contract of guaranty or suretyship?
2 Explain the difference between the liability of a surety and the liability of a guarantor.
3 What difference in form is there between a contract of suretyship and a contract of guaranty?
4 What right does a guarantor have against the principal by virtue of having paid the debt?
5 When does the right of contribution arise?
6 Why would a surety want to exercise the right of exoneration?
7 Why does a material alteration in the terms of the contract by the creditor without the surety's or guarantor's consent discharge the surety or guarantor?
8 What requirements must be met before a security interest can attach and become enforceable?
9 How is a security interest in equipment perfected?
10 What are the requirements for a sale of collateral by a seller after default?

Case Problems

LO1 1 George Bumila agreed to loan Keiser Homes of Maine, Inc. $300,000. Keiser executed a $300,000 promissory note which permitted assignment to Bumila and Bumila gave Keiser two checks. One check was a bank check and the other was from Pine Hill Estates Pension Plan and Trust. Edward Luck, Dorothy Luck, Robert Cross, Samuel Deegan, and Hanya Kandlis all shareholders and directors of Keiser Homes signed guaranties to George Bumila of all obligations of Keiser created by the $300,000 note. When Keiser's first payment was made to Bumila, he returned the check and asked that subsequent checks be made out to Pine Hill. Keiser's president executed a note payable to Pine Hill and Bumila returned the first note to Keiser. When Keiser later defaulted on the note Bumila sued the guarantors who alleged a material alteration of the obligation which discharged them. Was there a material alteration?

LO3 2 Vinod and Surekha Vashi leased a telephone system. The lease created a security interest. When the Vashis defaulted, General Electric Capital Corporation (GECC), the secured party, took possession of the equipment. GECC notified the Vashis it would sell the collateral, but GECC could not sell it because it was worthless. GECC obtained a deficiency judgment that gave the Vashis no credit for the equipment kept by GECC. The Vashis argued a court could not enter a deficiency judgment if GECC kept the collateral. Should the appellate court affirm the deficiency judgment?

LO3 3 Farmers & Merchants Bank of Long Beach loaned $35,400 to Frank Hoffer to finance his tractor and trailer. Hoffer gave Farmers a security interest in them, and Farmers gave him the titles, which had no binding notation of the liens. The vehicles were then registered with no notation of the liens on the titles. Hoffer filed a petition under Chapter 11 of the Bankruptcy Code, and Farmers sought to foreclose its security

Internet Resources for Business Law

Name	Resources	Web Address
Legal Information Institute (LII)—Bankruptcy Law Materials	The Legal Information Institute (LII), maintained by Cornell Law School, provides an overview of bankruptcy law, including the Federal Bankruptcy Code; rules in the Code of Federal Regulations (C.F.R.); state and federal court decisions; and state civil codes.	http://www.law.cornell.edu/topics/bankruptcy.html
11 USC Chapter 13—Adjustment of Debts of an Individual with Regular Income	LII provides Chapter 13, Adjustment of Debts of an Individual with Regular Income.	http://www.law.cornell.edu/uscode/11/ch13.html
Bankruptcy Act	The U.S. Congress provides the latest Bankruptcy Reform Act.	http://thomas.loc.gov/cgi-bin/query/z?c103:H.R.5116:
ABI World (American Bankruptcy Institute)	ABI World provides daily bankruptcy headlines, legislative news, and materials from the National Bankruptcy Review Commission (NBRC).	http://www.abiworld.org/
InterNet Bankruptcy Library	InterNet Bankruptcy Library, maintained by Bankruptcy Creditors' Service, Inc., provides bankruptcy data, news, and information.	http://bankrupt.com/
National Association of Consumer Bankruptcy Attorneys (NACBA)	NACBA, a national organization of over 600 attorneys, provides consumer bankruptcy information.	http://nacba.com/
11 USC Chapter 11—Reorganization	The Legal Information Institute (LII), maintained by Cornell Law School, provides a hypertext and searchable version of Chapter 11, Reorganization, of the U.S. Code.	http://www.law.cornell.edu/uscode/11/ch11.html
Bankruptcy Alternatives	Bankruptcy Alternatives, maintained by Mory Brenner, Attorney at Law, provides questions and answers about alternatives to bankruptcy.	http://www.debtworkout.com/

Part 8 Summary Cases

Risk-Bearing Devices

1 Robert McCloskey obtained a life insurance policy from New York Life Insurance Company. The medical questionnaire asked, "Have you ever consulted a physician or . . . had or been treated for . . . heart attack . . . or any other disorder of the heart or blood vessels . . . or diabetes?" McCloskey answered no. He in fact had diabetes and had had a heart attack. A paramedical examination had revealed he was overweight, so the policy New York issued required a higher premium than was standard. Within a month of the issuance of the policy, McCloskey died. New York refused to pay on the policy, alleging misrepresentation. Was there misrepresentation? *[McCloskey v. New York Life Insurance Company*, 436 A.2d 690 (Pa. Super. Ct.)]

2 Evelyn Vlastos carried a fire insurance policy on her building. The policy included a section labeled Endorsement No. 4 that was incorporated into the policy and stated: "Warranted that the third floor is occupied as Janitor's residence." The building was destroyed by fire, and the insurers refused to pay on the policy, charging breach of warranty. Vlastos sued the insurers alleging there was no proof the provision in Endorsement No. 4 was a warranty, implying it was a representation. Which was it, and what difference would it make? [*Vlastos v. Sumitomo Marine & Fire Insurance Company (Europe) Ltd.*, 707 F.2d 775 (3rd Cir.)]

3 Merrimack Mutual Fire Insurance Company issued a fire insurance policy to James and Loree Stewart as owners. There was a mortgage clause requiring payment upon loss to Portland Savings Bank as mortgagee. The clause provided: "the mortgagee . . . shall notify this Company of any change of ownership . . . or increase of hazard. . . ." Portland later foreclosed on the property, and after the Stewarts' redemption period expired, it became the owner. It did not notify Merrimack of the foreclosure and its ownership before there was a fire loss. Merrimack denied coverage because Portland had not notified it of the change in ownership. Was Merrimack liable under the policy? [*Hartford Fire Insurance Company v. Merrimack Mutual Fire Insurance Company*, 457 A.2d 410 (Me.)]

4 B. R. Justice owned a pickup truck that was insured by Government Employees Insurance Company. He bought a camper for use on the pickup. It was bolted on with chains and tighteners. Justice had an accident, and the pickup and camper were extensively damaged. Government refused to pay for the damage to the camper. The auto insurance policy provided coverage to "the automobile, including its equipment." Justice sued Government. Is Government liable for the damage to the camper? [*Justice v. Government Emp. Ins. Co.*, 597 P.2d 16 (Idaho.)]

5 On August 13, Dennis and Diane Rose borrowed $1,034.10 from Huntington National Bank. In order to obtain this unsecured loan the Roses omitted $2,900 in unsecured loans from the loan application. A month later, having made no payments on the loan, the Roses filed a petition under Chapter 13 of the Bankruptcy Code. Their plan called for them to pay the $220 difference between their monthly income and expenses to the trustee for three years and pay only 10 percent to unsecured creditors. Huntington objected to the plan on the ground of bad faith. Should Huntington recover only 10 percent? [*Matter of Rose*, 40 B.R. 178 (Bankr. S.D. Ohio)]

6 Sheila Kercher sued for dissolution of her marriage, and on November 3, the court issued an order restraining her husband "from transferring . . . or in any way disposing of any property except in the usual course of business or for the necessities of life." He

had a term life insurance policy on which Kercher was the beneficiary and which gave him the right to change the beneficiary. On November 11, he changed the beneficiary to his mother, Helen Tallent, and on December 11, committed suicide. Should Kercher or Tallent receive the proceeds of the life insurance? [*Metropolitan Life Insurance Company v. Tallent*, 445 N.E.2d 990 (Ind.)]

7 Huey Stewart had a homeowner's policy issued by Louisiana Farm Bureau Mutual Insurance Company on his mobile home. After the policy was in force, the original roof of the mobile home leaked, so Stewart nailed boards to the old roof decking, put in insulation, and put a new roof over the insulation. High winds damaged the roof Stewart had built on top of the original mobile home roof. The policy stated it did not cover "awnings, . . . shelters, cabanas, porches, completely enclosed additions, carports, or other structures and equipment . . . not part of the mobile home when purchased new." Farm Bureau denied coverage of the new roof and Stewart sued. Should damage to the new roof be covered? [*Stewart v. Louisiana Farm Bur. Mut. Ins. Co.*, 420 So.2d 1217 (La.App.)]

8 A car driven by James Hilton struck a parked trash truck that extended onto the travel lane of the highway. Two people in the Hilton car received severe head lacerations, and the car was considerably damaged. Joe Blakeney owned the truck and carried insurance with Safeco Insurance Company of America. At the scene, Blakeney saw the damage and injury, was issued a traffic summons, and was told by a police officer to file an accident report within 10 days. Seven weeks later, an attorney for the Hiltons wrote the insurance agent who had written the Safeco policy and advised him of the accident. He prepared an accident report form and sent it to Safeco. Its policy stated: "written notice . . . with respect to the time, place and circumstances . . . and the names and address of the injured and of available witnesses, shall be given by or for the insured to the company . . . as soon as practicable." Blakeney never notified anyone. Safeco denied coverage. Was it liable? [*Liberty Mutual Insurance Company v. Safeco Insurance Company*, 288 S.E.2d 469 (Va.)]

9 Devers Auto Sales financed its inventory with Thrift, Incorporated, which perfected its security interest in the inventory by filing a financing statement with the secretary of state in accordance with Article 9 of the UCC. The statement included a security interest in after-acquired inventory. A.D.E., Inc., agreed to sell three cars to Devers and gave it possession of them but not the titles. Thrift gave Devers the money for the cars, and Devers gave checks to A.D.E., but the checks were dishonored. Thrift took possession of Devers's inventory and demanded the titles from A.D.E. A.D.E. demanded the three cars. Did Thrift have a perfected security interest in the cars? [*Thrift, Inc. v. A.D.E., Inc.*, 454 N.E.2d 878 (Ind. Ct. App.)]

10 Smith sold a cruiser to Seal, who executed a security agreement and a note for $31,000 to the First National Bank of Linn Creek. The bank filed a financing statement. Seal decided not to keep the cruiser and asked Smith to sell it for him. Pieper bought it for $13,000 and his older boat. Smith applied the $13,000 to the note and told the bank it was received from the sale of the cruiser. Seal also told the bank he was going to sell the second boat. Five months later the bank repossessed the cruiser. Pieper sued for recovery of the cruiser. If the secured party has authorized a sale, the buyer obtains title free of any security interest. Was Pieper entitled to the cruiser? [*Pieper v. First National Bank of Linn Creek, Camdenton*, 453 S.W.2d 926 (Mo.)]

Part 9 Real Property

http://www.hud.gov

homes and communities

U.S. DEPARTMENT OF HOUSING AND URBAN DEVELOPMENT

translate | search/index

March 20, 2001

hud news
news releases
initiatives

homes
buying
selling
renting
homeless
home improvements
hud homes
fha refunds
foreclosure
consumer info

communities
your community
volunteering
organizing
what works
economic development

working with hud
grants
other funds
contracts
work online
about hud
hud jobs
local info
complaints

resources
library
handbooks/forms
common questions
most requested pages

tools
webcasts
mailing lists
federal clearinghouses
contact us
help

community news

The Fort Wayne, Indiana Neighborhood Tire Program allows City residents to actively participate in removing tires from their community, while also earning money for their respective neighborhoods. With the creation of the tire collection program, all 227 neighborhood associations within the City now have an outlet for tire disposal. The Allen County Solid Waste District pays for other costs such as the rent of semi-trailers to load, store and haul the tires away. Visit our What Works page.

hud highlights

- Daily message
- National Calendar of Events
- Blueprint for HUD
- HUD SuperNOFA released
- Visit our new Tenants page
- FHA 2001 Loan Limits
- Nominate a Best Practice
- Web Clinics for HUD Partners

at your service

- Learn how to buy a HUD home
- Learn how to apply for public housing and Section 8
- See if HUD owes you a refund on your FHA loan
- Find a HUD-approved lender in your area
- Talk to a housing counselor
- File a housing discrimination complaint
- Learn more about things you can do on HUD's site

Talk with us and others about issues important to you:

- Current discussions
- Suggest your own topic

Citizens
Homebuyers, Senior citizens, Veterans, Kids, Students, People with disabilities, Researchers, Landlords, Tenants, Farmworkers/colonias, Native Americans

Housing Industry
Lenders, Brokers, Housing authorities/tribes, Multifamily industry, Appraisers, Health care facilities providers

Other Partners
Grantees/non-profits, Elected officials, Small businesses, Fair housing, Investors, Auditors/investigators

homes for sale

Find homes for sale from HUD and other federal agencies.

now playing

View the Preventing Childhood Lead Poisoning in Multifamily Housing webcast in HUD's webcast library.

Visit FirstGov.gov

Content updated March 18, 2001

Back to Top

U.S. Department of Housing and Urban Development
451 7th Street S.W., Washington, DC 20410
Telephone: (202) 708-1112 TTY: (202) 708-1455

Privacy Statement

Real property includes not only real estate—land, buildings, and houses—but also wills and trusts. Laws about these issues can be very complex.

Transferring, buying, and selling real property involves the legalities of contracts, mortgages, deeds, titles, and many other factors. Even being a landlord or tenant has legal responsibilities. In addition, the transfer of real property to your heirs can be a complicated matter involving many legal issues, discussed in Chapter 45. If you're curious, CourtTV's Web site contains wills of famous people.

http://www.hud.gov
http://www.courttv.com/legaldocs/newsmakers/wills

41 Nature of Real Property

Learning Objectives

1. Define real property, and explain the rules about vegetation, running water, and fixtures.
2. Name the types of multiple ownership of property.
3. List the estates and other interests in real property.
4. Identify methods of acquisition exclusive to real property.

PREVIEW CASE

Walter Rogers, Ronald Rogers, and their corporation, Rogers Brothers, Inc., won a judgment against Charles Rogers in a federal bankruptcy court for not complying with his fiduciary responsibilities. They then secured a separate judgment on a different ground against Eleanor Rogers, Charles Rogers' wife, in a state trial court. Charles and Eleanor owned real estate as tenants by the entireties, and the judgment creditors asked the court to sell the real estate to satisfy the judgments. What does it mean to be a tenant by the entireties? What are the reasons this type of multiple ownership is used?

LO1 Real property rules

Real Property Land and permanent attachments to land

Real property consists of land, including the actual soil, and all permanent attachments to the land, such as fences, walls, other additions and improvements, timber, and other growing things. It also includes minerals under the soil and the waters upon it.

Distinguishing Real Property

Through court interpretations we have accumulated a definite set of rules to guide us in identifying real property and distinguishing it from personal property. The most important of these rules pertain to the following specific items of property:

1 Vegetation—trees and perennial crops
2 Waters—rivers and streams
3 Fixtures

TREES AND PERENNIAL CROPS

Vegetation may be real or personal property. Trees growing on the land, orchards, vineyards, and perennial crops, such as clovers, grasses, and others not planted annually and cultivated, are classed as real property until severed from the land. Annual crops and severed vegetation are personal property. When a person sells land, questions sometimes arise as to whether or not a particular item belongs to the land or constitutes personal property. The parties should agree before completing the sale just how to classify the item.

RIVERS AND STREAMS

If a nonnavigable river flows through property, the person who owns the property owns the riverbed but not the water that flows over the bed. The water cannot be impounded or diverted to the property owner's own use in such a way as to deprive any neighbors of its use. If the river or the stream forms the boundary line, then the owner on each side of the river owns the land to the middle of the riverbed.

In most states where navigable rivers form the boundary, the owner of the adjoining land owns the land only to the low-water mark.

FIXTURES

Personal property attached to land or a building that becomes a part of it is known as a **fixture**. To determine whether or not personal property has become real estate, one or more of the following rules may be applied:

Fixture
Personal property so securely attached to real estate that it becomes part of the real estate

1 How securely is it attached? If the personal property has become a part of the real estate and lost its identity, such as the boards or bricks making up a house wall, it constitutes a fixture. If it is so securely attached that it cannot be removed without damaging the real property to which it is attached, such as windows or light switches, then it also ceases to be personal property.
2 What was the intention of the one installing the personal property? No matter what one's intention, the personal property becomes real property if it cannot be removed

Facts: John Taylor bought a sewage treatment system that was manufactured by Multi-Flo, Inc. It was installed at Taylor's residence in August. In October he began to have problems with the system. Over the next three years, service and repairs were made by three different companies, and a few months later Taylor sued Multi-Flo, claiming the system was defective and had been since installation. In installing it, a hole was dug and the base leveled with sand. The unit was put into the hole and leveled. The inlet and outlet lines were hooked up and the wiring system installed from the aerator to the alarm box. Backfill was placed around the system.

Outcome: The court held that where the product has become a fixture, as here, the two-year statute of limitations for personal property does not apply.

without damaging the property. But, if it is loosely attached and the person installing the fixture indicates the intention to make the fixture real property, then this intention controls. Refrigerators have been held to be real property when apartments were rented unfurnished but contained refrigerators. In determining intention, courts frequently consider the purpose of the attachment and who did the attaching.

a. What is the purpose of attachment? The purpose for which the fixture is to be used may show the intention of the one annexing it.
b. Who attached the item? If the owner of a building installs personal property to the building, this usually indicates the intention to make it a permanent addition to the real property. If a tenant makes the same improvements, the court presumes that the tenant intended to keep the fixture as personal property unless a contrary intention can be shown.

Multiple Ownership

LO2
Multiple property ownership

One person can own property, or it can be owned by more than one person. When more than one person owns land, each person has the right to use and possess it. The most common ways real property can be owned by more than one person include:

1 Tenancy in common
2 Joint tenancy
3 Tenancy by the entirety
4 Community property

TENANCY IN COMMON

Tenancy in Common
Multiple ownership in which, at death, one owner's share passes as will directs or to heirs

A **tenancy in common** occurs when two or more persons own property and when one dies, that owner's interest in the property passes to a person named in the deceased's will or, if no will exists, to the deceased's heirs. In this type of ownership, the other owner or owners have no automatic right to the deceased's share of the property. Each owner determines who gets the share of the property at his or her death. A tenant in common has the right not only to determine who becomes the owner of the fractional share upon death but also to convey the property while alive. The property may be given away or sold. The new owner then becomes a tenant in common with the remaining owner or owners.

Facts: Theodore Beck and Harold Burbach owned a tract of land as tenants in common. Burbach transferred his interest to his wife, Bridgett Burbach. Later Sussex County Municipal Utilities Authority (SCMUA) secured a default judgment against Harold and Bridgett. SCMUA directed the sheriff to sell Bridgett's interest in the tract. While notice of the sale was sent to Bridgett and Harold, none was sent to Beck and SCMUA bought the property at the sale for a small sum. When Beck found out about the sale he notified SCMUA of his ownership interest and alleged the sale was void because the law required all owners of record to be notified and he had not been.

Outcome: The court held that since the title of each tenant in common is subject to the possessory right to the whole property of every other cotenant, each tenant in common is a record owner of the property.

The owners of property held as a tenancy in common each own an undivided fractional share of the property. For example, if two people equally own a piece of land, each tenant owns an undivided one-half interest in the land. Three people who own land equally each own an undivided one-third interest in the land. This means they do not own a specific portion of the land, but own a one-third interest in the entire piece of land. They thus have an interest in the entire property, but only to the extent of their percentage interest.

The property does not have to be owned equally. Two people could own a piece of property as tenants in common, and one could own a one-third interest and the other could own a two-thirds interest.

When more than one person takes title to property, the law presumes they hold the property as tenants in common. Thus when the type of ownership is not clearly spelled out, it will be held a tenancy in common.

JOINT TENANCY

Joint Tenancy
Multiple ownership in which, at death of one, that share passes to remaining owners

Right of Survivorship
Automatic ownership of property by survivors

A **joint tenancy** exists when two or more persons own property and upon the death of one, the remaining owners own the entire property free of any interest of the deceased. This means that a joint owner does not have the power to determine who owns the property at death. The remaining joint owner or owners automatically own the entire property. This automatic ownership of the entire property by the surviving owners is called the **right of survivorship**.

As in the case of a tenancy in common, each joint owner owns an undivided interest in the property. No joint owner owns a specific portion of the property.

The law does not favor the creation of a joint tenancy so there must be a clear intention to create one. The language normally used conveys the property "to X and Y as joint tenants with right of survivorship."

Facts: Lou Hill with his daughter, Louanne, executed a new signature card for his bank account at Garfield County Bank. They both signed the card which described the account as a "joint account, with right of survivorship." After Lou died, his son, Phil, alleged the account was part of Lou's estate while Louanne said that by right of survivorship the funds belonged to her.

Outcome: The court said that since the signature card expressly stated the account was a joint tenancy with right of survivorship and both Lou and Louanne had signed it, a joint tenancy had been created. At Lou's death, the account became the sole property of Louanne.

A joint tenancy can be destroyed by one joint tenant selling or giving that tenant's interest to another person. The new owner becomes a tenant in common of the interest conveyed. If there are three or more joint tenants and one sells his or her interest, the new owner is a tenant in common and the remaining, original joint tenants remain joint tenants as between themselves.

Partition
Suit to divide joint tenancy

A joint tenancy can also be destroyed by one joint tenant suing for a division of the property, called a suit for **partition**. Any joint tenant may sue for partition.

Because a joint tenant's interest in the property disappears at the joint tenant's death, a joint tenant cannot dispose of such an interest by will. If a joint tenant purports to dispose of an interest in jointly held property by will, the will has no effect with regard to such property.

TENANCY BY THE ENTIRETY

Tenancy by the Entirety
Co-ownership by husband and wife with right of survivorship

Similar to a joint tenancy, a **tenancy by the entirety** can exist only between a husband and wife. At the death of one, the other becomes the sole owner of the property. Almost half the states recognize this form of ownership. This type of tenancy is popular with married couples because most want the survivor to have title to the property and to get it without any court proceedings. Many couples also like this type of ownership because the creditors of just the husband or just the wife cannot claim the property. To have a claim against the property, a creditor must be a creditor of both spouses.

PREVIEW CASE REVISITED

Facts: Walter Rogers, Ronald Rogers, and their corporation, Rogers Brothers, Inc., won a judgment against Charles Rogers in a federal bankruptcy court for not complying with his fiduciary responsibilities. They then secured a separate judgment on a different ground against Eleanor Rogers, Charles Rogers' wife, in a state trial court. Charles and Eleanor owned real estate as tenants by the entireties, and the judgment creditors asked the court to sell the real estate to satisfy the judgments.

Outcome: The court stated that the two separate judgments did not impose joint liability on Charles and Eleanor so the judgment creditors could not force the sale of the real estate held as tenants by the entireties.

ETHICAL POINT
Is it really ethical for a married couple to own property in a tenancy by the entirety if the creditors of just one of the spouses cannot claim the property?

A joint tenancy differs in other ways from a tenancy by the entirety. In the case of property held as a tenancy by the entirety, neither the husband nor the wife alone may sell or otherwise dispose of it. Both parties must join in any conveyance of the property. A divorce changes the husband and wife from tenants by the entirety to tenants in common with respect to the property.

COMMUNITY PROPERTY

Community Property
Property acquired during marriage owned separately and equally by both spouses

Nine states, mostly in the west, recognize a form of ownership called **community property**. Community property is a type of ownership reserved for married couples, such that both spouses own a separate and equal share of the property no matter how titled. In these states, unless the parties agree it shall be separate property, property acquired by a husband and wife during their marriage constitutes community property. This is normally important if a couple divorces. In that case, each owns one-half of the

Facts: Robert and Joyce Hilke married and lived in a community property state. They bought a house conveyed to them as joint tenants. They later got a divorce, and before the divorce court determined a division of property, Joyce died. Robert argued that as joint tenants, upon Joyce's death, the house became his sole property.

Outcome: The court said once the divorce was entered, no matter how the house was titled, it constituted community property. Thus Robert owned only a one-half interest in the house.

property acquired during the marriage. Property owned by one spouse prior to the marriage normally is that spouse's separate property and not community property.

Estates in Property

LO3
Interests in property

An **estate** is the nature and extent of interest that a person has in real or personal property. The estate that a person has in property may be:

Estate
Interest in property

1 A fee simple estate
2 A life estate

FEE SIMPLE ESTATE

Fee Simple Estate
Largest, most complete right in property

A **fee simple estate** is the largest and most complete right that one may possess in property. A fee simple owner of property, whether real or personal, has the right to possess the property forever. The owner of a fee simple estate may also sell, lease, or otherwise dispose of the property permanently or temporarily. At the death of such an owner, the property will pass to the persons provided for in the owner's will or, if no will exists, to the heirs at law.

A fee simple owner of land has the right to the surface of the land, the air above the land "all the way to heaven," and the subsoil beneath the surface all the way to the center of the earth. The courts have held, however, that the right to the air above the land is not absolute. An individual cannot prevent an airplane from flying over the land unless it flies too low. It is possible for a person to own the surface of the land only and not the minerals, oil, gas, and other valuable property under the topsoil. A person may also own the soil but not the timber.

Life Estate
Estate for duration of a person's life

LIFE ESTATE

Life Tenant
Person owning property for a lifetime

Reversion
Interest of grantor in life estate that returns to grantor on death of life tenant

Remainder
Interest in life estate that goes to someone other than grantor on death of life tenant

One may have an estate in property by which the property is owned for a lifetime, known as a **life estate**. The person owning for the lifetime is called a **life tenant**. At the death of the life tenant, the title passes as directed by the original owner. The title may revert, or go back, to the grantor, the one who conveyed the life estate to the deceased. In this case, the interest of the grantor is called a **reversion**. Alternatively, the property may go to someone other than the grantor. Such an interest is called a **remainder**.

The life tenant has the exclusive right to use the property and may exclude the holder of the reversion or remainder during the life tenant's lifetime. However, while the life tenant has exclusive use of the property there is a duty on the life tenant to exercise ordinary care to preserve the property and commit no acts that would permanently harm the remainder interest.

Other Interests in Real Property

Although not classified as estates, other interests a person may have in real property exist. Two common ones are easements and licenses.

Easement
An interest in land for nonexclusive or intermittent use

An **easement** is a right to use land, such as a right-of-way across another's land or the use of another's driveway. An easement does not give an exclusive right to possession, but a right of permanent intermittent use. It is classified as an interest in land and created by deed or by adverse use for a period of time set by statute.

Facts: Herman and Jeanette Brown sold Marygaele Jaffe part of a tract of land which did not have direct access to a public road. The deed granted three easements including the use with others of the "main driveway, running in a generally southwesterly direction between South Ferry Road and the . . . residence." Two other easements were defined by measurements to the hundredth of a foot. Later Neda Young and her husband acquired the Brown's tract. They began construction of a large house, swimming pool, and tennis court. Jaffe had given oral consent to the changes including moving the driveway; however, she died before construction began. The Youngs had the driveway moved but it still ran "in a generally southwesterly direction between South Ferry Road and the . . . residence" and overlapped the original drive at some points. Roger Lewis obtained title to Jaffe's property and said he would agree to relocating the driveway if landscaping and other improvements were made. The Youngs agreed to do so when the house was completed. Several months later Lewis demanded that the improvements be made in 10 days or he would move the driveway back at Young's expense despite destruction of the tennis court. Lewis sued to determine his rights concerning the easement.

Outcome: The court held that the indefinite description of the right of way, particularly when two other easements were described so precisely, indicated an intention to allow the landowner to relocate the driveway. Since the relocation did not impair Lewis' use of the driveway the court approved Young's relocation.

License
Right to do certain acts on land

A **license** is a right to do certain acts on the land but not a right to stay in possession of the land. It constitutes a personal right to use property for a specific purpose. A licensor normally may terminate a license at will.

Facts: Monarch Associates owned an apartment complex. It contracted with James Todd giving Todd the exclusive, 10-year right to install and maintain laundry machines in the complex. The contract stated it bound the successors and assigns of the parties. Ronald Krolick and his partners obtained title to the complex. They asked Todd to remove the machines, so he sued for a court order preventing removal of them during the term of the contract with Monarch.

Outcome: The court stated that the contract granted a license, not an easement or lease. As a license, Krolick and his partners could revoke it, which they did.

Acquiring Real Property

LO4
Acquiring real property

Real property may be acquired in many of the same ways as personal property (Chapter 14). However, some ways exist in which real property, but not personal property, can be acquired. These include accretion and adverse possession.

ACCRETION

Accretion
Addition to land by gradual water deposits

Accretion is the addition to land as a result of the gradual deposit by water of solids. It takes place most commonly when a stream, river, lake, or ocean constitutes the boundary line of property. If one's land extends to the low-water mark of a navigable stream, title to some land may be acquired by the river's shifting its flow. This occurs slowly by the deposit of silt. Also, the accretion may be the result of dredging or channeling of the river. If the silt and sand are thrown up on the riverbank, thereby increasing the acreage of the land contiguous to the river, the added acreage belongs to the owner of the contiguous land.

ADVERSE POSSESSION

Adverse Possession Acquiring title to land by occupying it for fixed period

An individual may acquire title to real property by occupying the land owned by another for a period fixed by statute. This is known as **adverse possession** and basically means the original owner may no longer object to a trespass. The statutory period required varies from 7 years in some states to 21 in others. Occupancy must be continuous, open, hostile, visible, actual, and exclusive. It must be apparent enough to give the owner notice of trespass. In colonial times this was known as "squatter's rights." To get title by adverse possession, one had to go one step further than the "squatter" did; this meant the adverse possession had to continue for the statutory period.

Color of Title One's apparent title

Possession for the statutory period then gave clear title to all the land one's color of title described. **Color of title** is a person's apparent title. It usually arises, but does not have to, from some defective document purporting to be a deed or a will or even a gift.

Facts: Marvel L. Gaddis purchased a home. The property was described as a rectangular tract 295 feet north and south by 73 feet 8 inches east and west. On the north portion of the property was a horse barn, flower garden, and orchard all located partially on the property and partially on a 20-foot by 295-foot strip of land to the east. At the eastern edge of the strip was a drop-off to farmland beyond. The strip was never cultivated with the cropland. Gaddis assumed her property extended to the cropland and maintained and used the strip as an integral part of her property. A septic tank for the house was installed on it. Only Gaddis used or had possession of the strip since her purchase. Seventeen years later, a survey revealed that the strip was not part of her rectangular tract. The statutory period for adverse possession was 10 years. Nebraska State Bank, which held a deed to the strip, asked a court to declare it the owner.

Outcome: The court found Gaddis was in actual, continuous, exclusive, notorious, and hostile possession of the strip for 10 years. She owned it by adverse possession.

Questions

1. What items are included in the term *real property?*
2. What is the difference in ownership rights of a person whose property borders on a nonnavigable river and a person whose property borders on a navigable river?
3. May personal property ever become real property?
4. When a tenant in common dies, who becomes the owner of that tenant's share of the property?
5. When property is owned by more than one person, what type of ownership does the law presume they have?
6. a. Which types of multiple ownership of property give the owners the right of survivorship?
   b. What does the right of survivorship mean?
7. When a couple living in a community property state divorce how is their property divided?
8. Explain the difference between a fee simple estate and a life estate?
9. How is an easement created?
10. Who owns the land created by accretion?

Case Problems

LO1 1 Paul and Shelly Higgins owned a house that had an antique wood cook stove resting on a built-in brick platform in the master bedroom. The stove was not connected to the chimney flu and had no stove pipe with which to connect to the chimney. The chimney flu in that room had been blocked with a concrete plug. The Higginses sold the house to Jack Everitt who discovered when he took possession that the stove had been removed. When the Higginses refused to deliver the stove to him he sued alleging it was sold to him with the sale of the house. Was the stove a fixture that was sold with the house?

LO3 2 Claude Stephens conveyed a 110-acre tract used as an equestrian center to Laura Thorn but retained a life estate in a residence located on 5 of the acres. Thorn sued Stephens for access to the life estate area by real estate agents, brokers, and prospective purchasers of the tract. No right of entry was provided by the conveyance. Should Thorn have access to the life estate in order to market the entire tract?

LO2 3 Kohl, Metzger, Spotts, P.A. obtained a judgment against Shelman Morse. Kohl tried to get a court to order that a bank account that Morse and his wife held as tenants by the entireties could be taken to pay off the judgment. The bank signature card specifically designated the account as being held as tenants by the entireties. Shelman signed almost all the checks issued on the account, contributed the funds to it, and Mrs. Morse had a separate bank account. May Kohl obtain the funds in the account?

LO4 4 Some islands were formed as an accretion to the bed of the Missouri River. Continued accretion permanently joined them to the shore. The state of Iowa, as the owner of the bed of the river, claimed the land. As owners of land adjoining a navigable river, Harry Sorensen and other adjoining landowners owned only to the high-water mark. However, once the islands became attached to the shore, they were no longer part of the riverbed and were not necessary for navigation or commerce. The state brought a lawsuit to establish its title to the land. Discuss the rights of the parties to the land.

LO2 5 With her own funds, Nina Zarins purchased a condominium. The deed was made to Zarins and Teranis without mention of joint ownership with right of survivorship. Zarins was the only person who lived in the condominium and she paid all the maintenance, taxes, and utilities. She mortgaged the property and the mortgage show Zarins and Teranis as mortgagors. Teranis filed for bankruptcy and the trustee filed suit to sell the condominium to obtain Teranis' half ownership. Zarins alleged she was to be the sole owner while alive and Teranis was to obtain ownership only after Zarins' death. Is half the value of the condominium available to pay Teranis' debts?

LO4 6 In 1940 Harve Wright and Aitchey Wright each paid $100 down on a $2,000 farm. Harve died two years later and his wife and minor children lived on the farm for six years with Aitchey and his family. Aitchey and his wife, Lorene, farmed the property, paid off the mortgage, made substantial improvements, and paid all the taxes. Aitchey conveyed 8.6 acres to the county and warranted he had the right to sell and transfer the land. He also gave easements for construction purposes. In the 70's Aitchey's siblings had the title investigated, but were afraid to confront Aitchey with the allegation that he and Harve had owned the property in common. After Aitchey died, Lorene asked the court to declare she owned the whole property by adverse possession. Had Aitchey and Lorene possessed the property adversely to Aitchey's siblings?

LO1 7 Key Bank loaned William DiBiase $2,580,000 secured by a mortgage on real property and covering after-acquired fixtures. DiBiase had an inn built on the property and bought 90 heating and air-conditioning units, one for each of the rooms. The units were purchased from Lewiston Bottled Gas Co. (LBG), which retained a security interest in the units. Bolted to the walls, they became part of the walls of the building. Their removal would leave a large hole in the wall of each room. Key Bank foreclosed on the real property, and a court had to determine whether it or LBG had priority over the units. The issue was whether they were fixtures or remained personal property. What were they?

Internet Resources for Business Law

Name	Resources	Web Address
U.S. Department of Housing and Urban Development (HUD)	HUD provides information on real property and planning issues for both consumers and businesses. HUD also provides information on the Fair Housing Act and the Civil Rights Act.	http://www.hud.gov/
HUD USER	HUD USER, PD&R's information source for housing and community development researchers and policy makers, provides federal government reports and information on housing policy and programs, building technology, economic development, urban planning, and other housing-related topics.	http://www.huduser.org/
Legal Information Institute (LII)— Land-Use Law Materials	LII provides an overview of land-use law, links to statutes, federal and state judicial court decisions, and other materials.	http://www.law.cornell.edu/topics/land_use.html
American Bar Association's (ABA) Section of Real Property, Probate and Trust Law	The ABA's Section of Real Property, Probate, and Trust Law provides news, information, and links property.	http://www.abanet.org/rppt/home.html

42 Transfer of Real Property

Learning Objectives

1 Describe the means by which title to real estate is transferred.

2 Explain the provisions normally contained in a deed.

3 Summarize the steps taken to safely and effectively transfer title to real property after a deed is signed.

PREVIEW CASE

I. A. Rosenbaum conveyed land to T. S. McCaskey by quitclaim deed. The deed stated: "The grantor herein is to retain one-half of all oil, gas, and mineral rights in the above described lands. . . ." When this conveyance was made, Rosenbaum owned the surface and one-half of the mineral rights. After Rosenbaum died, his heirs sued to confirm title to the mineral rights. What did this deed convey to McCaskey? What is the impact of a quitclaim deed?

A sale constitutes the most common reason for transferring title to real estate. In the ordinary case, the parties sign a contract of sale, but the title is not transferred until the seller delivers a deed to the buyer. One may, by means of a lease, transfer a leasehold title giving the rights to the use and possession of land for a limited period. The provisions of the deed or the lease determine the extent of the interest transferred.

LO1 Means of transferring real estate

Even when the owner makes a gift of real property, the transfer must be evidenced by a deed. As soon as the owner executes and delivers a deed, title vests fully in the donee. Acceptance by the donee is presumed.

Deeds

Deed
Writing conveying title to real property

A **deed** is a writing, signed by the owner, conveying title to real property. The law sets forth the form that the deed must have, and this form must be observed. The parties to

Grantor
Person conveying property

Grantee
Person receiving title to property

the deed include the **grantor**, or original owner, and the **grantee**, or recipient. The two principal types of deeds are:

1 Quitclaim deeds
2 Warranty deeds

QUITCLAIM DEEDS

Quitclaim Deed
Deed that transfers whatever interest grantor has in property

A **quitclaim deed** is just what the name implies. The grantor gives up whatever interest he or she may have in the real property. However, the grantor makes no warranty that he or she has any claim to the property.

In the absence of a statute or an agreement between the parties requiring a warranty deed, a quitclaim deed may be used in making all conveyances of real property. A quitclaim deed transfers the grantor's full and complete interest as effectively as a warranty deed. When buying real property, however, one does not always want to buy merely the interest that the grantor has. A buyer wants to buy a perfect and complete interest so that the title cannot be questioned by anyone. A quitclaim deed conveys only the interest of the grantor and no more. It contains no warranty that the grantor has good title. In most real estate transactions, therefore, a quitclaim deed cannot be used because the contract will specify that a warranty deed must be delivered.

PREVIEW CASE REVISITED

Facts: I. A. Rosenbaum conveyed land to T. S. McCaskey by quitclaim deed. The deed stated: "The grantor herein is to retain one-half of all oil, gas, and mineral rights in the above described lands. . . ." When this conveyance was made, Rosenbaum owned the surface and one-half of the mineral rights. After Rosenbaum died, his heirs sued to confirm title to the mineral rights.

Outcome: The court stated a quitclaim deed was only a conduit that passed the grantor's interest to the grantee. To find out what interest passed, it is necessary to determine what interest the grantor had to convey and take from it anything reserved in the quitclaim deed. This deed reserved a one-half interest in the mineral rights and conveyed what was left—the surface.

WARRANTY DEED

Warranty Deed
Deed with guarantees

General Warranty Deed
Warrants good title free from all claims

Special Warranty Deed
Warrants grantor has right to convey property

A **warranty deed** not only conveys the grantor's interest in the real property but, in addition, makes certain warranties or guarantees. The exact nature of the warranty or guarantee depends upon whether the deed is a general warranty or a special warranty deed. A **general warranty deed** (see Illustration 42-1) not only warrants that the grantor has good title to the real property but further warrants that the grantee "shall have quiet and peaceable possession, free from all encumbrances, and that the grantor will defend the grantee against all claims and demands from whomsoever made." This warranty, then, warrants that all prior grantors had good title and that no defects exist in any prior grantor's title. The grantee does not have to assume any risks as the new owner of the property.

A **special warranty deed** warrants that the grantor has the right to sell the real property. The grantor makes no warranties of the genuineness of any prior grantor's

WARRANTY DEED

Know All Men by These Presents:

That Donald C. Coson and Millicent M. Coson, his wife
of Butler *County,* Ohio
in consideration of the sum of Forty-five Thousand Dollars ($45,000)
to them *in hand paid by* Eugene F. Acknor, the grantee, the receipt of which is hereby acknowledged,
do hereby **Grant, Bargain, Sell and Convey**
to the said Eugene F. Acknor
h is *heirs*
and assigns forever, the following described **Real Estate** *situated in the* City
of Hamilton *in the County of* Butler *and State of* Ohio
Lot No. 10, Section 14, Range 62, Randall Subdivision, being a portion of the estate of Horace E. Cresswell and Alice B. Cresswell *and all the* **Estate, Right, Title and Interest** *of the said grantors in and to said premises;* **To have and to hold** *the same, with all the privileges and appurtenances thereunto belonging, to said grantee,* his *heirs and assigns forever. And the Said* Donald C. Coson and Millicent M. Coson
do hereby **Covenant and Warrant** *that the title so conveyed is* **Clear, Free and Unencumbered,** *and that* they *will* **Defend** *the same against all lawful claims of all persons whomsoever.*

In Witness Whereof, *the said grantors have hereunto set* their *hands, this* first *day of* December *in the year A.D. two-thousand and —*

Signed and acknowledged in presence of us:

Micheal R. Wiser	Donald C. Coson
Antonia C. Patricelle	*Millicent M. Coson*

State of Ohio, Butler **County, ss-**

On this first *day of* December *A.D. 20* *, before me, a* Notary Public *in and for said County, personally came* Donald C. Coson and Millicent M. Coson
the grantor in the foregoing deed, and acknowledged the signing thereof to be their *voluntary act and deed.*

Witness *my official signature and seal on the day last mentioned.*

NOTARIAL SEAL
STATE OF OHIO

Sarah M. Evans

Sarah M. Evans
Notary Public, State of Ohio
My commission expires June 1, 20–

Illustration 42-1
General Warranty Deed

title. Trustees and sheriffs who sell land at a foreclosure sale use this type of deed. Executors and administrators also use such a deed. These officials should not warrant anything other than that they have the legal right to sell whatever interest the owner has.

When a builder sells a new house, most courts now impose an implied warranty of fitness not found in the deed. The warranty amounts to a promise that the builder designed and constructed the house in a workmanlike manner, suitable for habitation by the buyer.

Provisions in a Deed

LO2
Deed provisions

Unless statutes provide otherwise, a deed usually has the following provisions:

1. Parties
2. Consideration
3. Covenants
4. Description
5. Signature
6. Acknowledgment

PARTIES

The grantor and the grantee must be identified, usually by name, in the deed and the grantee must be a living or legal person. If the grantor is married, the grantor's name and that of a spouse should be written in the deed. If the grantor is unmarried, this fact should be indicated by using the word *single* or the phrase "a single person."

CONSIDERATION

The amount paid to the grantor for the property is the consideration. The payment may be in money or in money's worth. A deed usually includes a statement of the consideration, although the amount specified need not be the actual price paid. Some localities have a practice of indicating a nominal amount, such as one dollar, although a much larger sum was actually paid. The parties state a nominal amount as the consideration to keep the sale price from being a matter of public record.

COVENANTS

Covenant
Promise in a deed

Affirmative Covenant
Promise by grantee to do an act

Negative Covenant
Agreement by grantee not to do an act

A **covenant** is a promise contained in a deed. There may be as many covenants as the grantor and the grantee wish to include. **Affirmative covenants** obligate the grantee to do something, such as agreeing to maintain a driveway used in common with adjoining property. In **negative covenants** the grantee agrees to refrain from doing something. Such covenants frequently appear in deeds for urban residential developments. The more common ones prohibit the grantee from using the property for business purposes and set forth the types of homes that can or cannot be built on the property. Most covenants run with the land, which means they bind all future owners.

Facts: Capitol Housing Corporation (CHC) bought land containing a building from the Harrisburg Redevelopment Authority. The deed incorporated covenants restricting the building to residential private housing for 40 years. The Pennsylvania Higher Education Assistance Agency contracted to buy the property and obtained permission from the city of Harrisburg to rent the second, third, and fourth floors for government offices. A lawsuit ensued.

Outcome: The court held that using three floors of the building for government offices violated the covenants and prohibited the sale to PHEAA.

DESCRIPTION

The property to be conveyed must be correctly described. Any description that will clearly identify the property suffices. Ordinarily, however, the description used in the deed by which the present owner acquired the title should be used if correct. The description may be by lots and blocks if the property is in a city; or it may be by metes and bounds or section, range, and township if the property is in a rural area. If the description is indefinite, the grantor retains title.

Facts: Lake Minnewaska Mountain Houses, Inc. (LMMH) contracted to convey land to the Nature Conservancy. LMMH employed Albin Rekis and allowed him to live in a house located on five acres of the land. LMMH called Rekis to the office to sign some documents, including an agreement providing:

1. LMMH would execute a deed to real property to Rekis. LMMH would record it prior to the conveyance to the Nature Conservancy.
2. Rekis would execute a deed of property to LMMH. It would be recorded after the conveyance to the Nature Conservancy.

The parties executed the deeds. The deed Rekis signed contained no description of the property to be conveyed by the deed. Rekis later discovered that LMMH's contract with the Nature Conservancy excluded the five-acre parcel and stated LMMH agreed to convey that parcel to Rekis. He sued LMMH.

Outcome: The court held that since the deed Rekis signed had no description it was void.

SIGNATURE

The grantor should sign the deed in the place provided for the signature. A married grantor must have the spouse also sign for the purpose of giving up the statutory right of the spouse. In some states a witness or witnesses must attest the signatures. If the grantor cannot sign the deed, an agent, the grantor with assistance, or the grantor making a mark, may execute it as:

Maria Smith		His
Witness of the mark of	Henry	X	Finn
Henry Finn		Mark

ACKNOWLEDGMENT

The statutes normally require that the deed be formally acknowledged before a notary public or other officer authorized to take acknowledgments. The acknowledgment allows the deed to be recorded. After a deed has been recorded, it may be used as evidence in a court without further proof of its authenticity. Recording does not make a deed valid, but it helps give security of the title to the grantee.

Acknowledgment
Declaration grantor has stated execution of instrument is free act

The **acknowledgment** is a declaration made by the properly authorized officer, in the form provided for that purpose, that the grantor has acknowledged signing the instrument as a free act and deed. In some states the grantor must also understand the nature and effect of the deed or be personally known to the acknowledging officer. The officer attests to these facts and affixes an official seal. The certificate provides evidence of these actions.

Delivery

LO3
Steps taken after deed signed

A deed has no effect on the transfer of an interest in real property until it has been delivered. **Delivery** consists of the grantor intending to give up title, possession, and control

Delivery
Giving up possession and control

over the property. So long as the grantor maintains control over the deed and reserves the right to demand its return before delivery of the deed to the grantee, there has been no legal delivery. If the grantor executes a deed and leaves it with an attorney to deliver to the grantee, there has been no delivery until the attorney delivers the deed to the grantee. Since the attorney is the agent of the grantor, the grantor has the right to demand that the agent return the deed. If the grantor, however, delivers the deed to the grantee's attorney or agent, then there has been an effective delivery because releasing control constitutes evidence of intent that title pass. Once the grantor makes delivery, title passes.

Facts: Arthur Lynn made the highest bid for Janna Dodge's real estate at a sheriff's sale. The sheriff executed a deed to the property and delivered the deed to Lynn on April 5. The law gave Dodge one year to redeem the property from the sale. She formally sought to redeem the property on the following March 6.

Outcome: The court held that the sale of the property was effective on the date the deed was delivered, April 5, so Janna had exercised her right to redeem within one year after the sale.

Recording

Statutes in every state require grantees to file their deeds with a public official in the county in which the land lies. Any other instrument affecting title to real property in the county can also be filed. These public records of land transactions give notice of title transfers to all, particularly potential subsequent purchasers.

A deed need not be recorded in order to complete one's title. Title passes upon delivery of the deed. Recording the deed protects the grantee against a second sale by the grantor and against any liens that may attach to the property while still recorded in the grantor's name.

When the recording official receives a deed for recording, the law ordinarily requires that the deed be stamped with the exact date and time the grantee leaves the deed for recording.

Abstract of Title

Abstract of Title
History of real estate

Before one buys real estate, an abstract of title may be prepared. An abstract company normally does this, but an attorney may also do it. The **abstract of title** gives a complete history of the real estate. It also shows whether or not there are any unpaid taxes and assessments, outstanding mortgages, unpaid judgments, or other unsatisfied liens of any type against the property. Once an abstracting company makes the abstract, an attorney normally reads the abstract to see if it reveals any flaws in the title.

Title Insurance

Some defects in the title to real estate cannot be detected by an abstract. Some of the most common of these defects are forgery of signatures in prior conveyances; claims by adverse possession; incompetency to contract by any prior party; fraud; duress; undue influence; defective wills; loss of real property by accretion; and errors by title examiners, tax officials, surveyors, and many other public officials. A title insurance policy can be obtained that will cover these defects. The policy may expressly exclude any possible defects that the insurance company does not wish to be covered by the policy. The insured pays one premium for coverage as long as the property is owned. The policy does not benefit a subsequent purchaser or a mortgagee.

Questions

1 What interest in property does a quitclaim deed convey and how does it differ from a warranty deed?
2 What warranty does a special warranty deed make?
3 Does a deed always recite the actual consideration paid?
4 What is the difference between an affirmative covenant and a negative covenant?
5 What description of property is sufficient in a deed?
6 What is an acknowledgment and why is it necessary?
7 In order to have an effective delivery of a deed must the deed be delivered only to the grantee?
8 a. Is it necessary to record a deed in order to complete one's title to the land?
b. What does recording a deed do?
9 Why must a deed be recorded?
10 What is an abstract of title, and what is its significance when transferring real estate?

Case Problems

LO3 1 Virginia Evans executed a deed to real property to Charlie Evans. Charlie kept a notarized copy of it and Virginia kept the original for safekeeping. Charlie took possession of the property and after Virginia died Charlie told her executor about the deed and conveyance and gave him the copy of the deed. The executor voided the deed and told Charlie the property was not his. Charlie sued the executor alleging that delivery of the deed could be made by the executor of the grantor's estate when the deed is found in the grantor's safe deposit box. Did Virginia's behavior indicate an intent by her to give up title to the property?

LO2 2 Elton and Sonia Hudson owned a 4.11 acre tract of land. A deed from them to Carnes-Miller Gear Co., Inc. describing this tract was recorded. A year later, a deed by the Hudsons to Cossette Furr describing land including the 4.11 acres was recorded. A year after that, a deed by Cossett Furr to Piedmont and Western Investment Corp. describing land including the 4.11 acres was recorded. Piedmont sued Carnes-Miller for a declaration that it owned the 4.11 acres. Piedmont had been issued a corporate charter but the charter had been suspended 6 1/2 years before Furr's conveyance to it. State law provided that a corporation whose charter was not reinstated within five years of its suspension would be automatically dissolved. Carnes-Miller alleged Piedmont was not in existence at the time of the coveyance and could not have taken title to the 4.11 acres. Was the deed to Piedmont effective?

LO1 3 Edmund and Maude Clarke, husband and wife, owned a home. They had one child, Fleur Van Pelt. After Maude died, Edmund married Enid and they lived in the home. Van Pelt and her husband executed a quitclaim deed to Edmund and Enid for the recited purpose of giving up any claim to the property. Edmund died and his will did not specifically mention the property, so Van Pelt asked the court to determine its status. The court had to determine the effect of the quitclaim deed. What had that deed done to the title to the property?

LO3 4 A month after Alice Ramsey purchased a house she became very ill and did not expect to live. She had several children living at home and decided Allen Walters was an appropriate person to maintain her home for her children since she had no relatives. Ramsey executed a deed of the property to Walters and had it recorded even though she did not intend to give the home to Walters. She and her children continued to live in the house and she made all the payments including the taxes. Twenty years later, Robert Johnson got a judgment against Walters as a result of an automobile accident and the sheriff was going to seize the property to pay the judgment. Ramsey, who was still alive, sued to be declared the owner of the property. Had there been a valid delivery of the deed to Walters making him the owner of the property?

LO2 5 William Middleton owned a large tract of land that he conveyed in smaller parcels using deeds containing covenants restricting the land to residential use. The covenants stated they ran with the land. Two deeds, including one to Waldo Leynse, also specifically prohibited commercial logging on the property. Leynse divided his property and conveyed it to a number of people including Lawrence Holmes. Holmes Lumber Co. got approval from the state board of forestry for commercial logging on the property of Lawrence Holmes and others who had obtained their property from Leynse. Other owners of land originally in the Middleton tract filed suit against these landowners to prevent the logging, asking the court to enforce the restrictive covenants in the deeds. Should the court enforce the covenants?

LO1 6 Mary Genola executed an instrument with McHenry Browning by which he agreed to sell her a 6 1/2 acre tract of land. The instrument recited a price for the tract payable in monthly installments and reserved for Browning the right to cancel the contract. A year later, Mary's son, Alton Genola, was married. Two months later Browning executed a contract of sale of the tract to Alton and Leatrice Genola. In the contract Mary Genola renounced any right she had in her contract of sale of the tract. Twenty-six years later, Alton and Leatrice separated and Leatrice sued for a declaration that the tract was part of the property acquired by Alton and her during their marriage. Alton and Mary alleged Mary was the owner of the property because the document between Browning and her was a deed. Had Browning deeded the tract to Mary?

LO3 7 Martha Wisdom executed a deed conveying certain real property to her son, Charles Smith. Wisdom put the deed in an envelope and asked Smith to hide the envelope with other papers in a wall heater in Wisdom's house, which he did. Wisdom had told Smith she had made a deed of the house to him. At a later time when at Wisdom's home, Smith went through the papers and found the deed. After Wisdom died, Smith recorded the deed. Smith's sister, Mildred Cecil, filed a suit to have the deed set aside based on failure of Wisdom, the grantor, to deliver the deed. Should the court find a valid delivery?

Internet Resources for Business Law

Name	Resources	Web Address
Legal Information Institute (LII)—Land-Use Law Materials	LII provides an overview of land-use law, links to statutes, federal and state judicial court decisions, and other materials.	http://www.law.cornell.edu/topics/land_use.html
American Bar Association's (ABA) Section of Real Property, Probate and Trust Law	The ABA's Section of Real Property, Probate, and Trust Law provides news, information, and links property.	http://www.abanet.org/rppt/home.html
The Takings Issue in State Legislatures	The "Takings" Resource Guide, part of the Planning Commissioners Journal's Planning Web, provides articles, news, and analysis concerning eminent domain issues.	http://www.envpoly.org/stateleg/index.htm

43 Real Estate Mortgages

Learning Objectives

1. Define and discuss the effect of a mortgage.
2. List the duties and rights of a mortgagor.
3. Explain the rights of parties upon foreclosure, sale, and assignment of the mortgage.

PREVIEW CASE

Dianna Deppe and her husband, Mark Schaefer, borrowed $55,000 from Mark's parents to buy their home. They signed a note for $55,000 and orally promised to execute a mortgage, but made only one payment on the note. Several years later they were divorced and Dianna was given "all right, title, and interest, free and clear" of Mark to the home. The court ordered Dianna to take responsibility for all the debt on the home. A year later Dianna filed for bankruptcy. Under state law the full value of her home was exempt from payment of her debts. The parents sued her alleging they held a mortgage on the home. Did they? What form must a mortgage be in?

LO1
Effect of mortgage

Mortgage
Interest in real estate given to secure debt

Mortgagor
Person who gives mortgage

Mortgagee
Person who holds mortgage

A **mortgage** is an interest in real estate given to secure the payment of a debt. The mortgage does not constitute the debt itself but the security for the debt. If the debt is not paid the property may be sold to pay the debt. Land or any interest in land may be mortgaged. Land may be mortgaged separately from the improvements, or the improvements may be mortgaged apart from the land. A person who gives a mortgage as a security for a debt is a **mortgagor**. A person who holds a mortgage as security for a debt is a **mortgagee**.

The mortgagor normally retains possession of the property. In order for the mortgagee to obtain the benefit of the security, the mortgagee must take possession of the premises upon default or sell the mortgaged property at a foreclosure sale. In some states, the mortgagee may not take possession of the property upon default but may obtain the appointment of a receiver to collect the rents and income. If the sale of the property brings more than the debt and the costs, the mortgagor must be paid the balance.

The Mortgage Contract

A mortgage must be in writing. The contract, as a rule, must have the same form as a deed, which means it must be acknowledged. The mortgage, like all other contracts, sets forth the rights and the duties of the contracting parties (see Illustration 43-1). As a type of contract, mortgages are interpreted according to contract law rule.

PREVIEW CASE REVISITED

Facts: Dianna Deppe and her husband, Mark Schaefer, borrowed $55,000 from Mark's parents to buy their home. They signed a note for $55,000 and orally promised to execute a mortgage, but made only one payment on the note. Several years later they were divorced and Dianna was given "all right, title, and interest, free and clear" of Mark to the home. The court ordered Dianna to take responsibility for all the debt on the home. A year later Dianna filed for bankruptcy. Under state law the full value of her home was exempt from payment of her debts. The parents sued her alleging they held a mortgage on the home.

Outcome: The court held that since Dianna and Mark had only made an oral promise to execute a mortgage and had not executed a written document there could be no mortgage.

A mortgagor normally gives a mortgage to raise money for the purchase price of real estate, but it may be given for other reasons. One may borrow money for any reason and secure the loan by a mortgage. One may assume a contingent liability for another, such as becoming a surety, and receive a mortgage as security.

Lien
Encumbrance or claim against property

The effect of a mortgage is to be a lien against the mortgaged property. A **lien** is an encumbrance or claim against property. The lien of the mortgage attaches to the property described in the mortgage. A mortgage generally also provides that the lien attaches to additions thereafter made to the described property; for example, the lien of the mortgage attaches to personal property, which thereafter becomes a fixture. A clause purporting to make the security clause of a mortgage cover future debts will be valid if the parties intended it to cover future debts.

Recording

Depending upon the law of the state in which the land lies, the mortgage gives the mortgagee either a lien on the land or title to the land. The mortgagor's payment of the debt divests or destroys this title or lien. Recording the mortgage protects the mortgagee against subsequent creditors, since the public record normally constitutes notice to the whole world as to the mortgagee's rights. There may be both a first mortgage and subsequent mortgages. The mortgage recorded first normally has preference. This is

MORTGAGE

WITH POWER OF SALE (Realty)

KNOW ALL MEN BY THESE PRESENTS:

THAT Walter A. Righetti and Susan L. Righetti husband and wife, GRANTORS, for and in consideration of the sum of One Dollar ($1.00), to GRANTORS in hand paid, the receipt of which is hereby acknowledged, and in consideration of the premises hereinafter set forth, do hereby grant, bargain, sell and convey unto Third National Bank of Russellville, GRANTEE, (Whether one or more) and unto GRANTEE'S ~~heirs~~ (Successors) and assigns forever, the following property, situated in Pope County, Arkansas:

Lot 37 in GREENE HEIGHTS SUBDIVISION

TO HAVE AND TO HOLD the same unto the said GRANTEE, and unto GRANTEE's ~~heirs~~ (successors) and assigns forever, with all appurtenances thereunto belonging; and all rents, income, and profits therefrom after any default herein.

We ~~(I)~~ hereby covenant with the said GRANTEE, GRANTEE's ~~heirs~~ (successors) and assigns, that said lands are free and clear of all encumbrances and liens, and will forever warrant and defend the title to said property against all lawful claims. And, we, GRANTORS, Walter A. Righetti and Susan L. Righetti, for the consideration aforesaid do hereby release unto the said GRANTEE and unto GRANTEE's ~~heirs~~ (successors) and assigns forever, all our rights and possibility of dower, curtesy and homestead in and to the said lands.

The sale is on the condition, that whereas, GRANTORS are justly indebted unto said GRANTEE in the sum of Sixty Thousand and 00/100 Dollars ($ 60,000.00), evidenced by their promissory note dated October 17, 20–, in the sum of $ 60,000.00 bearing interest from date until due at the rate of 10 % per annum and thereafter until paid at the rate of 10 % per annum, payable as follows: $ 545 per month, due and payable on the first day of the month, beginning November 1, 20– and continuing for 25 years.

This mortgage shall also be security for any other indebtedness of whatsoever kind that the GRANTEE or the holders or owners of this mortgage may hold against GRANTORS by reason of future advances made hereunder, by purchase or otherwise, to the time of the satisfaction of this mortgage.

In the event of default of payment of any part of said sum, with interest, or upon failure of GRANTORS to perform the agreements contained herein, the GRANTEE, GRANTEE's ~~heirs~~ (successors) and assigns, shall have the right to declare the entire debt to due and payable; and

GRANTORS hereby covenant that they will keep all improvements insured against fire, with all other full coverage insurance, loss payable clause to holder and owner of this mortgage; that said improvements will be kept in a good state of repair, and waste will neither be permitted nor committed; that all taxes of whatever nature, as well as assessments for improvements will be paid when due, and if not paid GRANTEE may pay same and shall have a prior lien upon said property for repayment, with interest at the rate of 10% per annum; now,

THEREFORE, if GRANTORS shall pay all indebtedness secured hereby, with interest, at the times and in the manner aforesaid, and perform the agreements herein contained, then this conveyance shall be void. In case of nonpayment or failure to perform the agreements herein contained, the said GRANTEE, GRANTEE's ~~heirs~~ (successors) and assigns, shall have the right and power to take possession of the property herein conveyed and expel any occupant therefrom without process of law; to collect rents and profits and apply same on unpaid indebtedness; and with or without possession to sell said property at public sale, to the highest bidder for cash, (*or* ....), at the county courthouse of Pope County, Arkansas, public notice of the time, terms and place of sale having first been given twenty days by advertising in some newspaper published in said County, by at least three insertions, or by notices posted in five public places in the County, at which sale any of the parties hereto, their heirs (successors), or assigns may bid and purchase as any third person might do; and GRANTORS hereby authorize the said GRANTEE, GRANTEE's ~~heirs~~ (successors), or assigns to convey said property to anyone purchasing at said sale, and to convey an absolute title thereto, and the recitals of such conveyance shall be taken as *prima facie* true. The proceeds of said sale shall be applied, first to the payment of all costs and expenses attending said sale; second to the payment of all indebtedness secured hereby, with interest; and the remainder, if any, shall be paid to said GRANTORS. GRANTORS hereby waive any and all rights of appraisement, sale, redemption, and homestead under the laws of the State of Arkansas, and especially under the Act approved May 8, 1899, and acts amendatory thereof.

WITNESS our hand s and seal s this 17th day of October, 20–

Walter A. Righetti (seal)

Susan L. Righetti (seal)

(ACKNOWLEDGMENT BEFORE NOTARY FOLLOWS)

Illustration 43-1
Mortgage Contract

not true when actual notice of a prior mortgage exists. However, a purchase money mortgage has preference over other claims arising through the mortgagor. The mortgage is also recorded to notify subsequent purchasers that as much of the purchase price as is necessary to pay off the mortgage must be paid to the mortgagee. Recording must be proper, otherwise the purpose of the mortgagee providing notice to others cannot be accomplished.

Facts: Burl Brunson borrowed $50,000 from Howard Savings Bank securing the loan by a mortgage on real estate. This mortgage was properly recorded but not properly indexed. (The index is the alphabetical listing of the names of the mortgagors.) Two years later, Brunson conveyed the property by deed to Jesus and Celeste Ijalba, and the Ijalbas executed a mortgage on the property to Chrysler First Financial Services Corp. This mortgage was properly recorded and indexed. Chicago Title Insurance Co. conducted a thorough title search and, finding no mortgage under Brunson's name, issued a title insurance policy on the property to Chrysler. Six months later, Howard filed a foreclosure suit against Chrysler and Ijalba claiming its mortgage had priority.

Outcome: The court said the law requires recording to give notice to subsequent purchasers and encumbrancers of real estate. Because each county has thousands of record books, each with at least 1,000 pages, a mortgage cannot be duly recorded without being properly indexed. Howard's mortgage did not have priority over the one to Chrysler.

Duties of the Mortgagor

LO2 Duties and rights of mortgagor

The mortgagor assumes three definite duties and liabilities when placing a mortgage upon real estate. These pertain to:

1. Interest and principal
2. Taxes, assessments, and insurance premiums
3. Security of the mortgagee

INTEREST AND PRINCIPAL

The mortgagor must make all payments of interest and principal as they become due. Most mortgages call for periodic payments, such as monthly, semiannually, or annually. These payments are used to pay all accrued interest to the date of payment, and the mortgagee applies the balance on the principal. Other mortgages call for periodic payment of interest and for the payment of the entire principal at one time. In either case, a failure to pay either the periodic payments of interest and principal or of interest only constitutes a default. A default gives the mortgagee the right to foreclose. Most mortgages contain a provision that if the mortgagor does not make an interest or principal payment when due or within a specified time after due, the mortgagee may declare the entire principal immediately due. This is known as an **acceleration clause**.

Acceleration Clause Clause allowing entire principal to be due

If the mortgagor wishes to pay off the mortgage debt before the due date so as to save interest, that right must be reserved at the time the mortgage is given.

TAXES, ASSESSMENTS, AND INSURANCE PREMIUMS

The mortgagor, who is the owner of the land regardless of the form of the mortgage, must continue to make such payments as would be expected of an owner of land. The mortgagor must pay taxes and assessments. If the mortgagor does not, the mortgagee may pay them and compel a reimbursement from the mortgagor. If the mortgage contract requires the mortgagor to pay these charges, a failure to pay them becomes a default.

The law does not require the mortgagor to keep the property insured nor to insure it for the benefit of the mortgagee. This duty can be imposed on the mortgagor by the mortgage contract. Both the mortgagor and the mortgagee have an insurable interest in the property to the extent of each one's interest or maximum loss.

SECURITY OF THE MORTGAGEE

The mortgagor must do no act that will materially impair the security of the mortgagee. Cutting timber, tearing down buildings, and all acts that waste the assets impair the security and give the mortgagee the right to seek legal protection. Some state statutes provide that any one of these acts constitutes a default. This gives the mortgagee the right to foreclose. Other statutes provide only that the mortgagee may obtain an injunction in a court of equity enjoining any further impairment. Some states provide for the appointment of a receiver to prevent waste. Many state laws also make it a criminal offense to willfully impair the security of mortgaged property.

Facts: Alfred and Donna Allen and James and Patricia Simpson had executed a 20-year mortgage to Michael Bodwitch. It contained a provision "that no building on the premises shall be removed or demolished without the consent of the mortgagee." The city condemned the building on the mortgaged property as a safety hazard because part of it collapsed. It notified the Allens and Simpsons that they had to demolish the building. They, Bodwitch, and a demolition contractor signed a contract for the demolition. Bodwitch then sued the Allens and Simpsons alleging they had breached the mortgage agreement.

Outcome: The court said the purpose of the provision regarding demolition of a building was to protect the security of the mortgagee. However, in this case the mortgagee lost any security when the building collapsed, not from its demolition.

Rights of the Mortgagor

The mortgagor has several rights including:

1 Possession of the property
2 Rents and profits
3 Cancellation of lien
4 Redemption
5 Sale of the property

POSSESSION OF THE PROPERTY

As the owner of the property, the mortgagor usually has the right to retain possession of the mortgaged property. Upon default the mortgagee usually may take possession to collect rents and profits and apply them to the mortgage debt in compliance with a duty as a fiduciary to the mortgagor. In some states possession cannot be taken, but the appointment of a receiver to collect rents and profits may be obtained.

RENTS AND PROFITS

The mortgagor, as the owner of the property, has the right to rents and profits from the property. In the absence of an express agreement to the contrary, the mortgagor has the right to all rents and profits obtained from the mortgaged property. The mortgagor may retain the profits. This rule or any other rule may, of course, be superseded by a contract providing otherwise.

CANCELLATION OF LIEN

The mortgagor has the right to have the lien canceled on final payment. As soon as the mortgagee receives the mortgage, it becomes a lien upon the mortgaged real estate. The clerk in the recorder's office cancels a mortgage lien by entering a notation, usually on the margin, certifying that the debt has been paid and that the lien is canceled. The mortgagee, not the mortgagor, must have this done. If the mortgagee does not, the mortgagor may institute court action to have this cloud removed from the title so that there may be a clear title.

REDEMPTION

Redemption
Right to free property from lien of mortgage

The mortgagor has the right to free the mortgaged property from the lien of the mortgage after default, known as the right of **redemption**. Statutes in most states prescribe a specific time after the foreclosure and sale when this right may be exercised. In order to redeem the property, the mortgagor must pay the amount of the mortgage and the costs of the sale.

Usually only a person whose interests will be affected by foreclosure may exercise the right of redemption. This includes the executor or administrator and heirs of the mortgagor, and frequently a second mortgagee.

SALE OF THE PROPERTY

The mortgagor has a right to sell the property on which a mortgage exists. The purchaser may agree to "assume the mortgage," which means to be primarily liable for its payment. "Assuming" the mortgage differs from buying the property "subject to the mortgage." In the first case the buyer agrees to be liable for the mortgage obligation as fully as the original mortgagor. If the buyer takes the property "subject to the mortgage" and default occurs, the property may be lost, but no more.

A sale of the mortgaged property does not automatically release the original mortgagor whether the purchaser assumed the mortgage or bought it subject to the mortgage. The mortgagor remains fully liable in both cases.

To excuse the mortgagor from liability under a mortgage, a novation must take place. This can occur if the parties involved sign a written agreement releasing the

Facts: Carteret Savings Bank extended a home equity credit line to Mayer and Linda Weiner secured by a mortgage on their home. They each had access to the credit line by writing a check. They had marital difficulties. Linda tried to negotiate a check on the credit line and found that Mayer had closed the account. Mayer withdrew $12,000 after reopening the account. Linda closed the account. While it was closed, Carteret refused to honor a check by Mayer for $8,800. Carteret told Linda it had opened the account again, so she withdrew the balance of $9,000. The Weiners defaulted and Carteret sued them both for foreclosure. The trial court said closing the account constituted a termination of it. Reopening the account, that court found, constituted a new agreement.

Outcome: The appellate court said reopening the account at one party's request did not result in a novation. It did not constitute a new, written agreement by the parties or extend the time of payment of the debt.

mortgagor. Courts have also found novations if the mortgagee extends the time of payment for the purchaser of the property without the mortgagor's consent. Accepting an interest payment after the principal of the mortgage has become due constitutes an extension of the mortgage. If the mortgagee does this without the mortgagor's consent, a novation results and releases the mortgagor from all liability under the mortgage. However, the action of the mortgagee must amount to an extension of time of payment.

Foreclosure

LO3
Foreclosure and assignment of rights

Foreclosure
Sale of mortgaged property to pay debt

If the mortgagor fails to pay the debt secured by the mortgage when it becomes due, or fails to perform any of the other terms set forth in the mortgage, the mortgagee has the right to foreclose for the purpose of collecting the debt. **Foreclosure** usually consists of a sale of the mortgaged property. The sale is made under an order of a court and generally by an officer of the court. The mortgagor must be properly notified of the foreclosure proceedings.

Facts: Earnestine and Henry Henderson mortgaged their home to the Farmers Home Administration (FmHA) as security for a loan. They defaulted on the loan, so FmHA accelerated the debt and foreclosed on the property. When sued for eviction, the Hendersons alleged the notice of foreclosure FmHA sent them misrepresented the law regarding what they had to pay to avoid foreclosure. The law stated: "The debtor . . . may at any time before a sale . . . stop a threatened sale . . . by paying the amount actually past due . . . rather than the amount accelerated." The amount past due was $1,200. The notice from FmHA stated: "The indebtedness . . . consists of $8,585.77 plus interest of $477.77. . . . You are hereby notified that unless said indebtedness is paid in full within 20 days . . . the United States . . . will take action to foreclose. Any negotiation by the United States . . . of any remittance tendered by you . . . will not constitute a waiver of this acceleration or institution of foreclosure action."

Outcome: The court found this notice was faulty because it indicated that foreclosure could have been avoided only by payment of the entire amount owed. Notice is required to give debtors the opportunity to make the payments to avoid foreclosure. The incorrect notice negated the very reason for it.

Mechanics' Lien
Lien of people who have furnished materials or labor on property

Foreclosure literally means "a legal proceeding to shut out all other claims." A first mortgage may not necessarily constitute a first claim on the proceeds of the sale. The cost of foreclosure and taxes always takes precedence over the first mortgage. People who furnish materials for the construction of a house and workers who work on it have a claim under what is known as a **mechanics' lien**. A mechanics' lien takes precedence over unrecorded mortgages. The law varies somewhat among the states, but normally a mortgage recorded before a mechanics' lien attaches has priority. The foreclosure proceedings establish the existence of all prior claims and the order of their priority. Foreclosure proceedings are fixed by statutory law and therefore vary in different states.

If the proceeds of the sale of mortgaged property exceed the amount of the debt and the expenses of foreclosure, the surplus must be used to pay off any other liens such as second mortgages. Any money remaining belongs to the mortgagor.

If a deficiency results, however, the mortgagee may secure a deficiency judgment for this amount. In that case the unpaid balance of the debt will stand as a claim against the mortgagor until payment of the debt.

When the mortgagor has given a mortgage for the purpose of purchasing the property, some states limit the amount of a deficiency judgment. The deficiency cannot be greater than the amount by which the debt exceeds either the fair market value or the selling price, whichever amount is smaller. This gives protection to the mortgagor from the mortgagee buying the property at foreclosure for a very low price. For example, suppose *A* mortgages property to *B* for $50,000, and the value of the property declines to $40,000. *A* defaults and *B* forecloses. *B* buys the property at foreclosure for $30,000.

	Fair Market Value	Selling Price
Amount of debt	$50,000	$50,000
Less amount "received"	40,000	30,000
Deficiency	$10,000	$20,000

B may obtain a deficiency judgment of $10,000 because it is the lesser of the two amounts.

Assignment of the Mortgage

The rights of the mortgagee under the mortgage agreement may be assigned. The assignee, the purchaser, obtains no greater rights than the assignor had. To be protected, the assignee should require the assignor to produce an estoppel certificate signed by the mortgagor. This certificate should acknowledge that the mortgagor has no claims of any kind in connection with the mortgage. This would bar the mortgagor from subsequently claiming the right of offset.

The assignee of a mortgage should have this assignment recorded. In the event that the mortgagee assigns the mortgage to more than one party, the one who records an assignment first has preference. This can be important when the proceeds are not adequate to pay both assignees.

Deed of Trust

Deed of Trust
Deed that transfers property to trustee for benefit of creditor

Trustee
One who holds title to property for another

In a number of states, parties commonly use a deed of trust instead of a mortgage for securing a debt with real estate. A mortgage involves two parties, a debtor and a creditor. A **deed of trust** involves three parties. It conveys title to the property to a disinterested party, called a **trustee**. The trustee holds the property in trust for the benefit of the creditor. Most courts treat a deed of trust like a mortgage. If a default in payment occurs, the trustee forecloses on the property and applies the proceeds to the payment of the debt. The right to redeem under a deed of trust, when it exists, is similar to the right of redemption under a mortgage.

The advantage to the creditor in using a deed of trust instead of a mortgage is in the power held by the trustee. In the event a mortgagor defaults in the payments, the mortgagee who holds an ordinary mortgage can foreclose. In most states, however, the mortgagee must go into court and have a judicial foreclosure in order to have the mortgaged property sold to satisfy the debt. A trustee of a deed of trust may sell the mortgaged property at public auction if the debtor defaults. No time-consuming court foreclosure proceedings are necessary. Hence, the property can be sold more quickly at a trustee's sale.

Mortgage Insurance

Private companies and several agencies of the federal government insure or guarantee mortgages against default by the mortgagor. The insurance lasts for the term of the mortgage. The government agrees to pay in case of default by the mortgagor in order to make it easier for some people to obtain a mortgage. The most frequently used government programs are those administered by the Federal Housing Administration (FHA) and the Veterans Administration (VA).

FHA-insured mortgages require a smaller down payment than conventional mortgages. Anyone who meets the financial qualifications may obtain an FHA loan. Because FHA mortgages are insured, the interest rate is slightly less than for a conventional mortgage. The FHA sets a maximum amount that may be mortgaged. The FHA bases this amount on the average sale price in the area for a home. The mortgagor pays premiums for this mortgage insurance.

The VA guarantees mortgages for people who have served on active duty in the armed forces for a minimum period of time. The mortgage must be on owner-occupied property. The VA charges the mortgagor a percentage of the loan amount for its guarantee. It sets the interest rate charged. As a benefit to veterans, it sets this rate less than the market rate for conventional loans. A VA mortgage may be for up to 100 percent of the value of the real estate. This means no down payment is required. The maximum loan amount is $144,000.

Questions

1. Is a mortgage a debt? Explain.
2. What legal requirements are there regarding the form of a mortgage?
3. Do all mortgages require monthly payments of principal and interest?
4. Is a mortgagor required to keep mortgaged property insured?
5. Who has the right to rents and profits from mortgaged property?
6. How may the mortgagor redeem property after it has been sold under a foreclosure sale?
7. Does a sale of mortgaged property automatically release the original mortgagor? Explain.
8. What should the assignee of a mortgage do to be protected from possible claims by the mortgagor?
9. What is a deed of trust and how is it used?
10. Why does the government insure mortgages against default by the mortgagor?

Case Problems

LO1 1. New Panorama Development Corporation bought a tract of land from Robert Simpson and executed a mortgage for $654,000 covering only lot 126 of the land. New Panorama created lot 130 mostly from part of lot 126 but also with some of the unmortgaged acreage. The mortgage allowed for release of portions of the mortgaged property upon payment of $752,100 "divided by the total number of subdivided . . . lots." Lot 130 was ultimately sold to Caryn Woods. There was default on the mortgage and foreclosure. Woods sued alleging the mortgage was ambiguous. She asked the court to set a price based on acreage at which the portion of her lot taken from lot 126 could be released from the mortgage. What rules should the court use in interpreting the mortgage?

LO2 2. Michael and Drue Gisvold defaulted on their home mortgage and GMAC, the holder, began foreclosure proceedings. Several sales were held or attempted at which Randall Cudd and Jim Claycomb were the high bidders, but the Gisvolds prevented or delayed the sales or court confirmation of sales by filing bankruptcy petitions or objections. At the confirmation hearing of the second sale the court agreed to allow the Gisvolds until January 17 to redeem the property or the confirmation would be effective January 18. Cudd and Claycomb then had 10 days to pay the purchase price. Three hours before the redemption time expired Michael filed another bankruptcy petition. A week after the bankruptcy petition was dismissed the Gisvolds paid the amount due on the mortgage. Had they redeemed the property in time?

LO3 3 Victor Paulos, Dan Lamountt, and Stanley Stephen formed Westridge Court Joint Venture to build an apartment complex. Westridge borrowed $1.9 million secured by a deed of trust on the complex's property to finance construction. After construction, Paulos, Lamountt, and Stephen did not like the occupancy rate and sold the project to DFAI. DFAI defaulted on the loan and the mortgagee foreclosed. The mortgagee made the only bid at the foreclosure sale and purchased the project for $957,000. The court entered a deficiency judgment against DFAI for $1.9 million—the difference between the debt and the price bid at the foreclosure sale. Discuss the rights of the parties depending on whether or not the state has a law regarding the sufficiency of the sale price at a foreclosure.

LO2 4 Crossroads Inc. mortgaged land to First Interstate Bank of Texas to secure payment of a $3 million debt. The state condemned the land for a highway. A condemnation award of more than $6 million was made and the state and Crossroads objected to it, but the state deposited the $6 million with the court. Crossroads and the bank moved to withdraw the $6 million. Since no one objected, Crossroads got the money and paid its debt to the bank. The state and Crossroads finally agreed on a $3.5 million value for the property and the court ordered Crossroads to pay back the $2.5 million excess. Crossroads could not repay the excess so the state alleged the bank was liable for it. State law provided that when an award paid exceeded the finally determined value of the property "the court shall order the property owner to return the excess." The state alleged that a mortgagee was the owner of mortgaged property, therefore the bank had to pay the $2.5 million. Decide the case.

LO1 5 Turabo Shopping Center, Inc., owned and operated the Plaza del Carmen Shopping Center. In order to build it, Turabo had executed a mortgage to Chase Manhattan Bank. The mortgage provided that Chase was to be repaid by assignment of rent due Turabo from tenants of the Plaza. Chase instituted foreclosure proceedings and asked for the appointment of a receiver to manage the Plaza during the action. The value of the Plaza was probably not enough to cover the amount owed Chase, and three tenant companies run by the sister of Turabo's president paid no rent for a substantial time. Turabo allowed its lawyer to set up a restaurant without paying rent and withheld $100,000 in rent from Chase to defend the foreclosure action and get an appraisal to be used in that action. Should a receiver be appointed?

LO1 6 After mortgaging a piece of real property to Francis Barnett, Mr. and Mrs. Surjit Sethi sold it to Kaval Chandhok. Chandhok assumed the mortgage binding himself with the makers of the mortgage note ". . . to the full and final payment . . . of said note and of all the liabilities . . . expressed in said act of mortgage." When sued for payment of the mortgage, Chandhok alleged the agreement to purchase the property had conditioned his assumption of the Barnett mortgage on his being able to assume a different existing mortgage. Since Chandhok's application to assume that mortgage had been denied, and since Chandhok had not signed the mortgage to Barnett, Chandhok alleged he had no liability to Barnett. Decide.

LO3 7 Acting on behalf of the senior lienholder, Pacific Loan Management Corp. (PLMC) conducted a foreclosure sale of Dennis and Nina Armstrong's real estate. The U.S. Small Business Administration (SBA) purchased the property at the sale. SBA had a second mortgage on the property. After paying the senior mortgage, $31,000 remained. The Armstrongs and the SBA both claimed it. Who should get it and why?

LO1 8 The Henry S. Miller Company executed deeds of trust to Harold and Ruth Wood and Warren and Ruth Ann Wood to secure payment of notes. There was default, so the Woods foreclosed and bought the property at foreclosure. Later they paid taxes assessed during the term of the mortgage and sued Miller for reimbursement. The deeds of trust stated: "The undersigned shall have no personal liability for the payment of the note secured hereby, and in the event of default, the holder of said note shall have the mortgaged property alone as security for payment of said note." The deeds of trust also stated: "If the undersigned shall fail . . . to pay such taxes, . . . said taxes may be paid by the legal holder of said note, and sums so expended shall . . . become part of the debt hereby secured." Was Miller liable for reimbursement of the taxes?

Internet Resources for Business Law

Name	Resources	Web Address
U.S. Department of Housing and Urban Development (HUD)	HUD provides information on real property and planning issues for both consumers and businesses. HUD also provides information on the Fair Housing Act and the Civil Rights Act.	http://www.hud.gov/
HUD USER	HUD USER, PD&R's information source for housing and community development researchers and policy makers, provides federal government reports and information on housing policy and programs, building technology, economic development, urban planning, and other housing-related topics.	http://www.huduser.org/
Legal Information Institute (LII)—Land-Use Law Materials	LII provides an overview of land-use law, links to statutes, federal and state judicial court decisions, and other materials.	http://www.law.cornell.edu/topics/land_use.html
American Bar Association's (ABA) Section of Real Property, Probate and Trust Law	The ABA's Section of Real Property, Probate, and Trust Law provides news, information, and links property.	http://www.abanet.org/rppt/home.html

44
Landlord and Tenant

Learning Objectives

1. Explain the nature and formation of the landlord/tenant relationship.
2. Name the various types of tenancies.
3. List the rights and duties of tenants and landlords.
4. Explain how a lease may be terminated.

PREVIEW CASE

David Clark leased 13 acres of vacant property to American Pipe Threading. American built three buildings on the property and one on property owned by the Whiteheads which it had no right to use. Clark acquired American's assets and leased the Whiteheads' property for one year at $1,200 a month. The lease provided that if Clark held over after termination of the lease the rent would be $1,500. At the end of the lease term Clark held over and paid $1,500 a month for three months. He then gave notice of termination, but did not remove all his property, including large trucks and trash from the Whitehead property for several years. When sued for rent for the holdover period, Clark claimed he was a trespasser and not a holdover tenant. How is a tenancy terminated? Who has the right to determine the character of relief available to a landlord when a tenant holds over?

LO1 Nature and formation of relationship

A contract whereby one person agrees to lease land or a building to another creates the relationship of landlord and tenant. Such an agreement does not require special words or acts for creation unless the lease lasts for more than a year, in which case it must be in writing. The tenant's temporary possession of the premises and payment of rent for its use constitute the chief characteristics that determine the relationship of landlord and tenant. The landlord may retake possession of the property at the end of the lease period.

Landlord or Lessor Owner of leased property

Tenant or Lessee Possessor of leased property

The owner of the leased property is known as the **landlord**, or **lessor**. The person given possession of the leased property is the **tenant**, or **lessee**. The contract or agreement between the landlord and tenant is called a **lease** (see Illustration 44-1).

RENTAL AGREEMENT

1. Parties:
____***Richard T. Mowbray, Cincinnati, OH***________(Owner) and ____***Edward J. and Doris L. Caldwell, Cincinnati, OH***______________________(Tenant) hereby agree as follows:

2. Premises:
Owner rents to Tenant and Tenant rents from Owner for residential use only, the premises located at: ____***2669 Russell Road, Cincinnati, OH 45299*** together with the following furnishings, appliances, and fixtures: ____***stove, refrigerator, dishwasher, washer, and dryer***_ on the following terms:

3. Term:
This agreement shall begin on ____***May 1, 2002***_______________ and shall continue from that date
____A) on a month-to-month basis. This agreement will continue for successive terms of one month each until either owner or tenant terminate the tenancy by giving the other thirty (30) days written notice of an intention to terminate the tenancy. In the event such notice is given, tenant agrees to pay all rent up to and including the notice period.
X B) for a period of ____***12***_____ months, expiring on _***April 30, 2003***_____.

4. Rent:
Tenant shall pay Owner rent of ____***$775***_____ per month. Rent for each month is payable in advance on or before the first day of the month for which the rent is due. Rent shall be paid by personal check, money order, or cashier's check only, to the order of ____***Mowbray Apartments***______________ (Cash shall not be accepted).

5. Security Deposit:
Tenant shall deposit ____***$400***________ with Owner as security. Owner may use all or any part of this security deposit to remedy defaults in the payment of rent, to repair damage to the premises, to clean the premises, or for any other purpose allowed by law. This deposit shall be refunded to Tenant within three weeks (21 days) after vacating said apartment, if the following conditions have been satisfied:
a) Proper notice of termination has been given;
b) There is no default in the payment of rent and/or late charges;
c) The premises are left in clean, orderly condition, including the cleaning of carpets, refrigerator, stove, oven, etc.
d) There has been no damage to premises, equipment, or furnishings; and
e) All other terms and conditions of this agreement have been satisfied.
In the event Owner incurs expenses to remedy any default in this agreement, including but not limited to the above conditions, the cost may be deducted from the Security Deposit. If Owners' expenses exceed said deposit, Tenant shall be liable for excesses.

6. Utilities:
Tenant shall pay all utility charges related to his/her occupancy of the premises except ***trash collection services.***

7. Late Charges:
Tenant shall pay Owner a late charge of____***$100***_____ if rent is not received by Owner by 5:00 p.m. on the fifth day of the month for which it is due.

8. Habitability:
Tenant has examined the entire interior and exterior of the premises and acknowledges that the entire premises are in good, clean condition. Tenant, to the best of his/her ability, has examined all furnishings, appliances, and fixtures on the

Illustration 44-1
Lease

premises including plumbing, heating and electrical appliances, and fixtures and acknowledges that these items are in good working order with the following exceptions: ______________________________ Tenant shall immediately give Owner written notice upon discovery of any damage, defects, or dangerous conditions on or about the premises, including plumbing, heating and electrical appliances, and fixtures.

9. Disturbances:
Tenant shall not use the premises for any unlawful purpose, violate any law or ordinance, commit waste, or create a nuisance on or about the premises or permit such acts to occur. It shall be presumed that three disturbance complaints from other tenants in the building or occupants of nearby buildings during any consecutive sixty-day period shall constitute an irremediable breach of this agreement and Owner shall have the right to immediately terminate the tenancy.

10. Right of Entry:
Upon reasonable notice, Owner may enter the premises during reasonable hours for the purpose of making repairs, alterations, decorations or improvements, to supply services, to show the premises to others, or for any other purpose allowed by law. In an emergency, Owner may enter the premises at any time without prior notice to Tenant for the purpose of taking such action as is necessary to alleviate the emergency.

11. Smoke Detectors:
The premises are equipped with a smoke detection device(s), and Tenant shall be responsible for reporting any problems, maintenance, or repairs to Owner. Replacing batteries is the responsibility of the Tenant.

12. Termination of Tenancy:
A thirty-day notice of termination may be given by either Tenant or Owner at any time during the month and tenancy does not have to terminate at the end of the calendar month. Rent shall be due and payable up to and including the date of termination. When the thirty-day notice is given by Tenant, it may not be revoked or modified without written approval of the Owner. As a condition for the full refund of all of the security deposit Tenant shall do the following: a) completely vacate the premises, including any storage or other areas of the general premises which Tenant may be occupying or in which Tenant may have personal property stored; b) deliver all keys and other personal property furnished to Tenant during the term of this Agreement; c) and leave Tenant's forwarding address. Tenant shall cooperate in allowing the Manager to show Tenant's apartment at any reasonable time during this thirty-day period.

Tenant's and Co-Signer's Certificate and Acknowledgement of Receipt:

I hereby certify that I have read all provisions of this agreement, that I understand them, that I agree to abide by them, and that I acknowledge receipt of a copy of this agreement and all attachment to it.

April 18, 2002	Edward J. Caldwell
Date	Tenant
April 18, 2002	Doris L. Caldwell
Date	Tenant
April 18, 2002	Richard T. Mowbray
Date	Owner/Agent

Illustration 44-1
(continued)

Lease
Contract between landlord and tenant

Rent
Amount paid landlord for possession of property

The amount the tenant agrees to pay the landlord for the possession of the leased property is called the **rent**.

A tenant differs from a lodger or roomer in that the former has the exclusive legal possession of the property, whereas the latter has merely the right to use the premises subject to the control and supervision of the owner.

The Lease

The lease may be oral or written, express or implied, formal or simple, subject, however, to the general statutory requirement that a lease of land for a term longer than one year must be in writing to be enforceable. If a dispute arises between the tenant and the landlord over their rights and duties, the court will look to the terms of the lease and the general body of landlord and tenant law to determine the decision.

In order to avoid disputes, a lease should be in writing and should cover all terms of the contract. The parties should include such items as a clear identification of the property, the time and place of payment of rent, the notice required to vacate, the duration or the nature of the tenancy, and any specific provision desired by either party, such as the right of the landlord to show the property to prospective purchasers or an agreement requiring the landlord to redecorate.

Facts: Russell Ratliff rented a house to Johnny and Mary Gorman. The Gormans became delinquent in their rent to Ratliff and he asked them to vacate the house. The written lease provided that if the Gormans did not pay any rent when due, Ratliff "may, if desired, take immediate possession . . . removing and storing at the expense of said lessees all property contained therein." Relying on such provisions in the lease, Ratliff entered the house in the Gormans' absence, removed all their personal property, and put it in storage. State law provided that "carrying away the goods of the party in possession . . ." constituted the offense of forcible entry and detainer. The Gormans sued Ratliff.

Outcome: The court said that although the lease gave Ratliff the authority to take possession of the Gormans' property, state law invalidated that portion of the lease.

Types of Tenancies

LO2
Tenancy types

Four separate and distinct classes of tenancies exist, each of which has some rule of law governing it that does not apply to any other type of tenancy. The four classes of tenancies are:

1. Tenancy for years
2. Tenancy from year to year
3. Tenancy at will
4. Tenancy by sufferance

TENANCY FOR YEARS

Tenancy for Years
Tenancy for any definite period

A **tenancy for years** is a tenancy for a definite period of time, whether it is one month, 1 year, or 99 years. The lease fixes the termination date. However, by law most states limit the length of time a lease may last. A lease for a time greater than the statutory limit is void. The payment of the rent may be by the month even when a tenancy for a specified number of years exists. No notice to terminate the tenancy need be given by either party when the lease fixes the termination date. Most leases provide that they will continue to run on a year-to-year basis after the termination date, unless the tenant gives notice to the landlord not less than a specified number of days before the termination date that the tenant intends to leave on that date.

TENANCY FROM YEAR TO YEAR

Tenancy from Year to Year
Tenancy for indefinite period with yearly rent

A tenancy for an indefinite period of time with rent set at a yearly amount is known as a **tenancy from year to year**. Under such a tenancy, a tenant merely pays the rent periodically, and the lease lasts until proper notice of termination has been given. A tenancy of this kind may also be by the month or any other period agreed upon. If by the month, it is called *a tenancy from month to month.* The length of the tenancy is usually determined by the nature of the rent stated or paid, although there could be a tenancy from year to year with the rent paid quarterly or monthly.

Notice to terminate this type of tenancy must exactly follow the state law governing it. Notice must normally be in writing. In a tenancy from month to month, the law usually requires notice 30 days before a rent due date.

TENANCY AT WILL

Tenancy at Will
Tenancy for uncertain period

A **tenancy at will** exists when the tenant has possession of the property for an uncertain period. Either the tenant or the landlord can terminate the tenancy at will, since both must agree to the tenancy. This tenancy, unlike any of the others, automatically terminates upon the death of the tenant or the landlord, if the tenant attempts to assign the tenancy, or if the landlord sells the property.

TENANCY AT SUFFERANCE

Tenancy at Sufferance
Holdover tenant without landlord's permission

When a tenant holds over the tenancy after the expiration of the lease without permission of the landlord, a **tenancy at sufferance** exists until the landlord elects to treat the tenant as a trespasser or as a tenant. The landlord may treat the tenant as a trespasser, sue for damages, and have the tenant removed by legal proceedings. If the landlord prefers, payment of the rent due for another period may be accepted, and thus the tenant's possession may be recognized as rightful.

PREVIEW CASE REVISITED

Facts: David Clark leased 13 acres of vacant property to American Pipe Threading. American built three buildings on the property and one on property owned by the Whiteheads which it had no right to use. Clark acquired American's assets and leased the Whiteheads' property for one year at $1,200 a month. The lease provided that if Clark held over after termination of the lease the rent would be $1,500. At the end of the lease term Clark held over and paid $1,500 a month for three months. He then gave notice of termination, but did not remove all his property, including large trucks and trash from the Whitehead property for several years. When sued for rent for the holdover period, Clark claimed he was a trespasser and not a holdover tenant.

Outcome: The court pointed out that a landlord has the option of treating a lessee in possession after expiration of a lease as a trespasser or as a holdover tenant.

Rights of the Tenant

LO3
Tenant and landlord rights and duties

A lease gives the tenant certain rights, as follows:

1 Right to possession
2 Right to use the premises
3 Right to assign or sublease

RIGHT TO POSSESSION

By signing the lease, the landlord warrants the right to lease the premises and that the tenant shall have possession during the period of the lease. During the term of the lease, tenants have the same right to exclusive possession of the premises as if they owned the property. If someone questions the owner's right to lease the property, the landlord must defend the tenant's right to exclusive possession. Failure of the landlord to give possession on time or to protect the tenant's rights subjects the landlord to liability for damages.

A nuisance that disturbs the tenant's quiet enjoyment of the property often causes disputes between landlords and tenants. Courts have held that failure to remove dead rats from the wall, failure to stop disorderly conduct on the part of other tenants, and frequent and unnecessary entrances upon the property by the landlord or agents constitute acts that destroy the tenant's right to quiet enjoyment and constitute a breach of warranty on the part of the landlord.

If the nuisance existed at the time the tenant leased the property and the tenant knew of its existence, the right to complain would be deemed to have been waived. Also, if the landlord has no control over the nuisance, the tenant cannot avoid the contract even though the nuisance arose subsequent to the signing of the lease. If the landlord fails or refuses to abate a nuisance over which the landlord has control, the tenant not only may terminate the lease but may sue for damages. In other cases the tenant may seek an injunction compelling the landlord to abate a nuisance.

RIGHT TO USE THE PREMISES

Unless the lease expressly restricts this right, the tenant has the right to use the premises in any way consistent with the nature of the property. A dwelling cannot be converted into a machine shop, nor can a clothing store be converted into a restaurant. Damage to leased property other than that which results from ordinary wear and tear is not permissible. In the case of farming land, the tenant may cut wood for personal use but not to sell.

RIGHT TO ASSIGN OR SUBLEASE

Assignment
Transfer to another of tenant's rights

Sublease
Transfer of less than a tenant's full rights under a lease

If the tenant transfers all interest in the lease to another party who agrees to comply with its terms, including the payment of the rent to the landlord, there is an **assignment**. In an assignment, the assignee pays the rent directly to the landlord. Assignment must include the entire premises. In a **sublease**, the tenant transfers the premises for a period less than the term of the lease or transfers only a part of the premises. The tenant usually collects the rent from the subtenant and pays the landlord. Ordinarily a written lease prohibits assigning or subleasing the premises unless the lessor gives written consent thereto first. Residential leases commonly restrict the use of the premises to the tenant and the immediate family or to a certain number of persons. Unless the lease expressly prohibits both assignment and subleasing, either may be done. If the lease prohibits only subleasing, then the lease may be assigned.

Joint occupancy closely relates to subleasing. A provision in the lease prohibiting subleasing does not forbid a contract for a joint occupancy. In joint occupancy the tenant does not give up exclusive control of any part of the premises. The tenant merely permits another party to jointly occupy all or a part of the premises.

Duties of the Tenant

The lease imposes certain duties upon the tenant:

1 To pay rent
2 To protect and preserve the premises

TO PAY RENT

The tenant's primary duty is to pay the rent. This payment must be made in money unless the contract provides otherwise, such as a share of the crops. The rent is not due until the end of the term, but leases almost universally provide for rent in advance.

Landlords commonly appoint an agent for the purpose of collecting the rent. The death of the principal automatically terminates such a principal-agent relationship. Any rent paid to the agent after this termination and not remitted to the proper party must be paid again.

If the tenant fails to pay rent on time, the landlord may terminate the lease and order the tenant to vacate, or the landlord may permit the tenant to continue occupancy and sue for the rent. However, even if the landlord forces the tenant to vacate the property the tenant is still liable for the agreed rent. Under the common law the landlord could seize and hold any personal property found on the premises. This right has been either curtailed or abolished by statute.

TO PROTECT AND PRESERVE THE PREMISES

Traditionally, a tenant had to make repairs on the premises. This was because a tenant had a duty to keep the leased property in as good condition as the landlord had it when the lease began. Some states have enacted statutes requiring the landlord to make repairs. Other states find a warranty of habitability, which makes the landlord responsible for keeping the premises livable. Some statutes even give tenants a form of self-help. The tenant must notify the landlord of needed repairs. If the landlord does not make the repairs, the tenant may fix things and deduct the cost from the rent. Tenants, however, must repair damage caused by their negligence. In states in which statutes have not altered the traditional responsibility, tenants must repair damage except reasonable wear and tear and damage by the elements.

Facts: Bobenal Investment, Inc., leased 15,000 square feet of a 45,000-square-foot building to Giant Super Markets, Inc. The agreement between the parties allowed Giant to remove all its fixtures and equipment. When Giant moved out, it inadvertently removed a downspout, which resulted in flooding of the building. Within two days Giant mopped up and swept away the water and then had the floor scrubbed and cleaned by a professional janitorial contractor. Bobenal later filed a suit.

Outcome: The court found Giant had substantially repaired the damage caused by its error.

Rights of the Landlord

The landlord has three definite rights under the lease:

1 To regain possession
2 To enter upon the property to preserve it
3 To assign rights

TO REGAIN POSSESSION

Action of Ejectment
Action to have sheriff remove tenant

Upon termination of the lease, the landlord has the right to regain peaceable possession of the premises. If the tenant refuses this possession, the most common remedy is to bring an **action of ejectment** in a court of law. Upon the successful completion of this suit the sheriff will forcibly remove the tenant and any property.

When the landlord repossesses the property, all permanent improvements and fixtures may be retained. Courts determine whether or not the improvements have become a part of the real estate. If they have, they cannot be removed.

TO ENTER UPON THE PROPERTY TO PRESERVE IT

The landlord has a right to enter upon the property to preserve it. Extensive renovations that interfere with the tenant's peaceable occupancy cannot be made. If the roof blows off or becomes leaky, the landlord may repair it or put on a new roof. This occasion cannot be used to add another story. A landlord who enters the property without permission may be treated as a stranger. A landlord has no right to enter the premises to show the property to prospective purchasers or tenants unless the lease reserves this right.

TO ASSIGN RIGHTS

The landlord has the right to assign the rights under the lease to a third party. The tenant cannot avoid any duties and obligations by reason of the assignment of the lease. Like all other assignments, the assignment does not release the assignor from the contract without the consent of the tenant. If, for example, the tenant suffers injury because of a concealed but defective water main cover and the landlord knew of this condition, the landlord has liability even though rights under the lease were assigned before the injury.

Duties of the Landlord

The lease imposes certain duties upon the landlord:

1 To pay taxes and assessments
2 To protect the tenant from concealed defects
3 To mitigate damages upon abandonment by the tenant

TO PAY TAXES AND ASSESSMENTS

Although the tenant occupies and uses the premises, the landlord must pay all taxes and special assessments. Sometimes the lease provides that the tenant shall pay the taxes. In such event, the tenant has no liability for special assessments for sidewalks, street paving, and other improvements.

TO PROTECT THE TENANT FROM CONCEALED DEFECTS

The landlord has liability to the tenant if the tenant suffers injury by concealed defects that were known or should have been reasonably known to the landlord at the time of giving the tenant possession of the premises. Such defects might be contamination from contagious germs; concealed, unfilled wells; and rotten timbers in the dwelling. The tenant bears the risk of injury caused by apparent defects or defects reasonably discoverable upon inspection at the time that the tenant enters into possession. Most cities and many states have tenement laws that require the landlord to keep all rental property habitable and provided with adequate fire escapes. The question of the habitability of the property relates to major defects in the structure. Any damage due to a failure to observe these laws may subject the landlord to liability for damages.

TO MITIGATE DAMAGES UPON ABANDONMENT BY THE TENANT

Unless the landlord accepts the abandonment, a tenant who abandons leased property before the end of the lease term still has an obligation to pay the rent due through the end of the term. However, the landlord has a duty to mitigate the tenant's damages by attempting to secure a new tenant. If a new tenant occupies the premises, the landlord's damage from the first tenant abandoning the property equals the difference between the rent the original tenant had to pay and the rent the new tenant pays. In this way, the original tenant's obligation amounts to less than the original rent called for by the lease and the new tenant's payments mitigate the landlord's damage due from the original tenant.

Facts: The National Bank and Trust Company of South Bend leased some commercial real estate to Radio Distributing Company. Before the end of the lease term, Radio Distributing moved out. The bank allowed the Council for the Retarded to move into the building and remain in possession without paying any rent for several years. The bank had exercised reasonable efforts to relet the property and let the Council occupy it in order to maintain property and casualty insurance on it. When sued by National, Radio alleged the bank had not acted to mitigate its damages.

Outcome: The court said that as long as National had made reasonable efforts to relet the property and only let the Council use it in order to keep the property insured, National had carried out its obligation to mitigate damages.

Termination of the Lease

LO4 Lease termination

A lease for a fixed time automatically terminates upon the expiration of that period. The death of either party does not ordinarily affect the lease. If the leased property consists of rooms or apartments in a building and fire or any other accidental cause destroys them, the lease terminates without liability on the part of the tenant. In the case of leases of entire buildings, serious problems arise if fire, tornado, or any other cause destroys the property. Under the common law the tenant had to continue to pay rent even though the property was destroyed. Some states retain this rule; other states have modified it. A landlord who has a 10-year lease on a $100,000 building destroyed by fire one year after signing the lease would not be inclined to rebuild if fully covered by fire insurance. The landlord would find it more profitable to invest the $100,000 and

NOTICE TO LEAVE THE PREMISES

To Mr. C. Harold Whitmore

You will please take notice that I *want you to leave the premises you now occupy, and which you have rented of* me *, situated and described as follows:*

Suite 4

Lakeview Apartment

Lake Shore Drive at Overview Street

in Cleveland *County of* Cuyahoga *and State of* Ohio

Your compliance with this Notice July 31

will prevent legal measures being taken by me *to obtain possession of the same, agreeably to law.*

Yours respectfully,

H. B. Simpson

May 1 *20*–

Illustration 44-2

Landlord's Notice to Leave the Premises

continue to collect the rent. To prevent this, statutes may provide that if the landlord refuses to restore the property, the lease terminates. The lease itself may contain a cancellation clause. If it does not, the tenant can carry fire insurance for the amount of possible loss. Even when the lease will thus terminate, the tenant will probably wish to carry fire insurance for personal property and, if the premises are used for a business purpose, may carry insurance to indemnify for business interruption or loss of business income.

The landlord may agree to the voluntary surrender of the possession of the premises before the lease expires. An abandonment of the premises without the consent of the landlord does not constitute a surrender, however, but a breach of contract.

If the lease runs from year to year or from month to month, the party wishing to terminate it must generally give the other party a written notice of this intention (see Illustrations 44-2 and 44-3). Statutes prescribe the time and the manner of giving notice; they may also specify other particulars, such as the grounds for a termination of the tenancy.

If either party fails to give proper notice, the other party may continue the tenancy for another period.

EVICTION

Eviction
Expulsion of tenant from leased property

Tenants sometimes refuse to give up possession of the property after the expiration of the lease or fail to perform required duties. In such a case, a landlord may seek an **eviction** of the tenant. Eviction is the expulsion of the tenant from the leased property. The laws of the states vary, but all have some form of summary eviction law. The

January 2, 20 –

Mr. George A. Hardwick
1719 Glenview Road
St. Louis, Missouri 65337

Dear Mr. Hardwick

This is to notify you that on March 31, 20 –, I intend to vacate the premises now leased from you and located at 1292 Clarendon Road, St. Louis, Missouri. In accordance with the terms of our written lease, this letter constitutes notice of the termination of said lease as of March 31, 20 –.

Sincerely,

John N. Richter

JOHN N. RICHTER

Illustration 44-3
Tenant's Notice that the Tenant is Leaving the Premises

Forcible Entry and Detainer Action
Summary action by landlord to regain possession

summary action brought by the landlord is called a **forcible entry and detainer action**. The tenant has a right to written notice and a court hearing. However, the court will set an early date, usually 7 to 15 days after notification of the tenant, for the trial. If the landlord wins, law enforcement officers may enforce the eviction in a few days. The proceedings permit quick recovery of real property by the one legally entitled to it.

Improvements

Trade Fixtures
Fixtures used in business

Tenants frequently make improvements during the life of the lease. Many disputes arise as to the tenant's right to take these improvements after the lease is terminated. Courts must determine whether an improvement has become a fixture, which must be left on the land, or whether it remains personal property. If the improvements are **trade fixtures**, or fixtures used in business, and can be removed without substantial injury to the leased property, the tenant may remove them. If a farm tenant builds a fence in the normal way, the fence is a fixture, and the tenant has no right to remove it upon leaving. A poultry house built in the usual way is a fixture and cannot be removed. In a similar case a tenant built the poultry house on sledlike runners. When ready to leave, the tenant had the poultry house hauled away and took it when vacating. The court held the shed had not become a fixture but remained personal property.

Unless prohibited by law, one may freely contract away rights or may waive them, so the parties may agree as to how to treat fixtures. In one case a tenant built a permanent frame house on leased property with the landlord's agreement that the house could be moved at the end of the lease. The landlord was bound by this contract.

Discrimination

Federal law prohibits landlords from discriminating against tenants or proposed tenants because of race, color, religion, sex, familial status, or national origin. The term *familial status* refers to whether the tenant has children. Additionally, some states and even municipalities prohibit discrimination based on such aspects as physical or mental handicaps, age, or marital status.

Questions

1. What are the chief characteristics that determine the relationship of landlord and tenant?
2. What are the requirements regarding the form of a lease?
3. May a tenancy for years be for any length of time? Explain.
4. What rights does the tenant have when property is leased?
5. From what kinds of defects must a landlord protect a tenant?
6. a. If a hurricane breaks all the windows in a dwelling, must the tenant replace these windows?
   b. If leased property is destroyed by fire, must the tenant continue to pay rent?
7. Explain the duty of a landlord to mitigate damages.
8. If a tenant refuses to give up possession after the expiration of a lease, what may the landlord do?
9. If a tenant builds a garage on the property, may the garage be taken when the tenant moves? Explain.
10. What limitations does federal law place on landlords when selecting tenants?

Case Problems

LO3 1. Geraldine McAllister was a tenant in property owned by the Boston Housing Authority. Ice had accumulated on the outside stairs of the property from snow and cold weather. After McAllister slipped and fell on the ice, she sued alleging a breach of the warranty of habitability. Was the natural accumulation of ice and snow a breach of the warranty of habitability?

LO2 2. Cross Timbers owned property mortgaged to AgriBank FCB to secure payment of a note. Cross Timbers defaulted on the note and AgriBank foreclosed on the mortgage, buying the property at the foreclosure sale. Cross Timbers and AgriBank engaged in negotiations regarding the redemption or lease of the property by Cross Timbers, but no agreement was reached. Cross Timbers had remained in possession during the nine months of negotiations, but never paid rent. AgriBank sued for possession. Cross Timbers alleged that it had a tenancy at will and therefore AgriBank had to give it 60 days' notice of termination. Did a tenancy at will exist?

LO3 3 JBA, Inc., leased a commercial warehouse from Properties Investment Group of Mid-America (PIGOMA). Before the end of the term, JBA moved out and PIGOMA refused to accept termination of the lease. PIGOMA interviewed realtors to list the property for sale or lease and listed it with a realtor a month after JBA moved out. The realtor advertised and showed the property for a year. PIGOMA then retained a certified property manager for three months to assist it in selling or leasing the property and negotiated a sale itself that fell through. Other realtors also showed the property during those three months until PIGOMA signed another listing agreement with one. When PIGOMA sued JBA for unpaid rent, JBA alleged PIGOMA had not taken reasonable steps to mitigate its damages. Had it?

LO1 4 The lessee of a long-term lease for a radio broadcasting tower site assigned the lease to Towers of Texas, Inc. The lease's description of the site gave latitude and longitude coordinates and an elevation but also gave the lessee "exclusive use of the space on top of said Double Mountain." The original lessee built the tower on a flat place on top of the mountain because the coordinates described a single point on the side of the mountain not suitable in location or size for the tower and which did not coincide with the elevation given. The lessors built a second radio tower on the top of the mountain, and Towers sued them. Was Towers' lease limited to the coordinate-described point, or was that description ambiguous?

LO2 5 Anthony Manfredi, d.b.a. Manfredi Pizza, and Minnie Cesta entered into a lease of realty for five years. It obligated Manfredi in the first year to pay "yearly rent of $8,400, payable in equal monthly installments." The lease also provided that at the end of each year "the rent shall be increased by a percentage equal to the increase in the consumer price index for such 12-month period immediately preceding." Manfredi paid the rent during the first year and for January of the second year, but then paid no more. Cesta sued, claiming the lease created a year-to-year tenancy. Manfredi claimed the first year was on an annual term, but the last four years were a month-to-month tenancy. Which is it?

LO4 6 The East Harlem Pilot Block Building 1 Housing Development Fund Corp. leased an apartment for a specified period to Jose Serrano, who died during the term of the lease. The Fund then brought an eviction proceeding for nonpayment of rent against the deceased. To decide who the proper party defendant was in the proceeding the court had to decide whether the lease terminated with Serrano's death. Does a lease automatically terminate when the tenant of a tenancy for years dies?

Internet Resources for Business Law

Name	Resources	Web Address
Legal Information Institute (LII)—Landlord-Tenant Law Materials	LII provides an overview of landlord-tenant law, links to statutes, federal and state judicial court decisions, and other materials.	http://www.law.cornell.edu/topics/landlord_tenant.html
TenantNet	TenantNet, an informal network of tenants and tenant leaders in New York, provides news, information, and resources on landlord-tenant law.	http://tenant.net/

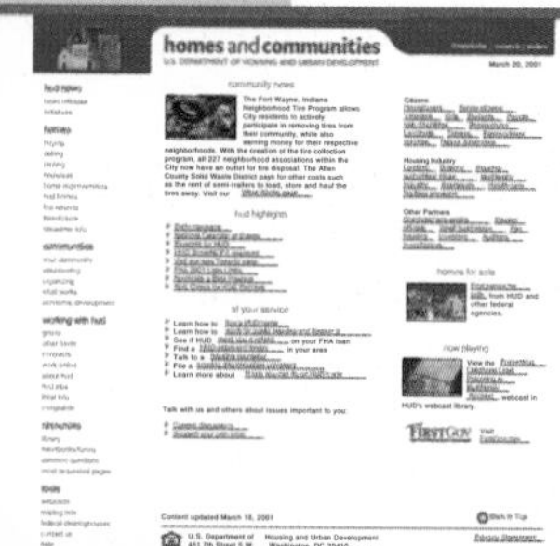

45

Wills, Inheritances, and Trusts

Learning Objectives

1 Describe a will, its characteristics, and the limitations on disposition of property.

2 Explain the normal formalities required for executing the various types of wills.

3 Name the ways in which a will may be changed or revoked.

4 Discuss the requirements for probate and administration.

5 Recognize a trust and the parties to a trust.

PREVIEW CASE

By the terms of her will, Eloise Williams devised her 103-acre "home place" to her nephews and nieces. The residue of the estate was bequeathed to the Masonic Home or Homes for Crippled Children. Three months before her death, Williams sold the "home place" and received an $80,000 note secured by a deed of trust. What effect does the sale of the property have on the devises? When specific property bequeathed by a will is no longer owned, what does the beneficiary receive?

LO1
Will characteristics

Will
Document providing disposition of property after death

Estate
Property left by a deceased

Testator (Testatrix)
Person making a will

Title to all property, both real and personal, may be transferred by a will. A **will** is an instrument prepared in the form prescribed by law that provides for the disposition of a person's property and takes effect after death. The property left by a person who has died is called the **estate**.

The person making the will is called a **testator** (**testatrix** if a woman). Testators do not have to meet as high a standard of capacity to make a will as a person does in order to make a contract. They must have the mental capability at the time of making the will to know the natural objects of their bounty, understand the nature and extent of their property, understand that they are making a will, and have the ability to dispose of their property by means of a plan they have formulated. Even if they do not have the mental capacity to carry on a business or if they make unusual provisions in the will, this does not necessarily mean that they do not have the capacity to make a will. An insane person lacks sufficient capacity; however, an insane person who has intervals of sanity has capacity during sane intervals to make a will. Any person, other than a minor, of sound mind ordinarily has the competence to make a will. In a few states minors can, under limited circumstances, make a will.

Facts: William and Alberta McQuady executed identical wills leaving everything to the survivor and upon the survivor's death to a cousin and Thomas Beavin, Alberta's brother. Alberta died and her estate went to William. William was blind and hired Mary Bye as his housekeeper. Two months later McQuady and Bye visited his lawyer and McQuady executed a new will leaving all but $100 to Bye. She had a garage built on McQuady's property and kept her car not McQuady's in it. McQuady's cousin and Beavin had Beavin appointed as a limited guardian for McQuady who was diagnosed with Alzheimer's disease. A petition to allow McQuady to marry Bye was filed and at a hearing McQuady said Bye had misled him about the content of the petition. He stated he did not want to marry Bye and was afraid of her. The judge denied the petition and Bye was fired. McQuady then executed a will that re-enacted the will he had executed with his wife. After McQuady died, Bye challenged the validity of the latest will alleging lack of testamentary capacity.

Outcome: The court stated that although McQuady suffered from Alzheimer's he was presumed to have had a lucid interval when the will was executed. McQuady's testimony during the hearing on the marriage petition showed he could have lucid intervals and that at that time he had a total grasp of the circumstances. Bye had to show he lacked capacity and she did not do that.

Limitations on Disposition of Property

The law places few restrictions on the right to dispose of property by will. However some restrictions include:

Right to Take Against the Will
Spouse's right to share of estate provided by statute if will leaves smaller share

1 A spouse may elect to take that share of property that would have been received had the deceased died without leaving a will, or the share provided by statute, if the spouse's will does not leave as large a share, called the **right to take against the will.**

Most state laws now provide that when an individual dies without leaving a will, a spouse has the right to a set portion of all the property the deceased spouse owned at the time of death. The spouse's portion varies depending on the number of children or other heirs who survive. The surviving spouse in some states may also claim an interest in property conveyed by the deceased spouse during the marriage without the consent of the surviving spouse.

The right to take against the will can be barred by actions of the surviving spouse. If the surviving spouse commits acts that would have justified the deceased in securing a divorce, the surviving spouse generally cannot elect to take against the will.

Except for the cases of a surviving spouse electing to take against the will and in some cases of a subsequent marriage, birth, or adoption, the testator may exclude or disinherit any person from receiving any portion of the estate. If the testator gives the entire estate to someone else, all persons who would inherit in the absence of a will are excluded. The testator does not even have to mention in a will those persons disinherited with the exception of children, nor does a nominal sum have to be left to those disinherited.

2 One cannot control by will the distribution of property in perpetuity (for all time). The common-law rule against perpetuities requires that an interest in property must vest, if at all, within 21 years after the death of persons living on the date the owner of the property creates the interest. When the interest is created by will, the date of death of the owner constitutes the date of creation.

Terms Common to Wills

Devisee
One receiving realty by will

Legatee
One receiving personal property by will

Devise
Realty left by will

A number of terms may refer to individuals named or gifts given in a will. The one receiving a gift of real estate (the beneficiary) is called the **devisee**; the beneficiary of personal property is a **legatee**. A **devise** is real property given by will. A **bequest**, or a **legacy**, is a gift by will of personal property. The person named in a will as the one to administer the estate is an **executor**. One who dies without having made a will is said to die **intestate**. A person appointed by a court to settle the affairs of an intestate is an **administrator** (man) or an **administratrix** (woman).

Distinguishing Characteristics of a Will

Bequest or Legacy
Personal property left by will

Executor
Person named in will to administer estate

Intestate
One who dies without a will

A will has the following outstanding characteristics that distinguish it from many other legal instruments:

1 The courts construe a will with less technical strictness than a deed or any other kind of written document.
2 A will devising real property must be executed in conformity with the law of the state in which the property is situated. The law of the state in which the testator was domiciled (had permanent residence) at the time of death governs a will bequeathing personal property.
3 A will may be revoked at any time during the life of the testator.

Formalities

LO2
Will formalities

Administrator or Administratrix
Person appointed by court to administer estate of intestate

Publication
Testator's informing witnesses that document is will

All states prescribe formalities for wills. These formalities must be strictly followed. A will almost always must be in writing and signed by the testator.

A will written in the testator's own handwriting and dated need not be witnessed in a number of states. In almost all states the will must be witnessed by at least two, and in some states three, disinterested witnesses regardless of how it is written. Usually, the witnesses and the testator must sign in the presence of each other. Many states also require the testator to inform the witnesses that the instrument being signed is the testator's will. This is called **publication**.

When the law requires subscribing witnesses, they must be available at the time of probate of the will to identify their signatures and the signature of the testator and to state that they were present when the testator signed the will. If the witnesses cannot be found, two persons must normally identify the signature of the testator on the will. They base their opinion regarding the testator's signature upon their experience through prior correspondence or business records involving the testator's signature. A will executed in another jurisdiction is valid if correctly executed in the other jurisdiction. If a person's will is not drawn according to the legal requirements, the court may disregard it and the property may be disposed of in a manner entirely foreign to the testator's wishes.

Special Types of Wills

Under special circumstances, testators can make valid wills that are less formal than usual. Three special types of wills include:

1. Holographic wills
2. Nuncupative wills
3. Soldiers' and sailors' wills

HOLOGRAPHIC WILLS

Holographic Will
Will written out by testator

Holographic wills are written entirely in longhand by the testator. Some states make no distinction between holographic and other wills. In other states variations of the general law of wills exist for holographic wills. In still other states holographic wills may not be recognized.

Facts: David Horwitz had a son, also named David, from a previous marriage. David Sr. died leaving two-thirds of his estate to Margaret, his wife, and one-third to David Jr. Margaret died 25 years later. A nephew found pages of writing paper, folded together, on Margaret's bedside table. The pages contained only Margaret's handwriting in several colors of ink, with interlineations, corrections, and marginal notations. The first page began, "Being of sound mind I, Margaret Macleod Horwitz, declare the following to be my last will and testament." The pages contained many numbered bequests to people including David Jr., his wife, and daughter. The last bequest gave the remainder of the estate to five nephews and listed their names. Margaret did not sign at the end. The court received the document for determination of its status.

Outcome: The court said that the document described itself as a will; it contained specific bequests and a residuary clause that disposed of all of Margaret's property; and it seemed reasonable and complete. Therefore the court found it a valid, holographic will.

NUNCUPATIVE WILL

Nuncupative Will
Oral will made during last illness

Nuncupative wills are oral wills declared by the testator in the presence of witnesses. Usually such a will can only be made during the testator's last illness. A nuncupative will only applies to personal property, and sometimes only a limited value of personal property may be so disposed. The witnesses frequently must reduce the will to writing within a specified number of days and they must agree as to how the deceased disposed of the property.

Facts: During the last of several hospital stays, Mr. Kay told Shirley Macow that he wanted to change his will. She called Mr. Engelhardt, his attorney, who went to see Kay at the hospital. While alone with Engelhardt, Kay told him what terms he wanted in his will. During this conversation, Kay did not tell Engelhardt that he was making an oral will. Engelhardt drafted a new will for Kay, but when he took it to Kay's office, Kay had had a heart attack and died. Mike Kay alleged the new will constituted a nuncupative will that revoked a prior will.

Outcome: The court found the alleged nuncupative will invalid because the law required three witnesses to agree to the words spoken by the deceased. Only Engelhardt heard Kay, and Kay did not indicate the words he spoke constituted his will.

SOLDIERS AND SAILORS

Most states make special provision for members of the armed forces. They are allowed to make oral or written wills of personal property without complying with the formalities required of other wills. These wills are in force even after the testator returns to civilian life. They must be revoked in the same manner as other wills.

The Wording of a Will

Any words that convey the intention of the testator suffice (see Illustration 45-1). No matter how rough and ungrammatical the language may be, if the intention of the

WILL OF FRANK JOSEPH ROSE

I, Frank Joseph Rose, of the City of Chicago and State of Illinois, revoke all prior wills and codicils and declare that this is my will.

FIRST: If she survives me, I give to my beloved daughter, Anna Rose, now residing in Crestwood, Illinois, that certain piece of real estate, with all improvements thereon, situated at 341 Hudson Avenue, Crestwood, Illinois. If my daughter predeceases me, I give this real estate to my brother, James Earl Rose, now residing in Crestwood, Illinois.

SECOND: All the remainder and residue of my property I give to my beloved wife, Mary Ellen Rose, if, she survives me. If my wife predeceases me, I give the remainder and residue of my property to my daughter, Anna. If both my wife and my daughter predecease me, I give the remainder and residue of my property to my brother, James.

THIRD: I hereby nominate and appoint my wife, Mary Ellen Rose, executrix of this will. If my wife is unable or unwilling to act as executrix, I nominate and appoint my daughter, Anna, executrix. I direct that neither Mary Ellen nor Anna be required to give bond or security for the performance of duties as executrix.

IN WITNESS WHEREOF, I have subscribed my name this tenth day of October, in the year two thousand–.

Frank Joseph Rose
Frank Joseph Rose

We, the undersigned, certify that the foregoing instrument was, on the tenth day of October, signed and declared by Frank Joseph Rose to be his will, in the presence of us who, in his presence and in the presence of each other, have, at his request, hereunto signed our names as witnesses of the execution thereof, this tenth day of October, 20–.

Constance O. Moore — 4316 Cottage Grove Avenue residing at Chicago, Illinois 60600

Sarah J. King — 1313 East 63 Street residing at Chicago, Illinois 60600

Stewart S. Samuels — 2611 Elm Street residing at Chicago, Illinois 60400

Illustration 45-1
Will

testator can be ascertained, the court will order that the provisions of the will be carried out. Since the court will order the terms of a will to be carried out exactly, the wording of the will should express the exact wishes of the testator.

Revocation

LO3
Will revocation and change

A will may be revoked at any time prior to the death of the testator. The revocation may take any one of several forms.

Codicils

Codicil
Writing that modifies a will

A **codicil** is a separate writing that modifies a will. Except for the part modified, the original will remains the same. A codicil must be executed with all the formalities of the original will.

DESTRUCTION OR ALTERATION

If the testator deliberately destroys a will, this constitutes a revocation. If the testator merely alters the will, this may or may not revoke it, depending upon the nature and the extent of the alteration. If the testator merely obliterates a part of the will, in most states this does not revoke the will.

MARRIAGE AND DIVORCE

If a single person makes a will and later marries, the marriage may revoke the will in whole or in part, or the will may be presumed to be revoked unless made in contemplation of the marriage or unless it made provision for a future spouse. In some states a marriage will not revoke a will completely, but only so that the spouse will get the estate that would have been received in the absence of a will. A divorce automatically revokes a will to the extent of the property left to the divorced spouse if the court orders a division of property; otherwise, a divorce usually in no way affects the will.

Facts: Grady Miles made a will leaving his "friend," Georgia Hall, his car and a life interest in his home. Georgia had rejected numerous marriage proposals from Grady. More than a year later, Grady and Georgia got married. Grady died seven months later without having changed his will. Georgia filed suit claiming the marriage revoked the will.

Outcome: The court said that while Grady did make some provision for Georgia in the will, he made no indication that the bequest was made in contemplation of marriage. In fact Georgia had refused to marry him many times and it took more than a year for Grady to persuade her to marry him. The will, not having been made in contemplation of marriage, was revoked by the marriage.

EXECUTION OF A LATER WILL

The execution of a later will automatically revokes a prior will if the terms of the second conflict with the first will. If the second will merely changes a few provisions in the first will and leaves the bulk of it intact, then a second revokes the first will only to the extent of such inconsistency.

AFTER-BORN CHILD

A child may be born or adopted after a person makes a will. If the original will does not provide for subsequent children or the testator makes no codicil to provide for the child, this revokes or partially revokes the will.

Abatement and Ademption

Abatement
Proportionate reduction in monetary bequest because of insufficient funds

Ademption
Failure of bequest because property not in estate

An **abatement** occurs when a testator makes bequests of money in the will and the estate does not have enough money to pay the bequests. The legatees will receive a proportionate share of the bequests.

An **ademption** occurs when a testator makes a bequest of specific property and the estate does not have the property at death. In this case, the legatee gets nothing.

If a testator leaves $20,000 to his son John, $10,000 to his sister Mary, and a painting to his brother Adam, there could be both an abatement and an ademption. If the estate has only $15,000 in cash left after paying all debts, the cash gifts to John and Mary will abate. Each will receive a proportionate share, in this case 50 percent, or $10,000 and $5,000 respectively. If the testator had sold the painting, given it away, or someone had stolen, destroyed, or lost the painting before the death of the testator, Adam would get nothing. The bequest to him is adeemed since the property was not in the estate at the testator's death. He has no right to its cash value or any other substitute item of property.

PREVIEW CASE REVISITED

Facts: By the terms of her will, Eloise Williams devised her 103-acre "home place" to her nephews and nieces. The residue of the estate was bequeathed to the Masonic Home or Homes for Crippled Children. Three months before her death, Williams sold the "home place" and received an $80,000 note secured by a deed of trust.

Outcome: The court held that the devise of the "home place" was adeemed by the sale, and the $80,000 note passed under the residuary clause of the will.

Probate of a Will

LO4
Requirements for administration

Probate
Court procedure to determine validity of a will

When a testator dies leaving a will, the will must be probated. **Probate** is the court procedure that determines the validity of a will. The will normally names an executor to preserve and handle the estate during probate and distribute it to the rightful individuals. An executor has liability to legatees, creditors, and heirs for loss to the estate as a result of negligence, bad faith, or breach of trust and must comply with any instructions in the will. A will may expressly direct the executor to continue a business owned by the deceased. If the will does not so provide, an executor frequently can obtain permission of the appropriate court to continue the business. With but few exceptions, anyone may be appointed executor. The testator may excuse the executor from furnishing a bond that would be an expense to the estate. If the will does not name an executor, then upon petition of one of the beneficiaries the court will appoint an administrator.

If a person contests the will, the court must hear the contest to determine the validity of the will. A contest of the will differs from litigation over the meaning or interpretation to be given the will. If the contest alleges and proves fraud, undue influence, improper witnessing, mental incapacity of the testator, revocation of the will, or any other infirmity in the will affecting its legality, the court will find the will nullified. It will then distribute the property of the testator according to the law of descent described later in this chapter.

When Administration Is Unnecessary

Of course, if an individual does not own any property at the time of death, no need for administration exists. Also, all property jointly owned with someone else who acquires the interest by right of survivorship does not require administration.

Some states have special statutes allowing the administration procedures to be shortened for very small estates. In many states all the persons interested in the estate, relatives and creditors, can agree on the share each one is to receive and can divide the estate without formal court proceedings.

Title by Descent

When a person dies intestate, the property is distributed in accordance with the state law of descent. Every state has such a law. Although these laws vary slightly, on the whole they provide as follows: The property of the intestate goes to any children subject to the rights of the surviving spouse. If no spouse, children, or grandchildren survive, the father and mother, as the next of kin, receive the property. If no parents survive, the brothers and sisters become the next of kin, followed by grandparents, aunts and uncles, and so on. Some statutes permit any person related by blood to inherit when no nearer related relative exists. Other statutes do not permit those beyond first cousins to inherit. In any case, if no proper person to inherit survives, the property passes to the state.

The administrator conveys title to real estate by means of an administrator's deed. When approved by the court, the grantee obtains good title to the property.

Per Capita and *Per Stirpes* Distribution

Per Capita
Per head

Per Stirpes
Distribution among heirs according to relationship to deceased

The lineal descendants of a decedent include the children and grandchildren. If all the children were living at the time of an intestate's death, and the spouse was dead, the property would be distributed ***per capita***, meaning per head, or equally to the children (see Illustration 45-2). If one child predeceased the intestate and left two surviving children, then the property would be divided into equal parts on the basis of the number of children the intestate had. The dead child's part would then be divided into two equal parts with one of these parts going to each of the grandchildren. This divides the property ***per stirpes*** (see Illustration 45-3). If the deceased child left no children or other lineal descendants, then the surviving children of the intestate would take the deceased child's share.

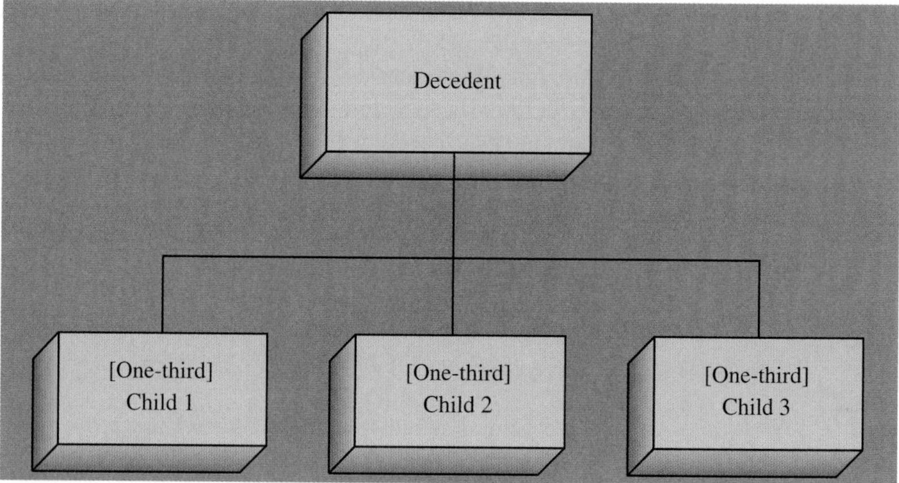

Illustration 45-2
Per Capita Distribution

Facts: In his will Samuel Dwight created a trust with the income to be paid to his children and upon the death of the last of the children the trust assets were to be distributed to the descendants of his "children as shall then be living in equal shares per stirpes." When the trust terminated, one child had three children living and the other had six children. The trustee filed suit to find out whether to divide the trust assets in nine parts so that each grandchild received an equal share or in two parts, one for each of the families of Dwight's children.

Outcome: The court held that per stirpes means by right of representation so that the descendants were to take as representatives of a parent.

Administrators

For the most part the duties and responsibilities of administrators resemble those of executors, with two significant differences. First, in the appointment of an administrator, some states have a clear order of priority. The surviving spouse has first priority, followed by children, grandchildren, parents, and brothers or sisters. Second, an administrator must in all cases execute a bond guaranteeing the faithful performance of the duties.

The prime duty of administrators is the same as that of executors—to preserve the estate and distribute it to the rightful parties. Administrators must act in good faith, with prudence, and within the powers conferred on them by law. If any part of the estate is a going business, with only a few exceptions the business must be liquidated. However, the administrator may obtain leave of court to continue the business for either a limited time or an indefinite time, depending largely upon the wishes of those entitled to receive the estate. Third parties dealing with administrators, as well as executors, must know of limitations upon their authority.

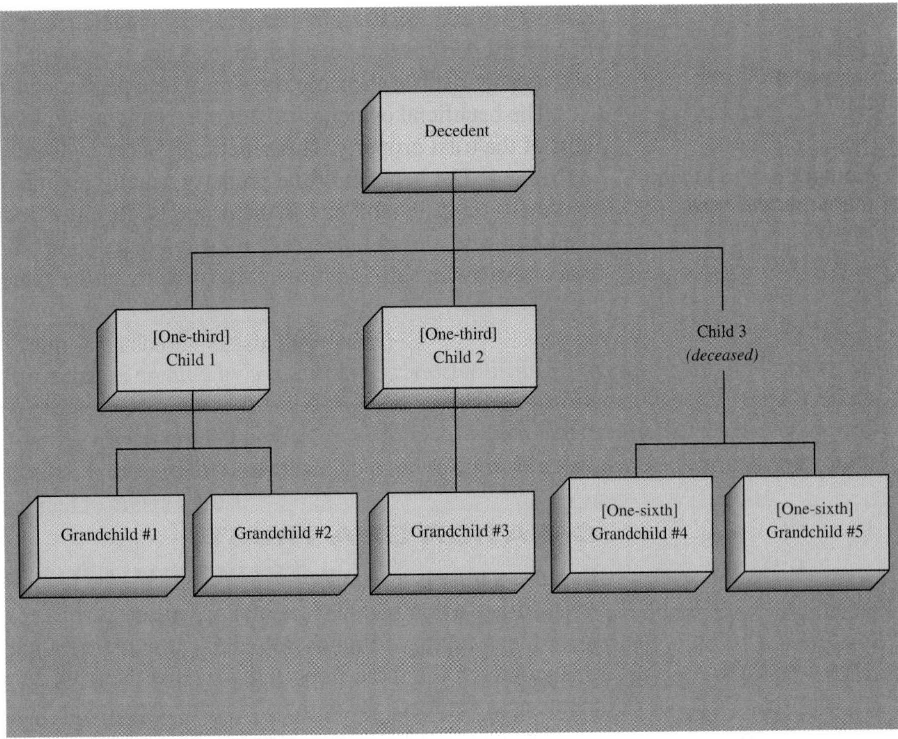

Illustration 45-3
Per Stirpes Distribution

Trusts

LO5
Trust and its parties

Trust
Contract by which one holds property for another

A **trust** is a form of contract by which one person or entity agrees to hold property for the benefit of another. Chapter 41, "Nature of Real Property," examined one way in which ownership of property may be divided between two owners. That chapter discussed the difference between a life estate, or income interest, and a remainder interest in property. This division in ownership separates the total ownership, or the fee simple estate, over time. The life tenant is the first owner and the holder of the reversion or remainder is the second after the death of the life tenant.

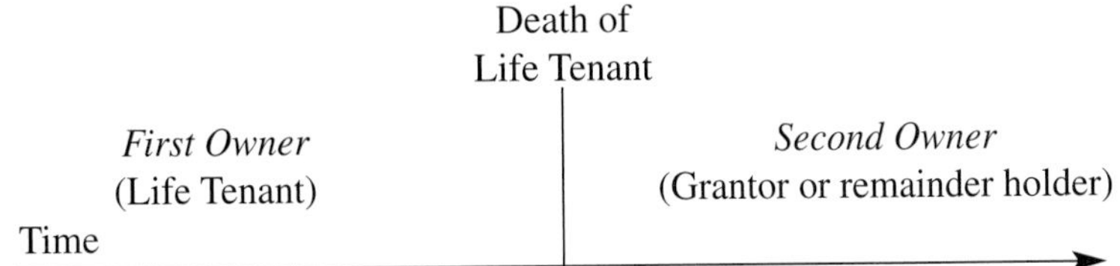

Ownership of property in trust can be described as a division at the same time of two ownership interests—the legal ownership and the beneficial ownership. The legal owner of trust property is the person or entity who holds title to the property and who has the

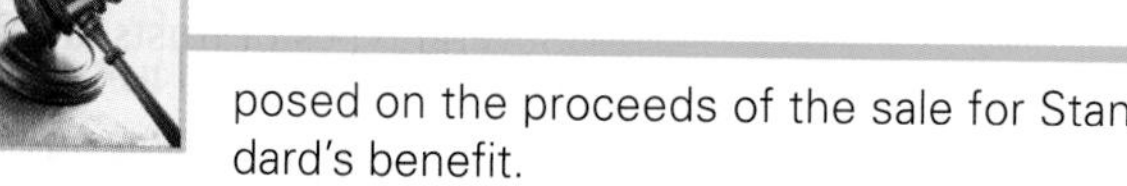

Facts: Over a period of about three years, Angela Bransom embezzled $480,000 from her employer, Standard Hardware. Some of the money was used to pay family expenses of Angela and her husband, Donald, including mortgage payments on their home. When the home was sold, Standard alleged a constructive trust should be imposed on the proceeds of the sale for Standard's benefit.

Outcome: The court held that it did not matter that Donald did not know of or have any fault with regard to Angela's wrongdoing—stolen funds are held in trust for the lawful owner of the funds.

An example is when a government official with authority to regulate a certain industry gives management of property to a trustee, so that there will be no conflict between the official's personal financial interests and official government duties. Wealthy members of Congress frequently use blind trusts so they will not know exactly what securities they own. Then when they vote on legislation they cannot know whether their vote helps the companies in which they have a personal financial interest.

TESTAMENTARY TRUST

Testamentary Trust
Trust created in will

A **testamentary trust** is a special form of express trust created by the will of a testator. Even though the trust will not actually be created until the death of the testator, it will become a valid trust at that time. The trustee may, but need not, be the same person or entity as the executor of the will. A trust created by a will is subject to the same rules as other trusts.

Consider, as an example, the will of Heinrich Heine, the famous nineteenth-century German poet. His will included the following provision for his wife: "I leave all my estate to my wife on the express condition that she remarry. I want at least one person to sincerely grieve my death." Does this language have the effect of placing the entire estate into a trust? Heine died in France, but if his will had been probated in the present-day United States, it is highly unlikely a court would enforce this provision because of the requirement that Heine's widow remarry. Instead, the property would most likely be distributed directly to Heine's widow, outright and free from trust.

Questions

1. What is the mental capacity required of persons in order to make a will?
2. What restrictions are there upon one's right to leave property by will to anyone desired?
3. What law governs bequests of real property and bequests of personal property by will?
4. How clearly and correctly must the wording of a will be?
5. What are the ways in which a will may be revoked?
6. To whom and for what does an executor of a will have liability?
7. a. What is the difference between distributing property *per capita* and *per stirpes*?
   b. When would a *per stirpes* distribution be required?
8. What is the prime duty of an administrator and how does it differ from that of an executor?
9. What two ownership interests does the ownership of property in trust divide?
10. What specific words are required to create an express trust?

Case Problems

LO2 1 Stanley Bernatowicz attempted to sign his name to his will but had difficulty signing in spite of making several attempts. He was very ill and died several hours later. Bernatowicz' attorney told Sherry Callara who was the named executrix and mother of a legatee under the will that she could help Bernatowicz by steadying his hand. The attorney told Callara she could not sign the will for Bernatowicz or move his hand and she assisted him in signing. After Bernatowicz' death Natalie Mack contested the will alleging Callara had controlled Bernatowicz rather than assisted him. Had Bernatowicz signed the will?

LO1 2 John Gerard executed a will naming his sister-in-law, Eva Gerard, executrix and making provision for his wife of two years, Violet. Gerard had told numerous people he wanted to provide for Violet and leave her his house. Gerard had cancer and was taking medicine that interfered with mental processes and caused confusion and forgetfulness. He was depressed and unable to make up his mind. His acquaintance, Joyce Crabtree, took Gerard to the doctor leaving Violet in the waiting room while Crabtree accompanied Gerard to see the doctor. Gerard began living with Joyce and her husband who would not let anyone else talk with him. Two weeks after Gerard's first will he executed a new one using a different lawyer and removing all mention of Violet. This will funded a trust that was amended several times. The final amendment made two days before Gerard's death was dictated to the lawyer by Joyce and put the Crabtrees in complete control of the trust eliminating Eva, Violet, and all other heirs. After Gerard's death Violet attacked the second will alleging he lacked testamentary capacity. Did he?

LO3 3 William Cole executed a will naming Catherine Jackson the sole beneficiary and executrix. He specifically did not leave any property to any of his brothers. Six months later, he married Catherine Jackson. He died about 25 years later. As his executrix, Catherine executed a deed of William's real estate to herself. Catherine's will left the real estate to St. Pius Church. A question arose about the validity of the church's title, so Laureen D'Ambra, Catherine's executrix, filed a suit to clear it up. The issue before the court involved whether William's marriage after execution of his will revoked it. Did it?

LO2 4 The attorney who prepared a will for Edwin Lubin inserted a clause that stated it relieved the executor from liability "for any loss or injury to the property . . . except . . . as may result from fraud, misconduct, or gross negligence." In a court proceeding relating to the will the validity of this provision arose. Is this provision in accordance with the liabilities and duties of an executor?

LO5 5 Maureen Sullivan gave up her career as a flight attendant to maintain a home for herself and James Rooney. Rooney continued to climb the career ladder as an attorney, while Sullivan's contributions were largely in the home. Rooney assured Sullivan that they owned their property together, although title to the home was taken in Rooney's name alone in order to obtain certain veteran's benefits. After the relationship turned sour, Sullivan sued Rooney for her share of the property. Should the court find a constructive trust?

LO4 6 Myrtice Hogue became pregnant by Archie Hearn, so they got married and had a daughter, Mallery Clotille Hearn. Archie had no contact with the child after she was a month old, and Myrtice obtained a divorce. Fourteen years later Archie married Mamie Slack and 40 years later Archie died. Archie's will named Mamie executrix and bequeathed her his entire estate. Mamie petitioned to probate the will alleging that Archie died leaving no lawful descendants. The estate was probated and Mamie got Archie's property. Six years after Archie died, Mallery filed suit alleging Archie's estate was probated based on false statements by Mamie because she knew about Mallery. Did Mamie owe any duty to Mallery?

LO5 7 Shortly before he died, Joseph Staples created several trusts. The trusts benefited Joseph during his life, and his children and grandchildren upon his death. He transferred most of his assets to those trusts. Upon his death, his wife, Elizabeth Staples, was left with virtually nothing. Furthermore, since the trust property did not pass by Joseph's will, Elizabeth could not elect her statutory share of the property. Elizabeth asked the court to impose a constructive trust for her benefit on the trust assets. Will the court help her?

LO2 8 To write out her will Frances Black used three copies of a stationer's form designed to be used for a one-page will. In the clause at the top of each page she filled in her signature and residence. She also filled in the name and gender of her executor and used the appropriate blanks on the last page to give her city and state of residence and the date. She dated the top of the first page. The rest of the printed language was either stricken or ignored by her. She used almost all the remaining area on all three pages for a specific disposition of her estate. No other person's handwriting appeared on the three pages. The court denied probate of the will because Black "incorporated" portions of the form in her will so it was not entirely in her own handwriting. Should the will be admitted to probate?

Internet Resources for Business Law

Name	Resources	Web Address
Legal Information Institute (LII)—Estates and Trusts Law Materials	LII, maintained by Cornell Law School, provides an overview of estates and trust law, including relevant sections from the U.S. Code and Code of Federal Regulation, court cases, the Uniform Probate Code, and links.	http://www.law.cornell.edu/topics/estates_trusts.html
Crash Course in Wills and Trusts	Crash Course in Wills and Trusts created by attorney and CFP Michael T. Palermo, is a practical guide to what everyone should know about the law of wills and trusts before an estate plan is designed.	http://www.mtpalermo.com/
Layne T. Rushforth's Estate Planning	Layne T. Rushforth's Estate Planning Page has basic and advanced articles on estate planning, links, and newsgroups.	http://www.rushforth.org/planning/
American Bar Association's Section of Real Property, Probate and Trust Law	The Real Property, Probate and Trust Law Section, with over 30,000 members, publishes the scholarly journal, *Real Property, Probate and Trust Law Journal,* and the practical bimonthly magazine, *Probate & Property.*	http://www.abanet.org/rppt/home.html
The American College of Trust & Estate Counsel (ACTEC)	The American College of Trust and Estate Counsel, a nonprofit association of lawyers and law professors, provides pamphlets on wills and estates.	http://www.actec.org/

Part 9 Summary Cases

Property

1 Frank Billotti owned two pieces of real estate as a joint tenant with right of survivorship with his wife, Carolyn. Frank murdered Carolyn and their daughters and was convicted of the murders. Frank conveyed the properties to his mother, Rose Billotti. State law stated that no one convicted of killing another could acquire any property from the person killed "by descent and distribution, or by will, . . . or otherwise." Carolyn's parents sued for the joint tenancy property. Did the words "or otherwise" in the statute include taking property under joint tenancy with right of survivorship? [*Lakatos v. Estate of Billotti*, 509 S.E.2d 594 (W.Va.)]

2 Honolulu Book Shops (HBS) leased real property from Hi Kai Investment. HBS assigned the lease to Aloha Futons that defaulted in the payment of the rent. Hi Kai sued for summary possession of the property, past rent, and future rent under the lease. Aloha alleged that Hi Kai could get summary possession of the property or future rent, but not both. May Hi Kai get both possession of the property and future rent or is its remedy limited to only one? [*Hi Kai Inv. v. Aloha Futons Beds*, 929 P.2d 88 (Hawai'i)]

3 Dillie McIntyre sold a tract of land to Russell and Sally Scarbrough reserving a life estate in 1.2 acres on which her mobile home sat. The reservation required McIntyre to maintain the 1.2 acres and pay the real estate taxes on it. Several years later, McIntyre had failed to pay the prior three years' real estate taxes. The Scarbroughs sued to terminate the life estate alleging McIntyre was also not maintaining the property. Should the life estate be terminated? [*McIntyre v. Scarbrough*, 471 S.E.2d 199 (Ga.)]

4 The Wade family owned the west half of Section 5, Township 7 North, Range 11 East in Newton County. Robert Grisson owned the east half of said section. Grisson claimed the west half by adverse possession and hired Jake Smith, Harvey Cleveland, and Bobby Gregory to cut timber from part of the west half. The timber was cut and delivered to Bay Springs Forest Products, Inc. The Wades sued Bay Springs to recover the value of the timber. Having determined that Grisson did not own the west half by adverse possession, the court had to consider what type of property the timber was. What was it? [*Bay Springs Forest Products, Inc. v. Wade*, 435 So. 2d 690 (Miss.)]

5 Cecil Carruth sent a letter to Paul McDaniel in which he agreed to deed McDaniel some land for $260,000. He stated that the deed would be delivered to McDaniel upon payment of the $30,000 down payment. Carruth later told McDaniel he was not going to sell him the land, and McDaniel filed suit for specific performance or conversion of his real estate. Carruth admitted he had told his lawyer to hold the deed until McDaniel paid the $30,000. McDaniel alleged a deed was executed and delivered for his benefit to the attorney and was either wrongfully taken or still in the possession of the attorney. Did the facts establish that McDaniel had title to the land? [*McDaniel v. Carruth*, 637 S.W. 2d 498 (Tex.)]

6 B-L-S Construction Company, Inc., orally agreed to lease property to St. Stephen Knitwear, Inc., for four months at $4,500 a month. The parties had planned to sign a written lease but did not. St. Stephen paid one month's rent and then abandoned the property. B-L-S sued for the rent remaining under the oral lease. Was there a valid lease? [*B-L-S Construction Company, Inc. v. St. Stephen Knitwear, Inc.*, 281 S.E.2d 129 (S.C.)]

7 Robert Daly died, and his will was offered for probate. The first witness, Ronald Witkowski, stated he was employed by Daly and was called into Daly's office and asked to sign a document. Witkowski did not know what he was signing and was not told it was Daly's will. Daly did not sign it in his presence. The second witness, Leo Hodge, was also employed by Daly and asked to witness a document. Hodge insisted on knowing what he was signing, so Daly showed him the front, which indicated it was Daly's will. Hodge was not sure whether Daly's signature was on the will or not. Daly's widow and three children, who were left very little by the will, filed objections to its probate alleging it was not properly executed. Was it? [*Matter of Will of Daly*, 402 N.Y.S.2d 747 (N.Y.)]

Glossary

A

Abandon: discard personal property with no intention to reclaim.

Abatement: proportionate reduction in monetary bequest because of an estate's insufficient funds.

Abstract of title: the history of a specific real estate property, including transfers and related legal procedings.

Acceleration clause: clause allowing entire principle to be due at a certain point in time.

Acceptance: assent to an offer resulting in a contract.

Acceptor: person who agrees to pay a draft, receive goods or assent to an order.

Accession: acquisition of title to property that is attached to property already owned.

Accretion: titled addition to land when owner's land built up by gradual water deposits and water's action on land.

Action of ejectment: action brought by landlord to have sheriff remove tenant.

Active fraud: party engages in action that causes the fraud.

Acknowledgement: declaration grantor has stated execution of instrument is free act.

Ademption: the inability to make a bequest of specific property because the property is not in the testator's estate.

Administrative agency: governmental boards or commissions with authority to regulate matters or implement laws.

Administrator or administratrix: person appointed by court to administer estate of deceased person.

Adverse possession: acquiring title to land by occupying it for a fixed period, typically a hostile acquisition.

Affirmative covenant: promise in a contract or deed to do an act.

Agency by estoppel: agency arising when person leads another to believe third party is the first person's agent.

An agency coupled with an interest: agency in which agent has the final stake in performance of agency because of having given consideration to principal.

Agent: person appointed to contract on behalf of another.

Alien corporation: corporatoin chartered in another country.

Allonge: paper so firmly attached to an instrument as to become part of it.

Alteration: unauthorized change or completion of negotiable instrument to modify obligation of a party.

Annual percentage rate (APR): amount charged for a loan as a percentage of the loan.

Annuity Insurance: contract that pays monthly income to an insured person while insured is alive.

Anonymous remailer: device that permits sending anonymous e-mail messages and software without the recipient knowing the source of the communication.

Answer or motion: the written response by defendant to a complaint's charges.

Antitrust laws: statutes that seek to promote competition among businesses, especially in the same industry.

Apparent authority: the authority an agent is believed by third parties to have because of the principal's behavior.

Appellate court: court that reviews the decision of another court, usually of a lower court.

Articles of incorporation: document stating facts about a corporation as required by law and for issuance of a charter.

Articles of partnership: a written partnership agreement.

Assessment mutual company: mutual insurance company in which losses are shared by policy holders in the ratio of their insurance to the company's total insurance in force.

Assignee: person to whom contract right is assigned.

Assignment: conveyance of personal property rights in a contract to a person not a party; transfer to another of tenant's rights.

Assignor: the person making an assignment.

Attorney in fact: general agent appointed by a written authorization.

Auction: the sale of property or goods to the highest bidder, or the bidder's agent, translated orally.

Automatic teller machine: electronic fund transfer terminal that performs routine banking services.

B

Bad check: a check the drawee bank refuses to pay for reasons such as insufficient funds or closed accounts.

Baggage: articles necessary for personal convenience while traveling on common carriers.

Bailee: the person in possession of bailed property.

Bailment: transfer of possession of personal property on condition property will be returned.

Bailor: the person who gives up possession of property when there is a bailment.

Balloon payment: a payment that is more than twice the normal installment payment.

Bank draft or teller's check: check drawn by one bank on another bank.

Bearer: payee of an instrument made payable to whomever is in possession of the instrument.

Bearer paper: commercial paper made payable to the bearer.

Beneficiary: the person who receives the proceeds of a life insurance policy; person entitled to income or enjoyment of trust property; a person who is given property by a will.

Bequest or legacy: a gift of personal property left to a party by a will.

Bidder: the person who makes an offer at an auction.

Bilateral contract: contract consisting of mutual exchange of promises to perform future acts.

Bill of exchange (draft): written order by one person directing another person to pay a sum or money to a third person.

Bill of lading: receipt and contract between consignor and carrier regarding terms of the contract of transportation.

Bill of rights: first 10 amendments of the U.S. constitution, enacted by the first Congress to protect the civil rights and liberties of citizens and states.

Bill of sale: written evidence of title transfership of tangible personal property.

Blank indorsement: indorsement that does not state to whom the instrument is to be paid.

Blanket policy: an insurance policy on many items in different places or different items in one place.

Blind trust: when the assets and administration of a trust are hidden from the grantor.

Blue-sky laws: statutes to protect the public by preventing the sale of worthless stocks and bonds.

Boarding housekeeper: a person in business to supply accommodations to permanent lodgers or boarders, as distinguished from transient guests.

Bond: a sealed, written contract obligation with essentials of note.

Bonding company: a paid surety.

Breach: failure or refusal to perform contractual obligations or agreements.

Broker: agent with job of bringing two contracting parties together.

Business crimes: crimes against a business or committed by using a business.

Business interruption insurance: insurance covering loss of profits while a damaged business building is repaired.

Business law: rules of conduct prescribed by government for the performance of business transactions.

Business tort: tort caused by or involving a business.

Bylaws: rules enacted by directors to govern a corporation's conduct.

C

Cancellation: an act indicating intention to destroy the validity of an instrument.

Capital stocks: declared value of outstanding stocks.

Carrier: a transporter of goods, people, or both.

Cashier's check: check drawn by a bank on its own funds and signed by the cashier or another official of the bank.

Caveat emptor: let the buyer beware.

Certificate of deposit: an acknowledgement by bank of receipt of money with engagement to repay it with interest.

Certified check: an ordinary check accepted by a bank's writing *Certified* on it.

Check: draft drawn on a bank and payable on demand.

Check truncation: shortening a check's trip from the payee to drawee bank and then the drawer.

Civil law: the body of law dealing with enforcement or protection of private rights.

Close or Closely held corporation: a corporation that has a very small number of shareholders.

Codicil: a writing that modifies a will.

Coguarantor or cosurety: one of two or more people jointly liable for another's debt, default, or obligation.

Coinsurance: a principle that the insured recovers in ratio of insurance to amount of insurance required.

Collateral note: a note secured by personal property.

Collective bargaining: a process by which employer and union negotiate and agree on terms of employment.

Color of Title: one's apparent title.

Commercial paper or negotiable instrument: the writing down in special form that can be transferred as a substitute for money or as an instrument of credit.

Commercial unit: an article, group of articles, or quantity regarded as a separate unit.

Common carrier: one that undertakes to transport without discrimination all who apply for service.

Common law: English custom recognized by courts as binding.

Common stock: stock that entitles owner to vote.

Communication: telling something to a third person.

Comparative negligence: the rule that contributory negligence reduces but does not bar recovery from a negligent person.

Compensatory damages: compensation amount equal to the loss sustained.

Complaint or petition: a written request to a court to settle a dispute.

Composition of creditors: when all multiple creditors settle in full for a fraction of the amount owed.

Comprehensive policy: an automobile insurance covering large number of miscellaneous risks.

Computer crimes: crimes that are committed with the aid of computers or because computers are involved.

Computer trespass: unauthorized use of, or access to, a computer.

Community property: property acquired during marriage that is owned separately and equally by both spouses.

Concealment: willful failure to disclose pertinent information.

Confusion of goods: the mixing of goods of different owners that under certain circumstances results in one of the owners becoming the owner of all the goods.

Confusion of source: representing goods or services as being those of another.

Consideration: what a promisor requires from another party as a price for a promise.

Consignment: the transfer of possession of personal goods for purpose of sale.

Consignor: one who ships goods by common carrier.

Consignee: one to whom goods are shipped.

Consolidation: combining two corporations into one.
Constitution: document that contains fundamental principles of a government.
Constructive bailment: bailment imposed when a person finds and takes control of lost property.
Constructive notice: information or knowledge the law assumes everyone knows.
Constructive trust: a trust created by a court to correct a wrong.
Consumer goods or services: goods or services primarily for personal, family or household use.
Contract to sell: an agreement to transfer the title of goods for a price.
Contribution: right of coguarantor to recover excess of proportionate share of debt from other coguarantor(s).
Conversion: unauthorized exercise of ownership rights; obtaining possession of property and converting it to one's own use.
Convict: a person found guilty by a court of a major criminal offense.
Counteroffer: offeree's response that rejects offer by varying terms of initial offer.
Corporation: an association of people created by law into an entity.
Coupon bond: a bond with detachable individual coupons representing interest payments.
Court of original general jurisdiction: court of record in which a criminal or civil case is first tried.
Court of record: court in which an official record of the proceedings is kept.
Covenant: a promise contained in a deed or conveyance relating to real estate; a solemn compact.
Creation: bringing property into actual being.
Creditor: party who receives guaranty.
Creditor beneficiary: person to whom promisee owes obligation, which is discharged if promisor performs.
Crime: an offense against society, the state, or a government; violation of a law.
Criminal law: law dealing with offenses against society.
Cumulative preferred stock: stock on which all dividends must be paid before common dividends can be paid.
Cumulative voting: stockholder votes for directors of corporation and has votes equal to company shares owned times the number of directors to be elected.
Customary authority: the authority an agent possesses by custom.

D

Damages: a sum of money a wrong-doer must pay to an injured party.
Debenture: an unsecured bond or note issued by a business.
Debt: obligation to pay in money or goods.
Deductible clause: insurance provision whereby insured pays damage up to specified amount; company pays excess up to policy limits.
Deed: writing conveying title to real property; an instrument by which the grantor (owner of land) conveys or transfers the title to a grantee.
Deed of trust: a deed that transfers land property to a trustee for the benefit of the creditor when real estate is used to secure payment of a debt; commonly used as a form of mortgage.
Default: breach of contractual obligation other than money.
Defendant: person against whom a legal case is filed.
Defense clause: policy clause in which insurer agrees to defend insured against damage claims.
Delegation: the transfer of duties from one person to another.
Delivery: intentional transfer of possession and control of something.
Devise: a gift of real estate made by will.
Devisee: a person receiving a gift of real estate by a will.
Disaffirmance: repudiation of a voidable contract.
Discovery: means of obtaining unprivileged information from other party before a trial.
Dishonor: when a presentment is made, but acceptance or payment not yet made.
Disparate impact: a policy disproportionately affecting a protected class of persons.
Disparate treatment: intentional discrimination against a particular individual because of membership in a protected class.
Dissolution: termination of corporation's operation except activities needed for liquidation of the corporation.
Dissolution of a partnership: a change in relation of partners by elimination of one partner.
Diversity jurisdiction: federal jurisdiction based on parties being from different states.
Document of title: document that shows ownership.
Domestic corporation: one chartered in the state of incorporation.
Domestic relations court: court that handles divorce and related cases.
Donor: person who makes a gift.
Donee: person who receives a gift.
Donee beneficiary: third-party beneficiary for whom performance is a gift.
Dormant or sleeping partner: partner unknown to public with no part in management.
Double indemnity rider: policy requiring insurer to pay twice the policy's ordinary face amount if death is by accidental means.
Draft: written order by one person directing another to pay sum of money to a third person or party.
Drawee: person ordered to pay a draft.
Drawer: person who executes a draft.
Durable power of attorney: a written appointment of agency that survives incapacity of principal.
Duress: obtaining consent by means of a threat.

E

Easement: an interest in land for nonexclusive or intermittent use; the right that on person has to use the land of another for a special purpose.
Electronic fund transfer: fund transfer initiated electronically, telephonically, or by computer.

Embezzlement: fraudulent appropriation of property by a person to whom it has been entrusted.

Employment at will: employment terminable by employer or employee for any reason.

Endowment insurance: decreasing term insurance policy combined with a savings account.

Equipment: goods for use in business.

Equity: justice system based on fairness; provides relief other than merely monetary damages.

Estate: an interest in property; property left by the deceased.

Estoppel: occurs when one party leads the second to a false conclusion that the second party relies on. The second party would be harmed if the first party were later allowed to show the conclusion was false.

Ethics: principles that determine the morality of one's conduct, motives, and duties.

Eviction: the expulsion of a tenant from leased property.

Executed contract: fully performed contract.

Executor: person named in will to administer estate.

Executory contract: a contract not fully carried out by all parties.

Existing goods: goods that are in being and owned by the seller.

Exoneration: the guarantor's right to have creditor compel payment of debt.

Express authority: the authority of agent stated in agreement creating agency.

Express contract: a contract with the terms of the agreement specified in words.

Express trust: a trust clearly established by clear action of the grantor.

Express warranty: statement of guarantee by seller.

Extended coverage: riders to a fire insurance policy covering loss from additional risks.

F

Face: the maximum amount insurer pays for loss.

Factor: bailee seeking to sell property on commission.

Factor del credere: factor who sells on credit and guarantees price will be paid.

False representation: the misstatement of material fact by the insured.

Federal Court of Appeals: court that hears appeals in the federal court system.

Federal District Court: Trial Court of a Federal Court system.

Fee Simple Estate: largest, most complete right in property.

Fellow Servant: employee with the same status and working with another worker.

Felony: a more serious crime that is punishable by confinement in prison or by death.

Fictious name registration statute: a law requiring operator of business under assumed name to register with the state.

Fidelity bond: suretyship for someone who handles another's money.

Fiduciary: a person in a relationship of trust and confidence.

Finance charge: total dollar amount borrower paid for credit.

Financing statement: writing with signatures and addresses of debtor and secured party and description of the collateral.

Firm offer: a merchant's signed, written offer to sell or purchase goods saying it will be held open.

Fixtures: personal property so securely attached to real estate that it becomes part of the real estate.

Floating policy: insurance coverage of property no matter where property is located at time of loss.

Forbearance: refraining from doing something.

Forcible entry and detainer action: summary action by landlord to regain possession of leased property.

Foreclosure: sale of mortgaged property to pay debt.

Foreign corporation: corporation chartered under the rules of another state.

Formal contract: contract with a special form or manner of creation.

Fraud: inducing another to contract as a result of an intentionally or recklessly false statement of a material fact.

Fraud in the execution: defrauded party did not intend to enter into a contract but false statement made by other party induce's contract signing.

Fraud in the inducement: defrauded party intended to make a contract but false statements were made about the terms or in obligations of the contract.

F.O.B. (free on board): designated point to which seller bears risk and expense of delivery.

Friendly fire: fire contained where intended.

Full warranty: warranty with unlimited duration of implied warranties, with an agreement to remedy any defects in products.

Fungible goods: goods of a homogeneous nature sold by weight or measure.

Future goods: goods not both existing and identified.

G

Gambling contract: agreement in which parties win or lose, based on chance.

General agent: Agent authorized to carry out particular kind of principal's business or all of principal's business at a certain place.

General partner: one actively and openly engaged in business.

General warranty deed: a deed that warrants good title in the grantee free from all claims.

Gift: transfer of ownership of property without consideration

Goods: movable personal property.

Grace period: 30 or 31-day-period in which late premium may be paid without policy lapsing.

Grantee: person receiving title to property.

Grantor: person conveying property; creator of trust.

Guarantor or surety: party who agrees to be responsible for obligation of another.

Guest: transient received by hotel for accommodations.

H

Hacker: unauthorized outsider who gains access to another's computer system.

Hazards: factors that contribute to uncertainty of insured loss.

Holder: person in possession of instrument payable to bearer.

Holder in due course: person who aquires rights superior to original owner; holder for value and in good faith with no knowledge of dishonor, defenses, or claims.

Holder through a holder in due course: holder subsequent to holder in due course.

Holographic will: will written by testator in the testator's own hand.

Homeowner's policy: coverage of many perils plus liability for owners living in their houses.

Hostile fire: fire outside of its normal place.

Hostile work environment: alteration of terms or conditions of employment by harassment and abuse based on employee's membership in a protected class.

Hot cargo agreement: agreement between a union and an employer that the employer will not use nonunion materials.

Hotelkeeper: one engaged in business of offering lodging to transients.

I

Identified goods: goods picked to be delivered to the buyer.

Implied authority: agent's authority to do things not specifically authorized in order to carry out express authority.

Implied contract: contract with major terms implied by the parties' conduct or implied or deduced from the facts.

Implied warranty: warranty imposed by law.

Incidental beneficiary: person who unintentionally benefits from performance of contract.

Incorporators: people initially forming a corporation.

Indemnity: right of guarantor to be reimbursed by principal; a compensation for loss sustained.

Independent contractor: one who contracts to do jobs and is controlled only by specifications of contract.

Indorsee: named holder of indorsed negotiable instrument.

Indorsement: signature of holder on back of instrument with any directions or limitations.

Indorser: payee or holder who signs back of the financial instrument.

Inferior courts: trial courts that hear only cases involving minor offenses and personal disputes.

Injunction: court's permanent order forbidding a specific action.

Injunctive powers: power to issue cease and desist orders.

Injurious falsehood: false statement of fact that degrades quality of another's goods or services.

Inland draft: draft drawn in one state and payable in the same or another state.

Innocent misrepresentation: false statement made in belief it is true.

Insider: officer, director, or owner of more than 10 percent of stock or any other class of securities of a corporation.

Insurable interest: an interest in the nonoccurrence of the risk insured against.

Insurance: contract that transfers risk of financial loss for a fee.

Insured: person protected against a loss.

Insurer: the company writing insurance policy or contract and that agrees to compensate a person for loss under policy terms.

Intestate: one who dies without having made a valid will.

Intangible personal property: evidences of ownership of personal property.

Inventory: articles purchased with intention of reselling or leasing.

Issue: first delivery of negotiable instrument by maker or drawer to give rights to another.

J

Joint and several contract: two or more people bound jointly and individually by contract and who are entitled to recover individually and as a unit.

Joint and survivor annuity: annuity contract paid out until the second of two insured people die.

Joint contract: contract obligating or entitling two or more people together to performance under the contract.

Joint-stock company: entity that issues shares of stock, but investors have unlimited liability; an association where the stock shares are transferable and control is delegated to a group or board.

Joint tenancy: multiple ownership of property in which, at death of one, that individual's share passes on to remaining owners.

Joint venture: business relationship similar to partnership, except existing only for a single transaction.

Judge: chief officer of a court

Judicial admission: fact acknowledged in a course of legal proceeding.

Jurisdiction: authority of a court to hear a case.

Justice of the peace: chief officer of an inferior court.

Juvenile court: court with jurisdiction over cases involving delinquent, dependent, and neglected children.

L

Lease: contract between landlord and tenant.

Landlord or lessor: owner of leased property.

Larceny: taking and carrying property away without consent of the person in possesion of the property.

Last clear chance rule: rule allowing negligent driver to recover if the other driver had one last clear chance to avoid the accident.

Law: governmental rule prescribing conduct and carrying a penalty for violation.

Law merchant: rules applied by courts set up by merchants in early England, prior to 1400.

Lawyers or attorneys: persons licensed to represent others in court.

Leasehold interest insurance: policy protecting property lessee from paying a higher rent after fire damages a leased building.
Legal rate of interest: interest rate applied according to statute when no rate specified and interest is to be paid.
Legal tender: any form of lawful money.
Legatee: one receiving personal property by a will's specification.
Lien: Encumbrance or claim against property as security for a debt.
License: right to do certain acts on another's land.
Life estate: estate for the duration of a person's life.
Life insurance: contract of an insurer to pay money upon the death of the insured.
Life tenant: person owning property for a lifetime.
Limited defense: defense that cannot be used against a holder in due course.
Limited liability: capital contribution is maximum loss.
Limited liability company: partnership-type organization with limited personal liabilities.
Limited partner: partner who takes no active part in management and who the public know know as a partner.
Limited partnership: partnership with partner whose liability is limited to capital contribution and who is not viewed as an active business manager.
Limited warranty: written warranty that is not a full warranty.
Liquidated damages: a sum fixed by contract in case of contractual breach where actual damages are difficult to measure.
Lost property: property unintentionally left with no intention to discard.

M

Magistrate: chief officer of an inferior court.
Maker: person who executes a promissary note.
Malpractice: failure to perform with ability and care normally exercised by people in the profession.
Marshal: executive officer of a federal court.
Maximum contract rate: highest legal rate of interest allowed.
Mechanics' lien: lien by people who have furnished materials or labor for property development or improvement.
Merchant: person who deals in goods of the kind or by occupation is considered to have particular knowledge or skill regarding goods involved.
Merger: one corporation absorbed by another.
Minor: person under the legal age to contract.
Misdemeanor: a less serious crime, neither treason nor a felony.
Misrepresentation: false statement of a material fact made innocently without any deceipt.
Model: replica of an article.
Money order: instrument issued by business indicating payee may receive financial instrument's indicated amount.
Mortgage: an interest in real estate given to secure debt.
Mortgagor: person who gives mortgage.
Mortgagee: person who holds mortgage.
Moveable personal property: all physical items except real estate.
Mutual insurance company: company of insurance policyholder-investors.
Mutual mistake: mistake by both parties to a contract.

N

Necessaries: items required for living at a reasonable standard.
Negative Covenant: agreement by grantee not to do an act.
Negligence: failure to exercise reasonable and prudent care.
Negotiability: transferability.
Negotiable instrument: document of payment, such as a check.
Negotiation: act of transferring ownership of negotiable instrument, by indorsement, delivery, or physical transfer.
No-fault insurance: insurance companies pay for their insured's injuries regardless of who is at fault.
No-par-value stock: stock without face value.
Nominal damages: small amount awarded when there is technical breach but no injury.
Nominal partner: person who pretends to be a partner or permits others to represent him/her as a partner.
Noncumulative preferred stock: stock on which current dividends must be paid before common dividends are paid.
Nonparticipating preferred stock: stock on which maximum dividend is stated percentage on the stock.
Nonresellable goods: specially-made goods not easily resellable.
Nontrading partnership: partnership devoted to professional services.
Not-for-profit corporation: one formed by private individuals for charitable, educational, religious, social, or fraternal purposes.
Notice and comment rule making: enacting administrative rules by publishing the proposed rule and then the final rule without holding formal hearings.
Novation: termination of a contract and substitution of new contract with same terms but a new party.
Nuncupative will: oral will made during last illness and in the presence of witnesses.

O

Offer: a proposal to make a contract.
Offeree: person to whom an offer is made.
Offeror: person who makes an offer.
Open policy: policy that requires insured party to prove the actual loss sustained.
Option: binding promise to hold an offer open.
Oral contract: contract with terms spoken.
Order bill of lading: contract allowing delivery of shipped goods to bearer.

Order paper: commercial paper payable to order of a named person.
Ordinances: laws enacted by cities.
Ordinary or general partnership: partnership with no limitation on rights and duties of partners.

P

Par-value stock: stock with an assigned face value.
Parol evidence: oral testimony.
Parole evidence rule: complete, written contract may not be modified by oral testimony unless upon evidence of fraud, accident or mistake.
Participating preferred stock: stock that shares with common stock in extra dividends.
Partner: member of partnership.
Partnership: association of two or more people to carry on business for profit.
Partition: suit to divide joint tenancy, filed by one joint tennant against the other.
Passive fraud: fraud caused by failure to disclose information when there is duty to do so.
Pawn: tangible personal property left as security for a debt.
Payee: party to whom instrument is payable.
***Per capita*:** per head.
***Per stirpes*:** distribution among heirs according to the relationship to deceased.
Per se violations: activities deemed illegal regardless of their effect.
Perfected security interest: seller's right to collateral that is superior to third party's right.
Personal property: movable property; interests less than complete ownership in land or rights to property.
Physical damage insurance: insurance for damage to car itself.
Piercing the corporate veil: a judicial ignoring of the corporate entity.
Pirated software: software copied illegally.
Plaintiff: person who brings action in a court.
Pledge: intangible property serving as a security for a debt.
Point-of-sale system: EFTs begun at retailers when customers pay for goods or services.
Policy: written contract of insurance.
Polygraph: a lie detector.
Postdated check: check drawn prior to its date.
Power of attorney: principal's writing appointing an agent.
Preauthorized credit: automatic deposit of funds to an account.
Preauthorized debit: automatic deduction of bill payment from checking account.
Precedent: court decision that determines the decision in a subsequent, similar case.
Preemptive right: right to purchase new shares in proportion to shares owned.
Preference: disallowed transfer to a creditor.
Preferred stock: stock given special advantage as to payment of dividends, upon liquidation or both.
Premium: consideration paid by insured for a policy.
Presentment: demand for acceptance or payment of commercial paper.
Price: consideration in a sales contract.
Prima facie: on the face of it.
Prima facie evidence: evidence sufficient on its face, if uncontradicted.
Primary liability: liability without conditions for commercial paper that is due.
Principal: person who appoints another to contract with third parties; party primarily liable to third person or creditor.
Private carrier: carrier that transports under special arrangements for a fee.
Private corporation: one formed to do non–governmental function.
Privity of contract: relationship between contracting parties.
Probate: court procedure to determine validity of a testator's will.
Probate court: court that handles individuals' estates and proves authenticity of testator's will.
Procedural law: laws specifying how actions are filed and what trial procedure to follow.
Profit corporation: one organized to run a business and earn money.
Promissory estoppel: substitute for consideration when another acts in reliance on promisor's promise.
Promissory note: unconditional written promise to pay sum of money to another.
Promoters: one who takes initial steps to form corporation.
Property: anything that may be owned.
Property insurance: contract by which insurer pays for damage to specified property.
Proprietor: owner of sole proprietorship.
Prosecutor or district attorney: government employee who brings criminal actions.
Prospectus: document giving specified information about a corporation.
Protected class: group protected by antidiscrimination laws.
Protest: certification of notice of dishonor by authorized official.
Proxy: person authorized to vote for another; written authorization to vote for another.
Proxy war: attempt by competing sides to secure majority of stockholders' votes.
Publication: testator's informing witnesses that document being signed is the testator's will.
Public corporation: one formed for governmental function.
Public liability insurance: insurance designed to protect third persons from bodily injury and property damage.
Punitive damages: amount paid to one party to punish the other in excess of those required to compensate the plaintiff for the wrong done.
Purchase: ownership by payment.

Q

Qualified indorsement: indorsement that limits liability of indorser.

Quasi contract: imposition of rights and obligations by law without a contract.

Quasi-public corporation: public body with powers similar to a corporations.

Quitclaim deed: deed where grantor gives up whatever interest grantor has in property, without specifying any particular interest is being transferred.

Quorum: minimum number of shares required to be represented to lawfully transact business.

R

Ratification: adult indicating contract made while a minor is binding; approval of unauthorized act.

Real estate mortgage note: note secured by mortgage on real estate.

Real property: land and things permanently attached to the land.

Receipt: taking possession of goods.

Recognizance: obligation entered into before a court to do an act required by law.

Redemption: right to free property from lien of mortgage; buying back one's property after default cleared.

Reformation: judicial correction of a contract.

Registered bond: bond payable to specific person, whose name is recorded by issuer.

Remainder: interest in life estate that goes to someone other than grantor on death of life tenant.

Renewable term insurance: term insurance renewable without physical examination.

Rent: amount paid landlord for possession and use of property.

Renunciation: unilateral act of holder giving up rights in the instrument or against a party to it.

Reporting form for merchandise inventory: policy allowing periodic reporting of inventory on hand to vary coverage amount.

Rescind: to set a contract aside or cancel.

***Respondeat superior*:** theory imposing liability on employers for torts of employees.

Restraining order: court's temporary order forbidding an action.

Restrictive indorsement: indorsement that restricts use of instrument.

Resulting or purchase money trust: resulting trust created when one person buys property but takes title in another person's name.

Reversion: interest of grantor in life estate that returns to grantor on death of estate's owner.

Rider: addition to insurance policy to modify, extend, or limit base contract.

Right of survivorship: automatic ownership of property by survivors.

Right to take against the will: spouse's right to share of estate provided by statute if the will leaves smaller share.

Risk or peril: danger or loss from which the insured is protected against, according to contract's terms.

Robbery: taking property by force.

Rogue program: set of software instructions that produces abnormal computer behavior.

S

Sale: transfer of title to goods for a price.

Sale on approval: sale that is not complete until buyer approves goods.

Sale or return: completed sale with the right to return goods.

Sample: portion of a whole mass that is the subject of transaction.

Secondary boycott: attempt by employees to stop third party to a labor dispute from dealing with employer.

Secondary liability: liability for a negotiable instrument that has been presented, dishonored, and notice of dishonor given.

Secondary meaning: special meaning of a mark that distinguishes goods, in such a way as to warrant trademark protection.

Secret partner: partner active in a business but unknown to the public.

Secured credit sale: sale in which seller retains right to repossess goods upon default.

Security agreement: written agreement signed by buyer that creditor has a security interest in collateral.

Set off: a claim by the party being sued against the party suing.

Several contracts: two or more people individually agree to perform obligation.

Share: unit of stock.

Shareholder or stockholder: person who owns stock.

Sheriff: court of record's executive officer.

Shop right: employer's right to use employee's invention without payment of royalty.

Shoplifting: taking unpurchased goods from a store.

Short-swing profits: profits made by insider buying and selling corporations stock in six-month period.

Sight draft: draft payable upon presentation of draft's holder.

Silent partner: partner who takes no active part in the management of a firm, whether known to the public or not.

Simple contract: contract that is not formal.

Sole proprietorship: business owned and carried on by one person.

Special agent: agent authorized to transact specific act or acts.

Special federal courts: federal trial courts with limited jurisdiction, such as the U.S. Tax Court.

Special indorsements: indorsement that designates particular person to whom payment is to be made.

Special warranty deed: warrants that a grantor has the right to convey or sell real property.

Specific performance: carrying out the terms of contract.

Specific policy: insurance that applies to only one item.

Stale check: check presented more than six months after its date.

***Stare decisis*:** principle that a court decision controls the decision of a similar future case.

State court of appeals: intermediate appellate courts.

State Supreme Court: highest court in most states.

Statute of frauds: law requiring certain contracts to be in writing in order to be binding or enforceable.

Statute of limitation: time within which right to sue must be exercised or lost.

Statutes: laws enacted by legislative bodies.

Stock corporation: one in which ownership is represented by stock.

Stock insurance company: corporation of policyholder–investors.

Stock option: right to purchase shares at set price during a set time.

Straight bill of lading: contract between shipper and carrier requiring delivery of shipped goods only to consignee.

Strict tort liability: manufacturer of product liable without proof of negligence for dangerous product.

Strike: temporary, concerted action of workers to withhold their services from an employer.

Sublease: transfer of less than a tenant's full rights under a lease to a third person.

Subrogation: right of insurer to assume rights of insured.

Subscriber: one who agrees to buy stock in proposed corporation.

Summons or process: notice of suit.

Supreme Court of the United States: the highest court in the United States.

T

Tangible personal property: personal property that can be seen, touched, and possessed.

Tenancy at sufferance: a holdover tenant remaining on landlord's property without landlord's permission.

Tenancy at will: tenancy for uncertain period that can be dissolved by the landlord or landlord and tennant acting together.

Tenancy by the entirety: property co-ownership by husband and wife, each with right of survivorship upon death of the spouse.

Tenancy for years: tenancy for a fixed period of time even though the time is less than a year.

Tenancy from year to year: tenancy for an indefinite period with yearly rent.

Tenancy in common: when two or more persons own property and one dies, that owner's interest in the property passes to a person named in the deceased's will or, if no will exists, to the deceased's heirs.

Tenancy in partnership: ownership of a partner in partnership property.

Tenant or lessee: possessor of leased property.

Tender of payment: offer and ability to pay money owed as specified by contract.

Tender of performance: offer to perform in satisfactory terms as specified in contract.

Term insurance: contract whereby insurer assumes risk of death of insured for a specified time period.

Testamentary trust: a trust created in a will.

Testator (testatrix): a man (woman) who makes a will.

Theft: taking another's property without consent.

Third party beneficiary: person not party to contract but whom parties intend to benefit.

Time draft: draft payable certain number of days or months after date or presentation.

Title: evidence of ownership of property.

Tort: private wrong for which damages may be recovered.

Tortfeasor: person whose action causes injury.

Trade acceptance: draft drawn by seller on purchaser of goods and accepted by purchaser.

Trade fixtures: fixtures in used in tenant's business and which have been attached to property by tenant.

Trademark: word, symbol, device, or combination of them used to identify and distinguish goods from other goods.

Trademark or trade name dilution: lessening the capacity of a famous mark to identify and distinguish goods.

Trademark or trade name infringement: unauthorized use or imitation or another's mark or name.

Trading partnership: one engaged in buying and selling merchandise.

Trailing edge: left side of front of check.

Treasury stock: stock reacquired by a corporation.

Trial court: court that conducts original trial of a case.

Trial Justice: court officer overseeing disposition of a case.

Trust: contract by which one person holds property for another person.

Trustee: one who holds title to property for another; legal owner of a trust property.

U

Ultra vires contract: contract exceeding a corporation's powers.

Uncured default: not all payments on an instrument fully made and not all made by due date.

Undue influence: person in special relationship causing another's action contrary to free will.

Unenforceable contract: agreement that is not currently binding but can be made so by the parties.

Unfair competition: total impression of product results in confusion as to product's origin.

Unilateral contract: contract calling for an act in consideration for a promise.

Unilateral mistake: mistake by one party to a contract.

Union shop: work setting in which all employees must be union members.

Unit pricing: price stated per unit of measurement.

Universal defense: defense against any holder.

Unjust enrichment: one benefiting unfairly at another's expense.
Unlimited liability: business debts payable from personal assets.
Usury: charging higher interest rate than law allows.

V

Valid contract: contract enforceable by the law.
Valued policy: fire insurance policy that fixes values for insured items of property.
Verdict: decision of a jury.
Void: of no legal effect.
Voidable contract: enforceable agreement that may be set aside by one party.
Voting trust: device whereby stock is transferred to trustee to vote its shares for two or more shareholders.
Voucher check: check with voucher attached.

W

Warehouse receipt: document of title issued by storage company for goods stored.
Warranty: assurance article conforms to a standard; statement of insured that relates to risk and appears in an insurance contract.
Warranty deed: deed with guarantees conveyed by grantor.
Watered stock: stock paid for with property of inflated value; stock issued by a corporation as being fully paid when in fact, it is not.
Will: document providing disposition of property after death.
Winding up: taking care of outstanding obligations of a partnership and distributing remaining assets.
With reserve: auction goods may be withdrawn after bidding starts.
Without reserve: auction goods may not be withdrawn after bidding starts.
Writ of certiorari: order to produce record of a case for review by a higher court.
Written contract: contract with terms in writing.

Index

A

B

D

N

O

P

Q

R

U

V

W